Psychological Perspectives on Lesbian, Gay, and Bisexual Experiences

Between Men ~ Between Women
Lesbian and Gay Studies

Lillian Faderman and Larry Gross, Editors

Psychological Perspectives on Lesbian, Gay, and Bisexual Experiences

Second Edition

Linda D. Garnets
and Douglas C. Kimmel
Editors

COLUMBIA   UNIVERSITY   PRESS   NEW   YORK

COLUMBIA UNIVERSITY PRESS
Publishers Since 1893
New York   Chichester, West Sussex

Library of Congress Cataloging-in-Publication Data

Pyschological perspectives on lesbian, gay, and bisexual experiences /
Linda D. Garnets and Douglas C. Kimmel, editors. — 2nd ed.
    p. cm. — (Between men — between women)
    Includes bibliographical references and index.
    ISBN 0-231-12412-0 (cloth : alk. paper) —
    ISBN 0-231-12413-9 (paper : alk. paper)
    1. Homosexuality — United States   2. Lesbians — United States —
Psychology.   3. Gays — United States — Psychology.   I. Garnets, Linda.
II. Kimmel, Douglas C.   III. Series.
HQ76.3.U5 P783 2002
305.9′0664′0973 — dc21   2002025717

Columbia University Press books
are printed on permanent and durable acid-free paper
Printed in the United States of America

c 10 9 8 7 6 5 4 3 2 1
p 10 9 8 7 6 5 4 3 2 1

Between Men ~ Between Women
Lesbian and Gay Studies

Lillian Faderman and Larry Gross, Editors

Advisory Board of Editors

Claudia Card
Terry Castle
John D'Emilio
Esther Newton
Anne Peplau
Eugene Rice
Kendall Thomas
Jeffrey Weeks

Between Men ~ Between Women is a forum for current lesbian and gay scholarship in the humanities and social sciences. The series includes both books that rest within specific traditional disciplines and are substantially about gay men, bisexuals, or lesbians and books that are interdisciplinary in ways that reveal new insights into gay, bisexual, or lesbian experience, transform traditional disciplinary methods in consequence of the perspectives that experience provides, or begin to establish lesbian and gay studies as a freestanding inquiry. Established to contribute to an increased understanding of lesbians, bisexuals, and gay men, the series also aims to provide through that understanding a wider comprehension of culture in general.

Contents

Part III: Identity Development and Stigma Management   217

Part IV: Diversity Among Lesbians, Bisexuals, and Gay Men   349

Part VIII: Status of Research, Practice, and Public Policy Issues in American Psychology   733

Contemporary Issue: What Do Lesbians, Gay Men, and Bisexuals Contribute to Society? Conversely, What Is the Cost to Society for the Various Forms of Legal Discriminations Against Bisexuals, Lesbians, and Gay Men?   736

Preface

Interest in lesbian, bisexual, and gay studies is growing rapidly. It is important that psychological perspectives be represented in this emerging field. This second edition of a book we first edited in 1993 reflects some of the best thinking in social science about psychological issues affecting lesbians, bisexuals, and gay men. While most of the articles are psychological in focus, anthropology, biology, economics, medicine, public policy, and sociology are included as well. We have revised, updated, and shortened the introduction and included a set of new articles, almost all of them published after the first edition.

Although the book is designed for upper-level undergraduate students with some experience in social science courses, it is also intended to be used in graduate psychology courses that focus on human diversity. Graduate students in clinical and counseling psychology, nursing, psychiatry, and social work, in particular, will find this book a useful introduction to issues relevant to professional practice.

General readers will find this book of interest because critical issues reflecting the contemporary relevance of each section are discussed. These are, in turn, the debate regarding choice versus no choice of sexual orientation; sexual prejudice, verbal abuse, physical harassment, and violence based on sexual orientation; the effects of historical differences between older and younger generations of lesbians, bisexuals, and gay men; racism in the gay, lesbian, and bisexual community; legal recognition of gay, lesbian, and bisexual relationships and families; the impact of acquired immune deficiency syndrome (HIV/AIDS) on adolescents and older persons;

barriers to health care for lesbians, gay men, and bisexuals; effects of state and national legislation and popular votes regarding sexual orientation issues on the psychological well-being of gay men, lesbians, and bisexuals; and benefits of bisexuals, lesbians, and gay men to society and to heterosexual women and men.

The origin of this book was an invited lecture at the American Psychological Association meetings in 1990 by the co-editors. Having developed this broad overview, we felt that the articles most central to the field should be collected and made available in one source. The articles selected for the second edition include overviews of contributions that helped define the field, seminal papers reflecting current thinking in the area, and some of the most recent publications reflecting future directions and guidelines for new research and practice. We have written a brief introduction to each of the nine sections to provide background and perspective.

Part 1, "The Meaning of Sexual Orientation," presents a broad perspective on psychology and sexual orientation. The first selection is a personal biography by the editors of a pioneer in the field, Evelyn Hooker. The second article is an overview of biological perspectives on sexual orientation. The third is a comprehensive review of theory and research on bisexuality, demonstrating the importance of including and integrating bisexuality into gay and lesbian psychology. The final selection is an empirical examination of diversity in the development of sexual orientation among young women. The contemporary issue discussed is the degree of choice versus no choice of sexual orientation and the implications of these viewpoints.

Part 2, "Psychological Dimensions of Prejudice, Discrimination, and Violence," focuses on the hostile social context in which lesbians, bisexuals, and gay men live in the United States. Instead of an individual pathology, sexual orientation is now seen as a source of stress because of external forces in society that reinforce hatred, prejudice, discrimination, and violence toward lesbians, gay men, and bisexuals. The first article presents some of the best thinking on the dynamics of sexual prejudice. The second selection discusses gender differences in attitudes toward sexual minority orientations. The third article focuses on the effects of hostile attitudes and prejudice in terms of violence and victimization of lesbians and gay men. The final selection provides a poignant personal statement about the effect of the murder of Matthew Shepherd, a gay man, on a social scientist. The contemporary issue focuses on sexual prejudice and the verbal abuse, physical harassment, and violence often linked to it.

Part 3, "Identity Development and Stigma Management," explores the process of individual development of a positive sexual identity in the social context of stigma about homosexuality and bisexuality. It includes articles that address self-disclosure to others, relations with parents, and the effects of disclosure in the workplace. The contemporary issue focuses on the effects of historical differences between older and younger generations of lesbians, bisexuals, and gay men with regard to identity and coming out.

Part 4, "Diversity among Gay Men, Lesbians, and Bisexuals," builds on the general process of identity development to explore differences among gay men, bisexuals, and lesbians based on racial and ethnic background, gender, class, age, physical challenges, hearing or visual impairment, and deviations from normative standards of beauty. Two cross-cultural examples are included to reflect the enrichment that can result from the study of other cultures. Both these articles illustrate ways that other cultures provide examples of gender diversity and highlight the influence of differing gender systems and different levels of social stratification on patterns of lesbian, gay male, and bisexual experiences. The final essay focuses on the issues of rural gays, lesbians, and bisexuals in the United States. The contemporary issue is the significance of racism within the gay, bisexual, and lesbian community.

Part 5, "Relationships and Families," summarizes research on characteristics of sexual and romantic relationships among bisexuals, lesbians, and gay men, and takes a broad perspective on couple relationships. This section also reviews research about gay men and lesbians who are parents and refutes myths and stereotypes about the children of lesbian and gay parents. The final article presents the heterosexual parents' perspective on having a lesbian or gay child from the point of view of Asian mothers. The contemporary issue focuses on the legal recognition of same-gender relationships and families.

Part 6, "Adolescence, Midlife, and Aging," provides a lifespan perspective on lesbian, gay male, and bisexual development. It addresses a wide range of issues that adolescents face in coping with the knowledge of being gay, bisexual, or lesbian. Moreover, the articles review research on adult development in midlife and include a major study of aging among lesbian and gay elders. The contemporary issue is the effect of the HIV/AIDS epidemic on adolescents and on those growing older with the disease.

Part 7, "Mental Health," begins with the historical perspective and evolution of the diagnosis of same-gender sexual attraction. The second article is the seminal article that helped greatly to reduce the widespread practice of sexual orientation conversion therapy. The third article focuses on the mental health effects of the stress of minority status on gay men. The contemporary issue is the effects of state and national legislation and popular votes regarding sexual orientation issues on the psychological well-being of gay men, lesbians, and bisexuals.

Part 8, "Status of Research, Practice, and Public Policy Issues in American Psychology," presents three examples of applications of the new paradigm of lesbian, gay, and bisexual psychology: a report that provides guidelines for avoiding heterosexist bias in psychological research; a set of guidelines for psychotherapy with lesbian, gay, and bisexual clients; and a review of the relationship between psychology and legislation on lesbian, bisexual, and gay male civil rights. The contemporary issue discusses some of the benefits of bisexuals, lesbians, and gay men to society and to heterosexual women and men.

This book was made possible through the generosity of authors and publishers who allowed articles to be reprinted without charge: the American Psychological Association, Blackwell Publishers, Columbia University Press, Haworth Press, Lawrence Erlbaum Associates, Sage Publications, Society for the Psychological Study of Lesbian, Gay, and Bisexual Issues, Society for the Psychological Study of Social Issues, and the Asian-American Study Center of the University of California, Los Angeles. Royalties from the sale of the book go to support the Malyon-Smith Memorial Research Fund of the Society for the Psychological Study of Lesbian, Gay, and Bisexual Issues — A Division of the American Psychological Association. This fund provides support for graduate student research. Columbia University Press has edited the articles here for style. The original sources should be consulted for any extended quotations.

We are indebted to Tony D'Augelli, Armando Estrada, Greg Herek, Ilan Meyer, Anne Peplau, Ken Pope, Esther Rothblum, Paula Rust, and Craig Waldo for their advice and reviews of the manuscript. Ann Miller, Anne McCoy, John Michel and Roy Thomas of Columbia University Press made the second edition of this book possible. Special thanks to Rita Bernard for her thorough and thoughtful copyediting of the anthology. The support of our partners, Barrie and Ron, who understood how important it has been for us to work together on this project, is deeply appreciated. Sadly, the book needs also to remember the contributions of those friends and colleagues, some of whose work is cited here, who did not live to see it published.

Psychological Perspectives
on Lesbian, Gay, and Bisexual Experiences

Introduction to the Second Edition

Lesbian, Gay Male, and Bisexual Dimensions in the Psychological Study of Human Diversity

Linda D. Garnets and Douglas C. Kimmel

Sexual orientation has become an aspect of the psychological study of human diversity during the last few years. Our basic assumption is that an understanding of sexual orientation will enhance psychological research and practice by reducing heterosexist bias, will increase the perception of similarity and appreciation of difference among those who differ in sexual orientation, and will support efforts to remove the stigma and discrimination against lesbians, gay men, and bisexual people.

Following a brief overview of the social context, we introduce this emerging field from the perspective of four main themes: (a) the definition of sexual orientation and new paradigms to understand it; (b) limitations and caveats of psychological research on sexual orientation; (c) why it is an important variable in the psychological understanding of people; and (d) historical and cultural perspectives.

Overview

In the last decade of the twentieth century, lesbians, bisexuals, and gay men have become much more visible in the fabric of American society. Instead of a focus on the cause of same-sex attraction, the perspective has shifted to dimensions of diversity. As a result, sexual orientation has been reframed from an atypical form of sexual behavior into a manifestation of gender diversity. On the one hand, this has meant that discrimination against lesbians and gay men has been seen as a subset of gender discrimination issues. On the other hand, the concept of sexual orientation has broadened to include not only lesbian and gay issues but also bisexual concerns and, increasingly, transgender interests.

In addition, the focus of public discussion about sexual orientation has shifted away from sexual behavior to a greater focus on love in terms of relationships, parenting, and marriage. Moreover, public attention has shifted from the view that sexual orientation is a private matter to be discussed only in hushed tones to a recognition that it represents a minority group that has political implications, power, and even humor.

In short, the 1990s have been a remarkable decade. Throughout this period the psychological perspective on lesbian, gay, and bisexual issues has remained in the forefront of positive changes through research, advocacy, and practice.

In contrast, until the 1970s most psychological research on homosexuality focused on its presumed pathological aspects. Morin (1977) documented the bias that dominated the field up to that time as "heterosexist bias," which he defined as "a belief system that values heterosexuality as superior to and/or more 'natural' than homosexuality" (p. 631). Only a few pioneers, such as Kinsey, Pomeroy, and Martin (1948), Kinsey, Pomeroy, Martin, and Gebhard (1953), Ford and Beach (1951), and Hooker (1957), stood out as questioning the dominant model of homosexuality as a sign of mental illness. A significant change occurred as a result of a concerted effort by gay-affirmative mental health professionals who called attention to the empirical data that led the American Psychiatric Association in 1973 to remove homosexuality per se from its list of mental disorders (Bayer 1981). The American Psychological Association (APA) supported this change and further urged mental health professionals to take the lead in removing the stigma that previously had been associated with homosexuality (Conger 1975; Kooden et al. 1979). Subsequent psychological research on homosexuality shifted from a preoccupation with the causes and pathology of homosexuality to a much greater focus on the characteristics and psychosocial concerns of lesbians, bisexuals, and gay men, including social attitudes about homosexuals (Watters 1986).

In recent years there has been much positive change within the field of psychology as a gay-affirmative perspective has emerged. Within this perspective homosexuality is viewed as a natural variant in the expression of erotic attractions and relationships; the adoption of a gay male, bisexual, or lesbian identity is considered to be a viable and healthy option; and many of the problems of living associated with being bisexual, lesbian, or gay are thought to result from negative social attitudes about homosexuality. However, a survey of a large and diverse sample of psychologists by an APA Committee on Lesbian and Gay Concerns Task Force (1990) showed that a wide range of negative biases and misinformation about homosexuality persisted that could affect therapy practice with lesbians, bisexuals, and gay men. The existence of these attitudes led to the development of guidelines for psychotherapy with lesbians, bisexuals, and gay men that were adopted by the APA Council of Representatives (February 26, 2000) and are included in this book.

Likewise, in recent years social attitudes have been affected by the increased visibility and political power of lesbians, bisexuals, and gay men. However, few aspects of human behavior evoke the intensity of opposition that homosexuality arouses in some circles. For example, empirical research has documented the persistence of institutional and personal hostility toward gay men and lesbians, and the mental health consequences of hate crimes, victimization, and verbal abuse (Garnets, Herek, and Levy 1990; Herek 1991). The APA has joined with other mental health organizations to submit amicus curiae briefs in many court cases, beginning with the removal of "sodomy" laws in New York state and including the U.S. Supreme Court decision regarding the Boy Scouts discrimination against members and leaders on the basis of sexual orientation (Bersoff and Ogden 1991; Melton 1989; Ogden, Ewing, and Bersoff 1986; Patterson and Redding 1996; Smith 2000).

The emergence of acquired immune deficiency syndrome (HIV/AIDS) focused considerable attention on gay male lifestyles and brought renewed stigma to and discrimination against lesbians, bisexuals, and gay men (Herek 1999). Psychology, to its credit, has played a leading role in the fight against the epidemic and the related discrimination against those people affected by the disease (cf. Backer, Batchelor, Jones, and Mays 1988). It has been a tragic episode and the end is not yet in sight. Certainly it has affected sexual behavior, intimate relationships, and the developmental experiences of bereaved survivors, but it is too soon to know the extent of the impact or the long-term consequences of this historical event. One positive outcome of the AIDS epidemic has been to reveal that gay men are in all walks of life when this tragic disease forced them to come out. After the death of many gay male community leaders, lesbian leaders emerged and gained prominence in many lesbian, gay, bisexual, transgender (LGBT) organizations. As a result of these interrelated events, social awareness of gay, lesbian, and bisexual concerns and their relevance in public life has increased, at least in the media, the federal government, and in many corporations.

Contrasting Perspectives to Define and Conceptualize Sexual Orientation

There have been significant shifts in recent years about the ways that sexual orientation has been conceptualized and defined. Specifically, the field has moved away from relying on a dichotomous model that fits people into rigid categories to a continuous, multidimensional approach that captures the complex nature of men's and women's sexualities and sexual orientations. This has resulted in a greater understanding of the complexity of sexuality and the recognition of bisexuality as a distinct sexual identity.

The prevailing view of sexual orientation in Western psychology has been dichotomous and unidimensional. There are four key features to this old model. First, sexual orientation is viewed as a bipolar construct — it exists only in two opposite, discrete forms: heterosexuality or homosexuality. That model makes bisexuality either nonexistent or a middle, transitory, or transitional state. As one bisexual man expressed it: "I'm simply trying to live a both/and life in an either/or world" (Bennett 1992:205) Second, sexual orientation is a unidimensional construct based solely on sexual activity; that is, what one does sexually defines one's sexual orientation. Third, sexual orientation is viewed as an enduring, unchanging disposition. It is assumed that sexual orientation forms at an early age, that it involves sexual attraction, and that it cannot be changed. Fourth, generalizations about sexuality and sexual orientation have taken male experiences as the norm for both men and women. Differences between homosexual versus heterosexual women and men are emphasized in this dichotomous model (Garnets and Kimmel 1991).

In the early 1980s researchers began to rethink approaches to sexuality. They realized that sexual orientation is more complex than either homosexuality or heterosexuality. A continuous, multidimensional model of sexual orientation emerged. There are four key features of this contemporary approach.

First, sexual orientation is a continuum (similar to a spectrum of colors as in a rainbow) that varies in degree, diversity, and intensity (Garnets and Kimmel 1991; Rothblum 2000). Sexual orientation reflects the affectional-erotic attractions and love toward the same gender, other gender, or both genders. It is the combination of an individual's relative homosexuality and heterosexuality, representing two separate and independent parallel dimensions. This, in turn, makes it possible to view bisexuality as a distinct sexual orientation and identity.

Second, sexual orientation encompasses multiple dimensions, in addition to sexual behavior. These include erotic-affectional behaviors and fantasies, emotional attachments, self-identification, and current relationship status. Thus sexual orientation may be conceptualized as aspects of an individual's unique "lovemap" (Money 1988). The lovemap reflects the wide range of sexual interests and attractive characteristics in one's idealized lover and emphasizes love instead of only sexual behavior. The concept of a lovemap views the core ingredients in sexual orientation as affectional and erotic desires, love, and relationships. Sexual orientation is viewed as diverse with each individual having a template of erotic and affectional feelings, fantasies, activity, and relationships that is as unique as one's fingerprint or voiceprint. Sexual orientation is therefore only one aspect of an individual's unique pattern of sexuality.

Sexual activity, fantasy, and identity are not always congruent, however. They can be varied, complex, and inconsistent (Baumeister 2000; Diamant et al. 1999). For example, a woman who identifies as a lesbian might develop a strong attraction to a man. Or an individual may engage in sexual acts or have sexual desires without self-identifying as a member of a particular sexual orientation. For example, a man may have strong attractions to both men and women but not identify as bisexual. In fact, many more people engage in same-gender sexual behavior than identify as gay, lesbian, or bisexual (Rothblum 2000). Moreover, some people identify themselves as gay, lesbian, or bisexual but do not engage in sexual activity at all. Others may use heterosexual fantasy to facilitate a homosexual encounter or vice versa. For example, a heterosexual woman may employ homoerotic fantasies when having sex with her male partner. It should be noted also that there is not a necessary relationship between biological gender, gender identity or role, and sexual orientation; they represent separate components of sexual identity (Larsen 1981; Ross 1987; Shively and DeCecco 1977).

Third, sexual orientations are potentially fluid, changeable over time, and vary across social contexts and cultures (Peplau and Garnets 2000). Considerable evidence indicates that nonexclusive attractions toward both women and men and change over time characterize the experience of some men and women who may, or may not, call themselves bisexual (Rust 2000). For example, American women who are not exclusively heterosexual are more likely to be bisexual rather than homosexual in their attractions and relationships (Laumann et. al. 1994; Williams and Pryor 1994). Moreover, identification as bisexual, gay/lesbian, or heterosexual and one's actual behavior may vary over time. It need not be the same at age fifteen, twenty-five, forty-five, or seventy. This does not mean that most men or women will actually exhibit change over time. At a young age, many people adopt enduring patterns of heterosexuality, homosexuality, or bisexuality that remain stable across their lifetime. The key points are that some people are capable of variation and change and that such fluidity is more characteristic of women than men (Baumeister 2000; Diamond 1998).

A related idea is that the patterning of men and women's sexuality may be expected to vary cross-culturally and in different historical contexts (Garnets and Peplau 2000; Peplau et al. 1999). There is mounting evidence that men's and women's sexuality and sexual relationships are influenced by cultural beliefs about gender and sexual desire, by kinship systems, and by men's and women's economic and social status (Blackwood 2000; Bohan 1996).

Fourth, the nature and development of sexualities and sexual orientations are different for women and men. Regardless of sexual orientation, there are important commonalities, as well as differences, in women's and men's sexualities. For example, girls and women tend to have a relational or partner-centered orientation to sexuality, whereas boys and men tend to have a recreational or body-centered orientation (Peplau and Garnets 2000).

In summary, heterosexuality, homosexuality, and bisexuality are aspects of an individual's unique pattern of sexual responsiveness. To reduce this complexity to a bipolar dichotomy of homosexuality versus heterosexuality is not only a gross oversimplification but also a reflection of Western religious beliefs and "either-or" logic. This simplistic perspective has led to a denial of similarity between and diversity within these supposedly dichotomous sexual orientations. It may also be observed that whereas our culture has emphasized the importance of this dimension of human sexuality, other cultures and historical eras have structured the meaning of homosexual behaviors and heterosexual behaviors differently (cf. Blackwood and Wieringa 1999; Greenberg 1988; Weinrich and Williams 1991).

Limitations and Caveats Regarding Research

Empirical research is the basis of the psychological understanding of sexual orientation, but it is complex for many reasons. Representative sampling of the population is problematic because many people will not disclose their sexual orientation, lack of funding makes it difficult to obtain samples other than those that are convenient, and much research is conducted with the aim of efficient completion of the project (e.g., dissertations). Therefore differing levels of confidence in research with regard to sexual orientation must be noted.

In general, research that focuses on refuting universal stereotypes about lesbians, bisexuals, and gay men does not require representative samples to be compelling, because it focuses on disproving these generalizations. For example, Hooker's (1957) study showed that homosexual men cannot be distinguished from heterosexual controls on the basis of psychological tests, and Masters and Johnson's (1979) laboratory study showed that homosexual men and homosexual women showed the same physiological sexual response as did heterosexual men and heterosexual women, respectively. In neither study was a representative sample used; yet both were convincing. Likewise, studies of patterns of aging among gay men (Kimmel 1978) may lead one to conclude that, contrary to stereotypes, there is considerable diversity — probably even more than was found among the limited sample — without claiming that the findings are representative of all gay men. Similarly, Rust's (1992) survey of women indicated that the categories of "lesbian" and "bisexual" are not clear-cut and that there is more fluidity and change over time in sexual orientation than had previously been thought.

In ordinary research, limited generalizations may be made from nonrepresentative samples if proper caution is taken. Because most research has focused on predominately white lesbian and gay male samples, we can be relatively comfortable describing this population, although noting that these volunteer samples tend to be better educated and more affluent than their age group as a whole (which does not imply that this is true for gay men and lesbians in general, because this is not a representative sample). Obvious biases, such as samples from gay bars or from GLBT community organizations, are typically noted. Clearly, however, such samples cannot be generalized to lesbians and gay men of color or to bisexual men or women; urban samples also cannot be generalized to rural groups, youthful samples to older adults, and so on.

Unless truly representative samples are used we cannot claim certainty regarding the proportion of respondents manifesting various characteristics. For example, we do not know how many gay men have children or how many lesbians are living in committed relationships with another woman. We do not know how many parents accept their son's or daughter's sexual orientation or whether bisexual men and women are more likely to be divorced than heterosexual men and women. Recently, however, survey researchers have developed techniques for representative sampling (e.g., using telephone surveys that inquire about sexual orientation and related themes).

Although problems exist, if limitations are specified, it may now become possible to describe some characteristics of the lesbian, gay male, and bisexual populations (cf. Herek and Capitanio 1999a, 1999b; Laumann, Gagnon, Michael, and Michaels 1994). For example, the General Social Survey has included questions on sexual behavior since 1988; it indicates that 5.6 percent of adults report bisexual behavior since the age of eighteen (Smith 1991). On the National Health and Social Life Survey, only 0.5 percent of women and 0.8 percent of men self-identified as bisexual (Laumann et al. 1994). The proportion identifying as lesbian and gay is 1.4 percent and 2.8 percent, respectively (Laumann et al. 1994).

Moreover, it is important that research be replicated before it is accepted with confidence. A study by Kolodny, Masters, Hendryx, and Toro (1971) showed that testosterone levels were lower in gay men than in heterosexual controls; this was not found in a careful replication study (Sanders, Bain, and Langevin 1985). Similarly, research by Gladue, Green, and Hellman (1984) that showed different gonadotropic hormone response in homosexual and heterosexual men was not replicated in a later study (Hendricks, Graber, and Rodriguez-Sierra 1989). More recent research on sexual orientation differences in brain structure or hearing abilities have not been replicated by independent studies, and so they are difficult to interpret.

An additional problem is that past research studies often included people with some heterosexual experience in the "homosexual" sample and rarely distinguished bisexuals as a distinct group. In that sense, as MacDonald (1983) and others have noted, "a little bit of lavender" — that is, a little same-gender sexual experience — can make an individual homosexual for research purposes.

We must be cautious, therefore, about placing either too little or too much confidence in the research on which we rely. Many findings have been replicated to a large extent in other studies and appear to be robust. However, most topics would benefit from additional research with different samples.

Sexual Orientation Is an Important Psychological Variable

Sexual orientation, similar to gender, age, race, and ethnicity, is an important psychological variable. The determinants of sexual orientation reflect a complex interaction of biology, culture, history, and psychosocial influences. The mix is unlikely to be identical for different individuals (Richardson 1987). The result is a mosaic of diversity in lifestyle, behavior, and adaptation.

Gender, economic, and class differences, chronological age, ethnic and racial variation, and whether one is a parent are among other relevant dimensions of diversity in gay, bisexual, and lesbian lives.

Several characteristics stand out for gay male, lesbian, and bisexual people within the context of Western society. These include the following:

1. Gay men, lesbians, and bisexual individuals discover their sexual orientation at a relatively late point in the process of identity development, often at the time sexual desire begins to be recognized. It is not recognized or acknowledged from birth but is an *achieved* instead of an *ascribed* status (cf. M. S. Weinberg and Williams 1974:288). Often there is a time lag between the discovery and owning of one's identity.

2. Sexual orientation is multiply determined by many influences. No single factor reliably predicts whether a man or woman is embarked on a path toward heterosexuality, homosexuality, bisexuality, or some other pattern. Moreover, there are multiple developmental pathways that lead to common outcomes (Diamond and Savin-Williams 2000; Savin-Williams and Diamond 2000). In contemporary society, the assertion that one is heterosexual, bisexual, or gay/lesbian may be based on quite diverse and nonlinear developmental patterns and trajectories. In addition, knowing that someone labels oneself as heterosexual, gay/lesbian, or bisexual does not necessarily inform us about the pattern of their life experiences or the nature of their current erotic thoughts and feelings (Peplau and Garnets 2000).

3. Lesbians, gay men, and bisexual women and men learn negative attitudes about homosexuality, bisexuality, gay men, lesbians, and bisexuals from others (both significant others and conventional society); do not imagine that such negative attitudes could apply to them; and then learn that they do indeed apply.

4. Because families of lesbians, gay men, and bisexuals typically are heterosexual, they do not provide useful role models for normal transitions and developmental periods of gay male, lesbian, and bisexual individuals' lives.

5. Family disruption often results when a gay, lesbian, or bisexual sexual orientation is revealed. Moreover, it may be revealed in different ways: by conscious decision, positive transition (a new relationship or the birth of a grandchild), or some negative circumstance (e.g., arrest, divorce, illness, or being outed by someone else).

6. Because lesbians, gay men, and bisexuals are diverse and the majority are not easily identifiable, most move in and out of gay/bisexual and straight identities, and many hide their sexual orientation from public view. In ad-

dition, they may be assumed to be gay/bisexual or not gay/bisexual as roles shift during the day or week, and often they are treated as if they were heterosexual.

7. Even when gay men, lesbians, and bisexuals are open about their sexual orientation, they do not automatically invalidate stereotypes about them because each individual can be discounted as an exception to the general pattern.

8. The lesbian, gay male, and bisexual community encompasses diversity in terms of gender, race, ethnicity, age, socioeconomic status, relationship status, parenthood, health, disabilities, politics, and sexual behavior. For many lesbians, gay men, and bisexuals, this community may introduce them to greater social diversity than they had experienced before coming out as gay or bisexual. Individuals who are both ethnic and sexual minorities may encounter sexual prejudice from both mainstream society, from their own racial/ethnic communities, and from the predominant Anglo gay, lesbian, and bisexual communities (Greene 2000; Rust 1996).

9. Gay, lesbian, and bisexual people have had little awareness of any community history until relatively recently. Although the gay, lesbian, and bisexual community has a history, it is not passed on through family traditions. Therefore few clear road maps exist, and each person tends to be an individual creation. The absence of expectations about positive gay, bisexual, and lesbian roles in society may lead to greater potential for innovation and for creating new and different norms. Brown (1989) termed this process *normative creativity*: "Lacking clear rules about how to be lesbian and gay in the world, we have made the rules as we go along" (p. 451).

10. Gay men, lesbians, and bisexuals are often encouraged or permitted by their deviance from accepted norms to explore androgynous gender role behavior, independence, self-reliance, and educational and occupational options.

11. Lesbians, gay men, and bisexual people raise issues that some members of the public may find potentially threatening, such as: (a) anyone can be gay or bisexual (stereotypes are inaccurate predictors); (b) same-sex sexual fantasies can be explored (everyone is not 100 percent heterosexual all the time); and (c) relationships and sexual relations need not be based on gender role constraints.

12. The experiences of gay men, lesbians, and bisexuals must be understood in the context of widespread prejudice against sexual minorities in our society. Bisexual men and women may encounter negative attitudes from both heterosexuals and homosexuals. This form of prejudice toward bisex-

uals is called monosexism (Ochs 1990). On the one hand, they may be seen as trying to avoid the stigma of being homosexual; on the other hand, they may be viewed as being less normal than a heterosexual. Similarly, individuals who are both ethnic and sexual minorities may encounter sexual prejudice from both mainstream society and from their own racial/ethnic communities (Rust 1996; Savin-Williams 1996).

In conclusion, for many different reasons, gay male, lesbian, and bisexual sexual orientations are important characteristics within the context of American culture at the present time. They represent complex psychosocial factors that affect heterosexuals as well as gay and bisexual men and women.

Historical Context: Changing Definitions of Sexual Orientation

Since the nineteenth century, the meaning of homosexuality has evolved from a purely sexual act to a personal identity (Foucault 1979; Hart and Richardson 1981; Weeks 1977; Weinberg 1983). Thus in American culture, as Herek has stated, "what a person *does* sexually defines who the person *is*" (Herek 1986:568). The social forces that have transformed the awareness and conditions of gay and lesbian life, in part through the homophile rights movement, to produce a greater recognition of group identity have been documented by social historians (Adam 1987; Altman 1981; Chauncey 1994; D'Emilio 1983, Loughery 1998). In addition, the feminist movement changed women's ideas about sexuality in general, raised questions about traditional gender roles, and reduced stigma surrounding lesbianism; this led to visible communities based on lesbian-feminist ideology (Faderman 1984; Krieger 1982; Lockard 1985).

The reconstruction of the meaning of homosexuality in Western history has represented a paradigm shift from an illness model to a minority group status. Today this minority group is seen as an aspect of human diversity and one that offers potential advantages. For example, when one "comes out" one also may "come in" to a community and be able to identify with a larger group of lesbian, bisexual, and gay people (Petrow 1990). Some observers are even holding up gay and lesbian relationships as a model of "peer marriage" suitable for other dual career couples (Schwartz 1994).

This paradigm shift suggests that to understand sexual orientation one must consider the historical period, cultural context, and social structure.

Several themes during the last decade of the twentieth century illustrate the importance of the historical context.

First, many prominent people have come out as gay, lesbian, or bisexual — sometimes as the result of the HIV/AIDS epidemic — and this has put a personal face on issues of sexual orientation. Sports, politics, and media have each contributed famous persons to this cause. The right-wing movement to oppose "gay rights" has also brought out many persons who would not stand for this intolerance and denial of civil rights. In Colorado, Oregon, California, and Maine neighbors, friends, and community leaders have become public about their sexual orientation or their support of civil rights as an ally. Moreover, the Clinton administration appointed a broad diversity of citizens to positions of power and prominence in the federal government, including open lesbians and gay men. One of President Bush's first appointments was an openly gay man to direct the office of AIDS research.

Second, every major social institution in our society — from organized religion to the military, including the workplace, government, the courts, and schools — have been challenged to rethink long-standing beliefs and policies concerning sexual behavior and sexual orientation. In particular, issues involving marriage, parenting, discrimination statues, and the popular media have made sexual orientation a widely discussed theme. One milestone in this process was when the U.S. Supreme Court ruled in 1996 that gay men and lesbians may not be singled out for official discrimination simply because of hostility or prejudice toward their sexual orientation (Savage 1996). This historic decision marked the first time the high court treated gay rights as a matter of civil rights. In addition, there have been signs of increasing tolerance toward gay men and lesbians, as shown, for instance, in the changing public opinion about employment discrimination. Over the past twenty years the percentage of persons in the United States endorsing equal employment for homosexuals has increased from 56 percent in 1977 to 71 percent in 1989 to 84 percent in 1998 (Berke 1998). Moreover, the growing public visibility of sexual minorities and their civil rights concerns has challenged the undisputed dominance of heterosexuality and led to increased expressions of discrimination and animosity at the institutional and personal levels (e.g., the enactment of "The Defense of Marriage Act" in 1996, which defines "marriage" for federal programs as a legal union between a man and a woman; this act also allows states the right not to recognize same-sex marriages performed in other states).

Third, Matthew Shepherd's death, the response of the media and many politicians to it, the role his mother played as an advocate of change in antigay ideologies, and his symbolic role as biblical-like martyr has made homophobia as unacceptable as racism or anti-Semitism. The murder of gay men in the armed services by fellow servicemen, the "don't ask, don't tell" policy of the military, the legal fight one lesbian had to wage to gain the right to oversee the medical care of her disabled female partner, and the Supreme Court case of the Boy Scout's ability to discriminate against openly gay leaders have raised the level of public awareness to the multiple levels of discrimination and intolerance in the United States.

Fourth, the decision by the Hawaii supreme court that laws banning same-sex marriages are a manifestation of gender discrimination, the enactment by Vermont of a "civil union" as equal to heterosexual marriage, and the emergence of gay and lesbian parenthood as a mainstream phenomenon have potentially altered the relationship of same-gender couples with the broader institutions of society. Only time will tell if these changes are permanent or are only a temporary window of opportunity. For reasons not well understood, some people feel they are threatened either personally or as a group by these changes. Similar attitudes also have impeded progress in racial attitudes and religious tolerance.

Finally, the attention of lesbian, gay, bisexual, and transgender communities has focused on the concerns of young people, especially those in school, pointing out antigay/lesbian harassment as a component of a general climate of violence and hostility and the lack of acceptance of diversity (Gainor 2000). For example, there have been heated debates about including gay and lesbian examples in diversity education in elementary and secondary schools, the access to student clubs such as the "gay-straight alliance," and the emergence of a national organization known as the Gay, Lesbian, and Straight Education Network (GLSEN). In addition, midlife issues have received more attention — both in terms of families rearing children and persons facing age-biased views and obstacles. Greater attention has also been focused on the needs of older persons, and retirement and long-term care facilities have begun to emerge.

Conclusions

The psychological study of lesbian, gay male, and bisexual issues has explored the ramifications of the social significance attributed to sexual orientation. Although homosexuality is no longer considered a form of mental illness, considerable attention has been given to a wide range of factors thought to predispose individuals to homosexuality. Nonetheless, today no more is known about the specific origins of sexual orientation than is known about the origins of other characteristics such as expertise in ballet, chess, or the violin. The best conclusion is that a complex set of factors interact, varying from individual to individual, to produce lesbian, gay, and bisexual adults. Likewise, the gay male, lesbian, and bisexual community is diverse and multiethnic and differs by gender and socioeconomic status, and few generalizations apply across cultural borders.

We have discussed the relevance of sexual orientation to new paradigms to conceptualize and define sexual orientation, limitations, and caveats of psychological research on sexual orientation, why it is an important variable in the psychological understanding of people, and historical perspectives. In concluding, we call attention to the salient issues for psychology in terms of practice, research, and public policy.

Sexual orientation and mental health practice has progressed through three distinct waves. Before the early 1970s the prevailing approach was an illness model of homosexuality — that is, heterosexuals were viewed as normal and mentally healthy; sexual minorities were seen as abnormal and psychologically impaired.

After the mental health professions rejected that model an affirmative approach emerged within psychology to guide practice. The affirmative model in psychology focuses on helping gay men, lesbians, and bisexuals to cope adaptively with the impact of stigma, minority status, and difference from the heterosexual mainstream. This second wave assisted gay men, lesbians, and bisexuals in understanding and accepting their sexual orientation as a natural part of themselves, helped them to develop strategies for coping and forming a positive sense of identity, and taught them the effect of negative social attitudes, prejudice, discrimination, and heterosexism on psychological functioning.

A third wave has now emerged and several themes are evident. A minority stress model is used to understand psychological well-being among lesbians, gay men, and bisexuals. Specifically, this model posits that lesbians, gay men, and bisexuals may be at increased risk for mental distress because of exposure to stressors related to social antigay attitudes. There has also been increased attention to understanding psychological resilience and the ways in which lesbians, gay men, and bisexuals successfully cope with stress and stigma. In addition, assertiveness as a positive psychological process is demonstrated by different aspects of coming out as a lesbian, gay man, or bisexual: identity commitment, identity disclosure, and community involvement (Herek 2000).

In this third wave, greater attention has been placed on ensuring that gay/ lesbian/bisexual affirmative concepts are more fully integrated into current personality theories and therapeutic approaches. Education, training, ethical and professional guidelines, and research are used to reduce bias in theories and practice. The promotion and dissemination of empirical testing of gay/ lesbian/bisexual affirmative modes and theories has been emphasized.

Finally, this third wave has also seen a shifting away from viewing sexual orientation from within a heterosexually dominated psychology. The result has been a defining of norms and terms based on lesbian, gay, and bisexual realities. This has led to an examination of the ways that gay, lesbian, and bisexual paradigms help to inform and reconceptualize broader psychological issues of sexuality, gender roles, identity, intimacy, family relationships, and life span development.

Psychological research has likewise shifted from removing the stigma of pathology from lesbians, gay men, and bisexuals to examining issues of implicit concern to them. Five major themes have emerged:

1. Research on mental health has documented that gay men, lesbians, and bisexuals, as individuals, couples, and a social community, do not show lower levels of adjustment than heterosexuals. Moreover, research has focused on the nature and impact of negative social attitudes toward lesbians, gay men, and bisexuals and has documented the pervasive effects of heterosexist bias and sexual prejudice within American society.

2. Research has shifted from viewing homosexuals as a group with definite characteristics to a recognition of the diversity that exists among lesbians and gay men. This view has led to an increased awareness of the similarity between heterosexuals and homosexuals, on the one hand, and, on the other, has called attention to the effects of gender, ethnicity, race, age, socioeconomic status, geographic locale, and lifestyle on salient characteristics of gay men, lesbians, and bisexuals.

3. Theoretical perspectives on homosexuality have shifted from attention to an illness model that emphasized origins and treatment to an affirmative model that examines how gay men and lesbians form and maintain their identity and manage ordinary problems of life span development.

4. The view that sexual orientation is an inherent characteristic of an individual has been broadened to include the role of social and historical influences in shaping the meaning and expression of homosexuality.

5. The relationship between gender roles and sexual orientation has received great attention. Research has indicated that gender is a central or-

ganizing factor for heterosexuals, lesbians, and gay men in personal experiences, values, and relationship styles.

New ways of conceptualizing sexual orientation and new empirical findings have had important implications for public policy in the arena of sexual orientation. Organized psychology has had an important role in making possible a public discourse which assumes that gay and bisexual people are normal and healthy and should therefore be treated equally and with respect. The APA has influenced public policy by participating with other professional organizations in a research and demonstration project on healthy, lesbian, gay, and bisexual students (Smith 2001); by disseminating social science research that demonstrates that same-gender sexual orientation is not pathological; and by educating other professionals and the public about the reality of gay, lesbian, and bisexual lives.

Finally, the importance of understanding sexual orientation for heterosexuals has become apparent. Social policy, legislative deliberations, and judicial decisions have increasingly recognized the legitimacy of gay male, lesbian, and bisexual issues, often encouraged by psychological research and perspectives. Moreover, all people can benefit from acknowledging the restrictive constraint of heterosexist bias that limits behavior to rigid gender roles, requires 100 percent heterosexuality, and defines one's value as a man or a woman by one's rejection of homosexuality. In particular, lesbians, gay men, and bisexuals can continue to make a contribution to a greater appreciation of human diversity and the benefits that result from examining predetermined constraints that limit the fulfillment of one's unique potential.

References

Adam, B. 1987. *The rise of a gay and lesbian movement*. Boston: Twayne.
Altman, D. 1981. *Coming out in the seventies*. Boston: Alyson.
American Psychological Association (APA) Committee on Lesbian and Gay Concerns. 1990. *Final Report of the Task Force on Bias in Psychotherapy with Lesbians and Gay Men*. Washington, D.C.: Author.
Backer, T. E., W. F. Batchelor, J. M. Jones, and V. M. Mays. 1988. Introduction to the special issue: Psychology and AIDS. *American Psychologist* 43:835–36.
Baumeister, R. F. 2000. Gender differences in erotic plasticity: The female sex drive as socially flexible and responsive. *Psychological Bulletin* 126:347–74.
Bayer, R. 1981. *Homosexuality and American Psychiatry: The Politics of Diagnosis*. New York: Basic Books.

Bennett, K. 1992. Feminist bisexuality: A both/and option for an either/or world. In E. R. Weise, ed., *Closer to Home: Bisexuality and Feminism*, pp. 205–31. Seattle, Wash.: Seal Press.

Berke, R. L. 1998. Chasing the polls on gay rights. The *New York Times*, August 2, WK3.

Bersoff, D. N., and D. W. Ogden. 1991. APA amicus curiae briefs furthering lesbian and gay male civil rights. *American Psychologist* 46(9):950–56.

Blackwood, E. 2000. Culture and women's sexualities. *Journal of Social Issues* 56(2):223–38.

Blackwood, E., and S. E. Wieringa. 1999. *Female Desires: Same-Sex Relations and Transgender Practices Across Cultures.* New York: Columbia University Press.

Bohan, J. S. 1996. *Psychology and Sexual Orientation.* New York: Routledge.

Brown, L. S. 1989. New voices, new visions: Toward a lesbian/gay paradigm for psychology. *Psychology of Women* 13:445–58.

Chancey, G. 1994. *Gay New York: Gender, Urban Culture, and the Making of the Gay Male World, 1890–1940.* New York: Basic Books.

Conger, J. J. 1975. Proceedings of the American Psychological Association, Incorporated, for the year 1974: Minutes of the annual meeting of the Council of Representatives. *American Psychologist* 30:620–51.

Diamant, A. L., M. A. Schuster, K. McGuigan, and J. Lever. 1999. Lesbians' sexual history with men. *Archives of Internal Medicine* 159:2730–36.

D'Emilio, J. 1983. *Sexual Politics, Sexual Communities: The Making of a Homosexual Minority in the United States, 1940–1970.* Chicago: University of Chicago Press.

Diamond, L. M. 1998. Development of sexual orientation among adolescent and young women. *Developmental Psychology* 34:1085–95.

Diamond, L. M., and R. C. Savin-Williams. 2000. Explaining diversity in the development of same-sex sexuality among young women. *Journal of Social Issues* 56(2):297–313.

Faderman, L. 1984. The "new gay" lesbian. *Journal of Homosexuality* 10(3–4):85–95.

Foucault, M. 1979. *The History of Sexuality.* London: Allen Lane.

Ford, C. S., and F. Beach. 1951. *Patterns of Sexual Behavior.* New York: Harper.

Gainor, K. A. 2000. Including transgender issues in lesbian, gay, and bisexual psychology: Implications for practice and training. In B. Greene and G. L. Croom, eds., *Education, Research, and Practice in Lesbian, Gay, Bisexual, and Transgendered Psychology*, pp. 131–60. Thousand Oaks, Calif.: Sage.

Garnets, L. D., and D.C. Kimmel. 1991. Lesbian and gay male dimensions in the psychological study of human diversity. In J. Goodchilds, ed., *Psychological Perspectives on Human Diversity in America*, pp. 137–92. Washington, D.C.: American Psychological Association.

Garnets, L., G. M. Herek, and B. Levy. 1990. Violence and victimization of lesbians and gay men: Mental health consequences. *Journal of Interpersonal Violence* 5:366–83.

Garnets, L. D., and L. A. Peplau. 2000. Understanding women's sexualities and sexual orientations. *Journal of Social Issues* 56(2):181–92.

Gladue, B. A., R. Green, and R. E. Hellman. 1984. Neuroendocrine response to estrogen and sexual orientation. *Science* 225:1496–99.

Greenberg, D. F. 1988. *The Construction of Homosexuality*. Chicago: University of Chicago Press.

Greene, B. 2000. Beyond heterosexism and across the cultural divide: Developing an inclusive lesbian, gay, and bisexual psychology: A look to the future. In B. Greene and G. L. Croom, eds., *Education, Research, and Practice in Lesbian, Gay, Bisexual, and Transgendered Psychology*, pp. 1–45. Thousand Oaks, Calif.: Sage.

Hart, J., and D. Richardson, eds. 1981. *The Theory and Practice of Homosexuality*. London: Routledge and Kegan Paul.

Hendricks, S. E., B. Graber, and J. F. Rodriguez-Sierra. 1989. Neuroendocrine responses to exogenous estrogen: No differences between heterosexual and homosexual men. *Psychoneuroendocrinology* 14:177–85.

Herek, G. M. 1986. On heterosexual masculinity: Some psychical consequences of the social construction of gender and sexuality. *American Behavioral Scientist* 29:563–77.

Herek, G. M. 1991. Stigma, prejudice, and violence against lesbians and gay men. In J. C. Gonsiorek and J. D. Weinrich, eds., *Homosexuality: Research Findings for Public Policy*, pp. 60–80. Newbury Park, Calif.: Sage.

Herek, G. M., ed. 1999. AIDS and stigma in the United States. *American Behavioral Scientist* 42(whole no. 7):1101–1243.

Herek, G. M., and J. P. Capitanio. 1999a. Sex differences in how heterosexuals think about lesbians and gay men: Evidence from survey context effects. *Journal of Sex Research* 36:348–60.

Herek, G. M., and J. P. Capitanio. 1999b. AIDS stigma and sexual prejudice. *American Behavioral Scientist* 42:1126–43.

Hooker, E. 1957. The adjustment of the male overt homosexual. *Journal of Projective Techniques* 21:18–31.

Kimmel, D.C. 1978. Adult development and aging: A gay perspective. *Journal of Social Issues* 34(3):113–30.

Kinsey, A. C., W. B. Pomeroy, and C. E. Martin. 1948. *Sexual Behavior in the Human Male*. Philadelphia: Saunders.

Kinsey, A. C., W. B. Pomeroy, C. E. Martin, and P. H. Gebhard. 1953. *Sexual Behavior in the Human Female*. Philadelphia: Saunders.

Kolodny, R. C., W. H. Masters, J. Hendryx, and G. Toro. 1971. Plasma testosterone and semen analysis in male homosexuals. *New England Journal of Medicine* 285:1170–74.

Kooden, H. D., S. R. Morin, D. I. Riddle, M. Rogers, B. E. Sang, and F. Strass-
    burger. 1979. *Removing the Stigma: Final Report of the Board of Social and
    Ethical Responsibility for Psychology's Task Force on the Status of Lesbian
    and Gay Male Psychologists*. Washington, D.C.: American Psychological
    Association.

Krieger, S. 1982. Lesbian identity and community: Recent social science literature.
    Signs 8:91–108.

Larsen, P. C. 1982. Gay male relationships. In W. Paul, J. D. Weinrich, J. C.
    Gonsiorek, and M. E. Hotvedt, eds., *Homosexuality: Social, Psychological, and
    Biological Issues*, pp. 219–32. Beverly Hills, Calif.: Sage.

Laumann, E. O., J. H. Gagnon, R. T. Michael, and S. Michaels. 1994. *The Social
    Organization of Sexuality: Sexual Practices in the United States*. Chicago: Uni-
    versity of Chicago Press.

Lockard, D. 1985. The lesbian community: An anthropological approach. *Journal
    of Homosexuality* 11(3–4):83–95.

Loughery, J. 1998. *The Other Side of Silence: Men's Lives and Gay Identities: A
    Twentieth Century History*. New York: Holt.

MacDonald, A. P., Jr. 1983. A little bit of lavender goes a long way: A critique of
    research on sexual orientation. *Journal of Sex Research* 19:94–100.

Masters, W. H., and V. E. Johnson. 1979. *Homosexuality in Perspective*. Boston: Lit-
    tle, Brown.

Melton, G. B. 1989. Public policy and private prejudice: Psychology and law on gay
    rights. *American Psychologist* 44:933–40.

Money, J. 1988. *Gay, Straight, and In-Between: The Sexology of Erotic Orientation*.
    New York: Oxford University Press.

Morin, S. 1977. Heterosexual bias in psychological research on lesbianism and male
    homosexuality. *American Psychologist* 32:629–37.

Ochs, R. 1996. Biphobia: It goes more than two ways. In B. Firestein, ed., *Bisexuality:
    The Psychology and Politics of an Invisible Minority*, pp. 217–39. Thousand
    Oaks, Calif.: Sage.

Ogden, D. W., M. F. Ewing, and D. N. Bersoff. 1986. *In the Supreme Court of the
    United States: Michael J Bowers, Attorney General of Georgia v. Michael
    Hardwick, and John and Mary Doe*. Brief of amici curiae. American Psycho-
    logical Association and American Public Health Association in Support of
    Respondents (nos. 85–140).

Patterson, C. J., and R. E. Redding. 1996. Lesbian and gay families with children:
    Implications of social science research for policy. *Journal of Social Issues*
    52(2):29–50.

Peplau, L. A., and L. D. Garnets. 2000. A new paradigm for understanding women's
    sexuality and sexual orientation. *Journal of Social Issues* 56(2):329–50.

Peplau, L. A., L. R. Spalding, T. D. Conley, and R. C. Veniegas. 1999. The develop-
    ment of sexual orientation in women. *Annual Review of Sex Research* 10:70–99.

Petrow, S. 1990. Together wherever we go. *The Advocate*, May, pp. 42–44.

Richardson, D. 1987. Recent challenges to traditional assumptions about homosexuality: Some implications for practice. *Journal of Homosexuality* 13(4):1–12.

Ross, M. W. 1987. A theory of normal homosexuality. In L. Diamant, ed., *Male and Female Homosexuality: Psychological Approaches*, pp. 237–59. Washington, D.C.: Hemisphere.

Rothblum, E. D. 2000. Sexual orientation and sex in women's lives: Conceptual and methodological issues. *Journal of Social Issues* 56(2):193–204.

Rust, P. C. 1992. The politics of sexual identity: Sexual attraction and behavior among lesbian and bisexual women. *Social Problems* 39:366–86.

Rust, P. C. 1996. Managing multiple identities: Diversity among bisexual men and women. In B. Firestein, ed., *Bisexuality: The Psychology and Politics of an Invisible Minority*, pp. 53–83. Thousand Oaks, Calif.: Sage.

Rust, P. C. 2000. Bisexuality: A contemporary paradox for women. *Journal of Social Issues* 56(2):205–21.

Sanders, R. M., J. Bain, and R. Langevin. 1985. Peripheral sex hormones, homosexuality, and gender identity. In R. Langevin, ed., *Erotic Preference, Gender Identity, and Aggression in Men: New Research Studies*, pp. 227–47. Hillsdale, N.J.: Erlbaum.

Savage, D. G. 1996. Supreme Court strikes down law targeting gays. *Los Angeles Times*, May 21, A1, A14.

Savin-Williams, R. C., and L. M. Diamond. 2000. Sexual identity trajectories among sexual-minority youths: Gender comparisons. *Archives of Sexual Behavior* 24:419–40.

Schwartz, P. 1994. *Peer Marriage: How Love Between Equals Really Works*. New York: The Free Press.

Shively, M. G., and J. P. DeCecco. 1977. Components of sexual identity. *Journal of Homosexuality* 3(1):41–48.

Smith, T. W. 1991. Adult sexual behavior in 1989: Number of partners, frequency of intercourse, and risk of AIDS. *Family Planning Perspectives* 23(3):102–7.

Smith, P. L. 2000. *In the Supreme Court of the United States: Boy Scouts of America and Monmouth council, Boy Scouts of America, Petitioners, v. James Dale*. Brief of amici curiae.

Smith, D. 2001. Assessing the needs of lesbian, gay, and bisexual youth. *APA Monitor on Psychology* 32(8):42–43.

Watters, A. T. 1986. Heterosexual bias in psychological research on lesbianism and male homosexuality (1979–1983), utilizing the bibliographic and taxonomic system of Morin. 1977. *Journal of Homosexuality* 13(1):35–58.

Weeks, J. 1977. *Coming Out: Homosexual Politics in Britain from the Nineteenth Century to the Present*. London: Quartet.

Weinberg, M. S., and C. Williams. 1974. *Male Homosexuals: Their Problems and Adaptations*. New York. Oxford University Press.

Weinberg, M. S., C. J. Williams, and D. W. Pryor. 1994. *Dual Attraction: Understanding Bisexuality*. New York: Oxford University Press.

Weinberg, T. S. 1983. *Gay Men, Gay Selves: The Social Construction of Homosexual Identities*. New York: Irvington.

Weinrich, J., and W. L. Williams. 1991. Strange customs, familiar lives: Homosexualities in other cultures. In J. C. Gonsiorek and J. D. Weinrich, eds., *Homosexuality: Research Findings for Public Policy*, pp. 44–59. Newbury Park, Calif.: Sage.

Part I

The Meaning of Sexual Orientation

Affectional, erotic, and sexual orientation can be understood only within the social milieu in which the individual is embedded at a particular historical moment. Sociohistorical changes have transformed the meaning of homosexuality from its medical classification in 1869 by Benkert as one of many forms of sexual perversion (Plummer 1984). Fifty years ago it was conceptualized as a minority status in Donald Webster Cory's 1951 book, *Homosexual in America* (Kameny 1971). More recently it has begun to be seen as a characteristic that defines a diverse, multiethnic, and multiracial community not only with a history but also with shared political and social concerns.

As a result of political activism and accumulating empirical evidence that failed to link homosexuality with mental illness or emotional instability (e.g., Hooker 1957), the American Psychiatric Association voted to remove homosexuality from the list of mental illnesses in 1973 (Bayer 1981). At the same time, a lesbian/gay affirmative approach in psychology emerged that promoted the view that same-gender sexual orientation is a natural variant in the expression of normal erotic attractions and emotional commitment (Gonsiorek 1988). Minority sexual orientations, no longer deemed an illness and expanded to include bisexuality, are now studied by psychologists to understand the characteristics, strengths, and problems of living associated with being lesbian, gay, or bisexual in a nonsupportive or hostile society.

The first selection describes these significant changes through a personal biography of Evelyn Hooker, the psychologist who conducted a pioneering empirical study finding that homosexuals were not mentally ill.

As long as sexual orientation is treated in our society as a dimension that overwhelms all other characteristics of the individual, the causes of this condition will be of concern. To date, it has been possible only to reframe the issue from a focus on the causes of homosexuality to the origins of sexual orientation in general. Even so, bisexual orientation has received little serious attention, and often persons with some homosexual erotic imagery or behavior are combined with the more exclusively homosexual sample.

The nature and origin of sexual orientation may be viewed within three major differing theoretical frameworks: essentialist, social constructionist, and interactionist. The *essentialist* view is that sexual orientation represents an inherent, immutable characteristic of an individual. Homosexuality, heterosexuality, or bisexuality are considered universal characteristics of human experience that have always existed across history and cultures. For example, a major contemporary view of sexual orientation development is that it reflects some sort of inborn predisposition to learn sexual-erotic responses and key experiences at critical times in development (Money 1988). A parallel with language development may be apt, because erotic feelings can operate as a kind of encoded language of sexuality and intimacy that frames the ways these experiences are conceptualized. Moreover, like language, more than one sexual orientation could be mastered.

In contrast to the essentialist view, the second perspective is that sexual orientation is a product of *social construction*; that is, regardless of the origin of one's sexual and affectional preferences, it is the social meaning attached to them that is critical. According to this view, sexual orientation is a product of particular historical and cultural understandings. Different societies organize human sexual relations in a variety of ways, and therefore the meaning of sexual orientation is specific to particular cultures. Moreover, an individual's sexual orientation is a concept of importance only because it was created by certain societies and emphasized by the social norms and values held by dominant groups in those societies. As Bohan (1996) explained: "If the culture did not define identity by the sex of one's partner, neither would we define ourselves in that manner" (p. xvi).

Some scientists have proposed a third approach to sexual orientation, the *interactionist* perspective, which would be a middle ground between the other two perspectives. It would combine elements of both the essentialist and constructionist views and focus on the process by which they interact. Herek (1994) noted:

Although this interactionist perspective has not yet been stated in a definitive form, its general assumption is that commonalities exist among cultures in patterns of sexual behavior and attraction: these commonalities have a biological basis to at least some extent. At the same time, the meanings associated with these patterns are acknowledged to vary widely among cultures, and the differences must be understood to recognize which aspects of human sexuality are universal and which are culturally specific. (p. 154)

The selection by Bailey on biological aspects of sexual orientation examines some of the most controversial elements of the essentialist perspective. Are there physical or genetic differences between homosexuals and heterosexuals? Does homosexuality occur more often in the families of gay men or lesbians? He helps us to understand the complex science involved in these studies that often make front-page news.

Bisexuals are a group that appears to be less restricted by gender in their sexual and affectional attractions than either homosexuals or heterosexuals; further, their development of sexual orientation appears to differ from that of gay men and lesbians. For example, an early study by Bell, Weinberg, and Hammersmith (1981) found that, unlike gay men, bisexual males tended not to report feeling sexually different in childhood; both male and female bisexuals were less likely to have established their adult sexual preference by age nineteen, and they were more likely to have been influenced by sexual learning than were lesbians and gay men. Moreover, some bisexual women and men are attracted to persons of both genders, attending more to the characteristics of the person than to his or her gender. Others are sequential bisexuals who alternate same- and other-gender affectional and sexual relationships (Blumstein and Schwartz 1977; Money 1988).

Another early study (Masters and Johnson 1979) provided interesting information about the interaction of gender and sexuality for persons they called "ambisexuals"; their study restricted the sample to those men and women who had equal sexual attraction to women and men and who reported no interest in a continuing emotional relationship with a partner. This atypical sample was paired with homosexual and heterosexual assigned partners and observed while engaging in assigned sexual interactions. No differences in physical sexual response were found among the ambisexual men and women between their heterosexual and homosexual experiences. Moreover, the patterns were similar to those displayed by the homosexual and heterosexual couples in other phases of the research. However, the procedure provided a fascinating laboratory for the study of gender differences in sexual behavior. For example, the same ambisexual men moved more quickly toward orgasm with heterosexual female partners than with homosexual male partners. Similarly, the same ambisexual women engaged in mutual "my turn, your turn" sexual interaction with homosexual female partners, but let the heterosexual male partners "set the pace throughout the entire sexual interaction" (p. 169). These sexual patterns were similar to those of gay men and lesbians in another part of the study with partners of the same gender and were similar to the pattern of heterosexuals with partners of the other gender.

The complex realities of bisexual lives have become better known since these early studies (Firestein 1996; Rust 2000; Weinberg, Williams, and Pryor 1994). In the 1990s gay and lesbian organizations welcomed bisexuals and often changed their name to indicate their inclusion. The selection by Fox summarizes the significant changes that have taken place and outlines several important research findings.

A new paradigm in understanding the meanings of sexual orientations and sexualities is emerging. This paradigm conceptualizes sexual orientations along a continuum similar to a spectrum of colors as in a rainbow, emphasizes that sexual orientation is multiply determined, and recognizes the highly individualized and personal process of arriving at a sexual identity for each person (Garnets 2001; Peplau and Garnets 2000). The selection by Diamond and Savin-Williams provides empirical support for this new paradigm by describing the diversity of same-sex attraction and variations of bisexuality among young women.

Western culture has made sexual orientation a major social concern. Perhaps this will change. Only a few decades ago (1967) the Supreme Court struck down laws that forbid interracial marriages. Before that time, persons who fell in love with someone of the wrong socially defined race were stigmatized in ways similar to that of bisexuals, lesbians, and gay men today who fall in love with persons of the same gender.

Contemporary Issue: Debate Concerning the Extent of Choice versus No Choice in the Nature of Sexual Orientation

Whether sexual orientation is, in some sense, as fixed and immutable as race, gender, and eye or hair color is of considerable interest in the political debate about the meaning of sexual orientation. The debate centers on the fact that in many states sexual orientation can be the basis for legal discrimination.

The no-choice position is that if sexual orientation is determined, perhaps as some essential part of oneself such as one's race, then civil rights protections would be granted more readily. In contrast, persons who believe sexual orientation is a matter of choice imply that people have voluntarily chosen to subject themselves to stigma and oppression and therefore do not require legal protections, since they could choose to conform to the majority position. Likewise, some religious leaders believe that homosexuality is a sinful behavior that can be changed through some kind of religious practice.

Conversely, if homosexuality is linked to a gene or seen as a "congenital physical disability" that may lead to corrective interventions, then the no-choice position could be used to stigmatize sexual minorities:

> Some people fear that biological research will be used to harm sexual minorities, as in the case of selective abortions. Some people are concerned about increased pressures for gay individuals to interpret their personal life experiences in biological terms, perpetuating the dichotomization of sexual orientation as homosexual versus heterosexual. Still others worry that the reliance on biological explanations communicates a disempowering message. (Veniegas and Conley 2000:279)

A middle point in the debate seems not to be widely recognized (Kimmel and Weiner 1995:355; Van Gelder 1991), namely, that sexual orientation is at least as stable and no more a matter of choice than one's religion, which is a protected category with regard to civil rights in the United States; for some, sexual orientation may be as immutable as one's race, which is also a protected category.

This issue touches off more, however. For example, when a careful scientific research project finds a difference between homosexual and heterosexual men or women in some biological study, media attention focuses on the possible significance of these findings. No matter how carefully phrased, with caveats and concerns about the need to replicate the research, suddenly it is assumed that a clue to the cause of homosexuality has been found. To understand the peculiarity of this, consider instead that the research had found a similar difference between persons who were gifted violinists and those who were without musical talent. Would attention suddenly focus on the no-choice origin of musical giftedness? Obviously the underlying theme is one of heterosexist bias and its belief that if the origin of homosexuality is found, then maybe it can be cured or prevented — unlike musical gifts, which we recognize as part of the mosaic of human diversity.

A final caution is in order regarding this debate. Essentially all the studies that have proposed some biological or biochemical difference between persons with a homosexual orientation and those with a heterosexual orientation have not been replicated successfully. The media reports the findings when they are first discovered, but the lack of replication is seldom reported as prominently and often goes unnoticed.

References

Bayer, R. 1981. *Homosexuality and American Psychiatry: The Politics of Diagnosis*. New York: Basic Books.

Bell, A. P., M. S. Weinberg, and S. K. Hammersmith. 1981. *Sexual Preference*. Bloomington: Indiana University Press.

Blumstein, P. W., and P. Schwartz. 1977. Bisexuality: Some social psychological issues. *Journal of Social Issues* 33:30–45.

Bohan, J. S. 1996. *Psychology and Sexual Orientation*. New York: Routledge.

Firestein, B. A., ed. 1996. *Bisexuality: The Psychology and Politics of an Invisible Minority*. Thousand Oaks, Calif.: Sage.

Garnets, L. D. 2001. Sexual orientations in perspective. Paper presented at the American Psychological Association National Multicultural Summit II, Santa Barbara, California, January 25.

Gonsiorek, J. C. 1988. Current and future directions in gay/lesbian affirmative mental health practice. In M. Shernoff and W. A. Scott, eds., *The Sourcebook on Lesbian/Gay Health Care*, pp. 107–13. Washington D.C.: National Lesbian and Gay Health Foundation.

Herek, G. M. 1994. Homosexuality. In R. J. Corsini, ed., *Encyclopedia of Psychology*, 2nd ed., pp. 151–55. New York: Wiley.

Hooker, E. 1957. The adjustment of the male overt homosexual. *Journal of Projective Techniques* 21:18–31.

Kameny, F. E. 1971. Homosexuals as a minority group. In E. Sagarin, ed., *The Other Minorities*, pp. 50–65. Waltham, Mass.: Ginn.

Kimmel, D.C., and I. B. Weiner. 1995. *Adolescence: A Developmental Transition*, 2nd ed. New York: Wiley.

Masters, W. H., and V. E. Johnson. 1979. *Homosexuality in Perspective*. Boston: Little, Brown.

Money, J. 1988. *Gay, Straight, and In-Between: The Sexology of Erotic Orientation*. New York: Oxford University Press.

Peplau, L. A., and L. D. Garnets. 2000. A new paradigm for understanding women's sexuality and sexual orientation. *Journal of Social Issues* 56(2):329–50.

Plummer, K. 1984. Sexual diversity: A sociological perspective. In K. Howells, ed., *The Psychology of Sexual Diversity*, pp. 219–53. Oxford: Basil Blackwell.

Rust, P. C. 2000. *Bisexuality in the United States: A Social Science Reader*. New York: Columbia University Press.

Van Gelder, L. 1991. The "born that way" trap. *Ms.*, May/June, 86–87.

Veniegas, R. C., and T. D. Conley. 2000. Biological research on women's sexual orientations: Evaluating the scientific evidence. *Journal of Social Issues* 56(2):267–82.

Weinberg, M. S., C. J. Williams, and D. W. Pryor. 1994. *Dual Attraction: Understanding Bisexuality*. New York: Oxford University Press.

1   What a Light It Shed: The Life of Evelyn Hooker

Douglas C. Kimmel and Linda D. Garnets

Evelyn Gentry was born into a farm family and grew up in the hard life on the plains of Nebraska and Colorado. In 1924 she entered the University of Colorado and majored in psychology, earning a bachelor's degree in 1928 and a master's degree in 1930. In 1932 she received her Ph.D. from The Johns Hopkins University. Some years later she moved to California to recover from tuberculosis and stayed two years in a sanitarium. In 1939 she became an adjunct faculty member at the University of California at Los Angeles (UCLA), where she taught through the extension program. While she and her second husband, Edward Hooker, a Distinguished Professor of History at UCLA, fought the anticommunist loyalty-oath issue of the 1950s, Evelyn began collecting the data that would change the psychological understanding of human sexuality. After her ground-breaking paper was presented at the annual meeting of the American Psychological Association (APA) in Chicago in 1955, one member of the audience commented, "What a light it shed" (Harrison and Schmiechen 1991).

When Hooker died at her home in Los Angeles on November 18, 1996, she was surrounded by awards and tributes to her work and by persons whose lives had been directly touched by her research four decades earlier. That research changed the meaning of same-gender love from an illness to a gift. She was, in many ways, the recipient of that gift and became an "honorary homosexual."

The authors of this brief review of the life of Hooker are among the direct beneficiaries of her work. We came to discover our same-gender attractions and love when the impact of the research and writings of Hooker and other pioneers began to offer a perspective different from the pathology, illness, deviance models that were prevalent in the 1950s and 1960s. By the time we entered our careers, Alfred Kinsey, Hooker, and William Masters and Virginia Johnson were as well known to us as B. F. Skinner, Carl Rogers, Virginia Satir, and Abraham Maslow. Hooker was then in the final period of her life: one of fame, awards, and a surprising bequest, but also a period of health problems and limitations. We begin with this period of her life, for we knew her well then. Then we focus on the specific details of her life in two parts: first, as a remarkable woman of her time; second, as a psychologist who was the fore-mother of the gay liberation movement. We conclude with a discussion of the lasting legacy of her contributions to psychology.

Two Personal Reflections on the Later Years

Hooker touched people in many different ways. She cared about people and attracted a circle of friends of all ages. She was a teacher, mentor, colleague, psychotherapist, and bon vivant. She enjoyed knowing everyone as an individual who had stories to share with a good listener.

Hooker's Kitchen Cabinet

The second author (LG) first met Hooker in 1986 at the home of Nora Weckler. Hooker had been given the first Outstanding Achievement Award from the APA Committee on Lesbian and Gay Concerns. She was unable to attend the convention, so we presented the award to her in Los Angeles. I was immediately impressed with her wit, incisive comments, and astute mind. I was thrilled to be in the presence of this woman whose research had given me such hope as I was coming out in the early 1970s. We became friends over the next several years, and I often visited her at her home in Santa Monica.

I had the good fortune to meet with Hooker regularly as part of what she called her "kitchen cabinet" — a group made up of Anne Peplau, Jackie Goodchilds, and me. We used to arrive at Hooker's apartment laden with food and wine and settle in for an afternoon of lively conversation and much good humor. We would sit in her living room, surrounded by books and awards she had received. Hooker was eager to discuss art, literature, politics, and the issues of the day; she was always open to new ideas. The conversations moved between intense intellectual and political debate to sharing intimate secrets about our lives. And when Hooker had sufficiently tired the three of us out, we would leave filled with this woman who conveyed such a great strength of character. She was smart, well-read, iconoclastic, opinionated, and able to have a good time.

One experience with Hooker exemplifies the kind of impact she had on my life. In the summer of 1995 my parents were visiting me and I wanted them to meet Hooker. We went to see her with my life partner and my uncle, who is gay. Earlier in the day, I had shown my parents *Changing Our Minds*, the film about Hooker's life and work. Eventually our conversation turned to a discussion about homosexuality. Hooker remarked that she believed homosexuality was genetic, at which point my father jumped up and exclaimed, "It's not my fault!" When he realized the effect of what he had said, he confided in Hooker, "You know, I've always wished that Linda was heterosexual, and I still do." Now it was Hooker's turn to jump out of her seat. She said, "Ira, how sad! Here you have a daughter who has done everything to make a parent happy. She has a loving, stable, long-term relationship; she's successful in her work; and she has a happy and fulfilling life. What more could any parent want?" What Hooker did for me that day is what her research has done for all of us.

Hooker's work and friendship encouraged me to pursue a career in gay, lesbian, and bisexual psychology. During the 1990s, when Hooker and I served on the review committee for the American Psychological Foundation's Wayne Placek Fund, we developed an important group ritual. The committee would first meet at my home to narrow down the applications. The next day we would go over to Hooker's to make the final decisions. I was continually impressed with how carefully Hooker (in her late eighties at this point) had reviewed each proposal and would engage us for hours in discussions of the nuances of the research and its implications for gay, lesbian, and bisexual psychology. She punctuated all her scholarly comments by regaling us with stories about when she was conducting her own research in the 1950s. For example, to learn about the gay community, Hooker not only interviewed people but she also went with friends to gay bars and parties. She made it clear that she enjoyed being the only woman at these events. And then she would lament one of her favorite refrains: "But alas, I am hopelessly heterosexual!"

She Knew My Work Before We Met

It was at the annual APA convention in San Francisco, on August 26, 1977, where the first author (DK) was chairing the meeting of the four-year-old Association of Gay Psychologists, that Hooker walked into the room. The business meeting was nearly over, so after asking a colleague if that in fact was Dr. Hooker, I introduced her. She was a tall woman with a distinctive voice, raspy from years of cigarette smoking. According to a report of the meeting, she said that "when she began her research 25 years ago she never dreamed that gay men and women would come together openly at a meeting of the American Psychological Association during her lifetime" (Kimmel 1978:1). This was greeted with a standing ovation in her honor. After the meeting adjourned, I met her in person and was overwhelmed: She began to give citations of papers I had written on gay male aging. I listened in amazement as others in the room met her for the first time and she cited their publications, and clearly had read them. At this time she was nearly seventy, retired from UCLA, and in private practice.

We corresponded occasionally over the years. One letter I received troubled me deeply, because she was apparently depressed when she wrote it. Later I learned she had struggled for many years with bipolar affective disorder and was often on medication for it.

My correspondence with her intensified when she received a bequest from one of the participants in her classic study. I offered my assistance in resolving the disposition of the moneys, which eventually became the Wayne Placek Fund of the American Psychological Foundation. I also was a member of the APA Board of Social and Ethical Responsibility for Psychology and, in that role, nominated her year after year for the award she eventually received from the APA. Although she was unable physically to be present at the award ceremony, a telephone hookup was arranged so she could listen as her paper was read the following year, and then she engaged in a long-distance audio discussion with the audience. The whole event was videotaped for her to view later.

By now we had become friends, and I visited her at her home on a few occasions. She was a delightful conversationalist, sharp and incisive in her wit and comments, and blessed with a good memory and sense of humor. As a bequest, she left me a watercolor portrait of a young man that had hung in her home, a gift to her from the artist, Don Bachardy; it is a treasured reminder of those visits. Eventually her health began to fail. During one particularly bad episode, I was able to reassure her that her memory would return, that she was suffering from the aftereffects of the acute illness and not from dementia. After one bad fall that made it no longer feasible for her to be alone, I contacted some gerontological psychology colleagues and they found a home care service. One of the key people at that service knew of Hooker's research and made a personal commitment that she be cared for with all the loving skill possible.

A Remarkable Woman of Her Time

It is important to understand Hooker's life and professional experiences in the social context of the status of women in society and psychology. As we look at some of the key aspects of her upbringing, education, and high-lights of her career, it becomes clear how she created many opportunities for herself, but she also encountered repeated instances of sexism. Hooker had the ability to focus on the opportunities and to surmount the obstacles she faced simply because she was female.

The sixth of nine children, Hooker began school in a succession of one-room schoolhouses. As a young girl she experienced the burden of social stigma — both for being poor and for being a girl: "Growing up for me was a very painful process. . . . I was very tall, very tall when I was an adolescent. I grew to be almost six feet . . . and girls at that time, especially in a small high school, were not favored, let us say we didn't learn to stand up straight for example" (Schmiechen and Haugland, interview with Evelyn Hooker, as cited in Boxer and Carrier 1998:5–6).

Hooker's mother was a pioneer of another sort who had crossed the plains in a covered wagon. Although her mother had only a third-grade education, she advised Hooker, "Get an education and they can never take it away from you" (Anonymous, 1992b:502). She moved the family to the county seat so that Hooker could attend a large high school, where she entered an honors program that included a course in psychology. At the urging of a female teacher to pursue a college education, Hooker entered the University of Colorado at Boulder in 1924 at the age of seventeen. To supplement her tuition scholarship, Hooker supported herself by doing housework — one of the few jobs then available for women. Later she became a teaching assistant and, working with Karl Muenzinger in her senior year, she was offered an instructorship.

Hooker completed a master's degree at Colorado, and the topic of her research — vicarious learning in rats — scarcely hinted at the career that lay ahead. When it came time for a Ph.D. program, Hooker chose Yale, but the male department chair at Colorado (whose doctoral degree was from Yale) refused to recommend a woman. So Hooker went to The Johns Hopkins University. After receiving her Ph.D., she held a succession of short-term positions, first at the Maryland College for Women and later at Whittier College in California. Her teaching was interrupted by a two-year bout with tuberculosis that began in 1934. After recovering, she had a fellowship to study in Germany (1937–38).

When Hooker applied for an appointment in the psychology department at UCLA, she experienced more sex discrimination. As she told the story, the department chair turned her down, explaining that the department already had three women, which were more than enough for his male colleagues. Instead, he only offered her an opportunity to teach through the UCLA Extension Program. She never joined the full-time faculty at UCLA, maintaining her affiliation as an adjunct with an NIMH (National Institute of Mental Health) Research Career Award until 1970 (Anonymous 1992b).

Hooker's determination and tenacity in dealing with the sexism she experienced as a student in the 1920s and 1930s and throughout her professional life make her a role model for all women psychologists. Hooker drew from her own life experiences an appreciation and awareness of social stigma: "The fact that I should end up studying an oppressed, a deprived people comes from my own experiences, in part, of being stigmatized" (quoted in Humphreys 1978:199).

"Another Eleanor Roosevelt": Foremother of the Lesbian and Gay Liberation Movement

When Hooker died in 1996, several major newspapers carried a full obituary. The *Los Angeles Times* article began, "Evelyn Hooker, the psychologist whose 1950s research showing that homosexuality is not a mental illness helped fuel gay liberation, has died" (Oliver 1996:A32). The *New York Times* lead was "Dr. Evelyn Hooker, a psychologist who defied conventional wisdom and greatly emboldened the fledgling gay rights movement in the 1950s by finding there was no measurable psychological difference between homosexual and heterosexual men, died on Monday at her home in Santa Monica, Calif. She was 89" (Dunlap 1996:D-19). D'Emilio (1996) in his obituary in the newsletter of the National Gay and Lesbian Task Force, reprinted in the APA *Monitor*, wrote, "I'm willing to lay odds that not many of us know who she is or what she did. Yet she deserves the status of hero in our community as a pioneering psychologist whose research has changed our world. Her career is also a fascinating case study of the potentially productive relationship between 'the expert' and a social movement."

A documentary film, *Changing Our Minds: The Story of Dr. Evelyn Hooker*, was selected as the best documentary in the 1992 San Francisco Lesbian and Gay Film Festival and was nominated for "best documentary feature" at the Sixty-fifth Academy Awards (Harrison and Schmiechen 1991). It was shown widely at film festivals, added to library collections, and distributed commercially.

Hooker received many awards from lesbian, gay, bisexual, and allied groups. In the documentary film, she is shown speaking at the award presentation for the Lesbian and Gay Community Services Center in Los Angeles. Her apartment proudly displayed awards from the Association of Lesbian and Gay Psychologists, the Gay Caucus of the American Psychiatric Association, and the Parents and Friends of Lesbians and Gays. In the film, she quotes one homophile leader who introduced her as "another Eleanor Roosevelt."

In 1991 Hooker received the APA Award for Distinguished Contribution to Psychology in the Public Interest. The citation was written by the first author (DK):

> When homosexuals were considered to be mentally ill, were forced out of government jobs, and were arrested in police raids, Evelyn Hooker courageously sought and obtained research support from the National Institute of Mental Health (NIMH) to compare a matched sample of homosexual and heterosexual men. Her pioneering study, published in 1957, challenged the widespread belief that homosexuality is a pathology by demonstrating that experienced clinicians using psychological tests widely believed at the time to be appropriate could not identify the nonclinical homosexual group. This revolutionary study provided empirical evidence that normal homosexuals existed, and supported the radical idea then emerging that homosexuality is within the normal range of human behavior. Despite the stigma associated with homosexuality, she received an NIMH Research Career Award in 1961 to continue her work. In 1967, she became chair of the NIMH Task Force on Homosexuality, which provided a stamp of validation and research support for other major empirical studies. Her research, leadership, mentorship, and tireless advocacy for an accurate

scientific view of homosexuality for more than three decades has been an outstanding contribution to psychology in the public interest. (Anonymous 1992b:501–2)

Until a few months before her death in 1996, Hooker continued to participate in professional activities related to the psychological study of lesbian and gay issues as a member of a review panel for the Placek Fund research awards.

The Research Project

As Hooker described in *Changing Our Minds* (also described in Boxer and Carrier 1998), she was teaching an undergraduate course at UCLA when one very good student, Sam From, sensing she could be trusted, befriended her and eventually confided to her that he and other friends to whom he had introduced her were homosexual. They took her to parties, clubs, and bars, where she was accepted as a heterosexual woman who was "in the know." Finally, they confronted her with the urgent request that she conduct scientific research to show that they were not abnormal or mentally ill. She refused, because she could not study this group objectively. Unconvinced, they introduced her at meetings of homophile organizations in Los Angeles where she could recruit participants she did not know. At one meeting she asked, "How many of you are married?" When many raised their hands, she was aghast, because she thought that meant they must be bisexual and not suitable for her study. It turned out, however, that they were in long-term, same-sex relationships. Thus she gathered a sample of exclusively homosexual men (although three had a few heterosexual experiences, all identified as homosexual) who were not in psychotherapy and did not show overt signs of disturbance.

It was difficult to find a matched comparison sample. Her study became known as "the fairy project," and no heterosexual man would want to be seen going to her office at UCLA. She used a building on the estate of her private home for conducting the interviews and projective tests. Her husband once commented that "no man is safe on Saltaire Avenue" (Harrison and Schmiechen 1991), because she needed to find a group of heterosexual men that matched (in terms of age, IQ, and educational level) the homosexual men recruited from the homophile organizations. In her published report (Hooker 1957) she described the process by which community leaders referred heterosexual participants, of whom any who had had more than a single postadolescent homosexual experience were eliminated from the study. Likewise, she attempted to exclude any who showed evidence of latent or covert homosexuality. As with the homosexual sample, none were in psychotherapy at the time of the study. They were matched with the homosexual sample pair-wise on age, Otis self-administered intelligence scale scores (Otis 1922), and educational level.

Funding was difficult to obtain. She once told the story of the site visit by the chief of extramural grants of the NIMH, John Eberhart, who, she said, wanted to meet this "kook" who claimed she had access to a large number of normal homosexual males. At that time, of course, the concept of "normal homosexual" was an oxymoron. She was a charming and strikingly attractive woman, and obviously convinced the NIMH to provide funding for the study.

Clinical psychology was in its infancy at the end of World War II, and the measures that were thought to be valid were projective tests. She shared an office with Bruno Klopfer, one of the foremost experts on the Rorschach test, and he, too, urged her to conduct the study. Klopfer scored the Rorschach protocols (Rorschach 1921) for the matched pairs of heterosexual and homosexual respondents. Edwin Shneidman, who had developed a projective test using cut-out figures called the Make-A-Picture-Story (MAPS) test (Shneidman 1947), scored those results. Mortimer Meyer scored the Thematic Apperception Test (TAT) (Murray 1943). Each test was scored by two judges. The protocols were then reviewed by three expert clinicians in Los Angeles who rated the individuals' overall adjustment. Finally, the three experts were presented with the thirty matched pairs and were asked to determine which of the pair was homosexual.

The then startling result was that the homosexual and heterosexual samples could not be distinguished from each other.

> Can you imagine what it was like when I examined the results of the three judges of the adjustment ratings from the projective techniques? I knew the men for whom the ratings were made, and I was certain as a clinician that they were relatively free of psychopathology. But what would these superb clinicians find? You know now that the two groups, homosexuals and heterosexuals, did not differ in adjustment or psychopathology. When I saw that, I wept with joy. I knew that the psychiatrists would not accept it then. But sometime! (Hooker 1993:452)

After the paper was presented at the 1955 APA meeting in Chicago, it was published in the *Journal of Projective Techniques* (Hooker 1957) with an unusual footnote by the editor: "A study such as Dr. Hooker's challenges several widespread and emotional convictions. In view of the importance of her findings it seemed desirable to the editors that they be made public, even in their preliminary form" (p. 18 n.). Several follow-up articles appeared in subsequent issues (Hooker 1958, 1959, 1960, 1961). Although the study was open to criticism on several empirical grounds, it did call into question the belief that homosexuality is a form of mental illness. As Hooker once commented, "After all, if Bruno Klopfer couldn't tell who was homosexual on the Rorschach, who could?" (Harrison and Schmiechen 1991).

In 1972 Siegelman replicated the Hooker study with a larger sample, using objective measures. "I wrote to him when I had read his article, saying that I wished I had done it. What Dr. Siegelman had demonstrated was that the results of my research were not dependent on projective tests. The results were not artifacts. They were true" (Hooker 1993:452).

NIMH Task Force on Homosexuality

Dr. Eberhard's successor at NIMH, Philip Sapir, encouraged Hooker and her work in countless ways, including extending her research grants until she received the Career Research Award (1961). In 1967 she was invited to form the NIMH Task Force on Homosexuality, which lasted until 1969. Bayer (1981) observed, "The Task Force placed enormous emphasis on the extent to which the misery of homosexuals could be alleviated through an end to the discriminatory social practices of the heterosexual world" (p. 53). Judd Marmor was a member; a few years later he would play an important role as a member of the Executive Committee, when the American Psychiatric Association made the decision to remove homosexuality from the revised third edition of the *Diagnostic and Statistical Manual of Mental Disorders* (American Psychiatric Association 1987). Although publication of the task force report was delayed on the election of Richard Nixon as U.S. president, it was circulated by homophile organizations. The task force also encouraged NIMH funding of important research projects on homosexuality.

Social Context of Hooker's Contribution

During the 1950s a repressive attitude was widespread regarding homosexuality. The U.S. armed services sought out and dishonorably discharged lesbians and gay men, and often engaged in witch hunts, forcing one suspect to reveal others, using deceit and undercover surveillance, and generally created an openly hostile atmosphere. U.S. Rep. Joseph McCarthy (R-WI), as chair of the House Un-American Activities Committee, specialized in uncovering secret homosexuals, especially in the government bureaucracy. The policy that homosexuals could not have high-level security clearance led to the firing of many government employees and to subsequent protests by those discharged.

Homosexual parties, private clubs, and public bars were sometimes raided by the police, and, if people were arrested, their names were published in the newspaper, often causing loss of employment, divorce, and public humiliation. These raids were especially likely to occur at the time of elections as a sign that the incumbent was intolerant of "sexual perversion."

Until the mid-1970s homosexuality was "treated" by mental health professionals with electroshock, hospitalization, hormone therapy, psychotherapy, and aversive conditioning. There was also a stigma applied to the mothers and fathers of homosexuals, who were portrayed as engaging in pathological parenting. Distinctions were blurred among homosexuality, cross-dressing, and pedophilia in both the public mind and the professional literature. Nearly all empirical research was based on clinical, hospitalized, or prisoner samples. Morin (1977) documented the heterosexist bias that dominated psychology during this period.

Impact of Hooker's Contributions

In the obituary for the *American Psychologist*, Shneidman (1998) wrote, "Many homosexual men have stated that they owe improvements in the attitudes of society and in their acceptance of themselves directly and indirectly to the work of Evelyn Hooker" (p. 481). An example of this impact is her entry in the 1968 *International Encyclopedia of the Social Sciences* (Hooker 1968):

The only obvious difference between homosexuals and heterosexuals is in psychosexual object choice. All experienced clinicians and research workers report that the personality differences among individual homosexuals are far more apparent than the similarities. Investigators who include the data on individual differences in their studies have found a great diversity of personality patterns. (p. 227)

Homosexual communities in large cities are made up of constantly changing aggregates of persons who are loosely linked by friendship and sexual interests in an extended and overlapping series of networks. Some network clusters form tightly knit cliques of friends and homo-sexually "married" pairs, while in others, informal groups or social organizations develop. The structure of the communication, friend-ship, and sexual network among members of the community is com-plex. (p. 231)

Female homosexual, or lesbian, communities apparently develop on a smaller scale, with informal groups, cliques, and special gathering places. But a formal organization of lesbians and an official publica-tion with national circulation indicate that the collective aspects of female homosexuality have some importance. No empirical studies of these aspects are currently available. Although homophile organiza-tions, whether male or female, constitute and represent a very small minority of the total homosexual population, they achieve social sig-nificance by the role they assume in openly protesting the status as-signed to homosexuals by the larger society. (p. 231)

These ideas were published one year before the sociopolitical event trig-gered by the 1969 police raid on the Stonewall Inn Bar in New York City. Word of the raid, the riot, and several days of civil disobedience that followed spread through an underground network and began the modern era of a gay, lesbian, and bisexual community identity.

Bayer (1981) noted,

The appearance of Hooker's work in the mid-1950s was of critical importance for the evolution of the homophile movement. Her find-ings provided "facts" that could buttress the position of homosexuals who rejected the pathological view of their conditions. She had met the psychiatrists on their own terms and provided their critics with clinical data with which to do battle. As important as her findings was her willingness to share them with the ordinary men and women of the homophile movement. . . . She became not only a source of ideo-logical support, but an active participant in the homosexual struggle. (p. 53)

On February 8, 1973, Charles Silverstein made a presentation to the Nomenclature Committee of the American Psychiatric Association urging that homosexuality be removed from the list of disorders. His presentation began with the work of Hooker, Kinsey, Clellan Ford, and Frank Beach (Bayer 1981). Silverstein concluded, "It is no sin to have made an error in the past, but surely you will mock the principles of scientific research upon which the diagnostic system is based if you turn your backs on the only objective evidence we have" (quoted in Bayer 1981:120).

The Silverstein presentation apparently made a significant impression on the committee, which undertook a serious review of the matter and announced it to the *New York Times*, which reported the event the next day, February 9. Opponents of the change also mobilized their supporters. On December 15, 1973, the Board of Trustees of the American Psychiatric Association met, and, in a vote of 13 to 0 with two abstentions, homosexuality was deleted and replaced with "sexual orientation disturbance." The trustees also approved a significant civil rights statement:

Whereas homosexuality in and of itself implies no impairment in judgment, stability, reliability, or vocational capabilities, therefore be it resolved, that the American Psychiatric Association deplores all public and private discrimination against homosexuals in such areas as employment, housing, public accommodation, and licensing, and declares that no burden of proof of such judgment, capacity, or reliability shall be placed upon homosexuals greater than that imposed on any other persons. Further, the APA supports and urges the enactment of civil rights legislation at local, state, and federal levels that would insure homosexual citizens the same protections now guaranteed to others. Further, the APA supports and urges the repeal of all legislation making criminal offenses of sexual acts performed by consenting adults in private. (American Psychiatric Association 1973, quoted in Bayer 1981:137)

The decision was supported in a subsequent referendum of the membership; 58 percent of the voters supported the board's decision.

In August 1973 a group of openly gay and lesbian psychologists met at the APA convention in Montreal to form the Association of Gay Psychologists. Two of the "demands" the group made to the APA Board of Directors were to establish a task force on homosexuality and to depathologize homosexuality. The task force was established in 1974 and the APA Council of Representatives adopted the following two resolutions in 1975 to remove the stigma of mental illness that had long been associated with homosexuality.

1. The American Psychological Association supports the action taken on December 15, 1973, by the American Psychiatric Association, removing homosexuality from that Association's official list of mental disorders. The American Psychological Association therefore adopts the following resolution:

Homosexuality per se implies no impairment in judgment, stability, reliability, or general social and vocational capabilities; Further, the American Psychological Association urges all mental health professionals to take the lead in removing the stigma of mental illness that has long been associated with homosexual orientations.

2. Regarding discrimination against homosexuals, the American Psychological Association adopts the following resolution concerning their civil and legal rights:

The American Psychological Association deplores all public and private discrimination in such areas as employment, housing, public accommodation, and licensing against those who engage in or have engaged in homosexual activities and declares that no burden of proof of such judgment, capacity, or reliability shall be placed upon these individuals greater than that imposed on any other persons. Further, the American Psychological Association supports and urges the enactment of civil rights legislation at the local, state, and federal level that would offer citizens who engage in acts of homosexuality the same protections now guaranteed to others on the basis of race, creed, color, etc. Further, the American Psychological Association supports and urges the repeal of all discriminatory legislation singling out homosexual acts by consenting adults in private. (Conger 1975:633)

Many additional resolutions by professional organizations have followed.

Within the APA, the Committee on Lesbian, Gay, and Bisexual Concerns was established in 1980 and an official division, called the Society for the Psychological Study of Lesbian and Gay Issues (Division 44 of the APA) was approved in 1985. Hooker was a discussant at the symposium entitled, "From Mental Illness to an APA Division: Homosexuality and Psychology," presented by the new division at the 1986 APA convention (Kimmel and Browning 1999).

Her Legacy

Hooker's research has had far-ranging impact. It has affected psychological science by encouraging a new generation of researchers to study the lives of gay men and lesbians, and her demonstration that homosexuality is not a form of mental illness cleared the way for researchers to ask new questions. In 1978, with the support of Jackie Goodchilds, then editor of the *Journal of Social Issues*, a special issue on "psychology and the gay community" was a landmark. This issue was an outgrowth of the APA Task Force on the Status of Lesbian and Gay Male Psychologists. Steve Morin and Dorothy Riddle were the editors of this special issue. As Hooker wrote in her epilogue to the volume, "This is a first in publishing in the social and behavioral sciences," noting that "the entire issue is devoted to social issues which are problematic for gay/lesbian individuals, and not to clinical problems" (Hooker 1978:132).

Her research has directly affected psychological practice. She laid the groundwork for a new affirmative approach that has as its premise that being gay or lesbian is a capacity, an ability — not a disability — and that focuses on finding ways to enhance the functioning of gay and bisexual men and lesbian and bisexual women. Both authors are personally aware of the trail blazed by Hooker as we worked over the past twenty years on boards and committees within the APA that have been addressing issues of concern for gay men and lesbians. We have seen the ways that organized psychology has taken steps to remove the stigma and to advance an affirmative psychology for lesbians and gay men.

The APA has influenced public policy by participating in amicus curiae briefs concerning the civil rights of lesbians and gay men, by disseminating social science research that demonstrates that same-gender sexual orientation is not pathological, and by educating other professionals and the public about the reality of gay and lesbian lives. Moreover, the APA Council of Representatives has passed numerous policy statements on gay and lesbian issues, including discrimination against homosexuals, child custody, hate crimes, sodomy laws, gay and lesbian youth, treatments to alter sexual orientation, and same-sex marriage benefits. Hooker helped legitimate gay, lesbian, and bisexual research as well as gay, lesbian, bisexual, and heterosexual researchers conducting investigations in this field. Hooker was greatly pleased in her later years by the growing numbers of gay and lesbian psychologists and the development within the APA of a division devoted to the study of gay, lesbian, and bisexual issues. Hooker took great satisfaction in knowing that she helped to launch these new directions within psychology.

Her legacy lives on in several concrete ways. The University of Chicago established the Evelyn Hooker Center for the Mental Health of Gays and Lesbians in 1992. Through its interdisciplinary research programs and multidisciplinary training programs, the center contributes new knowledge about lesbians and gay men and applies that knowledge through clinical services. An Evelyn Hooker archive has been established in the Division of Special Collections of the UCLA Library (Boxer and Carrier 1998).

In 1992 Hooker received a telephone call from a bank in Nebraska informing her that she had been named to head a committee entrusted to distribute the Wayne F. Placek bequest. Wayne Placek was one of the participants in Hooker's classic 1957 study. She had worked with Placek for only two days and remembered him as someone who expressed unhappiness at being gay. Placek's explicit goals for this fund were to support research, to increase information, and to change attitudes and beliefs about lesbians and gay men. Hooker said, "It is highly unlikely that a half million dollars will ever again be available for research on homosexual orientation. This bequest makes possible a sustained research attack on homophobia, the most serious problem facing gays and lesbians today" (Anonymous 1992a:1).

Since 1994 the American Psychological Foundation's (APF) Wayne Placek Trust has been awarding annual research grants to meet these important goals. In 2000 APF created the Evelyn Hooker Programs to include the Placek Trust and all other APF funds dealing with gay, lesbian, and bisexual issues. Through the Evelyn Hooker Center and through the Evelyn Hooker Programs and the APF, the values and goals that Hooker practiced and encouraged remain as vital reminders of her work and contributions.

Most important, Hooker's legacy lives on in the improved quality of lives for so many sexual-minority individuals. Hooker cherished the letters, cards, and calls that she received over the years from gay men and lesbians who let her know how directly and deeply she had affected their lives. One such letter is quoted (Hooker 1993:453).

DEAR DR. EVELYN HOOKER, FEB. 20, 1992, BERLIN

My boyfriend and I just saw the documentary about you at the Berlin Film Festival. We want to say thank you for all the work you did. We're pretty sure that life would have been a lot different and a lot worse for us if you hadn't done your research.

I asked a close, straight friend of mine, who is a medical student at Berlin, why you wanted to do this work. I mean, it just didn't make sense. Why did this straight lady care about gays? My friend replied that it was probably because you felt that it had to be done by somebody, sooner or later. He said that you must have thought that the studies you undertook would help people in some way. He called it scientific altruism.

Well, whatever the reason is, I think that your work was more than just doing a good turn for man. I think you did it because you knew what love was when you saw it and you knew that gay love was like all other love. No better, no worse.

So I guess if we are thanking you, we should thank you not for the work itself, but for your desire to show to the world what you had already understood, or at least suspected, on your own.

With much respect and admiration. . . .

Conclusion

For more than forty years, Hooker used the methods of her discipline of empirical psychology to advance knowledge of same-gender sexual and erotic attraction, which she often termed "love"; and to change scientific and public misconceptions about lesbians, gay men, and bisexual persons. Her work has had major impact in four interrelated areas.

1. Her research and its replication is often cited in amicus curiae briefs presented to courts making determinations about child custody and adoption, laws prohibiting same-sex sexual behavior between consenting adults in private, the integration of lesbians and gay men into the U.S. armed services, in cases of discrimination on the basis of sexual orientation, and in same-gender marriage cases in Hawaii and Vermont.

2. Her research and personal mentorship have stimulated a generation of researchers and research topics that are based on sexual orientation as one dimension of human diversity, not as a pathology to be explained.

3. Her research and professional influence helped to create the practice of gay-affirmative psychotherapy, which she also practiced after retiring from her research career at UCLA.

4. Her research, combined with the cultural impact of the 1969 Stonewall

Uprising and the emergence of the contemporary lesbian and gay movement, produced a paradigm shift in the psychological view of homosexuality from a mental illness to a lesbian, gay, or bisexual identity that links one with others — locally, nationally, internationally, and also historically. It is not an individual's illness or condition but a natural variant of sexual expression that provides some individuals a community with which to identify.

References

American Psychiatric Association. 1987. *Diagnostic and statistical manual of mental disorders*, 3rd rev. ed. Washington. D.C.: Author.

Anonymous. 1992a. Fall). APF receives $510,000 trust: Largest gift in foundation's history. *American Psychological Foundation* 4 (fall):1.

Anonymous. 1992b. Awards for distinguished contribution to psychology in the public interest. *American Psychologist* 47:498–503.

Bayer, R. 1981. *Homosexuality and American Psychiatry: The Politics of Diagnosis*. New York: Basic Books.

Boxer, A.M., and J. M. Carrier. 1998. Evelyn Hooker: A life remembered. *Journal of Homosexuality* 36(1):1–17.

Conger, J. J. 1975. Proceedings of the American Psychological Association, Incorporated, for the year 1974: Minutes of the annual meeting of the Council of Representatives. *American Psychologist* 30:620–651.

D'Emilio, J. 1996. Evelyn Hooker: Unsung hero. *National Gay and Lesbian Task Force Newsletter*. Reprinted in *APA Monitor*.

Dunlap, D. W. 1996. Evelyn Hooker, 89, is dead: Recast the view of gay men. *New York Times*, November 22, D-19.

Harrison, J. (producer) and Schmiechen, R. (director). 1991. *Changing Our Minds: The Story of Dr. Evelyn Hooker* (Film/Video). Distributed by Frameline, 346 Ninth Street, San Francisco, California 94103; http://www.framline.org.

Hooker, E. 1957. The adjustment of the male overt homosexual. *Journal of Projective Techniques* 21:18–31.

Hooker, E. 1958. Male homosexuality in the Rorschach. *Journal of Projective Techniques* 22:33–54.

Hooker, E. 1959. What is a criterion? *Journal of Projective Techniques* 23:278–81.

Hooker, E. 1960. The fable. *Journal of Projective Techniques* 24:240–45.

Hooker, E. 1961. The case of El: A biography. *Journal of Projective Techniques* 25:252–67.

Hooker, E. 1968. Sexual behavior: Homosexuality. *International Encyclopedia of the Social Sciences*, pp. 222–33. New York: Crowell Collier and Macmillan.

Hooker, E. 1978. Epilogue. *Journal of Social Issues* 34(3):131–35.

Hooker, E. 1993. Reflections of a 40-year exploration: A scientific view on homosexuality. *American Psychologist* 48:450–53.

Humphreys, L. 1978. An interview with Evelyn Hooker. *Alternative Lifestyles* 1(2):191–206.

Kimmel, D.C. 1978. Kimmel reports on convention activities. *Association of Gay Psychologists Newsletter* 1(3):1.

Kimmel, D.C., and C. Browning. 1999. A history of Division 44 (Society for the psychological study of lesbian, gay, and bisexual issues). In D. A. Dewsbury, ed., *Unification Through Division:Histories of the Divisions of the American Psychological Association*, 4:129–50. Washington, D.C.:American Psychological Association.

Morin, S. 1977. Heterosexual bias in psychological research on lesbianism and male homosexuality. *American Psychologist* 32:629–37.

Murray, H. A. 1943. *Thematic apperception test pictures and manual.* Cambridge, Mass.: Harvard University Press.

Oliver, M. 1996. Evelyn Hooker: Her study fueled gay liberation. *Los Angeles Times*, November 22, A32.

Otis, A. S. 1922. *Otis self-administering tests of mental ability.* Yonkers, N.Y.: World.

Rorschach, H. 1921. *Psychodiagnostik.* Berne, Switzerland: Birchen.

Shneidman, E. S. 1947. The make-a-picture story (MAPS) projective personality test. *Journal of Consulting Psychology* 11:315–25.

Shneidman, E. S. 1998. Obituaries: Evelyn Hooker, 1907–1996. *American Psychologist* 53:480–81.

2 Biological Perspectives on Sexual Orientation

J. Michael Bailey

The question of "biological" influences on human sexual orientation remains immensely controversial (see Barinaga 1991). This stems, in part, from the inconclusive nature of the empirical evidence; however, the ambiguity of the scientific answers is only part of the problem. The question "Is homosexuality 'biological'?" has been subjected to many interpretations, often not clearly specified. Thus this chapter has two main goals: first, to clarify different meanings that have been attached to "biological" in the context of research on human sexual orientation and, second, to summarize research findings for the most pertinent meanings.

Before we consider alternative meanings of "biological," it is important to specify what is meant by sexual orientation and related terms such as *heterosexual* and *homosexual*. I use the term *sexual orientation* to refer to one's pattern of sexual attraction, to men or to women. Thus men who are sexually attracted to women and women who are sexually attracted to men are "heterosexual" in their sexual orientation. Men who are attracted to men and women who are attracted to women have a "homosexual" orientation. Those who are attracted to both men and women have a "bisexual" orientation. Note that these are psychological rather than behavioral definitions. Thus, for example, the behaviorally heterosexual man who is attracted to both his wife and her brother is considered bisexual, and the teenage male prostitute who sells his body only for the purpose of buying gifts for his female love interest is heterosexual in orientation.

This is not the only possible meaning of sexual orientation. Some men who are sexually attracted to other men call themselves heterosexual. Some

sexual orientat'n - one's pattern of sexual orientation

[handwritten: sexual identity = what the decide they want 2 associate w/]

women who are less sexually attracted to women than to men call themselves lesbians. They are using these words to label what I call their "sexual identity," which I understand to be the identity they desire for reasons other than the relative intensity of the sexual feelings for men versus women. For instance, a man who prefers sex with men may still identify himself as heterosexual, because he prefers heterosexual marriage or other aspects of lifestyle more common to heterosexuals (e.g., rearing children). A woman who prefers sex with men may adopt a lesbian identity as an expression of her emotional and political solidarity with lesbian feminists. In these cases *sexual orientation* and *sexual identity*, as these terms are used herein, are discordant. Some writers have emphasized the frequency of discordance between sexual identity, sexual orientation, and sexual behavior (Klein 1990). In my research experience, however, men and women who label themselves "heterosexual" have almost always admitted to far greater sexual feelings toward and activity with the opposite sex. The opposite pattern has been true for those who call themselves "homosexual," particularly regarding recent patterns of feelings and behavior (as opposed, e.g., to feelings and behavior during adolescence). Nevertheless, these observations are based only on my own research experiences. The degree of concordance between sexual orientation, sexual identity, and sexual behavior is an important question that deserves far more systematic attention that it has received. I chose a psychological definition of sexual orientation for this chapter because it seems likely that sexual attraction is more closely linked to potential biological mechanisms than either sexual identity or sexual behavior, which are more susceptible to social processes (Le Vay 1993). It also seems plausible that sexual orientation is more longitudinally stable than either sexual identity or sexual behavior; however, this remains an uninvestigated empirical question.

Alternative Construals of the "Biological" Question

Biological Determinism Versus Free Will

The argument over whether homosexuality is "biological" or "freely chosen" is perhaps the most common and least productive version of the biology debate. It is common because participants on both sides believe that crucial moral answers hinge on its outcome. For instance, they argue that if homosexuality is biologically determined, and hence homosexuals could not have chosen heterosexuality, then it is unfair to judge their sexual behavior morally. The argument is unproductive for at least two reasons. First, its resolution is primarily a philosophical rather than an empirical matter, and scholars who have considered it at length generally (and legitimately) take a strong position independent of evidence (e.g., Money 1988; Le Vay 1993). Second, the rational link between the position that homosexuality is biologically determined and a sympathetic view of homosexuality is much more tenuous than commonly assumed. This is because all behavior is biologically determined, in one fundamental sense. Thus if homosexuality (or heterosexuality) is excused on the grounds that it is biologically determined, all behavior must be excused, including behavior that should not be excused, such as dishonesty, theft, homophobia, or even genocide. These behaviors are also biologically determined, in the sense I now elaborate.

Most scientists are both (strict) determinists and materialists. Determinism, in its strict sense, implies that all present events (including mental states and behaviors) are completely caused by past events. Equivalently, given a configuration of events at Time A, there can be exactly one configuration of events at later Time B. Materialists believe that all causes and effects obtain in the material world, as opposed, for instance, to a nonmaterial "soul." Thus a materialistic determinist acquainted with modern neuroscience believes (as I do) that all behavior is most proximately caused by brain states, and thus behavioral differences must be caused by brain differences. This is true even for socially acquired traits. For instance, there must be relevant brain differences between the group of people who have learned the quadratic theorem and the group who has not yet acquired this knowledge, though of course those brain differences are undoubtedly subtle. Future recitation of the theorem depends on activating the brain's "representation" of it. Thus all behaviors are "biologically determined" in the sense that all events are caused, and behavioral events are caused by brain states, which are "biological." By these assumptions, the mere fact that Le Vay (1991) found a brain difference between homosexual and heterosexual men was unsurprising; such a difference has to exist. Because we are biological organisms, everything about us is traceable to biology. As John Money (1988) incisively noted: "The postnatal determinants that enter the brain through the senses by way of social communication and learning are also biological, for there is a biology of learning and remembering. That which is not biological is occult, mystical, or, to coin a term, spookological" (p. 50). To be sure, there are some more meaningful and interesting construals of the question "Is homosexuality 'biological'?" — some of which are considered in the following. To encourage more responsible usage, I recommend referring to "biological" causes, influences, theories, or explanations (i.e., with quotation marks). This draws attention to the problematic term that has both numerous connotations and an uninformative literal meaning.

Innate Versus Acquired

Most people participating in the "biology" debate have this version of the issue in mind, at least part of the time. As Lehrman (1970) noted, there are at least two interpretations of "innate." The interpretation of innate as genetic or heritable is the more restrictive of the two, and a discussion of that sense is deferred to the next section. A behavior is also said to develop innately to the extent that it develops in a uniform or fixed pattern without being learned. In this sense, innate signals an independence from, or perhaps a resistance to, psychosocial influences.

Studies in comparative psychology and ethology have shown that behaviors cannot simply be divided into those that are innate versus those that are acquired. For instance, Mineka et al. (1984) showed that rhesus monkeys acquired a fear of snakes by observing other monkeys react fearfully to a snake, and thus the fear is acquired. However, another study (Cook and Mineka 1989) demonstrated that the monkeys did not acquire a fear of flowers, even though they had observed monkeys reacting fearfully to them (through videotape manipulation). They suggested that because snakes are dangerous to monkeys and flowers are not, rhesus monkeys have become "evolutionarily prepared" to learn fear of snakes easily through observation. Furthermore, since snakes are common in the monkeys' natural habitat, they are virtually guaranteed to acquire snake fear. Thus, in a sense, snake fear in rhesus monkeys is highly innate.

Given these complications, it is tempting to dismiss discussion of whether a characteristic such as homosexuality is "innate" or "acquired" as misguided and, instead, to focus on elaborating the process of development. While it is certainly true that obtaining a full picture of development is more illuminating than determining the degree of innateness, the latter goal is also useful for organizing research to accomplish the former. Thus diverse processes of acquisition, such as operant and classical conditioning, imitation, and persuasion, can be theoretically and empirically pitted against such innate processes as heredity and prenatal neuroendocrine development.

Genes Versus Environment

The question "Is homosexuality 'biological'?" is often asked in the form "Is homosexuality genetic?" That the question is often not meant literally was recently evidenced on an American talk show in which a gay man with a heterosexual identical twin argued emphatically that sexual orientation is "genetic," seemingly oblivious to the contradictory nature of his own personal evidence. In fact, many people say "genetic" when they mean "innate," a problematic equation. For instance, if massive androgen injections given prenatally to a female fetus altered her sexual orientation, this would be an innate influence, but it would be entirely environmental. Conversely, there are conceivable developmental routes that involve the genes but that most people would not consider innate. For instance, suppose a gene existed for feminine beauty and, furthermore, that boys with this trait were relatively likely to be treated in a way that fostered homosexuality. A quantitative genetic analysis would find homosexuality to be heritable, but the necessary developmental step would be psychosocial. A phenotypic (observable) difference between organisms is genetic, or heritable, to the extent that it is attributable to genetic differences between them, regardless of the intervening steps from genotype to phenotype.

Essentialism Versus Social Constructionism

During the past decade perhaps the most contentious version of the "biology" debate has been whether sexual orientation is a category universal (in some way) to every culture or merely an arbitrary categorization that says more about the observer (or constructor) than the observed (e.g., Halperin 1989). Social constructionists make much of historical accounts of Greece and Rome, in which sexual acts between men appear to have been much more common than they are in contemporary Western societies. Furthermore, they argue that there was no equivalent categorization in the ancient societies. In contrast, those labeled by the social constructionists as essentialists argue that there have probably been people whom we could identify as homosexual, bisexual, and heterosexual in all times and places. Boswell (1980, 1989, 1990) has argued persuasively that these categories have been recognized throughout the recorded history of Western civilization.

The essentialism-constructionist debate is fueled, in part, by the different ways that the two sides use "homosexuality." Social constructionists empha-

size cultural variation in incidence of homosexual behavior and in the way
sexuality is treated linguistically. These issues are actually more pertinent to
the social construction of sexual identity and sexual behavior than that of
sexual orientation. Boswell (1990), however, has generally emphasized homosexuality and bisexuality as psychological attraction patterns.

But even granting the social constructionist premise that homosexuality
(or, for that matter, heterosexuality) occurs in only some societies, it does not
follow, as some constructionists believe (e.g., De Cecco 1990), that "biological" investigations into sexual orientation are misguided. Given a society that
has constructed the sexual categories "heterosexual" and "homosexual," there
is still the question of why people may adopt one or the other label (or are so
labeled by others). The categories "priest," "Sumo wrestler," and "Fortune 500
executive" are surely more socially constructed than "homosexual" or "heterosexual," but within any society in which they are meaningful, there are
probably "biological" (i.e., innate or genetic) factors that contribute to the
likelihood that one will be categorized within any one of them.

"Biological" Explanations of Sexual Orientation: The Empirical Evidence

The Neuroendocrine View

Background   The most influential "biological" theory of sexual orientation
is motivated by the observation that homosexuals have a sexual orientation
identical to that of opposite-sex heterosexuals. Gay men and heterosexual
women are sexually attracted to men; lesbians and heterosexual men are
sexually attracted to women. The neuroendocrine theory of sexual orientation then, in simplistic and general form, is that the brains of gay men have
something in common with those of heterosexual women, and similarly for
lesbians and heterosexual men. Furthermore, according to this view, the
relevant brain differences between men-preferring and women-preferring
individuals are relatively innate, depending less on postnatal experience such
as parental socialization than on patterns of hormonal exposure.

Before examining the neuroendocrine theory in detail, let us consider its
plausibility on a priori grounds. First, children who become homosexual
adults appear to display some behaviors more typical of the opposite sex.
Gay men frequently (but not invariably) remember being relatively gender
nonconforming in childhood — for example, being teased for being "sissies,"

preferring female playmates, and shunning rough sports (Bell et al. 1981; Grellert et al. 1982; Harry 1983; Whitam 1977). Prospective studies have shown that this association is not because of memory bias. A majority of extremely gender atypical boys become gay or bisexual adults (Green 1987; Zuger 1978), a far higher proportion than would be expected by chance. Similarly, lesbians recall being more masculine during childhood compared to heterosexual women (Bell et al. 1981), though there have unfortunately been no prospective longitudinal studies of tomboys. For both men and women, the association between sexual orientation and (recalled) childhood gender nonconformity is strong (though somewhat less so for women) (Bailey and Zucker 1993). This supports the idea that homosexuals have been subject to some influences more typical of the opposite sex and is thus consistent with a neuroendocrine hypothesis.

Doubtless some readers will cringe at the implication that a sexual orientation difference mirroring a sex difference is consistent with a "biological" theory. Are human sex differences in behavior not caused by socialization differences? In fact, an immense body of research describes differences in the ways that boys and girls are socialized by parents, other adults, and peers. However, the vast majority of these studies cannot claim to show more than that boys and girls are treated differently. They cannot claim to show that this differential treatment makes *any* difference, much less that it makes *all* the difference. (The human sex differences literature is limited primarily by the difficulty of doing definitive research on etiological questions about sex differences, since it is rarely possible to separate "biological" and social influences; e.g., typical females are both "biologically" female and treated as females.) My own intuition is that both social and "biological" factors will be found necessary to account for many behavioral sex differences. In any case, advocates of neither nature nor nurture can honestly claim to have excluded the other side's explanation for any behavioral sex difference. Hence the possibility of innate sex differences remains viable.

Indeed, sexual orientation may be an especially strong candidate for "biological" causation. This is because the most familiar social influences cannot plausibly be operating. Homosexuals are attracted to members of their own sex despite their (usually) heterosexual parents' example and despite the punishment that they endure from peers and many other enforcers of social norms. Furthermore, prehomosexual boys are often gender nonconforming despite being socialized to the contrary and despite the punishment that often follows such behavior in males. Although some psychological theories circumvent these problems by emphasizing subtle aspects of parenting (e.g., Lidz 1968), these theories have generated remarkably little empirical support (Bell et al. 1981; Siegelman 1981). Moreover, insofar as such theories have garnered support, the direction of causation is ambiguous. For instance, consistent with Freudian theory, homosexual males do appear to have poorer childhood relationships with their fathers than do male heterosexuals (Bell et al. 1981). However, as Bell et al. have pointed out, it is possible that the fathers are reacting to the atypical childhood behaviors of the prehomosexual boys.

The Theory   The neuroendocrine theory of sexual orientation (Byne and Parsons 1993; Ellis and Ames 1987; Meyer-Bahlburg 1984) posits that the sexual differentiation of brain structures affecting sexual orientation proceeds roughly analogously to the differentiation of morphological structures such as the external genitalia. Both male and female embryos start development identically. Sexual differentiation begins when the undifferentiated gonads develop into either ovaries or testes; male development is triggered by the sex determination gene on the Y chromosome. Later, the testes of the male fetus secrete two hormones that further masculine differentiation. Müllerian inhibiting substance (MIH) prevents the growth of the uterus and related structures, and in this sense is a defeminizing substance. In contrast, testosterone and other closely related substances (generally speaking, androgens) masculinize relevant structures, forming both the internal male sex organs and the external genitalia. For the most part, masculine development requires androgens, and without the action of androgens, feminine development occurs. This is evidenced most dramatically in 46, XY androgeninsensitivity syndrome, in which genetic males lack a gene needed to utilize androgens effectively, despite normal androgen levels. Individuals with this syndrome are evidently typical females, both anatomically and psychologically, with the exception of the internal reproductive organs, whose formation was blocked by MIH (Money 1988).

The neuroendocrine theory of homosexuality hypothesizes that there are brain structures that sexually differentiate during prenatal and possibly early postnatal development and that these structures determine sexual orientation toward males or toward females. Presumably, masculinization of the relevant brain structures in heterosexual men and homosexual women occurs because of relatively high levels of androgens, whereas development in a feminine direction requires a relative dearth of androgens (or relatively low sensitivity to androgens). The neuroendocrine view stresses the role of organizational, as opposed to activational, hormones; that is, androgens are

les ♀ men = ↑ androgen which makes them masculine

hypothesized to affect the sexual differentiation of brain structures during critical periods of development. For instance, one cannot necessarily predict that in a homosexual man the differentiation of a brain structure in a feminine direction will be associated with a low level of circulating testosterone during adulthood. Indeed, that hypothesis is untenable given a large number of studies that show otherwise (Meyer-Bahlburg 1984). It should be noted that the neuroendocrine theory makes rather strong predictions about the existence of relevant neural structures affecting sexual orientation in men and women. While the account of morphological differentiation provided above is generally accepted, the causes and extent of sexual differentiation of the human brain remain speculative.

Fortunately the neuroendocrine theory does not merely rest on the analogy with morphological sexual differentiation. Four general areas of research have been used to support a neuroendocrine view of homosexuality: studies manipulating the sexual behavior of nonhuman animals, studies of humans with unusual patterns of hormone exposure, studies relating sexual orientation to traits thought to be innately sexually dimorphic, and direct neurophysiological studies of human sexual orientation.

Studies of Nonhuman Animals   The study of other species, particularly rodents, has been immensely important in the development of a "biological" view of homosexuality (Adkins-Regan 1988; Byne and Parsons 1993; Meyer-Bahlburg 1984). Perhaps the most influential animal model has been the rat. Typical female rats exhibit a posture called "lordosis" during sexual receptivity in response to appropriate tactile stimulation; lordosis allows male rats to achieve intromission and ejaculation. Typical male rats, in contrast, show high rates of mounting behavior. However, genetic males can be made to display lordosis by (surgically or chemically) castrating them prenatally or perinatally and then administering appropriate hormones during adulthood to activate the behavior. Similarly, genetic females can be made to exhibit a male pattern of sexual behavior by the perinatal administration of androgens and subsequent replacement of sex hormones in adulthood. The sexual differentiation of these behaviors has been shown to involve the preoptic, anterior, and ventromedial portions of the hypothalamus.

There is an important limitation of the rat findings as support for a neuroendocrine model for human sexual orientation (Atkins-Regan 1988; Byne and Parsons 1993; Meyer-Bahlburg 1984). Human homosexuals do not clearly display a pattern of copulatory behavior typical of the opposite sex, with the exception of their sexual orientation. Homosexual men do not appear to show decreased mounting behavior nor homosexual women an increase in mounting behavior, compared to their heterosexual counterparts. Conversely, the large majority of the rat studies have failed to assess preference for males versus females. Thus the rat studies have focused on a dimension of behavior that is not clearly relevant to human sexual orientation. As Byne and Parsons (1993) have noted, when a neonatally castrated rat displays lordosis in response to mounting by another male, it is the mounted animal that has provoked the interest of psychoneuroendocrinologists, not the animal that initiated the contact. Yet if rat sexual behavior were directly analogous to human sexual orientation, the male who mounted the treated animal would be equally worthy of an explanation. There have, in fact, been experimental studies of the origins of preference for males versus females in rats (Brand et al. 1991, 1992) and ferrets (Martin and Baum 1986; Stockman, Callaghan, and Baum 1985; see also the review of this issue by Adkins-Regan 1988). These studies have explored the consequences of either blocking the effects of androgens in male animals or administering androgens to female animals, prenatally or perinatally. In general, treated adult animals spend less time with animals of the opposite sex and more time with animals of the same sex. Though the behaviors in these studies appear to have more relevance to human sexual orientation than do studies of mounting or lordotic behavior, they are still uncomfortably distant from establishing a consistent interest in sexual contact with same-sex conspecifics.

What, then, has been the value, if any, of neuroendocrine studies of rodents and other nonhuman species? As Ruse (1988) has noted, these studies have had immense heuristic value in the specification of models for human sexual orientation. It was largely results of animal work that led researchers such as LeVay (1991) to focus on the anterior hypothalamus as the most promising area of the human brain to be causally related to sexual orientation. On the other hand, some scientists argue that some researchers have assumed too close a correspondence between the sexual behavior and related brain organization of rats and humans, thus leading themselves (and the field) astray (Gooren 1990; Byne and Parsons 1993). The ultimate gauge of the value of animal models for human sexual orientation will be the number of theoretically interesting, replicable findings they generate, using human subjects.

Studies of Prenatal Influences in Humans   For obvious reasons experimental studies of the effects of prenatal hormonal manipulations on humans are impossible. However, in some rare circumstances humans have been inadvertently exposed to unusual patterns of hormones in utero, as a result of either medical intervention or genetic anomalies. These "natural experiments" are potentially informative regarding the effects of hormones on the development of sex-dimorphic behavior such as sexual orientation.

Perhaps the most extensively studied condition has been congenital adrenal hyperplasia (CAH). CAH is a genetic autosomal recessive condition that prevents the production of sufficient quantities of cortisol to inhibit the release of adrenocorticotropic hormone (ACTH) and subsequent adrenal steroid synthesis. Affected individuals are thus exposed to high levels of androgens. The level of androgens is sufficient to cause some degree of masculinization of genitals in most females with the condition, enough so that the sex of the child is frequently ambiguous at birth. Some of these females have been reared as males, particularly before the 1950s, before corrective surgery was available or because diagnosis of the condition was late. However, the large majority of such women are now assigned as females and given early surgery to feminize their genitals and ongoing hormonal therapy to prevent virilization.

A neuroendocrine theory of sexual orientation is supported by, and indeed seems to require, a finding of increased homosexuality among CAH females reared as women. There have been several studies of this issue. Ehrhardt, Evers, and Money (1968) reported that as many as half of their twenty-three CAH female subjects were bisexual (depending on the criteria). None was exclusively homosexual. This study was problematic because it included late-treated patients, who were notably masculine in appearance. In contrast, a study of eighteen late-treated CAH women found no reports of homosexual fantasy or experience (Lev-Ran 1974). However, subjects in this study were from the Soviet Union, where intolerance of homosexuality was particularly high, possibly making subjects less open. Money et al. (1984) studied thirty women with early-treated CAH and found results similar to those of Ehrhardt et al. Of those for whom sexual history data were available, 48 percent were bisexual with respect to fantasy or behavior, significantly higher than a control group. The largest study to date on sexuality among CAH women, by Mulaikal et al. (1987; this paper contains some subjects studied by Money et al. 1984), found a 5 percent (4/80) rate of self-identification as "homosexual" or "bisexual." Unfortunately these authors did not report the incidence of homosexual attraction, as distinct from behavior. Furthermore, fully 38 percent of the women in this sample gave insufficient data to ascertain sexual orientation. It is possible that those with homosexual feelings may have been overrepresented in that group. Dittmann et al. (1992) found increased homosexual versus heterosexual interest in thirty-four female CAH patients, compared to fourteen control sisters. Finally, in a recent abstract Zucker et al. (1992) reported that a sample of twenty-nine CAH women had significantly less attraction to men and significantly more attraction to women than a control group consisting of their female relatives.

There is another body of CAH research which, though not directly concerned with sexual orientation, is quite relevant. This is the study of gender atypicality of female children with CAH. Since gender atypicality or gender nonconformity is a strong predictor of adult homosexuality, a finding that girls with CAH are, for instance, more tomboyish would provide indirect support for a neuroendocrine theory of homosexuality. Several studies have provided results suggesting that CAH girls are tomboyish in certain respects, particularly regarding play patterns (Berenbaum and Hines 1992; Ehrhardt et al. 1968; Ehrhardt and Baker 1974). The most methodologically rigorous of these studies, by Berenbaum and Hines, compared CAH girls and boys to young male and female relatives on a free play paradigm, in which "feminine," "masculine," and "neutral" toys were equally available. CAH girls and boys and unaffected control boys were all much more likely to play with "masculine" toys and less likely to play with "feminine" toys than were control girls.

The literature regarding CAH and sexual orientation is inconclusive. Although most of the studies have found some evidence for increased homosexuality in CAH women, the largest study (Mulaikal et al. 1987) found relatively low rates. The link between CAH and some aspects of childhood gender nonconformity is more compelling, but this provides only indirect evidence for a neuroendocrine view of homosexuality. Furthermore, some have argued that even if CAH women have higher rates of homosexuality (or childhood gender nonconformity), a neuroendocrine interpretation is unnecessary (Byne and Parsons 1993; Bleier 1984). This is because CAH females are often born with masculinized genitals that might very well affect parental attitudes or self-concept in important ways. However, it should be noted that Berenbaum and Hines found the degree of masculine toy preference in their CAH girls to be unrelated to the degree of genital virilization reported at diagnosis. Furthermore, parents of CAH and normal girls did not differ in their reports of behavior toward their daughters. Although studies of CAH have provided some promising results, and therefore may eventually provide definitive data on the question, they cannot now be invoked as conclusive evidence for either nature or nurture. For more conclusive findings, it will be necessary to study large samples of CAH females (as

Mulaikal et al. did), comparing them to large control samples on detailed measures of sexual attraction (as some of the smaller studies did).

I have focused on CAH because it has been studied relatively frequently and because, of all the hormonal anomalies, it is closest to the neuroendocrine model of homosexual etiology. Other conditions have been mentioned as relevant for theories of sexual orientation, including androgen insensitivity, 5-alpha reductase deficiency, and prenatal exposure to synthetic hormones with androgenizing effects. However, androgen insensitivity and 5-alpha reductase deficiency are far less convincing than CAH as "natural experiments," because they do not clearly separate hormonal and experiential influences (Byne and Parsons 1993; Money 1988). For instance, androgen-insensitive XY individuals are effectively female in their hormonal influences. They are also raised as females, thus confounding social and "biological" influences. Female offspring of hormonally treated pregnancies are less problematic in this interpretive respect, but the results of relevant studies have been highly inconclusive (Byne and Parsons 1993).

Sexually Dimorphic Traits and Sexual Orientation   Another strategy for studying neuroendocrine hypotheses has been to compare homosexuals and heterosexuals on traits that are sexually dimorphic. Findings that homosexuals are somewhat intermediate between heterosexual men and women on these traits provide some support for a neuroendocrine theory of homosexuality, particularly if the relevant traits are plausibly thought to be innately sexually dimorphic. The rationale, often unstated, is that a pattern of hormonal influences causing a brain to differentiate homosexually is likely to have more general effects. These should result in a more gender atypical pattern of neural organization in some other respects, as well.

One characteristic that seemed promising in this respect was the luteinizing hormone (LH) response. Female rats show a surge of LH following secretion of estrogen, which triggers ovulation. In contrast, estrogen inhibits LH secretion in male rats. In rats this sex difference has been found to depend on the organizational effects of prenatal androgens (Gorski 1966). Humans also show a sex difference in LH secretion following estrogen injections. Thus great excitement initially greeted two reports that homosexual (but not heterosexual) men show a partial LH surge to the administration of estrogen (Dörner et al. 1975; Dörner 1988; Gladue et al. 1984). These findings supported the possibility that male homosexuals have a "feminine brain."

However, it now appears that the LH data may be problematic as support for a neuroendocrine theory of homosexuality. Other studies have failed to replicate the finding of a partial LH surge in male homosexuals (Gooren 1986a; Hendricks et al. 1989). These failures, by themselves, are not a fatal blow to the LH data, because they were all small studies, with insufficient statistical power to guarantee replication. More problematic is the work of Gooren (1986a, 1986b), who has demonstrated that the human sex difference in LH release is unlikely to reflect differences in neural organization. In an elegant series of experiments, Gooren studied male-to-female and female-to-male transsexuals, before and after hormonal therapy and sex reassignment surgery. He found that these individuals showed a pattern of LH response appropriate to their hormonal and/or gonadal sex; thus LH response appears to be a function of circulating androgens; that is, pretreatment female-to-male and post-treatment male-to-female transsexuals showed the LH surge, whereas pretreatment male-to-female and post-treatment female-to-male transsexuals did not. Indeed, the same individuals showed two different patterns of LH response in two different phases of their treatment. Gooren thus demonstrated that LH response patterns are unlikely to provide information about the masculine or feminine neural organization of homosexuals or heterosexuals. Because two independent studies found an association between sexual orientation and LH response, and since no one has convincingly explained away these findings, they cannot be entirely rejected. Nor, on the other hand, can they be considered strong evidence for a neuroendocrine theory of homosexuality.

A second line of research has focused on sexually dimorphic characteristics thought to be related to cerebral lateralization (Geschwind and Galaburda 1985), including spatial ability and handedness. Lateralization refers to the tendency of certain brain functions to be specialized in either the right or left cerebral hemisphere. Males are more lateralized than females, and right-handers are more lateralized than left-handers, on average, for both verbal and spatial functions (McGlone 1980). Somewhat paradoxically, males are more likely than females to be left-handed, but this is thought by some scientists to result from a sex difference in timing of cerebral development (Geschwind and Galaburda 1985). Men tend to have higher spatial abilities relative to verbal abilities, and this pattern has been hypothesized to be related to sex differences in lateralization. It is also noteworthy that CAH has been associated with both increased left-handedness (Nass et al. 1987) and higher spatial scores (Resnick et al. 1986) among women.

Several studies have reported homosexual men to have a higher incidence of left-handedness than heterosexual men (McCormick et al. 1990; Lindesay 1987; Götestam et al. 1992). Relatedly Watson (1991) found an increased rate of left-handedness among male-to-female transsexuals, and Gooren (1991) obtained similar results in a combined sample of male-to-female and female-to-male transsexuals. On the other hand, two recent reports on large samples both failed to find an increase in left-handedness among homosexual men (Satz et al. 1991; Marchant-Haycox et al. 1991). McCormick et al. (1990) also found an increased rate of left-handedness among homosexual women, the only report to focus on women to date, and Tkachuk and Zucker (1991) found a higher incidence of left-handedness in a combined sample of homosexual males and females. Thus there is some indication that both male and female homosexuals have an increased rate of left-handedness. (Because high levels of fetal testosterone are hypothesized to be associated with left-handedness, it is counterintuitive that male homosexuality is associated with sinistrality. James [1989] offers an intriguing explanation of this apparent paradox, suggesting that male homosexuality may arise from a different pattern of timing of prenatal androgen surges, with high androgen levels occurring when handedness is affected and low levels occurring when sexual orientation is affected.)

Regarding spatial ability, several studies have suggested that homosexual men score lower than heterosexual men on spatial tests (Sanders and Ross-Field 1986; Gladue et al. 1990; McCormick et al. 1991; Tkachuk and Zucker 1991). Similarly gender-nonconforming boys, who are likely to become homosexual men, also have been found to perform less well than controls on spatial tests (Finegan et al. 1982; Grimshaw et al. 1991). The one study focusing on women, however, found lesbians to obtain lower scores than heterosexual women (Gladue et al. 1990), a finding difficult to reconcile with a neuroendocrine theory.

Thus a reasonable number of studies suggest that there may be lateralization differences between homosexuals and heterosexuals, particularly among men (who have been studied more often). Nevertheless, they cannot be considered definitive proof for a neuroendocrine theory of sexual orientation. This is partly because of the mixed findings. It is troubling, for instance, that the largest studies of handedness found no association with sexual orientation. But, more important, neuroendocrine theories of both sexual orientation and lateralization are currently insufficiently specified to allow strong predictions, and hence confirmations, of either. Furthermore, the causes of the sex difference in spatial ability, particularly, remain controversial, with both "biological" and psychosocial explanations being offered (Linn and Petersen 1985).

Human Neuroanatomical Studies   Potentially the most persuasive type of evidence for a neuroendocrine theory of sexual orientation is finding neuroanatomical differences between homosexuals and heterosexuals in areas of the brain hypothesized to be involved in sexual or related behavior. Studies of nonhuman animals have implicated the hypothalamus as the most likely site of interest. However, any part of the brain that is sexually dimorphic is of interest, given the likelihood that an influence affecting sexual differentiation of the hypothalamus would affect other areas of the brain as well.

Careful, systematic research on sex differences in the human brain has only recently begun, and studies of neuroanatomical correlates of human sexual orientation are rare indeed. Before this literature is evaluated, it is useful to put it into a methodological context. Neuroanatomical studies are typically enormously painstaking enterprises. Because of this, a research team usually investigates several brain locations of interest. Sometimes a difference is discovered after the researchers, looking at one part of the brain, notice a potential pattern elsewhere. Both these factors increase the probability of type 1 error, that is, the possibility that a difference occurs merely as a result of chance sample fluctuations. Hence, while replication in science is always important, replication of neurophysiological findings is especially so. By the same token, failures to replicate with small samples should not be considered definitive disconfirmation of initial findings, since small samples are associated with a high type 2 error rate. *with small findings*

Three highly publicized reports of brain structures are related to sexual orientation. The first, by Swaab and Hofman (1990), found the suprachiasmatic nucleus of the hypothalamus to be 1.7 times larger in homosexual than in heterosexual men. This nucleus is thought to be involved in the regulation of circadian rhythms and, as such, is a surprising location in which to find a sexual orientation difference. These authors also examined a nucleus that their research group (Swaab and Fliers 1985) had previously found to be sexually dimorphic, but found no difference between homosexuals and heterosexuals. The sexual orientation difference in the suprachiasmatic nucleus has not yet been replicated.

The most noted finding of a brain difference between homosexuals and heterosexuals was reported by LeVay (1991). LeVay investigated two hypothalamic nuclei that had previously been reported to be sexually dimorphic (Allen et al. 1989). He studied the brains of eighteen homosexual men, all of whom had died of acquired immune deficiency syndrome (HIV/AIDS), a comparison group of sixteen men whose sexual orientations were unknown but presumed to be heterosexual, and a group of six women. One of the nuclei was not even found by LeVay to be sexually dimorphic. However, the third interstitial nucleus of the anterior hypothalamus (INAH-3) was less than half as large in the women as in the heterosexual men, replicating the previous researchers' findings. Furthermore, the nuclei of the homosexual men were also less than half the size of the heterosexual men's, and were indistinguishable from those of the women.

LeVay's findings have been subjected to intense scrutiny. For instance, it has been noted that the findings could be owing to the effects of AIDS rather than sexual orientation. However, LeVay demonstrated that his findings were robust even when the analysis was restricted to those heterosexual men who had died of AIDS. Another criticism has been that LeVay did not know for certain that his "heterosexual" group contained no homosexuals. However, any misclassification of subjects would diminish the obtained effect size relative to the true effect size. Finally, it should be emphasized that LeVay was studying a nucleus that had been found *twice* (counting LeVay's own demonstration) to be sexually dimorphic. Thus the a priori justification for his search was strong. Like all important findings, LeVay's should be replicated. The INAH-3 remains the most promising road to confirmation of a neuroendocrine theory of sexual orientation.

The most recent brain study, by Allen and Gorski (1992), demonstrated sex and sexual orientation differences in the anterior commissure (AC) of the corpus collosum, with heterosexual women's ACs being larger than heterosexual men's, but with homosexual men's the largest of all. Their search was motivated by a previous finding of a sex difference in the AC (Allen and Gorski 1991) and thus was well justified. Though apparently sexually dimorphic, the AC is not thought to be involved in sexual behavior. So this finding may reflect the generalized effects of neuroendocrine influences that also affect the areas of the brain that directly regulate sexual orientation.

Current Status of the Neuroendocrine View   The neuroendocrine theory of sexual orientation is currently the most influential etiological theory of sexual orientation. Its empirical support, however, is largely indirect. The most careful and definitive studies of hormonal influence on sexually dimorphic sexual behavior have used nonhuman animals whose species-typical mating behaviors do not map directly onto ours. Rats do not seem to have a sexual orientation in the same way humans do, and it is controversial whether the behaviors that have been studied (primarily lordosis and mounting) are relevant at all. The most replicated relevant finding in humans, that sexual orientation is related to childhood gender atypicality, is not clearly a biological phenomenon, though it does suggest that homosexuals and opposite-sex heterosexuals have been subject to similar influences, as predicted by a neuroendocrine view. Individuals who have been exposed to atypical levels · of hormones are, in principle, quite relevant to the neuroendocrine theory; however, results of research on such persons have been mixed. Studies of sexually dimorphic traits related to brain lateralization such as spatial ability and handedness have also provided a complicated empirical picture. Furthermore, the neuroendocrine theory does not make strong predictions about the relationship between these traits and sexual orientation. Perhaps the most promising findings have been the demonstrations of neuroanatomical differences between heterosexual and homosexual men. If these findings are replicated (and extended to women), they may provide the long sought-after proof of neuroendocrine routes to human sexual orientation.

Genetics and Sexual Orientation

Human behavior genetics has produced evidence for substantial genetic factors in a wide variety of behavioral traits (Plomin 1990), from different types of psychopathology to personality and intelligence, even to characteristics such as religiosity (Waller et al. 1990). Indeed, failures to find significant heritability for well-measured traits in large sample studies have been exceedingly rare. Viewed from this perspective, it is hardly daring to hypothesize that sexual orientation may be heritable as well. However, sexual orientation is significantly different from the aforementioned characteristics. Homosexuals have presumably always been at a reproductive disadvantage compared to heterosexuals. (With respect to recent history, this disadvantage is demonstrably severe. Bell and Weinberg [1978; Tables 17.1 and 17.13] showed that both male and female homosexuals reported less than one-quarter of the number of children as same-sex heterosexuals.) If sexual orientation is somewhat heritable, this means that some genes predispose individuals to homosexuality. How have those genes resisted elimination by the inevitable engine of natural selection? Even at its lowest estimated base rates, homosexuality occurs far more frequently than the highest known mutation rates; thus mutation alone cannot account for the persistence of "gay genes," if they exist. The paradox of relatively high incidence and low fertility of homosexuals makes sexual orientation a likely candidate for low or zero heritability.

It is genuinely surprising, therefore, that the available evidence is more consistent with moderate to high heritability for both male and female sexual orientation (though relevant evidence is more plentiful for men). Before reviewing this evidence, it will be useful to explicate some basic genetic concepts.

Heritability   If a trait is at least partially genetic, then it should be familial. Therefore the first step in a behavioral genetic investigation is generally to find if the trait of interest runs in families. Although necessary, familiality is not sufficient to justify a genetic conclusion, because traits can be familial for genetic or environmental reasons. Therefore more sophisticated approaches are needed subsequently, and these might be termed "heritability studies," because they have one common goal of providing a heritability estimate for the trait.

Heritability is the proportion of phenotypic variance that is explicable by genetic variance. Represented by a number ranging from 0 to 1, heritability is estimated in several ways, though the most intuitive is the intraclass correlation of monozygotic (MZ) twins who were reared separately in environments assigned at random. This method of estimating heritability is used infrequently, because of the extreme rarity of MZ twins who were reared apart. There are, for instance, only six separated MZ pairs with homosexuality (i.e., at least one twin is homosexual) in the literature (Eckert, Bouchard, Bohlen, and Heston 1986).

Perhaps the most widely used design for estimating heritability of human behavioral traits is the classical twin study, in which MZ and dizygotic (DZ) twins are compared for their degree of phenotypic similarity. The rationale is as follows: MZ twins are genetically identical (with rare exceptions), but DZ twins are not. MZ and DZ twins were both reared together and thus had equally similar rearing environments. Thus if MZ twins are more similar than DZ twins for a trait, it must reflect the increased genetic similarity. An important assumption on which the classical twin method depends is the "equal environments assumption," that the relevant environments are no more similar for MZ than for DZ twins. Although this assumption has been criticized (e.g., Lewontin et al. 1984), it seems to be accurate for traits studied so far (Plomin et al. 1989). Unfortunately it has not been specifically examined within the context of sexual orientation.

Because heritabilities may be different for different populations (e.g., Asians versus whites), and because heritability estimates typically have substantial standard errors around them, they should be viewed as approximations. I use the following very rough scale: less than .25 is low, .25 to .50 is moderate, and greater than .50 is high heritability. Note, however, that even a "low" heritability of .16 implies a correlation of .40 between genotype and phenotype. Furthermore, provided the assumptions required to compute heritability are valid, this correlation may be interpreted causally, that is, individual differences in genotype cause individual differences in phenotype. Given our present ignorance about causes of sexual orientation, one would be delighted to find a causal connection so large. On the other hand, if heritability were .16, environmentality would be .84, implying a correlation between relevant environment and phenotype of nearly .92. In this case environmental causes would dwarf genetic ones, though even the latter would be important enough to be interesting.

Familiality of Sexual Orientation   Hirschfeld (1936) remarked more than fifty years ago that homosexuality appeared to run in families. However, rigorous confirmation of Hirschfeld's informal observations has taken a long time. In a landmark study Pillard and Weinrich (1986) demonstrated the plausibility of doing family genetic studies of homosexuality. Using newspaper advertisements they recruited fifty-one homosexual male and fifty heterosexual male probands, who were blind to the purpose of the study. During the interview they asked about the sexual orientation of all siblings. Furthermore, they asked (and received, to a large degree) permission to contact siblings. This was generally done through the mail, but some phone interviews were necessary. In the sibling questionnaires or interviews, several questions were asked about sexual orientation. Pillard and Weinrich showed that probands predicted their siblings' orientations with a high degree of accuracy. They also found substantially more gay brothers among gay male probands than among heterosexual male probands, 20 to 4 percent, respectively. This is roughly consistent with another family study of male homosexuality. Bailey et al. (1991) obtained estimates of the number of brothers "known" to be homosexual from heterosexual male and female probands, as well as homosexual male probands, finding a 10 percent rate among the brothers of homosexual men compared to a 2 percent rate among the brothers of heterosexual men and women. Although brothers were not contacted to verify their sexual orientations, the results of Pillard and Weinrich suggest that this is unnecessary.

Is female sexual orientation also familial? There have now been two reasonably large studies of this question. Pillard (1990) found a 25 percent rate of homosexuality or bisexuality among sixty sisters of bisexual or homosexual female probands, compared to a rate of 11 percent for sisters of fifty-three heterosexual female probands. It is interesting that they also found a marginally significant elevation of homosexual brothers among their homosexual female probands. If replicated, this finding would have important implications for theories of sexual orientation: a common mechanism in the development of male and female homosexuality. Bailey and Benishay (1993) also reported significant familiality. Of the ninety-nine sisters of the homosexual probands, 12 percent were homosexual compared to 2 percent of the eighty-three sisters of the heterosexual probands. Although a slightly higher percentage of brothers of the homosexual probands were also homosexual (7 to 1 percent), this difference was not significant. Both Pillard (1990) and Bailey and Benishay (1993) obtained verification of probands' reports of their siblings' sexual orientation in the majority of cases, and both found such reports to be highly accurate.

Genetic Studies   The first noteworthy genetic study of sexual orientation was done by Kallmann (1952a, 1952b), who found a 100 percent concordance rate for thirty-seven male MZ twin pairs compared to a 15 percent rate for twenty-six dizygotic male DZ pairs. Kallmann's study has been justifiably criticized for its methodology, particularly its reliance on sampling from correctional and psychiatric institutions, its lack of detail regarding zygosity diagnosis, and its anomalous findings. Most important, results of several case studies and small twin series (reviewed by Rosenthal 1970) suggest that the true MZ concordance rate, although appreciable, is substantially less than 100 percent. Because of these problems, the study is generally held in low regard. Nevertheless, no one has offered a plausible alternative to genetic influence to account for Kallmann's strikingly different concordance rates.

A fascinating report of MZ twins raised separately (Eckert et al. 1986) was consistent with a high heritability for male sexual orientation. Both the two male pairs included were concordant for homosexual feelings (though one of the twins classified himself as a heterosexual anyway). In contrast, in the same study none of four female pairs was concordant. Obviously the sample size of this study was too small to justify strong conclusions.

Given the promising results obtained by Kallmann, it is somewhat surprising that almost forty years passed before the question of heritability was again investigated using large samples. Seemingly by coincidence, four reasonably large studies have been reported in the last year. All four obtained samples through advertisements in gay publications. For instance, the first and largest, by Bailey and Pillard (1991), used advertisements that asked for gay men with either male twins or adoptive brothers. (Adoptive brothers are biologically unrelated males reared as siblings to the probands.) Eligible and interested subjects called the investigators and were interviewed, usually in person, about their sexual orientations and related traits. They were also asked about their brothers' sexual orientation and, finally, for permission to contact their co-twins or adoptive brothers. As Pillard and Weinrich (1986) found, sibling reports were highly related to proband reports. The rates of homosexuality (including bisexuality) among the relatives were 52 percent (29/56) for MZ co-twins; 22 percent (12/54) for DZ co-twins; and 11 percent (6/57) for adoptive brothers. This pattern is consistent with moderate to strong heritability for male sexual orientation. Under varying assumptions, heritability estimates ranged from .31 to .74. The lowest estimates came from models that assumed a base rate of 10 percent for homosexuality. Recent reports suggest that the lower base rate of 4 percent is more appropriate (Johnson et al. 1992; ACSF 1992). All heritabilities computed assuming a 4 percent rate exceeded .50. One anomalous finding of the study was a lower than expected rate of homosexuality among the biological non-twin brothers of 9 percent. Genetic theory predicts that this rate should be equal to that for DZ twins and higher than that for adoptive brothers.

Because I have defined "sexual orientation" as sexual attraction rather than either identity or behavior, it is important to address one methodological issue of this study. Both probands and relatives were classified according to sexual identity, that is, whether they called themselves "gay/bisexual" or "heterosexual." This was done for three reasons. First, this was the easiest way to write the advertisements used to recruit probands. Second, in both groups sexual identity was closely related to both sexual behavior and sexual attraction patterns, as measured by the seven-point Kinsey scale (Kinsey et al. 1948). Third, probands' ratings of their relatives were used when relatives' self-ratings were unavailable, and it was believed that the concordance between probands' ratings and relatives' self-ratings would be higher for the broader categories of sexual identity than for the more specific Kinsey scores. Indirectly supporting this belief was the finding that although probands were almost perfect at predicting whether their relatives would identify as "heterosexual" versus "gay/bisexual," they did poorly at predicting whether a nonheterosexual relative would call himself "gay" or "bisexual." This method of classifying sexual orientation was also used in the female family study by Bailey and Benishay (1993) mentioned previously and in the genetic study of female sexual orientation by Bailey, Pillard, Neale, and Agyei (1993) discussed later.

The second genetic study, restricted to twins, was reported by King and

McDonald (1992). Using recruitment methods similar to those of Bailey and Pillard, they found a sample of forty-six homosexuals with twins (thirty-eight male; eight female). The reported concordances, 25 percent for MZ twins compared to 12 percent for DZ twins, appear to conflict with the higher rates obtained by Bailey and Pillard. However, King and McDonald's sample was considerably smaller, so that the difference might largely be owing to sampling error. Furthermore, it is unclear how zygosity was diagnosed in this study, nor were co-twins contacted to verify orientations, nor were results reported separately for men and women. Finally, it is noteworthy that five of seven respondents considered their co-twins entirely heterosexual despite an apparently prolonged incestuous homosexual relationship. The third study, by Whitam et al. (1992) found even higher concordances than did Bailey and Pillard — 66 percent for MZ versus 30 percent for DZ pairs.

A fourth study (Bailey et al. 1993) focused exclusively on female sexual orientation. The methodology was identical to that of Bailey and Pillard's (1991) genetic study of males. Probands were homosexual or bisexual women with twins or adoptive sisters. Of the relatives whose sexual orientation could be confidently assessed, 48 percent (34/71) of MZ co-twins, 16 percent (6/37) of DZ co-twins, and 6 percent (2/35) of adoptive sisters were homosexual. Probands also reported that 14 percent (10/73) of their non-twin biological sisters were homosexual, a rate quite similar both to the DZ twin rate and to the rate found by Bailey and Benishay (1993) in their family study of female sexual orientation. Heritabilities were significant under a wide range of assumptions about the population base rate of homosexuality and ascertainment bias, and they were of the same order as those obtained by Bailey and Pillard for male sexual orientation (1991).

Thus the available genetic evidence suggests that both male and female sexual orientations are moderately heritable. However, the limitations of this literature must be recognized. All the genetic studies discussed herein used a method of subject ascertainment that may be susceptible to serious biases; that is, if gay men with gay co-twins are more likely than gay men with heterosexual co-twins to volunteer for such studies, the concordance rates will be artifactually higher. Bailey and Pillard (1991), however, demonstrated that this kind of bias cannot lead to spurious findings of heritability unless it is greater for MZ than for DZ twins. Given the general consistency of the picture obtained from family studies, the small study of twins reared apart (at least for men), and the four large twin studies, all of which found higher MZ than DZ concordance, it seems likely that the heritability findings are robust. However, large population-based twin studies (for a small version, see Buhrich et al. 1991) or systematically obtained (and hence representative) samples of gay twins are necessary to address such methodological issues.

One striking result of the more recent genetic studies is the high rate of discordance among the MZ twins. Except for Kallmann's study, concordances have been well under 100 percent. This shows that environment exerts an influence on sexual orientation. It should be remembered, however, that "environment" refers simply to all nongenetic influences, biological or social. There is presently no good candidate for an environmental factor not shared by MZ co-twins that might affect sexual orientation.

Even if it could be demonstrated with certainty that sexual orientation were substantially heritable, the question would remain of what, exactly, the relevant genes are doing. Although most genetic researchers have been influenced by the neuroendocrine theory, a finding of nonzero heritability is merely consistent with it. Such a finding does not provide direct support for a neuroendocrine view because alternative genotype-to-phenotype routes involving social environmental factors are imaginable (see, e.g., Byne and Parsons 1993). Only if either a specific gene affecting sexual orientation or a genetic marker associated with it were identified could genetic data strongly confirm a neuroendocrine theory.

The Paradox of "Gay Genes" Revisited   I have delayed discussion of possible explanations for the persistence of genes for sexual orientation until a consideration of the genetic data. While ultimately inconclusive, the genetic data seem strong enough to justify serious consideration of mechanisms by which "gay genes" might be maintained.

Several explanations have been proposed. A necessary feature of any such explanation is that, although the relevant genes detract from a gay individual's reproductive output, they facilitate reproduction in other carriers. One possible model, proposed by Hutchinson (1959), is that of heterozygote superiority, of which sickle-cell anemia is an example. Heterozygote superiority occurs when individuals homozygous for either of two alleles at a genetic locus (i.e., those who have two copies of either gene) have decreased reproductive success compared to heterozygotes (who have one copy of each). This model explains the persistence of genes for sickle-cell anemia, because heterozygotes are better protected against malaria than individuals without any sickling genes. Although plausible, this model is not very useful without a specification of the alleged advantage for heterozygotes.

The second explanation considered here is an application of an immensely important concept in evolutionary theory, namely, kin selection

(Hamilton 1964; Wilson 1978). Applied to sexual orientation, kin selection theory suggests that while homosexuals do not themselves reproduce at high rates, their sacrifice enables kin (most likely siblings and parents) to reproduce more than they otherwise would. Kin selection requires that this increased benefit be substantial: Siblings or parents must total at least two extra children for every one foregone by the homosexual individual. What is the specific mechanism by which homosexuals aid kin in reproduction? It has been proposed that homosexuals may be particularly likely to aid in rearing and to invest resources in their nieces and nephews (Weinrich 1987; Wilson 1978). This theory could be supported either by demonstrating increased fertility of relatives of homosexuals or by examining specific behaviors of homosexuals toward their relatives. Unfortunately no empirical studies of this theory have been attempted, so it remains unfounded speculation.

Related Phenotypes: Bisexuality and Transsexualism

Bisexuality   In "biological" studies of sexual orientation, there are generally two approaches to bisexuals: They are either classified with homosexuals or they are excluded. Which approach is more justifiable?

From the vantage of a neuroendocrine theory, bisexuality need not be particularly problematic. Attraction to women means that sexual orientation has been masculinized. However, some unknown physiological process has prevented behavioral defeminization, and thus attraction to men occurs simultaneously. In this view it makes most sense to treat bisexuals as intermediate between heterosexuals and homosexuals. Until a neuroendocrine account of bisexuality garners scientific support, however, the etiological relationship between bisexuality and either homosexuality or heterosexuality remains an open, empirical question. Relevant evidence consists of whether bisexuals are more like homosexuals or heterosexuals with respect to relevant variables. For instance, Bell et al. (1981) found bisexual women to be intermediate between heterosexual and homosexual women in recollections of childhood gender nonconformity. No such pattern was reported for men. Consistent with the null finding for men, Freund (1974) found that men who self-labeled as bisexual were aroused to homosexual but not heterosexual erotic stimuli.

One empirical strategy, as yet untapped, would be to see whether patterns of familiality differed between bisexuals and homosexuals. For example, do bisexuals and homosexuals differ in their rates of homosexual siblings? Do

MZ co-twins of bisexual probands have a different distribution of sexual orientation from MZ co-twins of homosexual probands? One problem with doing such studies is that bisexuals appear to be somewhat rare, comprising a minority of nonheterosexuals in most samples. Bailey and Pillard (1991) obtained results supporting the hypothesis that homosexuality and hetero-sexuality may be more categorically than dimensionally distinct, with bisexuality a relatively rare occurrence. Verifying this observation could have important implications for understanding the development of sexual orientation.

Transsexualism   Transsexualism is a rare phenotype characterized by a persistent dissatisfaction with one's anatomical sex (gender dysphoria) and a desire to change it. Blanchard (1987, 1989) has shown that there are two independent types of transsexualism, which he distinguishes as homosexual and heterosexual transsexualism. The former is characterized by attraction to the same sex, an early history of childhood gender nonconformity, early onset of gender dysphoria, and a fairly even sex ratio. The latter type of transsexuals are heterosexual without a history of childhood gender nonconformity and are nearly always male. Heterosexual transsexuals usually have a history of fetishistic cross-dressing (transvestism), which, in adulthood, evidently transforms into the desire to change sex. It is homosexual transsexualism that seems likely to be etiologically related to homosexuality. Besides the obvious similarities of a homosexual orientation and childhood gender nonconformity, Blanchard and colleagues have demonstrated other non-obvious similarities in homosexuality and homosexual transsexualism (Blanchard and Sheridan 1992a), including a sibling sex ratio biased toward males and a relatively late average birth order. On the other hand, they failed to find a high percentage of homosexual siblings among homosexual transsexuals (Blanchard and Sheridan 1992b).

Future Directions

There is much work to be done in articulating the "biological" mechanisms involved in the development of sexual orientation. Indeed, even most researchers who are engaged in, or otherwise sympathetic to, a biological research program freely admit that neuroendocrine or genetic hypotheses about sexual orientation have not been supported to a degree of certainty that would justify their acceptance. Nor can critics of these hypotheses reasonably claim that they have been adequately falsified. There are roughly three broad programs of research that would further illuminate both the strengths and weaknesses of "biological" theories of sexual orientation: research on basic nonbiological questions of interest to homosexology in general, research designed to replicate the most important "biological" findings, and, given the results of the replication attempts, research aimed at elaborating promising "biological" findings.

All researchers studying sexual orientation are impeded by the absence of knowledge about some very basic facts. Foremost are incidence figures for sexual feelings, identification, and behavior. It is symptomatic of the sorry present state of knowledge that we still look to Kinsey's (1948, 1953) data to estimate these figures, despite the facts that those data are decades old, had severe sampling biases that Kinsey acknowledged at the time, and are cited by different writers to support a wide range of estimates. For example, many people are fond of citing a 10 percent figure for homosexuality in the general population; this figure derives from Kinsey's data. Gebhard (1972), however, used Kinsey's data to estimate the incidence of female homosexuality at 1.5 percent or less. Although these differences are partly explicable by use of different criteria for "homosexuality," Kinsey's data cannot yield trustworthy, specific current estimates. Successful future studies will attempt representative sampling, obtain high cooperation rates, and ask specific and detailed questions about both sexual feelings and behavior. Though a hostile political environment has impeded progress, at least three large relevant surveys are in progress (one American, one British, and one French). These studies were most immediately motivated by the need to obtain information relevant to the epidemiology of sex practices likely to transmit HIV. Let us hope, however, that the need to focus on specific sexual behaviors will not prevent the surveys from inquiring about sexual orientation and other psychological issues as well.

To illustrate the importance of knowing incidence figures more precisely, let us consider two examples. First, suppose one interviewed a large cohort of gay men and found the rate of homosexuality among their brothers to be 12 percent. If one accepts the high estimate of 10 percent for the base rate of homosexuality in the general population, then one will conclude that familial factors make only a trivial contribution to the development of sexual orientation in men. This is because brothers of gay men, in this case, do not have much of an increased rate of homosexuality. They are only 1.2 times more likely to be gay than is a man sampled randomly from the general population. In contrast, if one accepts Gebhard's (1972) estimate of 4 percent, then this is triple the expected rate, a fairly substantial increase. As a second example, consider the possibility suggested by unsystematic research (e.g., Friday 1991) that homosexual fantasies may be quite common among women who identify themselves as heterosexuals. If such fantasies were similar in nature, frequency, and intensity to those of homosexually identified women, then it would seem unlikely that sexual identity merely reflected sexual feelings, per se. Why would only a relatively small minority of the women capable of homosexual arousal call themselves "lesbian" and mate more or less exclusively with other women? I emphasize that this example is hypothetical, and many of us who take a biological approach believe that heterosexual and homosexual women's sexual feelings differ in important respects. But we do not know this.

Another kind of research that is needed in homosexology, generally, is a systematic study of homosexuality across many diverse cultures. The research with which I am most familiar (e.g., Bailey and Pillard 1991; Bailey et al. 1993) primarily used white Americans as subjects, because they volunteered most frequently. Cross-cultural differences in the causes of sexual orientation are certainly conceivable and could illuminate the role of the social environment. Alternatively, it is possible, as Whitam and Mathy (1986) have suggested, that homosexuality develops similarly across cultures that seem to differ in important respects. If so, this would provide more support for a "biological" view.

The second broadly defined research program previously endorsed concerns replication. Many of the findings considered important for "biological" research were obtained in studies that had important methodological limitations. I have attempted to note the most serious limitations in the relevant sections of this paper. My purpose here is merely to emphasize that it is crucial to demonstrate beyond a reasonable doubt the validity of findings on which a theory rests. As Zubin (1987) pithily expressed it, "It ain't ignorance that causes all the trouble. It's knowing things that ain't so!" The most important study to replicate, in my view, is LeVay's (1991). If possible, it would be highly desirable to examine brains of lesbians as well. Furthermore, areas with mixed findings, such as the CAH literature, could greatly benefit from a large, controlled, and, one would hope, definitive study.

Provided that careful studies replicate the most promising findings supporting the neuroendocrine and genetic theories of sexual orientation, such as LeVay's neuroanatomical study and Bailey and Pillard's genetic study of male sexual orientation, the next phases of research should attempt to elaborate their deeper meanings. Thus, for example, does the INAH-3 affect sexual orientation, or is it noncausally associated with sexual orientation but masculinized along with causally relevant brain structures? A number of techniques from contemporary neuroscience may be useful in answering such questions, including immunohistochemistry, hybridization histochemistry, positron emission tomography (PET), and magnetic resonance imaging (MRI). Assuming that careful studies replicate the heritability findings, the questions of which genes are involved and what they are doing remains. Methodologies such as linkage analysis are useful in theory for the identification of genes affecting a trait, and there is reason to hope that they will someday illuminate sexual orientation. As our knowledge of the genome progresses exponentially, so will the power of these techniques. However, to date they have not been very useful in studying behavioral characteristics, perhaps because these characteristics are typically etiologically complex (Plomin 1990). Even so, behavior genetics methods can be used to study genetic and environmental mechanisms indirectly.

For example, as I have noted previously, the high rate of discordance among the MZ twins shows that environment must exert an influence on sexual orientation. Furthermore, the effective environment for sexual orientation largely appears to include aspects of experience (social or biological) that differ between MZ twins who have been reared together. No current theories of sexual orientation would predict frequent discordance between MZ co-twins. Given the possibility of prenatal influences on sexual orientation, it would be useful to know whether aspects of the prenatal environment such as hormonal exposure often differ between MZ co-twins. The equivalent question on the psychosocial side is whether parental treatment of twins differs in ways likely to foster differences in sexual orientation.

Genetic mechanisms can be illuminated by identifying differences between probands of concordant MZ pairs and those of discordant MZ pairs. Probands of concordant pairs should have relatively high genetic loadings compared to those of discordant pairs. Bailey and Pillard (1991), for example, found that male MZ probands who had been gender atypical during childhood were neither more nor less likely than other probands to have gay co-twins. Hence childhood gender atypicality does not appear to be a marker of genetic influence on sexual orientation. This finding should be replicated, and other candidate markers should be investigated in this manner.

Future research should also attempt to integrate different "biological" approaches. For example, neuroanatomical studies of MZ twins discordant for homosexuality could illuminate the nature of environmental influences, while analogous studies comparing MZ homosexual probands from concordant versus discordant pairs could provide valuable information about the routes by which genes exert their influence.

Conclusion

The present state of biological research on biological influences on sexual orientation is one of inconclusive complexity. My own view is that the general area is an exciting and promising one. A theory can be considered promising for only a limited time, however. Without conclusive results, it will eventually be dismissed as disappointing, having failed to fulfill its original promise. The time is ripe for biological theories of sexual orientation to fulfill theirs.

Acknowledgment

I thank Sheri Berenbaum, Tony D'Augelli, Joan Linsenmeier, Charlotte Patterson, and Miriam Wolfe for their insightful comments on a previous version of this paper.

References

ACSF Investigators. 1992. AIDS and sexual behaviour in France. *Nature* 360:407–9.

Adkins-Regan, E. 1988. Sex hormones and sexual orientation in animals. *Psychobiology* 16:335–47.

Allen, L. S., M. Hines, J. E. Shryne, and R. A. Gorski. 1989. Two sexually dimorphic cell groups in the human brain. *Journal of Neuroscience* 9:497–506.

Allen, L. S., and R. A. Gorski. 1991. Sexual dimorphism of the anterior commissure and massa intermedia of the human brain. *Journal of Comparative Neurology* 312:97–104.

Allen, L. S., and R. A. Gorski. 1992. Sexual orientation and the size of the anterior commissure of the human brain. *Proceedings of the National Academy of Sciences* 89:7199–7202.

Bailey, J. M., and D. Benishay. 1993. Familial aggregation of female sexual orientation. *American Journal of Psychiatry* 150:272–77.

Bailey, J. M., and K. J. Zucker. 1993. Childhood gender identity/role and sexual orientation: A conceptual analysis and quantitative review. Unpublished manuscript.

Bailey, J. M., L. Willerman, and C. Parks. 1991. A test of the maternal stress hypothesis of human male homosexuality. *Archives of Sexual Behavior* 20:277–93.

Bailey, J. M., and R. C. Pillard. 1991. A genetic study of male sexual orientation. *Archives of General Psychiatry* 48:1089–96.

Bailey, J. M., R. C. Pillard, M. C. Neale, and Y Agyei. 1993. Heritable factors influence female sexual orientation. *Archives of General Psychiatry* 50:217–23.

Barinaga, M. 1991. Is homosexuality biological? *Science* 253:956–57.

Bell, A. P., and M. S. Weinberg. 1978. *Homosexualities: A study of diversity among men and women.* New York: Simon and Schuster.

Bell, A. P., M. S. Weinberg, and S. K. Hammersmith. 1981. *Sexual preference: Its development in men and women.* Bloomington: Indiana University Press.

Berenbaum, S. A., and M. Hines. 1992. Early androgens are related to childhood sex-typed toy preferences. *Psychological Science* 3:203–6.

Blanchard, R. 1987. Heterosexual and homosexual gender dysphoria. *Archives of Sexual Behavior* 16:139–52.

Blanchard, R. 1989. The classification and labeling of nonhomosexual gender dysphorias. *Archives of Sexual Behavior* 18:315–34.

Blanchard, R., and P.M. Sheridan. 1992a. Sibling size, sibling sex ratio, birth order, and parental age in homosexual and nonhomosexual gender dysphorics. *Journal of Nervous and Mental Disorders* 180:40–47.

Blanchard, R., and P.M. Sheridan. 1992b. Proportion of unmarried siblings of homosexual and nonhomosexual gender-dysphoric patients. *Canadian Journal of Psychiatry* 37:163–67.

Bleier, R. 1984. *Science and gender: A critique of biology and its theories on women.* New York: Pergamon.

Boswell, J. 1980. *Christianity, Social Tolerance, and Homosexuality: Gay People in Western Europe from the Beginning of the Christian Era to the Fourteenth Century.* Chicago: University of Chicago Press.

Boswell, J. 1989. Revolutions, universals, and sexual categories. In M. B. Duberman, M. Vicinus, and G. Chauncey Jr, eds., *Hidden from History: Reclaiming the Gay and Lesbian Past*, pp. 17–36. New York: New American Library.

Boswell, J. 1990. Sexual categories, sexual universals: A conversation with John Boswell. In L. D. Mass, ed., *Homosexuality as Behavior and Identity*, pp. 202–33. Binghamton, N.Y.: Harrington Park.

Brand, T., E. J. Houtsmuller, and A. K. Slob. 1992. Organization of adult "sexual orientation" in male rats. Paper presented at Annual Meeting, International Academy of Sex Research, Prague, Czechoslovakia.

Brand, T., J. Kroonen, J. Mos, and A. K. Slob. 1991. Adult partner preference and sexual behavior of male rats affected by perinatal endocrine manipulations. *Hormones and Behavior* 25:323–41.

Buhrich, N. J., J. M. Bailey, and N. G. Martin. 1991. Sexual orientation, sexual identity, and sex-dimorphic behaviors in male twins. *Behavior Genetics* 21:75–96.

Byne, W., and B. Parsons. 1993. Human sexual orientation: The biologic theories reappraised. *Archives of General Psychiatry* 50:228–39.

Cook, M., and S. Mineka. 1989. Observational conditioning of fear to fear-relevant versus fear-irrelevant stimuli in rhesus monkeys. *Journal of Abnormal Psychology* 98:448–59.

De Cecco, J. P. 1990. Confusing the actor with the act: Muddled notions about homosexuality. *Archives of Sexual Behavior* 19:409–12.

Dittmann, R. W., M. E. Kappes, and M. H. Kappes. 1992. Sexual behavior in adolescent and adult females with congenital adrenal hyperplasia. *Psychoneuroendocrinology* 17:153–70.

Dörner, G. 1988. Neuroendocrine response to estrogen and brain differentiation in heterosexuals, homosexuals, and transsexuals. *Archives of Sexual Behavior* 17:57–75.

Dörner, G., W. Rohde, F. Stahl, L. Krell, and W. G. Masius. 1975. A neuroendocrine predisposition for homosexuality in men. *Archives of Sexual Behavior* 4:1–8.

Eckert, E. D., T. J. Bouchard, J. Bohlen, and L. L. Heston. 1986. Homosexuality in monozygotic twins reared apart. *British Journal of Psychiatry* 148:421–25.

Ehrhardt, A. A., K. Evers, and J. Money. 1968. Influence of androgen and some aspects of sexually dimorphic behavior in women with late-treated adrenogenital syndrome. *The Johns Hopkins Medical Journal* 123:115–22.

Ehrhardt, A. A., and S. W. Baker. 1974. Fetal androgens, human central nervous system differentiation, and behavior sex differences. In R. C. Friedman, R. M. Richart, and R. L. Vande Wiele, eds., *Sex Differences in Behavior*, pp. 33–51. New York: Wiley.

Ellis, L., and M. A. Ames. 1987. Neurohormonal functioning and sexual orientation: A theory of homosexuality-heterosexuality. *Psychological Bulletin* 101:233–58.

Finegan, J. K., K. J. Zucker, S. J. Bradley, and R. W. Doering. 1982. Patterns of intellectual functioning and spatial ability in boys with gender identity disorder. *Canadian Journal of Psychiatry* 27:135–39.

Freund, K. W. 1974. Male homosexuality: An analysis of the pattern. In J. A. Loraine, ed., *Understanding Homosexuality: Its Biological and Social Bases*, pp. 25–81. New York: Elsevier.

Friday, N. 1991. *Women on Top*. New York: Simon and Schuster.

Gebhard, P. 1972. Incidence of overt homosexuality in the United States and western Europe. In J. M. Livingood, ed., *National Institute of Mental Health Task Force on Homosexuality: Final Report and Background Papers*. Washington, D.C.: U.S. Government Printing Office (DHEW Publication No. HSM 72–9116), pp. 22–29.

Geschwind, N., and A.M. Galaburda. 1985. Cerebral lateralization, Part 1: *Archives of Neurology* 42:428–59.

Gladue, B. A., W. W. Beatty, Larson, and R. D. Staton. 1990. Sexual orientation and spatial ability in men and women. *Psychobiology* 18:101–8.

Gladue B. A., R. Green, and R. E. Hellman. 1984. Neuroendocrine response to estrogen and sexual orientation. *Science* 225:1469–99.

Gooren, L. 1986a. The neuroendocrine response of luteinizing hormone to estrogen administration in heterosexual, homosexual, and transsexual subjects. *Journal of Clinical Endocrinology and Metabolism* 63:583–88.

Gooren, L. 1986b. The neuroendocrine response of luteinizing hormone to estrogen administration in humans is not sex specific but dependent on the hormonal environment. *Journal of Clinical Endocrinology and Metabolism* 63:589–93.

Gooren, L. 1990. Biomedical theories of sexual orientation: A critical examination.

In D. P. McWhirter, S. A. Sanders, and J. M. Reinisch, eds., *Homosexuality/ Heterosexuality: Concepts of Sexual Orientation*, pp. 71–87. New York: Oxford University Press.

Gooren, L. 1991. New pathways into the biological research of gender dysphoria. Paper presented at Annual Meeting, International Academy of Sex Research, Barrie, Ontario.

Gorski, R. A. 1966. Localization and sexual differentiation of the nervous structures which regulate ovulation. *Journal of Reproduction and Fertility* 1 (suppl):67–88.

Götestam, K. O., T. J. Coates, and M. Ekstrand. 1992. Handedness, dyslexia, and twinning in homosexual men. *International Journal of Neuroscience* 63:179–86.

Green, R. 1987. *The "Sissy Boy Syndrome" and the Development of Homosexuality*. New Haven: Yale University Press.

Grellert, E. A., M. D. Newcomb, and P.M. Bentler. 1982. Childhood play activities of male and female homosexuals and heterosexuals. *Archives of Sexual Behavior* 11:451–78.

Grimshaw, G., K. J. Zucker, S. J. Bradley, C. B. Lowry, and J. N. Mitchell. 1991. Verbal and spatial ability in boys with gender identity disorder. Paper presented at the International Academy of Sex Research, Barrie, Ontario.

Halperin, D. M. 1989. Sex before sexuality: Pederasty, politics, and power in classical Athens. In M. B. Duberman, M. Vicinus, and G. Chauncey Jr., eds., *Hidden from History: Reclaiming the Gay and Lesbian Past*, pp. 37–53. New York: New American Library.

Hamilton, W. D. 1964. The genetical evolution of social behavior. In G. C. Williams, ed., *Group Selection*, pp. 23–43. Chicago: Aldine.

Harry, J. 1983. Defeminization and adult psychological well-being among male homosexuals. *Archives of Sexual Behavior* 12:1–19.

Hendricks, S. E., B. Graber, and J. F. Rodriguez-Sierra. 1989. Neuroendocrine responses to exogenous estrogen: No differences between heterosexual and homosexual men. *Psychoneuroendocrinology* 14:177–85.

Hirschfeld, M. 1936. Homosexuality. In I. Bloch and M. Hirschfeld, eds., *Encyclopaedia sexualis*, pp. 321–34. New York: Dingwall-Rock.

Hutchinson, G. E. 1959. A speculative consideration of certain possible forms of sexual selection in man. *American Naturalist* 93:81–91.

James, W. H. 1989. Foetal testosterone levels, homosexuality, and handedness: A research proposal for jointly testing Geschwind's and Dörner's hypothesis. *Journal of Theoretical Biology* 136:177–80.

Johnson, A.M., J. Wadsworth, K. Wellings, S. Bradshaw, and J. Field. 1992. Sexual lifestyles and HIV risk. *Nature* 360:410–12.

Kallmann, F. J. 1952a. Twin and sibship study of overt male homosexuality. *American Journal of Human Genetics* 4:136–46.

Kallmann, F. J. 1952b. Comparative twin study on the genetic aspects of male homosexuality. *Journal of Nervous and Mental Disease* 115:283–98.

Kinsey, A. C., W. B. Pomeroy, and C. E. Martin. 1948. *Sexual Behavior in the Human Male*. Philadelphia: Saunders.

Kinsey, A. C., W. B. Pomeroy, C. E. Martin, and P. H. Gebhard. 1953. *Sexual Behavior in the Human Male*. Philadelphia: Saunders.

King, M., and E. McDonald. 1992. Homosexuals who are twins: A study of 46 probands. *British Journal of Psychiatry* 160:407–9.

Klein, F. 1990. The need to view sexual orientation as a multivariable dynamic process: A theoretical perspective. In D. P. McWhirter, S. A. Sanders, and J. M. Reinisch, eds., *Homosexuality/Heterosexuality: Concepts of Sexual Orientation*, pp. 277–82. New York: Oxford University Press.

Lehrman, D. S. 1970. Semantic and conceptual issues in the nature-nurture problem. In L. R. Aaronson and E. Tobach, eds., *Development and Evolution of Behavior*, pp. 17–52. San Francisco: Freeman.

LeVay, S. 1991. A difference in hypothalamic structure between heterosexual and homosexual men. *Science* 253:1034–37.

LeVay, S. 1993. *The Sexual Brain*. Cambridge, Mass.: MIT Press.

Lev-Ran, A. 1974. Sexuality and educational levels of women with the late-treated adrenogenital syndrome. *Archives of Sexual Behavior* 3:27–32.

Lewontin, R. C., S. Rose, and L. J. Kamin. 1984. *Not in Our Genes*. New York: Pantheon.

Lidz, T. 1968. *The Person: His Development Throughout the Life Cycle*. New York: Basic Books.

Lindesay, J. 1987. Laterality shift in homosexual men. *Neuropsychologia* 25:965–69.

Linn, M. C., and A. C. Petersen. 1985. Emergence and characterization of sex differences in spatial ability: A meta-analysis. *Child Development* 56:1479–98.

Marchant-Haycox, S. E., I. C. McManus, and G. D. Wilson. 1991. Left-handedness, homosexuality, HIV infection, and AIDS. *Cortex* 27:49–56.

Martin, J. T., and M. T. Baum. 1986. Neonatal exposure of female ferrets to testosterone alters sociosexual preferences in adulthood. *Psychoneuroendocrinology* 11:167–76.

McCormick, C. M., S. F. Witelson, and E. Kingstone. 1990. Left-handedness in homosexual men and women: Neuroendocrine implications. *Psychoneuroendocrinology* 15:69–76.

McGlone, J. 1980. Sex differences in human brain asymmetry: A critical survey. *Behavioral and Brain Sciences* 3:215–27.

Meyer-Bahlburg, H. 1984. Psychoendocrine research on sexual orientation: Current status and future options. In G. J. De Vries, J.P.C. De Bruin, H.M.B. Uylings, and M. A. Corner, eds., *Progress in Brain Research*, 61:375–98. Amsterdam: Elsevier.

Mineka, S., M. Davidson, M. Cook, and R. Keir. 1984. Observational conditioning of snake fear in rhesus monkeys. *Journal of Abnormal Psychology* 93:355–72.

Money, J. 1988. *Gay, Straight, and In-Between*. Oxford: Oxford University Press.

Money, J., M. Schwartz, and V. G. Lewis. 1984. Adult erotosexual status and fetal hormonal masculinization and demasculinization. *Psychoneuroendocrinology* 9:405–14.

Mulaikal, R. M., C. J. Migeon, and J. A. Rock. 1987. Fertility rates in female patients with congenital adrenal hyperplasia due to 21-hydroxylase deficiency. *New England Journal of Medicine* 316:178–82.

Nass, R., S. Baker, P. Speiser, R. Virdis, A. Balsamo, E. Cacciari, A. Loche, M. Dumic, and M. New. 1987. Hormones and handedness: Left-hand bias in female congenital adrenal hyperplasia patients. *Neurology* 37:57–77.

Pillard, R. C. 1990. The Kinsey Scale: Is it familial? In D. P. McWhirter, S. A. Sanders, and J. M. Reinisch, eds., *Homosexuality/Heterosexuality: Concepts of Sexual Orientation*, pp. 88–100. New York: Oxford University Press.

Pillard, R. C., and J. D. Weinrich. 1986. Evidence of familial nature of male homosexuality. *Archives of General Psychiatry* 43:808–12.

Plomin, R. 1990. The role of inheritance in behavior. *Science* 248:183–88.

Plomin, R., J. C. DeFries, and G. E. McClearn. 1989. *Behavioral Genetics: A Primer*. New York: Freeman.

Resnick, S., S. A. Berenbaum, I. I. Gottesman, and T. J. Bouchard. 1986. Early hormonal influences on cognitive functioning in congenital adrenal hyperplasia. *Developmental Psychology* 22:191–98.

Rosenthal, D. 1970. *Genetic Theory and Abnormal Behavior*. New York: McGraw-Hill.

Ruse, M. 1988. *Homosexuality*. Oxford: Basil Blackwell.

Sanders, G., and L. Ross-Field. 1986. Sexual orientation and visuo-spatial ability. *Brain and Cognition* 5:280–90.

Satz, P., E. N. Miller, O. Selnes, W. Van Gorp, and L. F. D'Elia. 1991. Hand preference in homosexual men. *Cortex* 27:295–306.

Siegelman, M. 1981. Parental backgrounds of homosexual and heterosexual men: A cross-national replication. *Archives of Sexual Behavior* 10:505–20.

Stockman, E. R., R. S. Callaghan, and M. J. Baum. 1985. Effects of neonatal castration and testosterone propionate treatment on sexual partner preference in the ferret. *Physiology and Behaviour* 34:409–14.

Swaab, D. F., and E. Fliers. 1985. A sexually dimorphic nucleus in the human brain. *Science* 228:1112–15.

Swaab, D. F., and M. A. Hofman. 1990. An enlarged suprachiasmatic nucleus in homosexual men. *Brain Research* 537:141–48.

Tkachuk, J., and K. J. Zucker. 1991. The relation among sexual orientation, spatial ability, handedness, and recalled childhood gender identity in women and men. Paper presented at Annual Meeting, International Academy of Sex Research, Barrie, Ontario.

Waller, N. G., B. A. Kojetin, B. A., Bouchard, T. J., Lykken, D. T., and Tellegen, A. 1990. Genetic and environmental influences on religious interests, attitudes, and values: A study of twins reared apart and together. *Psychological Science* 1:138–42.

Watson, D. B. 1991. Laterality and handedness in adult transsexuals. *SIECCAN Journal* 6 (spring):22–26.

Weinrich, J. D. 1987. *Sexual Landscapes*. New York: Scribner's.

Whitam, F. L. 1977. Childhood indicators of male homosexuality. *Archives of Sexual Behavior* 6:89–96.

Whitam, F. L., M. Diamond, and J. Martin. 1992. Homosexual orientation in twins: A report on 61 pairs and three triplet sets. Paper presented at Annual Meeting, International Academy of Sex Research, Prague, Czechoslovakia.

Whitam, F. L., and R. M. Mathy. 1986. *Male Homosexuality in Four Societies: Brazil, Guatemala, the Philippines, and the United States*. New York: Praeger.

Wilson, E. O. 1978. *On Human Nature*. Cambridge, Mass.: Harvard University Press.

Zubin, J. 1987. Closing comments. In H. Häfner, W. F. Gattaz, and W. Janzarik, eds., *Search for the Causes of Schizophrenia*, pp. 359–65. Berlin: Springer-Verlag.

Zucker, K. J., S. J. Bradley, G. Oliver, J. E. Hood, J. Blake, and S. Fleming. 1992. Psychosexual assessment of women with congenital adrenal hyperplasia: Preliminary analyses. Paper presented at Annual Meeting, International Academy of Sex Research, Prague, Czechoslovakia.

Zuger, B. 1978. Effeminate behavior in boys from childhood: Ten additional years of follow-up. *Comprehensive Psychiatry* 19:363–69.

3 Bisexual Identities

Ronald C. Fox

Scholarly and scientific understanding of sexual orientation has been hindered by two assumptions: that homosexuality is an indication of psychopathology and that sexual orientation is dichotomous. The movement toward a descriptive, multidimensional approach has greatly facilitated understanding of the complexity of sexual orientation and sexual identity and brought theory and research on both homosexuality and bisexuality into focus.

The theoretical and research literature on the development of lesbian and gay identities emerged following the American Psychiatric Association's 1973 decision to remove homosexuality as a clinical diagnostic category. The literature on bisexual identities, however, is more recent. This is a result of the historical polarization of sexual orientation into heterosexuality and homosexuality, as well as the variety of ways in which the term *bisexuality* has been used and defined in theory, clinical practice, and research.

In fact, bisexuality has existed as a concept and descriptive term in the literature since Freud and his contemporaries first conceptualized the process of psychosexual development. For example, bisexuality has been used as a theoretical construct to explain aspects of evolutionary theory, psychosexual development, psychopathology, masculinity and femininity, and homosexuality. The designation *bisexual* has been used as a descriptive term to refer to individuals with heterosexual and homosexual attractions or relationships, just as the designations *gay* and *lesbian* have referred to individuals with homosexual attractions or relationships. Finally, individuals themselves have used the self-designations *homosexual, lesbian, gay,* and *bisexual* to describe their sexual orientations. This paper examines how bisexuality has appeared in the literature as a concept, a descriptive term, a sexual orientation category, and a sexual identity, and compares theory and research on bisexual, gay, and lesbian identities.

Bisexuality in Psychoanalytic Theory

The view that homosexuality is a mental illness has been part of medical and psychological writing since the late nineteenth century. Early theorists found the concept of bisexuality useful in understanding homosexuality from the perspective of evolutionary theory (Ellis [1905] 1942; Krafft-Ebing [1886] 1965; Moll [1897] 1933; Weininger [1903] 1908). They believed that the human species evolved from a primitive hermaphroditic state to today's gender-differentiated physical form and that the physiological and psychological development of the individual parallels this evolutionary process.

Freud, who was familiar with evolutionary theory, incorporated the concept of bisexuality as a basic element of his theory of psychosexual development (Freud [1905] 1962; Ritvo 1990; Sulloway 1979). Like his contemporaries, he used the concept of bisexuality to account for homosexuality, which he saw as an indication of arrested psychosexual development (Freud [1925] 1963). At the same time, he emphasized that all individuals have some homosexual feelings: "The most important of these perversions, homosexuality . . . can be traced back to the constitutional bisexuality of all human beings. . . . Psychoanalysis enables us to point to some trace or other of a homosexual object-choice in everyone" (pp. 71–72). Other psychoanalysts, in particular Stekel ([1922] 1946a), expressed the view that bisexuality is normative during childhood, and adult sexual orientation results from repression that occurs during the developmental process:

> All persons originally are bisexual in their predisposition. There is no exception to this rule. Normal persons show a distinct bisexual period up to the age of puberty. The heterosexual then represses his homosexuality. . . . If the heterosexuality is repressed, homosexuality comes to the forefront. (p. 39)

Freud and his contemporaries used *invert* and *homosexual* as generic clinical and descriptive terms to refer to persons with any same-gender sexual attractions or behavior. At the same time, Freud ([1905] 1962) differentiated three types of homosexuals, including persons with both same- and opposite-gender sexual attractions or behavior:

> (a) They may be absolute inverts. In that case their sexual objects are exclusively of their own sex. . . . (b) They may be amphigenic inverts, that is psychosexual hermaphrodites. In that case their sexual objects may equally well be of their own or of the opposite sex. . . . (c) They may be contingent inverts. In that case, under certain external conditions . . . they are capable of taking as their sexual object someone of their own sex and of deriving satisfaction from sexual intercourse with him. (pp. 2–3)

Havelock Ellis ([1905] 1942) differentiated individuals on the basis of sexual attractions. He saw bisexuals as a distinct category of individuals who are attracted to persons of both genders, concluding that "there would thus seem to be a broad and simple grouping of all sexually functioning persons into three comprehensive divisions: the heterosexual, the bisexual, and the homosexual" (pp. 87–88).

Freud ([1937] 1963) later used the term *bisexual* to refer to persons with both homosexual and heterosexual attractions or behavior:

> It is well known that at all times there have been, as there still are, human beings who can take as their sexual objects persons of either sex without the one trend interfering with the other. We call these people bisexual and accept the fact of their existence without wondering much at it. . . . But we have come to know that all human beings are bisexual in this sense and that their libido is distributed between objects of both sexes, either in a manifest or a latent form. (pp. 261–62)

Most psychoanalysts maintained that the theory of bisexuality is an essential conceptual reference point for understanding psychosexual development (Stekel [1922] 1946a; [1922] 1946b), masculinity and femininity (Stoller 1972), psychopathology (Katan 1955; Khan and Masud 1974; Kubie 1974; Nunberg 1947; Weiss 1958), and homosexuality (Alexander 1933; Limentani 1976; Nunberg 1938). Some psychoanalysts challenged the utility of the concept of bisexuality, arguing that transferring the concept from evolutionary biology to psychology was inappropriate. Their position was that the individual's adaptational responses to family influences are the relevant etiological factors in the development of homosexual behavior as well as masculine and feminine characteristics (Bieber et al. 1962; Kardiner, Karesh, and Ovessey 1959; Rado 1940).

Other authors argued with the term *bisexual* as a descriptive category referring to individuals with both homosexual and heterosexual attractions or behavior. For example, Bergler (1956) viewed sexual orientation in strictly dichotomous terms and believed that those who consider themselves bisexual are denying their homosexual orientation:

> Bisexuality — a state that has no existence beyond the word itself — is an out-and-out fraud. . . . The theory claims that a man can be — alternatively or concomitantly — homo and heterosexual. . . . Nobody can dance at two different weddings at the same time. These so-called bisexuals are really homosexuals with an occasional heterosexual excuse. (pp. 80–81)

The polarization of sexuality into heterosexual (normal) and homosexual (abnormal) was basic to the illness model of homosexuality and lent support to the position that the diagnostic category *homosexuality* was appropriate for individuals with *any* same-gender sexual attractions or behavior. This approach was maintained and further articulated by many authors in the fields of psychoanalysis and psychiatry (Bergler 1956; Bieber et al. 1962; Caprio 1954, 1955; L. J. Hatterer 1970; Ruitenbeek 1963, 1973; Socarides 1972, 1978). The goal of psychoanalytic psychotherapy with individuals with homosexual attractions or behavior was an exclusively heterosexual orientation.

However, traditional psychoanalytic attitudes toward homosexuality were not universally accepted in the psychiatric community (Bayer 1981). Prominent authors in the field (Green 1972; Hoffman 1968; Hooker 1956, 1965; Marmor 1965, 1972; Szasz 1965, 1970; G. Weinberg 1972) challenged the prevailing position on homosexuality based on evidence from several areas: surveys of sexual behavior; ethnographic data on the incidence and integration of homosexual behavior in other cultures; criticism of clinical assessment and treatment based on the illness model; and critiques of research claiming support for hormonal, genetic, and family of origin etiologies for homosexuality. The 1973 American Psychiatric Association decision to remove homosexuality as a diagnostic category signaled a move away from the illness model and toward a more affirmative approach to homosexuality.

Bisexuality in Lesbian and Gay Identity Development Theory

The first descriptions in the literature of the lives of lesbians and gay men from other than an illness model perspective appeared in ethnographic reports on urban gay and lesbian communities (Achilles 1967; Gagnon and Simon 1968; Hooker 1956, 1965; Leznoff and Westley 1956; Ponse 1978, 1980; Simon and Gagnon 1967; Warren 1974, 1980; D. G. Wolf 1979). These and other authors found that the expression *coming out* was used to signify acknowledging one's homosexual attractions (Cory and LeRoy 1963; Cronin 1974; Dank 1971; Gagnon and Simon 1968, 1973; Ponse 1978, 1980; D. G. Wolf 1979), making contact with the lesbian and gay communities (Gagnon and Simon 1968, 1973; Hooker 1965; Saghir and Robins 1973), and identifying oneself to other people as being gay or lesbian (Hooker 1965; Ponse 1978, 1980; D. G. Wolf 1979).

Several authors have elaborated significant events involved in *coming out* into a sequence of stages leading to the formation of positive lesbian and gay identities (Cass 1979, [1983] 1984; Coleman 1982b; Dank 1971; de Monteflores and Schultz 1978; Plummer 1981; Troiden 1979, 1988). The typical developmental sequence proceeds from a point of departure (first homosexual attractions) through a set of intermediate experiences (seeking out similar others, initiating same-gender sexual experiences and relationships, identifying oneself as gay or lesbian, and disclosing one's sexual orientation to others) to an endpoint (exclusively homosexual relationships and an integrated lesbian or gay identity). Disclosing one's sexual orientation to significant others and community participation are both seen as necessary in maintaining positive gay and lesbian identities. For these authors, the term *coming out* refers to the entire developmental process, including but not limited to, disclosing one's sexual orientation to others. Troiden (1988) believed that "homosexual identities are most fully realized . . . when self-identity, perceived identity, and presented identity coincide; that is, where an accord exists among who people think they are, who they claim they are, and how others view them" (p. 31).

Cass (1984) followed up her theoretical formulation with a study designed to assess the validity of her developmental stages. Although she found evidence for the general order of milestone events, she also found that some individuals did not follow the exact sequence she had proposed, and others moved through more than one stage at the same time. These findings are in accord with similar variations found in research on lesbian identity development (Chapman and Brannock 1987; Sophie [1985] 1986) and support the perspective that stage theories give a general rather than exact outline of events involved in the coming-out process (Coleman 1982b; Troiden 1988).

As with other developmental models, theorists have explained deviations from the proposed direction or sequence of events. For example, in her first formulation, Cass (1979) considered a bisexual self-identification as an example of identity foreclosure, delaying or preventing the development of a positive homosexual identity. From this point of view, a bisexual self-identification and persistent heterosexual attractions, behavior, or relationships are all transitional phenomena some individuals experience as they proceed toward permanent monosexual lesbian and gay identities. More recently, however, Cass (1990) has described a bisexual identity differently, as a viable sexual identity, with a separate developmental pathway distinct from that characteristic of a homosexual identity. Coleman (1982b) suggested that the developmental stages he articulated for the coming-out process might apply to bisexuals as well. Troiden (1988) also saw bisexuality as a valid sexual orientation category. However, he believed that the general lack of recognition of bisexuality affects the individual's ability to sustain a bisexual identity:

> The unwillingness of people in general, and significant others in particular, to acknowledge bisexual preferences makes it more difficult to maintain and validate these preferences than heterosexual identities, which are supported continuously by sociocultural institutions, or homosexual identities, which are recognized and reinforced by institutional arrangements within the homosexual community. (p. 82)

In summary, the emergence of lesbian and gay identity theory represented an important shift in emphasis in developmental theory away from the concern with etiology and psychopathology characteristic of the illness model toward articulation of the factors involved in the formation of positive gay and lesbian identities. While theories of lesbian and gay identity development initially saw bisexuality as a transitional phenomenon, over time the focus has shifted away from a strictly dichotomous view of sexual orientation toward a more inclusive perspective in which bisexuality is regarded as a distinct sexual orientation and identity.

Bisexuality in Sexual Orientation Theory and Assessment

The theoretical and research literature on gay and lesbian identities emerged after psychiatry and psychology moved to consider homosexuality from a more affirmative point of view. The predominance of a dichotomous view of sexual orientation, however, constrained the development of a comparable theoretical and research literature on bisexuality and bisexual identities. Examination and critique of this model led to the development of a multidimensional approach to sexual orientation, which allows for more accurate representation of the complexity of sexual orientation and acknowledgment of bisexuality as a sexual orientation and sexual identity.

Kinsey and his associates (Kinsey, Pomeroy, and Martin 1948; Kinsey, Pomeroy, Martin, and Gebhard 1952) considered human sexuality from a descriptive rather than a clinical point of view, and they emphasized the inadequacy of dichotomous concepts for describing the diversity of human sexual experience (Kinsey et al. 1948):

> Males do not represent two discrete populations, heterosexual and homosexual. The world is not divided into sheep and goats. Not all things are black nor all things white. It is a fundamental of taxonomy that nature rarely deals with discrete categories. Only the human mind invents categories and tries to force facts into separated pigeon-holes. The living world is a continuum in each and every one of its aspects. The sooner we learn this concerning human sexual behavior the sooner we shall reach a sound understanding of the realities of sex. (p. 639)

They were aware that the term *bisexual* had been used to refer to individuals with both heterosexual and homosexual attractions or behavior. It was their view, however, that moving from two categories (heterosexual and homosexual) to three categories (heterosexual, bisexual, and homosexual) did not represent the continuum of human sexual behavior as accurately as their 7-point scale.

Other authors have viewed heterosexuality and homosexuality as independent aspects of sexual orientation, which they saw as the individual's physical and affectional preferences for relationships with members of the same and/or opposite biological sex (Shively and DeCecco 1977; Storms 1980). Sexual orientation was seen as one of four components of sexual identity, along with biological sex, gender identity, and social sex role (Shively and De Cecco 1977). The research literature included a variety of criteria for defining sexual orientation, among which the most frequently used were sexual behavior, affectional attachments (close relationships), erotic fantasies, arousal, erotic preference, and self-identification as bisexual, heterosexual, or homosexual (Shively, Jones, and De Cecco [1983] 1984).

The Klein Sexual Orientation Grid (Klein, Sepekoff, and Wolf 1985; Klein 1990) provided a more encompassing approach to assessing sexual orientation by including not only sexual attraction, fantasy, and behavior but emotional preference, social preference, heterosexual-bisexual-homosexual lifestyle, and self-identification as well. Individuals are asked to rate themselves on a 7-point heterosexual-bisexual-homosexual scale for each of these variables for past, present, and ideal time frames, which provides a more accurate picture of the factors involved in an individual's sexual orientation over time.

The Assessment of Sexual Orientation (Coleman 1987, 1990) was designed to facilitate clinical interviews in which the presenting issues include sexual orientation concerns. The client indicates current relationship status, sexual orientation self-identification, desired future identification, and level of comfort with present orientation. A series of circles are also marked, in terms of both "up to the present" and "ideal" time frames, to indicate physical identity, actual and fantasized gender identity, sex-role identity, as well as sexual, fantasy, and emotional aspects of sexual orientation.

In summary, a multidimensional view of sexual orientation has evolved, which takes into consideration factors such as emotional and social preferences, lifestyle, self-identification, and changes in identity over time, as well as sexual attraction, fantasy, and behavior. This has led to the development of more comprehensive tools for assessing sexual orientation and a wider acknowledgment of bisexuality as a distinct sexual orientation and identity.

Theoretical Perspectives on Bisexuality and Bisexual Identities

Lesbian and gay identity theory developed out of the more affirmative approach to homosexuality that followed its removal as a diagnostic category. The discourse on bisexual identities has developed out of the more positive attitude toward bisexuality that has resulted from a critique of the dichotomous view of sexual orientation and the emergence of a multidimensional perspective. Several typologies of bisexual behavior have been elaborated, and similarities and differences between the development of bisexual, gay, and lesbian identities have been examined.

Psychoanalytic theorists used the concept of bisexuality in discussing psychosexual development in terms of evolutionary theory and in explaining homosexual attractions and behavior. The viewpoint that bisexuality is an intrinsic factor in psychosexual development was shared by Wolff (1971): "We certainly are bisexual creatures, and this innate disposition is reinforced by the indelible memory of childhood attachments, which know no limitation of sex" (pp. 45–46). She also believed that the psychoanalytic assumption of an inherent bisexuality has lent support to a greater acknowledgment of bisexuality as a sexual orientation (Wolff 1979).

Although most psychoanalytic theorists used the concept of bisexuality to account for homosexual attractions and behavior, they believed that exclusive heterosexuality is the only normal outcome of the developmental process. Klein (1978, 1993) challenged this belief, as well as the position that sexual relationships with both women and men indicate immaturity and psychopathology. He maintained that awareness and expression of both heterosexual and homosexual attractions can enhance the individual's experience of intimacy and personal fulfillment.

Other authors also have approached bisexuality from an affirmative perspective and have emphasized that bisexuality challenges several assumptions of a dichotomous view of sexual orientation: that heterosexuality and homosexuality are mutually exclusive; that gender is the primary criterion for sexual partner selection; and that sexual orientation is immutable (Fox 1993; Hansen and Evans 1985; Klein et al. 1985; MacDonald 1981, 1982, 1983; Morrow 1989; Nichols 1988; Paul [1983] 1984, 1985; Ross and Paul 1992; Rust 1992, 1993; Schuster 1987; Weise, 1992; Zinik 1985). Stereotypes of bisexuality in the literature have been based on these assumptions. One misconception is that bisexuality is only a transition on the way to either exclusive homosexuality or heterosexuality. Another is that bisexuals are in denial, that is, they have not come out all the way and are trying to avoid the stigma of a gay identity. The impact of these stereotypes has been that many bisexual men and women feel marginal to both the heterosexual and homosexual communities.

Several typologies of bisexuality have been elaborated, based on the extent and timing of past and present heterosexual and homosexual behavior. Klein (1978, 1993) distinguished four kinds of bisexuality: transitional, historical, sequential, and concurrent. For some individuals, bisexuality represents a stage in the process of coming out as lesbian or gay, while, for others, a gay or lesbian identity is a step in the process of coming out bisexual (transitional bisexuality). Some individuals, whose sexual lives are presently heterosexual or homosexual, have experienced both same- and opposite-gender sexual attractions or behavior in the past (historical bisexuality). Other individuals have had relationships with both women and men, but with only one person during a particular period of time (sequential bisexuality), while others have had relationships with both men and women during the same time period (concurrent bisexuality). Other authors (Berkey, Perelman-Hall, and Kurdek 1990; Boulton and Coxon 1991; Weinberg, Williams, and Pryor 1994) have developed similar typologies. Other factors that are relevant in considering bisexual behavior and identity have also been identified (Doll, Peterson, Magana, and Carrier 1991): the social context in which the person lives (heterosexual, homosexual, or both); the relationship(s) in which the individual is involved; and how open the person is with others about being bisexual.

Ross (1991) described several patterns of bisexual behavior relative to identity and in terms of the circumstances in which homosexual behavior takes place. For example, a person may be hiding a homosexual orientation, exploring homosexuality, or in transition to a gay or lesbian identity (defense bisexuality). When a society provides no alternatives to marriage, homosexual behavior may take place away from the family environment (married bisexuality). Homosexual behavior may be prescribed for some or all members of a society, as in Melanesia (ritual bisexuality). For some people, gender is not a criterion for sexual attraction or partner selection (equal bisexuality). In other cases, a male who takes only the inserter role in anal intercourse with another male is considered heterosexual (*Latin* bisexuality). Homosexual behavior may be circumstantial, taking place only once or a few times (experimental bisexuality) or only when there are no heterosexual outlets (secondary bisexuality). Homosexual behavior also may occur as part of male or female prostitution (technical bisexuality).

Bisexual identity formation has not been conceptualized as a linear process with a fixed outcome, as in theories of lesbian and gay identity formation. The development of bisexual identities has been viewed as a more complex and open-ended process in light of the necessity of considering patterns of homosexual *and* heterosexual attractions, fantasies, behaviors, and relationships that occur during any particular period of time and over time (Coleman 1987, 1990; Klein et al. 1985; Shively and De Cecco 1977; Shively et al. [1983] 1984).

Several authors have examined bisexual identity development empirically and have discussed the coming-out process on the basis of their research findings (Fox 1993; Rust 1992, 1993; Twining 1983; Weinberg et al. 1994). Twining (1983) identified several issues that bisexual women face in the coming-out process: self-acceptance, resolving societal homophobia, developing a support network, deciding to whom disclosures of sexual orientation would be made, and coping with concerns about disclosure in professional contexts. She concluded that "an initial formulation of a conceptual theory of bisexual identity development seems to call for a task model rather than a phase or stage model" (p. 158). In contrast, based on the results of their 1983, [1984] 1985, and 1988 studies, Weinberg, Williams, and Pryor (1994) outlined the stages they believed were involved in the development of bisexual identities: initial confusion, finding and applying the label, and settling into the identity. They conceptualized bisexuality as an "add-on" to an already established heterosexual identity. The authors also proposed a fourth stage, continued uncertainty, which they saw as a common experience of many bisexuals. They related this to the general lack of social validation for bisexual identities compared to lesbian and gay identities, which are more effectively supported by visible, well-established lesbian and gay communities.

Rust (1992, 1993) and Fox (1993) have emphasized that multiple factors influence the development of bisexual identities, and dichotomous and linear conceptual approaches to sexual identity formation do not adequately describe the coming-out experiences of many individuals. The results of both their studies indicate that, although many men and women develop a bisexual identity after first considering themselves heterosexual, others arrive at a bisexual identity from an established lesbian or gay identity. These findings strongly suggest that sexual identity is not as immutable for all individuals as some theorists and researchers have assumed. Rust (1993) concluded that bisexual, lesbian, and gay identities may be viewed from the point of view of a more encompassing conceptual framework in which sexual identity development is an *ongoing* process with changes in sexual identities being "a normal outcome of the dynamic process of identity formation that occurs as mature individuals respond to changes in the available social constructs, the sociopolitical landscape, and their own positions on that landscape" (p. 74).

In summary, theory on bisexuality and bisexual identities has evolved on the basis of an ongoing critique of the illness model and the dichotomous view of sexual orientation. Bisexuality has been examined in terms of the variety of contexts and circumstances in which sexual attractions and behavior occur. A multidimensional theoretical approach to bisexual identity formation has developed which acknowledges that individuals arrive at their sexual identities by several possible routes and that sexual identity may remain constant or change as a normal response to both personal and social influences.

Bisexuality in Research on Homosexuality

Information about bisexuality first appeared in the research literature in the results of anthropological studies and ethnographic and survey studies on homosexuality, which consistently included many individuals with both heterosexual and homosexual attractions and relationships. In cross-cultural research, bisexuality has been used primarily as a descriptive term referring to the sexual behavior of individuals in particular cultures. In ethnographic research on gay and lesbian communities, and in survey research on homosexuality, bisexuality has also been used to refer to sexual attractions and behavior as well as to signify sexual orientation or sexual identity.

Anthropological Perspectives

The cross-cultural incidence of homosexual behavior has been well documented (Adam 1985; Blackwood 1985; Carrier 1980; Churchill 1967; Davenport 1977; Ford and Beach 1951; Herdt 1990; Mead 1961; Opler 1965). However, only a few anthropologists who have reported on cultures in which some individuals exhibit both homosexual and heterosexual behavior have framed the homosexual behavior as a component of the bisexuality characteristic of sexual expression in that culture.

Based on their examination of cross-cultural patterns of sexual behavior, Ford and Beach (1951) noted the human potential for bisexuality and the inadequacy of a dichotomous view of sexuality:

> When it is realized that 100 per cent of the males in certain societies engage in homosexual as well as heterosexual alliances, and when it is understood that many men and women in our own society are equally capable of relations with partners of the same or opposite sex, ... then it should be clear that one cannot classify homosexual and heterosexual tendencies as being mutually exclusive or even opposed to each other. (p. 242)

This perspective was also expressed by Mead (1975), who believed that bisexuality is normal, but that social attitudes about sex and love constrain the
expression of bisexual attractions in sexual behavior and relationships:

> Even a superficial look at other societies and some groups in our own
> society should be enough to convince us that a very large number of
> human beings — probably a majority — are bisexual in their potential
> capacity for love. Whether they will become exclusively heterosexual
> or exclusively homosexual for all their lives and in all circumstances
> or whether they will be able to enter into sexual and love relationships
> with members of both sexes is, in fact, a consequence of the way they
> have been brought up, of the particular beliefs and prejudices of the
> society they live in and, to some extent, of their own life history. (p. 29)

The integration of bisexuality into a particular culture is exemplified by the
coexistence of heterosexual and homosexual behavior in one Melanesian
society (Davenport 1965):

> Not all [men] become exclusively heterosexual at marriage. There is
> no doubt that some do, but most do not. . . . He need not forego ped-
> erasty as long as this does not prevent him from giving sexual satisfac-
> tion to his wife. In other words, this is a society that quite frankly
> expects and accepts some bisexual behavior in most men, although
> there is nothing odd or deviant about an exclusively heterosexual male.
> (pp. 201–2)

Concurrent homosexual and heterosexual behavior also characterizes another Melanesian society (Herdt 1984):

> The Sambian male . . . has the opportunity for direct experience of
> both homosexual and heterosexual relations and the opportunity to
> compare and evaluate them. Shared communications about the rela-
> tive qualities of all sexual activities are an ordinary part of male dis-
> course. . . . The self-esteem of bisexuals in Melanesia is relatively high
> and their bisexuality ego-syntonic. Neither they nor their fellows are
> out to lobby for or against their bisexuality. Bisexuals bear no stigma.
> (p. 59)

Mexican bisexuality has been examined by Carrier (1985), and Tielman, Carballo, and Hendriks (1991) have provided an overview of cross-cultural patterns of bisexual behavior as part of a research effort designed to understand more fully transmission of the human immunodeficiency virus (HIV) from a global perspective and to develop more effective health intervention and prevention strategies.

Bisexuality in Research on Lesbian and Gay Male Communities

While early ethnographic reports on lesbian and gay communities focused on the coming-out process and the importance of community for maintaining homosexual identities, such efforts did not address the issue of bisexual identities. Later research, however, has provided some information on attitudes in the lesbian community toward bisexual women (Golden 1987; Ponse 1978; Rust 1992, 1993; D. G. Wolf 1979). While some lesbian respondents in these studies had never experienced heterosexual attractions or behavior, others had been involved in sexual relationships with men. Ponse (1978) and Golden (1987) called the former "primary" lesbians and the latter "elective" lesbians. Some respondents were accepting of women who admitted ongoing sexual attractions to men or who considered themselves bisexual, but many believed such women were not "real" lesbians or had not yet completed the coming out process. Warren (1974) reported similar reactions toward bisexual men from respondents in her study of a gay male community.

Research has also been conducted on situational homosexual behavior, in environments where opposite-gender partners are unavailable or relatively inaccessible (e.g., in prison or in the military) and where homosexual behavior occurs as an occupational or clandestine activity (e.g., prostitution or tearoom sex). Although respondents in such research typically identify themselves as homosexual or heterosexual, some consider themselves bisexual, for example, in studies of sex in prison (Wooden and Parker 1982), male prostitution (Reiss 1961), gay bars (Read 1980), and sex in public places (Humphreys 1970).

Bisexuality in Survey Research on Sexuality

The results of the research conducted by Kinsey and his associates (Kinsey et al. 1948, 1952) presented an early challenge to the belief that adult homosexuality is a rare phenomenon. Furthermore, a significant proportion of participants in these studies reported both heterosexual and homosexual behavior. Many researchers since then also have found some respondents reporting adult sexual experiences with both women and men. Researchers have differed greatly, however, in their interpretations of how the sexual behavior of such individuals relates to their sexual orientation or identity.

For example, Hunt (1974) believed that only a very limited number of American males are bisexual, or potentially so, in their adult lives. His perspective on the bisexual behavior reported by some of his respondents was that "some self-styled bisexuals . . . are basically homosexual but seek to minimize their conflicts and sense of deviance by having occasional heterosexual episodes. Others have had a bisexual period, . . . though they eventually recognized that their real orientation was toward same-sex partners" (p. 324). Likewise, Saghir and Robins (1973) took the position that the previous heterosexual attractions and relationships that some of their gay and lesbian respondents reported were not a sign of bisexuality. This was also the contention of Spada (1979) concerning reports of his gay male respondents' past and current relationships with women:

> It might be argued that these men are not homosexual but bisexual. It is thus significant that such a large number of men who sufficiently consider themselves gay to respond to this survey have sexual relations with women. (p. 215)

In contrast, other researchers took a more neutral or affirmative position in presenting information about the bisexual attractions and behavior of respondents. For example, Hite (1976, 1981) and Jay and Young (1976) took a descriptive approach, including respondents' comments about their bisexuality, and the Playboy Readers' Sex Survey (1983) contrasted results of respondents based on both identity and behavior.

The illness model approach toward homosexuality was rejected by Weinberg and Williams (1974), who also questioned the polarization of sexual orientation into heterosexuality and homosexuality: "By defining heterosexuality as the norm, there also has been the tendency to view persons as either heterosexual or homosexual. This . . . poses the danger of ignoring the great range and heterogeneity of homosexuals" (p. 4). One-fifth of their combined San Francisco and New York samples rated themselves other than exclusively or predominantly homosexual on the Kinsey scale. The authors differentiated between "nonexclusive homosexuals" and "exclusive homosexuals" in their data analysis. Compared to the more exclusively homosexual men, the bisexual men were more involved with heterosexuals, more concerned with passing as heterosexual, and less recognized as being "homosexual." They had more frequent and enjoyable sex with women and were more likely to have been married. The authors found no support for the argument that bisexuals are confused about their sexual identities, although their bisexual respondents evidenced greater guilt, shame, and anxiety about being "homosexual," feelings that did not appear to generalize to other psychological problems.

In their survey of the sexual experiences and psychological and social adjustment of lesbians and gay men, Bell and Weinberg (1978) noted:

> It would not be unreasonable to suppose that a fairly strong heterosexual element is to be found in about one-third of those homosexual men most likely to participate in surveys of this kind. Even larger numbers of comparable homosexual women are apt to exhibit a "partial bisexual lifestyle." (p. 61)

In presenting their research findings, however, the authors did not differentiate between bisexual and homosexual respondents, even though their sample included substantial proportions of men and women who rated themselves in the midrange on the Kinsey scale for sexual feelings and behavior. The criticism has been made that combining bisexual and homosexual respondents in this way obscures information specific to both components of the sample and greatly limits the ability to generalize about either component from the study results (MacDonald 1981, 1982, 1983).

The authors of a study of lesbian and gay male psychologists found that one-fifth of their female respondents and one-third of their male respondents considered themselves bisexual (Kooden et al. 1979). While the general responses of the bisexual psychologists were similar to those of the lesbian and gay psychologists, the bisexual respondents seemed to lack the social support networks that characterized the gay and lesbian respondents. Furthermore, the authors found that "the bisexual respondents appeared to have all of the stresses of the closeted gay respondents, but did not report having the positive experiences that were reported by the gay respondents who were generally open" (p. 68). The bisexual psychologists were more likely to be heterosexually married and less likely to be involved in the gay movement.

In their study of the development of sexual preference, Bell, Weinberg, and Hammersmith (1981) classified respondents who scored in the midrange on the Kinsey scale as bisexual. They differentiated bisexuals from exclusive homosexuals in their data analysis and found that "among the bisexuals, adult sexual preference is much less strongly tied to pre-adult sexual feelings" (p. 200). The authors concluded that "exclusive homosexuality tends to emerge from a deep-seated predisposition, while bisexuality is more subject to influence by social and sexual learning" (p. 201).

In summary, the evidence provided by ethnographic and survey studies of human sexuality indicates that many participants in such research have experienced heterosexual *and* homosexual attractions, behavior, or relationships. Based on ratings of past and current sexual attractions, sexual behavior, and self-identification, at least some of these individuals could be considered bisexual. When bisexual and homosexual respondents in sexuality research have been combined for the purposes of data analysis, information about each of these groups has been obscured. When respondents have been more adequately differentiated by sexual orientation, a more accurate characterization of both groups has been possible.

Research on Bisexuality and Bisexual Identities

Research on bisexuality has been strongly influenced by the assumptions of both the illness model and a dichotomous view of sexual orientation. Early studies addressed questions about the validity and viability of bisexuality as a sexual orientation and sexual identity as researchers examined issues such as psychological adjustment, the relationship between sexual identity and sexual behavior, and bisexuality in the context of heterosexual marriage. Just as a more affirmative approach to homosexuality led to a focus on factors involved in the development of positive lesbian and gay identities, the greater acknowledgment of bisexuality resulting from the elaboration of a multidimensional approach to sexual orientation has allowed more recent research to focus on factors involved in the development of positive bisexual identities.

Psychological Adjustment

The research demonstrating that homosexuality is not associated with psychopathology in nonclinical populations was an important part of the scientific evidence that influenced the American Psychiatric Association to remove homosexuality as a diagnostic category (Bayer 1981; Gonsiorek

1982). While this action contributed to a more affirmative view of homosexuality, the dichotomization of sexual orientation into heterosexuality and
homosexuality remained, supporting the belief that bisexuals were psychologically maladjusted. As in comparable research on lesbians and gay men,
however, research on nonclinical samples of bisexual women and men
found no evidence of psychopathology or psychological maladjustment
(Harris 1977; LaTorre and Wendenberg 1983; Markus 1981; Masters and
Johnson 1979; Nurius 1983; Ross 1983; Twitchell 1974; Weinberg and Williams 1974; Zinik 1984). In fact, some researchers found that self-identified
bisexuals were characterized by high self-esteem (Galland 1975; Rubenstein
1982), self-confidence and autonomy (Galland 1975), a positive self-concept
independent of social norms (Twining 1983), assertiveness (Bode 1976), and
cognitive flexibility (Zinik 1984).

Identity and Sexual Behavior

Another major research focus has been the relationship between identity
and sexual behavior. Some researchers approached this issue with the belief
that heterosexuality and homosexuality are irreconcilable opposites. Anything other than exclusively heterosexual or homosexual behavior was seen
as a case of incongruence between sexual behavior and sexual orientation.
Individuals who considered themselves bisexual were seen as confused about
their sexual orientation, and a bisexual identity was considered a transitional
phenomenon some individuals go through in coming to terms with an underlying gay or lesbian sexual orientation (Fast and Wells 1975; H. L. Ross 1971;
Miller 1979; Schafer 1976).

Other researchers proceeded from a more neutral perspective and focused on collecting descriptive data on the experiences of self-identified
bisexual women and men (Blumstein and Schwartz 1976a, 1976b, 1977;
Bode 1976; Fox 1993; Galland 1975; George 1993; Harris 1977; Hurwood
1974; Klein 1978; Klein et al. 1985; Little 1989; Morse 1989; Reinhardt
1985; Rubenstein 1982; Rust 1992, 1993; Saliba 1980; Twining 1983; Weinberg et al. 1994; Wolff 1979). Blumstein and Schwartz (1976a, 1976b, 1977)
addressed the subject of identity and sexual behavior in an interview study
of bisexual and homosexual women and men. They found that a variety of
sexual behaviors were associated with bisexual, lesbian, and gay identities.
Although some of their self-identified bisexual respondents did have sexual
relationships with both men and women during a particular period of time,

others did not. Furthermore, while some respondents who considered themselves lesbian or gay had exclusively homosexual relationships, others also had heterosexual relationships. Along these lines, in examining data from the Playboy study (Playboy Readers' Sex Survey 1983), Lever, Rogers, Carson, Kanouse and Hertz (1992) found that one-third of the male respondents with adult bisexual behavior reported a bisexual identity, but a much larger proportion considered themselves heterosexual or gay.

Several studies have found that, for some individuals, identity appears to be related to factors other than current sexual behavior: whether a person is in a heterosexual or homosexual relationship, fear of being known as gay or bisexual, or political reasons such as loyalty to the gay or lesbian communities (Blumstein and Schwartz 1976a, 1976b, 1977; Golden 1987; Rust 1992, 1993). The research literature also indicates that bisexual women and men arrive at their sexual identities by several possible sequences. While some individuals move from a heterosexual identity to a bisexual identity, others first consider themselves lesbian or gay before they consider themselves bisexual (Golden 1987; Fox 1993; Rust 1992, 1993). These findings suggest that self-ratings of sexual attractions, fantasy, and behavior may vary significantly for bisexual individuals *and* for lesbian, gay, and heterosexual individuals and that ratings on these factors, including self-identification, change over time.

On the other hand, several researchers have found that most self-identified bisexuals rated themselves in the middle of the Kinsey scale for ideal behavior but tended to fall at either the heterosexual or homosexual ends of the scale when rating themselves on actual current behavior (Fox 1993; George 1993; Klein et al. 1985; Reinhardt 1985). Sexual behavior appears to be constrained by the structure and dynamics of the current relationships in which individuals are engaged. This suggests that, although identity does change for some individuals, there is continuity in identity for *many* individuals, whether or not bisexual attractions are expressed in terms of sexual behavior or relationships during a particular period of time.

Homosexuality and Bisexuality in Heterosexual Marriages

The homosexual attractions and behavior of heterosexually married men and women have been the subject of extensive discussion in the literature. The traditional psychiatric position was that homosexual attractions or behavior in heterosexually married men are an indication of psychopathology

(Allen 1961; Bieber 1969; Imielinski 1969; L. J. Hatterer 1970; Thornton 1948). One writer viewed the spouses of such individuals as disturbed as well (M. S. Hatterer 1974).

Several authors have portrayed mixed-orientation marriages as problematic at best, with separation as the typical outcome, and a necessary step for the husband in the process of coming out as a gay man (Bozett 1982; H. L. Ross 1971; Hill 1987; Maddox 1982; Malone 1980; Miller 1979). Some authors have described the adjustments that some couples have made in order to continue their marriages (Deabill 1987; Gochros 1989; Latham and White 1978; Nahas and Turley 1979; M. W. Ross 1979; Whitney 1990). The argument that married men who consider themselves bisexual are actually gay, and are attempting to avoid the stigma of a homosexual label, was examined by M. W. Ross (1983). He concluded that there was not sufficient evidence to support the assertion that the bisexual self-identification reported by some such men does not accurately reflect their sexual orientation.

Other authors who have viewed bisexuality as a valid sexual orientation and identity, rather than solely as a transitional state, have described typical characteristics of the marriages of bisexual men (Brownfain 1985; Coleman 1982a, 1985b; D. Dixon 1985; Matteson 1985; T. J. Wolf 1985) and bisexual women (Coleman 1985a; J. K. Dixon 1984, 1985; Reinhardt 1985). Several researchers have identified factors that contribute to a successful marriage with a bisexual partner: open communication between partners (Coleman 1982a, 1985b; Reinhardt 1985; T. J. Wolf 1985); acceptance of, and discussion about, the bisexual partner's homosexual feelings (Coleman 1982a; T. J. Wolf 1985); commitment to making the relationship work (Coleman 1982a; T. J. Wolf 1985); the spouse's maintenance of a sense of worth outside the context of the relationship; and agreement by both partners to some degree of open relationship, if sexual contact outside the relationship was desired by the bisexual partner (Coleman 1982a). The impact that the husband's disclosure of sexual orientation may have on his spouse and the marriage relationship also has been examined (Buxton 1994; Gochros 1989; Hays and Samuels 1989).

The degree to which bisexuals disclose their homosexual attractions or behavior to their spouses varies widely. Brownfain (1985) found that most respondents in his nonclinical sample of bisexual married men were able to sustain a fulfilling family life, whether or not they disclosed their bisexuality to their spouses and whether or not they acted on their sexual attractions to other men. Matteson (1985) found that respondents who had disclosed to their spouses were more accepting of their homosexual experiences and bisexuality than those who had not disclosed, regardless of whether the couple was together or separating. He also found that husbands in together couples already had substantial homosexual experience and felt less need to act on current attractions to men. Husbands in separating couples had less homosexual experience and/or were more interested in relationships with men and involvement in the gay community. Reinhardt (1985) found that lack of sexual satisfaction with their husbands was not a significant factor in the decision of her bisexual respondents to pursue sexual relationships with women in addition to their marital relationships.

Research on Milestone Events in Bisexual Identity Development

Extensive data have been collected for lesbians and gay men on the "developmental milestone events" described in theoretical formulations of homosexual identity formation: first sexual attractions, behavior, and relationships; self-identification as gay or lesbian; and disclosure of sexual orientation to other people. Data have also been collected on these aspects of the process of coming out bisexual. This information allows for identification of patterns particular to bisexual identity development and clarifies similarities and differences in the formation of bisexual, lesbian, and gay identities.

First Heterosexual Attractions, Behavior, and Relationships

Bisexual men and women both experience their first heterosexual attractions at about the same ages, in their early teens, as shown in Table 3.1. This is somewhat earlier than for gay men and lesbians who have experienced heterosexual attractions, as shown in Table 3.2 and as found by Saghir and Robins (1973) and Bell et al. (1981).

Bisexual women have their first sexual experiences with men somewhat earlier than bisexual men have their first sexual experiences with women, in their middle to late teens, as Table 3.1 indicates. This is about the same as for lesbians and gay men who have had sexual experiences with persons of the opposite gender, as shown in Table 3.2 and as found by Saghir and Robins (1973) and Bell et al. (1981).

Bisexual women have their first heterosexual relationships about two years earlier than bisexual men, in their late teens, as Table 3.1 shows. The ages for bisexual men are about the same as for gay men who have had a heterosexual relationship (Table 3.2). No comparable data on the ages of first heterosexual relationships were found for lesbians.

First Homosexual Attractions, Behavior, and Relationships

Bisexual men experience their first sexual attractions toward other men in their early to middle teens, whereas bisexual women experience their first sexual attractions toward other women in their middle to late teens (Table 3.1). This is later, by about two to three years, than for gay men and lesbians (Table 3.2). The earlier ages for bisexual men compared to bisexual women are strikingly parallel to the earlier ages for gay men compared to lesbians, as shown in Tables 3.1 and 3.2 and as found by Saghir and Robins (1973) and Bell et al. (1981).

Bisexual men have their first sexual experiences with other men in their middle to late teens, whereas bisexual women have their first sexual experiences with other women in their early twenties (Table 3.1). This is somewhat later than for gay men and lesbians (Table 3.2). As with homosexual attractions, the earlier ages for homosexual behavior in bisexual men compared to bisexual women are strikingly parallel to the earlier ages for gay men compared to lesbians, as shown in Tables 3.1 and 3.2 and as found by Saghir and Robins (1973), Bell and Weinberg (1978), and Bell et al. (1981).

Bisexual women and men have their first homosexual relationships at about the same ages, in their early twenties (Table 3.1). This is about the same as for lesbians and gay men (Table 3.2).

First Bisexual, Lesbian, and Gay Self-Identifications

Most research has found that bisexual men and women first consider themselves bisexual at about the same ages, in their early to middle twenties (Table 3.1). This is about two to three years later than first homosexual self-identification for gay men and lesbians (Table 3.2). For those bisexual men and women who have considered themselves gay or lesbian, the men self-identified as gay earlier than the women self-identified as lesbian, in their early twenties (Table 3.1). This parallels the earlier homosexual self-identification of gay men compared to lesbians (Table 3.2).

TABLE 3.1 Average Ages at Milestone Events in Research on Bisexual Identity Development

Research	Date	N	Age	First Opposite Gender			First Same Gender			Identity as	
				Attraction	Behavior	Relationship	Attraction	Behavior	Relationship	Gay	Bi
Bisexual Women											
Harris	1977	10	28.0	—	21.1	—	—	22.2	—	—	25.8
Klein	1978	41	28.5	11.3	15.5	—	17.0	23.0	—	—	24.4
Kooden et al.	1979	17	—	—	—	—	16.0	22.0	24.9	27.9	—
Zinik	1984	63	31.8	10.8	—	—	16.9	—	—	—	—
Morse	1989	16	35.0	11.5	16.5	—	—	21.6	—	—	23.7
George	1993	121	30.6	—	—	—	—	—	—	—	23.2
Rust	1993	60	32.5	—	—	—	18.1	—	—	24.5	25.0
Fox	1993	486	30.3	11.1	15.1	18.0	15.8	20.0	22.4	22.8	22.5
Weinberg et al.	1994	44[a]	—	11.6	14.7	—	16.9	21.4	—	—	26.8
		96[b]	—	10.9	15.1	—	18.5	23.5	—	—	27.0

Bisexual Men

Harris	1977	15	34.9	—	20.1	—	—	14.5	—	27.3
Klein	1978	103	32.4	13.1	16.0	—	16.0	17.8	—	24.2
Kooden et al.	1979	64	—	—	—	—	12.6	13.9	19.1	22.3
Zinik	1984	72	36.2	11.9	—	—	16.2	—	—	—
Wayson	1985	21	—	—	19.8	—	—	18.6	—	—
Fox	1993	349	34.8	11.4	16.6	20.0	13.7	16.4	23.5	21.6
Weinberg et al.	1994	49[a]	—	11.7	17.3	—	13.5	16.3	—	27.2
		116[b]	—	12.8	15.9	—	17.1	17.2	—	29.0

[a] These figures are from the authors' 1983 study.

[b] These figures are from the authors' 1984/1985 study.

TABLE 3:2 Average Ages at Milestone Events in Research on Lesbian and Gay Identity Development

Research	Date	N	Age	First Opposite Gender			First Same Gender			Identity as Lesbian/Gay
				Attraction	Behavior	Relationship	Attraction	Behavior	Relationship	
Lesbians										
Kenyon	1968	123	36.4	—	—	—	16.1	21.5	—	—
Schafer	1976	151	26.2	—	18.5	—	14.5	19.8	—	20.7
Vance	1977	43	27.7	—	15.5	—	14.2	18.5	—	—
Califia	1979	286	27.5	—	—	—	—	20.0	—	20.5
Kooden et al.	1979	63	—	—	—	—	13.8	19.9	22.8	23.2
Ettore	1980	201	30.3	—	—	—	13.1	21.8	—	22.6
Fitzpatrick	1983	112	37.4	—	—	—	13.9	23.1	—	22.0
Zinik	1984	54	29.0	13.2	—	—	14.0	—	—	—
Chapman/Brannock	1987	197	34.0	—	16.8	—	—	20.6	—	22.5
Rust	1993	342	31.2	—	—	—	15.4	—	—	21.7
Weinberg et al.	1994	94[a]	—	14.3	16.4	—	16.4	20.5	—	22.5

Gay Men

Dank	1971	182	32.5	—	—	—	13.5	—	—	19.3
Danneker/Reiche	1974	581	27.5	—	—	—	—	16.7	—	19.0
Weinberg, T.S.	1977	30	—	—	18.3	—	—	14.1	—	19.9
Lehne	1978	47	22.8	—	—	—	—	16.0	—	—
Kooden et al.	1979	138	—	—	—	—	12.8	14.9	21.9	21.1
Troiden	1979	150	30.0	—	—	—	—	14.9	23.9	21.3
McDonald	1982	199	31.0	—	—	—	13.0	15.0	21.0	19.0
Sommers	1982	97	29.5	—	—	—	10.8	—	—	18.4
Benitez	1983	178	32.0	—	18.9	20.3	12.3	19.5	23.2	20.2
Cohen-Ross	1985	93	27.9	—	14.7	—	9.0	14.4	—	16.8
Wayson	1985	58	—	—	20.6	—	—	11.0	—	—
Zinik	1984	61	27.5	14.3	—	—	11.4	—	—	—
Edgar	1987	148	35.4	—	—	—	12.1	16.9	—	—
Prine	1987	51	35.1	—	—	—	15.2	17.7	—	—
Weinberg et al.	1994	186[a]	—	14.5	17.7	—	11.5	14.7	—	21.1

[a]These figures are from the authors' 1984/1985 study.

Age Cohort Group Differences

Differences in the average ages at which younger and older persons first self-identify as bisexual or gay have been addressed in one study of bisexual men and women (Fox 1993) and in three studies of gay men (Dank 1971; McDonald 1982; Troiden and Goode 1980). Significant differences for bisexual men and women in four age cohort groups (under twenty-five, twenty-five through thirty-four, thirty-five through forty-four, and forty-five and older) were found for first bisexual self-identification (Fox 1993). These results parallel similar differences found between different age cohort groupings of gay men: for men under and over thirty years of age (Dank 1971); for men in their twenties, thirties, and forties (McDonald 1982); and for men in their early twenties, late twenties, early thirties, and late thirties (Troiden and Goode 1980). Significant age cohort differences were also found for other typical coming-out milestone events for bisexual women and men, suggesting that the entire coming-out process is occurring earlier for younger bisexuals (Fox 1933). These kinds of age-group differences in samples of gay men and bisexual men and women have been seen as being related to the increased accessibility of information on sexuality and sexual orientation and the development of visible bisexual and gay communities as support systems for individuals involved in the coming-out process.

Self-Disclosure of Sexual Orientation

Lesbian and gay identity theory emphasizes the importance of disclosure of sexual orientation for the development of integrated lesbian or gay identities. Information on the ages of first disclosures to other people has been collected in two studies of bisexual men and women and several studies of gay men and lesbians. Bisexual women and men first disclose their sexual orientation to another person at about the same ages, at about the same time they first consider themselves bisexual. Respondents in one large sample first disclosed their bisexuality in their early twenties (Fox 1993), whereas respondents in two smaller samples first disclosed their bisexuality in their middle to late twenties (Weinberg et al. 1994). Lesbians first disclose in their middle twenties (Fitzpatrick 1983), and gay men first disclose in their early to middle twenties (Benitez 1983; Bilotta 1987; Cody 1988; Edgar 1987; McDonald 1982). Bisexual women and men first disclose to a family member in their middle twenties (Fox 1993), as do gay men (Benitez 1983; Bilotta

1987; Edgar 1987). Bisexual men and women first disclose to their father, mother, brother, or sister in their middle twenties (Fox 1993), whereas gay men first disclose to these family members in their late twenties (Cody 1988). No comparable information on the ages of first self-disclosures to family members was found for lesbians.

Fox (1993) and Weinberg et al. (1994) found that the persons to whom the greatest proportions of respondents had disclosed their bisexuality were friends and relationship partners, including spouses. Fox (1993) found that a substantial proportion of respondents had also disclosed to a therapist, whereas smaller proportions of respondents had disclosed to individual family members (mother, father, sister, or brother) or to people at work or school. A greater proportion of women than men had disclosed to a female friend or male relationship partner, or to a family member, a therapist, or someone at work or at school. These disclosure patterns are similar to those found in research on lesbians (Bell and Weinberg 1978; Chapman and Brannock 1987; Etorre 1980; Fitzpatrick 1983; Hencken 1984; Jay and Young 1979; Kooden et al. 1979; Loftin 1981; Weinberg et al. 1994) and gay men (Bell and Weinberg 1978; Benitez 1983; Cody 1988; Cramer and Roach 1988; Edgar 1987; Hencken 1984; Jay and Young 1979; Kooden et al. 1978; Weinberg et al. 1994). The proportions of bisexual respondents who had disclosed their sexual orientation to persons other than friends and relationship partners were smaller than those of lesbian and gay male respondents who had done so in comparable research.

Gender Differences in Coming Out Bisexual

The data for first sexual attractions, behavior, and bisexual self-identification, as shown in Table 3.1, reveal what appear to be different normative patterns for bisexual women and men. Most bisexual women experience their first heterosexual attractions and behavior *before* their first homosexual sexual attractions and behavior. In contrast, a greater proportion of bisexual men than bisexual women experience their first homosexual attractions and behavior earlier or at about the same ages as their first heterosexual behavior. Most bisexual women move from their first homosexual attractions to a bisexual identity more quickly than bisexual men, many of whom experience concurrent heterosexual and homosexual attractions and behavior at an earlier age than bisexual women and for a longer period of time before their first bisexual self-identification.

Counseling Issues

For bisexual men and women, the predominance of a polarized view of sexual orientation and the relative lack of a visible bisexual community complicate the task of coming to terms with concurrent heterosexual and homosexual attractions. As for many lesbians and gay men, psychotherapy has been helpful for many bisexual women and men in facing the issues involved in the coming-out process. Several issues that bisexual women and men typically bring into psychotherapy have been identified (Coleman 1982a; Lourea 1987; Matteson 1987; Nichols 1988; T. J. Wolf 1987, 1992): uncertainty about how to interpret their sexual attractions to both women and men; isolation, based on not knowing other bisexual women or men; alienation, feeling different from both heterosexuals and gay men or lesbians; apprehension about disclosure of their bisexuality to other people in their lives; and concerns about relationships and how to proceed with new or existing relationships while being open about sexual-orientation issues. Psychotherapy can assist an individual in coming to terms with these issues by facilitating greater self-acceptance and the courage to move from isolation to connection with a community of similar others. Autobiographical accounts also can be helpful by illustrating how other bisexual women and men have experienced and successfully moved through the coming out process (Falk 1975; Geller 1990; Hutchins and Kaahumanu 1991; Kohn and Matusow 1980; Norris and Read 1985; The Off Pink Collective 1988; Scott 1978; Weise 1992; Wolff 1979).

Community

Gay and lesbian identity theory has emphasized that friendships and relationships with other gay men and lesbians, and participation in the gay and lesbian communities, are important factors in developing integrated gay and lesbian identities. While numerous descriptive accounts of gay and lesbian communities appeared in the early literature, such has not been the case regarding bisexuality. Until recently, the only information in the literature on bisexuality in the context of community was found in research on homosexuality and lesbian and gay male communities. However, a few accounts of bisexual groups in urban communities do exist (Barr 1985; Mishaan 1985; Rubenstein and Slater 1985). Although the literature does not yet reflect the current growth of bisexual community groups and organizations on local, regional, and national levels, the development of community suggested by the emergence of these groups and organizations is indicated by a dramatic increase in the number of entries in successive editions of the *International Directory of Bisexual Groups* (Ochs 1994). This represents a major increase in the degree of access for bisexual women and men to a community of similar others during the coming-out process and on an ongoing basis.

Discussion

The illness model of homosexuality made a sharp distinction between normal (heterosexual) and abnormal (homosexual) sexual attractions and behavior. When homosexuality was removed as a diagnostic category, homosexual attractions and behavior were no longer officially considered an indication of psychopathology. This allowed for an important shift in emphasis in psychiatry and psychology away from the etiology of homosexuality and toward the development of theory and research on the formation of positive lesbian and gay identities.

Thinking about sexual orientation and sexual identity, however, continued to be based on the assumption of monosexuality, or exclusivity of heterosexual or homosexual "object choice." Looking through the lens of this dichotomous model, bisexuality appeared anomalous. For some authors, bisexuality and bisexuals simply did not exist. They believed that few people, if any, had equal attractions to men and women, and even a slight preference for one gender or the other was taken as "evidence" that the "real" orientation was homosexual *or* heterosexual. For others, *any* homosexual attractions or behavior indicated a homosexual orientation, and individuals who claimed a bisexual identity were seen as psychologically and socially maladjusted just as lesbians and gay men were considered maladjusted from the point of view of the illness model.

At the same time, the results of research on human sexuality clearly indicated that many individuals have experienced both heterosexual and homosexual attractions and behavior. Furthermore, research found no indication of psychopathology in nonclinical samples of bisexual women and men, just as prior research had found no evidence of psychopathology in nonclinical samples of lesbians and gay men.

No single pattern of homosexual and heterosexual attractions, behavior, and relationships characterizes self-identified bisexual men and women. Individuals arrive at their sexual identities by various routes. For some women and men, sexual identity remains constant, whereas for others, sexual identity varies in response to changes in sexual and emotional attractions, behavior, and relationships and the social and political contexts in which these occur. Finally, one of the main differences between bisexual men and women and gay men and lesbians is in the degree to which a visible community of similar others exists and serves to support the individual in the coming-out process. The extensive support networks that have developed in many communities have served this purpose for lesbians and gay men. While bisexual men and women often have looked to gay and lesbian communities for support and understanding regarding their homosexual interests and sexual minority status, the bisexual groups and organizations now emerging may be able to support them more effectively in the process of coming out bisexual and in their efforts to affiliate with other bisexual women and men.

Directions for Future Research

Multiple factors influence the development of bisexual identities, just as for heterosexual, gay, and lesbian identities. Gender, age, ethnicity, social class, and environment affect the experience and presentation of bisexual identities as well as other factors that theory and research have found to be relevant to identity: biological sex; gender identity; social sex roles; sexual attractions, fantasies, and behavior; emotional and social preferences; and lifestyle as well as prior lesbian, gay, and heterosexual identities.

As has been the case with most research on gay men and lesbians, research on bisexual men and women has been based on retrospective reports. Furthermore, in any particular study, respondents differ in age and in their qualitative experience of bisexuality and the coming-out process. In-depth longitudinal research is needed to understand better how bisexual identities develop over time.

Questions also remain regarding the representativeness of samples in existing research on bisexual, lesbian, and gay identities that are particular to surveys of stigmatized and partly invisible populations. The largest proportion of participants in most studies have been young, middle-class, white women and men. Research is needed on older bisexuals, working-class bisexuals, and bisexual people of color, who have been underrepresented, as have been people with bisexual behavior but other sexual orientation self-identifications.

Extensive research has been conducted on relationships in which one partner is heterosexual and the other is bisexual; however, research on re-lationships in which the partners are bisexual and gay or lesbian or both bisexual would add to our understanding of the relationships in which bi-sexual women and men are involved, as would research on triad and other multiple-partner relationships. Likewise, while research has been done on the transition from heterosexual to bisexual identity and on the transition from heterosexual to bisexual to gay identity, little research exists on the transition from lesbian and gay identities to a bisexual identity or on tran-sitions involving multiple sexual orientation self-identification sequences.

Although research has been conducted on attitudes of heterosexuals to-ward gay men and lesbians and on homophobia, very little research has been done on attitudes of heterosexuals, gay men, and lesbians toward bisexuals or on biphobia. Finally, research on how the coming-out process and the maintenance of positive bisexual identities are affected by the emergence and presence of a visible bisexual community could certainly augment our understanding of changes in the process of coming out bisexual that have occurred as a function of time and the development of community.

Conclusion

The evolution of theory and research on homosexuality and bisexuality has involved significant shifts in perspective. The movement from the het-erocentric illness model to a more affirmative approach to homosexuality, and the movement from a dichotomous model to a multidimensional model of sexual orientation, both have refocused the discourse on homosexuality and bisexuality toward examination of factors involved in the development of positive lesbian, gay, and bisexual identities.

The results of research on bisexuality indicate that there are similarities and differences in coming out bisexual and coming out gay or lesbian. Like lesbians and gay men, bisexual women and men need to acknowledge and validate their homosexual attractions and relationships to achieve positive and integrated sexual identities. In this respect, current models of gay and lesbian identity development are particularly helpful in understanding the homosex-ual component of bisexual identity development. Bisexual women and men, however, need to acknowledge and validate both the homosexual and the heterosexual components of their identities, regardless of the degree to which either or both of these are actualized in sexual behavior or relationships.

The development of a theoretical perspective that takes into consideration the diverse patterns of homosexual and heterosexual attractions and relationships of bisexual men and women has been essential in accurately conceptualizing bisexual identity development. The multidimensional view of sexual orientation and sexual identities on which this is based can further inform theory and research, and contribute to a fuller understanding of lesbian, gay, and bisexual identities.

References

Achilles, N. 1967. The development of the homosexual bar as an institution. In J. Gagnon and W. Simon, eds., *Sexual Deviance*, pp. 228–44. New York: Harper and Row.

Adam, B. D. 1985. Age, structure, and sexuality: Reflections on the anthropological evidence on homosexual relations. *Journal of Homosexuality* 11(3/4):19–34.

Alexander, F. 1933. Bisexual conflict in homosexuality. *Psychoanalytic Quarterly* 2:197–201.

Allen, C. 1961. When homosexuals marry. In I. Rubin, ed., *The Third Sex*, pp. 58–62. New York: New Book.

Barr, G. 1985. Chicago bi-ways: An informal history. *Journal of Homosexuality* 11(1/2):231–34.

Bayer, R. 1981. *Homosexuality and American Psychiatry: The Politics of Diagnosis.* New York: Basic Books.

Bell, A. P., and M. S. Weinberg. 1978. *Homosexualities: A Study of Diversity among Men and Women.* New York: Simon and Schuster.

Bell, A. P., M. S. Weinberg, and S. K. Hammersmith. 1981. *Sexual Preference: Its Development in Men and Women.* Bloomington: Indiana University Press.

Benitez, J. C. 1983. The effect of gay identity acquisition on the psychological adjustment of male homosexuals. Doctoral dissertation, Northwestern University 1982. *Dissertation Abstracts International* 43(10):3350B.

Bergler, E. 1956. *Homosexuality: Disease or Way of Life.* New York: Collier.

Berkey, B., T. Perelman-Hall, and L. A. Kurdek. 1990. Multi-dimensional scale of sexuality. *Journal of Homosexuality* 19(4):67–87.

Bieber, I. 1969. The married male homosexual. *Medical Aspects of Human Sexuality* 3(5):76–84.

Bieber, I., H. J. Dain, P. R. Dince, M. G. Drellich, R. H. Gunlach, M. W. Kremer, A. H. Rifkin, C. B. Wilbur, and T. B. Bieber. 1962. *Homosexuality: A Psychoanalytic Study.* New York: Random House.

Bilotta, G. J. 1987. Gay men coming out to their families of origin: An exploratory-descriptive investigation. Doctoral dissertation, United States International University 1987. *Dissertation Abstracts International* 48(4):1026A.

Blackwood, E. 1985. Breaking the mirror: The construction of lesbianism and the anthropological discourse on homosexuality. *Journal of Homosexuality* 11(3/4): 1–18.

Blumstein, P., and P. Schwartz. 1976a. Bisexuality in men. *Urban Life* 5(3):339–58.

Blumstein, P. W., and P. Schwartz. 1976b. Bisexuality in women. *Archives of Sexual Behavior* 5(2):171–81.

Blumstein, P. W., and P. Schwartz. 1977. Bisexuality: Some Social Psychological Issues. *Journal of Social Issues* 33(2):30–45.

Bode, J. 1976. *View from Another Closet: Exploring Bisexuality in Women.* New York: Hawthorne.

Boulton, M., and T. Coxon. 1991. Bisexuality in the United Kingdom. In R.A.P. Tielman, M. Carballo, and A. C. Hendriks, eds., *Bisexuality and HIV/AIDS: A Global Perspective*, pp. 65–72. Buffalo, N.Y.: Prometheus.

Bozett, F. W. 1982. Heterogeneous couples in heterosexual marriages: Gay men and straight women. *Journal of Marital and Family Therapy* 8(1):81–89.

Brownfain, J. J. 1985. A study of the married bisexual male: Paradox and resolution. *Journal of Homosexuality* 11(1/2):173–88.

Buxton, A. P. 1994. *The Other Side of the Closet: The Coming Out Crisis for Straight Spouses and Families.* New York: Wiley.

Califia, P. 1979. Lesbian sexuality. *Journal of Homosexuality* 4(3):255–66.

Caprio, F. S. 1954. *Female Homosexuality: A Psychodynamic Study of Lesbianism.* New York: Grove.

Caprio, F. S. 1955. *The Adequate Male.* New York: Medical Research Press.

Carrier, J. M. 1980. Homosexual behavior in cross-cultural perspective. In J. Marmor, ed., *Homosexual Behavior: A Modern Reappraisal*, pp. 100–122. New York: Basic Books.

Carrier, J. M. 1985. Mexican male bisexuality. *Journal of Homosexuality* 11(1/2): 75–86.

Cass, V. C. 1979. Homosexual identity formation: A theoretical model. *Journal of Homosexuality* 4(3):219–35.

Cass, V. C. [1983] 1984. Homosexual identity: A concept in need of definition. *Journal of Homosexuality* 9(2/3):105–26.

Cass, V. C. 1984. Homosexual identity formation: Testing a theoretical model. *Journal of Sex Research* 20(2):143–67.

Cass, V. C. 1990. The implications of homosexual identity formation for the Kinsey model and scale of sexual preference. In D. P. McWhirter, S. A. Sanders, and J. M. Reinisch, eds., *Homosexuality/Heterosexuality: Concepts of Sexual Orientation*, pp. 239–66. New York: Oxford University Press.

Chapman, B. E., and J. C. Brannock. 1987. Proposed model of lesbian identity development: An empirical examination. *Journal of Homosexuality* 14(3/4):69–80.

Churchill, W. 1967. *Homosexual Behavior among Males: A Cross-Cultural and Cross-Species Investigation.* New York: Hawthorn.

Cody, P. J. 1988. The personal development of gay men: A study of the relationship of length of time "out of the closet" to locus of control, self-concept, and self-actualization. Doctoral dissertation, California Institute of Integral Studies 1988. *Dissertation Abstracts International* 49(7):2847B.

Cohen-Ross, J. L. 1985. An exploratory study of the retrospective role of significant others in homosexual identity development. Doctoral dissertation, California School of Professional Psychology, Los Angeles 1984. *Dissertation Abstracts International* 46(2):628B.

Coleman, E. 1982a. Bisexual and gay men in heterosexual marriage: Conflicts and resolutions in therapy. *Journal of Homosexuality* 7(2/3):93–104.

Coleman, E. 1982b. Developmental stages of the coming out process. *Journal of Homosexuality* 7(2/3):31–44.

Coleman, E. 1985a. Bisexual women in marriages. *Journal of Homosexuality* 11(1/2):87–100.

Coleman, E. 1985b. Integration of male bisexuality and marriage. *Journal of Homosexuality* 11(1/2):189–208.

Coleman, E. 1987. Assessment of sexual orientation. *Journal of Homosexuality* 14(1/2):9–24.

Coleman, E. 1990. Toward a synthetic understanding of sexual orientation. In D. P. McWhirter, S. A. Sanders, and J. M. Reinisch, eds., *Homosexuality/Heterosexuality: Concepts of Sexual Orientation*, pp. 267–76. New York: Oxford University Press.

Cory, D. W., and J. P. LeRoy. 1963. *The Homosexual and His Society: A View from Within*. New York: Citadel.

Cramer, D. W., and A. J. Roach. 1988. Coming out to mom and dad: A study of gay males and their relationships with their parents. *Journal of Homosexuality* 15(3/4):79–91.

Cronin, D. M. 1974. Coming out among lesbians. In E. Goode and R. R. Troiden, eds., *Sexual Deviance and Sexual Deviants*, pp. 268–77. New York: Morrow.

Dank, B. M. 1971. Coming out in the gay world. *Psychiatry* 34:180–97.

Dannecker, M., and R. Reiche. 1974. *Der gewohnliche Homosexualle*. Frankfurt: Fisher.

Davenport, W. 1965. Sexual patterns and their regulation in a society of the Southwest Pacific. In F. A. Beach, ed., *Sex and Behavior*, pp. 164–207. New York: Wiley.

Davenport, W. 1977. Sex in cross-cultural perspective. In F. A. Beach, ed., *Human Sexuality in Four Perspectives*, pp. 115–63. Baltimore: The Johns Hopkins University Press.

Deabill, G. 1987. An investigation of sexual behaviors in mixed sexual orientation couples: Gay husband and straight wife. Unpublished doctoral dissertation, Institute for Advanced Study of Human Sexuality, San Francisco.

de Monteflores, C., and S. J. Schultz. 1978. Coming out: Similarities and differences for lesbians and gay men. *Journal of Social Issues* 34(3):59–72.

Dixon, D. 1985. Perceived sexual satisfaction and marital happiness of bisexual and heterosexual swinging husbands. *Journal of Homosexuality* 11(1/2):209–22.

Dixon, J. K. 1984. The commencement of bisexual activity in swinging married women over age thirty. *Journal of Sex Research* 20:71–90.

Master
    t
Mattes
    a
Mattes
    a
    M
McDor
    In
Mead, I
    an
    W
Mead, N
Miller, I
Mishaar
    11
Moll, A.
    Ver
    Am
Morrow,
    2:28
Morse, C
    Mas
Nahas, R.
    Seav
Nichols, N
    apy.
    Circ
Norris, S.,
    Bisex
Nunberg,
    Psych
Nunberg, I
    of Psy
Nurius, P.
    Resea
Ochs, R. 19
    Mass.:
Off Pink C
Opler, M. I
    Marm
    23. Ne

Hoc
Hu
Hu
Hu
Hu

Imi

Jay,

Kar

Kat

Kei

Kha

Kir

Kir

Kle

Kle

Kle
Kle

Ko

Ko

Kr

Dixon, J. K. 1985. Sexuality and relationship changes in married females following the commencement of bisexual activity. *Journal of Homosexuality* 11(1/2): 115–34.

Doll, L., J. Peterson, J. R. Magana, and J. M. Carrier. 1991. Male bisexuality and AIDS in the United States. In R.A.P. Tielman, M. Carballo, and A. C. Hendriks, eds., *Bisexuality and HIV/AIDS: A Global Perspective*, pp. 27–40. Buffalo, N.Y.: Prometheus.

Edgar, T. M. 1987. The disclosure process of the stigmatized: Strategies to minimize rejection. Doctoral dissertation, Purdue University, West Lafayette, Indiana 1986. *Dissertation Abstracts International* 47(9):3238A.

Ellis, H. [1905] 1942. *Studies in the Psychology of Sex*, vol. 1. New York: Random House.

Ettore, E. M. 1980. *Lesbians, Women, and Society*. London: Routledge and Kegan Paul.

Falk, R. 1975. *Women Loving: A Journey Toward Becoming an Independent Woman*. New York: Random House.

Fast, J., and H. Wells. 1975. *Bisexual Living*. New York: Pocket Books.

Fitzpatrick, G. 1983. Self-disclosure of lesbianism as related to self-actualization and self-stigmatization. Doctoral dissertation, United States International University 1982. *Dissertation Abstracts International* 43(12):4143B.

Ford, C. S., and F. A. Beach. 1951. *Patterns of Sexual Behavior*. New York: Harper and Row.

Fox, R. C. 1993. Coming out bisexual: Identity, behavior, and sexual orientation self-disclosure. Unpublished doctoral dissertation, California Institute of Integral Studies, San Francisco.

Freud, S. [1905] 1962. *Three Essays on the Theory of Sexuality*. Translated by J. Strachey. New York: Basic Books.

Freud, S. [1925] 1963. *An Autobiographical Study*. Translated by J. Strachey. Rev. ed. New York: Norton.

Freud, S. [1937] 1963. Analysis terminable and interminable. In P. Rieff, ed., *Therapy and Technique*, pp. 233–72. New York: Collier.

Gagnon, J. M., and W. Simon. 1968. Homosexuality: The Formulation of a Sociological Perspective. In M. Lefton, J. K. Skipper Jr., and C. H. McGaghy, eds., *Approaches to Deviance: Theories, Concepts, and Research Findings*, pp. 349–61. New York: Appleton-Century-Crofts.

Gagnon, J. M., and W. Simon. 1973. *Sexual Conduct: The Social Sources of Human Sexuality*. Chicago: Aldine.

Galland, V. R. 1975. Bisexual women. Doctoral dissertation, California School of Professional Psychology, San Francisco 1975. *Dissertation Abstracts International* 36(6):3037B.

Geller, T., ed. 1990. *Bisexuality: A Reader and Sourcebook*. Ojai, Calif.: Times Change.

Paul, J. P. 1984. The bisexual identity: An idea without social recognition. *Journal of Homosexuality* 9(2/3):45–64.

Paul, J. P. 1985. Bisexuality: Reassessing our paradigms of sexuality. *Journal of Homosexuality* 11(1/2):21–34.

Playboy readers' sex survey, part 3. 1983. *Playboy Magazine*, May, pp. 126–28, 136, 210–20.

Plummer, K. 1981. Going gay: Identities, lifestyles, and life cycles in the male gay world. In J. Hart and D. Richardson, eds., *The Theory and Practice of Homosexuality*, pp. 93–110. London: Routledge and Kegan Paul.

Ponse, B. 1978. *Identities in the Lesbian World: The Social Construction of Self*. Westport, Conn.: Greenwood.

Ponse, B. 1980. Lesbians and their worlds. In J. Marmor, ed., *Homosexual Behavior: A Modern Reappraisal*, pp. 157–75. New York: Basic Books.

Prine, K. A. 1987. Gay men: The open behavioral expression of sexual orientations and descriptions of psychological health. Doctoral dissertation, University of Cincinnati 1987. *Dissertation Abstracts International* 48(4):1185B.

Rado, S. 1940. A critical examination of the concept of bisexuality. *Psychosomatic Medicine* 2(4):459–67.

Read, K. E. 1980. *Other Voices: The Style of a Male Homosexual Tavern*. Novato, Calif.: Chandler and Sharp.

Reinhardt, R. U. 1985. Bisexual women in heterosexual relationships: A study of psychological and sociological patterns. Doctoral dissertation, The Professional School of Psychological Studies, San Diego 1985. *Research Abstracts International* 11(3):67.

Reiss, A. J. 1961. The social integration of queers and peers. *Social Problems* 9:102–20.

Ritvo, L. B. 1990. *Darwin's Influence on Freud: A Tale of Two Sciences*. New Haven: Yale University Press.

Ross, H. L. 1971. Modes of adjustment of married homosexuals. *Social Problems* 18:385–93.

Ross, M. W. 1979. Heterosexual marriage of homosexual males: Some associated factors. *Journal of Sex and Marital Therapy* 5:142–50.

Ross, M. W. 1983. *The Married Homosexual Man: A Psychological Study*. London: Routledge and Kegan Paul.

Ross, M. W. 1990. Toward a synthetic understanding of sexual orientation. In D. P. McWhirter, S. A. Sanders, and J. M. Reinisch, eds., *Homosexuality/Heterosexuality: Concepts of Sexual Orientation*, pp. 267–76. New York: Oxford University Press.

Ross, M. W. 1991. A taxonomy of global behavior. In R.A.P. Tielman, M. Carballo, and A. C. Hendriks, eds., *Bisexuality and HIV/AIDS: A Global Perspective*, pp. 21–26. Buffalo, N.Y.: Prometheus.

Ross, M. W., and J. P. Paul. 1992. Beyond gender: The basis of sexual attraction in bisexual men and women. *Psychological Reports* 71:1283–90.

Masters, W. H., and V. E. Johnson. 1979. *Homosexuality in Perspective*. Boston: Little, Brown.

Matteson, D. R. 1985. Bisexual men in marriage: Is a positive homosexual identity and stable marriage possible? *Journal of Homosexuality* 11(1/2):149–72.

Matteson, D. R. 1987. Counseling bisexual men. In M. Scher, M. Stevens, G. Good, and G. A. Eichenfeld, eds., *Handbook of Counseling and Psychotherapy with Men*, pp. 232–49. Newbury Park, Calif.: Sage.

McDonald, G. J. 1982. Individual differences in the coming out process for gay men: Implications for theoretical models. *Journal of Homosexuality* 8(1):47–60.

Mead, M. 1961. Cultural determinants of sexual behavior. In W. C. Young, ed., *Sex and Internal Secretions*, vol. 2, 3rd ed., pp. 1433–79. Baltimore: Williams and Wilkins.

Mead, M. 1975. Bisexuality: What's it all about? *Redbook*, January, pp. 6–7.

Miller, B. 1979. Gay fathers and their children. *The Family Coordinator* 28:544–52.

Mishaan, C. 1985. The bisexual scene in New York City. *Journal of Homosexuality* 11(1/2):223–26.

Moll, A. [1897] 1933. *Libido Sexualis: Studies in the Psychosexual Laws of Love Verified by Clinical Sexual Case Histories*. Translated by D. Berger. New York: American Ethnological Press.

Morrow, G. D. 1989. Bisexuality: An exploratory review. *Annals of Sex Research* 2:283–306.

Morse, C. R. 1989. Exploring the bisexual alternative: A view from another closet. Master's thesis, University of Arizona 1989. *Master's Abstracts* 28(2):320.

Nahas, R., and M. Turley. 1979. *The New Couple: Women and Gay Men*. New York: Seaview.

Nichols, M. 1988. Bisexuality in women: Myths, realities, and implications for therapy. In E. Cole and E. Rothblum, eds., *Women and Sex Therapy: Closing the Circle of Sexual Knowledge*, pp. 235–52. New York: Harrington Park.

Norris, S., and E. Read. 1985. *Out in the Open: People Talking about Being Gay or Bisexual*. London: Pan.

Nunberg, H. 1938. Homosexuality, magic, and aggression. *International Journal of Psychoanalysis* 19:1–16.

Nunberg, H. 1947. Circumcision and problems of bisexuality. *International Journal of Psychoanalysis* 28:145–79.

Nurius, P. S. 1983. Mental health implications of sexual orientation. *Journal of Sex Research* 19(2):119–36.

Ochs, R. 1994. *The International Directory of Bisexual Groups*. 11th ed. Cambridge Mass.: Bisexual Resource Center.

Off Pink Collective. 1988. *Bisexual Lives*. London: Off Pink.

Opler, M. 1965. Anthropological and cross-cultural aspects of homosexuality. In J. Marmor, ed., *Sexual Inversion: The Multiple Roots of Homosexuality*, pp. 108–23. New York: Basic Books.

Paul, J. P. 1984. The bisexual identity: An idea without social recognition. *Journal of Homosexuality* 9(2/3):45–64.

Paul, J. P. 1985. Bisexuality: Reassessing our paradigms of sexuality. *Journal of Homosexuality* 11(1/2):21–34.

Playboy readers' sex survey, part 3. 1983. *Playboy Magazine*, May, pp. 126–28, 136, 210–20.

Plummer, K. 1981. Going gay: Identities, lifestyles, and life cycles in the male gay world. In J. Hart and D. Richardson, eds., *The Theory and Practice of Homosexuality*, pp. 93–110. London: Routledge and Kegan Paul.

Ponse, B. 1978. *Identities in the Lesbian World: The Social Construction of Self.* Westport, Conn.: Greenwood.

Ponse, B. 1980. Lesbians and their worlds. In J. Marmor, ed., *Homosexual Behavior: A Modern Reappraisal*, pp. 157–75. New York: Basic Books.

Prine, K. A. 1987. Gay men: The open behavioral expression of sexual orientations and descriptions of psychological health. Doctoral dissertation, University of Cincinnati 1987. *Dissertation Abstracts International* 48(4):1185B.

Rado, S. 1940. A critical examination of the concept of bisexuality. *Psychosomatic Medicine* 2(4):459–67.

Read, K. E. 1980. *Other Voices: The Style of a Male Homosexual Tavern.* Novato, Calif.: Chandler and Sharp.

Reinhardt, R. U. 1985. Bisexual women in heterosexual relationships: A study of psychological and sociological patterns. Doctoral dissertation, The Professional School of Psychological Studies, San Diego 1985. *Research Abstracts International* 11(3):67.

Reiss, A. J. 1961. The social integration of queers and peers. *Social Problems* 9:102–20.

Ritvo, L. B. 1990. *Darwin's Influence on Freud: A Tale of Two Sciences.* New Haven: Yale University Press.

Ross, H. L. 1971. Modes of adjustment of married homosexuals. *Social Problems* 18:385–93.

Ross, M. W. 1979. Heterosexual marriage of homosexual males: Some associated factors. *Journal of Sex and Marital Therapy* 5:142–50.

Ross, M. W. 1983. *The Married Homosexual Man: A Psychological Study.* London: Routledge and Kegan Paul.

Ross, M. W. 1990. Toward a synthetic understanding of sexual orientation. In D. P. McWhirter, S. A. Sanders, and J. M. Reinisch, eds., *Homosexuality/Heterosexuality: Concepts of Sexual Orientation*, pp. 267–76. New York: Oxford University Press.

Ross, M. W. 1991. A taxonomy of global behavior. In R.A.P. Tielman, M. Carballo, and A. C. Hendriks, eds., *Bisexuality and HIV/AIDS: A Global Perspective*, pp. 21–26. Buffalo, N.Y.: Prometheus.

Ross, M. W., and J. P. Paul. 1992. Beyond gender: The basis of sexual attraction in bisexual men and women. *Psychological Reports* 71:1283–90.

Rubenstein, M. 1982. An in-depth study of bisexuality and its relationship to self-esteem. Unpublished doctoral dissertation, Institute for Advanced Study of Human Sexuality, San Francisco.

Rubenstein, M., and C. A. Slater. 1985. A profile of the San Francisco Bisexual Center. *Journal of Homosexuality* 11(1/2):227–30.

Ruitenbeek, H. M. 1963. The male homosexual and the disintegrated family. In H. M. Ruitenbeek, ed., *The Problem of Homosexuality in Modern Society*, pp. 80–93. New York: Dutton.

Ruitenbeek, H. M. 1973. The myth of bisexuality. In H. M. Ruitenbeek, ed., *Homosexuality: A Changing Picture*, pp. 199–204. London: Souvenir.

Rust, P. C. 1992. The politics of sexual identity: Sexual attraction and behavior among lesbian and bisexual women. *Social Problems* 39(4):366–86.

Rust, P. C. 1993. "Coming out" in the age of social constructionism: Sexual identity formation among lesbian and bisexual women. *Gender and Society* 7(1):50–77.

Saghir, M. T., and E. Robins. 1973. *Male and Female Homosexuality: A Comprehensive Investigation*. Baltimore: Williams and Wilkins.

Saliba, P. A. 1980. Variability in sexual orientation. Unpublished master's thesis, San Francisco State University.

Schafer, S. 1976. Sexual and social problems of lesbians. *Journal of Sex Research* 12(1):50–79.

Schuster, R. 1987. Sexuality as a continuum: The bisexual identity. In The Boston Lesbian Psychologies Collective, ed., *Lesbian Psychologies: Explorations and Challenges*, pp. 56–71. Urbana: University of Illinois Press.

Scott, J. 1978. *Wives Who Love Women*. New York: Walker.

Shively, M., and J. DeCecco. 1977. Components of sexual identity. *Journal of Homosexuality* 3(1):41–48.

Shively, M. G., C. Jones, and J. P. DeCecco. 1984. Research on sexual orientation: Definitions and methods. *Journal of Homosexuality* 9(2/3):127–36.

Simon, W., and J. H. Gagnon. 1967. The lesbians: A preliminary overview. In J. H. Gagnon and W. Simon, eds., *Sexual Deviance*, pp. 247–84. New York: Harper and Row.

Socarides, C. W. 1972. Homosexuality: Basic concepts and psychodynamics. *International Journal of Psychiatry*, 10(1):118–25.

Socarides, C. W. 1978. *Homosexuality*. New York: Jason Aronson.

Sommers, M. A. 1982. The relationship between present social support networks and current levels of interpersonal congruency of gay identity. Doctoral dissertation, California School of Professional Psychology, Los Angeles 1982. *Dissertation Abstracts International* 43(6):1962B.

Sophie, J. 1986. A critical examination of stage theories of lesbian identity development. *Journal of Homosexuality* 12(2):39–51.

Spada, J. 1979. *The Spada Report: The Newest Survey of Gay Male Sexuality*. New York: New American Library.

Stekel, W. [1922] 1946a. *Bi-sexual Love*. New York: Emerson.

Stekel, W. [1922] 1946b. *The Homosexual Neurosis*. New York: Emerson.

Stoller, R. J. 1972. The "bedrock" of masculinity and femininity: Bisexuality. *Archives of General Psychiatry* 26:207–12.

Storms, M. D. 1980. Theories of sexual orientation. *Journal of Personality and Social Psychology* 38(5):783–92.

Sulloway, F. J. 1979. *Freud, Biologist of the Mind: Beyond the Psychoanalytic Legend*. New York: Basic Books.

Szasz, T. S. 1965. Legal and Moral Aspects of Homosexuality. In J. Marmor, ed., *Sexual Inversion: The Multiple Roots of Homosexuality*, pp. 124–39. New York: Basic Books.

Szasz, T. S. 1970. *The Manufacture of Madness: A Comparative Study of the Inquisition and the Mental Health Movement*. New York: Dell.

Thornton, N. 1948. Why American homosexuals marry. *Neurotica* 1(1):24–28.

Tielman, R.A.P., M. Carballo, and A. C. Hendriks, eds. 1991. *Bisexuality and HIV/AIDS: A Global Perspective*. Buffalo, N.Y.: Prometheus.

Troiden, R. R. 1979. Becoming homosexual: A model of gay identity acquisition. *Psychiatry* 42:362–73.

Troiden, R. R. 1988. *Gay and Lesbian Identity: A Sociological Analysis*. Dix Hills, N.Y.: General Hall.

Troiden, R. R., and E. Goode. 1980. Variables related to the acquisition of a gay identity. *Journal of Homosexuality* 5(4):383–92.

Twining, A. 1983. Bisexual women: Identity in adult development. Doctoral dissertation, Boston University School of Education 1983. *Dissertation Abstracts International* 44(5):1340A.

Twitchell, J. 1974. Sexual liberality and personality: A pilot study. In J. R. Smith and L. G. Smith, eds., *Beyond Monogamy: Recent Studies of Sexual Alternatives in Marriage*, pp. 230–45. Baltimore: The Johns Hopkins University Press.

Vance, B. K. 1977. Female homosexuality: A social psychological examination of attitudinal and etiological characteristics of different groups. Doctoral dissertation, Oklahoma State University 1977. *Dissertation Abstracts International* 39:451B.

Warren, C.A.B. 1974. *Identity and Community in the Gay World*. New York: Wiley.

Warren, C. 1980. Homosexuality and Stigma. In J. Marmor, ed., *Homosexual Behavior: A Modern Reappraisal*, pp. 123–41. New York: Basic Books.

Wayson, P. D. 1985. Personality variables in males as they relate to differences in sexual orientation. *Journal of Homosexuality* 11(1/2):63–74.

Weinberg, G. 1972. *Society and the Healthy Homosexual*. New York: St. Martin's.

Weinberg, M. S., and C. J. Williams. 1974. *Male Homosexuals: Their Problems and Adaptations*. New York: Penguin.

Weinberg, M. S., C. J. Williams, and D. W. Pryor. 1994. *Dual Attraction: Understanding Bisexuality*. New York: Oxford University Press.

Weinberg, T. S. 1977. Becoming homosexual: Self-discovery, self-identity, and self-maintenance. Doctoral dissertation, University of Connecticut 1977. *Dissertation Abstracts International* 38(1):506A.

Weininger, O. 1908. *Sex and Character.* London: Heinemann; New York: Putnam's.

Weise, E. R., ed. 1992. *Closer to Home: Bisexuality and Feminism.* Seattle: Seal.

Weiss, E. 1958. Bisexuality and ego structure. *International Journal of Psychoanalysis* 39:91–97.

Whitney, C. 1990. *Uncommon Lives: Gay Men and Straight Women.* New York: Plume.

Wolf, D. G. 1979. *The Lesbian Community.* Berkeley: University of California Press.

Wolf, T. J. 1985. Marriages of bisexual men. *Journal of Homosexuality* 11(1/2): 135–48.

Wolf, T. J. 1987. Group counseling for bisexual men. *Journal for Specialists in Group Work* 11:162–65.

Wolf, T. J. 1992. Bisexuality: A counseling perspective. In S. H. Dworkin and F. J. Gutierrez, eds., *Counseling Gay Men and Lesbians: Journey to the End of the Rainbow,* pp. 175–87. Alexandria, Va.: American Association for Counseling and Development.

Wolff, C. 1971. *Love Between Women.* New York: St. Martin's.

Wolff, C. 1979. *Bisexuality: A Study.* London: Quarter Books.

Wooden, W., and J. Parker. 1982. *Men Behind Bars: Sexual Exploitation in Prison.* New York: Plenum.

Zinik, G. A. 1984. The relationship between sexual orientation and eroticism, cognitive flexibility, and negative affect. Doctoral dissertation, University of California, Santa Barbara 1983. *Dissertation Abstracts International* 45(8):2707B.

Zinik, G. A. 1985. Identity conflict or adaptive flexibility? Bisexuality reconsidered. *Journal of Homosexuality* 11(1/2):7–19.

4 Explaining Diversity in the Development of Same-Sex Sexuality Among Young Women

Lisa M. Diamond and Ritch C. Savin-Williams

Models of sexual identity development typically posit a sequence of feelings, experiences, and events through which individuals progressively realize, understand, and accept a nonheterosexual (or *sexual-minority*) identity. Because most of these "coming-out" models are based on men, they portray as normative a sequence of feelings and experiences that may be entirely foreign to a sexual-minority woman: early "precursors" such as gender atypicality or feelings of differentness, late childhood and early adolescent same-sex attractions, lack of sexual interest in the other sex, subsequent same-sex experimentation, and, finally, adolescent self-labeling as lesbian, gay, or bisexual.

In fact, the developmental trajectories of most sexual-minority women violate this "master narrative" in at least one way. Some sexual-minority women have no childhood or adolescent recollections of same-sex attractions (Kitzinger and Wilkinson 1995) but assert that their same-sex attractions were triggered in adulthood by exposure to lesbian, gay, or bisexual ideas or individuals (Golden 1996) or the formation of an unusually intense emotional attachment to one particular woman (Cassingham and O'Neil 1999; Kitzinger and Wilkinson 1995; Shuster 1987). Others report abrupt changes in their sexual attractions over time (Weinberg, Williams, and Pryor 1994).

Such cases run counter to the conventional view of sexual orientation as a stable, early-appearing trait. Yet these cases have typically been considered few in number and exceptional in nature — unwanted noise in the "data" of normative sexual identity development. The results of our intensive investigations of adolescent and young adult sexual-minority women directly challenge this view (Diamond 1998, 2000a, 2000b; Diamond and Dubé 2000;

Savin-Williams, in preparation; Savin-Williams and Diamond 2000). Our findings lead us to propose that variability in the emergence and expression of female same-sex desire during the life course is normative rather than exceptional. In other words, the cases noted above are *not* noise in the data; rather, they are the data with potentially the most to tell us about female sexual development.

In this article we review major findings from our ongoing program of research, integrate them with existing knowledge on female sexuality, and articulate a conceptual approach to the study of female same-sex sexuality that aims to explain, and not simply describe, the diverse developmental trajectories we have observed. Our goal is not to replace a single model of development with an ever increasing number of ideosyncratic models but to highlight the conditions and processes that *produce* multiple developmental trajectories. Toward this end, our main points are as follows:

1. Because of the prevalence of nonexclusivity and fluidity in women's attractions, there is considerable variation in the quality and relative distribution of women's same-sex and other-sex attractions, as well as the context in which these attractions are experienced.

2. The timing of a woman's first same-sex attractions does not systematically predict their quality or exclusivity, nor does it predict the stability of her sexual identity.

3. Variability in both sexual-minority and heterosexual women's sexual development is best explained by interactions between personal characteristics and environmental contexts.

Although we here emphasize women's development, the approach we advocate would also enhance research on men's sexual development (Savin-Williams 1998). Yet we believe it holds particular promise for research on women given the prevalence of nonexclusivity and fluidity in women's attractions (Baumeister 2000), as well as the documented tendency for social and environmental factors to exert stronger influences on female than male sexual behavior (Udry, Talbert, and Morris 1986).

Sample and Methods

We here review findings from two independent, ongoing studies (for clarity, Study A and Study B). Study A is a longitudinal study of the sexual attractions, behaviors, and identities of eighty-nine sexual-minority and eleven heterosexual women who were first interviewed in 1995 when they were between the ages of sixteen and twenty-three (Diamond 1998). These women were reinterviewed two years later in 1997 (Diamond 2000a, 2000b) and are currently undergoing a third round of interviews. This is the first prospective study of female sexual-minority youth ever undertaken and therefore offers a unique opportunity to observe the long-term course of sexual identity development. Study B is an interview study of the childhood and adolescent experiences of seventy-eight female and eighty-six male sexual minorities between the ages of seventeen and twenty-five (Savin-Williams 1998, in press; Savin-Williams and Diamond, in press). Because this study uses a standardized, qualitative interview protocol, it permits systematic examination of the quality and context of sexual identity milestones and not just their timing.

Participants for both projects were recruited from similar sites: lesbian/gay/bisexual community events and youth support groups in central New York, college classes on gender and sexuality, campus social and political organizations, and Internet list-serves (for more detail, see publications cited above). This wide-ranging recruitment strategy was undertaken to ensure diversity in women's histories of same-sex attractions and behaviors and to recruit women who decline to identify as lesbian or bisexual but acknowledge same-sex attractions. Of the participants in Study A, 34 percent identified as lesbian, 26 percent as bisexual, 20 percent as "unlabeled" or "questioning" (collectively denoted *unlabeled*), and 10 percent as heterosexual (heterosexual participants were recruited on the basis of having consciously reflected on their sexual identity at some point and thus cannot be considered representative of most heterosexual women). Of the female participants in Study B, 38 percent identified as lesbian, 42 percent as bisexual, and 20 percent as unlabeled. Both samples overrepresent highly educated, middle-class white women; about 25 percent of the women were working-class, and 20 percent were women of color. A primary goal for the ongoing expansion of both studies involves recruitment of greater numbers of ethnic-minority and working-class women.

The interview questions for both studies were modeled on those represented in existing survey and interview data on sexual identity development (Golden 1996; Rust 1992, 1993; Savin-Williams 1998; Weinberg et al. 1994). Topics included childhood experiences such as gender atypicality and feelings of differentness, early sexual and emotional attractions, sexual and romantic relationship history, and antecedents and processes of sexual questioning (for more details, see publications cited above).

Will the Real Sexual Minorities Please Stand Up?

Studying Bisexual and Unlabeled Women

Both studies include notable proportions of bisexual and unlabeled women, who have been traditionally underrepresented in research on sexual minorities. In fact, many researchers intentionally exclude such individuals from their samples because they are difficult to categorize. As a journal reviewer for one of our recent manuscripts queried: "How can you be sure of their true sexual orientation? It would make for a cleaner study if you took them out."

The implicit assumption is that openly identified lesbians are the most prototypical group of sexual-minority women and therefore the most valid basis for generalizations about the development of same-sex sexuality. Yet this assumption is questionable. Data from a random, representative sample of American men and women (Laumann et al. 1994) showed that 84 percent of women with same-sex attractions or behavior identify as heterosexual. Given that research on female sexual minorities has focused exclusively on openly identified lesbian/bisexual women, it appears that our current understanding of the female sexual-minority life course is based on the smallest, least representative subset of this population. In our view, any explanation of female sexual development that does not account for the full range of sexual-minority women is no explanation at all. For this reason, we begin with a discussion of two phenomena that critically influence variability in women's developmental trajectories: nonexclusivity and fluidity in women's attractions.

Nonexclusivity

Contrary to conventional wisdom, exclusive same-sex attractions are the exception rather than the norm among sexual-minority women. Laumann et al. (1994) found that 4.4 percent of American women reported experiencing same-sex attractions, and 94 percent of these women were also attracted to men. In fact, nearly two-thirds were *predominantly* attracted to men. Similarly, two-thirds of the lesbian women in Study A reported experiencing periodic attractions to men. The prevalence of nonexclusivity in sexual-minority women's attractions suggests that other-sex attractions and relationships remain an ever present possibility for most sexual-minority women, a fact that creates multiple opportunities for discontinuity and inconsistency in the female sexual-minority life course. For example, nearly one-fourth of lesbians in Study A listed a high school boyfriend as one of the strongest attractions they had ever experienced, yet many of these women reported that they no longer experienced other-sex attractions (Diamond 1998). An altogether different subset of lesbians (again, approximately one-fourth) pursued other-sex sexual contact between the first and second interviews (Diamond 1998, 2000b).

Such experiences may explain why so many women in Study A changed identity labels over time. Contrary to the notion that most sexual minorities undergo a one-time discovery of their true identities, 50 percent of the respondents had changed their identity label more than once since first relinquishing their heterosexual identity (Diamond 2000b). Rust (1993) ably identified nonexclusive attractions as a key factor in such transitions. She argued that women with nonexclusive attractions may comfortably adopt a lesbian *or* bisexual identity, depending on such factors as the relative intensity of their attractions, perceived prospects for same-sex and other-sex relationships, and their social network. When one of these factors or its importance changes, identity may change as well. It is possible that by the time women in Study A reach late adulthood, a majority will have reconsidered or changed their sexual-minority identity in the process of navigating the multiple possibilities engendered by nonexclusive attractions.

What about heterosexual women? If most sexual-minority women retain a capacity for other-sex attractions, do most heterosexual women retain a capacity for same-sex attractions? A reliable answer to this question is elusive, given the stigma that prevents heterosexual women from readily acknowledging same-sex attractions, yet Laumann et al. (1994) found that 7.3 percent of heterosexually identified women admitted experiencing same-sex attractions or behavior. As they noted, sporadic same-sex attractions and fantasies among heterosexuals may never culminate in same-sex behavior or identity change. Yet in order to interpret their developmental significance, *both* same-sex and other-sex attractions, fantasies, and behaviors should be routinely assessed in studies of female sexual development.

Sexual Fluidity

One of the most significant challenges to traditional notions of sexual orientation is posed by heterosexual women who report experiencing sexual desire (sometimes culminating in sexual contact) for one and only one woman, typically an extremely close friend. Such stories are often greeted with a wink and a knowing smile, implying a tacit understanding that there is, of course, no such thing as *one* same-sex attraction. However, the experiences of several heterosexual women interviewed for Study A suggest that unusually intense emotional bonds sometimes spill over into authentic, albeit temporary, same-sex sexual desire.

We attribute this phenomenon to *sexual fluidity*, defined as a capacity for situation dependence in some women's erotic responses. The notion that female sexuality is more situation dependent than male sexuality has been noted by many researchers (Dixon 1985; Kitzinger and Wilkinson 1995; Pillard 1990; Shuster 1987; Weinberg et al. 1994) and has recently been the subject of an extensive review and theoretical treatment by Baumeister (2000). However, notions of fluidity have not been systematically integrated into models of female sexual identity development, perhaps because sexual fluidity is thought to pose a de facto challenge to any systematic developmental model of same-sex sexuality. However, this is not the case: Fluid sexual responsiveness is not the same as random sexual responsiveness. Across a wide variety of cultures and historical periods, the situations that trigger unexpected same-sex eroticism among ostensibly heterosexual women are remarkably similar, allowing for some speculation regarding the underlying mechanisms, limiting parameters, and even evolutionary bases of sexual fluidity (Baumeister 2000; Diamond 2000c).

One of the most common triggers for sexual fluidity is an intense, emotionally intimate relationship. For example, an unlabeled participant in Study A was interviewed shortly after becoming sexually involved with her best friend: "We've known each other since we were twelve and we've always been really affectionate, but last Tuesday it just sort of kept going. . . . Right now I only have these feelings for her, and I don't know if that'll change. I don't know if I'm a lesbian. I just know I want to be with her, forever." One might be tempted to characterize this woman as a budding lesbian who was not quite ready to embrace her true identity. Two years later, however, she reported that she and her best friend had gone back to being platonic friends. Neither one ever experienced attractions for other women nor could they recall prior "repressed" same-sex attractions (to their disappointment, actually). Both continue to identify as heterosexual. Similarly, a lesbian in Study A unexpectedly fell in love with a close *male* friend between the first and second interviews and felt this relationship was "an exception."

In our view, neither one of these women's experiences is fully interpretable without an appreciation for nonexclusivity and fluidity in women's attractions, and we maintain that these phenomena should be integrated into models of *all* women's sexual development. Yet by blurring distinctions among lesbian, bisexual, and heterosexual women, they make it difficult to discern exactly who we have been (and should be) sampling in research on sexuality. How should we distinguish a latent bisexual from a curious heterosexual? At what point in a woman's development can we reliably sort her into one of these categories?

In truth, the answer may be never. One of the unavoidable implications of nonexclusivity and sexual fluidity is that no heterosexual woman can be unequivocally assured that she will never desire same-sex contact, just as no lesbian woman can be unequivocally assured that she will never desire other-sex contact. Of course, not all women appear equally fluid, and the question of individual differences in fluidity deserves substantive attention. For now, we argue that it is both logistically impossible and theoretically misguided to study female same-sex sexuality by seeking out "true" sexual minorities and assessing the process by which they came out. The notion of "true" sexual minorities presumes categories where there may be continua, and "coming out" presumes a single outcome where there may be several.

We advocate replacing traditional assessments of identity labels with descriptive data on women's actual feelings and behaviors in different circumstances and replacing the traditional focus on coming out with a focus on *sexual questioning*. The advantage of focusing on sexual questioning is that it shifts attention to the process, rather than the outcome, of sexual development. Unlike coming out, sexual questioning can be initiated by any woman, can be repeated multiple times, and might never culminate with the adoption of a lesbian or bisexual identity. The advantage of focusing on specific experiences of same-sex attractions and behavior rather than identity labels is that it broadens the scope of our investigations to include women who do not subscribe to the set of sexual identity categories defined by (historically male) researchers. This allows us to begin modeling not "lesbian identity development" but *female sexual development*, a process that possibly involves varying degrees of same-sex and other-sex eroticism at different points in the life course.

Although we define the population of sexual minorities fairly broadly, we consider their defining characteristic to be same-sex attractions. Sexual attractions have generally been considered the most reliable indicator of an individual's sexual orientation (Cohen 1999; Marmor 1980). Yet our research suggests that accurate models of female sexual development may have to jettison traditional assumptions about when and how same-sex attractions emerge. Specifically, the notion that the timing of a woman's first same-sex attractions predicts the future course of her sexuality requires substantial revision. It is this topic to which we turn next.

First Same-Sex Attractions: What's Age Got to Do with It?

I should probably tell you that I'm not one of those people who knew they were gay from when they were very little. I didn't know at all until I was twenty! Listen, I'm probably not a very good example of a gay person, and I don't want to mess up your study or anything, so it's okay if you don't want to interview me after all.

— twenty-one-year-old bisexual

Perhaps the most common question posed to sexual minorities by friends, family members, and social scientists is this: "When were you first attracted to the same sex?" The most common answer, especially among women, is, "When I was young, although I didn't interpret it that way at the time." Most studies (including our own) find that individuals' earliest recollections of same-sex attractions take place around age ten (see McClintock and Herdt 1996, for a review); an important note is that this is also the age at which heterosexual children first recall experiencing sexual feelings (Knoth, Boyd, and Singer 1988) and has been linked to adrenal maturation (McClintock and Herdt 1996).

Yet rarely are these early feelings interpreted at the time as same-sex attractions, especially among women. The respondents in Study A reported that their first *conscious* same-sex attraction occurred at a mean age of fifteen, and they did not consider the relevance of these feelings for sexual identity until a mean age of sixteen. Once the full range of variability is taken into account, some women show disjunctures of ten to twenty years between their first recollected *experience* and their first recollected *awareness* of same-sex attractions. These gaps are typically attributed to the fact that women receive more ambiguous cues of sexual arousal from their bodies than do men and are not socialized to monitor such cues as rigorously as men are (Baldwin and Baldwin 1997). Nonetheless, the attractions are presumed to be "in there" all along, and sexual minorities often search their memories for such prescient childhood desires in the process of sexual questioning.

"Early Onset" and "Late Onset" Subtypes

What if they cannot find any? Is it possible that such individuals develop authentic same-sex attractions in adulthood, with no prior warning? This notion runs directly counter to the popular conceptualization of sexual orientation as an early-appearing trait. Perhaps for this reason women with late-appearing same-sex attractions are often characterized as less essentially or exclusively attracted to the same sex than those with early-appearing same-sex attractions and more likely to question their sexual identities for ideological rather than sexual reasons. This conceptual framework contrasts *born*, *primary*, or *exclusive* lesbians with *elective, political,* or *bisexual* lesbians (Burch 1993; Ettore 1980; Golden 1996; Ponse 1978). The underlying presumption is that a woman who recalls being sexually attracted to women from the age of ten is more essentially, consistently, and exclusively attracted to the same sex than a woman whose first attractions emerged in a Women's Studies class at age twenty.

Despite its intuitive appeal, our research finds no support for this view. Study A subdivided sexual-minority women into *primary* and *elective* subgroups to determine whether this distinction fell along lesbian/bisexual lines. The *primary* group contained women who reported a childhood feeling or event that presaged their eventual sexual orientation (prepubertal same-sex attractions, childhood gender atypicality, or "feelings of differentness"), experienced clear-cut same-sex attractions *before* questioning their sexuality, and reported stability in their attractions over time. The *elective* group contained any woman who did not meet these criteria. As it turned out, there were equal proportions of lesbian, bisexual, and unlabeled women in each group, and there was no link between group membership and a woman's degree of same-sex attractions (Diamond 1998). Since then, follow-up assessments have established that women in the *primary* group are just as likely to report changes in their sexual attractions or sexual identities over time as women in the *elective* group. One important implication of these findings, which we teased out with follow-up analyses, is that prior inconsistencies do not necessarily foreshadow later inconsistencies and prior stability does not necessarily foreshadow later stability. Women who reported at the first interview that their attractions had previously changed were not more likely to undergo *subsequent* changes in either their attractions or their sexual identity.

These findings cast doubt not only on the notion of primary/elective subtypes but also on the view that the timing of a woman's same-sex attractions gives us critical information about the nature of her sexual orientation.

Study B provides further evidence to this effect: Neither the age of first same-sex attractions nor the recollection of childhood experiences such as gender atypicality was associated with subsequent features of sexual identity development, including the timing of first same-sex sexual contact, the timing of first sexual-minority identification, the sequencing of first sex and first identification, the total length of time of the questioning process, or the selection of a lesbian versus bisexual versus unlabeled identity.

In our minds, these counterintuitive findings spotlight two critical questions. First, what did we think "age of first attractions" had to do with the rest of sexual identity development to begin with? Were we assuming that earlier attractions represented stronger attractions? More exclusive attractions? A more authentic same-sex orientation? A more self-aware individual? These are all plausible and testable hypotheses, but the simple truth is that few studies assessing age of first attractions articulate a theoretical rationale for doing so, relying instead on a collective, implicit intuition that it has *some* developmental relevance.

In our view, this vague notion of developmental relevance needs to be clarified and reconsidered. We think the timing of same-sex attractions *is* relevant but not for the reasons some have thought. Specifically, we believe that it taps general features of sexual development (such as whether the sexual system is "on line" and the availability of various eliciting stimuli) rather than predicting or explaining variation in developmental trajectories. This does not mean that the childhood feelings of heterosexual and sexual-minority women are necessarily identical, only that the comparative *timing* of their same-sex and other-sex attractions may be less informative than their comparative *quality*. Thus rather than simply assessing the age at which heterosexuals and sexual minorities first experienced same-sex and other-sex attractions, we should assess the experiential context of these attractions, their strength, their physiological and affective correlates, their frequency, and their capacity to motivate behavior.

Will the Real Same-Sex Attractions Please Stand Up?

This brings us to a second question: When respondents report "age of first attractions," what are they counting as an attraction? It is implicitly assumed that researchers, study participants, and readers have comparable conceptualizations of sexual attractions and that we all "know them when we feel them." Yet for many of the women in Study A, a significant component of their questioning process involved trying to determine just what qualified as a sexual attraction. As one sixteen-year-old noted, "When I look at a beautiful woman I'm not sure if I want her or if I want to *be* her." Another young woman was unsure whether she had ever experienced an authentic sexual attraction to *either* sex. Such reports challenge the notion that same-sex and other-sex attractions are unambiguous, easily recognizable experiences.

This becomes particularly clear when one attempts to interpret a sexual-minority woman's most intense same-sex friendships. Nearly half the young women in Study A (Diamond 2000a) reported having participated in a platonic same-sex friendship characterized by high levels of emotional passion, devotion, exclusivity, and physical affection. Such relationships typically occurred in early adolescence, often long before sexual questioning, and appeared remarkably similar to the unusually affectionate bonds that have been documented between young women in a variety of cultures and historical periods (Faderman 1981; Gay 1985; Sahli 1979; Smith-Rosenberg 1975). In most cases, the intense feelings that developed were not considered sexual (Diamond 2000a; Faderman 1981).

Should we consider such relationships early manifestations of same-sex attractions? After all, even if women did not experience their feelings as explicitly sexual, it seems plausible that sexual-minority women might unconsciously desire more intense and affectionate same-sex friendships than do heterosexual women and might find such relationships particularly rewarding even when they do not involve explicit sexual interest or activity. At the same time, Faderman (1981) convincingly argued that we are too eager to apply our contemporary cultural notions of same-sex sexuality to such passionate friendships — in many cases, they may be authentically nonsexual attachments.

In truth, the affectional component of sexuality has been drastically undertheorized in studies of both sexual minorities and heterosexuals, creating a notable stumbling block for efforts to understand the uniqueness of women's experiences. How common are passionate, platonic friendships among sexual-minority *and* heterosexual women? To what extent does a young woman's sexual orientation prefigure experiences of emotional bonding? In our view, research on the development of sexual orientation must begin to explore systematically processes of emotional bonding and attachment formation to understand better how these processes shape sexual desires and behaviors. Toward this end, we have begun to explore associations between the specific quality and context of sexual minorities' first same-sex attractions and their subsequent development.

Do Quality and Context Matter?

When asked to describe their first same-sex attraction, interviewees listed a wide range of divergent experiences. Examples included "wanted all the girls to take their clothes off," "fixation on the popular girls in school," "loved to look at pretty women," "moved my cot next to this one girl and wanted to be napping with her," "platonic crushes on girls — wanted to get to know them," "wanted to touch Wonder Woman's breasts," "terribly upset when best friend moved away, couldn't stop crying." The men in Study B, too, listed a wide range of experiences, but their descriptions were more consistently linked to the concrete experience of sexual arousal.

We coded interviewees' descriptions into three basic groups: The *sexual* group included individuals who described this experience as involving explicit sexual thoughts or sexual activity (for example, "wanted to touch Wonder Woman's breasts"). The *emotional* group included individuals who described their attractions as involving only emotional feelings (for example, "terribly upset when best friend moved away"). The *ambiguous* group included individuals who described this experience in terms that were neither explicitly sexual nor emotional (such as "fixation on the popular girls in school"). The following discussion focuses on the sexual and emotional categories, as these were the primary sites for gender differences. The ambiguous category is clearly a fascinating one, but we suspect it houses several meaningful subcategories, and we are holding off on interpreting "ambiguous" attractions until we can tease them apart. Inter-rater reliability for the existing coding scheme was assessed by calculating Cohen's kappa on a subset of cases (n = 86), and this value was .86.

Although nearly two-thirds of young men recalled an explicitly sexual context for their first same-sex attraction, just over one-third of the young women did so. In contrast, women were five times as likely as young men to recall an exclusively emotional basis for their first same-sex attraction (Savin-Williams and Diamond, in press). Quite frequently these were emotional "crushes" on peers, teachers, or coaches. The quality of a young man's or woman's same-sex attractions was not associated with the age at which those attractions were experienced or with the age at which he/she first had same-sex sexual contact. Among women, however, the quality of first attractions was associated with the *context* of first same-sex contact. Women who described their first same-sex attractions as exclusively emotional were more likely to have their first same-sex contact within an established same-sex romantic relationship (a pattern characteristic of nearly 70 percent of the women and only 5 percent of the men). Furthermore, women who had their first same-sex sexual contact within a relationship were more likely to self-identify as sexual minorities before or soon after this experience, and they reported shorter absolute latencies between first sex and first self-labeling. To the contrary, the majority of sexual-minority men had their first same-sex sexual contact several years before self-labeling.

We observed that some young women whose first sexual contact took place within a relationship appeared to undergo a compressed version of sexual identity development, moving quickly through self-labeling, first sex, first relationship, and first disclosure during the course of a single, transformative romance. One possibility is that such women are only comfortable acknowledging and acting on sexual feelings when these feelings have an intimate emotional context. Alternatively, they may be disproportionately sensitive to emotional cues, such that sexual attractions achieve greater strength, intensity, and motivational force when they occur in an intimate emotional context. At the present time we are simply unable to discriminate between such possibilities. We now offer a number of suggestions on how future research might address these questions.

Individual Differences and Person-Context Interactions

In our review of research on processes of sexual identity development, we are struck by what the extant data do *not* address: individual differences in women's personal characteristics and environmental/situational contexts. By personal characteristics, we mean factors such as personality, attachment style, sexual attitudes and expectations, self-efficacy, self-control, social skills, and even physical attractiveness. By environmental/situational context, we mean factors such as a woman's family relationships (including her degree of involvement in, and supervision by, the family), friendship and local community ties, ethnic background, social class, access to educational and work opportunities, access to information about sexuality, and opportunities for both same-sex and other-sex friendships and romantic relationships.

Such factors have been exhaustively investigated in studies of *heterosexual* feelings and behaviors during adolescence (see, for example, Feldman et al. 1995; Goodson, Evans, and Edmundson 1997; and Udry 1988), yet have been almost entirely ignored by researchers investigating same-sex sexuality, with the exception of ethnicity and social class. Even when ethnicity and social class are addressed, the unfortunate tendency has been to emphasize group differences at the expense of individual differences.

Our suggestion that researchers pay greater attention to person-context interactions is far from revolutionary: Such interactions have long been a chief concern in developmental psychology. Yet investigations of sexual identity development have been strangely myopic on this front. This may have been justifiable in the earliest phases of research on sexual orientation, but it is no longer tenable. To understand why women with similar feelings and experiences follow radically different sexual identity trajectories, we must begin to assess factors *other* than sexual orientation that impinge on their participation in (and subjective experience of) sexually and emotionally intimate relationships.

For example, research on heterosexual adolescents has identified a wide range of environmental factors that reliably influence the age at which an adolescent becomes sexually active, ranging from peers' sexual attitudes and behavior (Udry 1990) to mothers' coerciveness and love withdrawal (Miller et al. 1997). An adolescent's personal characteristics also play a role, such as independence, restlessness, achievement motivation, aggressiveness, tolerance for deviance, risk taking, and religiosity (R. Jessor et al. 1983; S. L. Jessor and R. Jessor 1974; Udry et al. 1995). Then there is basic sexual motivation. It is well known that some individuals are more arousable than others (Bancroft 1989), have more difficulty recognizing feelings of sexual arousal (Heiman 1975; Knoth et al. 1988), and are more likely to initiate sexual behavior than others (Cyranowski and Andersen 1998). These differences are obviously related to social factors (Udry et al. 1986), but they also show associations with individual differences in hormonal status and personality (Andersen and Cyranowski 1995) and are reliably associated with sexual behavior (Udry 1990).

How might our interpretation of a "late onset" lesbian change if we discovered that she has a generally low sex drive, is fairly inhibited, and has had the same boyfriend throughout high school? Such a woman might only become aware of same-sex attractions if and when she encounters a situation that makes it extraordinarily easy to do so, such as a Women's Studies class or having a lesbian roommate. She might only *act* on those attractions if the opportunity practically falls in her lap, and this is probably more likely to occur if she is socially and physically attractive, has plenty of female friends, is comfortable with intimacy, and enjoys some degree of privacy. Conversely, a woman with unusually high arousability, low self-restraint, a tendency to approach novel situations, and a history of early heterosexual behavior might begin experimenting with same-sex sexual contact at a fairly early age, even in environments that are less conducive to this behavior. It is important to recognize that the difference between these two women's trajectories might have nothing to do with the quality or exclusivity of their same-sex attractions.

As if this is not complicated enough, we must also consider the fact that sexual arousal and desire are not the only motivations for sexual behavior. Youths also engage in sexual behavior to discharge negative affect, to achieve status, to attain intimacy, to procure companionship, or to experience excitement (Cooper, Shapiro, and Powers 1998). The long-term implications of same-sex sexual behavior for sexual identity development likely depends on these initial motivations. For example, one interviewee in Study A indicated that although her "gut level" attractions for men were stronger than her attractions for women, she consistently achieved greater levels of emotional intimacy with women than men. Because this was more important to her, she eventually identified as lesbian. To characterize this woman as "in denial" of her bisexual orientation would be not only dismissive but wrong. Yet in order to make sense of her identity development, we must move beyond models of sexual orientation that assume clean, stable matches between attractions, behavior, and identity toward models that acknowledge the multiple factors shaping *all* women's experiences and interpretations of same-sex and other-sex desires and relationships.

Conclusion

The incredible variability in the developmental trajectories of sexual minorities, especially sexual-minority women, has received little systematic attention. Instead, researchers have focused disproportionately on discerning whether milestones such as "age of first same-sex attractions" predict the adult course of sexual orientation. The findings from our research suggest that this approach may be of limited usefulness. The quality, timing, and interpretation of same-sex *and* other-sex erotic responses (and their manifestation in sexual behavior) are multiply determined phenomena. This is anything but a new argument (Kinsey, Pomeroy, and Martin 1948), but it seems to have been forgotten in the rush to describe and explain the unique experiences of gay, lesbian, and bisexual men and women. As a result, researchers commonly treat sexual minorities as a homogeneous class of people whose differences from heterosexuals (owing to their sexual orientation) outweigh differences among themselves.

This reification of sexual identity categories has long been the subject of criticism, particularly by feminist theorists who argue that the very notion of essential, traitlike sexual predispositions is a historically specific social construction (Kitzinger 1987; Rust 1993). An early blow against sexual categorization was struck by Rich (1980), who argued in a now classic article that *all* women occupy a "lesbian continuum" ranging from passionate, platonic same-sex friendships to explicit same-sex sexual affairs. Rich's notion of a lesbian continuum has been most influential as an ideological vision, yet our research demonstrates that it is also an empirical reality with substantive implications for understanding the course of female sexual development.

For this reason, we argue that future research on sexual minorities should undertake a large-scale shift from classifying individuals into sexual identity categories to describing the full range of men's and women's same-sex and other-sex desires, affections, and behaviors. This requires more complex and labor-intensive research strategies, yet there is no alternative. Our failure to study systematically the development of individuals who challenge our traditional notions of same-sex and other-sex sexuality is, at a basic level, unscientific. Asking *all* adolescents about the quality and context of their same-sex and other-sex sexuality, and questioning our own assumptions about what experiences do and do not "count" as developmentally relevant, is a necessary first step toward building models that both describe *and* explain diversity in human sexuality.

References

Andersen, B. L., and J. M. Cyranowski, J. M. 1995. Women's sexuality: Behaviors, responses and individual differences. *Journal of Consulting and Clinical Psychology* 63:891–906.

Baldwin, J. D., and J. I. Baldwin. 1997. Gender differences in sexual interest. *Archives of Sexual Behavior* 26:181–210.

Bancroft, J. H. 1989. Sexual desire and the brain. *Sexual and Marital Therapy* 3:11–27.

Baumeister, R. F. 2000. Gender differences in erotic plasticity: The female sex drive as socially flexible and responsive. *Psychological Review* 126:347–74.

Brown, L. 1995. Lesbian identities: Concepts and issues. In A. R. D'Augelli and C. Patterson, eds., *Lesbian, Gay, and Bisexual Identities over the Lifespan*, pp. 3–23. New York: Oxford University Press.

Burch, B. 1993. *On Intimate Terms: The Psychology of Difference in Lesbian Relationships*. Chicago: University of Illinois Press.

Cassingham, B. J., S. M. and O'Neil. 1999. *And Then I Met This Woman*. Freeland, Wash.: Soaring Eagle.

Cohen, K. M. 1999. The biology of male sexual orientation: Relationship among homoeroticism, childhood sex-atypical behavior, handedness, and spatial ability. Unpublished manuscript. University of Detroit-Mercy, Detroit, Michigan.

Cooper, M. L., C. M. Shapiro, and A.M. Powers. 1998. Motivations for sex and risky sexual behavior among adolescents and young adults: A functional perspective. *Journal of Personality and Social Psychology* 75:1528–58.

Cyranowski, J. M., and B. L. Andersen. 1998. Schemas, sexuality, and romantic attachment. *Journal of Personality and Social Psychology* 74:1364–79.

Diamond, L. M. 1998. Development of sexual orientation among adolescent and young women. *Developmental Psychology* 34:1085–95.

Diamond, L. M. 2000a. Passionate friendships among adolescent sexual-minority women. *Journal of Research on Adolescence* 10:191–209.

Diamond, L. M. 2000b. Sexual identity, attractions, and behavior among young sexual-minority women over a two-year period. *Developmental Psychology* 36:241–50.

Diamond, L. M. 2000c. Variability in same-gender sexuality: A model emphasizing evolved processes underlying human mating. Paper presented at the annual meeting of the Society for Research on Adolescence, March, Chicago, Illinois.

Diamond, L. M., and E. M. Dubé. 2000. Friendship and attachment among heterosexual and sexual-minority youths: Does the gender of your friend matter? Manuscript under review.

Dixon, J. K. 1985. Sexuality and relationship changes in married females following the commencement of bisexual activity. *Journal of Homosexuality* 11(1/2):115–33.

Ettore, E. M. 1980. *Lesbians, Women, and Society.* London: Routledge.

Faderman, L. 1981. *Surpassing the Love of Men.* New York: Morrow.

Feldman, S. S., D. R. Rosenthal, N. L. Brown, and R. D. Canning. 1995. Predicting sexual experience in adolescent boys from peer rejection and acceptance during childhood. *Journal of Research on Adolescence* 5:387–411.

Gay, J. 1985. "Mummies and babies" and friends and lovers in Lesotho. *Journal of Homosexuality* 11(3/4):97–116.

Golden, C. 1996. What's in a name? Sexual self-identification among women. In R. C. Savin-Williams and K. M. Cohen, eds., *The Lives of Lesbians, Gays, and Bisexuals: Children to Adults*, pp. 229–49. Fort Worth: Harcourt Brace.

Goodson, P., A. Evans, and E. Edmundson. 1997. Female adolescents and onset of sexual intercourse: A theory-based review of research from 1984 to 1994. *Journal of Adolescent Health* 21:147–56.

Heiman, J. R. 1975. The physiology of erotica: Women's sexual arousal. *Psychology Today* 8:90–94.

Jessor, R., F. Costa, L. Jessor, and J. E. Donovan. 1983. Time of first intercourse: A prospective study. *Journal of Personality and Social Psychology* 44:608–26.

Jessor, S. L., and R. Jessor. 1974. Transition from virginity to nonvirginity among youth: A social-psychological study over time. *Developmental Psychology* 11:473–84.

Kinsey, A. C., W. B. Pomeroy, and C. E. Martin. 1948. *Sexual Behavior in the Human Male*. Philadelphia: W. B. Saunders.

Kitzinger, C. 1987. *The Social Construction of Lesbianism*. London: Sage.

Kitzinger, C., and S. Wilkinson. 1995. Transitions from heterosexuality to lesbianism: The discursive production of lesbian identities. *Developmental Psychology* 31:95–104.

Knoth, R., K. Boyd, and B. Singer. 1988. Empirical tests of sexual selection theory: Predictions of sex differences in onset, intensity, and time course of sexual arousal. *Journal of Sex Research* 24:73–89.

Laumann, E. O., J. H. Gagnon, R. T. Michael, and F. Michaels. 1994. *The Social Organization of Sexuality: Sexual Practices in the United States*. Chicago: University of Chicago Press.

Marmor, J. 1980. *Homosexual Behavior: A Modern Reappraisal*. New York: Basic Books.

McClintock, M. K., and G. Herdt. 1996. Rethinking puberty: The development of sexual attraction. *Current Directions in Psychological Science* 5:178–83.

Miller, B.C., M. C. Norton, T. Curtis, E. J. Hill, P. Schvaneveldt, and M. H. Young. 1997. The timing of sexual intercourse among adolescents — Family, peer and other antecedents. *Youth and Society* 29:54–83.

Pillard, R. C. 1990. The Kinsey Scale: Is it familial? In D. P. McWhirter, S. A. Sanders, and J. M. Reinisch, eds., *Homosexuality/Heterosexuality: Concepts of Sexual Orientation*, pp. 88–100. New York: Oxford University Press.

Ponse, B. 1978. *Identities in the Lesbian World: The Social Construction of Self*. Westport, Conn.: Greenwood.

Rich, A. 1980. Compulsory heterosexuality and lesbian existence. *Signs* 5:631–60.

Rust, P. 1992. The politics of sexual identity: Sexual attraction and behavior among lesbian and bisexual women. *Social Problems* 39:366–86.

Rust, P. 1993. Coming out in the age of social constructionism: Sexual identity formation among lesbians and bisexual women. *Gender and Society* 7:50–77.

Sahli, N. 1979. Smashing: Women's relationships before the fall. *Chrysalis* 8:17–27.

Savin-Williams, R. C. 1998. " . . . *And Then I Became Gay": Young Men's Stories*. New York: Routledge.

Savin-Williams, R. C. In preparation. " . . . *And Then I Kissed Her": Young Women's Stories*. New York: Routledge.

Savin-Williams, R. C., and L. M. Diamond. 2000. Sexual identity trajectories among sexual-minority youths: Gender comparisons. *Archives of Sexual Behavior* 29:419–40.

Shuster, R. 1987. Sexuality as a continuum: The bisexual identity. In Boston Lesbian Psychologies Collective, ed., *Lesbian Psychologies*, pp. 56–71. Urbana: University of Illinois Press.

Smith-Rosenberg, C. 1975. The female world of love and ritual: Relations between women in nineteenth-century America. *Signs* 1:1–29.

Udry, J. R. 1988. Biological predispositions and social control in adolescent sexual behavior. *American Sociological Review* 53:709–22.

Udry, J. R. 1990. Hormonal and social determinants of adolescent sexual initiation. In J. Bancroft and J. M. Reinisch, eds., *Adolescence and Puberty*, pp. 70–87. New York: Oxford University Press.

Udry, J. R., J. Kovenock, N. M. Morris, and B. J. Vandenberg. 1995. Childhood precursors of age at first intercourse for females. *Archives of Sexual Behavior* 24:329–37.

Udry, J. R., L. M. Talbert, and N. M. Morris 1986. Biosocial foundations for adolescent female sexuality. *Demography* 23:217–30.

Weinberg, M. S., C. J. Williams, and D. W. Pryor. 1994. *Dual Attraction: Understanding Bisexuality*. New York: Oxford University Press.

Part II

Psychological Dimensions of Sexual Prejudice, Discrimination, and Violence

As psychology began to view gay, lesbian, and bisexual people as members of a minority group rather than as mentally ill, a corresponding shift occurred from research on the causes of homosexuality toward research on the pathology of sexual prejudice. A major line of study has identified the nature and impact of negative social attitudes toward lesbians, gay men, and bisexuals and has documented the pervasive effects of heterosexist bias, prejudice, and discrimination. Herek (2000a) defined *sexual prejudice* as: "Negative attitudes toward an individual because of her or his sexual orientation. It is used to characterize heterosexuals' negative attitudes toward (a) homosexual behavior; (b) people with a homosexual or bisexual orientation; and (c) communities of gay, lesbian, and bisexual people" (p. 19).

An important concept for understanding sexual prejudice is the idea of a *master status*. Western societies have adopted sexual orientation as a characteristic of great importance. As a result, homosexuality and bisexuality have been defined as an overarching social master status that takes precedence over everything else about an individual, so that even gender, race, and age become subordinate to the person's sexual orientation. This master status devalues the individual and is used as a foil to enforce heterosexual norms. Individuals come to be defined solely by what they do, or what they would like to do, in the privacy of their own affectional and sexual lives. Thus, when they come out to others, they are perceived as "flaunting their private lives" — when, in fact, all they are doing is revealing the gender of the persons they love, or would like to love, and their sexual-minority status.

Sexual prejudice implies that heterosexuality is the only acceptable sexual orientation and that any nonheterosexual form of behavior, identity, relationship, or community is denied, denigrated, and stigmatized (Herek 1990). This attitude legitimizes both individual and institutional prejudice and discrimination. On the one hand, assuming that all people are or should be heterosexual excludes the needs, concerns, and life experiences of gay, lesbian, and bisexual people from social awareness and recognition. Such heterosexist bias perpetuates the invisibility of gay, lesbian, and bisexual existence. For example, a lesbian was dying in a hospital and her partner of twelve years had to pose as her sister in order to get in to see her. As a lesbian partner, she was not considered "immediate family" according to the hospital's visitation rules.

On the other hand, when the existence of gay, lesbian, and bisexual people is recognized, sexual prejudice leads to institutional and personal hostility. One result is tacit permission by the heterosexist society to commit violence against lesbians, gay men, and bisexuals, to express disgust in public about them and their behavior, and to avoid endorsement of their civil rights by calling them "special rights." Moreover, sexual minorities may lose their jobs; lose custody of their children; face eviction from their homes; be subjected to verbal harassment; and be alienated from, and rejected by, their families, friends, and coworkers.

Bisexual men and women often encounter negative attitudes from homosexuals as well as heterosexuals, a form of prejudice called *monosexism* (Eliason 1997; Istvan 1983; Ochs 1996). They may be seen as trying to avoid the stigma of being homosexual and they may be viewed as being less trustworthy than heterosexuals (Rust 1993). Examples of these negative attitudes include the belief that bisexuality does not exist, that bisexuals are promiscuous, and that bisexuals should identify as either heterosexual or gay/lesbian (Spalding and Peplau 1997).

The first article in this section by Herek explores the dynamics of sexual prejudice in contemporary society. As a leading researcher in this area, he often contributes important perspectives that focus the issues of lesbians, gay men, and bisexuals within the framework of broader social psychology — in this case, the study of prejudice.

Despite considerable progress over the past twenty-five years, substantial barriers remain for gay, lesbian, and bisexual people. There are continuing efforts to turn back political and social progress by conservative groups who portray lesbians, gay men, and bisexuals as threats to the family or to marriage. Although attempts were made to change military policy, discrimination still clearly exists in the current "Don't Ask, Don't Tell" policy. Although thirty-nine states no longer criminalize adult homosexual activity, eleven continue to do so. Although many religious institutions have welcomed gay members, most continue to stigmatize homosexuality and ban ceremonies of commitment or marriage. Although sexual minorities have made tremendous strides in private sector policies about workplace discrimination, only nine states provide legal protection against overt discrimination in employment, housing, or access to public accommodations; more than two hundred municipalities do so, however. Progress has clearly been made in family law, creating precedents for the rights of gay men and lesbians as parents. However, lesbians and gay men must battle to achieve the same rights as heterosexual couples in issues of child custody, adoption, and foster care.

For gay, lesbian, and bisexual people, sexual prejudice creates a conflict between the fear of discrimination and harassment if they disclose their sexual orientation and invisibility of their true selves if they do not. Many people opt for nondisclosure as a way to avoid stigma, discrimination, and violence, especially if they want to adopt or rear children, hold a high profile job, or enter public life. Because gay men, lesbians, and bisexuals are diverse and not easily identifiable, most can pass as heterosexual. This invisibility of sexual orientation obscures the true diversity in the lives of sexual-minority persons and contributes to widespread misconceptions about them. It also creates stress for the individual. A strong connection between gender role beliefs and antigay attitudes has been documented, reflecting a link between sexism and heterosexism. Distrust of gender role violation is often reflected in antigay attitudes among heterosexuals (Hyde and Jaffee 2000). In addition, heterosexuals with negative attitudes toward gay people are more likely to express traditional, restrictive attitudes about gender and family roles, and to report less approval of equality between the sexes (Herek 1988; Kite and Whitley 1996). Moreover, there are gender differences in the degree of hostility and prejudice that heterosexual people feel and express toward lesbians and gay men. It has been found that heterosexual men manifest more antigay attitudes on average than heterosexual women do and that heterosexual females' attitudes toward lesbians and gay men in general do not differ in intensity, whereas heterosexual males hold more negative attitudes toward gay men than toward lesbians (Herek 2000b; Kite 1994). Kite and Whitley's article in this section reviews differences in women's and men's attitudes toward homosexuality and examines the underlying sources for these gender differences in the attitudes of heterosexuals.

Clearly the interpersonal costs of sexual prejudice are high. It is harmful to heterosexuals as well as to lesbians and gay men because it keeps everyone "in their place" by raising fears that deviation from traditional gender roles will lead to one being seen as a "fag" or "lezzie." Attempts to avoid the stigma of being labeled gay may inhibit the ability of heterosexual men and women to form close, intimate relationships with members of their own gender or to develop skills that are not typical for their gender.

Research has demonstrated that when we look more closely at the content of antigay or antilesbian stereotypes, we discover that they are tied to gender stereotypes. Specifically gay men are presumed to have characteristics that are culturally defined as nonmasculine, and lesbians are believed to manifest nonfeminine characteristics (Kite 1994; Kite and Deaux 1987). In addition, gay men and lesbians who violate stereotypic expectations of gender roles by appearing effeminate or butch are more disliked than those who do not (Laner and Laner 1979; Storms 1978). In reality, sexual orientation is not inherently related to gender role conformity or nonconformity (Peplau and Garnets 2000; Peplau, Spalding, Conley and Veniegas 1999).

Moreover, fear of being labeled gay is a powerful socialization influence in our society, which has negative consequences for both heterosexual and homosexual individuals. Women and men who manifest characteristics inconsistent with those culturally prescribed for their gender, regardless of their sexual orientation, are likely to be denigrated as gay (Deaux and Lewis 1984; Storms et al. 1981). For example, a young woman may be labeled as lesbian if she exhibits autonomous or self-assertive behavior, fights for her rights as a woman, enjoys the company of other women, works at a nontraditional job, or objects to sexual advances by males. Similarly an adolescent male who avoids contact sports, excels in music or drama, does not brag about sexual conquests, and defends the rights of all minorities, including gays, is likely to be perceived as gay. Thus traditional stereotyped gender roles are enforced to a large extent through the stigma of homosexuality. As a result, heterosexuals often restrict their gender role behavior for fear of being stigmatized. This influence appears to be especially strong among men (Herek 1991; Pleck 1981).

Today *gay* and *faggot* are the most prevalent terms of derision in schools and represent one of the most virulent forms of sexual prejudice among adolescents and children. Tolerance of it by peers, teachers, and school staff is unacceptable. It is linked with other forms of bullying and contributes to a general climate of intimidation and intolerance of differences, as well as perpetuating rage and violence in schools (Safe Schools Coalition of Washington 1999; www.safeschools-wa.org).

Sexual prejudice contributes to antigay behavior, including antilesbian and antigay violence. Reports of violence based on sexual orientation have increased dramatically in recent years (Cogan 1996). Many young gay males, for example, are abused by their families for being feminine or because their sexual orientation is revealed (Harry 1990). Some may even be driven to suicide. The article by Garnets, Herek, and Levy summarizes the mental health consequences of hate crimes on the victim and suggests treatment concerns for the survivor, significant others, and the broader gay and lesbian community.

The article by Savin-Williams is a personal reflection on the impact Matthew Shepard's murder had and shows how this hate crime is inextricably linked to society's hostile environment toward sexual minorities.

Contemporary Issue: Sexual Prejudice, Verbal Abuse, Physical Harassment, and Violence Based on Sexual Orientation

A substantial number of lesbian, gay, and bisexual people experience victimization in the form of verbal abuse, physical harassment, and violence based on sexual orientation. Harassment and violence against lesbians, gay men, and bisexuals is an extension of sexual prejudice; that is, lesbians, bisexuals, and gay men are targeted for attack specifically because of their sexual orientation. Pervasive sexual prejudice promotes antigay violence and an environment in which it is sanctioned and accepted. A cultural climate of denigration allows widespread violence against sexual minorities to go largely unpunished, conveying the message that gay, lesbian, and bisexual people do not deserve full legal protection and justice.

Violence and harassment are endemic in the lives of youth, starting in elementary school. Research suggests that young lesbians, bisexuals, and gay males are often the target of assaults in their schools and homes, and in community settings (Bradford, Ryan, and Rothblum 1994; Dean, Wu, and Martin 1992; Hunter 1992; Pilkinston and D'Augelli 1995; Rivers and D'Augelli 2001).

Several studies have found that such victimization has correlated with psychological distress and has had a negative impact on mental health (Herek, Gillis, and Cogan 1999; Hershberger and D'Augelli 1995; Otis and Skinner 1996). Compared to other recent crime victims, hate-crime survivors manifested significantly more symptoms of anxiety, depression, anger, and posttraumatic stress. These survivors also displayed more crime-related fears and beliefs, lower sense of mastery, and attributions of their personal setback to sexual prejudice than did nonbias-crime victims (Herek, Gillis, and Cogan 1999).

The principal risk associated with victimization based on sexual orientation is that the survivor links his or her homosexuality with the newly heightened sense of vulnerability that normally follows victimization. The most profound psychological effects of hate crimes are heightened feelings of personal danger and vulnerability, perceptions of the world as malevolent, and a linkage of these perceptions to one's personal identity based on sexual orientation. This linkage can be harmful because sexual orientation is such an important part of self-identity.

The gay, lesbian, and bisexual community has taken steps to reduce and prevent antigay bias crimes. They have provided services to assist survivors, promoted and improved an official response to the problem, and mobilized the community to take an active stance against it (Wertheimer 1990). Some approaches have used community organizing to mobilize sexual minorities in order to confront these antigay bias crimes as a community problem. To get at the root of the problem, namely, sexual prejudice, primary prevention efforts have been aimed at redefining social norms to create a safe climate for lesbians, gay men, and bisexuals to be open about their identities without fear or violence (e.g., Cogan 1996).

References

Bradford, J., C. Ryan, and E. D. Rothblum. National Lesbian Health Care Survey: Implications for mental health care. *Journal of Consulting and Clinical Psychology* 62:228–242.

Cogan, J. 1996. The prevention of anti-lesbian/gay hate crimes through social change and empowerment. In E. D. Rothblum and L. A. Bond, eds., *Preventing Heterosexism and Homophobia*, pp. 219–38. Thousand Oaks, Calif.: Sage.

Deaux, K. and L. L. Lewis. 1984. Structure of gender stereotypes: Interrelationships among components and gender label. *Journal of Personality and Social Psychology* 46:991–1004.

Dean, L., S. Wu, and J. L. Martin. 1992. Trends in violence and discrimination against gay men: 1984 to 1990. In G. M. Herek and K. Berrill, eds., *Hate Crimes*, pp. 19–45. Thousand Oaks, Calif.: Sage.

Deaux, K. and L. L. Lewis. 1984. Structure of gender stereotypes: Interrelationships among components and gender label. *Journal of Personality and Social Psychology* 46:991–1004.

Eliason, M. J. 1997. The prevalence and nature of biphobia in heterosexual undergraduate students. *Archives of Sexual Behavior* 26:317–26.

Harry, J. 1990. Conceptualizing anti-gay violence. *Journal of Interpersonal Violence* 5:350–58.

Herek, G. M. 1988. Heterosexuals' attitudes toward lesbians and gay men: Correlates and gender differences. *Journal of Sex Research* 25:451–77.

Herek, G. M. 1990. The context of anti-gay violence: Notes on cultural and psychological heterosexism. *Journal of Interpersonal Violence* 5:316–33.

Herek, G. M. 1991. Stigma, prejudice, and violence against lesbians and gay men. In J. D. Gonsiorek and J. D. Weinrich, eds., *Homosexuality: Research Implications for Public Policy*, pp. 60–80. Newbury Park, Calif.: Sage

Herek, G. M. 2000a. The psychology of sexual prejudice. *Current Directions in Psychological Science* 9:19–22.

Herek, G. M. 2000b. Sexual prejudice and gender: Do heterosexuals' attitudes toward lesbians and gay men differ? *Journal of Social Issues* 56(2):251–66.

Herek, G. M., J. R. Gillis, and J. C. Cogan. 1999. Psychological sequelae of hate-crime victimization among lesbian, gay, and bisexual adults. *Journal of Consulting and Clinical Psychology* 67:945–51.

Hershberger, S. L., and A. R. D'Augelli. 1995. The impact of victimization on the mental health and suicidality of lesbian, gay, and bisexual youth. *Developmental Psychology* 31:65–74.

Hunter, J. 1992. Violence against lesbian and gay male youth. In G. M. Herek and K. Berrill, eds., *Hate Crimes*, pp. 76–82. Thousand Oaks, Calif.: Sage.

Hyde, J. S., and S. R. Jaffee. 2000. Becoming a heterosexual adult: The experiences of young women. *Journal of Social Issues* 56(2):283–96.

Istvan, J. 1983. Effects of sexual orientation on interpersonal judgment. *Journal of Sex Research* 19:173–91.

Kite, M. E. 1994. When perceptions meet reality: Individual differences in reactions to gay men and lesbians. In B. Greene and G. Herek, eds., *Lesbian and Gay Psychology: Theory, Research, and Clinical Applications*, pp. 25–53. Thousand Oaks, Calif.: Sage.

Kite, M. E., and K. Deaux. 1987. Gender belief systems: Homosexuality and the implicit inversion theory. *Psychology of Women Quarterly* 11:83–96.

Kite, M. E., and B. E. Whitley. 1996. Sex differences in attitudes toward homosexual persons, behaviors, and civil rights: A Meta-analysis. *Personality and Social Psychology Bulletin* 22:336–56.

Laner, M. R., and R. H. Laner. 1979. Personal style or sexual preference: Why gay men are disliked. *International Review of Modern Sociology* 9:215–28.

Ochs, R. 1996. Biphobia: It goes more than two ways. In B. Firestein, ed., *Bisexuality: The Psychology and Politics of an Invisible Minority*, pp. 217–39. Thousand Oaks, Calif.: Sage.

Otis, M. D., and W. F. Skinner. 1996. The prevalence of victimization and its effect on mental well-being among lesbian and gay people. *Journal of Homosexuality* 30(3):93–121.

Peplau, L. A., and L. D. Garnets. 2000. A new paradigm for understanding women's sexuality and sexual orientation. *Journal of Social Issues* 56(2):329–50.

Peplau, L. A., L. R. Spalding, T. D. Conley, and R. C. Veniegas. 1999. The development of sexual orientation in women. *Annual Review of Sex Research* 10:70–99.

Pilkington, N. W., and A. R. D'Augelli. 1995. Victimization of lesbian, gay, and bisexual youth in community settings. *Journal of Community Psychology* 23:33–56.

Pleck, J. H. 1981. *The Myth of Masculinity*. Cambridge, Mass.: MIT Press.

Rivers, I., and A. R. D'Augelli. 2001. The victimization of gay, lesbian, and bisexual youths. In A. R. D'Augelli and C. J. Patterson, eds., *Lesbian, Gay, and Bisexual Identities and Youth*, pp. 199–223. New York: Oxford University Press.

Rust, P. C. 1993. Neutralizing the political threat of the marginal woman: Lesbians' beliefs about bisexual women. *Journal of Sex Research* 30:214–28.

Spalding L. R., and L. A. Peplau. 1997. The unfaithful lover: Heterosexuals' perceptions of bisexuals and their relationships. *Psychology of Women Quarterly* 21:611–25.

Storms, M. D. 1978. Attitudes toward homosexuality and femininity in men. *Journal of Homosexuality* 3(3):257–63.

Storms, M. D., M. L. Stifers, S. M. Lambers, and C. A. Hill. 1981. Sexual scripts for women. *Sex Roles* 3:257–63.

Wertheimer, D. M. 1990. Treatment and service interventions for lesbian and gay male crime victims. *Journal of Interpersonal Violence* 5:384–400.

5   The Psychology of Sexual Prejudice

Gregory M. Herek

In a six-month period beginning late in 1998 Americans were shocked by the brutal murders of Matthew Shepard and Billy Jack Gaither. Shepard, a twenty-one-year-old Wyoming college student, and Gaither, a thirty-nine-year-old factory worker in Alabama, had little in common except that each was targeted for attack because he was gay. Unfortunately their slayings were not isolated events. Lesbians, gay men, and bisexual people — as well as heterosexuals perceived to be gay — routinely experience violence, discrimination, and personal rejection. In all, 1,102 hate crimes based on sexual orientation were tallied by law-enforcement authorities in 1997. Because a substantial proportion of such crimes are never reported to police, that figure represents only the tip of the iceberg (Herek, Gillis, and Cogan 1999).

People with homosexual or bisexual orientations have long been stigmatized. With the rise of the gay political movement in the late 1960s, however, homosexuality's condemnation as immoral, criminal, and sick came under increasing scrutiny. When the American Psychiatric Association dropped homosexuality as a psychiatric diagnosis in 1973, the question of why some heterosexuals harbor strongly negative attitudes toward homosexuals began to receive serious scientific consideration.

Society's rethinking of sexual orientation was crystallized in the term *homophobia*, which heterosexual psychologist George Weinberg coined in the late 1960s. The word first appeared in print in 1969 and was subsequently discussed at length in a popular book (Weinberg 1972).[1] Around the same time, *heterosexism* began to be used as a term analogous to sexism and racism, describing an ideological system that casts homosexuality as inferior to heterosexuality.[2] Although usage of the two words has not been uniform, homophobia has typically been employed to describe individual antigay attitudes and behaviors, whereas heterosexism has referred to societal-level ideologies and patterns of institutionalized oppression of nonheterosexual people.

By drawing popular and scientific attention to antigay hostility, the creation of these terms marked a watershed. Of the two, *homophobia* is probably more widely used and more often criticized. Its critics note that homophobia implicitly suggests that antigay attitudes are best understood as an irrational fear and that they represent a form of individual psychopathology rather than a socially reinforced prejudice. As antigay attitudes have become increasingly central to conservative political and religious ideologies since the 1980s, these limitations have become more problematic. Yet *heterosexism*, with its historical macro-level focus on cultural ideologies rather than individual attitudes, is not a satisfactory replacement for *homophobia*.

Thus scientific analysis of the psychology of antigay attitudes will be facilitated by a new term. I offer *sexual prejudice* for this purpose. Broadly conceived, sexual prejudice refers to all negative attitudes based on sexual orientation, whether the target is homosexual, bisexual, or heterosexual. Given the current social organization of sexuality, however, such prejudice is almost always directed at people who engage in homosexual behavior or label themselves gay, lesbian, or bisexual. Thus, as used here, the term *sexual prejudice* encompasses heterosexuals' negative attitudes toward (a) homosexual behavior, (b) people with a homosexual or bisexual orientation, and (c) communities of gay, lesbian, and bisexual people. Like other types of prejudice, sexual prejudice has three principal features: It is an attitude (i.e., an evaluation or judgment); it is directed at a social group and its members; and it is negative, involving hostility or dislike.

Conceptualizing heterosexuals' negative attitudes toward homosexuality and bisexuality as sexual prejudice — rather than homophobia — has several advantages. First, sexual prejudice is a descriptive term. Unlike homophobia, it conveys no a priori assumptions about the origins, dynamics, and underlying motivations of antigay attitudes. Second, the term explicitly links the study of antigay hostility with the rich tradition of social psychological research on prejudice. Third, using the construct of sexual prejudice does not require value judgments that antigay attitudes are inherently irrational or evil.

Prevalence

Most adults in the United States hold negative attitudes toward homosexual behavior, regarding it as wrong and unnatural (Herek and Capitanio 1996; Yang 1997). Nevertheless poll data show that attitudes have become more favorable over the past three decades. For example, whereas at least two-thirds of respondents to the General Social Survey (GSS) considered homosexual behavior "always wrong" in the 1970s and 1980s, that figure declined noticeably in the 1990s. By 1996, only 56 percent of GSS respondents regarded it as always wrong (Yang 1997).

Much of the public also holds negative attitudes toward individuals who are homosexual. In a 1992 national survey more than half the heterosexual respondents expressed disgust for lesbians and gay men (Herek 1994). Respondents to the ongoing American National Election Studies have typically rated lesbians and gay men among the lowest of all groups on a 101-point feeling thermometer, although mean scores increased by approximately 10 points between 1984 and 1996 (Yang 1997).

Despite these examples of negative attitudes, most Americans believe that a gay person should not be denied employment or basic civil liberties. The public is reluctant to treat homosexuality on a par with heterosexuality, however. Most Americans favor giving same-sex domestic partners limited recognition (e.g., employee health benefits and hospital visitation rights), but most oppose legalizing same-sex marriages. And whereas the public generally supports the employment rights of gay teachers, they do not believe that lesbians and gay men should be able to adopt children (Yang 1997).

Unfortunately most studies have not distinguished between lesbians and gay men as targets of prejudice. The available data suggest that attitudes toward gay men are more negative than attitudes toward lesbians, with the difference more pronounced among heterosexual men than women (Herek and Capitanio 1996; Kite and Whitley 1998). This pattern may reflect sex differences in the underlying cognitive organization of sexual prejudice (Herek and Capitanio 1999).

Correlates

Laboratory and questionnaire studies have utilized a variety of measures to assess heterosexuals' attitudes toward gay men and lesbians (e.g., Davis,

Yarber, Bauserman, Schreer, and Davis 1998). Consistent with findings from public opinion surveys, they have revealed higher levels of sexual prejudice among individuals who are older, less educated, living in the U.S. South or Midwest, and living in rural areas (Herek 1994). In survey and laboratory studies alike, heterosexual men generally display higher levels of sexual prejudice than heterosexual women (Herek and Capitanio 1999; Kite and Whitley 1998; Yang 1998).

Sexual prejudice is also reliably correlated with several psychological and social variables. Heterosexuals with high levels of sexual prejudice tend to score higher than others on authoritarianism (Altemeyer 1996; Haddock and Zanna 1998). In addition, heterosexuals who identify with a fundamentalist religious denomination and frequently attend religious services typically manifest higher levels of sexual prejudice than do the nonreligious and members of liberal denominations (Herek and Capitanio 1996). Since the 1980s political ideology and party affiliation have also come to be strongly associated with sexual prejudice, with conservatives and Republicans expressing the highest levels (Yang 1998).

Sexual prejudice is strongly related to whether a heterosexual knows gay people personally. The lowest levels of prejudice are manifested by heterosexuals who have gay friends or family members, describe their relationships with those individuals as close, and report having directly discussed the gay or lesbian person's sexual orientation with him or her. Interpersonal contact and prejudice are reciprocally related. Not only are heterosexuals with gay friends or relatives less prejudiced, but heterosexuals from demographic groups with low levels of sexual prejudice (e.g., women, highly educated people) are more likely to experience personal contact with an openly gay person (Herek and Capitanio 1996).

Relatively little empirical research has examined racial and ethnic differences. Sexual prejudice may be somewhat greater among heterosexual African-Americans than among heterosexual whites, mainly because of white women's relatively favorable attitudes toward lesbians and gay men. The correlates of sexual prejudice may vary by race and ethnicity. Interpersonal contact may be more important in shaping the attitudes of whites than of blacks, for example, whereas the belief that homosexuality is a choice may be a more influential predictor of heterosexual blacks' sexual prejudice (Herek and Capitanio 1995).

Underlying Motivations

Like other forms of prejudice, sexual prejudice has multiple motivations. For some heterosexuals, it results from unpleasant interactions with gay individuals, which are then generalized to attitudes toward the entire group. This explanation probably applies mainly to cases in which interpersonal contact has been superficial and minimal. For other heterosexuals, sexual prejudice is rooted in fears associated with homosexuality, perhaps reflecting discomfort with their own sexual impulses or gender conformity. For still others, sexual prejudice reflects influences of in-group norms that are hostile to homosexual and bisexual people. Still another source of prejudice is the perception that gay people and the gay community represent values directly in conflict with one's personal value system.

These different motivations can be understood as deriving from the psychological functions that sexual prejudice serves, which vary from one individual to another. One heterosexual's sexual prejudice, for example, may reduce the anxiety associated with his fears about sexuality and gender, whereas another heterosexual's prejudice might reinforce a positive sense of herself as a member of the social group "good Christians." Such attitudes are functional only when they are consistent with cultural and situational cues, for example, when homosexuality is defined as inconsistent with a masculine identity or when a religious congregation defines hostility to homosexuality as a criterion for being a good Christian (Herek 1987).

Prejudice and Behavior

Hate crimes and discrimination are inevitably influenced by complex situational factors (Franklin 1998). Nevertheless sexual prejudice contributes to antigay behaviors. In experimental studies sexual prejudice correlates with antigay behaviors, although other factors often moderate this relationship (Haddock and Zanna 1998; Kite and Whitley 1998). Voting patterns on gay-related ballot measures have been generally consistent with the demographic correlates of sexual prejudice described earlier (Strand 1998). Recognizing the complex relationship between sexual prejudice and antigay behavior further underscores the value of anchoring this phenomenon in the scientific literature on prejudice, which offers multiple models for understanding the links between attitudes and behavior.

Conclusion and Directions for Research

Although more than a quarter of a century has passed since Weinberg first presented a scholarly discussion of the psychology of homophobia, empirical research on sexual prejudice is still in its early stages. To date, the prevalence and correlates of sexual prejudice have received the most attention. Relatively little research has been devoted to understanding the dynamic cognitive processes associated with antigay attitudes and stereotypes, that is, how heterosexuals think about lesbians and gay men. Nor has extensive systematic inquiry been devoted to the underlying motivations for sexual prejudice or the effectiveness of different interventions for reducing sexual prejudice. These represent promising areas for future research.

In addition, there is a need for descriptive studies of sexual prejudice within different subsets of the population, including ethnic and age groups. Given the tendency for antigay behaviors to be perpetrated by adolescents and young adults, studies of the development of sexual prejudice early in the life span are especially needed. Finally, commonalities and convergences in the psychology of sexual prejudice toward different targets (e.g., men or women, homosexuals or bisexuals) should be studied. Much of the empirical research in this area to date has been limited because it has focused (implicitly or explicitly) on heterosexuals' attitudes toward gay men.

Stigma based on sexual orientation has been commonplace throughout the twentieth century. Conceptualizing such hostility as sexual prejudice represents a step toward achieving a scientific understanding of its origins, dynamics, and functions. Perhaps most important, such an understanding may help to prevent the behavioral expression of sexual prejudice through violence, discrimination, and harassment.

Notes

1. Although Weinberg coined the term *homophobia*, it was first used in print in 1969 by Jack Nichols and Lige Clarke in their May 23 column in *Screw* magazine (J. Nichols, personal communication, November 5 1998; G. Weinberg, personal communication, October 30 1998).

2. The term *heterosexism* was used as early as July 10 1972, in two separate letters printed in the *Great Speckled Bird,* an alternative newspaper published in Atlanta, Georgia. I thank Joanne Despres of the Merriam Webster Company for her kind assistance with researching the origins of this word.

Acknowledgments

Preparation of this article was supported in part by an Independent Scientist Award from the National Institute of Mental Health (K02 MH01455).

Recommended Reading

Herek, G. M., ed. 1998. *Stigma and Sexual Orientation: Understanding Prejudice against Lesbians, Gay Men, and Bisexuals.* Newbury Park, Calif.: Sage.

Herek, G. M., and K. Berrill, eds. 1992. *Hate Crimes: Confronting Violence against Lesbians and Gay Men.* Thousand Oaks, Calif.: Sage.

Herek, G. M., D.C. Kimmel, H. Amaro, and G. B. Melton. 1991. Avoiding heterosexist bias in psychological research. *American Psychologist* 46:957–63.

Herman, D. 1997. *The Antigay Agenda: Orthodox Vision and the Christian Right.* Chicago: University of Chicago Press.

Rothblum, E., and L. Bond, eds. 1996. *Preventing Heterosexism and Homophobia.* Thousand Oaks, Calif.: Sage.

References

Altemeyer, B. 1996. *The Authoritarian Specter.* Cambridge, Mass.: Harvard University Press.

Davis, C. M., W. L. Yarber, R. Bauserman, G. Schreer, and S. L. Davis, eds. 1998. *Handbook of Sexuality-Related Measures.* Thousand Oaks, Calif.: Sage.

Franklin, K. 1998. Unassuming motivations: Contextualizing the narratives of antigay assailants. In G. M. Herek, ed., *Stigma and Sexual Orientation: Understanding Prejudice Against Lesbians, Gay Men, and Bisexuals*, pp. 1–23. Newbury Park, Calif.: Sage.

Haddock, G., and M. Zanna. 1998. Authoritarianism, values, and the favorability and structure of antigay attitudes. In G. M. Herek, ed. *Stigma and Sexual Orientation: Understanding Prejudice Against Lesbians, Gay Men, and Bisexuals*, pp. 82–107. Newbury Park, Calif.: Sage.

Herek, G. M. 1987. Can functions be measured? A new perspective on the functional approach to attitudes. *Social Psychology Quarterly* 50:285–303.

Herek, G. M. 1994. Assessing attitudes toward lesbians and gay men: A review of empirical research with the ATLG scale. In B. Greene and G. M. Herek, eds., *Lesbian and Gay Psychology*, pp. 206–28. Thousand Oaks, Calif.: Sage.

Herek, G. M., and J. Capitanio. 1995. Black heterosexuals' attitudes toward lesbians and gay men in the United States. *Journal of Sex Research* 32:95–105.

Herek, G. M., and J. Capitanio. 1996. "Some of my best friends": Intergroup contact, concealable stigma, and heterosexuals' attitudes toward gay men and lesbians. *Personality and Social Psychology Bulletin* 22:412–24.

Herek, G. M., and J. P. Capitanio. 1999. Sex differences in how heterosexuals think about lesbians and gay men: Evidence from survey context effects. *Journal of Sex Research* 36:348–60.

Herek, G. M., J. Gillis, and J. Cogan. 1999. Psychological sequelae of hate crime victimization among lesbian, gay, and bisexual adults. *Journal of Consulting and Clinical Psychology* 67:945–51.

Kite, M. E., and B. E. Whitley Jr. 1998. Do heterosexual women and men differ in their attitudes toward homosexuality? A conceptual and methodological analysis. In G. M. Herek, ed., *Stigma and Sexual Orientation: Understanding Prejudice Against Lesbians, Gay Men, and Bisexuals*, pp. 39–61. Newbury Park, Calif.: Sage.

Strand, D. 1998. Civil liberties, civil rights, and stigma: Voter attitudes and behavior in the politics of homosexuality. In G. M. Herek, ed., *Stigma and Sexual Orientation: Understanding Prejudice Against Lesbians, Gay Men, and Bisexuals*, pp. 108–37. Newbury Park, Calif.: Sage.

Weinberg, G. 1972. *Society and the Healthy Homosexual*. New York: St. Martin's.

Yang, A. 1997. Trends: Attitudes toward homosexuality. *Public Opinion Quarterly* 61:477–507.

Yang, A. 1998. *From Wrongs to Rights: Public Opinion on Gay and Lesbian Americans Moves Toward Equality*. Washington, D.C.: National Gay and Lesbian Task Force Policy Institute.

6 Do Heterosexual Women and Men Differ in Their Attitudes Toward Homosexuality? A Conceptual and Methodological Analysis

Mary E. Kite and Bernard E. Whitley Jr.

Gender Role Analysis of Sex Differences in Attitudes Toward Homosexuality

A gender role analysis of sex differences in attitudes toward homosexuality is based on the assumption that heterosexuals' evaluations of gay men and lesbians are rooted in a broader belief system about women, men, and their appropriate roles (Deaux and Kite 1987; Kite 1994). This belief system has two consequences relevant to attitudes toward homosexuality. First, gender-associated beliefs appear to be inextricably linked; that is, people expect others' gender-associated characteristics to form a coherent package. They believe, for example, that people who possess stereotypically masculine traits also adopt stereotypically masculine roles and possess stereotypically masculine physical characteristics and, similarly, that those who possess feminine characteristics on one dimension are likely to be feminine on other dimensions (e.g., Deaux and Lewis 1984; Rajecki, De Graaf-Kaser, and Rasmussen 1992). Evidence that this belief system is tied to heterosexuals' perceptions of gay people comes from demonstrations that men who are described as having feminine characteristics are judged likely to be homosexual, whereas women described as having masculine characteristics are judged likely to be lesbian (e.g., Deaux and Lewis 1984; Martin 1990; McCreary 1994). People likewise infer that gay men have the gender-associated characteristics of heterosexual women and that lesbians have the gender-associated characteristics of heterosexual men (e.g., Kite and Deaux 1987; Taylor 1983). It is noteworthy, however, that the association between lesbianism and attributed masculinity appears to be much weaker than the association between gay male homosexuality and attributed femininity (e.g., Deaux and Lewis 1984; Kite and Deaux 1987; Martin 1990; McCreary 1994).

The second consequence of the gender belief system as relevant to antigay prejudice stems from people's evaluations of those who contradict traditional gender roles. In general, people who engage in role behaviors associated with the other sex (e.g., Costrich et al. 1975; Jackson and Cash 1985) or who possess characteristics associated with the other sex (e.g., Laner and Laner 1979, 1980) are not viewed positively. This may be particularly true for gay people, who, as discussed above, are stereotypically perceived as having cross-sex traits, roles, and physical characteristics and who are apparently disliked as a result (e.g., Laner and Laner 1979, 1980), particularly by those with traditional gender role attitudes (e.g., Krulewitz and Nash 1980). Men, for example, report that the worst possible insult that can be hurled at a man is "homosexual"; women list this label as the second worst insult for a man (Preston and Stanley 1987).

These two aspects of the gender belief system may work to produce men's greater intolerance of homosexuality compared to women's. First, even though people expect consistency in others' gender-associated characteristics, these expectations appear to be more firmly held for men than for women. Research suggests that male gender roles are particularly nonpliant compared to female roles (see Stockard and Johnson 1979). For example, gender-associated traits and gender-associated physical characteristics are more narrowly defined for men than for women (Hort, Fagot, and Leinbach 1990). Second, violation of the traditional male gender role is seen as more egregious than violation of the traditional female gender role (see Herek 1986; Kite and Whitley 1996). People react more negatively to boys who possess female-typed traits than to girls who possess male-typed traits (Feinman 1981).

If male gender roles are so clearly delineated, it follows that tolerance for those who are perceived as violating those roles (e.g., gay men) would be actively discouraged. This is particularly true for heterosexual men, for whom gender role conformity is acutely defined by American society (Bem 1993). Men, more than women, are pushed to suppress any aspect of the self that might be associated with femininity (Herek 1986). As a result, heterosexual men are especially likely to be pressured toward displaying antigay prejudice. That society responds differently to men's and women's gender role nonconformity can be explained by the generally higher status associated with the American male gender role compared to the American female gender role (Bem 1993; Hogg and Turner 1987; Lewin and Tragos 1987; but see McCreary 1994, for another viewpoint). Men, then, may simply have more to lose by overstepping their gender role boundaries and engaging in or endorsing homosexual behavior. In contrast, the cultural gender script allows greater flexibility for the female gender role; hence women are allowed to hold more tolerant attitudes toward gender role violators. Similarly it follows that heterosexuals of both sexes should be less likely to perceive lesbianism as a clear gender role violation; if women's roles are generally viewed as lower status, prejudice toward lesbians or engaging in lesbian behavior should not be as strongly culturally sanctioned. That lesbianism is largely invisible in American society, except as part of male-oriented eroticism (discussed below), highlights this perspective (see also Bem 1993).

Psychodynamic Processes

Psychodynamic theories propose that prejudice stems from ego-defensiveness and the need to deny certain aspects of one's personality (Duckitt 1992). From this viewpoint, heterosexuals' negative attitudes toward lesbians and gay men stem from a denial of sexual impulses in general or denial of attraction to same-sex others more specifically. The failure to recognize latent homosexual impulses purportedly produces irrational, negative responses toward gay people. The often-used (and often-misused) term *homophobia*, defined as an irrational, persistent fear or dread of homosexuals (MacDonald 1976), has its roots in this perspective.

Relatively little research has directly explored the relationship between repressed homosexual impulses and attitudes toward gay men or lesbians. However, the finding that male heterosexuals have aversive reactions to depictions of the male body (e.g., Morin and Garfinkle 1978) is typically explained by a psychodynamic perspective. Recently Adams, Wright, and Lohr (1996) found that homophobic men in their sample showed greater physical arousal to consensual male homosexual activity than did nonhomophobic men, although the self-reported arousal of these individuals did not vary, suggesting that these homophobic men were repressing same-sex attraction. Moreover, homophobic and nonhomophobic men showed similar arousal levels to other types of erotica, including consensual female homosexual activity. Franklin (1998) has also provided evidence that, for at least a few men, antigay violence stems from a defensive reaction to their discomfort with their own sexual attraction to men.

Within the antigay prejudice literature, most research taking a psychodynamic perspective has focused on the relationship between psychodynamic personality characteristics such as dogmatism, gender role rigidity, religious conservatism, and, most commonly, authoritarianism and negative attitudes toward homosexuality (see Herek 1984, for a review). In general, individuals who score high on these dimensions manifest the highest levels of antigay prejudice. Whether sex of respondent accounts for additional variance remains unresolved. Outside the literature on attitudes toward homosexuality, there has been little discussion of sex differences in authoritarianism (see Christie 1991, for a review) or of sex differences in prejudice toward other social groups (see Ashmore and Del Boca 1981; Duckitt 1992). Pratto et al. (1994) found sex differences in authoritarianism, but Altemeyer (1988) did not. If there are no generalized sex differences in psychodynamic personality traits, it appears that to account adequately for sex differences in heterosexuals' attitudes toward homosexuality, theorists with a psychodynamic outlook must assume that such attitudes are a special case, with sex differences emerging because homosexuality raises a particular kind of threat that is specific to heterosexual men (e.g., Morin and Garfinkle 1978). One possible source of this threat is that heterosexual men, who are unaccustomed to rejecting sexual advances (e.g., McCormick 1979), feel more anxiety than do heterosexual women over the possibility of an invitation for same-sex relations. Heterosexual women, in contrast, have more readily available strategies for rejecting offers of sex (McCormick 1979) and so may be relatively less threatened by the possibility of a same-sex approach. Supporting this idea, LaMar and Kite (1998) found that heterosexual women and men reported similar levels of discomfort at the idea of a sexual advance from a member of their sex but that men were significantly less likely than women to agree that they would know how to respond to such a proposition. As Franklin (1998) has suggested, the anxiety produced by the threat of rejecting unwanted sexual advances may result in the defense mechanism of reaction formation; that is, heterosexual men may substitute feelings of anger and resentment toward gay men for the anxiety associated with unwanted sexual advances. Women's lower anxiety in similar situations would not necessitate such a defensive reaction.

The Sexualization of Lesbianism by Heterosexual Men

A third theoretical explanation for sex differences in attitudes toward homosexuality addresses the more specific finding that heterosexual men hold less negative attitudes toward lesbians than toward gay men, whereas heterosexual women hold approximately the same attitudes toward both groups (see Kite and Whitley 1996). This explanation derives from heterosexual men's sexualization of women in American society (e.g., DeLamater 1987; Sprecher and McKinney 1993). As DeLamater (1987) has noted, "Generally, men seem more likely than women to perceive persons of the opposite sex in sexual terms" (p. 134). For example, a number of studies (reviewed by Sprecher and McKinney 1993) have found that men are much more likely than women to attribute sexual intent to friendly behavior by members of the other sex. In addition, surveys have consistently found that men are more likely to be consumers of erotica in all its forms than are women (Fisher 1983). Heterosexual men's tendency to view women in sexual terms may lead them to eroticize the idea of a woman making love to another woman. The positive erotic value thus assigned to lesbianism by heterosexual men may counteract the general stigma associated with homosexuality, resulting in attitudes toward lesbians that are less negative than those toward gay men. Because heterosexual women tend not to sexualize men in the same way, however, they may not sexualize male homosexuality and may therefore hold similar attitudes toward lesbians and gay men.

Although a number of writers have alluded to the idea that lesbianism has erotic value for heterosexual men (e.g., Reiss 1986), researchers have conducted only a few studies to address this question. These researchers have used two methodological approaches to investigate this issue. Some have had participants rate slides or films that depict heterosexual and homosexual sexual activity (e.g., Gaughan and Gaynor 1973; Greendlinger 1985; Hatfield, Sprecher, and Traupmann 1978; Levitt and Brady 1965; Turnbull and Brown 1977). Turnbull and Brown's (1977) results are typical: Although both male and female respondents rated homosexual acts more negatively than heterosexual acts, men rated lesbian sexual activity more positively than did women; there was no sex difference for ratings of gay male sexual activity. Using the other methodological approach, Nyberg and Alston (1977) asked their respondents to rate the ideas of men making love to men and of women making love to women as being either erotic or nonerotic. Their results show that only 7 percent of both male and female respondents found the idea of a man making love to another man erotic. However, 33 percent of their male respondents found the idea of a woman making love to another woman erotic compared to only 10 percent of their female respondents.

These studies demonstrate that lesbianism does hold erotic value for at least some heterosexual men. But is this erotic value related to attitudes toward lesbians? Louderback and Whitley (1997) assessed male and female heterosexual respondents' ratings of the erotic value of male and female homosexuality and their attitudes toward lesbians and gay men. Consistent with the results of previous research, female respondents reported attitudes toward lesbians that were similar to their attitudes toward gay men, whereas male respondents reported less negative attitudes toward lesbians than toward gay men. Furthermore, male respondents' ratings of the erotic value of lesbianism were much higher than their ratings of the erotic value of male homosexuality and much higher than female respondents' ratings of the erotic value of either male or female homosexuality. With perceived erotic value of homosexuality controlled, men's attitudes toward lesbians were more negative than before controlling for perceived erotic value and were similar to their attitudes toward gay men; women's attitudes toward both lesbians and gay men were essentially unaffected by controlling for the perceived erotic value of homosexuality. These results are consistent with the hypothesis that heterosexual men's less negative attitudes toward lesbians stem at least in part from the erotic value they attribute to lesbianism.

We have described three theoretical perspectives on sex differences in attitudes toward homosexuality, each of which offers a plausible explanation for heterosexual men's greater negativity toward gay people. Connections across these perspectives, however, should not be overlooked. Herek's (1984, 1986) work on attitude functions, for example, points to a link between defensiveness toward homosexuality and gender role issues. Specifically, Herek argues that heterosexual male insecurity about homosexuality may stem from an inability to meet gender role expectations. Similarly the sexualization of lesbianism may stem from the belief that women's deviation from prescribed gender roles is less serious than men's, or from more generalized beliefs about gender roles. Duckitt (1992) has argued that although the capacity for prejudice may exist in all humans, cultural conditions may determine both an individual's propensity to be prejudiced and the targets of those prejudicial reactions. Humans, then, may be predisposed to hold defensive attitudes toward threatening groups, but societal shaping of cultural roles may heavily influence the choice of the derogated out-group, as well as the direction and strength of prejudice toward that group.

Meta-Analysis of Sex Differences in Attitudes Toward Homosexuality

We conducted a meta-analysis of the available literature on sex differences in attitudes toward homosexuality through September 1993 (Kite and Whitley 1996). Our analysis was based on 112 studies and included a total of 46,966 male and 53,858 female respondents. From these studies, we obtained 167 effect sizes. We further classified these effect sizes as representing attitudes toward homosexual persons, attitudes toward homosexual behavior, and attitudes toward gay people's civil rights. We based our predictions on the gender role analysis of sex differences in attitudes toward homosexuality described earlier and on the proposition that, because different types of judgments about an attitude object can be based on different sources of information (e.g., Esses, Haddock, and Zanna 1993), these judgments need not be consistent. Finally, within each category, to the extent possible, we considered moderators of the effect sizes.

Attitudes Toward Homosexual Persons

We predicted a sex difference in heterosexuals' attitudes toward homosexual persons, arguing that men's more rigid adherence to gender roles would lead to their more negative attitude. This prediction was borne out. The average correlation between sex and attitude was $r = .19$.[1] (Positive correlations indicate that men hold more negative attitudes.) We further expected, however, that men's negativity would be particularly acute when the attitude object was a gay man or a person of unspecified sex rather than a lesbian. This prediction, too, held. Sex differences were largest when the person being rated was a gay man ($r = .25$) or of unspecified sex ($r = .27$). For the latter category, it is likely that the perceivers assumed the questions referred to gay men (see Black and Stevenson 1984; Haddock, Zanna, and Esses 1993). In contrast, the sexes did not differ when the attitude object was a lesbian ($r = .00$). We explained these findings by noting that gay men may be viewed as violators of the male gender role, leading heterosexual men to evaluate them particularly negatively. In contrast, heterosexual men may be less likely to view lesbianism as a gender role violation, and hence are less derogatory toward those individuals. If female gender roles are less constrained, however, heterosexual women might be free to express greater acceptance of both gay men and lesbians. The sexualization of lesbianism, described earlier, provides a more detailed explanation for how gender roles might account for this finding.

Attitudes Toward Homosexual Behavior

Our prediction of sex differences in attitudes toward homosexual behavior also relied on a gender role analysis. Specifically we reasoned that if sexuality more generally is an important aspect of the gender belief system (Deaux and Kite 1987), heterosexual men might be more likely to view homosexual behavior as inappropriate and would therefore hold more negative attitudes toward that behavior than women would. We were more tentative about this prediction, however, because men generally hold more permissive attitudes toward sexual behavior than women do (e.g., Oliver and Hyde 1993). The average effect size ($r = .13$) indicated that men were more negative than women toward homosexual behavior, although the size of this difference was significantly smaller than that for attitudes toward homosexual persons. Apparently heterosexual men's permissive sexual attitudes do not extend to homosexuality.

Attitudes Toward Gay People's Civil Rights

Although the results described above provide clear evidence for heterosexual men's greater negativity toward homosexuality, we did not expect these results to generalize to all types of attitudes toward homosexuality, because attitudes toward a particular group need not be consistent (e.g., Esses et al. 1993). Herek's (1991) review of national opinion poll data showed greater acceptance of gay civil rights than of either homosexual behavior or homosexual people (see also Strand 1998). Moreover, national surveys rarely have found sex differences in this area (but see Herek and Capitanio 1995; Herek and Glunt 1993). We therefore reasoned that heterosexual women and men might differ in their attitudes toward homosexuality and still hold similar views about gay people's civil rights.

Our meta-analysis found essentially no overall sex difference in heterosexuals' attitudes toward the civil rights of lesbians and gay men ($r = .02$). However, four of the sixteen studies found that men held more negative attitudes than women, with an average difference of about one-third of a standard deviation. The twelve studies that found no sex difference were all conducted as part of the General Social Survey (Wood 1990) and dealt with free speech rights, asking respondents, for example, whether they would allow a "homosexual" to give a speech in their community. In contrast, the four studies that found sex differences included questions about rights that could be construed as related to gender role: military service, homosexual marriage, and adoption. The results of a Gallup Poll published after completion of our meta-analysis fit the same pattern: Men expressed more negative attitudes than women did on the issue of gays serving in the military (Moore

1993). These results are consistent across national probability samples and convenience samples of college students (e.g., Harris and Vanderhoof 1995). Thus, as with heterosexuals' attitudes toward homosexual persons and behavior, gender role issues may be a key to understanding sex differences in attitudes toward gay civil rights. Men are more negative than women on gender role-related issues, whereas there is no difference on gender role-neutral issues.

Additional new data suggest that the pattern changes slightly when gay male and lesbian targets are considered separately (LaMar and Kite 1998; but see Harris and Vanderhoof 1995). Heterosexual college students' ratings of gender role-related civil rights differed both by the sex of the rater and the sex of the person being rated. Heterosexual men reported less acceptance for gay men's than for lesbians' civil rights, but heterosexual women's acceptance did not differ by the sex of the person being rated. This pattern mirrors the comparisons of attitudes toward gay men and lesbians found in our meta-analysis. Finally, heterosexual men were more willing to accept discrimination (e.g., housing, job, etc.) against gay men than against lesbians, but heterosexual women's acceptance of this type of discrimination was similar for gay men and lesbians. Attitudes toward free speech were not assessed. Because no other studies we know of have examined heterosexuals' attitudes toward the civil rights of gay men and lesbians separately, it is difficult to know whether the results emerged because of the specific use of target labels (i.e., heterosexual men will derogate gay men almost regardless of the question asked), because of methodological issues such as study population (discussed below), or because a gender role analysis cannot account for all aspects of heterosexuals' attitudes toward gay people's civil rights. Given the current political landscape and recent legislative attempts to restrict the rights of gay men and lesbians, this issue is crucial and deserves considered investigation.

Study Population as a Moderator of Effect Size

In the case of both attitudes toward homosexual persons and attitudes toward homosexual behavior, we were able to consider whether study population (e.g., college students versus other adults) moderated the sex difference in attitudes toward homosexuality. In both cases, sex differences were smallest for nonprofessional adults and largest for college students. Our analysis of attitudes toward homosexual persons also included graduate students and professionals; the effect size for this group fell between college students and other adults. Analysis of attitudes toward homosexual behaviors also included high school students, for whom the sex difference was largest.

Interpretation of these population differences is difficult because many factors co-occur with the study population (e.g., age, education) (see Whitley and Kite 1995, for a discussion). Other confounds also obscure interpretation of these results. For example, the majority of studies on sex differences in attitudes toward homosexual persons and behavior used convenience samples of college students. In contrast, most studies using national or regional probability samples of adults have assessed only attitudes toward the civil rights of gay men; when other dependent variables were used, they were usually measured with single items of unknown validity. To determine how well the research using college students generalizes to the population at large, survey researchers must use well-validated measures of attitudes toward homosexual persons and behavior. Studies that have done so have obtained inconsistent results. Herek and Glunt (1993) found sex differences of about the same magnitude as the average effect size for studies using college student samples, and Herek and Capitanio (1995) found a similar sex difference with an African-American sample. However, additional data collected by Herek and Capitanio (1996) were consistent with the majority of prior survey studies finding no sex difference in attitudes toward either lesbians or gay men. The question of the generalizability of the research conducted with college students is therefore still unresolved.

Gender Roles and Attitudes Toward Homosexuality

The gender role approach to understanding sex differences in attitudes toward homosexuality implies that gender role attitudes should mediate those sex differences; that is, when sex differences in gender role attitudes are controlled, sex differences in attitudes toward homosexuality should disappear. Statistically, the hypothesis predicts that there should be correlations between respondent sex and gender role attitudes, between respondent sex and attitudes toward homosexuality, and between gender role attitudes and attitudes toward homosexuality, and that the partial correlation between respondent sex and attitudes toward homosexuality should be near zero when gender role attitudes are controlled (Baron and Kenny 1986).

Before examining the data on this question, it is important to note that the concept of gender role is an example of what Carver (1989) has called a multifaceted construct. It is composed of several related components, each of which can have different relationships to another variable, such as attitudes toward homosexuality. Three components of gender role have been studied in relation to heterosexuals' attitudes toward homosexuality (Whitley 1987). Gender role self-concept is assessed through self-reports of gender role-related personality traits, such as those included in Spence, Helmreich, and Stapp's (1975) Personal Attributes Questionnaire (PAQ). These scales typically provide two scores: one for traits stereotypically associated with men (variously labeled as masculine, instrumental, or agentic) and another for traits stereotypically associated with women (variously labeled as feminine, expressive, or communal). Gender role behavior is assessed through self-reports of the frequency of behaviors that men and women engage in at different rates, such as those included in Orlofsky, Ramsden, and Cohen's (1982) Sex Role Behavior Scale. Finally, gender role attitudes are assessed by the degree to which respondents endorse statements that reflect traditional or nontraditional gender roles, such as those included in Spence and Helmreich's (1972) Attitudes Toward Women Scale (AWS).

In order for any of these gender role constructs to mediate sex differences in attitudes toward homosexuality, scores on measures of the constructs must correlate with scores on measures of attitudes toward homosexuality. In a meta-analysis of ten studies of the relationship between gender role self-concept and attitudes toward homosexuality, Whitley (1995) found a mean correlation of $r = .00$ for male-associated traits and a mean correlation of $r = -.09$ for female-associated traits, indicating that these constructs could have no mediating effect. Similarly, in the only study that included gender role behaviors, Whitley (1987) found a correlation of only $r = .10$ between self-reports of male-associated behaviors and attitudes toward homosexuality and a correlation of only $r = -.06$ between self-reports of female-associated behaviors and such attitudes. In contrast, our meta-analysis found that scores on measures of gender role attitudes had a mean correlation of $r = .44$ with scores on measures of attitudes toward homosexuality. We also found that when sex differences in gender role attitudes were controlled (men holding more traditional attitudes), the average partial correlation between gender role attitudes and attitudes toward homosexuality was only $r = .02$. These results indicate that sex differences in attitudes toward homosexuality are related to differences in gender role attitudes but not to sex differences in gender role self-concept or gender role behaviors.

We must place a qualification on the conclusions just stated. Recent research suggests that men who score higher on extreme gender role involvement, a trait that Mosher (1991) has called *hypermasculinity*, also express more negative attitudes toward homosexuality (e.g., Mosher 1991; Patel et al. 1995), even though hypermasculinity scores are relatively independent of gender role attitudes as assessed by the AWS (Mosher 1991). Thus hyper-gender-role involvement may be related to heterosexuals' attitudes toward homosexuality independent of respondents' gender role attitudes. Although a parallel hyperfemininity scale has been developed for women (Murnen and Byrne 1991), no research has reported its relation to attitudes toward homosexuality.

Conservative Gender Role Attitudes or General Conservatism?

Although the gender role interpretation of sex differences in attitudes toward homosexuality is appealing, one might ask whether it is the gender role relatedness of those attitudes or their reflection of generally conservative versus liberal social and political viewpoints that leads them to be correlated with attitudes toward homosexuality. For example, scores on measures of sexism (endorsement of traditional gender role beliefs), racism, and antigay attitudes are all intercorrelated (Bierly 1985; Qualls, Cox, and Schehr 1992). Scores on measures of authoritarian and conservative attitudes correlate with scores on measures of both racism and sexism (e.g., Altemeyer 1988; Pratto et al. 1994) and have an average correlation of $r = .41$ with scores on measures of antigay attitudes (Whitley 1997).

It is therefore possible that sexism, racism, and antigay attitudes are all facets or manifestations of the higher-order construct of authoritarian conservatism, at least for the predominantly white, heterosexual respondent samples used in the research. This possibility raises the question of whether the specific construct of sexism has a relationship to antigay attitudes beyond that generated by the relationship between the general construct of authoritarian conservative attitudes. We were able to locate only two studies that addressed this issue by examining the correlation of traditional sex role attitudes with attitudes toward homosexuality, controlling for conservative beliefs (Agnew et al. 1993; Whitley 1987). Although these studies found significant partial correlations, indicating that both conservatism and sexism had an independent relationship to attitudes toward homosexuality, their attitude measures did not distinguish among attitudes toward homosexual persons, behavior, and civil rights. Given the complexity of attitudes toward homosexuality, replication and extension of this research is needed to provide a complete answer to the question posed in the above section heading.

Moreover, preliminary data analysis in our laboratory (LaMar and Kite 1996) suggests that when attitudes toward women's roles (as assessed by the FEM scale; Smith, Ferree, and Miller 1975) are controlled for, attitude toward the male gender role (as assessed by the Attitudes about Masculinity Scale; Brannon and Juni 1984) makes an independent contribution to heterosexuals' attitudes toward gay people, suggesting another avenue for further study.

Other Gaps in the Research Literature

Despite the large number of studies on sex differences in heterosexuals' attitudes toward homosexuality, significant gaps exist in the research literature. In addition to those already suggested, some possible directions for future research include making greater use of behavior as a dependent variable and studying responses to lesbians and gay men as individuals rather than as social groups.

Behavior Toward Lesbians and Gay Men

Although there has been a great deal of research on sex differences in expressed attitudes toward lesbians and gay men, few studies have used behavior toward lesbians and gay men as a dependent variable. In making this statement, we define behavioral dependent variables rather narrowly as direct observation of positive or negative actions, self-reports of positive or negative actions, and what Aronson et al. (1990) have called *behavioroid* measures — having research participants make a commitment to perform an action, even if that action is not carried out. These variables include such behaviors as self-reports of antigay aggression, observation of interpersonal distance in laboratory interactions with persons described as being gay, and agreeing to meet with a person described as being gay. We take this narrow approach because it seems to us that other types of behavioral measures — such as self-reports of desired levels of intimacy with lesbians or gay men, nonverbal behaviors, and the content of conversations — bear less resemblance to the types of negative behaviors that lesbians and gay men experience in their everyday lives (e.g., Berrill 1990; Herek 1993).

Behavioral studies are important because the attitude-behavior relationship can be very weak and can vary as a function of other variables in the research situation (e.g., Eagly and Chaiken 1993). In fact, of the five studies that used a dependent variable that met our definition of behavioral (Karr 1978; Kite 1992; Lord, Lepper, and Mackie 1984; Patel et al. 1995; San Miguel and Millham 1976), only Karr's found a simple attitude-behavior relationship. However, two of the studies did identify variables that moderated the attitude-behavior relationship. Lord et al. (1984) found a moderate relationship when the target person's reported traits fully matched the respondents' personal stereotypes of gay men but no relationship when the target person's traits only partly fit the stereotype. San Miguel and Millham (1976) found a relationship when the target person was similar to the respondent but not when he was dissimilar, and when the outcome of an interaction was negative but not when it was positive. The other studies found no relationship between antigay attitudes and behavior. Thus, like other attitude-behavior relationships, that between heterosexuals' attitudes toward homosexuality and their behavior toward lesbians and gay men can vary as a function of situational factors (e.g., Kite 1994). For example, Franklin (1998) has suggested that negative attitudes toward lesbians and gay men can lead people to perceive negative actions directed at lesbians and gay men to be permissible. However, she further notes that additional, situational factors — such as youthful thrill seeking, peer group norms, and the felt need to exercise masculine power — must be present before the negative attitudes are expressed as negative behaviors. Consequently one should not generalize from sex differences in antigay attitudes to sex differences in antigay behavior.

Unfortunately all five studies assessed only men's behavior, four using only gay male targets, so there is almost no information in the research literature on sex differences in behavior toward lesbians and gay men, although research on antigay violence shows that it is most commonly perpetrated by men (e.g., Berrill 1990). Research is therefore clearly needed to answer a number of questions. Are there sex differences in heterosexuals' behavior directed toward lesbians and gay men? If so, what variables, especially sex of target person, moderate that relationship? Are there sex differences in the attitude-behavior relationship? If so, what psychological processes cause that difference? The answers to questions such as these can give direction to interventions aimed at reducing antigay behavior in society.

Attitudes Toward Individuals Versus Attitudes Toward Social Groups

Most studies of sex differences in attitudes toward lesbians and gay men assess respondents' attitudes toward lesbians and gay men as social groups rather than as individuals. However, when interacting with lesbians and gay men, heterosexuals are responding to concrete individuals in all their complexity, rather than to abstract and perhaps simplistically construed social groups. People's responses may differ in these two situations because presenting respondents with a social group as an attitude object calls their stereotypes of the group to mind, which are usually negative with respect to lesbians and gay men (e.g., Lord et al. 1984). Not surprisingly, then, several studies have shown that people respond more negatively to lesbians and gay men presented in a stereotypical manner than when they are presented as "average" people (Laner and Laner 1979, 1980; Lord et al. 1984).

Therefore the question arises of whether the sex differences that are found when heterosexuals rate lesbians and gay men as social groups are also found when they rate individual lesbians and gay men who behave in a non-stereotypical manner. The results of this type of research are mixed. Only one study found the typical outcome in which male respondents rate gay men more negatively than lesbians and rate gay men more negatively than do female respondents (Cuenot and Fugita 1982). Three studies found no effects related to the sex of the respondent or to the sex of the target (Kite 1992, 1994; Shaffer and Wallace 1990). One pair of related studies found that men rated lesbians and gay men similarly but rated gay men more negatively than did women (Laner and Laner 1979, 1980). Another study found that men rated both heterosexual and homosexual men more negatively than women did (Gross et al. 1980). Finally, San Miguel and Millham (1976) found that men's reactions to a gay man varied as a function of their attitudes toward homosexuality (see also Kite 1992), the extent to which they perceived the gay man to be similar to themselves, and whether their interaction with the gay man was positive or negative.

Clearly more research is needed on how heterosexual men and women respond to individual lesbians and gay men and on what factors affect those responses. The answers to questions such as these are especially important given that classroom presentations by lesbians and gay men, either live or on videotape, are commonly used as attitude-change interventions in colleges and universities (Stevenson 1988). Such research must, however, be carefully designed to maximize its generalizability to real-life interactions. For example, only two of the studies described above (Cuenot and Fugita 1982; San Miguel and Millham 1976) had research participants interact with another person; participants in the other studies either read summaries of information about the people they evaluated or viewed a videotape of a simulated interview. Research of the latter variety lacks much of the richness of the face-to-face interactions of everyday life.

The ways in which interacting with "average" lesbians and gay men affect respondents' stereotypes also need to be assessed, given that people often see members of social groups who do not fit their stereotypes as "exceptions to the rule" and so maintain the stereotype for the social group as a whole (Brewer 1988), resulting in little real attitude change. For example, Herek and Capitanio (1996) found that heterosexuals who had contact with only one lesbian or gay man held attitudes similar to those who had never had contact with someone they knew to be gay; however, heterosexuals who knew two or more gay people had more favorable attitudes. As Rothbart and John (1985) have suggested, a person who knows more than one member of a group may find it difficult to dismiss their behavior as atypical.

Distinguishing Between Attitudes Toward Lesbians and Attitudes Toward Gay Men

In closing, we wish to reiterate a point that others have made before us (e.g., Herek 1994): It is essential to distinguish between attitudes toward lesbians and attitudes toward gay men. Our meta-analysis found that only 7 percent of the studies reviewed specifically examined attitudes toward lesbians and that all these studies were limited in that they assessed only the "persons" component of the attitude and used only college student respondent samples. In contrast, 59 percent of the studies simply described the attitude object using the term *homosexual*, which, as noted earlier, many interpret as meaning *gay man*. Another 18 percent of the studies specified gay men as the attitude objects, and 16 percent of the studies assessed attitude toward both lesbians and gay men but combined these responses into a single attitude score. Consequently little is known about the ways in which attitudes toward lesbians are similar to and different from attitudes toward gay men.

Making a distinction between the two sets of attitudes is important both empirically and theoretically. Empirically our meta-analysis found a clear interaction between sex of respondent and sex of attitude object: Men and women held similar attitudes toward lesbians, but men were more negative toward gay men. Consequently researchers must control both sex of respondent and sex of attitude object to get an accurate picture of the meaning of their results. Research conducted with only male or only female respondents rating only lesbians or only gay men may not generalize to other combinations of respondents and attitude objects. Theoretically the processes underlying men's and women's attitudes toward lesbians and gay men may differ. For example, we earlier noted the possibility that men's less negative attitudes toward lesbians may result from men's sexualization of lesbianism.

Both theoretical and empirical requirements therefore indicate the necessity of distinguishing between attitudes toward lesbians and attitudes toward gay men. Such well-focused research and theory can only better our understanding of attitudes toward both lesbians and gay men and point to better interventions aimed at alleviating the negative aspects of those attitudes.

Notes

1. Our theoretical analysis concerns *heterosexuals'* attitudes toward gay men and lesbians. In describing our own research and that of others, however, we describe the findings more generally. Although the majority of the respondents in these studies are likely heterosexual, few researchers specifically exclude gay men, lesbian, and bisexual participants. Although the impact of this inclusion is likely minimal, it is not completely correct to assume that these data reflect only heterosexuals' viewpoints. Certainly a literature based on respondents who report exclusive heterosexuality would provide clearer tests of our hypotheses.
2. Kite and Whitley (1996) reported effect sizes as *d*. However, to make results more accessible, we have converted those effect sizes to *r* in this presentation. This conversion has no effect on the interpretation of the results.

References

Adams, H. E., L. W. Wright, and B. A. Lohr. 1996. Is homophobia associated with homosexual arousal? *Journal of Abnormal Psychology* 105:440–45.

Agnew, C. R., V. D. Thompson, V. A. Smith, R. H. Gramzow, and D. P. Currey. 1993. Proximal and distal predictors of homophobia: Framing the multivariate roots of out-group rejection. *Journal of Applied Social Psychology* 23:2013–42.

Altemeyer, B. 1988. *Enemies of Freedom: Understanding Right-Wing Authoritarianism.* San Francisco: Jossey-Bass.

Aronson, E., P. C. Ellsworth, J. M. Carlsmith, and M. H. Gonzales. 1990. *Methods of Research in Social Psychology.* 2nd ed. New York: McGraw-Hill.

Ashmore, R. D., and F. K. Del Boca. 1981. Conceptual approaches to stereotypes and stereotyping. In D. L. Hamilton, ed., *Cognitive Processes in Stereotyping and Intergroup Behavior*, pp. 1–35. Hillsdale, N.J.: Erlbaum.

Baron, R. M., and D. A. Kenny. 1986. The mediator-moderator variable distinction in social psychological research: Conceptual, strategic, and statistical considerations. *Journal of Personality and Social Psychology* 51:1173–82.

Bem, S. L. 1993. *The Lenses of Gender: Transforming the Debate on Sexual Inequality.* New Haven, Conn.: Yale University Press.

Berrill, K. T. 1990. Anti-gay violence and victimization in the United States. *Journal of Interpersonal Violence* 5:274–94.

Bierly, M. M. 1985. Prejudice toward contemporary outgroups as a generalized attitude. *Journal of Applied Social Psychology* 15:189–99.

Black, K. N., and M. R. Stevenson. 1984. The relationship of self-reported sex-role characteristics and attitudes toward homosexuality. *Journal of Homosexuality* 10(1–2):83–93.

Brannon, R., and S. Juni. 1984. A scale for measuring attitudes about masculinity. *Psychological Documents* 14:6–7.

Brewer, M. B. 1988. A dual process model of impression formation. In T. K. Srull and R. S. Wyer, eds., *Advances in Social Cognition*, 1:1–36. Hillsdale, N.J.: Erlbaum.

Carver, C. S. 1989. How should multifaceted personality constructs be tested? Issues illustrated by self-monitoring, attributional style, and hardiness. *Journal of Personality and Social Psychology* 56:577–85.

Christie, R. 1991. Authoritarianism and related constructs. In J. P. Robinson, P. R. Shaver, and L. S. Wrightsman, eds., *Measures of Personality and Social Psychological Attitudes*, 1:501–71. New York: Academic Press.

Costrich, N., L. Feinstein, L. Kidder, J. Marecek, and L. Pascale. 1975. When stereotypes hurt: Three studies of penalties for sex-role reversals. *Journal of Experimental Social Psychology* 11:520–30.

Cuenot, R. G., and S. S. Fugita. 1982. Perceived homosexuality: Measuring heterosexual attitudinal and nonverbal reactions. *Personality and Social Psychology Bulletin* 8:100–106.

Deaux, K., and M. E. Kite. 1987. Thinking about gender. In B. B. Hess and M. M. Ferree, eds., *Analyzing Gender: A Handbook of Social Science Research*, pp. 92–117. Newbury Park, Calif.: Sage.

Deaux, K., and L. L. Lewis. 1984. Structure of gender stereotypes: Interrelationships among components and gender label. *Journal of Personality and Social Psychology* 46:991–1004.

DeLamater, J. 1987. Gender differences in sexual scenarios. In K. Kelley, ed., *Females, Males, and Sexuality: Theories and Research*, pp. 127–39. Albany: State University of New York Press.

Duckitt, J. 1992. Psychology and prejudice. *American Psychologist* 47:1182–93.

Eagly, A. H., and S. Chaiken. 1993. *The Psychology of Attitudes*. Fort Worth: Harcourt Brace Jovanovich.

Esses, V. M., G. Haddock, and M. P. Zanna. 1993. Values, stereotypes, and emotions as determinants of intergroup attitudes. In D. M. Mackie and D. L. Hamilton, eds., *Affect, Cognition, and Stereotyping: Interactive Processes in Group Perception*, pp. 137–66. New York: Academic Press.

Feinman, S. 1981. Why is cross-sex-role behavior more approved for girls than for boys? A status characteristics approach. *Sex Roles* 7:289–300.

Fisher, W. A. 1983. Gender, gender-role identification, and response to erotica. In E. R. Allgeier and N. B. McCormick, eds., *Changing Boundaries: Gender Roles and Sexual Behavior*, pp. 261–84. Mountain View, Calif.: Mayfield.

Franklin, K. 1998. Unassuming motivations: Contextualizing the narratives of anti-gay assailants. In G. M. Herek, ed., *Stigma and Sexual Orientation: Understanding Prejudice Against Lesbians, Gay Men, and Bisexuals*, pp. 1–23. Thousand Oaks, Calif.: Sage.

Gaughan, E. J., and M. W. Gaynor. 1973. College student ratings of arousal value of pornographic photographs. *Proceedings of the Annual Convention of the American Psychological Association* 8:409–10.

Greendlinger, V. 1985. Authoritarianism as a predictor of response to heterosexual and homosexual erotica. *High School Journal* 68:183–86.

Gross, A. E., S. K. Green, J. T. Storck, and J. M. Vanyur. 1980. Disclosure of sexual orientation and impressions of male and female homosexuals. *Personality and Social Psychology Bulletin* 6:307–14.

Haddock, G., M. P. Zanna, and V. M. Esses. 1993. Assessing the structure of prejudicial attitudes: The case of attitudes toward homosexuals. *Journal of Personality and Social Psychology* 65:1105–18.

Harris, M. B., and J. Vanderhoof. 1995. Attitudes towards gays and lesbians serving in the military. *Journal of Gay and Lesbian Social Services* 3(4):23–51.

Hatfield, E., S. Sprecher, and J. Traupmann. 1978. Men's and women's reactions to sexually explicit films: A serendipitous finding. *Archives of Sexual Behavior* 7:583–92.

Herek, G. M. 1984. Beyond "homophobia": A social psychological perspective on attitudes toward lesbians and gay men. *Journal of Homosexuality* 10(1–2):1–21.

Herek, G. M. 1986. On heterosexual masculinity: Some psychical consequences of the social construction of gender and sexuality. *American Behavioral Scientist* 29:563–77.

Herek, G. M. 1988. Heterosexuals' attitudes toward lesbians and gay men: Correlates and gender differences. *Journal of Sex Research* 25:451–77.

Herek, G. M. 1991. Stigma, prejudice, and violence against lesbians and gay men. In J. C. Gonsiorek and J. D. Weinrich, eds., *Homosexuality: Research Implications for Public Policy*, pp. 60–80. Newbury Park, Calif.: Sage.

Herek, G. M. 1993. Documenting prejudice against lesbians and gay men on campus: The Yale Sexual Orientation Survey. *Journal of Homosexuality* 25(4):15–29.

Herek, G. M. 1994. Assessing heterosexuals' attitudes toward lesbians and gay men: A review of empirical research with the ATLG scale. In B. Greene and G. M. Herek, eds., *Lesbian and Gay Psychology: Theory, Research, and Clinical Applications*. Thousand Oaks, Calif.: Sage.

Herek, G. M., and J. P. Capitanio. 1995. Black heterosexuals' attitudes toward lesbians and gay men in the United States. *Journal of Sex Research* 32:95–105.

Herek, G. M., and J. P. Capitanio. 1996. "Some of my best friends": Intergroup contact, concealable stigma, and heterosexuals' attitudes toward gay men and lesbians. *Personality and Social Psychology Bulletin* 22:412–24.

Herek, G. M., and E. K. Glunt. 1993. Interpersonal contact and heterosexuals' attitudes toward gay men: Results from a national survey. *Journal of Sex Research* 30:239–44.

Hogg, M. A., and J. C. Turner. 1987. Intergroup behaviour, self-stereotyping, and the salience of social categories. *British Journal of Social Psychology* 26:325–40.

Hort, B. E., B. I. Fagot, and M. D. Leinbach. 1990. Are people's notions of maleness more stereotypically framed than their notions of femaleness? *Sex Roles* 23:197–212.

Jackson, L. A., and T. F. Cash. 1985. Components of gender stereotypes: Their implications for inferences on stereotypic and nonstereotypic dimensions. *Personality and Social Psychology Bulletin* 11:326–44.

Karr, R. G. 1978. Homosexual labeling and the male role. *Journal of Social Issues* 34(3):73–83.

Kite, M. E. 1992. Individual differences in males' reactions to gay males and lesbians. *Journal of Applied Social Psychology* 22:1222–39.

Kite, M. E. 1994. When perceptions meet reality: Individual differences in reactions to lesbians and gay men. In B. Greene and G. M. Herek, eds., *Lesbian and Gay Psychology: Theory, Research, and Clinical Applications*. Thousand Oaks, Calif.: Sage.

Kite, M. E., and K. Deaux. 1987. Gender belief systems: Homosexuality and the implicit inversion theory. *Psychology of Women Quarterly* 11:83–96.

Kite, M. E., and B. E. Whitley Jr. 1996. Sex differences in attitudes toward homosexual persons, behavior, and civil rights: A meta-analysis. *Personality and Social Psychology Bulletin* 22:336–53.

Krulewitz, J. E., and J. E. Nash. 1980. Effects of sex role attitudes and similarity on men's rejection of male homosexual. *Journal of Personality and Social Psychology* 38:67–74.

LaMar, L. M., and M. E. Kite. 1996. Male and female gender role attitude and sex differences in attitudes toward homosexuality. Unpublished raw data.

LaMar, L. M., and M. E. Kite. 1998. Sex differences in attitudes toward homosexuality: A multi-dimensional perspective. *The Journal of Sex Research* 35:189–96.

Laner, M. R., and R. H. Laner. 1979. Personal style or sexual preference: Why gay men are disliked. *International Review of Modern Sociology* 9:215–28.

Laner, M. R., and R. H. Laner. 1980. Sexual preference or personal style? Why lesbians are disliked. *Journal of Homosexuality* 5(4):339–56.

Levitt, E. E., and J. P. Brady. 1965. Sexual preferences in young adults and some correlates. *Journal of Clinical Psychology* 21:347–54.

Lewin, M., and L. M. Tragos. 1987. Has the feminist movement influenced adolescent sex role attitudes? A reassessment after a quarter century. *Sex Roles* 16:125–35.

Lord, C. G., M. R. Lepper, and D. Mackie. 1984. Attitude prototypes as determinants of attitude-behavior consistency. *Journal of Personality and Social Psychology* 46:1254–66.

Louderback, L. A., and B. E. Whitley Jr. 1997. Perceived erotic value of homosexuality and sex-role attitudes as mediators of sex differences in heterosexual college students' attitudes toward lesbians and gay men. *Journal of Sex Research* 34:175–82.

MacDonald, A. P. Jr. 1976. Homophobia: Its roots and meanings. *Homosexual Counseling Journal* 3(1):23–33.

Martin, C. L. 1990. Attitudes and expectations about children with nontraditional and traditional gender roles. *Sex Roles* 22:151–65.

McCormick, N. B. 1979. Come-ons and put-offs: Unmarried students' strategies for having and avoiding sexual intercourse. *Psychology of Women Quarterly* 4:194–211.

McCreary, D. R. 1994. The male role and avoiding femininity. *Sex Roles* 31:517–31.

Morin, S. F., and E. M. Garfinkle. 1978. Male homophobia. *Journal of Social Issues* 34(1):29–47.

Moore, D. W. 1993. Public polarized on gay issue. *Gallup Poll Monthly*, April, pp. 30–34.

Mosher, D. L. 1991. Macho men, machismo, and sexuality. *Annual Review of Sex Research* 2:199–247.

Murnen, S. K., and D. Byrne. 1991. Hyperfemininity: Measurement and initial validation of the construct. *Journal of Sex Research* 26:479–89.

Nyberg, K. L., and J. P. Alston. 1977. Homosexual labeling by university youths. *Adolescence* 12:541–46.

Oliver, M. B., and J. S. Hyde. 1993. Gender differences in sexuality: A meta-analysis. *Psychological Bulletin* 114:29–51.

Orlofsky, J. L., M. W. Ramsden, and R. S. Cohen. 1982. Development of the revised Sex Role Behavior Scale. *Journal of Personality Assessment* 46:632–38.

Patel, S., T. E. Long, S. L. McCammon, and K. L. Wuensch. 1995. Personality and emotional correlates of self-reported antigay behaviors. *Journal of Interpersonal Violence* 10:354–66.

Pratto, F., J. Sidanius, L. M. Stallworth, and B. F. Malle. 1994. Social dominance orientation: A personality variable predicting social and political attitudes. *Journal of Personality and Social Psychology* 67:741–63.

Preston, K., and K. Stanley. 1987. "What's the worst thing . . . ?" Gender-directed insults. *Sex Roles* 17:209–19.

Qualls, R. C., M. B. Cox, and T. J. Schehr. 1992. Racial attitudes on campus: Are there gender differences? *Journal of College Student Development* 33:524–29.

Rajecki, D. W., R. De Graaf-Kaser, and J. L. Rasmussen. 1992. New impressions and more discrimination: Effects of individuation on gender-label stereotypes. *Sex Roles* 27:171–85.

Reiss, I. L. 1986. *Journey into Sexuality: An Exploratory Voyage.* Englewood Cliffs, N.J.: Prentice-Hall.

Rothbart, M., and O. P. John. 1985. Social categorization and behavioral episodes: A cognitive analysis of the effects of intergroup contact. *Journal of Social Issues* 41(3):81–104.

San Miguel, C. L., and J. Millham. 1976. The role of cognitive and situational variables in aggression toward homosexuals. *Journal of Homosexuality* 2(1):11–27.

Shaffer, D. R., and A. Wallace. 1990. Belief congruence and evaluator homophobia as determinants of the attractiveness of competent homosexual and heterosexual males. *Journal of Psychology and Human Sexuality* 3(1):67–87.

Smith, E. R., M. M. Ferree, and F. D. Miller. 1975. A short scale of attitudes toward feminism. *Representative Research in Social Psychology* 6:51–58.

Spence, J. T., and R. L. Helmreich. 1972. The Attitudes Toward Women Scale: An objective instrument to measure attitudes toward the rights and roles of women in contemporary society. *JSAS Catalog of Selected Documents in Psychology* 2:66 (ms. no. 153).

Spence, J. T., R. L. Helmreich, and J. Stapp. 1975. Ratings of self and peers on sex role attributes and their relations to self-esteem and conceptions of masculinity and femininity. *Journal of Personality and Social Psychology* 32:29–39.

Sprecher, S., and K. McKinney. 1993. *Sexuality.* Newbury Park, Calif.: Sage.

Stevenson, M. R. 1988. Promoting tolerance for homosexuality: An evaluation of intervention strategies. *Journal of Sex Research* 25:500–511.

Stockard, J., and M. M. Johnson. 1979. The social origins of male dominance. *Sex Roles* 5:199–218.

Strand, D. A. 1998. Civil liberties, civil rights, and stigma: Voter attitudes and behavior in the politics of homosexuality. In G. M. Herek, ed., *Stigma and Sexual Orientation: Understanding Prejudice Against Lesbians, Gay Men, and Bisexuals,* pp. 108–37. Thousand Oaks, Calif.: Sage.

Taylor, A. 1983. Conceptions of masculinity and femininity as a basis for stereotypes of male and female homosexuals. *Journal of Homosexuality* 9(1):37–53.

Turnbull, D., and M. Brown. 1977. Attitudes toward homosexuality and male and female reactions to homosexual and heterosexual slides. *Canadian Journal of Behavioral Science* 9:68–80.

Whitley, B. E. Jr. 1987. The relationship of sex-role orientation to heterosexuals' attitudes toward homosexuals. *Sex Roles* 17:103–13.

Whitley, B. E. Jr. 1995. Sex-role orientation and attitudes toward homosexuality: A meta-analysis. Unpublished manuscript, Ball State University, Department of Psychological Science, Muncie, Indiana.

Whitley, B. E. Jr. 1997. Authoritarian/conservative attitudes and attitudes toward homosexuality. Paper presented at the annual meeting of the Eastern Psychological Association, April, Washington, D.C.

Whitley, B. E. Jr., and M. E. Kite. 1995. Sex differences in attitudes toward homosexuality: A comment on Oliver and Hyde. 1993. *Psychological Bulletin* 117:146–54.

Wood, F. W., ed. 1990. *An American Profile: Opinions and Behavior 1972–1989.* Detroit, Mich.: Gale Research.

7   Violence and Victimization
of Lesbians and Gay Men: Mental Health
Consequences

*Linda D. Garnets, Gregory M. Herek,
and Barrie Levy*

Like other survivors of the violence that pervades American
society, lesbian and gay male crime victims must confront the difficulties
created by victimization. And, as members of a stigmatized group, lesbians
and gay men face numerous psychological challenges as a consequence of
society's hostility toward them. When individual victimization and societal
prejudice converge in antigay hate crimes, lesbian and gay male survivors
face additional, unique challenges. Those challenges are the principal focus
of this article.

Owing to the widespread prevalence of antigay prejudice in the United
States (Herek 1990, 1991) and the large number of lesbian and gay male
victims of hate crimes in this country (Berrill 1990; Herek 1989), American
gay people as a group might be expected to manifest significantly higher
levels of psychological distress and impairment than heterosexuals. Yet this
is not the case; the lesbian and gay male community does not differ significantly in mental health from the heterosexual population (Gonsiorek 1982;
Gonsiorek and Weinrich 1991). Obviously antigay victimization does not
inevitably lead to psychological dysfunction.

This article treats antigay victimization as creating a crisis for the survivor,
with opportunities for subsequent growth as well as risks for impairment (e.g.,
Caplan 1964). This conceptualization does not deny or minimize the negative consequences of victimization, both physical and psychological, immediate and long-term. But nor does it relegate lesbian and gay male targets
of hate crimes to passivity. Instead, it should encourage researchers and
mental health practitioners to view the survivors of antigay victimization as

active, problem-solving individuals who are potentially capable of coping with the aftermath of the attack and using the experience as an opportunity for growth.

The Psychological Aftermath of Victimization

In addition to dealing with the physical consequences of injury and the practical aftermath of having one's possessions stolen or damaged, crime victims often experience a variety of psychological symptoms. Common behavioral and somatic reactions to victimization include sleep disturbances and nightmares, headaches, diarrhea, uncontrollable crying, agitation and restlessness, increased use of drugs, and deterioration in personal relationships (e.g., Frieze, Hymer, and Greenberg 1984; Janoff-Bulman and Frieze 1983a). Victimization creates psychological distress for several reasons. First, it dramatically interferes with everyday processes of denial through which people are able to feel secure and invulnerable, that "it can't happen to me" (Janoff-Bulman and Frieze 1983b). The world suddenly seems less predictable; people seem more malevolent. Because their victimization did not result from accidental or natural forces but was intentionally perpetrated against them, survivors are likely to feel a reduction in their previous level of basic trust (Bard and Sangrey 1979).

Second, the experience of victimization interferes with perceptions of the world as an orderly and meaningful place. Survivors often try to restore some sense of meaning and predictability by asking, "Why me?" and many respond to the question with self-blame. This is not necessarily maladaptive. Blaming specific behaviors related to the victimization (*behavioral self-blame*) may constitute an effective coping strategy, because it helps survivors feel a sense of control over their own lives and provides strategies for avoiding revictimization (Janoff-Bulman 1979, 1982). In contrast, blaming one's victimization on perceived character flaws (*characterological self-blame*) is associated with low self-esteem, depression, and feelings of helplessness (Janoff-Bulman 1979). Although behavioral self-blame may sometimes be adaptive, observers may react more negatively to victims who blame themselves than to victims who attribute their circumstances to chance factors (Coates, Wortman, and Abbey 1979), thereby exacerbating survivors' psychological distress.

A third reason why victimization creates psychological distress is that it often leads people to question their own worth. Survivors may devalue them-

they may feel self worth bcuz they feel violated *they have feelings of helplessness & need relly on peep-4 help*

selves because they perceive they have been violated and because they experience a loss of autonomy, first at the hands of the perpetrator and subsequently as they must rely on others to help them recover from the victimization (Bard and Sangrey 1979). Survivors also may internalize the social stigma associated with being a victim. Others often react negatively to them, seeing them as weak or inferior, of having failed in the basic task of protecting themselves, of somehow deserving their fate (e.g., Coates et al. 1979). Such social reactions may lead survivors to feel ashamed or embarrassed at their perceived "failure."

Severe psychological responses to victimization may be of short or prolonged duration, and may be immediate in their onset or delayed by years after the victimization. Severe reactions are diagnosed as Posttraumatic Stress Disorder, or PTSD (American Psychiatric Association 1987; Frederick 1987), indicated by the persistence of three types of symptoms for at least one month consequent to victimization: (a) persistent reexperiencing of the victimization (e.g., via memories, intrusive thoughts, dreams, or intense distress from activities or events triggering recollection of the event); (b) persistent avoidance of trauma-associated stimuli or a numbing of general responsiveness (e.g., diminished interest in significant activities, feelings of detachment from others, restricted affect, sense of foreshortened future); and (c) persistent symptoms of increased arousal (e.g., sleep disturbances, exaggerated startle response, difficulty concentrating).

The crisis following victimization is likely to create different challenges as time passes (e.g., Tsegaye-Spates 1985). Bard and Sangrey (1979), for example, highlighted three important stages: (a) an *impact* phase, when victims typically feel vulnerable, confused, helpless, and dependent on others for even the simplest decisions; (b) a *recoil* phase, characterized by mood swings and a "waxing and waning" of fear, rage, revenge fantasies, and displacement of anger (often onto loved ones); and (c) a *reorganization* phase, when survivors assimilate their painful experience, put it into perspective, and get on with their lives. Most victims successfully negotiate these stages of recovery, although not necessarily in a linear sequence and often only after a period of several years (Sales, Baum, and Shore 1984). The victimization is not likely ever to be entirely forgotten, however; the self can no longer be regarded as invulnerable. Survivors must nevertheless reestablish a perception of the world as not entirely threatening, as a meaningful place in which most events make sense. Additionally they must regain self-perceptions as worthy, strong, and autonomous (Janoff-Bulman and Frieze 1983b).

Psychological Consequences of Heterosexist Stigma

In addition to the victimization for which all Americans are at risk, lesbians and gay men are targeted for attack specifically because of their sexual orientation (Berrill 1990). The psychological consequences of antigay hate crimes must be examined against the background of cultural heterosexism. Heterosexism is an ideological system that denies, denigrates, and stigmatizes any nonheterosexual form of behavior, identity, relationship, or community (Herek 1990). American culture is pervaded by a heterosexist ideology that simultaneously makes lesbians and gay men invisible and legitimizes hostility, discrimination, and even violence against them (Herek 1990). Heterosexist stigma also creates two interrelated challenges that lesbians and gay men must confront in the course of their psychosocial development: overcoming internalized homophobia and coming out.

Because most children internalize society's ideology of sex and gender at an early age, gay women and men usually experience some degree of negative feeling toward themselves when they first recognize their own homosexuality in adolescence or adulthood. This sense of *internalized homophobia* often creates a "basic mistrust for one's sexual and interpersonal identity" (Stein and Cohen 1984, p. 61) and interferes with the process of identity formation (Malyon 1982). Coming out[1] becomes a process of reclaiming disowned or devalued parts of the self, and developing an identity into which one's sexuality is well integrated (Malyon 1982; Stein and Cohen 1984).

In the course of coming out, most lesbians and gay men successfully overcome the threats to psychological well-being posed by heterosexism. Psychological adjustment appears to be highest among men and women who are committed to their gay identity and do not attempt to hide their homosexuality from others (Bell and Weinberg 1978; Hammersmith and Weinberg 1973). As with other stigmatized minorities, gay men and lesbians probably maintain self-esteem most effectively when they identify with, and are integrated into, the larger gay community (Crocker and Major 1989). Conversely people with a homosexual orientation who have not yet come out, who feel compelled to suppress their homoerotic urges, who wish they could become heterosexual or who are isolated from the gay community, may experience significant psychological distress, including impairment of self-esteem (Bell and Weinberg 1978; Hammersmith and Weinberg 1973; Malyon 1982; Weinberg and Williams 1974; see also Hodges and Hutter

1979). Chronically hiding one's sexual orientation can create a painful discrepancy between public and private identities (Humphreys 1972; see also Goffman 1963), feelings of inauthenticity, and social isolation (Goffman 1963; Jones et al. 1984).[2]

Victimization of Lesbians and Gay Men

Consequences for the Victim

When people are attacked because they are perceived to be gay, the consequences of victimization converge with those of societal heterosexism to create a unique set of challenges for the survivor. Perhaps most important is that the victim's homosexuality becomes directly linked to the heightened sense of vulnerability that normally follows victimization. One's homosexual orientation consequently may be experienced as a source of pain and punishment rather than intimacy, love, and community. Internalized homophobia may reappear or be intensified. Attempts to make sense of the attack, coupled with the common need to perceive the world as a just place, may lead to feelings that one has been justifiably punished for being gay (Bard and Sangrey 1979; Lerner 1970). Such characterological self-blame can lead to feelings of depression and helplessness (Janoff-Bulman 1979), even in individuals who are comfortable with their sexual orientation.

The aftermath of victimization probably is affected by the survivor's stage in the coming-out process (e.g., Cass 1979; Troiden 1988). Those who have come out have already faced a major threat to their self-esteem and have emerged intact and possibly stronger for the experience. Additionally lesbians and gay men in the course of coming out may develop coping skills (i.e., a "crisis competence"; Kimmel 1978), which they subsequently can use when new life crises occur. Coming out does not "prepare" gay men and women for subsequent victimization, but it does provide them with tools they can use in coping: supportive social networks, community resources, and nonheterosexist interpretations of the victimization experience. Lesbian and gay male survivors, who are in the later stages of coming out before their assault, have the benefit of being able to balance their victimization experience against many other positive experiences associated with being gay.

Women and men who are still in the early stages of coming out, in contrast, are unlikely to have the requisite social support and strongly developed gay identity that can increase their psychological resilience and coping skills (Miranda and Storms 1989). Like closeted gay men with AIDS, closeted survivors of victimization face the prospect of a double disclosure — that they are gay and that they were victimized or have AIDS — with increased risks for stigmatization (e.g., Herek and Glunt 1988). If the survivor's homosexuality becomes known, heterosexual family members or friends may blame the victimization on it. Lacking a more positive interpretation and feeling especially vulnerable to others' influence, the survivor may well accept this characterological attribution (e.g., Bard and Sangrey 1979) and its attendant feelings of helplessness, depression, and low self-esteem. If closeted survivors can avoid public disclosure of their sexual orientation in such a potentially hostile setting as a police station, they are likely not to report the victimization. They may even minimize or deny its impact to themselves, a tactic that can intensify and delay the resolution of psychological and physical problems (Anderson 1982; Koss and Burkhart 1989; Myers 1989).

Sexual Assault

Antigay sexual assault may give rise to unique problems in addition to the reactions described above. Lesbians may be directly targeted for sexual assault by antigay attackers, or raped "opportunistically" (i.e., when the perpetrator of another crime inadvertently discovers that his victim is a lesbian).[3] Rapists often verbalize the view that lesbians are "open targets" and deserve punishment because they are not under the protection of a man. Because many lesbians are not accustomed to feeling dependent on or vulnerable around men, a sexual attack motivated by male rage at their lifestyle constitutes a major assault on their general sense of safety, independence, and well-being. Any physiological response by the victim during the assault or the decision not to resist can raise doubts later regarding her complicity or her sexuality. Such doubts may be exacerbated by reactions from significant others when she describes details of, or feelings about, the victimization experience.

In addition to the humiliation and degradation that are common components of all sexual victimization, antilesbian rape may also include attempts by the perpetrator to degrade lesbian sexuality. For example, a lesbian couple sought counseling from one of the authors (Levy) after they were forced at gunpoint to engage in sexual behaviors together, then raped. When behaviors that formerly were expressions of love become associated with humiliation, violence, and victimization, lesbian partners can experience serious difficulty redefining their sexuality positively.

Male-male sexual assault is largely an invisible problem in contemporary American society, often assumed to occur only in prisons and similar settings. The few reports that have been published, however, indicate that it is a serious problem outside institutions (Anderson 1982; Kaufman et al. 1980; Myers 1989). As with rape of females by males, male-male rape is a crime of violence — often antigay violence — rather than a crime of sexuality (Anderson 1982; Groth and Burgess 1980; Kaufman et al. 1980). Contrary to popular stereotype, the perpetrators of male rape often identify themselves as heterosexual (Groth and Burgess 1980). Whereas the feminist movement has made important gains in sensitizing law enforcement personnel, caregivers, and society at large to the problems faced by female rape survivors, male rape survivors remain hidden and isolated. Although victims of male-male rape may be either heterosexual or gay, we focus here on the special mental health consequences for gay men.

Male gender-role socialization creates distinct problems for gay male rape survivors. Because most men have internalized the societal belief that sexual assault of men is beyond the realm of possibility, the male victim's sudden confrontation with "his own vulnerability, helplessness, and dependence on the mercy of others" can be devastating (Anderson 1982, p. 150). Men may have trouble accepting their rape experience as real, not only because it happened to them but because it happened at all. This may interfere with their subsequent recovery. If internalized homophobia resurfaces or is intensified, gay male survivors may interpret the rape as punishment for their sexual orientation, with all the attendant problems detailed above. If a man did not resist, he may later blame himself and wonder whether he somehow was complicitous in the rape. Self-doubts are especially likely to follow when the assailant successfully forces the victim to ejaculate in the course of the assault (Groth and Burgess 1980). The victim may retrospectively confuse ejaculation with orgasm and may interpret his own physiological response as a sign of personal consent to the rape. Paralleling the experience of some lesbian rape victims, gay men may experience their sexual assault as an attempt to degrade gay male sexuality, which may later give rise to fearful or aversive feelings associated with their normal sexual behavior.

Words Can Never Hurt Me? Consequences of Verbal Victimization

Most discussions of antigay hate crimes focus on physical and sexual assaults. Yet verbal harassment and intimidation are the most common forms of victimization of lesbians and gay men; most survey respondents report that they have been the target of antigay verbal abuse (Berrill 1990). Although researchers, practitioners, and policy makers alike may be tempted to recall the children's chant that "sticks and stones may break my bones," the potentially damaging effects of "mere" words should not be minimized.

Most people in American society find epithets such as *nigger* and *kike* to be offensive precisely because they convey raw hatred and prejudice. Such words have been used historically by oppressors to remind the oppressed of their subordinate status (Unger 1979). Similar levels of hatred are conveyed by words such as *faggot, dyke,* and *queer,* and the threats of violence (implicit and explicit) that accompany them. Such antigay verbal abuse constitutes a symbolic form of violence and a routine reminder of the ever present threat of physical assault. Its "cost" to the perpetrator in time, energy, and risk is minimal, yet it reinforces the target's sense of being an outsider in American society, a member of a disliked and devalued minority, and a socially acceptable target for violence.

Like hate-motivated physical violence, antigay verbal assault challenges the victim's routine sense of security and invulnerability, making the world seem more malevolent and less predictable. The psychological effects of verbal abuse may be as severe as those following physical assaults, and possibly more insidious because victims of verbal abuse may find its "psychic scars" more difficult to identify than physical wounds. It affects how one feels about oneself with no physical injury to which to attribute the feelings. Two of us (Garnets and Levy) have observed that victims often minimize the impact of a hate-motivated verbal attack and subsequently do not understand the reason for their feelings of fear or self-hatred.

Because verbal abuse may be experienced as a near encounter with violence, it can seriously restrict day-to-day behaviors of lesbians and gay men. Most gay respondents to victimization surveys indicate that their public behavior is affected by their fear of physical attack (Berrill 1990). Verbal harassment and intimidation reinforce this climate of fear. Not knowing whether a specific instance of verbal harassment is likely to culminate in physical violence, many gay women and men probably follow the adaptive strategy of avoiding possible occasions of verbal abuse just as they avoid potential assault situations. Consequently their day-to-day behaviors are restricted, and they lose considerable control over their lives. Victims who are more closeted may experience heterosexist verbal abuse as an involuntary public disclosure of their sexual orientation. They may respond by withdrawing even further into the closet.

Consequences of Victimization for Others

In the aftermath of antigay violence, victims turn to significant others for social support. A lover, family, and friends can greatly enhance a survivor's coping resources (Bard and Sangrey 1979). Yet these others also must deal with the victimization experience. In cases of murder, they must cope with the physical loss of the victim; with other crimes, they must deal with the survivor's immediate reactions (including her or his displaced feelings of anger). They must make sense of the event for themselves and deal with their own self-blame. Same-sex partners are at special risk for secondary victimization (Berrill and Herek 1990) as they assist the survivor in seeking services. They may be denied access to hospital visitation, for example, because they are not considered "immediate family." They are likely not to be eligible for, or recognized by, social workers or victim assistance agencies. Indeed, much of the post-attack experience may serve to remind a gay couple that the larger society is hostile to them as gay people.

In addition to the victim's significant others, the entire gay community is victimized by antigay assaults. Hate crimes create a climate of fear that pressures lesbians and gay men to hide their sexual orientation. Needing to reduce their own feelings of vulnerability, some members of the community are likely to blame the victims of violence, often focusing on "obvious" behavior, gestures, or clothing. Such victim blaming reinforces key aspects of the cultural ideology of heterosexism, such as the prescription that men and women should conform to highly restrictive norms of gender-appropriate behavior[4] and the belief that being gay is wrong and deserves punishment (Herek 1990). Victim-blaming also may discourage observers from taking precautions for reducing their risk of victimization — both personal precautions, such as taking a self-defense class, and community precautions, such as organizing neighborhood street patrols.

Suggestions for Mental Health Practitioners

As a crisis, antigay victimization creates opportunities for growth, both at the individual and community levels. Survivors who cope successfully may infuse their lives with greater meaning or purpose than before and enjoy a strengthened sense of self-worth. They may take control of parts of their lives that they previously had not been able to manage while at the same time accepting that some events are beyond their control (Burt and Katz 1987).

They may redefine previous setbacks they experienced as the result of prejudice rather than personal failings, thereby increasing their self-esteem (e.g., Crocker and Major 1989). Previously complacent survivors may become outraged by the injustice of their victimization and may become politically militant (e.g., Birt and Dion 1987), with a subsequent increase in feelings of self-efficacy and empowerment. Violence may shock community members into taking collective action that channels their feelings of helplessness and anger (for an example, see Wertheimer 1990). Perhaps the most famous example of a positive community response to victimization was the 1969 "Stonewall Rebellion," which followed a police raid on a Greenwich Village gay bar and marked the beginning of the modern movement for gay rights (e.g., D'Emilio 1983).

Mental health practitioners can help gay male and lesbian victims of hate crimes maximize the positive aspects of their response. Before working with lesbian or gay male victims, however, professional caregivers must be aware of their own heterosexist biases and assumptions, and should be familiar with current and accurate information about gay male and lesbian identity, community, and mental health concerns. Among the basic assumptions to be avoided are that a homosexual identity or lifestyle is negative and unhealthy, that all clients are heterosexual unless they identify themselves as gay, and that biological family members necessarily constitute a client's significant others. In reality, homosexuality is not correlated with psychopathology; many crime victims are gay but do not choose to come out; and gay clients may define their family in terms of a same-sex lover and gay friends (Cohen and Stein 1986; Gonsiorek and Weinrich 1991; Morin and Charles 1983). Professionals should carefully respect confidentiality concerning clients' sexual orientation. In most jurisdictions, gay people whose sexual orientation becomes known to others can lose their jobs or apartments, lose custody of their children, and even be liable to criminal prosecution (Berrill and Herek 1990). Professionals who fail to understand these potentially negative consequences can themselves become secondary victimizers (e.g., by inadvertently revealing a client's sexual orientation to law enforcement personnel).

Practitioners should be aware of the different needs and experiences of gay men and lesbians from different sectors of the gay community. Although space limitations do not permit its consideration here, the mental health consequences of antigay victimization are likely to vary according to the survivor's race, age, and social class, among other variables.

For heuristic purposes, mental health interventions with gay male and lesbian survivors can be conceptualized according to the *impact, recoil,* and *recovery* phases described by Bard and Sangrey (1979). Crisis interventions are necessary in the *impact* phase, when the first concern is whether the victim is safe from further attacks and whether she or he requires immediate medical care. The focus of the crisis intervention is assessing the meaning that the victim is deriving from her or his experience, feelings about self, and the degree to which the victimization is equated with being gay or lesbian. Additionally, the mental health professional should assess internal and external coping resources: (a) learned coping skills; (b) support networks, such as a lover, family, or friends who can assist the victim in meeting immediate needs; and (c) existing or potential involvement in gay and lesbian community networks. Previously effective coping skills usually are not adequate to deal with the shock and fear of this stage of the reaction to physical or sexual violence. Assessment will suggest, to victim and practitioner alike, ways to build on previous coping resources or the need to develop new ones.

In the *recoil* phase, mental health professionals can help greatly by allowing survivors to ventilate the horror and terror that the victimization evokes. By listening empathically, the professional can give the survivor, who is feeling alienated and isolated, a sense of connection to another person. The therapeutic goal at this stage is to support victims as they regain their self-confidence and sense of competence and wholeness, and while their feelings of guilt, shame, helplessness, and embarrassment diminish.

Reducing the Negative Affect

Survivors should be encouraged to feel and express anger toward the assailant(s), especially survivors who are blaming themselves or are depressed (Bard and Sangrey 1979; Bohn 1984). Anger can be constructively directed, for example, by encouraging involvement in activist groups organized against antigay violence or in self-defense classes. Intervening to prevent self-blaming and guilt feelings involves helping the survivor to review decisions made before, during, and after the assault. In order to combat the distorted retrospective perceptions that lead to self-blame, survivors need to remember that their decisions were based on their perceptions and knowledge *at the time of the attack,* in a life-threatening situation. The aim is for survivors to see that they responded the best they could under the circumstances (Levy and Brown 1984).

Victims who manifest the symptoms of posttraumatic stress disorder may benefit from recently developed strategies that aim to reexpose the survivor to the memory of the traumatic event. These strategies include systematic desensitization, flooding or implosive therapy, and stress inoculation. Reexposure is accompanied by techniques of cognitive restructuring of false assumptions about oneself and the world (e.g., self-blame and the view of the world as malevolent; Fairbank, Gross, and Keane 1983; Frank et al. 1988; Steketee and Foa 1987). The cognition that "bad things happen because I am gay" can be reformulated to "bad things happen."

Gay male and lesbian survivors of hate violence often have to cope with negative feelings specifically about their sexual identity. If victimization has forced premature disclosure of the survivor's gay identity, it may have amplified the feelings of vulnerability, alienation, and exposure that often are part of the coming-out process. These feelings must be explored with the aim of separating the victimization experience from the coming-out experience. In addition, the survivor must be helped to feel the positive effects of disclosing her or his identity that are also part of coming out. When survivors who are in the later stages of coming out question their homosexuality as a result of the assault, the practitioner should review the bases for the client's coming-out decisions of the past, with the aim of reestablishing her or his positive identity as a lesbian or gay man.

Facilitating a Positive Affect

Self-confidence can be mended through consciousness raising, which can help survivors to locate their victimization in a social context. Understanding that the crime was based on global hatred that has its roots in a heterosexist society can relieve the survivor's feelings of being personally targeted and blameful. As Bohn (1984) noted, group work may be especially valuable for gay survivors because it permits identification with other lesbian and gay male victims and helps them to realize that they are not alone. Gay survivors in groups can share their reactions to victimization, express their anger, and develop analyses of their victimization that bond them to the larger gay community and its support systems.

Survivors inevitably are faced with the question of whether to report their victimization. At some point in the recovery process, this decision must be explored. In addition to its importance for the criminal justice system, reporting the incident has several potential benefits for the survivor. It can offer a constructive channel for anger, increase feelings of efficacy, and pro-vide the satisfaction of helping to protect other members of the community from the sort of victimization one has experienced. At the same time, sur-vivors should not be led to believe that reporting the crime necessarily will lead to arrest and prosecution of the attackers; indeed, such a result is un-likely in many cases (e.g., Bard and Sangrey 1979). The practitioner assists the survivor in weighing the benefits and risks in reporting, and ensures that the survivor makes her or his own decision. Because reporting also may lead to secondary victimization by insensitive or prejudiced criminal justice per-sonnel (Berrill and Herek 1990), an increase in the survivor's sense of power-lessness can be prevented if the practitioner helps the survivor to become adequately prepared and to develop a good support system.

Working through these many issues and feelings eventually permits the survivor to integrate the experience of victimization into her or his larger worldview and to get on with life. This *reorganization* process may require considerable time to complete, especially if a victim denies or represses awareness of the victimization for months or even years after it occurs (Koss and Burkhart 1989; Myers 1989). Greater involvement with the gay com-munity is likely to be particularly helpful in achieving reorganization.

Interventions After Sexual Assault

Survivors of antigay sexual assault need to separate the victimization from their experience of sexuality and intimacy, and develop positive feelings about sexual expression that are not intruded upon by images of the assault. Gay male survivors are at special risk for phobic or aversive feelings toward male sexuality because their normal sexual behavior will superficially resem-ble the sexual assault (if for no other reason than that both involve another male). Lesbian survivors also may experience fear reactions and flashbacks to the assault triggered by normal sexual contact. Practitioners must support survivors (and their partners) to allow healing time for the fear to diminish. Survivors should be encouraged to initiate sexual contact in stages and to determine their own readiness for gradually increasing sexual involvement. The aim is to regain a sense of being in charge of one's own body, in contrast to the powerlessness and fear experienced during the assault.

Practitioners should be aware of the heterosexist bias that sexual assault survivors may experience if they come in contact with the criminal justice or medical systems. For example, police may not believe that male-male rape occurs, may be hostile, or may assume that, because he is gay, the victim deserved or brought on the attack (Anderson 1982). Physicians and emergency room staff may assume that a lesbian rape victim is heterosexual, and consequently display insensitivity in asking questions about previous sexual experience, contraception, and significant others (Orzek 1988). Practitioners play an important role by advocating for survivors, helping them to advocate more effectively for themselves, and educating other professionals about sensitive responses to gay male and lesbian clients.

Interventions with Significant Others

Lovers, family, and friends also must deal with the losses and hardships imposed by the victimization, make sense of it, and regain a perception of the world as a stable and predictable place. Sometimes a lover or best friend will also have been victimized in the attack. In cases where the victims cannot provide each other with primary support as they ordinarily would, both survivors may need assistance in expanding their support networks.

Mental health professionals must respond to the needs of significant others while at the same time helping them to respond, in turn, to the victim's needs. Professionals may need to educate the significant others about the dynamics of violence, defuse their fears, and encourage their support for the primary victim. Significant others might benefit from exposure to educational materials (printed, audio, video) about homosexuality, victimization, and hate crimes. When internalized homophobia among significant others (gay and lesbian as well as heterosexual) makes it difficult for them to be supportive, professionals should assist the survivor in handling others' negative or nonsupportive reactions (e.g., through role playing).

Conclusion

The trauma associated with antigay victimization may become linked to survivors' homosexuality. Although this often results in intensification of psychosocial problems associated with being gay or lesbian, it also may lead to further consolidation of the survivor's gay or lesbian identity and involvement with her or his community. Mental health practitioners can play an important role by assisting lesbian and gay male survivors, their significant others, and their communities in successfully reconstructing survivors' lives and mobilizing confrontation of hate crimes as a community problem. Researchers have an important role to play in filling gaps in information about the mental health consequences of antigay hate crimes, and the effectiveness of individual and community-based intervention strategies. Most important, mental health practitioners and researchers should work with the lesbian and gay community to develop public awareness and comprehensive programs to prevent hate-motivated violence.

Notes

1. *Coming out* (a shortened form of *coming out of the closet*) refers to the sequence of events through which individuals recognize their own homosexual orientation and disclose it to others. Conversely, being *in the closet* or *closeted* refers to passing as heterosexual (e.g., Dynes 1985). Coming out is a continuous process: After coming out to oneself, one is continually meeting new people to whom one's sexual orientation must be disclosed. Consequently different gay people are out to varying degrees.

2. Attempting to pass as heterosexual may increase some individuals' risk for victimization. Men who are hiding their homosexuality may be more prone to victimization when they seek sexual partners outside the relative safety of the gay community (e.g., Harry 1982; Miller and Humphreys 1980; for an autobiographical account, see Bauman 1980). Additionally, because of the stigma attached to homosexuality and because discrimination against lesbians and gay men remains legal in most jurisdictions (see Herek 1990), closeted lesbians and gay men alike can be blackmailed with threatened involuntary revelation of their sexual orientation to family, employers, or others (Bell and Weinberg 1978; Harry 1982; Rofes 1983).

3. Currently operational definitions of hate crimes exclude male-female sexual assault unless the perpetrator can be shown to have attacked some aspect of the victim's identity other than her gender (e.g., her race, religion, or sexual orientation). Because space limitations prevent us from considering this definitional issue in detail, we focus here on the mental health consequences of male-female sexual assaults in which the victim is a lesbian and is targeted because of her sexual orientation (for more general discussions of the aftermath of sexual assault, see, e.g., Brownmiller 1975; Burgess 1985; Ledray 1986).

4. Heterosexuals, too, are victimized by antigay hate crimes (Berrill 1990). The threat of victimization probably also causes many heterosexuals to conform to gender roles and to restrict their expressions of (nonsexual) physical affection for members of their own sex (e.g., Herek 1986).

References

American Psychiatric Association. 1987. *Diagnostic and Statistical Manual of Mental Disorders*. 3rd rev. ed. Washington, D.C.: Author.

Anderson, C. L. 1982. Males as sexual assault victims: Multiple levels of trauma. *Journal of Homosexuality* 7(2/3):145–62.

Bard, M., and D. Sangrey. 1979. *The Crime Victim's Book*. New York: Basic Books.

Bauman, R. 1986. *The Gentleman from Maryland: The Conscience of a Gay Conservative*. New York: Arbor House.

Bell, A. P., and M. S. Weinberg. 1978. *Homosexualities: A Study of Diversity Among Men and Women*. New York: Simon and Schuster.

Berrill, K. T. 1990. Violence and victimization of lesbians and gay men: Mental health consequences. *Journal of Interpersonal Violence* 5(3):274–94.

Berrill, K. T., and G. M. Herek. 1990. Primary and secondary victimization. *Journal of Interpersonal Violence* 5(3):401–13.

Birt, C. M., and K. L. Dion. 1987. Relative deprivation theory and responses to discrimination in a gay male and lesbian sample. *British Journal of Social Psychology* 26:139–45.

Bohn, T. R. 1984. Homophobic violence: Implications for social work practice. In R. Schoenberg and R. S. Goldberg, eds., *With Compassion Toward Some: Homosexuality and Social Work in America*. New York: Harrington Park.

Brownmiller, S. 1975. *Against Our Will: Men, Women, and Rape*. New York: Simon and Schuster.

Burgess, A. W., ed. 1985. *Rape and Sexual Assault: A Research Handbook*. New York: Garland.

Burt, M. R., and B. L. Katz. 1987. Dimensions of recovery from rape: Focus on growth outcomes. *Journal of Interpersonal Violence* 2:57–81.

Caplan, G. 1964. *Principles of Preventive Psychiatry*. New York: Basic Books.

Cass, V. 1979. Homosexual identity formation: A theoretical model. *Journal of Homosexuality* 4(3):219–35.

Coates, D., C. B. Wortman, and A. Abbey. 1979. Reactions to victims. In I. H. Frieze, D. Bar-Tal, and J. S. Carroll, eds., *New Approaches to Social Problems*, pp. 21–52. San Francisco: Jossey-Bass.

Cohen, C., and T. Stein. 1986. *Psychotherapy with Lesbians and Gay Men*. New York: Plenum.

Crocker, J., and B. Major. 1989. Social stigma and self-esteem: The self-protective properties of stigma. *Psychological Review* 96:608–30.

D'Emilio, J. 1983. *Sexual Politics, Sexual Communities: The Making of a Homosexual Minority in the United States, 1940–1970*. Chicago: University of Chicago Press.

Dynes, W. 1985. *Homolexis: A Historical and Cultural Lexicon of Homosexuality*. New York: Gay Academic Union.

Fairbank, J. A., R. Gross, and T. M. Keane. 1983. Treatment of posttraumatic stress disorder. *Behavior Modification* 7:557–67.

Frank, E., B. Anderson, B. D. Stewart, C. Danou, C Hughes, and D. West. 1988. Efficacy of cognitive behavior therapy and systematic desensitization in the treatment of rape trauma. *Behavior Therapy* 19:403–20.

Frederick, C. J. 1987. Psychic trauma in victims of crime and terrorism. In G. VandenBos and B. Bryant, eds., *Cataclysms, Crises, and Catastrophes: Psychology in Action*, pp. 59–108. Washington, D.C.: American Psychological Association.

Frieze, I. H., S. Hymer, and M. S. Greenberg. 1984. Describing the victims of crime and violence. In A. Kahn, ed., *Victims of Crime and Violence: Final Report of the APA Task Force on the Victims of Crime and Violence*, pp. 19–78. Washington, D.C.: American Psychological Association.

Goffman, E. 1963. *Stigma: Notes on the Management of Spoiled Identity*. Englewood Cliffs, N.J.: Prentice-Hall.

Gonsiorek, J. C. 1982. Results of psychological testing on homosexual populations. *American Behavioral Scientist* 25:385–96.

Gonsiorek, J. C., and J. D. Weinrich. 1991. *Homosexuality: Social Psychological and Biological Issues*. 2nd ed. Newbury Park, Calif.: Sage.

Groth, A. N., and A. W. Burgess. 1980. Male rape: Offenders and victims. *American Journal of Psychiatry* 137:806–10.

Hammersmith, S. K., and M. S. Weinberg. 1973. Homosexual identity: Commitment, adjustment, and significant others. *Sociometry* 36:(1):56–79.

Harry, J. 1982. Derivative deviance: The cases of extortion, fag-bashing, and shakedown of gay men. *Criminology* 19:546–64.

Herek, G. M. 1986. On heterosexual masculinity: Some psychical consequences of the social construction of gender and sexuality. *American Behavioral Scientist* 29:563–77.

Herek, G. M. 1989. Hate crimes against lesbians and gay men: Issues for research and policy. *American Psychologist* 44:948–55.

Herek, G. M. 1990. The contents of anti-gay violence: Notes on cultural and psychological heterosexism. *Journal of Interpersonal Violence* 5:316–33.

Herek, G. M. 1991. Stigma, prejudice, and violence against lesbians and gay men. In J. Gonsiorek and J. Weinrich, eds., *Homosexuality: Social, Psychological, and Biological Issues*, 2nd ed. Newbury Park, Calif.: Sage.

Herek, G. M., and E. K. Glunt. 1988. An epidemic of stigma: Public reactions to AIDS. *American Psychologist* 43:886–91.

Hodges, A., and D. Hutter. 1979. *With downcast gays: Aspects of homosexual self-oppression*. 2nd ed. Toronto: Pink Triangle.

Humphreys, L. 1972. *Out of the Closets: The Sociology of Homosexual Liberation*. Englewood Cliffs, N.J.: Prentice-Hall.

Janoff-Bulman, R. 1979. Characterological versus behavioral self-blame: Inquiries into depression and rape. *Journal of Personality and Social Psychology* 37:1798–1809.

Janoff-Bulman, R. 1982. Esteem and control bases of blame: "Adaptive" strategies for victims versus observers. *Journal of Personality* 50:180–92.

Janoff-Bulman, R., and I. H. Frieze, eds. 1983a. Reactions to victimization [Special issue]. *Journal of Social Issues* 39(2).

Janoff-Bulman, R., and I. H. Frieze. 1983b. A theoretical perspective for understanding reactions to victimization. *Journal of Social Issues* 39(2):1–17.

Jones, E. E., A. Farina, A. H. Hastorf, H. Markus, D. T. Miller, and R. A. Scott. 1984. *Social Stigma: The Psychology of Marked Relationships.* New York: Freeman.

Kaufman, A., P. DiVasto, R. Jackson, D. Voorhees, and J. Christy. 1980. Male rape victims: Noninstitutionalized assault. *American Journal of Psychiatry* 137(2): 221–23.

Kimmel, D.C. 1978. Adult development and aging: A gay perspective. *Journal of Social Issues* 34(3):113–30.

Koss, M. P., and B. R. Burkhart. 1989. A conceptual analysis of rape victimization: Long-term effects and implications for treatment. *Psychology of Women Quarterly* 13:27–40.

Ledray, L. E. 1986. *Recovering from Rape.* New York: Holt, Rinehart, and Winston.

Lerner, M. J. 1970. The desire for justice and reactions to victims. In J. Macaulay and L. Berkowitz, eds., *Altruism and Helping Behavior*, pp. 205–29. New York: Academic Press.

Levy, B., and V. Brown. 1984. Strategies for crisis intervention with victims of violence. In S. Saunders, A. Anderson, C. Hart, and G. Rubenstein, eds., *Violent Individuals and Families: A Handbook for Practitioners*, pp. 57–68. Springfield, Ill.: Charles C Thomas.

Malyon, A. K. 1982. Psychotherapeutic implications of internalized homophobia in gay men. *Journal of Homosexuality* 7(2/3):59–69.

Miller, B., and L. Humphreys. 1980. Lifestyles and violence: Homosexual victims of assault and murder. *Qualitative Sociology* 3(3):169–85.

Miranda, J., and M. Storms. 1989. Psychological adjustment of lesbians and gay men. *Journal of Counseling and Development* 68:41–45.

Morin, S., and K. Charles. 1983. Heterosexual bias in psychotherapy. In J. Murray and P. R. Abramson, eds., *Bias in Psychotherapy*, pp. 309–38. New York: Praeger.

Myers, M. F. 1989. Men sexually assaulted as adults and sexually abused as boys. *Archives of Sexual Behavior* 18:203–15.

Orzek, A.M. 1988. The lesbian victim of sexual assault: Special considerations for the mental health professional. *Women and Therapy* 8(1/2):107–17.

Rofes, E. E. 1983. *"I Thought People like That Killed Themselves": Lesbians, Gay Men, and Suicide.* San Francisco: Grey Fox.

Sales, E., M. Baum, and B. Shore. 1984. Victim readjustment following assault. *Journal of Social Issues* 40(1):117–36.

Stein, T. S., and C. J. Cohen. 1984. Psychotherapy with gay men and lesbians: An examination of homophobia, coming out, and identity. In E. S. Hetrick and T. S. Stein, eds., *Innovations in Psychotherapy with Homosexuals*, pp. 60–73. Washington, D.C.: American Psychiatric Press.

Steketee, M. S., and E. B. Foa. 1987. Rape victims: Post-traumatic stress responses and their treatment. *Journal of Anxiety Disorders* 1:69–86.

Troiden, R. 1988. *Gay and Lesbian Identity: A Sociological Analysis*. New York: General Hall.

Tsegaye-Spates, C. R. 1985. The mental health needs of victims: An introduction to the literature. In A. W. Burgess, ed., *Rape and Sexual Assault: A Research Handbook*, pp. 35–45. New York: Garland.

Unger, R. 1979. *Female and Male: Psychological Perspectives*. New York: Harper and Row.

Weinberg, M. S., and C. J. Williams. 1974. *Male Homosexuals: Their Problems and Adaptations*. New York: Oxford University Press.

Wertheimer, D. M. 1990. Treatment and service intervention for lesbian and gay male crime victims. *Journal of Interpersonal Violence* 5(3):384–400.

8 Matthew Shepard's Death: A Professional Awakening

Ritch C. Savin-Williams

Silence killed Matthew Shepard . . . A young man's heart has
ceased to beat. Hear the silence of that awful truth. It is the
silence of death. It is the silence that descends on us like a
shroud . . . Our fear comes in many forms but it always comes
silently. A whispered joke. A glance to look away from the truth.
A quick shake of the head to deny any complicity in the pain of
others. These silent acts of our own fear of homosexuality are
acted out on this campus every day, just as they are acted out
every day in Wyoming. Through silence, we give ourselves
permission to practice what we pretend to abhor. With silence,
we condemn scores of our neighbors to lie in the shadows of
hate. In silence, we observe the suffering of any group of people
who have been declared expendable by our society.
–Rt. Rev. Steven Charleston
Chaplain, Trinity College
Hartford, Connecticut

Sixty-eight percent of North Americans believe the attack
against college freshman Matthew Shepard could have happened in their
community (Time/CNN Poll 1998). Within a week of the Wyoming murder,
a Colorado State University fraternity mocked Matthew's death in their
homecoming parade float by hanging a beaten scarecrow from a fence with
a sign, "I am Gay." A lesbian student at St. Cloud State University in Minnesota suffered cuts and bruises after two men attacked her, just hours after
an antihate crimes campus vigil honoring Matthew Shepard ("Lesbian College Student" 1998). Leonard "Lynn" Vines, a gay drag queen, was shot six
times by a group of Baltimore youths who shouted that they did not allow

"no drag queen faggot bitches" in their neighborhood. Leonard survived, but many do not. Liz Seaton, executive director of the Free State Justice Campaign, said in a press release:

> What happened in Wyoming is happening everywhere and it is happening here. It is time for people to wake up, to recognize that bias does lead to violence, and to take action. Fair-minded citizens must take a stand that anti-gay bias is not acceptable under any circumstances. (Seaton 1998)

Could Matthew's murder and the violence against Leonard, the Minnesota lesbian, and many other lesbian, gay, bisexual, and transgender individuals have been prevented? Perhaps. This violence has its roots in our culture's tolerance of children calling each other "faggot" and "dyke," of teachers who do not correct or stop gay-related name calling, and of parents who do not admonish children who have destructive stereotypes and myths about gay people. One need not be a perpetrator of violence to be a murderer. The bystander plays an important role in facilitating expressions of hatred and violence. Several years before Matthew's murder by two Laramie, Wyoming, young adult men, a local billboard advertising guns had been altered from "Shoot a day or two" to "Shoot a gay or two." For more than a month, hundreds, if not thousands, of residents had remained silent, until a visiting gay activist had it erased (New York Times News Service 1998). How many well-educated, liberal, scholarly men and women had passed the billboard and chose to do nothing? Perhaps a few social scientists were among those who decided to ignore the "humor."

In our silence we contribute to the figurative and, at times, literal deaths of sexual-minority family members, friends, clients, and colleagues. We perpetuate myths and hatred, if not directly, then by assuming the role of passive bystander. In this paper, my intent is to illustrate instances of silence within our scholarly lives and to suggest alternatives that demonstrate our commitment to enhancing the lives of gay, lesbian, bisexual, and transgender individuals and their communities.

Professional Awakening

My first realization that it was not going to be an easy task to increase the sensitivity and understanding of my scholarly colleagues came several years ago after I was asked to review a manuscript on the sexual experiences of adolescents for one of our most reputable journals. The authors asserted that they had conducted a definitive study on adolescent sexual behavior. About midway through my review, it became apparent that they had neglected to assess sexual behavior between same-sex individuals. It was as if the authors had assumed in their research design that adolescent girls and boys — regardless of their sexual orientation — never date, kiss, make out, or have genital contact with someone of the same sex. Furthermore, the authors wrote that "puberty makes females sexually attractive to males." Aside from the sexist nature of this statement, the authors apparently did not consider the possibility that puberty also makes females sexually attractive to other females. The implicit message of the research was clear — to be sexual was to be heterosexual, at least in behavior.

In response to my review, the senior author sent a letter to the editor to convey to me that he saw little substance to my criticism, was not going to apologize for the heterosexist nature of his study, and requested that I never again review his work. However, he had conceded to insert the word *hetero-sexual* in the title of the paper. In nearly twenty-five years of reviewing man-uscripts, this remains the only letter I have received criticizing a review. Indeed, the author insisted that if I wanted changes in the manuscript, I had to demonstrate to him how his "failure to identify the small number of homosexually oriented males and females in the sample would bias our conclusions."

I was stunned by the arrogance and insensitivity of this scholar, by his refusal to acknowledge that his research was biased against adolescents with same-sex attractions and behavior, and by his belief in the preeminence of heterosexuality. I had not requested an apology, and I have little desire to review his work again — I simply wanted him to acknowledge the existence of "homosexually oriented" youths and to be more inclusive of diversity when investigating adolescent sexual behavior.

I learned two things from this experience: (a) Merely pointing out defi-ciencies in research designs that perpetuate the silence and stereotypes of sexual-minority youths is insufficient, and (b) those who profess knowledge and have highly positioned academic jobs are not necessarily the same in-dividuals who do what is right. Although this saddens me, even angers me at times, writing this guest editorial for *Applied Developmental Science* attests to my commitment to "keep trying." In the following pages I enumerate several ways in which scholars can be less "heterocentric" — that is, assuming heterosexuality is the central element of sexuality and interpreting all references to sexuality in this light — and more inclusive of nonheterosexuality. I hope that the readers of this volume, an audience I assume to be well-meaning and receptive to change, will find these relatively modest suggestions helpful. The consequences of your positive actions may very well save the lives of other Matthew Shepards.

Include Sexual-Minority Relevant Variables in Research

The visibility of sexual minorities has exploded in popular culture but remains elusive within scientific pursuits. It is relatively easy and often rewarding (e.g., simplifying research designs) to ignore nonheterosexuality or to rationalize the exclusion of sexual minorities in our research and teaching. And, indeed, it is extraordinarily rare to read research reports that are "gay sensitive" or anything but blatantly *heterosexist* — a term used to denote discriminatory language and actions against nonheterosexuals. A recent example illustrates this blindness, whether intended or not I cannot say. A study purported to be "Canada's most comprehensive survey on sex and relationships" (Sonmor 1998:59) defined sexual activity as heterosexual sexual intercourse, dating as a relationship between a man and a woman, and relationships as heterosexual. It is unclear how someone with same-sex behaviors and desires is to respond to these questions. Must two women mock heterosexual intercourse through the use of a dildo before they are classified as having "sexual activity"? Is it inconceivable that two women or two men could date each other — to go out for dinner and catch a movie? Although those of the same sex cannot yet legally marry, many are committed to their romantic partner and treat their relationship as if they were married.

Investigators often explore the effects of gender, social class, religion, race, intelligence, and countless other human qualities in their empirical investigations but rarely is sexual orientation or identity included. Reasons for this exclusion may be "reasonable" — refusal of funding agencies to support controversial topics, subject recruitment sites (such as public schools) objecting to nonheterosexual survey or interview questions, and university human subjects committees eliminating such variables so as not to "endanger" heterosexual participants by exposing them to the harmful effects of answering questions regarding sexual orientation. But barriers can be hurdled. One exercise in ingenuity was demonstrated by the National Longitudinal Study of Adolescent Health, which overcame political threats (Jesse Helms) to withhold financial support by omitting all references to sexual orientation, sexual identity, and homosexual sexual behavior in the survey. However, they included the variable, "ever had same-sex romantic attractions or relationships" (Blum and Rinehart 1997). Hence considerable information is now available from a representative sample of adolescents who may or may not identify as lesbian, gay, or bisexual but who nevertheless have attractions to same-sex others. Many more of these creative solutions are necessary if research is to be more inclusive of sexual minorities and hence raise the visibility of those uninterested or uninspired by heterosexuality. By acknowledging the presence of same-sex attractions and behavior, nonheterosexuality is normalized, homosexuality becomes less of a polemical topic for discourse, and, with any luck, sexual minorities become less likely to be the objects of attack.

At Cornell we are attempting more than mere recognition of same-sex desires; we are exploring the significance of sexual orientation in many domains of human behavior. Unfortunately so little past research has attended to sexual identity-orientation issues that it is nearly impossible to hypothesize with precision the ways that sexual-minority populations differ from, or are similar to, heterosexuals. We have found in some domains that sexual orientation is a nonpredictor of human behavior, even where it is thought to be a decisive consideration. For example, some researchers have maintained, with a limited empirical base, that gay men are biologically distinguishable from heterosexual men in that they have an earlier onset of puberty (because gay brains were "inverted" in utero and thus they have the pubertal timing of the opposite sex). Others sample gays and lesbians in clinical settings and discover that "homosexuals" are psychologically deficient and have horrific relationships with others, especially parents. Research at Cornell during the last decade counters these claims: no difference in pubertal onset, equal self-esteem levels, little difference in suicide attempts, typical shifts in attachment from parents to peers during adolescence, comparable abilities to form and maintain romantic relationships, and very low percentages of parents rejecting their gay, lesbian, and bisexual children.

In other areas where lesbians, gays, and bisexuals are thought to resemble heterosexuals, we have empirically documented that sexual orientation influences cognitive abilities, the establishment and interpretation of same-sex friendships, ethnic identity, relations with family members, and developmental trajectories. Furthermore, even when sexual orientation sometimes appears to be a critical variable, as is generally believed for suicide attempts among adolescents, factors other than but related to sexual orientation are the strongest predictors. For example, peer harassment because of gender atypicality (often associated with being gay or lesbian), subject selection (eliciting early identifiers who are "out" in high school and thus at increased risk for mental health problems), and instrumentation (failure to distinguish false from true suicide attempts) explain a larger percentage of the variance; that is, it is not sexual orientation per se that leads to suicidal ideation and attempts but cultural reactions to a same-sex identification. By challenging agenda-oriented antigay research studies, refuting myths and modifying stereotypes, and providing accurate information, researchers can contribute to the accurate representation of sexual minorities—and thus perhaps decrease the conditions that lead to hate-based violence toward people like Matthew Shepard.

Incorporate Sexual-Minority Issues into Courses and Textbooks

Although I appreciate colleagues' efforts to be inclusive when they ask me to give "the gay lecture" in their courses, my strong preference would be for my colleagues to give the lecture themselves. This would indicate to me a deeper level of personal and professional investment and commitment to sexual-minority concerns. Even more appealing than having a "special" lecture or a reading on relevant sexual-minority issues is for teachers to integrate the lives of sexual-minority individuals throughout a course. For example, the topic of adolescent homosexuality is usually confined to a late chapter in adolescent textbooks, under headings titled "Sexuality," "Sexual Self," and "Sex and Dating" — as if being lesbian, bisexual, gay, or transgender is only about sex. If sexual minorities differ in physical growth characteristics, such as their physical shape and size, then these facts should be discussed in the "Physical Growth" chapter. If gay and lesbian adolescents disproportionately face particular difficulties in schools, are harassed by peers, or abuse substances, then these should be discussed in appropriate chapters. If sexual-minority youths have special intellectual or creative abilities and have made significant contributions to our culture, these, too, should be included. If two adolescents of the same sex fall in love, then the possibility ought to be acknowledged — and a photograph portraying their love should be included as well.

As with many adolescents, sex is important to these youths, but they are more than their sexual preferences, identities, and orientation. The aspect of Matthew that carried the most import to his murderers was his sexual orientation. Matthew, the Minnesota lesbian, and the drag queen are similar to all other adolescents but at the same time different, because of their sexuality. For example, all youths growing up in North America are aware that the worst putdown is to be called "dyke" or "faggot" and that many parents want their child to be anything but gay. A child with same-sex attractions living under these conditions has to be affected. It affects relations with family, peers, and, perhaps most important, the self. In our classrooms and scholarship we must recognize that sexual-minority individuals are unique as a group, perhaps for biological (brain organization) and environmental (growing up in a homonegative culture) reasons, but also that they differ among themselves in their life trajectories and in countless other ways (Savin-Williams 1998; Savin-Williams and Diamond 1997). Whether the course or text is on adolescence or on relationships, infancy, cognition, public policy, or psychopathology, sexual minorities and their lives should neither be ignored nor confined to a single lecture or reading but integrated within the spectrum of scholarly work. It is the representation of this wholeness that demonstrates the humanity of nonheterosexuals.

Extend Invitations to Experts on Sexual-Minority Issues

Complacency and sins of omission are omnipresent. Another example from my professional life is illustrative. The Society for Research on Adolescence (SRA) has never invited a speaker to their national conference to discuss any scholarly aspect of growing up gay or lesbian in today's world, and their widely distributed *Journal of Research on Adolescence* has not devoted a special issue to research on sexual-minority youths. In a correspondence with a highly placed officer of SRA about my forthcoming *SRA Newsletter* article in which I advocate that the organization take a proactive stance and include conversations about sexual-minority youths, the officer argued, "SRA is not an advocacy organization nor, in my opinion, should it be. . . . Although advocating on issues we care deeply about may enhance our moral credibility, more often than not it diminishes our scientific credibility." I disagree — SRA and many other professional organizations are advocates, if even for the status quo; thus SRA's silence regarding sexual-minority issues is a moral posture. I believe it is within the purview of science and its professional organizations to single out areas, perhaps for moral or ethical considerations, for research attention. Consequently research on ethnic-racial minorities and women has escalated, in large part because scientific organizations assumed a stance that this needed to be done. I argue that increasing our knowledge about sexual-minority individuals and their communities is one of those worthy areas.

It is my strong belief that it is unconscionable to delay addressing critical scientific concerns of sexual-minority populations simply because no one has volunteered to submit research articles or to give keynote addresses at professional conferences. Rather, those in positions of power must take a *proactive* stance and invite speakers and writers to submit their work. *Applied Developmental Science* has begun the process with this invitation for a guest editorial, and the "highly placed" SRA officer has recommended that I continue to "push" the SRA and the *Journal of Research on Adolescence* to be more inclusive. I only wish that it were not always necessary for members of oppressed groups (including women, racial-ethnic, and religious groups) to ensure that their representation is accurately and fairly presented to those in the majority.

Fight Homonegativity at All Levels of Our Scholarly Lives

When you witness heterocentric or homonegative language or actions, do not turn away. They occur at all levels of discourse, from interpersonal relationships to institutional policies and structures. If your institution does not have an antidiscrimination policy, a resource office or center, faculty or staff groups, courses, library materials, or visibility for sexual-minority populations, choose to change the status quo. Efforts can include active lobbying, organizing, and networking with highly placed officials who share your views. Class announcements about upcoming lectures, meetings, and social events that are of concern to sexual minorities can be very effective in communicating your openness. So, too, nonheterocentric, inclusive language conveys an acceptance of sexual diversity and allows nonheterosexual individuals to feel less alienated. Statements on course syllabi or at the beginning of courses about your nontolerant stance toward antigay acts and your inclusive attitude will help end the silence that was partially responsible for Matthew's death.

In an ideal world, all of us would challenge in whatever ways possible the presumption that sexual minorities are invisible, worthy of denigration, and that "heterosexual allies" do not exist or will not speak up. Failure to do so is to become a bystander — the silent perpetrator who passes, without acting, the billboard that advocates killing gay people.

Have Hope

Few sexual minorities want special rights, only adequate rights. They want the right not to be psychologically and physically harmed. They want to lead their lives as we all do. They want to see the murders of young people stopped, regardless of the victim's sexuality, race-ethnicity, social class, or sex. Gay activists alone cannot fulfill these aspirations. As professionals, we are afforded an invaluable opportunity to contribute to this struggle for justice by the way we conduct research, teach courses, and confront heterosexism and homonegativitiy.

There is hope. An editor of a book on adolescent relationships recently requested that contributors be sensitive to the relationships formed by lesbian, gay, and bisexual youths. He added that if they were not sure whether they had succeeded in this endeavor, they should "send it to Ritch" for review. More noteworthy, the University of Wyoming's football players are wearing a commemorative symbol on the side of their helmets for the remainder of the season — for peace, tolerance, and Matthew Shepard. It is too late for Matthew to have a full and productive life, to live his dreams, and to love those who loved him. My earnest hope is that it is not too late for other gay youths.

References

Blum, R. W., and P.M. Rinehart. 1997. Reducing the risk: Connections that make a difference in the lives of youth. Monograph based on findings from the *National Longitudinal Study on Adolescent Health*. Bethesda, Md.: Burness Communications.

Lesbian college student beaten in Minnesota. 1998. *Reuters Newswire*, October 21, St. Cloud, Minn.

New York Times News Service. 1998. Like victim, suspects in gay murder lived on margins of society. *Syracuse Herald American*, October 18, p. D10.

Savin-Williams, R. C. 1998. " . . . *and Then I Became Gay": Young Men's Stories.* New York: Routledge.

Savin-Williams, R. C., and L. M. Diamond. 1997. Sexual orientation as a developmental context for lesbians, gays, and bisexuals: Biological perspectives. In N. L. Segal, G. E. Weisfeld, and C. C. Weisfeld, eds., *Uniting Psychology and Biology: Integrative Perspectives on Human Development*, pp. 217–38. Washington, D.C.: American Psychological Association.

Seaton, E. 1998. *Person shot six times in anti-gay, anti-drag violence in Baltimore.* Free State Justice Campaign press release, November 5.

Sonmor, J. 1998. In the bedrooms of the nation: Canada's most comprehensive survey on sex and relationships. *The Toronto Sunday Sun,* October 25, pp. 58–63.

Time/CNN Poll. 1998. Poll: Gay attack could have happened anywhere. *Syracuse Herald American,* October 18, p. D10.

Part III

Identity Development and Stigma Management

A normal part of adolescence in Western cultures is the development of a sense of individual identity. The enduring personal sense of self that is continuous over time involves, among other aspects, a commitment to one's stance with regard to sexual, affectional, and erotic relationships with others (D'Augelli and Patterson 1995; Kimmel and Weiner 1995). Thus the development of a sense of identity is complicated for lesbians, gay men, and bisexuals since heterosexist biases devalue same-gender erotic and affectional feelings.

The process of developing a positive sense of identity in the social context of negative values about a core aspect of oneself has received considerable attention in the psychological literature (cf. Kimmel and Weiner 1995:210–19, 405–14). The primary task involves the transformation of a negative, stigmatized identity into a positive one. Gay male, lesbian, or bisexual identity development is a complex sequence of events through which individuals acknowledge, recognize, and label their sexual orientation, conceptualize it in positive terms, and disclose it to others throughout their lives. "The final stage . . . implies the acceptance of one's own identity, a committed attitude against oppression, and an ability to synthesize the best values of both perspectives and to communicate with members of the dominant group" (Espin 1987:39).

Gay male, bisexual, and lesbian identity development, or *coming out*, involves realization of one's own homosexuality or bisexuality as well as disclosure of this realization to selected others. Coming out has been conceptualized as a rite of passage during which one constructs one's own sense of self within the context of contemporary society (Herdt 1989; Savin-Williams 1995). Zimmerman (1984) discussed the power of shared story-telling of lesbians through telling their coming-out experiences: "The personal narrative, particularly the coming-out story, forms our 'tribal lore,' our myth of origins" (p. 674). Whenever gay men, bisexuals, and lesbians meet, sooner or later they get around to practicing this ritual of telling their coming-out stories.

Self-labeling as gay or lesbian, accepting this label, self-disclosing, and feeling accepted by others have been found to be strongly related to psychological adjustment (Bell and Weinberg 1978; Miranda and Storms 1989). Similarly a more positive gay male or lesbian identity has been found to be correlated with significantly fewer symptoms of neurotic or social anxiety, higher ego strength, less depression, and higher self-esteem (Hammersmith and Weinberg 1973; Savin-Williams 1989; Schmitt and Kurdek 1987). Further, studies have revealed no evidence of psychological maladjustment in bisexual men and women (Fox 1996).

Today one can also speak about *coming in*: the realization of having entered into a community and the process of identifying with a larger group of gay, bisexual, and lesbian people (Petrow 1990). Recognizing the ways that its members are differently advantaged by their diversity enriches this community. Moreover, gays, lesbians, and bisexuals have developed relationship patterns such as "peer marriage" that are being adopted as models by the heterosexual culture (Schwartz 1994).

For many years various stage theories have been employed to describe the process of sexual identity development. Common to these theories is the view that the coming-out process is a linear sequence that involves a specific ordering of events. These models have been useful in describing some of the commonalities, milestones, and barriers to coming out; they have also highlighted some of the significant events that are integral to the process. As with all stage theories, however, individual variation, gender differences, and the interaction with ethnic and cultural minority status complicate the theory and have not been adequately represented by most of the general stage models (Reynolds and Hanjorgiris 2000; Rust 1996; Savin-Williams 2001). In more recent years, the stage sequential models have been challenged (Garnets and Peplau 2002; Savin-Williams and Diamond 2000; Weinberg, Williams, and Pryor 1994). A new perspective has emerged that offers a nonlinear approach and incorporates the concept of different developmental pathways. This perspective suggests that there are multiple trajectories for the development of a lesbian, gay, bisexual, or heterosexual identity (Diamond 1998; Peplau and Garnets 2000; Rust 1993). In this approach, coming out is defined more like a spiral than as a straight line: "In common with other aspects of adult development, one may traverse the same psychological territory again and again, albeit at different 'elevations.' Moreover, some events do not happen to everyone and, if they do occur, they happen in different ways" (Garnets and Kimmel 1991:155).

Thus individuals may come out at any point in the life span. Sexual identity can also evolve over time; it may be constructed and reconstructed by the individual and not be the same at age forty-five or seventy as it was at age fifteen or twenty-five (e.g., Kitzinger and Wilkinson 1995). Rust's selection summarizes this topic and addresses similarities and differences between lesbian, gay, and bisexual experiences in identity formation.

Same-gender affectional and sexual relationships have different meanings in various cultures (Blackwood 2000; Ross 1989). Thus the experiences of gay men, bisexuals, and lesbians of color living in the United States often do not parallel Anglo experience. Often they must create a *dual identity* reflecting their minority culture and sexual orientation; women may need to form a *triple identity* to include their gender, cultural, and sexual orientation. The challenges for lesbian, gay men, and bisexual people of color is to integrate multiple identities, each of which can be disparaged and can result in social disadvantage (Garnets 2001).

Once a dual or triple individual identity is formed, integrating these potentially compartmentalized aspects of oneself requires an ongoing management of conflicting allegiances between those groups that represent the expression of intimacy and those that provide ethnic foundation. Audre Lorde (1990) wrote: "As a Black lesbian feminist comfortable with the many different ingredients of my identity, and a woman committed to racial and sexual freedom from oppression, I find I am constantly being encouraged to pluck some one aspect of myself and present this as the meaningful whole, eclipsing or denying other aspects of myself" (p. 285).

Other social and cultural variations may also be important. For example, in many urban areas a visible lesbian, gay, and bisexual community exists. This community of support is not available in most rural areas and thus represents another difference in the identity formation process. Moreover, some support groups for women provide a kind of community that differs in its acceptance of same-gender self-affirmation than is true in many male communities. This difference reflects both the emergence of the feminist movement and the dual oppression of lesbians as members of stigmatized minorities based on gender and sexual orientation.

An important step in the complex sequence of events involved in coming out is identity disclosure, a lifelong process of explicitly revealing one's sexual identity to others. Managing *outness*, that is, one's openness about one's gay, bisexual, or lesbian identity, is an important aspect of managing potentially stigmatizing information concerning one's sexual orientation. Coming out to others is usually a relatively late event in gay, lesbian, and bisexual identity formation. It has no counterpart in the lives of nongay people, although some parallels may exist, such as disclosing previously hidden identities or private experiences.

Since sexual orientation is often a characteristic that can be concealed, special dynamics of living with a concealable stigma may be involved. For example, there are parallels with children of mixed Asian ethnicity where to reveal one's ancestry may affect one's marriage, job, and future opportunities. In that context Murphy-Shigematsu (1999:492) noted:

> Some endure considerable and constant psychological stress in maintaining their secret. They live with the awareness that they are not presenting themselves honestly to others. . . . In a society like Japan's, where the presentation of self is extremely controlled and self-censored, and where being different is a major cause of exclusion, there is good reason for the great fear of going public.

An ongoing dilemma of whether to tell frequently faces gay men, bisexuals, and lesbians in situations where heterosexuality is assumed. In deciding whether to tell, lesbians, bisexuals, and gay men must weigh problems presented by their marginal status that reflect the social realities and risks of their environment. Balancing the costs and benefits of identity disclosure is a multifaceted, lifelong process of decision making. The principle of *rational outness* is usually the pragmatic solution: "to be as open as possible, because it feels healthy to be honest, and as closed as necessary to protect against discrimination" (Bradford and Ryan 1987:77).

Lesbians, gay, and bisexual individuals often function in two distinct worlds in order to avoid the stigma associated with homosexuality. They separate the heterosexual from the gay or bisexual and place clear boundaries between them. A variety of strategies are often employed to manage the stigma and to cross this boundary between the two worlds. Ideally the process of coming out eradicates the boundary so that one may be known as lesbian, gay, or bisexual in all major areas of life, including family and work.

Even when gay, lesbian, and bisexual individuals accept their sexual identity and are open in most aspects of daily life, there remain good reasons for them to conceal under some circumstances (Cain 1991). Realistic costs and benefits exist when coming out so that many gay men, lesbians, and bisexual men and women are out in certain areas of their lives but not in others. Typical examples might be in situations where there is the threat of anti-lesbian or antigay violence or where being assumed to be heterosexual would have short-term beneficial consequences in family or social interactions. Nonetheless, individuals in positions of public prestige and importance who choose to remain closed about their sexual identity risk having it revealed as a result of their perceived impact on lesbian, gay, and bisexual issues.

Herek's selection describes these general principles of coming out to others and applies this information to experiences of sexual minority individuals who are prohibited from disclosing their sexual orientation in the U.S. military.

Disclosure to parents and other significant relatives often precipitates a period of turmoil for the family. In many respects a family's process of coming to terms with their child's being gay, lesbian, or bisexual parallels the stages of coming out that individual lesbians, gay men, and bisexuals experience.

When a person of color discloses a gay, lesbian, or bisexual identity to their family, they risk several types of criticism (Garnets 2001). Like other sexual minorities, they may be criticized for rejecting the path of heterosexuality that their family expects. But, in addition, they may be seen as selfishly placing personal desires above the needs of their family or ethnic community. For example, they may be perceived as if they are betraying their own people, their disclosure viewed as a sign of assimilation into white mainstream culture.

Resolution of the family issues that result from disclosure by a son or daughter is often a complex and sometimes lengthy process. Some parents join a local group affiliated with a national peer support group known as Parents and Friends of Lesbians and Gays (www.PFLAG.org). The selection by Savin-Williams discusses these complex family issues in detail.

Since lesbians, gay men, and bisexuals generally work in settings that reflect heterosexual norms of interaction, they learn to manage their identity at work. Decisions about workplace openness involve the process of vocational choice, career development, management of identity, and coping with stigma at the work setting (Croteau et al. 2000; Fassinger 1995; Prince 1995).

Coming out at work involves a complicated assessment of the relative safety, sanctions, interpersonal support, and potential negative consequences. Nonetheless, lesbians and gay men who disclose their sexual orientation at work report that it allows the possibility of integration into the workplace with less anxiety and greater self-confidence. The selection by Badgett is an insightful review of these pragmatic and difficult issues.

Contemporary Issue: The Effects of Historical Differences Between Older and Younger Generations of Lesbians, Bisexuals, and Gay Men

A few years ago only a small number of lesbians, gay men, and bisexuals felt comfortable coming out, especially at work or in the family. Those who did often were in stigmatized occupations stereotypically associated with gay men and lesbians. Today lesbians, gay males, and bisexuals are openly demanding domestic partner health benefits, equal access to all social institutions, full recognition as couples, families, and workers, and other similar rights.

This sudden and dramatic historic shift has affected different generations of lesbians, gay men, and bisexuals differently. Not surprisingly younger persons benefited earlier in life from these changes, and many have little experience with the kind of stigma and hiding that was typical only a generation or two ago. One potential outcome of this cohort difference between older and younger generations of gay men, lesbians, and bisexuals could be a wedge between the young, proud, open, assertive groups and the older, secretive, stigmatized survivors of the old days. Some have even expressed an envy of being young and gay today. This envy came to an abrupt end, however, with the beginnings of the AIDS epidemic that clearly struck the younger segment of the population most severely.

Today it appears that the younger generation is beginning also to think of themselves as survivors and is looking to the older generation for clues to survivorship and a greater sense of historical continuity. Thus the potential exists for forming new bonds across generations. The older generation is, of course, benefiting from the changes, and the benefits for them are in many ways as profound as for younger people. Thus, as conditions are improving for all lesbians, gay men, and bisexuals, all generations are profiting and are freer to provide support and comfort openly to one another.

References

Bell, A. P., and M. S. Weinberg. 1978. *Homosexualities: A Study of Diversity among Men and Women.* New York: Simon.

Blackwood, E. 2000. Culture and women's sexualities. *Journal of Social Issues* 56(2):223–38.

Bradford, J., and C. Ryan. 1987. *National Lesbian Health Care Survey: Mental Health Implications.* Washington D.C.: National Lesbian and Gay Health Foundation.

Cain, R. 1991. Stigma management and gay identity development. *Social Work* 36(1):67–73.

Croteau, J. M., M. Z. Anderson, T. M. Distefano, and S. Kampa-Kokesch. 2000. Lesbian, gay, and bisexual vocational psychology: Reviewing foundations and planning construction. In R. M. Perez, K. A. DeBord, and K. J. Bieschke, eds., *Handbook of Counseling and Psychotherapy with Lesbian, Gay, and Bisexual Clients*, pp. 383–408. Washington D.C.: American Psychological Association.

D'Augelli, A. R., and C. J. Patterson. 1995. *Lesbian, Gay, and Bisexual Identities over the Lifespan.* New York: Oxford University Press.

Diamond, L. M. 1998. Development of sexual orientation among adolescent and young women. *Developmental Psychology* 34:1085–95.

Espin, O. M. 1987. Issues of identity in the psychology of Latina lesbians. In the Boston Lesbian Psychologies Collective, eds., *Lesbian Psychologies: Explorations and Challenges*, pp. 35–51. Urbana-Champaign: University of Illinois Press.

Fassinger, R. E. 1995. From invisibility to integration: Lesbian identity in the workplace. *Career Development Quarterly* 44:149–67.

Fox, R. C. 1996. Bisexuality in perspective: A review of theory and practice. In B. A. Firestein, ed., *Bisexuality: The Psychology and Politics of an Invisible Minority*, pp. 3–50. Newbury Park, Calif.: Sage.

Garnets, L. D. 2001. Sexual orientations in perspective. Paper presented at the American Psychological Association National Multicultural Conference and Summit II, Santa Barbara, California, January 25.

Garnets, L. D., and D.C. Kimmel. 1991. Lesbian and gay male dimensions in the psychological study of human diversity. In J. D. Goodschilds, ed., *Psychological Perspectives on Human Diversity in America*. pp. 143–92. Washington, D.C.: American Psychological Association.

Garnets, L. D., and L. A. Peplau. 2002. A new paradigm for women's sexual orientation: Implications for therapy. *Women in Therapy* 24 (1/2): 111–121.

Hammersmith, S. K., and M. S. Weinberg. 1973. Homosexual identity: Commitment, adjustments, and significant others. *Sociometry* 36(1):56–78.

Herdt, G. 1989. Gay and lesbian youth, emergent identities, and cultural scenes at home and abroad. *Journal of Homosexuality* 17(1–4):1–42.

Kimmel, D.C., and I. B. Weiner. 1995. *Adolescence: A Developmental Transition.* 2nd ed. New York: Wiley.

Kitzinger, C., and S. Wilkinson. 1995. Transitions from heterosexuality to lesbianism. *Developmental Psychology* 31:95–104.

Lorde, A. 1990. Age, race, class, and sex: Women redefining difference. In R. Ferguson, M. Gever, T. Minh-ha, C. West, eds., *Out There: Marginalization and Contemporary Cultures*, pp. 281–87. New York: The New Museum of Contemporary Art.

Miranda, J., and M. Storms. 1989. Psychological adjustment of lesbians and gay men. *Journal of Counseling and Development* 68:41–45.

Murphy-Shigematsu, S. 1999. Clinical work with minorities in Japan: Social and cultural context. *American Journal of Orthopsychiatry* 69:482–94.

Peplau, L. A., and L. D. Garnets. 2000. A new paradigm for understanding women's sexuality and sexual orientation. *Journal of Social Issues* 56(2):329–50.

Petrow, S. 1990. Together wherever we go. *The Advocate*, May, pp. 42–44.

Prince, J. P. 1995. Influences upon the career development of gay men. *Career Development Quarterly* 44:168–77.

Reynolds, A. L., and W. F. Hanjorgiris. 2000. Coming out: Lesbian, gay, and bisexual development. In R. M. Perez, K. A. DeBord, and K. J. Bieschke, eds., *Handbook of Counseling and Psychotherapy with Lesbian, Gay, and Bisexual Clients*, pp. 35–55. Washington D.C.: American Psychological Association.

Ross, M. W. 1989. Gay youth in four cultures: A comparative study. *Journal of Homosexuality* 17(1–4):299–314.

Rust, P.C.R. 1993. Neutralizing the political threat of marginal woman: Lesbians beliefs about bisexual women. *Journal of Sex Research* 30:214–28.

Rust, P.C.R. 1996. Managing multiple identities: Diversity among bisexual women and men. In B. A. Firestein, ed., *Bisexuality: The Psychology and Politics of an Invisible Minority*, pp. 53–83. Newbury, Calif.: Sage.

Savin-Williams, R. C. 1989. Coming out to parents and self-esteem among gay and lesbian youth. *Journal of Homosexuality* 18(1–2):1–35.

Savin-Williams, R. C. 1995. Lesbian, gay male, and bisexual adolescents. In A. R. D'Augelli and C. J. Patterson, eds., *Lesbian, Gay, and Bisexual Identities over the lifespan*, pp. 152–65. New York: Oxford University Press.

Savin-Williams, R. C. 2001. Differential developmental trajectories. *Mom, Dad. I'm Gay: How Families Negotiate Coming Out*, pp. 7–21. Washington D.C.: American Psychological Association.

Savin-Williams, R. C., and L. M. Diamond. 2000. Sexual identity trajectories among sexual-minority youths: Gender comparisons. *Archives of Sexual Behavior* 29:419–40.

Schmitt, J. P., and L. A. Kurdek. 1987. Personality correlates of positive identity and relationship involvement in gay men. *Journal of Homosexuality* 13(4):101–9.

Schwartz, P. 1994. *Peer Marriage: How Love Between Equals Really Works*. New York: The Free Press.

Weinberg, M. S., C. J. Williams, and D. W. Pryor. 1994. *Dual Attraction: Understanding Bisexuality*. New York: Oxford University Press.

Zimmerman, B. 1984. The politics of transliteration: Lesbian personal narratives. *Signs* 9:663–82.

9   Finding a Sexual Identity and Community: Therapeutic Implications and Cultural Assumptions in Scientific Models of Coming Out

Paula C. Rust

Coming out, as the term is commonly used, is the process by which individuals come to recognize that they have romantic or sexual feelings toward members of their own gender, adopt lesbian or gay (or bisexual) identities, and then share these identities with others. Coming out is made necessary by a heterosexist culture in which individuals are presumed heterosexual unless there is evidence to the contrary. Because of this heterosexual presumption, most lesbians, gay men, and bisexuals grow up with heterosexual parents who expect them to be heterosexual and socialize them as heterosexual. Thus they are raised with default heterosexual identities. Coming out as lesbian, gay, or bisexual involves replacing that default identity — one so taken for granted that it is rarely recognized as an identity — with a new lesbian, gay, or bisexual identity that is not at all taken for granted but rather is stigmatized.

Because identity is the link connecting the individual to the social world, this change in sexual identity usually leads to changes in the individual's relationships with others and with society as a whole. As a newly self-identified lesbian, gay, or bisexual person, one holds a very different position in society than one held as a presumed heterosexual. This refers to more than the fact that one is now socially marginalized and potentially rejected by friends and family — the very people most of us turn to for help in hard times; it also means that one has a different relationship to social institutions. For example, heterosexuals and LesBiGays[1] have very different positions vis-à-vis the institution of marriage. Heterosexuals are expected to marry and

usually expect themselves to marry, whereas lesbian, gay, and bisexual individuals are denied the right to marry their same-gender partners and are
therefore excluded from this institution and deprived of the social and legal
privileges that married couples enjoy.[2] Lesbian, gay, and bisexual people also
discover that the culture they grew up in is, to a great extent, irrelevant to
their needs because the norms, values, and traditions of that culture assume
and facilitate heterosexuality. For example, same-gender friendships are
predicated on the assumption that these friendships lack romantic potential,
as evidenced by the discomfort sometimes displayed by individuals who discover that a same-gender friend is lesbian or gay and fear that this friend
might be attracted to them. Conversely, on the presumption that they are
heterosexual, young people learn to initiate and participate in a heterosexual
romance; they do not learn how to establish a romantic same-gender relationship or even how to find another person who would be open to such a
relationship. They have abundant role models for heterosexual relationships,
but they do not know the norms, values, and traditions of gay culture. So
coming out means not only adopting a lesbian, gay, or bisexual identity but
also losing familiar social and cultural connections, finding a new community of people with similar sexual identities, and becoming resocialized
to the norms, values, and traditions of that community.

Because coming out often involves extensive psychological and social
changes, and because during these changes individuals might be unable to
rely on their usual sources of support, it can be a period of psychological
vulnerability during which lay and professional support is needed. It is therefore important for counselors to understand the process of coming out and
the issues that arise for individuals going through this process. Much of the
research on the coming-out process was done in the 1970s, when, in the
aftermath of the removal of *homosexuality* per se from the *Diagnostic and
Statistical Manual* (DSM) of the American Psychiatric Association, researchers turned their attention away from etiological questions and toward
issues of concern to lesbians and gay men. Researchers asked lesbian and
gay male subjects about their coming-out experiences, and subjects typically
described coming out as a linear developmental process of self-discovery in
which they had replaced a false, socially imposed heterosexual identity with
a lesbian or gay identity that reflected their true, essential selves. They told
about the milestone events that marked turning points or progress in their
coming-out experiences, including their first experience of feeling same-
gender attraction, their first same-gender sexual experience, the first time
they labeled themselves homosexual or gay, the first time they told another

person about their homosexuality, and their first encounter with a gay community. Based on these accounts, scientists proposed linear developmental models of coming out that closely mirrored the coming-out stories told by lesbians and gay men.

These models are both useful and dangerous when applied to therapeutic settings. They are useful because they accurately describe the way some individuals experience the process of coming out, and for these individuals they pinpoint the issues that arise at each stage of the process and suggest ways in which a counselor or friend can help. But they can also be dangerous because they make assumptions about the nature and development of sexual identity that are not true for all individuals — assumptions that are borrowed from popular sexual ideology. Thus they can also obscure or invalidate issues that arise for certain types of individuals. In particular, these models assume that coming out is a linear goal-oriented process, a conception that more accurately reflects the way individuals view their coming out in retrospect than the way they actually experienced it; they are based on Euro-American concepts of sexuality that are not necessarily meaningful to individuals from a variety of cultural backgrounds; and they are based on a dichotomous understanding of sexuality that does not validate the possibility of bisexual identity as a mature outcome.

This chapter is divided into two sections. In the first section I discuss linear developmental models of coming out and the useful suggestions these models hold for counselors whose clients are questioning their sexuality. In the second section I point out the assumptions these models make and show how these assumptions can lead to a misunderstanding of the issues some clients face. The arguments I make in this latter section draw partially on the findings of two research studies that I did in 1986 and 1993–96. The first was a study of lesbian- and bisexual-identified women's identities, sexual experiences, and attitudes toward bisexuality. The second is an ongoing international study of the construction of bisexual identities, communities, and politics. For methodological details and sample descriptions, see Rust (1992) for the first study, and Rust (1996b) for the second study.

Linear Models of Coming Out — What They Reveal

Typical examples of linear models of coming out are those proposed by Cass (1979), Coleman (1982), and McDonald (1982). Each of these models consists of a series of stages or steps, with the last stage constructed as a "goal" toward which movement through the other stages is directed. Cass's model centers on the individual's psychological development. In this model each stage of coming out is characterized by a psychological inconsistency that causes tension, pushing the individual toward a resolution and propelling her or him into the next stage. The models by Coleman and McDonald center on particular events that occur as an individual comes out, although both Coleman and McDonald also discuss the psychological issues surrounding each event. None of these authors discussed the therapeutic applications of the coming-out models, but each model highlights different issues that arise for their individual who is coming out, and I will use the models as a starting point for discussing the role that counselors and friends can play in supporting individuals who are coming out.

In Cass's (1979) model, the goal of coming out is "to acquire an identity of 'homosexual' fully integrated within the individual's overall concept of self" (p. 220). Psychological integration is characterized by consistency between one's perceptions of one's own behavior and one's self, and between one's private and public identities. The model consists of six stages: Identity Confusion, Identity Comparison, Identity Tolerance, Identity Acceptance, Identity Pride, and Identity Synthesis.

Individuals in the *Identity Confusion* stage begin to perceive that their behavior might be called homosexual, a perception that contrasts with their heterosexual identity, and they begin to wonder if they are homosexual. Cass argues that the individual reacts to this dilemma either by seeking information about homosexuality to resolve the identity question or by denial. Denial can involve either inhibiting the behavior that could be called homosexual or reinterpreting the behavior as nonhomosexual by attributing it to, for example, experimentation or drunkenness, or by considering it a means to another end such as money.

Individuals at the Identity Confusion stage of development usually have not yet sought counseling, so there is little a counselor can do within the traditional context of counseling practice. But today, nearly two decades after Cass described this stage, there is a great deal that can be done to ensure that individuals experiencing Identity Confusion have access to positive, accurate information that will decrease the chances of a denial reaction and lead to a healthy resolution of the identity question. Denial can be both physically and psychologically damaging, because it might include denial of the risks involved in unsafe sexual practices. Positive LesBiGay images reduce the chances of a denial reaction by reducing internalized homophobia. Individuals at this stage gather information from the mainstream media, including television, libraries, and the classroom; therefore it is important that these media present positive and accurate images of lesbian, gay, and bisexual people.

Unfortunately efforts to include positive LesBiGay images in the media are often frustrated by the counterefforts of people who believe, usually on the basis of religious teachings, that sexuality should only be expressed within the context of heterosexual marriage and who wish to impose this belief on others via the control of information. Schools and libraries that want to make positive LesBiGay materials available to students and the public are sometimes forced by political pressure to eliminate these materials or make them less accessible; the controversy over the Rainbow Curriculum in New York City schools is a case in point. Therefore efforts to make positive LesBiGay images available as positive heterosexual images need the support of all interested community members, especially members of the helping professions. Go to your local public library to find out what young people in your area would find if they looked up *homosexuality*. Is there any information at all, and will this information be helpful or harmful? Ask your local school how the curriculum is taking the needs of lesbian, bisexual, and gay students into account and how the school is teaching students to respect sexual diversity. Write letters supporting television shows that include positive LesBiGay characters; the producers of and advertisers on these shows receive many letters calling for the elimination of such characters.

In Cass's second stage, *Identity Comparison*, individuals begin to think that they might be homosexual while continuing to present a heterosexual identity to others. During this stage, individuals might confide in trusted friends or counselors, making it possible for these confidants to provide them with one-on-one support. Cass described this stage as an opportunity for individuals to consider the implications of identifying as homosexual, that is, to "try on" the identity themselves before presenting it to others and risking negative reactions. De Monteflores and Schultz (1978) noted that individuals usually have to cognitively transform the category "homosexual" to dispel the negative meanings ascribed to homosexuality before they can place themselves in that category. Other issues that arise at this stage include social alienation stemming from the difference between how one views oneself and how others view one, and from the sense of being different from others; the realization that norms, ideals, and expectations based on the presumption of heterosexuality are no longer applicable; and the stress involved in utilizing passing strategies that involve concealment, deception, avoidance, and role distancing. Cass also noted that at this stage individuals lose a sense of continuity between the past, present, and future, because they are no longer the persons they thought they were; this constitutes a psychological break with the past.

An issue Cass did not discuss is that at this stage individuals have to try out the gay identity in their mind's eye not only to see what the social implications of that identity would be but also to see what the psychological implications of adopting a gay identity would be for the rest of their self-concept. One's sexual identity is intertwined with one's gender, racial/ethnic, religious, and other identities; a change in one implies changes in others. For example, a man who thinks he might be gay but thinks gays are effeminate might wonder what kind of man he could be if he were gay. A Latina, for whom part of being a woman is being heterosexual, getting married, and becoming a mother, might wonder what kind of woman she is. African-Americans who are told that gayness is a "white disease," or Vietnamese Americans whose ethnic communities believe that Vietnamese become gay only when they are seduced by whites, might wonder how they could maintain their ethnic identities if they came out as lesbians or gay men. An African-American respondent in the author's recent survey wrote, "When I came out, it was made clear to me that my being queer was in some sense a betrayal of my 'blackness.' . . . I spent a lot of years thinking that I could not be me and be 'really' black too." A Mexican-American woman in the same study wrote that she has "felt like . . . a traitor to my race when I acknowledge my love of women. I have felt like I've bought into the white 'disease' of lesbianism." The phenomenon of homosexuality being perceived as a "white" thing among particular racial and ethnic groups is discussed by Carrier, Nguyen, and Su (1992), Chan (1989), Espín (1987), H. (1989), Icard (1986), Matteson (1994), Morales (1989, 1990), Tremble, Schneider, and Appathurai (1989), and Wooden, Kawasaki, and Mayeda (1983).

Individuals at this stage of coming out can be facilitated in the process of trying out their new sexual identities. Even though actual social relationships have not yet been lost, the individual can mentally rebuild these relationships and establish new relationships that are consistent with their developing LesBiGay identities. Friends and counselors can help the individual envision her- or himself as a LesBiGay person relating to others by asking questions such as, "If you came out, how would your mother/father/best friend/girl- or boyfriend/wife or husband/children/religious leader/employer react and how would you respond? Do you have any friends who you think would be supportive? How would you handle a situation in which peers expected you to take a date of the other gender to the prom/to the company holiday party? What would be the implications for your marriage, and how would you feel about that?" Envisioning themselves with this identity can help individuals realistically assess whether LesBiGay identity — and its attendant social position — is a "good fit" and reduce the sense of social alienation by helping individuals reestablish in their own minds the social connections that are threatened by the switch from heterosexual to LesBiGay identity. For those individuals who do proceed to adopt a LesBiGay identity, the next step of revealing that identity to others will feel less like jumping off a cliff if they have been able to imagine that they will still be able to relate socially to others as LesBiGay people.

As heterosexual identity is replaced by LesBiGay identity, and social relationships are psychologically lost and rebuilt, individuals are also realizing that heterosexual norms, ideals, and expectations no longer apply. They might need time to grieve the loss of heterosexual identity and social relationships as well as the previously taken-for-granted sense of belonging to mainstream society and culture. But some things they assume are lost might not really be lost. For example, they might mourn the family they expected to have; this expectation needs to be readjusted, not relinquished, via reassurance that LesBiGays can have lifetime partners and children. Although individuals in the Identity Comparison stage might not be ready to seek out gay social scenes, at this point they might appreciate knowing that a community exists in which being LesBiGay is normal and in which the norms and expectations are suited to LesBiGays, not to heterosexuals.

Because coming out as LesBiGay can disrupt one's sense of continuity between the past, present, and future, individuals who are coming out often look back at their pasts to find early signs of their LesBiGayness so as to reestablish a sense of continuity. De Monteflores and Schultz (1978) call this process "recasting the past." To recast the past, individuals might need to reinterpret early (same-gender) experiences; for example, a kiss with a girlfriend that was previously interpreted as "experimentation" might be reinterpreted as an early expression of same-gender attraction. Recasting the past also involves a reexamination of previous heterosexual experiences. Some individuals might feel that they cannot be lesbian or gay because they have had pleasurable heterosexual experiences; individuals struggling to reconcile these other-gender experiences with a developing lesbian or gay identity can be reassured that many lesbians and gay men have had heterosexual experiences and, in fact, remain attracted to the other gender even after coming out. For example, in my earlier study, I found that 91 percent of lesbian-identified women had had heterosexual relationships at some point in their lives; this figure is similar to findings obtained by other researchers, such as Chapman and Brannock (1987), Hedblom (1973), and Saghir and Robins (1973). I also found that 43 percent of lesbian-identified women had had a heterosexual romantic or sexual relationship *since* coming out as a lesbian, and only one-third reported that they were 100 percent attracted to women; two-thirds reported that 5 percent to 50 percent of their feelings of sexual attraction were toward men (Rust 1992).

Despite the ubiquity of other-gender experience among lesbians and gay men, or perhaps because of it, once individuals come into contact with a lesbian or gay community, they will probably be encouraged to construct their other-gender experiences as irrelevant to their true sexuality (Rust 1995). For example, they might be told that their heterosexual experiences were the result of social pressure toward heterosexuality and not authentic feelings on their part. They can be reassured that if these experiences were meaningful to them at the time, they need not discredit them in order to adopt a *lesbian* or *gay* identity. You can also suggest that *bisexual* might be a better way to describe their sexuality than lesbian or gay; if they have both same-gender and other-gender feelings, they need not invalidate one or the other in the process of deciding whether they are heterosexual or lesbian/gay. Although they might not take the suggestion immediately, it provides them the option of identifying as bisexual after they become comfortable enough with their sexuality to adopt an identity — bisexual — that has even less social support than do lesbian and gay identities.

Integrating one's sexual identity with the rest of one's self-concept requires challenging stereotypes, for example, the stereotypes that gay men are effeminate or that there are no black gays. Role models can also help; a counselor should be aware of any organizations in the local area for LesBiGays, including groups specifically for LesBiGays of color or Jewish LesBiGays. Bear in mind that the mainstream LesBiGay community is predominantly Euro-American. Because of racism — the same racism that permeates heterosexual culture — LesBiGays of color often do not receive the same psychological support from this community as Euro-American LesBiGays do. Moreover, the norms, expectations, and identities available in the Euro-American LesBiGay community may not suffice as a replacement for the heterosexual but ethnically relevant norms, expectations, and identities that the person of color risks losing by coming out (Greene 1994; Icard 1986; Rust 1996a). It is therefore particularly important to provide LesBiGays of color with ethnically relevant resources.

The written word can be an excellent resource, especially if local groups for LesBiGays of color do not exist. A number of books have been written by and for Asian-American, African-American, Latin, and Native American LesBiGays. These include *Living the Spirit* (Roscoe 1988) and *The Spirit and the Flesh* (Williams 1986) for Native Americans; *Sister/Outsider* (Lorde 1984), *In the Life* (Beam 1986), and *Brother to Brother* (Hemphill 1991) for African-Americans; *Loving in the War Years* (Moraga 1983) and *Chicana Lesbians* (Trujillo 1991) for Latinas; *The Very Inside* (Lim-Hing 1994) and *A Lotus of Another Color* (Ratti 1993) for Asian-Americans; *The Great Mirror of Male Love* (Saikaku 1990) and *Passions of the Cut Sleeve* (Hinsch 1990) about homosexuality in Japanese and Chinese history, respectively; *Talking Black* (Mason-John 1995) for lesbians of Asian and African descent; and *Piece of My Heart: A Lesbian of Colour Anthology* (Silvera 1991). Some of the anthologies published by and for bisexuals in recent years include essays by bisexuals of color, for example, *Closer to Home* (Weise 1992) and *Bi Any Other Name* (Hutchins and Kaahumanu 1991).

Counselors should also be aware that different norms for the expression of sexuality exist in different cultures and that the coming-out process, including the potential for integration of a sexual identity with an ethnic identity, therefore differs cross-culturally. For discussions of ways in which counselors can help LesBiGay people integrate their sexual identities with their racial or ethnic identities, and the particular issues that arise for LesBiGays of color, see Chan (1989, 1992), Comas-Díaz and Greene (1994), Espín (1987), Greene (1994), Gutiérrez and Dworkin (1992), Loiacano (1989), Morales (1992), Rust (1996a), Tafoya and Rowell (1988), Tremble et al. (1989), and Wooden et al. (1983).

The third stage, *Identity Tolerance*, is characterized by greater commitment to gay identity. In Cass's model, the individual is still passing as heterosexual to others. Today, however, tolerance of gayness has increased and the concept of gay pride is more widespread. It is likely that individuals today come out to others earlier, relative to their own degree of commitment to LesBiGay identity, because the risks of coming out before one's LesBiGay identity is firmly established have lessened somewhat and, conversely, the likelihood that by coming out one will find that support for the process of LesBiGay identity development has increased. It is in this stage that the individual is likely to seek out a LesBiGay community. In past decades LesBiGays often found their way into the LesBiGay community through the gay bar, because it was, as Hooker (1967) characterized it, the "tip of the iceberg," that is, the publicly visible corner of a much larger underground gay community. In the 1990s, however, there are gay community centers, political groups, recreational groups, student groups, coffeehouses, book-stores, and a variety of other publicly visible social contexts in which a person can meet other LesBiGays and find the LesBiGay community. Local LesBiGay organizations can often be found in the telephone book under *gay* or *lambda*.

In the *Identity Acceptance* stage, individuals increase their contact with other LesBiGays and accept LesBiGayness as normal and valid. By now, individuals have begun disclosing their identities to other people to reduce the inconsistency between their perceptions of themselves and others' per-ceptions of them. Reduction of this inconsistency leads to another inconsis-tency: that between one's concept of one's LesBiGay self as completely ac-ceptable and others' intolerance of that self. Resolution of this inconsistency is the task of the *Identity Pride* stage, during which one might devalue het-erosexuals' opinions or become politically active in the struggle against het-erosexism or both. One issue that confronts individuals at this stage is the conflict between their desire to be completely out and the reality that it is difficult to be out in some situations.

Cass argued that individuals finally reach the *Identity Synthesis* stage, in which the distinction between "us" (accepting LesBiGays) and "them" (in-tolerant heterosexuals) is muted, and individuals experience consistency be-tween their perceptions of self and others' perceptions of them.

Whereas Cass's model of coming out focuses on intrapsychic changes, Coleman's (1982) model focuses on the process of coming out to other people. Coleman notes that telling others is an important step in achieving self-acceptance via external validation. Others' reactions are critical, because those reactions are the mirror in which the LesBiGay individual sees her or his LesBiGay identity reflected and they influence the form that the LesBiGay identity takes. The impact of these reactions depends on the importance of the other person; the reactions of one's parents or best friend, for example, will have greater impact than the reaction of a stranger. Friends and counselors can help an individual who is coming out predict others' responses and make healthy choices about when and to whom to come out during the vulnerable period when one's LesBiGay identity can still be profoundly affected by others' reactions and when one might not have the skills and self-confidence to de-fend oneself against psychologically abusive reactions.

Coleman suggests that it might be wise to build up positive responses from others before telling family members, such as parents, who might react negatively. In my experience, however, a growing number of young people want to tell their parents early in the process. They suspect that their parents would otherwise be upset, feeling insufficiently trusted to be informed sooner. But despite increases in social tolerance of LesBiGayness, some people do react violently to the news that a friend or family member is LesBiGay. Parents do sometimes physically attack their children, throw them out of the house, disown them, or cut off financial support. For a minor child or a young adult in college, dependent on parents' tuition payments, this withdrawal of support can be very serious. If an individual thinks her or his parents might have such a reaction, the possibility of coming out to them should be considered very carefully indeed.

A number of books and other resources are available for people who are coming out, and for their parents. For example, *Coming Out to Parents* (Borhek 1983) is written for gay daughters and sons, and *Now That You Know* (Fairchild and Hayward 1979) addresses itself to the parents of gay daughters and sons. Rafkin's *Different Daughters: A Book by Mothers of Lesbians* (1987) can be useful for both mothers and daughters. Sometimes parents need to come out to their children; a book like *Different Mothers: Sons and Daughters of Lesbians Talk About Their Lives* (Rafkin 1990) could be helpful. Parents and Friends of Lesbians and Gays (P-FLAG) is an organization dedicated to increasing understanding between LesBiGay individuals and their families; it offers support to all family members during the adjustment process. P-FLAG is not just for parents and friends, as its name implies; many LesBiGay individuals join to find support in their struggles with their parents. Meeting the accepting parents of other LesBiGays can offer individuals hope for their own parents, strategies for dealing with their parents, and even parental substitutes who will listen to them when their own parents will not listen.

Because there are cross-cultural differences in the ways families function, coming out to one's family raises different issues for individuals belonging to different racial/ethnic groups. In some strong family-centered cultures, for example, part of being a woman or man is fulfilling one's family role by marrying and parenting children (Chan 1989, 1992; Sue, Schneider, and Appathurai 1981; Tremble et al. 1989). Because the family is the cornerstone of ethnic culture, fulfilling one's family role is also an ethnic obligation and an important aspect of one's ethnic identity. Individuals belonging to such cultures might find that their parents interpret their coming out as LesBiGay as a rejection of the family and of their ethnicity; parental pressure toward heterosexuality must therefore be understood as partially motivated by a desire to preserve ethnic identity (Rust 1996a). Although individuals in such cultures often experience greater familial control over their sexual expression and identity because the interests of the family supersede those of the individual, they usually also experience greater security in the knowledge that they will not be rejected by their family or deprived of family support (e.g., Carballo-Diéguez 1989). Facilitating the coming-out process of such an individual requires knowledge of that individual's culture to understand both the unique issues facing that individual and the particular cultural resources — such as family ties that do not break — available to the individual to confront these issues.

Two steps in Coleman's coming-out model are *Exploration* and *First Relationship*. Exploration is the stage in which LesBiGays begin sexual and social activities with other LesBiGay people. It is a period of sexual discovery and resocialization to gay subculture, including the development of interpersonal skills necessary to socialize with others in the LesBiGay community. But processes of identity formation, sexual discovery, and sociosexual socialization are processes that people typically go through during adolescence; if the LesBiGay person is coming out when an adult, the experience of feeling like an adolescent again can be disconcerting. The experience of a first relationship can also be difficult; although first relationships are usually learning experiences, the fact that there are few role models and a lack of social support for same-gender relationships — not to mention social and legal pressures *against* same-gender relationships — makes it even more difficult for individuals to build workable same-gender relationships. Therefore an individual, who is experiencing her or his first same-gender relationship or who is confronting adolescent developmental tasks again as an adult, might need extra support and encouragement.

In summary, traditional linear models of coming out do shed light on the issues that many lesbians, gay men, and bisexual people face during the coming-out process. The models reflect the ways in which many people understand their own coming-out experiences — as developmental processes consisting of steps toward an end stage or goal — and therefore provide a starting point for understanding and supporting the individual who is coming out. But, like all models, linear models of coming out highlight some aspects of the process by concealing others. They direct our attention toward those issues that are predicted by the model and cause us to overlook other issues or other ways of understanding coming out. The next section of this chapter discusses the biases that linear models of coming out introduce into our understanding of the coming-out process and thereby into our perception of people who are coming out and their needs.

A Critique of Coming-Out Models — What They Conceal

Although models are developed to *describe* psychological and social phenomena, when they are used in efforts to predict or facilitate the processes
they describe, they become *prescriptive*. This is especially true of linear or
developmental models in which the observation that many people have followed a particular path of change through time, ending in a particular state
of being, becomes transformed into the expectation that other people will
follow the same path and reach the same state of being. Within the context
of such an expectation, people who do not follow the process as described
come to be seen as deviating from a "normal" path, and people who do not
achieve the expected end state — or who achieve other states of being — are
perceived as not finishing the process. When the process being described is
a sociopsychological one, the end state is generally conceptualized as a state
of "maturity," with the implication that people who do not finish or have
not yet finished the process are still in a state of immaturity and those who
have finished the process are mature and will not change further. The transformation from description to prescription makes the model a moral one;
movement toward the end state is defined as progress, whereas movement
in the other direction is defined as regression.

So it is with linear developmental models of the coming-out process. In
all such models presented in the literature, homosexual or gay — and sometimes lesbian — identity is posited as the end stage of the coming-out process.
The implication is that other outcomes, such as bisexual identity or a refusal
to adopt a sexual identity, reflect immaturity. An individual who remains
bisexual-identified or nonidentified for any length of time is suspected of
having underlying psychopathological issues, such as internalized homophobia, that are preventing her or him from completing the coming-out
process. Cass (1979), for example, acknowledges the existence of bisexuality
and casts it as the "ambisexual strategy" used by some people during the
Identity Comparison stage to cope with feelings of alienation, because it
allows them to perceive themselves as *potentially* heterosexual. Schäfer
(1976) and Chapman and Brannock (1987) characterize bisexuality as a
stepping-stone on the way to homosexual identity, used by people who are
not yet ready to acknowledge their true lesbian or gay identity. Coleman
(1992) did suggest that "many individuals are not exclusively heterosexual
or homosexual" (p. 40), thereby implying that bisexual identity could be a

legitimate final step in the coming-out process; but the last stage in the model he presents is nevertheless "positive gay identity."

Scientific descriptions of bisexuality as a phase some people go through while coming out reflect popular understandings of bisexuality in the lesbian and gay communities. For example, within the lesbian community, bisexual identity is considered a normal phase in the process of coming out as a lesbian. Women who identify themselves as bisexual are assumed to be "really lesbians," and if they persist in identifying as bisexual for lengthy periods of time, they are criticized for not having the courage to acknowledge their "true" lesbian identity. They are also accused of being political cowards or fence-sitters who reap the benefits of the lesbian community while keeping a foot in the door of the privileged heterosexual world and shirking their responsibility for fighting lesbian oppression (Blumstein and Schwartz 1974; Bode 1976; MacDonald 1981; Ponse 1978, 1980; Rust 1993b, 1995). Many bisexual-identified individuals report that they are confused by their bisexuality because they are constantly trying to figure out which they "really" are — straight or gay.

Contrary to these characterizations of bisexual identity as a sign of psychological immaturity or denial, a bisexual identity for many individuals is psychologically healthy. Numerous studies demonstrate that a substantial proportion of the U.S. population has experienced feelings of attraction to both women and men or has had sexual experiences with both women and men. In fact, this proportion is larger than the proportion of the population that is exclusively same-gender oriented.[3] Why should individuals have to dismiss their feelings for one gender or the other to fit themselves into either the heterosexual or the lesbian/gay categories that are socially available? If an individual feels authentically attracted to both women and men, then bisexual identity might be the most psychologically healthy identity for that individual, because it does not deny the authenticity of either same-gender or other-gender inclinations. Whereas such individuals are often socially pressured into identifying as lesbian or gay by peers who perceive their bisexual identity as a symptom of internalized homophobia, politically minded bisexual-identified individuals are reconstructing this social pressure as an example of *biphobia*.

That linear coming-out models have invariably cast bisexuality as a state of immaturity does not mean that they must necessarily do so. Linear models could easily be modified to include the possibility of bisexual identity as a legitimate end stage. In fact, in recent years, preliminary attempts have been made to describe the process of coming out as bisexual (e.g., Fox 1991). But simply multiplying the number of identities that can serve as coming-out goals does not address the assumption that coming out is fundamentally a linear process in which there is an end state and that movement toward that end state is morally desirable.

Most theorists who proposed linear developmental models of coming out recognized this assumption and attempted to address it by acknowledging that not everyone goes through all the steps they described, nor does everyone go through the steps in the same order or achieve the end stage; nevertheless, they constructed these variations as deviations from an underlying linear path of development rather than reconceptualizing coming out as a nonlinear process (Rust 1993a). Coleman (1982) furthermore recognized the danger that his descriptive model might be used as a prescription and cautioned against it. But it is difficult not to measure one's progress against a model produced via scientific research, especially when that model coincides with our "common sense" understanding of the coming-out process. For example, imagine a man who is married to a woman, identifies as heterosexual, and engages in secretive sex with men on the side. Most LesBiGay-positive people would look at this man and say that he is denying the implications of his same-gender behavior; if he is not denying these implications, then he must be experiencing tension because his sexual identity is inconsistent with his behavior. We empathize with his difficulty; if he comes out, he might anger and lose his wife, but everything else being equal, would he not be happier and healthier if he could openly admit his same-gender attraction and come out? This is, in fact, the implication of coming-out models whose end stage is identity integration, that is, that one cannot be psychologically mature until one reveals one's LesBiGay identity to others. To achieve maturity, therefore, the man in question needs to confront the internalized homophobia that is presumably preventing him from identifying as gay or bisexual and share this knowledge with his wife and other people who are significant in his life.

That this is an accurate interpretation of the situation for some men does not change the fact that for others it contains inappropriate assumptions. These assumptions are especially problematic if we try to apply them cross-culturally. Different cultures construct sexuality differently; what is considered homosexuality in contemporary Euro-American culture is not necessarily considered homosexuality in, for example, Mexican or Chicano culture. What might appear to be incongruence between an individual's sexual identity — in this case, heterosexual — and her or his sexual behavior — in this case, same-gender — might reflect not internalized homophobia but merely a different way of understanding sexuality. In Euro-American culture sexual orientation is defined in terms of the genders of the people to whom one is romantically or sexually attracted. In contrast, the Chicano who identifies himself as heterosexual might do so because he takes the insertive or *activo* role with his partners, be they men or women; in Mexican culture the homosexual is the man who plays the receptive, or *pasivo*, role.[4] Or it might reflect the fact that sexuality is not a basis for identity; in some cultures people derive personal identity from their roles in the family, not from the sexual encounters they might have outside the family. Individuals who resist adopting a sexual identity, like those who adopt bisexual identities or identities that appear inconsistent with their behavior, should not be assumed a priori to have unresolved psychological issues anymore than individuals who readily adopt lesbian, gay, or heterosexual identities would be so assumed.

Most of us would agree that for reasons of physical health, if nothing else, the heterosexually married man who engages in same-gender activity should at least practice safe sex and be honest with his wife about his extramarital affairs. Men who identify as heterosexual but have secretive, anonymous sex with other men are perceived to be at increased risk of becoming infected with the virus associated with acquired immune deficiency syndrome (HIV/AIDS) and transmitting it to their sexual partners. The standard explanation for the presumed increased risk of these men is twofold. First, it is argued that they identify as heterosexual because internalized biphobia or homophobia prevents them from developing a positive bisexual or gay identity, and this same self-loathing underlies their willingness to engage in risky sex. Second, it is argued that safer sex messages aimed at "gay men" or, more recently, at "gay and bisexual men," fail to reach these men because they do not identify themselves as bisexual or gay. Both explanations imply that these men would be more likely to practice safer sex if they could be encouraged to develop positive bisexual or gay identities. This implication is not applicable cross-culturally, however. For example, the Latino who identifies as heterosexual probably does so because the Latin concept of masculine heterosexuality can accommodate *activo* same-gender activity; such a man's heterosexual identity does not necessarily reflect internalized homophobia or biphobia or any other form of self-loathing that would predispose him to take health risks. If, because he identifies as heterosexual, he is not receptive to safer-sex messages aimed at gay and bisexual men, then it seems more appropriate to design safer-sex messages that will speak to his situation rather than ask him to alter his identity so that ethnocentric Euro-American messages will be meaningful to him.

This discussion of cross-cultural differences reveals another bias inherent in linear models of coming out, that is, that they do not adequately account for the role of social constructs in shaping sexuality. Social constructs limit the possible outcomes of coming out by limiting the interpretations we are able to give our experiences and the self-labels available to us. But linear developmental models describe coming out as a journey experienced by an individual person; at best, they describe it as a journey in which that person interacts with others (e.g., Richardson and Hart 1981). They therefore focus our attention on the individual and on how that individual can manage her or his interactions with others to facilitate the coming-out process. Although they recognize that some identities are socially encouraged whereas others are socially discouraged, they focus on how both external and internalized social pressures (e.g., homophobia) inhibit an individual's journey toward recognition of her or his true essence. They fail to encourage us to look at the broader social forces that map out the terrain across which this journey takes place. For example, they fail to recognize that today lesbian and gay identities usually signify more than sexual orientation; these identities also have political meanings. Sometimes, as I will discuss below, individuals adopt sexual identities to represent their political commitments, not their sexual feelings or behaviors.

McDonald (1982) began to recognize that same-gender identities have political meanings by asserting that a *gay* identity reflects a more advanced stage of identity development than a *homosexual* identity does, but he failed to recognize the role of social constructive processes in shaping the concept of *gay*, such that a gay identity can signify a more positive self-concept. The fact is that the terms available for the description of sexual identity change over time and hold different meanings for different people. Some men reject the label *gay*, not because they feel any shame over their same-gender in-clinations but because the term is political and they do not share these politics. They prefer to describe themselves as homosexual because it is an accurate description of their feelings and behaviors. For them, *homosexual* is an accurate and affectively neutral term, whereas *gay* is a negative one — they are not necessarily any less psychologically mature than men with gay identities. To conclude, from the observation that men with gay identities use the term *gay* because they find it to be a more positive term than *homosexual*, that men who identify themselves as homosexual therefore feel less positively about their sexuality is to privilege one political interpretation of these terms over another.

Similarly, since the 1970s, many women have rejected a *gay* identity in favor of a *lesbian* identity because they find that when most people say or hear the word *gay*, they think of gay *men*. They use *lesbian* to make themselves visible as women. Therefore, for these women, *lesbian* is a more positive identity than *gay*. More recently, in the mid-1980s, the growth of Queer Nation stimulated many LesBiGays to reclaim the word *queer*, and many women and men now find *queer* identity more positive and affirming than either *lesbian* or *gay* identities. *Queer* is a decidedly political term that, for many people, symbolizes a challenge to traditional category boundaries. Any person with same-gender desires can be queer because they challenge traditional heterosexual notions of gendered sexuality. Likewise, a lesbian and a gay man who are attracted to each other might call themselves queer because they challenge more recent notions of what it means to be lesbian or gay, and transgendered people might identify as queer because they challenge the gender categories on which traditional notions of heterosexuality and homosexuality are based. For many people who adopt queer identity, it symbolizes not only their sexuality but also the challenge their sexuality poses to socially constructed sexuality, gender, or both. Yet, for other people, the term *queer* retains its pejorative connotations; for these people a queer identity would not reflect a positive self-image.

With the growth of the bisexual and queer political movements, the number of socially available sexual identities has exploded. Many of the newer identities are still only socially available within the queer community, because members of mainstream heterosexual society have not yet become aware of the great variety and political nuances that exist within the queer community. It is therefore worth noting some of these newer identities. In my current research study the most common sexual identities among women, after bisexual and queer, are *lesbian-identified bisexual* and *bisexual lesbian*. Similar identities are *bi dyke* and *byke*. These identities are often used by women for whom lesbian and bisexual identities each accurately reflect some aspects of their sexuality but do not completely describe their sexuality. Most commonly, these identities are used by women who feel attracted to both women and men but who, for political reasons often related to feminism or personal reasons involving their emotional feelings about women and men, choose to express these feelings only toward women. Other women use these identities because they previously identified as lesbian and retain the lesbian identity as a reflection of their political commitment to women or to the lesbian community. For them, the term *bisexual* is a more sexual and apolitical term than *lesbian*, so bisexual identity alone would not suffice to express the political meaning of their sexuality. But they feel attracted to both women and men and might be open to or actively engaged in either same-gender or other-gender activity, so they also use the term *bisexual* to express their sexual "essence." As the bisexual movement grows, the term *bisexual* is taking on political meaning, and some women drop the lesbian aspect of their identities because it is no longer needed to politicize their identities.

Another identity that will probably become less common as bisexual identity becomes more socially available and political is the *lesbian who has sex with men* identity. One woman who uses this identity explained, "Sexual identity has more to do with self-perception than actual sexual activity." For her, the fact that she has sex with men does not contradict her lesbian identity. She *is* a lesbian — who also happens to have sex with men. She does not think of herself as bisexual and, like many other lesbians, might believe that bisexuality does not exist as an authentic sexual orientation (Rust 1995).

Other increasingly common identities are *gay bisexual* among men, and *bisensual, polysexual, polyamorous,* and *polyfidelitous* among both women and men. *Bisensual* is used by people who dislike the cultural privileging of genital sex and the sharp distinction drawn between sexuality and other forms of human relating, and who feel that *sensuality* better describes the range of feelings they want to express via identity. *Polysexual* and *polyamorous* are used by people who recognize that the term *bisexual* reifies the gender dichotomy that underlies the distinction between heterosexuality and homosexuality, implying that bisexuality is nothing more than a hybrid combination of these two gendered sexualities, and who wish to define their sexuality independently of these gender and sexual dichotomies. As one polysexual respondent put it, "I dislike the dualistic dichotomy of 'bi.' . . . My sexuality is diffuse." *Polyfidelity* is the practice of fidelity within a group of three or more people, in contrast to monogamy, which involves fidelity between only two people. In short, the point is that the meanings ascribed to sexuality and the language available to express these meanings change over time, and therefore no particular sexual identity should be identified as more mature or morally desirable than any other sexual identity. Instead, the emphasis should be on encouraging each individual to choose or create an identity that feels satisfactory to her or him at a given point in time and within a given social and political context.

Another criticism of linear models is that they fail to acknowledge that coming out is a continuous, lifetime process. Within the context of traditional linear models of coming out, identity change is an indication that one has not yet completed the coming-out process, and achievement of the end stage — in which identity accurately reflects essence, and the individual *[handwritten margin note top: "coming out prob never changing) peep r"]*

therefore has no further motivation to change — is characterized by identity stasis. The existence of an end stage implies that the process can be "finished." But coming out is never a process that is finished, for two reasons. The first is apparent from the foregoing discussion of historical changes in sexual politics; when we take into account the social factors that shape the terrain across which one's coming-out journey takes place, we see that this terrain continues to change even after a given individual has "completed" the coming-out process. Therefore, even after they develop an identity that they find comfortable and that they feel reflects their sexuality accurately, individuals might find that they have to go through other identity change processes as the available identity terms change in meaning.

[handwritten margin note: "sexual politics never stop, process never stops"]

The second reason that coming out is a lifetime process is that whenever LesBiGays enter new situations, they have to decide whether to come out in that situation. Regardless of how out an individual is in other contexts of her or his life, every time she or he encounters a new person (outside specifically LesBiGay settings), that other person will assume that the individual is heterosexual, and the LesBiGay person will have to decide once again whether to correct the assumption and deal with whatever reaction the other person might have or to let the assumption persist and thereby present her- or himself as heterosexual in that encounter.

[handwritten margin note: "u always have dif situat'n have 2 decide whether 2 come out or not"]

Coming out, then, is not a singular process with an attainable end stage but rather an ongoing process of attempting to maintain an accurate self-description of one's sexuality in a world of sexual meanings that vary over time and across context. Maturity is not synonymous with stasis, and change is not an indication of immaturity. Rust (1993a) presents a nonlinear model of coming out that incorporates this understanding of identity change.

Similarly linear models of coming out do not allow for the possibility of multiple changes in sexual orientation. Linear models lead people to expect that once they come out as LesBiGay they have discovered their "true" sexuality, and it therefore will not change again. This expectation is subculturally reinforced for lesbians and gay men, who are encouraged by peers to perceive their early heterosexual experiences as merely responses to socialization or social pressure and their current lesbian or gay identity as the *true* identity that they finally discovered, in spite of all the odds, through hard work. Many people do experience changes in their sexual feelings and behaviors during their lives, however. Less than 4 percent of respondents in my current study report that they have been at the same point on an 11-point scale of sexual attraction all their lives. Fifty-eight percent have moved 5 scale points or more; a change of 5 points reflects movement from exclusive attraction to one gender

[handwritten margin note bottom: "model say once u come out u coin't go back. But sexuality is fluid."]

to 50:50 attraction to both genders, or from predominant attraction to one gender (e.g., 70:30 in favor of women) to predominant attraction to the other gender (e.g., 20:80 in favor of men). Numerous researchers provide other evidence that sexual orientation can change over the life course (e.g., Blumstein and Schwartz 1977; Dixon 1984).

Such changes can be very confusing to people who think they have already finished the coming-out process. For example, lesbian- or gay-identified persons who experience renewed heterosexual attraction might wonder whether they came to the wrong conclusion the first time they came out. This potentially undermines the work they did to come out, throwing it all into question. This new change might thereby lead them to invalidate their lesbian/gay feelings, just as their first coming out as lesbian or gay might have led them to invalidate the heterosexual feelings they had previously. In this way, the second identity change experience becomes an entirely new coming out that potentially invalidates another whole section of these individuals' lives, rather than a further evolution of their sexual identities that can build on the lessons learned from their first coming-out experience.

Individuals who are experiencing changes in their sexual feelings or be- *sexuality* haviors can be encouraged to think of these changes as part of an ongoing *is fluid* process of sexual discovery and can be reassured that many people change their sexual identities more than once over the course of their lives. In my current study of people who have experienced attraction to both women and men, 20 percent of women and men identified themselves as heterosexual again after coming out as lesbian, gay, or bisexual. Of those who came out initially as lesbian, gay, or homosexual, 91 percent of women and 68 percent of men later called themselves bisexual, and of those who came out as bisexual, 39 percent of women and 35 percent of men later identified as lesbian or gay. Individuals who are coming out for the first time can be informed that sexuality often changes during the life course, so that they will not be taken by surprise and find their sexual sense of self undermined if they do experience such changes later.

Scientific models have methodological implications; scientists' perceptions of a phenomenon have direct bearing on how they choose to study it. The findings produced by their methodologies, in turn, tend to reinforce the models that generated them. Linear models of coming out encourage scientists to calculate *average ages* at which individuals achieve each of a series of milestone events. For example, McDonald (1982) determined that men first identified themselves as homosexual at an average age of 19 years and became involved in their first homosexual relationship at an average age of 21 years. A problem arises, however, when these data are interpreted as suggesting that individuals necessarily experience these milestone events in a particular order—in the case of McDonald's data, that individuals self-identify as homosexual two years before their first involvement in a homosexual relationship. Such simplistic application of aggregate statistics to individuals introduces two errors into our thinking about individual experiences.

First, the average age at which a number of individuals experience a certain event might bear no relationship to the age at which any of those individuals actually experienced that event. To take an extreme example for the purpose of illustration, if half a sample first experienced same-gender attraction at age 12, and the other half first experienced same-gender attraction at age 34, then the average would be 23, an age that bears no resemblance to the actual experience of any one individual. Figures 9.1 through 9.4 show the range and distribution of ages at which the women and men in my current survey experienced each of four milestone events. These figures show that there are modal ages at which these events are experienced; for example, women and men are more likely to first experience same-gender attraction between the ages of 10 and 15 than at any other age (Figure 9.1), and they are more likely to realize that they are not heterosexual in their mid- to late teens than at any other age (Figure 9.2). But the most striking feature of each figure is the breadth of the range of ages at which individuals have experienced a given event. Individuals report having experienced same-gender attraction for the first time at ages as young as the beginning of childhood memory and as old as age 52. If the sample had included a larger number of elderly people, we would probably find people experiencing same-gender attraction for the first time at even older ages. Note also that the *average* age at which women in this sample first experienced same-gender attraction is 16.7 years, an age that is outside the modal range in which individual women were actually most likely to first experience same-gender attraction. This is because, relative to the mode, the average is biased upward by the fact that women continue to come out throughout the life span. Average ages conceal a great deal of individual variation and do not necessarily reflect any individual's actual experience. They are therefore poor bases for predicting or evaluating the experiences of someone who is in the process of coming out.

Second, that one average age is lower than another does not mean that any given individual experiences one event before another. As noted by McDonald (1982), individuals experience milestone events in varying orders.

we don't

The age

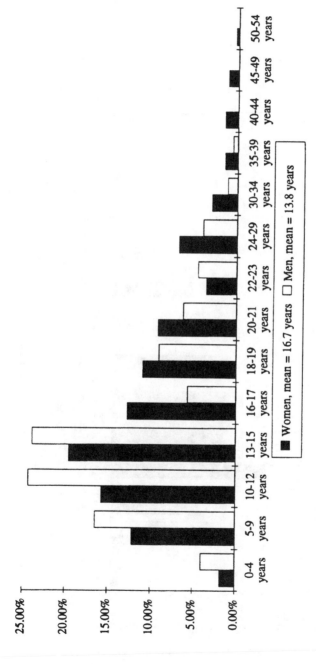

FIGURE 9.1 Ages at Which Women and Men First Experienced Same-Gender Attraction.

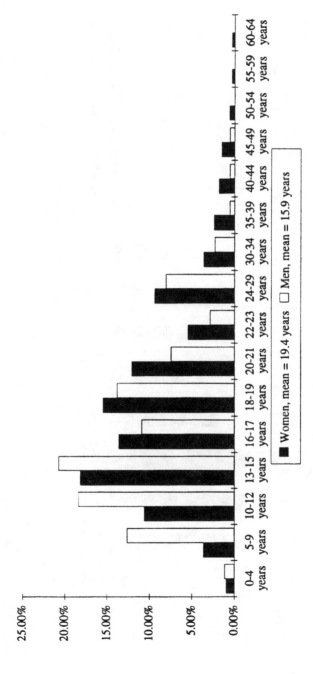

FIGURE 9.2 Ages at Which Women and Men First Realized They Were Not Heterosexual.

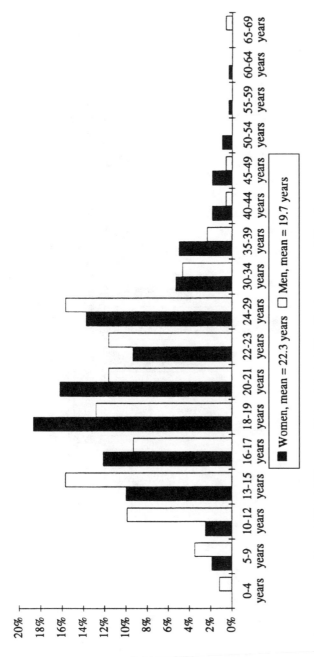

FIGURE 9.3 Ages at Which Women and Men Adopted First Nonheterosexual Identity.

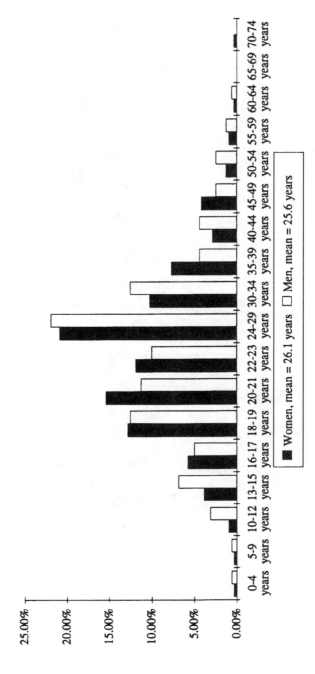

FIGURE 9.4 Ages at Which Women and Men Adopted Their Current Sexual Identities.

For example, linear models of coming out typically lead to the finding that the average age at which individuals first experience same-gender attraction is lower than the average age at which they adopt a lesbian or gay identity. This makes sense superficially; one would expect people to label themselves lesbian or gay only after they have had the experience of same-gender attraction to which the lesbian or gay label presumably refers. But it is not always true. In my earlier study I discovered that one-fourth of lesbian-identified respondents had identified themselves as lesbians *before* ever feeling attracted to women (Rust 1993a). Probably these women adopted a lesbian identity for political reasons, as an expression of a feminist commitment to women and a belief that a lesbian identity is more consistent with feminism than a heterosexual identity is; they are the *political lesbians* of the 1970s and early 1980s.

The coming-out process experienced by these women is misrepresented by descriptions of coming out based on average ages, and none of the linear models of coming out that exist in the literature could have predicted the issues they faced while coming out. For example, some of these women felt the anxiety of wanting desperately to experience an attraction to women that would validate their desired and already adopted lesbian identities; such an issue cannot be predicted by a model that assumes that the normal course is for an individual to experience same-gender attraction and then label it. *Political lesbians* also faced criticism and distrust from *real lesbians* — that is, those whose lesbian identities were based on same-gender attractions — who, ironically, were the very same lesbian feminists who had only a little while earlier exhorted them to identify as lesbians in expression of their feminist commitment to women. This issue also could not have been predicted by linear developmental models that focus on individual self-discovery while failing to consider the social and political context within which this "discovery" is taking place.

Researchers calculating average ages based on a linear understanding of coming out also have "determined" that some groups of people tend to come out at different ages and different speeds than other groups of people. For example, their calculations suggest that women come out at later ages, and more slowly, than men do; that is, women experience given events at higher average ages and have longer time lags between successive milestone events (Bell, Weinberg, and Hammersmith 1981; Cronin 1974; De Monteflores and Schultz 1978; Riddle and Morin 1977). One study that included bisexuals suggested that bisexual-identified individuals come out more slowly than lesbian- or gay-identified individuals (Kooden et al. 1979). Figures 9.1

through 9.4 confirm that women experience each milestone event at a higher average age than men do, but the figures also show that there is considerable overlap in the ages at which women and men experience each event. For example, there is a 2.9-year difference in the average ages at which women and men first experience same-gender attraction, but there is approximately a 35-year overlap in the range of ages at which women and men can have this experience; both women and men can first experience same-gender attraction as early as the beginning of childhood memory and both can experience it at least as late as their mid-30s (Figure 9.1). Thus, in terms of understanding a particular individual's experiences of coming out, the similarities between women and men are greater than the differences.

Besides highlighting difference at the expense of similarity, the use of average ages to compare groups of people with one another can produce findings that actually are empirically false. My previous research demonstrates that the apparent finding that bisexual women come out more slowly than lesbians reflects the failure to recognize that women experience events in varying orders. If we exclude from the analysis women who questioned their heterosexuality and identified themselves as lesbians *before* feeling attracted to women, the findings change dramatically. A comparison of lesbians who experienced same-gender attraction before questioning their heterosexuality with bisexuals who had these experiences in the same order reveals that bisexual women actually question their heterosexuality *sooner* after their first experience of same-gender attraction than lesbians do, not later (Rust 1993a). Thus the earlier finding is a statistical artifact produced by statistical procedures chosen based on linear understandings of coming out.

Specific Comments on Bisexuality

Because bisexuality has been neglected in the literature on coming out, as it has been neglected generally in the literature on sexual difference, a discussion of issues particular to bisexuals is in order. The first issue confronting individuals who have both same-gender and other-gender feelings or sexual experiences is the problem of finding an identity that suffices to represent their sexuality. Because the dominant conceptualization of sexuality in northwestern European and North American societies is a dichotomous one that authenticates only heterosexuality and homosexuality, individuals with both same-gender and other-gender feelings or experiences often attempt to fit themselves into one of these socially available categories.

They might discredit same-gender feelings and experiences to maintain a heterosexual identity or they might discredit other-gender feelings and experiences and come out as lesbian or gay. For some people this is a satisfactory resolution; many people with same-gender experience happily remain heterosexually identified, and many lesbian- and gay-identified people report extensive other-gender experience. But other people find that both their same-gender and other-gender feelings and experiences are important and ego-syntonic. These individuals cannot or do not want, and should not be encouraged, to deny any part of their sexuality in order to fit into either a heterosexual or a lesbian/gay identity.

Often the difficulties for these individuals are compounded because their emotional feelings for women and men differ from their sexual feelings. For example, one might feel emotionally closer to women and more capable of forming lasting romantic attachments with them but more sexually attracted to men. Someone trying to fit into either a lesbian/gay or a heterosexual category might wonder whether she or he should give greater weight to emotional or sexual feelings. Such individuals can benefit from reassurance not only that it is possible and common for individuals to feel attracted to both women and men but also that there are many dimensions to sexuality and that these dimensions vary independently of one another. The Klein Sexual Orientation Grid (KSOG), for example, includes seven dimensions — sexual attraction, sexual behavior, sexual fantasies, emotional preference, social preference, self-identity, and lifestyle (Klein, Sepekoff, and Wolf 1985). Each dimension is represented by a 7-point scale, ranging from "other sex only" to "same sex only." A given individual can be at different positions on each of these seven dimensions. For example, a woman might feel sexually attracted equally to women and men but emotionally closer to women than men while fantasizing mostly about men, having sex only with women, identifying as bisexual, and socializing within a lesbian community. Moreover, an individual's position on these dimensions can change over the life course. Knowing that sexuality is multidimensional gives individuals the validation necessary to recognize the complexity of their feelings, eliminating the need to figure out which feelings are real and which are not in order to fit themselves into preestablished categories. Of course, the number of dimensions is limited only by one's imagination; once individuals free themselves from conceptualizing sexuality as dichotomous or unidimensional, they will probably discover additional dimensions that contribute to their own senses of sexuality or sensuality.

Although multidimensional scalar models of sexuality can give individuals the freedom to recognize the complexity of their sexuality, these models are usually not satisfactory bases for sexual identity. Because sexuality is considered a basis for identity in contemporary northwestern European and dominant North American cultures, most individuals will feel a need to develop a particular sexual identity. Imagine, however, trying to form an identity around the concept of oneself as a "sexual 2.0, an emotional 5.4, and a behavioral 3.1." For many individuals, bisexual identity can encompass the range of their various feelings for, and experiences with, women and men.

But the lack of social recognition given to bisexual identity makes it difficult to develop and sustain a bisexual identity. Because others retain dichotomous conceptualizations of sexuality, they are likely to believe either that bisexuality does not exist at all or that it exists as a hybrid form of sexuality, combining heterosexual and homosexual elements. Others' beliefs that bisexuality does not exist have obvious implications for the formation of bisexual identity, given the importance of others' reactions to the development of sexual identity. Individuals who are repeatedly told that they cannot be bisexual because there is no such thing, or that they are really lesbian or gay and should overcome their internalized homophobia and finish coming out, might have difficulty maintaining a bisexual identity. These individuals need reassurance that bisexuality is, indeed, an authentic sexual orientation.

The implications of conceptualizing bisexuality as a hybrid are more subtle. Some people believe that bisexuality has to consist of exactly equal parts of heterosexuality and homosexuality; that is, that a person has to be a "perfect hybrid" to qualify as bisexual. In this view, anyone who feels more strongly about one gender or the other should identify as lesbian/gay or heterosexual accordingly. But sexual attraction is difficult, if not impossible, to gauge: How is one to determine if one's feelings for women and men are equal in strength, especially if one's sexual and emotional feelings differ? Such a definition of bisexuality, although appearing to acknowledge bisexuality as an authentic orientation, effectively makes it impossible for any individual to find a secure sense of self in bisexual identity. Figure 9.5 shows that most bisexuals reject this narrow definition of bisexuality; women and men who identify themselves as bisexual cover almost the entire spectrum of sexual feeling, ranging from those who feel 100 percent attracted to women to those who feel 90 percent attracted to men. In fact, fewer than one in four reports feeling equally attracted to women and men.

Another implication of the hybrid concept of bisexuality concerns the relationship between homosexuality and heterosexuality. As a combination

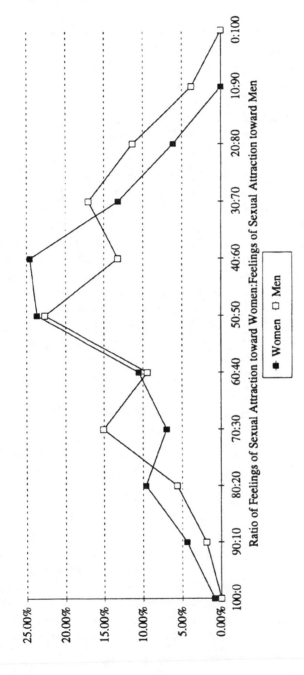

FIGURE 9.5 Range of Feelings of Attraction Toward Women and Men Among Bisexuals of Both Genders.

of homosexuality and heterosexuality, bisexuality is a combination of attractions to women and men. But women and men are constructed as cultural opposites — as in "the opposite sex" — and therefore attractions to women and men are typically thought of as opposite, even contradictory, attractions. Scalar models of sexual orientation, such as the KSOG, illustrate this. On most such scalar models, attraction to women and attraction to men occupy two ends of the same scale, implying that as one becomes more attracted to women, one must become less attracted to men, and vice versa. Bisexuality, then, consists of two forms of sexuality that are diametrically opposed to each other. If it were possible to combine them at all, the result would be conflict between these two opposing desires. Therefore bisexuality is stereotyped as an unstable form of sexuality, one that most likely is a transitional phase during coming out. Others expect bisexuals either to flip-flop between heterosexuality and homosexuality or settle into either heterosexuality or homosexuality but not to remain consistently bisexual. These expectations are tautologically confirmed as soon as the bisexual becomes romantically involved with another person, because that person is usually either a woman or a man. This relationship, therefore, is either same-gendered or other-gendered, and the bisexual is then said to have revealed her or his true sexuality, which is either lesbian/gay or heterosexual. Because it can be difficult and exhausting to explain to others that one has not *become* lesbian/gay or heterosexual just because one's current partner is of a particular gender, and because some bisexuals — who, after all, exist in the same sexual culture as do lesbian/gays and heterosexuals — also consider themselves either lesbian/gay or heterosexual whenever they are involved with a person of a particular gender, many bisexuals identify themselves as either lesbian/gay or heterosexual while they are romantically involved. Blumstein and Schwartz (1976) observed that there are people who maintain a bisexual identity only during periods in which they are romantically uninvolved.

If conceptualizing bisexuality as a hybrid form of sexuality is problematic because it undermines the potential for a stable bisexual identity, what is the alternative? Many bisexual-identified people prefer to conceptualize bisexuality as the ability to be attracted to people *regardless* of gender or to be attracted to people on the basis of a number of criteria, only one of which might be gender. Bisexuals, in this view, are not attracted to women *and* men but to *people*, whose gender may or may not be relevant to the attraction. Thus bisexuality is not a hybrid combination of two gender-exclusive sexualities but a holistic sexuality that is not gender-exclusive. When such a bisexual becomes involved with another person, this involvement is always an expression of bisexuality, not an expression of either "homosexuality" or "heterosexuality" just because of the other person's gender. Unfortunately the word *bisexual*, because of the prefix, tends to promote the concept of bisexuality as a hybrid form of sexuality, and hence the proliferation of alternative identities such as polysexual.

Although bisexual identity still does not have the cultural legitimacy accorded heterosexual and lesbian/gay identities, it is receiving increasing recognition for two reasons. One is the recent rapid growth of the bisexual political movement, which has bisexual visibility as a primary goal. The other is that the AIDS epidemic has dramatically demonstrated the inadequacy of dichotomous models of sexuality in which behavior is assumed to be consistent with identity. Heterosexuals, fearing that bisexuals would be the gateway through which HIV would spread from gay men to the heterosexual population, became very aware of the existence of bisexuality during the 1980s. Indeed, bisexuality has become a hot topic in the media, particularly on talk shows. Unfortunately the media usually choose to sensationalize bisexuality. Besides portraying bisexuals as people who spread HIV, the media promote images of bisexuals as men who cheat on their wives with other men and as people who have simultaneous female and male lovers. The problem is not that these images are available — they are accurate portrayals of some bisexuals — but that they overshadow all other images of bisexuality. The message conveyed is that bisexuality consists of having sexual relations with *both* women and men, a message rooted squarely in the concept of bisexuality as a hybrid form of sexuality.

These media images have negative effects on individuals who are coming out as bisexual. First, negative portrayals of bisexuals as cheating disease carriers can indeed make it difficult to form a positive bisexual identity. Second, they promote a concept of bisexuality defined in terms of behavior; that is, a bisexual is one who *behaves* bisexually by having simultaneous sexual relationships with both women and men. People who are coming to grips with the fact that they are attracted to both women and men have limited role models for being bisexual and might conclude, on the basis of the evidence at hand, that they are doomed to a life of shallow relationships, cheating, or, at best, serial monogamy. Sometimes people who identify as bisexual feel as if they have not fully come out until they have had sexual relationships with people of both genders, which creates pressure on them to find people of both genders with whom to have sex just to validate their sexual identity. This is dangerous because it encourages people to have sex simply to conform to an image they have applied to themselves, a situation not conducive to making psychologically or physically healthy choices about sexual behavior.

Individuals who are struggling with feelings for both women and men or who are coming out as bisexual need to know that having sexual feelings does not mean that these feelings must be acted on. They need to know that bisexuality need not be defined in terms of behavior but that being bisexual can also mean being attracted to members of both genders or to people regardless of gender. A person does not have to have sex with both women and men either to "prove" she or he is bisexual or to validate those feelings. The feelings are valid in themselves.

Bisexuals often encounter rejection in both heterosexual society and lesbian/gay communities. That bisexuals experience rejection from lesbians and gay men comes as a surprise to many heterosexuals, who lump bisexuals together with lesbians and gay men, in a process analogous to the racist "one drop" rule of racial classification, and therefore assume that bisexuals, lesbians, and gay men similarly lump themselves together. Although efforts have been made to create unity among lesbians, gay men, bisexuals, and transgenderists within the queer community, there are also intensely emotional divisions between these different groups. Bisexuals within the lesbian community are sometimes accused of being traitors or of wanting to hang on to heterosexual privilege. They are told to stop hiding behind the relatively "safe" bisexual identity, to come out as lesbians and shoulder their share of the burden of being part of an oppressed group. My earlier research documented lesbians' attitudes toward bisexual women. It showed, for example, that 75 percent of lesbian respondents believed that bisexual identity was a transitional identity, 60 percent believed that bisexuals are not as committed to other women as lesbians are, and the vast majority avoided dating bisexual women (Rust 1993b, 1995). Not all lesbians have negative opinions of, or negative feelings toward, bisexual women, but enough do to create an unwelcoming environment in some lesbian groups. In recent years controversies have erupted over the inclusion of the word *bisexual* in the names of lesbian and gay community centers and pride marches, either because some lesbians and gay men do not recognize bisexuality as a distinct sexual orientation or because they do not want bisexuals included in lesbian and gay communities. Examples are the controversies over the names of the Northampton Pride March and the 1993 March on Washington.

The kinds of issues that exclusion from lesbian and gay communities raise for people coming out as bisexual depend on whether they are coming out from a heterosexual identity or from a lesbian or gay identity. People who are coming out as bisexual from a heterosexual identity might expect to be accepted by lesbians and gay men. They probably will be accepted for a time, because lesbians and gay men will expect them to finish coming out and eventually adopt a lesbian or gay identity. But if they persist in identifying as bisexual, they are likely to find this acceptance replaced by criticism. They then face the choice of either adopting a lesbian or gay identity or being marginalized within a community from which they had expected and temporarily received acceptance. People who are coming out from a lesbian or gay identity, on the other hand, are familiar with the politics surrounding bisexual identity in the lesbian and gay communities. Knowing these politics, many conceal their emerging other-gender feelings from their lesbian and gay friends. Bisexual activist Robyn Ochs speaks of being the "bisexual confessor" for countless lesbian-identified women, who tell her about their attractions to men while professing a lesbian identity to others. For anyone coming out as bisexual, *Bi Any Other Name: Bisexual People Speak Out* (Hutchins and Kaahumanu 1991) can be an important source of validation, and for women coming out as bisexual from a lesbian identity, *Closer to Home: Bisexuality and Feminism* (Weise 1992) will have particular relevance.

The bisexual community is much smaller and less politically powerful than the lesbian and gay communities. Although the bisexual political movement grew at an astonishing rate during the late 1980s and early 1990s and is remarkably well organized, it has limited resources and numbers. Many bisexuals living outside large cities have no access to bisexual support groups, let alone bisexual political organizations or cultural institutions. Some rely on electronic mail to communicate with other bisexuals or see other bisexuals only when they attend conferences sponsored by national or regional bisexual organizations. Some eagerly await the arrival of their favorite bisexual magazine or newsletter, such as *Anything That Moves: Beyond the Myths of Bisexuality*, published by the Bay Area Bisexual Network; *Bi Women*, published by the Boston Bisexual Women's Network; or *North Bi Northwest*, published by the Seattle Bisexual Women's Network. Others seek support within the lesbian and gay communities. Because bisexual organizations often do not have dedicated phone lines, they can be more difficult to locate than lesbian or gay organizations. One way to find bisexual organizations is through the *Bisexual Resource Guide* (Ochs 1995), which is updated regularly and lists not only bisexual and bisexual-inclusive organizations around the world but also bi-related books and films.[5] BiNet USA is a national bisexual network that publishes *BiNet Newsletter* and holds national and regional conferences. These resources can provide individuals coming out as bisexual with positive bisexual role models and validation for their emerging bisexual identities.

The Importance of Prevention: Easing the Coming-Out Process by Eliminating Heterosexism

Coming out can be an exciting but difficult process. Individuals going through this process face many psychological and social issues, and they often face these issues without adequate support from others. Ironically, at a time when they most need support, many people are afraid to ask for it for fear of receiving rejection instead of support. Although social attitudes toward lesbians and gay men are becoming more positive, and lesbians and gay men themselves are becoming more visible, homophobia and heterosexism still pervade both our culture and our social, legal, and political systems. Moreover, despite the increasing visibility of lesbians and gay men, bisexuals still remain largely invisible.

Therefore individuals who are coming out are often in need of supportive friends and counselors who understand the process of coming out. Linear models of coming out, both those codified in scientific literature and the popular versions on which these scientific models are based, provide insight into coming out as it is experienced by some individuals. But they also lend a moral quality to the process of coming out by casting it as a developmental process leading toward certain forms of sexual identity, thereby privileging these sexual identities over others. In so doing they blind us to the legitimacy of other sexual identities, to the possibility that refusing to adopt a sexual identity might be a healthy choice, and to the reality that, for many people, coming out is a lifelong process of recurrent self-creation and self-discovery, not a singular goal-oriented process of self-classification. Moreover, because most research on coming out was done using Euro-American subjects, this research sheds little light on coming out as it is experienced by members of other cultural groups. Views of sexuality, and of the relationships between sexuality, gender, and the family, differ cross-culturally, causing profound differences in the issues members of different cultural groups face when they are coming out.

But the entire process of coming out is made necessary by the fact of heterosexism, in particular, the usually unspoken assumption that individuals are heterosexual. Although it is necessary to provide support for individuals who are coming out in a heterosexist society, it is perhaps even more important to attack the problem at its root by dismantling heterosexism. This work needs to be done at all levels, including the individual, social, and legal levels. Individually each of us should work on eliminating our own heterosexual assumptions. For example, instead of asking a new acquaintance "Are you married?" which, in a country in which same-gender relationships are not legally sanctioned as marriages, assumes heterosexuality, ask "Do you have a partner?" If you are heterosexual, recognize your heterosexual privilege and use it to undermine the heterosexism that gave you that privilege. For example, notice that you can casually mention your other-gender spouse or partner without other people noticing that you have just revealed your heterosexuality; this is because they already assumed you were heterosexual. In contrast, a lesbian or gay person cannot casually mention a same-gender partner, because such a mention constitutes an announcement of that person's sexuality. Try disrupting others' heterosexual assumptions by referring to your partner in gender-neutral terms.

Socially we need to work on making lesbianism, gayness, and bisexuality as visible as heterosexuality. Besides the obvious visibility provided heterosexuality by the disproportionate media attention given to it, heterosexuality is made visible through subtle means that are taken for granted by heterosexuals but appear blatant to lesbians, gay men, and bisexuals. For example, the wearing of gold wedding bands, heterosexual personal classified ads, and the announcement of engagements in the local paper all celebrate and normalize other-gender relationships in ways that same-gender relationships are rarely celebrated or normalized. Bisexuality, in particular, is rendered invisible because even those of us who are cognizant of the existence of same-gender relationships tend to deduce a person's sexual orientation from the gender of her or his partner. For example, both individuals in an other-gender couple are assumed to be heterosexual and both individuals in a same-gender couple are assumed to be lesbian or gay; rarely do we consider the possibility that either or both members of the couple might be bisexual. Work on avoiding assumptions about any individual's sexuality, and when others make such assumptions, point it out to them.

Lesbians, gay men, and bisexuals do not enjoy the same legal rights as heterosexuals do, and partners in same-gender relationships do not receive the same legal rights as partners in other-gender marriages do, for example, next-of-kin rights, certain property rights, and the right to joint custody of children. Even individuals who are comfortable with their own lesbianism, gayness, or bisexuality often hesitate to come out to others because of fear that they will lose their jobs or apartments because of discrimination; most states and cities offer no protection from discrimination based on sexual orientation. Ironically legislators often want proof that sexual orientation discrimination occurs before they will support legislation to outlaw it; such proof can be difficult to provide, because the victims of this discrimination fear suffering discrimination again if they come out publicly. Use your voice to educate others about sexual orientation discrimination and to convince legislators that it should be illegal. Support organizations such as the Lambda Legal Defense and Education Fund or the Human Rights Campaign Fund, whose purposes are to acquire legal and political equality for lesbians, gay men, and bisexuals. Educate yourself about the laws affecting lesbians, gay men, and bisexuals in your city and state and, whether you are heterosexual, lesbian, gay, or bisexual, consider it your responsibility to help end hetero-sexism at the legal level as much as at the individual and social levels. If we succeed in eliminating heterosexism at all levels, the difficult process of coming out will be no more necessary for the lesbians, gay men, and bisex-uals of the future than it is for the heterosexuals of today, and we will have faced as a society the most difficult coming-out issue of all.

Notes

1. *LesBiGay* refers to "lesbian, bisexual, and gay" or "lesbian, bisexual, or gay."
2. As of this writing, the *Baehr v. Lewin* case in Hawaii might lead to the extension of marriage rights to same-gender couples. If it does, other states would theo-retically be obliged to recognize these same-gender marriages because of the *full faith and credit* clause of the Constitution. In some states, however, radical religious-right groups are attempting to pass laws that would preempt this rec-ognition. [*Editors' Note:* The Hawaii State Supreme Court ruled that there was no compelling reason for the existing ban on gay and lesbian unions under the state constitutional protection from discrimination on the basis of sex or gender. In response, the state legislature passed a law exempting marriage from this constitutional protection. Many other states, and the U.S. Congress, also en-acted laws preventing the recognition of same-sex marriages.]
3. For statistics on the incidence of homosexual and bisexual behavior, see Dia-mond 1993; Hunt 1974; Janus and Janus 1993; Kinsey, Pomeroy, and Martin 1948; Kinsey et al. 1953; Laumann et al. 1994; and Rogers and Turner 1991.
4. For information about the construction of sexuality in Latin cultures, see Al-maguer 1993; Alonso and Koreck 1993; Carballo-Diéguez 1989; Carrier 1976, 1985; and Magaña and Carrier 1991.
5. The *Bisexual Resource Guide* is available from the Bisexual Resource Center, P.O. Box 639, Cambridge, Massachusetts 02140.

References

Almaguer, T. 1993. Chicano men: A cartography of homosexual identity and be-havior. In H. Abelove, M. A. Barale, and D. M. Halperin, eds., *The Lesbian and Gay Studies Reader*, pp. 255–73. New York: Routledge and Kegan Paul.

Alonso, A.M., and M. T. Koreck. 1993. Silences: "Hispanics," AIDS, and sexual practices. In H. Abelove, M. A. Barale, and D. M. Halperin, eds., *The Lesbian and Gay Studies Reader*, pp. 110–26. New York: Routledge and Kegan Paul.

Beam, J., ed. 1986. *In the Life: A Black Gay Anthology*. Boston: Alyson.

Bell, A. P., M. S. Weinberg, and S. K. Hammersmith. 1981. *Sexual Preference: Its Development in Men and Women*. Bloomington: Indiana University Press.

Blumstein, P., and P. Schwartz. 1974. Lesbianism and bisexuality. In E. Goode and R. R. Troiden, eds., *Sexual Deviance and Sexual Deviants*, pp. 278–95. New York: Morrow.

Blumstein, P., and P. Schwartz. 1976. Bisexuality in men. *Urban Life* 5(3):339–58.

Blumstein, P., and P. Schwartz. 1977. Bisexuality: Some social psychological issues. *Journal of Social Issues* 33(2):30–45.

Bode, J. 1976. *View from Another Closet: Exploring Bisexuality in Women*. New York: Hawthorn.

Borhek, M. V. 1983. *Coming Out to Parents: A Two-way Survival Guide for Lesbian and Gay Men and Their Parents*. New York: Pilgrim.

Carballo-Diéguez, A. 1989. Hispanic culture, gay male culture, and AIDS: Counseling implications. *Journal of Counseling and Development* 68:26–30.

Carrier, J., B. Nguyen, and S. Su. 1992. Vietnamese American sexual behaviors and HIV infection. *The Journal of Sex Research* 29:547–60.

Carrier, J. M. 1976. Cultural factors affecting urban Mexican male homosexual behavior. *Archives of Sexual Behavior* 5:103–24.

Carrier, J. M. 1985. Mexican male bisexuality. In F. Klein and T. J. Wolf, eds., *Two Lives to Lead: Bisexuality in Men and Women*, pp. 75–85. New York: Harrington Park.

Cass, V. C. 1979. Homosexual identity formation: A theoretical model. *Journal of Homosexuality* 4(3):219–35.

Chan, C. S. 1989. Issues of identity development among Asian-American lesbians and gay men. *Journal of Counseling and Development* 68:16–21.

Chan, C. S. 1992. Cultural considerations in counseling Asian-American lesbians and gay men. In S. Dworkin and F. Gutiérrez, eds., *Counseling Gay Men and Lesbians: Journey to the End of the Rainbow*, pp. 115–24. Alexandria, Va.: American Association for Counseling and Development.

Chapman, B. E., and J. D. Brannock. 1987. Proposed model of lesbian identity development: An empirical examination. *Journal of Homosexuality* 14(3/4):69–80.

Coleman, E. 1982. Developmental stages of the coming-out process. *Journal of Homosexuality* 7(2/3):31–43.

Comas-Diaz, L., and B. Greene, eds. 1994. *Women of Color: Integrating Ethnic and Gender Identities in Psychotherapy*. New York: Guilford.

Cronin, D. M. 1974. Coming out among lesbians. In E. Goode and R. R. Troiden, eds., *Sexual Deviance and Sexual Deviants*, pp. 268–77. New York: Morrow.

De Monteflores, C., and S. J. Schultz. 1978. Coming out: Similarities and differences for lesbians and gay men. *Journal of Social Issues* 34(3):59–72.

Diamond, M. 1993. Homosexuality and bisexuality in different populations. *Archives of Sexual Behavior* 22(4):291–310.

Dixon, J. K. 1984. The commencement of bisexual activity in swinging married women over age thirty. *The Journal of Sex Research* 20:71–90.

Espin, O. 1987. Issues of identity in the psychology of Latina lesbians. In Boston Lesbian Psychologies Collective, eds., *Lesbian Psychologies: Explorations and Challenges*, pp. 35–51. Urbana: University of Illinois Press.

Fairchild, B., and N. Hayward. 1979. *Now That You Know: What Every Parent Should Know About Homosexuality*. New York: Harcourt Brace Jovanovich.

Fox, A. 1991. Development of a bisexual identity: Understanding the process. In L. Hutchins and L. Kaahumanu, eds., *Bi Any Other Name: Bisexual People Speak Out*, pp. 29–36. Boston: Alyson.

Greene, B. 1994. Ethnic-minority lesbians and gay men: Mental health and treatment issues. *Journal of Consulting and Clinical Psychology* 62:243–51.

Gutiérrez, F. J., and S. H. Dworkin. 1992. Gay, lesbian, and African-American: Managing the integration of identities. In S. H. Dworkin and F. Gutiérrez, eds., *Counseling Gay Men and Lesbians: Journey to the End of the Rainbow*, pp. 141–55. Alexandria, Va.: American Association for Counseling and Development.

H., P. 1989. Asian-American lesbians: An emerging voice in the Asian-American community. In Asian Women United of California, eds., *Making Waves: An Anthology of Writings by and about Asian-American Women*, pp. 282–90. Boston: Beacon.

Hedblom, J. H. 1973. Dimensions of lesbian sexual experience. *Archives of Sexual Behavior* 2:329–41.

Hemphill, E., ed. 1991. *Brother to Brother: New Writings by Black Gay Men*. Boston: Alyson.

Hinsch, B. 1990. *Passions of the Cut Sleeve: The Male Homosexual Tradition in China*. Berkeley: University of California Press.

Hooker, E. 1967. The homosexual community. In J. H. Gagnon and W. Simon, eds., *Sexual Deviance*, pp. 167–84. New York: Harper and Row.

Hunt, M. 1974. *Sexual Behavior in the 1970s*. Chicago: Playboy Press.

Hutchins, L., and L. Kaahumanu, eds. 1991. *Bi Any Other Name: Bisexual People Speak Out*. Boston: Alyson.

Icard, L. 1986. Black gay men and conflicting social identities: Sexual orientation versus racial identity. *Journal of Social Work and Human Sexuality* 4(1/2):83–92.

Janus, S. S., and C. L. Janus. 1993. *The Janus Report on Sexual Behavior*. New York: Wiley.

Kinsey, A. C., W. B. Pomeroy, and C. E. Martin. 1948. *Sexual Behavior in the Human Male*. Philadelphia: Saunders.

Kinsey, A. C., W. B. Pomeroy, C. E. Martin, and P. H. Gebhard. 1953. *Sexual Behavior in the Human Female*. Philadelphia: Saunders.

Klein, F., B. Sepekoff, and T. J. Wolf. 1985. Sexual orientation: A multi-variable dynamic process. *Journal of Homosexuality* 11(1/2):35–49.

Kooden, H. D., S. F. Morin, D. I. Riddle, M. Rogers, B. E. Sang, and F. Strassburger. 1979. *Removing the Stigma: Final Report of the Board of Social and Ethical Responsibility for Psychology's Task Force on the Status of Lesbian and Gay Male Psychologists.* Washington, D.C.: American Psychological Association.

Laumann, E. O., J. H. Gagnon, R. T. Michael, and S. Michaels. 1994. *The Social Organization of Sexuality: Sexual Practices in the United States.* Chicago: University of Chicago Press.

Lim-Hing, S., ed. 1994. *The Very Inside: An Anthology of Writing by Asian and Pacific Islander Lesbian and Bisexual Women.* Toronto: Sister Vision.

Loiacano, D. K. 1989. Gay identity issues among black Americans: Racism, homophobia, and the need for validation. *Journal of Counseling and Development* 68:21–25.

Lorde, A. 1984. *Sister/Outsider.* Freedom, Calif.: Crossing.

MacDonald, A. P., Jr. 1981. Bisexuality: Some comments on research and theory. *Journal of Homosexuality* 6(3):21–35.

Magaña, J. R., J. M. and Carrier. 1991. Mexican and Mexican-American male sexual behavior and spread of AIDS in California. *The Journal of Sex Research* 28:425–41.

Mason-John, V., ed. 1995. *Talking Black: Lesbians of African and Asian Descent Speak Out.* New York: Cassell.

Matteson, D. R. 1994. Bisexual behavior and AIDS risk among some Asian-American men. Unpublished manuscript.

McDonald, G. J. 1982. Individual differences in the coming-out process for gay men: Implications for theoretical models. *Journal of Homosexuality* 8(1):47–60.

Moraga, C. 1983. *Loving in the War Years: Lo que nunca pasó por sus labios.* Boston: South End.

Morales, E. S. 1989. Ethnic minority families and minority gays and lesbians. *Marriage and Family Review* 14:217–39.

Morales, E. S. 1990. HIV infection and Hispanic gay and bisexual men. *Hispanic Journal of Behavioral Sciences* 12:212–22.

Morales, E. S. 1992. Counseling Latino gays and Latina lesbians. In S. H. Dworkin and F. Gutiérrez, eds., *Counseling Gay Men and Lesbians: Journey to the End of the Rainbow,* pp. 125–39. Alexandria, Va.: American Association for Counseling and Development.

Ochs, R., ed. 1995. *The Bisexual Resource Guide.* Cambridge, Mass.: The Bisexual Resource Center.

Ponse, B. 1978. *Identities in the Lesbian World: The Social Construction of Self.* Westport, Conn.: Greenwood.

Ponse, B. 1980. Finding self in the lesbian community. In M. Kirkpatrick, ed., *Women's Sexual Development: Explorations of Inner Space,* pp. 181–200. New York: Plenum.

Rafkin, L., ed. 1987. *Different Daughters: A book by Mothers of Lesbians.* San Francisco: Cleis.

Rafkin, L., ed. 1990. *Different Mothers: Sons and Daughters of Lesbians Talk About Their Lives*. San Francisco: Cleis.

Ratti, R., ed. 1993. *A Lotus of Another Color: An Unfolding of the South Asian Gay and Lesbian Experience*. Boston: Alyson.

Richardson, D., and J. Hart. 1981. The development and maintenance of a homosexual identity. In J. Hart and D. Richardson, eds., *The Theory and Practice of Homosexuality*. London: Routledge and Kegan Paul.

Riddle, D., and S. Morin. 1977. Removing the stigma: Data from institutions. *APA Monitor*, August, pp. 16–28.

Rogers, S. M., and C. R. Turner. 1991. Male-male sexual contact in the U.S.A.: Findings from five sample surveys 1970–1990. *The Journal of Sex Research* 28(4):491–519.

Roscoe, W., ed. 1988. *Living the Spirit: A Gay American Indian Anthology*. New York: St. Martin's.

Rust, P. C. 1992. The politics of sexual identity: Sexual attraction and behavior among lesbian and bisexual women. *Social Problems* 39:366–86.

Rust, P. C. 1993a. "Coming out" in the age of social constructionism: Sexual identity formation among lesbian and bisexual women. *Gender and Society* 7:50–77.

Rust, P. C. 1993b. Neutralizing the political threat of the marginal woman: Lesbians' beliefs about bisexual women. *The Journal of Sex Research* 30:214–28.

Rust, P. C. 1995. *Bisexuality and the Challenge to Lesbian Politics: Sex, Loyalty, and Revolution*. New York: New York University Press.

Rust, P. C. 1996a. Managing multiple identities: Diversity among bisexual women and men. In B. Firestein, ed., *Bisexuality: The Psychology and Politics of an Invisible Minority*, pp. 53–83. Thousand Oaks, Calif.: Sage.

Rust, P. C. 1996b. Monogamy and polyamory: Relationship issues for bisexuals. In B. Firestein, ed., *Bisexuality: The Psychology and Politics of an Invisible Minority*, pp. 127–48. Thousand Oaks, Calif.: Sage.

Saghir, M. T., and E. Robins. 1973. *Male and Female Homosexuality*. Baltimore: Williams and Wilkins.

Saikaku, I. 1990. *The Great Mirror of Male Love*. Stanford, Calif.: Stanford University Press.

Schäfer, S. 1976. Sexual and social problems of lesbians. *The Journal of Sex Research* 12:50–69.

Silvera, M., ed. 1991. *Piece of My Heart: A Lesbian of Colour Anthology*. Toronto: Sister Vision.

Sue, D. W., ed. 1981. *Counseling the Culturally Different: Theory and Practice*. New York: Wiley.

Tafoya, T., and R. Rowell. 1988. Counseling gay and lesbian Native Americans. In M. Shernoff and W. A. Scott, eds., *The Sourcebook on Lesbian/Gay Health Care*. Washington, D.C.: National Lesbian/Gay Health Foundation.

Tremble, B., M. Schneider, and C. Appathurai. 1989. Growing up gay or lesbian in a multicultural context. *Journal of Homosexuality* 17(1–4):253–67.

Trujillo, C., ed. 1991. *Chicana Lesbians: The Girls Our Mothers Warned Us About.* Berkeley, Calif.: Third Woman.

Weise, E. R., ed. 1992. *Closer to Home: Bisexuality and Feminism.* Seattle: Seal.

Williams, W. L. 1986. *The Spirit and the Flesh: Sexual Diversity in American Indian culture.* Boston: Beacon.

Wooden, W. S., H. Kawasaki, and R. Mayeda. 1983. Lifestyles and identity maintenance among gay Japanese-American males. *Alternative Lifestyles* 5:236–43.

10 Why Tell If You're Not Asked? Self-Disclosure, Intergroup Contact, and Heterosexuals' Attitudes Toward Lesbians and Gay Men

Gregory M. Herek

The United States military's principal justification for its policies concerning homosexual personnel has very little to do with the actual abilities or characteristics of gay men and lesbians. The Department of Defense (DoD) has virtually abandoned its past arguments that homosexual men and women are psychologically impaired, a security risk, or incapable of performing their duties, and therefore are inherently unfit for military service (Herek 1993). Instead, the DoD now concedes that lesbians and gay men can serve honorably and capably, and acknowledges that they have done so in the past. Indeed, the current policy ("Don't Ask, Don't Tell, Don't Pursue") allows service by gay people provided that they keep their sexual orientation a secret.

Thus current policy is less about homosexuality than it is about heterosexuals' reactions to homosexuality and to persons who are gay or lesbian. The DoD argues that heterosexual personnel would be unwilling to work with or obey orders from a gay man or lesbian, that they would be unwilling to share sleeping quarters or latrines with them, and that the presence in a unit of an individual known to be gay would reduce cohesion and thereby impair performance. These arguments boil down to a concern about information; how gay people manage information about their sexual orientation, and how heterosexuals react to information that another service member is gay.

In this paper I review theory and research from the behavioral and social sciences to provide an understanding of the processes whereby gay people — as members of a stigmatized minority group — manage information about their status, how and why they disclose this information to others (popularly referred to as *coming out of the closet*, or simply *coming out*), and the effects of receiving such information on members of the heterosexual majority group. I also explain why self-disclosure about one's sexual orientation — undertaken either as an end in itself or incidentally to achieving other goals — is important for an individual's well-being, regardless of whether that individual is a heterosexual, homosexual, or bisexual. I argue that the current policy imposes unequal restrictions on the speech and conduct of different military personnel by placing minimal constraints on heterosexuals' disclosure of information about their sexual orientation while prohibiting gay men and lesbians from doing the same.

Because many issues to be addressed here concern social interaction and interpersonal disclosure, the paper begins with a brief discussion of scientific research relevant to those topics. Next, basic aspects of sexual orientation are discussed as a prelude to considering self-disclosure about sexual orientation by heterosexuals. Then the asymmetries of experience between heterosexuals and homosexuals are described, followed by discussion of the reasons why gay men and lesbians — despite societal sanctions — come out to others. Then data are presented concerning the impact of such disclosure on heterosexuals. Finally, the implications of current military policy are considered in light of the foregoing discussion.

Self-Disclosure and Stigma

Coming out to another person is a form of *self-disclosure*, which is defined here as the communication by one individual to another of information about himself or herself that otherwise is not directly observable. By this definition, revealing one's height, weight, gender, or eye color does not usually constitute self-disclosure because such characteristics are apparent to the casual observer in most circumstances. In contrast, revelations about one's political beliefs, religious affiliation, personal income, family background, or sexual orientation would usually be classified as self-disclosure.

For the present discussion, four points about self-disclosure are particularly relevant. First, self-disclosure is an integral component of normal social interaction. Even casual conversations with strangers typically involve self-disclosures about, for example, one's marital or parental status, occupation, or opinions about a television program or sports team or politician. An extensive body of research indicates that self-disclosure is an integral component in the formation and maintenance of ongoing social relationships with

Self disclosure 272 is normal

friends, coworkers, neighbors, and others (Altman and Taylor 1973; Derlega and Berg 1987). Willingness to self-disclose is generally beneficial to one's social life and friendships, whereas patterns of consistent nondisclosure are linked to loneliness and social isolation (e.g., Davis and Franzoi 1986; Franzoi and Davis 1985; Franzoi, Davis, and Young 1985; Stokes 1987).

disclosure varies. Diff types of disclosure

Second, self-disclosure can vary in its level of intimacy. Ongoing interpersonal relationships generally are closer to the extent that they involve more intimate self-disclosures. Developing a relationship with someone — getting to know that person — is often analogous to the process of peeling away the layers of an onion, with the uncovering of each successive layer corresponding to revelations of progressively more intimate information about the self. Such information is more personal or intimate to the extent that it (1) promotes broad generalizations about one's personality; (2) distinguishes oneself from others; (3) reveals a characteristic not readily observable to others; (4) reveals a characteristic that the larger society regards as undesirable; (5) reveals a characteristic that may be perceived as a vulnerability; and (6) is associated with high levels of emotion or feeling (Archer 1980; see also Altman and Taylor 1973).

disclosure is reciprocal u give, I give back

Third, the level of intimacy in a relationship is usually reciprocal, that is, the parties to a relationship expect each other to share roughly equal amounts of personal information, and to disclose information that is of approximately the same level of intimacy (e.g., Berg and Derlega 1987; Derlega, Harris, and Chaiken 1973). Lack of reciprocity in the intimacy of self-disclosure — whether one party is perceived as disclosing too much or not enough — is likely to strain a relationship (Fitzpatrick 1987; Baxter 1987).

disclosure is complicated for many peeps who had stigma(s)

Finally, the process of self-disclosure is complicated considerably for people who possess a concealable stigma. As used here, *stigma* refers to a pattern of serious social prejudice, discounting, discrediting, and discrimination that an individual experiences as a result of others' judgments about her or his personal characteristics or group membership (e.g., Goffman 1963; Jones et al. 1984). Whereas some stigmatized characteristics are readily visible to others (e.g., skin color, physical disability), others can often be concealed (e.g., membership in an ostracized religious or political group, homosexuality). Having a concealable stigma means that otherwise routine self-disclosures can place one at heightened risk for negative sanctions, that others are likely to regard such disclosures as highly — often inappropriately — intimate, and that reciprocity of disclosure is difficult to maintain in a personal relationship.

In the most influential theoretical account of stigma, Goffman (1963) observed that the primary challenge in social interactions faced by persons with a concealable stigma is to control who knows about their stigmatized status. He referred to persons with a concealable stigma as the *discreditable* to highlight the importance of such information management. As the term *discreditable* suggests, having one's stigma revealed to others often carries negative consequences, ranging from having social stereotypes inaccurately applied to oneself, through social ostracism and discrimination, to outright physical attack. Once an individual's stigma is revealed, according to Goffman (1963), she or he becomes one of the *discredited* and her or his primary task in social interaction shifts from managing personal information to attempting to influence how others use that information in forming impressions about the individual.

Gay men and lesbians frequently find this task complicated by the widespread perception that acknowledgment of their homosexual orientation is perceived as a highly intimate disclosure, unlike acknowledgment of heterosexuality. Self-disclosing gay people are likely to be regarded as inappropriately flaunting their sexuality, whereas heterosexuals' self-disclosures about their sexual orientation are usually considered unnoteworthy because everyone is presumed to be heterosexual. This asymmetry creates difficulties in maintaining reciprocal levels of self-disclosure in social interactions between heterosexuals and homosexuals.

The foregoing discussion suggests that hiding their stigmatized status may be the safest strategy for gay men and lesbians. Successfully preventing others from learning about their stigma, however, requires considerable effort. *Passing* as a nonstigmatized person requires constant vigilance and a variety of strategies. These strategies include *discretion* (i.e., simply refraining from disclosing personal information to others), *concealment* (actively preventing others from acquiring information about oneself), and *fabrication* (deliberately providing false information about oneself to others; Zerubavel 1982). Whichever strategy is used, passing requires the individual to lead a kind of double life (e.g., Ponse 1976). It interferes with normal social interaction, creates a multitude of practical problems, and requires psychological as well as physical work.

Moreover, attempts to pass are not always successful. Lesbians and gay men often find that others have acquired information about their homosexuality from a third party, through astute observation, or simply by guessing. Even when they are able to pass, many gay people find the process personally objectionable for a variety of reasons. Consequently they reveal their stigma to one or more other persons. Before elaborating further on these points, it is important to clarify the meaning of sexual orientation.

Sexual Orientation, Heterosexuality, and Homosexuality

Although heterosexual and homosexual behaviors alike have been common throughout human history, the ways that cultures have made sense of these behaviors and the rules governing them have varied widely. For at least a century in the United States and Europe, human sexuality has been popularly understood in terms of a dichotomy between two types of people: those who are attracted to their same gender (*homosexuals*) and those who are attracted to the other gender (*heterosexuals*). (Individuals whose behavior crosses these categories have usually been labeled *bisexual* or have had their behavior explained as the product of situational or developmental factors such as, respectively, a sex-segregated environment or an age-specific stage of sexual experimentation.)

This classification system differs from other possible ways of understanding sexuality in that its focus is the individual rather than the behavior. Instead of conceiving of people as capable of a wide range of sexual attractions and behaviors, the heterosexual-homosexual dichotomy creates two ideal *types* that, depending on the individual, correspond more or less to actual experience and behavior (for historical perspectives on the heterosexual-homosexual dichotomy, see Duberman, Vicinus, and Chauncey 1989; and Katz 1983; for cross-cultural perspectives, see Herdt 1984).

Sexual orientation is not simply about sex. Because sexual attraction and expression are important components of romantic relationships, sexual orientation is integrally linked to the close bonds humans form with others to meet their personal needs for love, attachment, and intimacy. These bonds are not based only on specific sexual acts. They also encompass nonsexual physical affection, shared goals and values, mutual support, and ongoing commitment. In addition, one's sexual orientation is closely related to important personal identities, social roles, and community memberships. For heterosexuals, the identities and roles include those of *husband, wife, father,* and *mother.* Most heterosexuals experience their sexuality, their romantic and affectional relationships, and their social roles and community memberships based on those relationships as a central component of who they

Sexual orientation affects how we socialize

are, that is, their sense of self or identity. For homosexual persons, being *gay* or *lesbian* is itself an important personal identity, one commonly associated with membership in a minority community, as elaborated below.

Although heterosexual and homosexual orientations alike encompass interpersonal relationships, personal identity, and community memberships, an asymmetry exists in U.S. society between the experiences of heterosexuals and gay people. U.S. culture promotes an assumption of heterosexuality: Normal sexuality is equated with heterosexuality, and people are assumed to be heterosexual unless evidence is provided to the contrary (e.g., Herek 1992; Hooker 1965; Ponse 1976). Consequently heterosexuals need not disclose their sexual orientation for its own sake but are free to do so incidentally to pursuing other goals. Gay men and lesbians, in contrast, routinely face negative social sanctions if their sexual orientation becomes public knowledge, with the consequence that disclosing it often becomes an important act of self-affirmation as well as a vehicle for meeting other needs. This asymmetry is briefly explored below.

Heterosexuality and Normalcy

Society's institutions and customs routinely elicit and convey information about individuals' heterosexuality. Advertisements and other messages in mass media explicitly convey the assumption that the audience consists of heterosexuals, many of whom are preoccupied with meeting, marrying, living with, or having sexual relations with someone of the other gender. Employers, schools, hospitals, and government institutions often request information about one's marital status, spouse, and children. People routinely are publicly identified as part of a heterosexual relationship, whether as a fiancé, spouse, or widow. Wedding rituals and anniversaries are important family and community events.

Patterns of normal social interaction also reflect the heterosexual assumption. Heterosexuals are (correctly) assumed to be heterosexual without ever explicitly revealing their sexual orientation to others; they need not come out of the closet. Nonetheless, most heterosexuals regularly make statements and provide information to others about their relationship status, attractions, and even their problems with establishing or maintaining heterosexual relationships. Wearing a wedding ring or displaying a photograph of one's spouse, fiancé or (opposite-sex) romantic partner, for example, publicly identify oneself as heterosexual.

Some term) is not play a social role like husband

Such affirmations of heterosexuality, however, are not commonly inter-preted as statements about private sexual conduct. Rather, they identify an individual as occupying a particular role in society. These roles — husband or wife, father or mother — are largely *desexualized* (Herek 1992); that is, they are interpreted by others primarily as indicators of social duties and behaviors; further, they are not perceived to be associated primarily or ex-clusively with sexual behaviors, even though they recognize private sexual conduct (and, in the case of marriage, legitimize such conduct).

When a man says he is married or a woman says she is a mother, for example, the recipient of this information could make assumptions about the individual's private sexual behavior with a high likelihood of being ac-curate. Presumably the married man has, at some time, engaged in hetero-sexual intercourse with his wife (although the frequency of such intercourse is not revealed by such a statement), and the mother can be presumed to have engaged in heterosexual intercourse at least once (although she might possibly have conceived her child through artificial insemination or adopted a child). Yet marriage and parenthood are not usually construed primarily in sexual terms. Even at the time of a wedding — when assumptions about sexual conduct are perhaps most explicit — sex is widely understood to be merely one part of a larger picture. Friends and relatives may expect that newlyweds will engage in sexual intercourse (and some wedding rituals in-clude serious or joking references to this fact), but most do not regard the marriage in exclusively or primarily sexual terms. Indeed, advice to the newly married often stresses the many responsibilities and obligations associated with marital status, rather than romance and sex (e.g., see Slater 1963).

Because of the desexualized nature of heterosexual social roles, disclosures that identify one as heterosexual are not perceived as an inappropriate com-munication of information about private sexual conduct. Thus the act of re-ferring to one's heterosexual spouse in conversation or of introducing that spouse to one's coworkers is not regarded as a flaunting of one's sexuality. Family members or friends may approve or disapprove of the particular spouse's character, physical appearance, race, religion, occupation, or social class. They may be happy that their friend or relative has settled down, or they may feel that he or she should have waited longer before marrying. They may speculate about whether the couple's relationship is likely to endure over time. However, that a man's spouse is a woman or that a woman's spouse is a man does not often elicit surprise or comment. Rather, a heterosexual orientation is unremarkable, usually unproblematic, and is taken for granted.

Homosexuality, Invisibility, and Stigma

By contrast, homosexuality is stigmatized in the United States. Historically, the *homosexual* has been defined as a counterpart to the *normal person*:
People identified as homosexual have been regarded as abnormal and deviant, and have accordingly been stigmatized as sinners, criminals, and psy-
chopaths (Sarbin 1996). Stigma persists to the present day (for a review, see
Herek 1995). Opinion surveys since the 1970s have consistently shown that
roughly two-thirds of U.S. adults condemn homosexuality or homosexual
behavior as morally wrong or a sin (Herek 1996). Only a plurality of Americans feel that homosexual relations between consenting adults should be
legal (Herek 1996). In addition, more than half U.S. heterosexual adults feel
that homosexual relations — whether between women or men — are disgust-
ing, and about three-fourths regard homosexuality as unnatural (Herek and
Capitanio 1996). Public revelation that one is a homosexual can have
serious negative consequences, including personal rejection and isolation,
employment discrimination, loss of child custody, harassment, and violence
(Badgett 1995; Berrill 1992; Herek 1995; Levine 1979a; Levine and Leonard
1984; Patterson 1992). Heterosexuality not only remains the statistical
norm; it is also the only form of sexuality regarded by society as natural and
legitimate.

Like heterosexuals, most individuals with a homosexual identity experience their sexual orientation as a core part of the self. Unlike heterosexuals,
however, most lesbians and gay men also experience their sexual orientation
as problematic — to at least some extent — for several reasons. First, society's
assumption of heterosexuality means that most gay people were raised with
the expectation that they would be heterosexual. Not conforming to this
expectation, they had to discover and actively construct their homosexual
identity against a backdrop of societal disapproval, usually without access to
parental or familial support or guidance (Herdt 1989; Martin 1982; Savin-
Williams 1994). Because most people internalize society's negative attitudes
toward homosexuality, the discovery that one is gay often involves overcoming denial and then integrating one's homosexuality into the rest of one's
identity in a positive way; this is the process of coming out to oneself (Malyon
1982; Stein and Cohen 1984).

Second, like heterosexuality, a homosexual orientation is closely related
to important personal identities, social roles, and community memberships.
But because homosexuality has historically been defined as deviant and ab-

normal, homosexuals' identities and roles have been of an oppositional nature, that is, they represent the viewpoint of an outsider. Defining oneself
personally and socially as *gay* or *lesbian* — or, more recently, *queer* — provides entry to alternative communities that have developed in the United
States and elsewhere (Levine 1979b; Murray 1979; Warren 1974) but frequently prevents one from participating in "normal" community activities.

Third, whereas the public roles that assert one's heterosexuality (e.g.,
husband, wife) are desexualized, the roles associated with homosexuality are
sexualized. Heterosexual relationships are widely understood as involving
many components — including romantic love, commitment, and shared
goals, as well as sexual attraction — but same-sex relationships are widely
perceived only in sexual terms, even though they are very similar to heterosexual relationships in that they are primarily about love, affection, and commitment (Blumstein and Schwartz 1983; Kurdek 1994; Kurdek and Schmitt
1986; Peplau 1991; Peplau and Cochran 1990). Consequently, whereas a
man and woman holding hands in a public setting are likely to be regarded
fondly ("All the world loves a lover"), a similar public expression of affection
between two men or two women is usually perceived as an inappropriate
flaunting of sexuality.[1]

Despite these problems, a homosexual identity forms and develops
through the same process as do other aspects of identity and the self: social
interaction (Erikson 1963; Mead 1934). By verbally stating "I am gay" or "I
am lesbian" or "I am a homosexual" (or making such assertions through
symbolic speech or other conduct), an individual affirms her or his identity
and integrates it with other facets of the self. This process of affirmation and
integration is generally recognized as an important component of the process
of identity formation and psychological health (Malyon 1982; Stein and
Cohen 1984).

Thus stigmatization of homosexuality creates a dilemma for lesbians and
gay men. If they allow themselves to be perceived as heterosexual (or actively
work to pass as heterosexual), they must lead a double life that requires
considerable effort and carries psychological costs. If, however, they identify
themselves as homosexual (or allow others to learn of their homosexuality),
they are likely to be perceived as inappropriately flaunting their sexuality
and they risk ostracism, discrimination, and even physical violence. Despite
the risks, many gay men and lesbians today choose to come out to at least
some heterosexuals. Others have their sexual orientation revealed without
their consent. Some negative and positive consequences of being out of the
closet are discussed in the next section.

Coming Out: Disclosure of Homosexuality

Although some gay individuals (including some active-duty military personnel) have disclosed their sexual orientation by going public — for example, by appearing on national television or having their homosexuality reported in a major newspaper — survey research conducted with national probability samples suggests that this pattern is not common. In a 1991 national telephone survey of attitudes and opinions that I conducted with John Capitanio, approximately 45 percent of the heterosexual respondents who knew at least one gay person reported that they first learned about the individual's sexual orientation directly from that person herself or himself (Herek and Capitanio 1996). Another 16 percent initially learned about it through a third party or guessed but subsequently discussed it directly with the gay or lesbian friend or relative.

When we examined the types of relationships in which direct disclosure was made, we found that such disclosure almost always occurred between close friends and immediate family members, rarely occurred between distant relatives, and occurred slightly more than half the time between acquaintances or casual friends. Because this study was conducted with a nationally representative sample, we can conclude that approximately 61 percent of U.S. adult heterosexuals who know gay men or lesbians were told directly by at least one gay friend or relative about his or her homosexuality, and that such revelations occur more often in close relationships than in distant relationships.

Some revelations, of course, are out of the person's control; information about her or his homosexuality is circulated by a third party without the individual's consent. In recent years such third-party disclosures have been referred to as "outing" (Gross 1993; Johansson and Percy 1994). In 32 percent of the relationships with a gay person reported by heterosexuals in the national sample (note that respondents could report more than one relationship), the respondent initially learned through a third party that the friend, relative, or acquaintance was homosexual. In another 30 percent of the relationships, the respondent initially guessed that the friend, relative, or acquaintance was gay.

In summary, the majority of heterosexuals who know gay people have been told directly by at least one person that he or she is gay. At the same time, gay people often are outed involuntarily or have their sexual orientation guessed by a heterosexual. Nevertheless some gay men and lesbians keep their sexual orientation hidden from all or most of their social circles. In a 1989 national telephone survey of four hundred lesbians and gay men, for example, between 23 percent and 40 percent of the respondents (depending on geographical region) had *not* told their family of their sexual orientation, and between 37 percent and 59 percent had *not* told their co-workers ("Results of poll" 1989).

The Effects of Being Out on Social Perceptions

As noted previously, homosexuality's stigmatized status means that people who are identified as gay or lesbian are likely to encounter differential treatment by others, including ostracism, discrimination, and violence. In addition to these dramatic negative consequences, being identified as homosexual also has subtle effects on the ways heterosexuals perceive gay men and lesbians. Once a person is known to be homosexual, that fact is regarded by others as the most (or one of the most) important pieces of information they possess about that individual. In other words, homosexuality represents a master status (Becker 1963). Knowledge of one's homosexuality colors all other information about the person, even information that is totally unrelated to sexual orientation. Consequently once a man or woman is labeled by others as a homosexual, all her or his actions — regardless of whether they are related to sexual orientation — are likely to be interpreted in light of that person's sexual orientation. The master status of homosexuality has at least three important consequences.

First, gay-identified people are regarded by heterosexuals primarily in sexual terms. This sexualization of the individual is evident in the DoD's equation of disclosing that one is homosexual with acknowledgment that one has engaged in or intends to engage in homosexual behavior. Such assumptions are not necessarily accurate, however. A public statement about one's psychological identity and community membership may not reveal a great deal about one's private sexual behavior. A heterosexual who has never had sexual contact with another person (e.g., as a consequence of choosing to wait until marriage, taking a vow of celibacy, or lacking a suitable partner) or has not had sex for a long time (e.g., as a consequence of choice, aging, loss of a spouse, lack of a partner) is nevertheless a heterosexual. By the same logic, an individual may self-identify as homosexual, gay, or lesbian and yet not be engaging in sexual acts with others for a variety of reasons.

Second, gay-identified individuals are likely to experience problems establishing a satisfactorily reciprocal level of intimacy in daily social relations. Using Archer's (1980) previously described criteria, revealing information about one's homosexuality is likely to be perceived as a highly intimate self-disclosure. That one is gay or lesbian is a characteristic that invites broad generalizations, is distinctive and not readily evident in normal social interaction, and whose disclosure can be an affect-laden event. Revealing that one is heterosexual, in contrast, is not regarded as an intimate self-disclosure. Indeed, as noted above, revelation about one's heterosexual relationships or one's marital status is routine in casual interactions with strangers. Derlega, Harris, and Chaikin (1973), for example, found that a woman's disclosure of being caught by her mother in a sexual encounter was judged to be more intimate when the encounter was described as being with another woman than with a man.

A third important consequence of coming out is to have popular stereotypes about homosexuals applied to oneself (Sarbin 1996). A *stereotype* is a fixed belief that all or most members of a particular group share a characteristic that is unrelated to their group membership. Examples of widespread and enduring stereotypes are the beliefs that blacks are lazy and Jews are greedy. Some stereotypes of gay men and lesbians also are commonly applied to other disliked minority groups in this and other cultures. These include the stereotypes that members of the minority are hypersexual; a threat to society's most vulnerable members (e.g., children); secretive, clannish, and untrustworthy; and physically or mentally sick (Adam 1978; Gilman 1985). Other stereotypes are more specific to homosexuality, such as the beliefs that gay men are effeminate and lesbians are masculine (e.g., Kite and Deaux 1987).

When people hold stereotypes about the members of a group, they tend to perceive and remember information about the group in a way that is consistent with their stereotypes. Heterosexuals who hold stereotypes about lesbians and gay men are more likely than others to engage in *selective perception* and *selective recall*; that is, they tend to selectively notice behaviors and characteristics that fit with their preconceived beliefs about gay men or lesbians while failing to notice behaviors and characteristics that are inconsistent with those beliefs (e.g., Gross et al. 1980; Gurwitz and Marcus 1978). And when they are trying to remember information about a gay person, their recollections and guesses about that individual tend to fit with their preconceived beliefs (e.g., Bellezza and Bower 1981; Snyder and Uranowitz 1978).

Stereotypical thinking is difficult to overcome, even for people who have consciously decided that they do not wish to be prejudiced. Even though the latter are likely to experience guilt, discomfort, or other negative feelings when they realize that they have been thinking stereotypically about a particular group, they do it nevertheless (Devine and Monteith 1993). Stereotypical thinking is resistant to change for several reasons. The use of stereotypes appears to be fairly automatic when thinking about members of a social outgroup. In other words, using stereotypes is like a habit. To break the stereotype habit, one must break out of the automatic mental processes that one usually uses and consciously take control of one's thinking. Such a change requires cognitive effort. It also requires acquisition of new skills — one must learn new ways of (nonstereotypical) thinking (Devine and Monteith 1993). Another reason stereotypical thinking is difficult to overcome is that people tend to use whatever information is most accessible to them when they are making judgments and decisions (Tversky and Kahneman 1973). Stereotypical beliefs often represent the most readily available information about the members of a social outgroup. Finally, stereotypes persist because they tend to be reinforced by other members of one's own group. Someone who expresses a stereotypical belief about an outgroup is likely to be rewarded by members of the ingroup (e.g., in the form of acceptance or liking), whereas someone who expresses a counter-stereotypical belief may be punished (in the form of disagreement, discounting, ridicule, or even rejection and ostracism).

Why Do Lesbians and Gay Men Come Out?

Given the prevalence of stigma and the negative consequences of being labeled a homosexual, one might ask why lesbians and gay men ever voluntarily reveal their sexual orientation to anyone. At least three broad categories of why gay men and lesbians tell others about their sexual orientation can be identified.

Improving Interpersonal Relationships Withholding information about oneself from friends, coworkers, and acquaintances often disrupts social relationships — or hinders their development — and arouses suspicions about an individual's private life. As noted above, disclosure of information about oneself is an important component of forming and maintaining interpersonal relationships, with more extensive and intimate disclosures characterizing closer relationships. Because sexual orientation is so central to personal identity, keeping it a secret from another person necessarily requires withholding a substantial amount of information about oneself. This information is central to many of the topics people commonly discuss in a close relationship. Examples include the joys and stresses of one's romantic relationships or search for such relationships, feelings of fulfillment or loneliness, and mundane or momentous experiences with one's partner. In most such discussions, the gender of one's partner (and, consequently, information about one's sexual orientation) is revealed simply through the accurate use of masculine or feminine pronouns. Thus, when an individual actively conceals his or her sexual orientation from another, the two cannot have an honest discussion of such matters. As a result, spontaneity and personal disclosure are necessarily limited, which inevitably impoverishes the relationship.

Keeping one's sexual orientation a secret also creates a variety of practical problems (e.g., ensuring that one's heterosexual acquaintances do not see one entering a gay club or church or do not learn about the gender of one's lover) and ethical problems (e.g., lying and deception; e.g., Plummer 1975). Some gay people disclose to others as a way of eliminating or reducing these problems. Or anticipating that others will find out anyway, some gay people disclose as a way of exercising some degree of control over others' perceptions (e.g., Davies 1992; for examples of similar types of disclosure by members of other stigmatized groups, see Miall 1989, and Schneider and Conrad 1980, concerning, respectively, infertile adoptive mothers and epileptics). In either case, such disclosures represent an attempt to exercise control over the way another person learns of one's stigma when such revelation is inevitable, and to frame that information in a positive light. Thus coming out makes the gay person's life simpler and makes honest relationships with others possible (Wells and Kline 1987).

Enhancing One's Mental and Physical Health   Past research on stigma has documented the use of self-disclosure as a strategy for relieving the stress associated with concealment of one's stigma while also enhancing one's self esteem and overcoming the negative psychological effects of stigmatization (Schneider and Conrad 1980). Such *therapeutic disclosure* usually requires an audience that is supportive, encouraging, empathetic, and nonjudgmental (Schneider and Conrad 1980; but see Herman 1993). Hence it is most likely to occur with immediate family members or individuals who are considered close friends (e.g., Miall 1989). By disclosing to such individuals, the stigmatized person can reduce or eliminate the negative feelings about himself or herself that often accompany secrecy and isolation while also developing a new, shared definition of his or her stigmatized attribute as normal and ordinary (Schneider and Conrad 1980).

Gay people often disclose to others as a strategy for promoting their own well-being. As mentioned earlier, lesbians and gay men have been found to manifest better mental health to the extent that they feel positively about their sexual orientation and have integrated it into their lives through coming out and participating in the gay community (Bell and Weinberg 1978; Hammersmith and Weinberg 1973; Herek and Glunt 1995; Leserman et al. 1994). In contrast, closeted gay women and men may experience a painful discrepancy between their public and private identities (Humphreys 1972; see, generally, Goffman 1963; Jones et al. 1984; for a discussion of AIDS stigma and passing, see Herek 1990). They may feel inauthentic or that they are living a lie (Jones et al. 1984). Although they may not face direct prejudice against themselves, they face unwitting acceptance of themselves by individuals who are prejudiced against homosexuals (Goffman 1963). Passing also can create considerable strain for lesbian and gay male couples, who must actively hide or deny their relationship to family and friends. This denial can create strains in the relationship and, when it prevents the partners from receiving adequate social support, may have a deleterious effect on psychological adjustment (Kurdek 1988; Murphy 1989).

Coming out also may promote physical health. Psychologists have long hypothesized that hiding or actively concealing significant aspects of the self can have negative effects on physical health, whereas disclosure of such information to others can have positive health consequences (e.g., Jourard 1971). Empirical research has generally supported these hypotheses. Larson and Chastain (1990), for example, found that survey respondents high in self-concealment manifested significantly more bodily symptoms, depression, and anxiety than did respondents who were low in self-concealment. The negative health correlates of self-concealment appear to be independent of an individual's degree of social support (Larson and Chastain 1990; Pennebaker and O'Heeron 1984). Recent empirical research points to the physiological mechanisms underlying such relationships, indicating that ongoing inhibition of behavior—as is involved in active deception or concealment—requires physical effort and is accompanied by short-term physiological changes, such as increased electrodermal activity (Fowles 1980). Pennebaker and Chew (1985), for example, observed an increase in skin conductance levels when experimental subjects (following the experimenter's instructions) actively deceived another individual.

Long-term behavioral inhibition may lead to stress-related disease (Pennebaker and Susman 1988), and, conversely, disclosure of previously concealed personal information appears to be associated with better physical health. Pennebaker et al. (1988), for example, found that individuals who wrote a series of essays in which they disclosed highly personal information about upsetting experiences subsequently displayed better immune functioning, lower blood pressure, fewer medical visits, and less subjective distress than did members of a control group who wrote essays about trivial topics. Esterling et al. (1994) observed lower levels of Epstein-Barr Virus (EBV) antibody titers (indicating better immune system functioning) among experimental subjects who verbally disclosed personal information about a stressful event, compared to subjects who disclosed such information in a written essay. The latter group, in turn, displayed lower EBV antibody titers than subjects in a control group (Esterling et al. 1994).

In summary, coming out appears to be associated with enhanced mental health. In addition, although empirical research has not directly assessed whether deceiving others about one's sexual orientation can lead to physical health problems, such a conclusion is consistent with existing research.

Changing Society's Attitudes   As Goffman (1963) noted, some stigmatized individuals devote considerable energy and resources to self-disclosure in order to change societal attitudes and to help others who share their stigma (see also Anspach 1979; Kitsuse 1980). Some of them *go public*, that is, make their status a matter of public record through, for example, a speech, media interview or legal proceeding (Lee 1977).

Like members of other stigmatized groups (see, for example, Schneider and Conrad [1980] for epileptics, and Gussow and Tracy [1968] for persons with Hansen's Disease [leprosy]), gay people often come out to others in order to educate them about what it means to be gay and to affect their actions toward gay people as a group. Indeed, many gay men and lesbians regard coming out as a political act that is a necessary prelude to changing society's treatment of them (Humphreys 1972; Kitsuse 1980). Perhaps the most noted political leader to advocate this strategy was Harvey Milk, San Francisco's first openly gay supervisor, who was assassinated in 1978. For example, in a message that he had recorded to be played in the event of his death, Milk expressed the belief that coming out would eliminate prejudice: "I would like to see every gay lawyer, every gay architect come out, stand up and let the world know. That would do more to end prejudice overnight than anybody could imagine" (Shilts 1982:374).

Social science theory and data suggest that coming out is indeed likely to have a positive effect on heterosexuals' attitudes toward gay people as a group. This prediction is based on the *contact hypothesis*, which states that intergroup hostility and prejudice can be reduced by personal contact between majority and minority groups in the pursuit of common goals (Allport 1954; Sarbin 1996). A large body of empirical data (e.g., Amir 1976; Brewer and Miller 1984; Stephan 1985) indicates that intergroup contact can indeed change attitudes, provided that the contact meets the conditions originally specified by Allport (1954), for example, that the interacting individuals share equal status and that the two groups share superordinate goals.

Most empirical research using the contact hypothesis has focused on interracial and interethnic prejudice (for reviews, see Amir 1976; Brewer and Miller 1984; Stephan 1985). Social psychologists recognize, however, that common psychological processes underlie all forms of intergroup prejudice, regardless of the specific outgroup involved. The same theories and methods have been applied to understanding heterosexuals' antigay attitudes as have been used for, say, whites' anti-black attitudes (for examples, see Herek 1987a, 1987b). It would thus be reasonable to assume that the contact hypothesis is applicable to the case of heterosexuals' attitudes toward lesbians and gay men, even in the absence of data.

Supporting data, however, are indeed available. Survey research conducted with nationally representative probability samples (Herek and Capitanio 1995, 1996; Herek and Glunt 1993; Schneider and Lewis 1984) and with nonrepresentative convenience samples (Doran and Yerkes 1995; Gentry 1987; Herek 1988; Millham, San Miguel, and Kellogg 1976; Weis and Dain 1979) has consistently shown that heterosexuals who report personal contact with gay men or lesbians express significantly more favorable attitudes toward gay people as a group than do heterosexuals who lack contact experiences. In a 1988 national telephone survey of 937 adult U.S. residents, for example, Eric Glunt and I asked respondents, "Have any of your female or male friends, relatives, or close acquaintances let you know that they were homosexual?" We found that individuals who responded affirmatively had significantly lower scores on a measure of prejudice against gay men (Herek and Glunt 1993). Furthermore, we observed that contact was associated with less prejudice regardless of a respondent's demographic characteristics (including gender, age, educational background, level of religiosity, marital status, number of children, and geographic region). We also found that contact was the best statistical predictor of respondents' attitudes toward gay men, that is, the contact variable explained a greater proportion of variance in attitudes than any other demographic or social variable that we assessed.

I subsequently replicated and expanded on these findings in my previously mentioned research with Dr. John Capitanio (Herek and Capitanio 1996). In a 1990–91 national telephone survey of 538 adult heterosexuals, we asked respondents if they had "any male or female friends, relatives, or close acquaintances who are gay or homosexual." Respondents who reported contact experiences with at least one gay person (roughly one-third of the sample) manifested significantly more favorable attitudes toward gay men compared to respondents without contact experiences. As in my study with Eric Glunt, we found that this pattern held across demographic and social groups, and that contact was the most powerful predictor of attitudes.

In a follow-up survey one year later we asked the same respondents about their attitudes toward lesbians and found the same patterns. In both surveys we also asked questions about the nature of respondents' contact experiences: how many lesbians or gay men they knew, the type of relationship they had, and how they learned that a friend or relative was gay. Consistent with the contact hypothesis, we found that having a close relationship with a gay individual (e.g., a close friend or a member of one's immediate family) was associated with more favorable attitudes toward gay people generally than was having a more distant relationship (e.g., an acquaintance or distant relative). We also found that contact exerted an additive effect on attitudes: Respondents who knew three gay people generally had more favorable attitudes than those who knew two, and the latter, in turn, had more favorable attitudes than those who knew one.

The few attitude studies conducted with nonrepresentative samples of military personnel indicate that the relationship between contact experiences and favorable attitudes observed among civilians also holds for military personnel. Naval hospital personnel who reported having more than one gay friend manifested significantly less negative attitudes toward gay people generally (Doran and Yerkes 1995) and army personnel who believed that a gay man or lesbian was serving in their unit were more willing than others to allow homosexuals to serve in the military (Miller 1993, cited in National Defense Research Institute 1993:chap.7). In another survey of Army personnel conducted by Miller (1994), having gay friends was a significant predictor of opposition to the military's ban on homosexual personnel.

Yet another finding from my own national survey (Herek and Capitanio 1996) concerned the effects of self-disclosure on others' attitudes. We found that respondents who had been told directly by a gay friend or relative about the latter's homosexuality had more favorable attitudes toward gay people as a group compared to respondents who had guessed about a friend or relative's homosexuality or had been told by a third party. This effect also appeared to be additive: Respondents' attitudes tended to be more favorable to the extent that they had been the recipient of self-disclosures from a greater number of gay or lesbian individuals (Herek and Capitanio 1996).

Of course, correlational data do not indicate causality. However, our analyses of the relationships between reports of contact in the first survey (referred to here as Wave 1) and the same respondents' attitudes one year later in the follow-up survey (Wave 2) indicated that heterosexuals who knew a gay man or lesbian in 1990–91 were likely to develop more positive attitudes toward gay people as a group in the following year. Wave 1 contact explained a significant amount of variance in Wave 2 attitudes, even when Wave 1 attitudes were statistically controlled. At the same time we also observed that heterosexuals who reported favorable attitudes toward gay men and lesbians in 1990–91 were more likely than other respondents to experience contact with a gay person in the subsequent year; that is, Wave 1 attitudes explained a significant amount of variance in Wave 2 contact, even controlling for Wave 1 contact, probably because lesbians and gay men tend to reveal their sexual orientation to heterosexuals whom they expect to react favorably (see also Wells and Kline 1987). In summary, then, not only does contact with gay people affect heterosexuals' attitudes, but a heterosexual person's attitudes (or gay men and lesbians' perceptions of them) probably affects the likelihood that she or he will knowingly experience contact with gay people.

What are the psychological processes through which contact experiences influence heterosexuals' attitudes? In a close relationship, a gay or lesbian individual's direct disclosure about her or his homosexuality can provide the heterosexual with the necessary information and motivation to restructure her or his attitudes toward gay people as a group. This seems most likely to occur when the gay man or lesbian carefully manages the disclosure process so that the heterosexual can receive information (e.g., about what it means to be gay, about the gay person's similarity to other gay people) in the context of a committed relationship. For example, the gay person may self-disclose in a series of gradual stages, frame the disclosure in a context of trust and caring, explain why she or he did not disclose earlier, answer the heterosexual person's questions, and reassure the heterosexual that her or his past positive feelings and favorable judgments about the gay friend or relative are still valid.

Such interactions may help the heterosexual to keep in mind the other person's homosexual identity while observing behaviors that are inconsistent with stereotypes about gay people. Such a juxtaposition can facilitate the rejection of those stereotypes while fostering attitude change. If this experience leads the heterosexual person to accept that the friend or relative is indeed representative of the larger community of gay people — in other words, the friend or relative is not regarded as an anomaly — the heterosexual is likely to experience cognitive dissonance: On the one hand, she or he has strong positive feelings toward the gay friend or relative; on the other hand, she or he probably has internalized society's negative attitudes toward homosexuality. If the dissonance is resolved in favor of the friend or relative — an outcome that is more likely when the gay person plays an active role in imparting information about her or his stigmatized status — the heterosexual's attitudes toward gay people as a group are likely to become more favorable. The probability of favorable attitudes resulting from contact appears to be greater to the extent that a heterosexual has contact with more than one lesbian or gay man. Knowing multiple members of a stigmatized group is probably more likely to foster recognition of that group's variability than knowing only one group member (Wilder 1978). Knowing multiple members of a group may also reduce the likelihood that their behavior can be discounted as atypical (Rothbart and John 1985).

Summary   In summary, gay men and lesbians have a variety of reasons for disclosing their sexual orientation to others. Coming out affirms a core component of one's identity and facilitates the integration of one's homosexual identity with other aspects of the self. It permits honesty and openness in personal relationships with others, thereby enhancing and maintaining those relationships and creating a relational context in which other kinds of self-disclosure can occur. It permits the individual to feel authentic and to enjoy enhanced social and psychological functioning, while also possibly reducing stress and psychogenic symptoms. And it represents a political act through which an individual can attempt to change societal attitudes. Conversely, the negative consequences of staying in the closet include feelings of inauthenticity, impaired social relationships and interactions, increased strain on one's intimate relationships, and psychological and physical distress.

Conclusions and Implications for the U.S. Military

The foregoing discussion has several implications for current U.S. military policy. First, it demonstrates that the current policy — by codifying society's norms about disclosure of sexual orientation — establishes different rights of expression for heterosexual and homosexual personnel. Heterosexual personnel are permitted to declare their sexual orientation publicly whereas homosexual personnel are not. A married heterosexual soldier, for example, can freely disclose information about her or his marital status, can publicly display a photograph or letter from the spouse, and can even publicly display affection for the spouse (e.g., holding hands, embracing, kissing) — all without negative sanctions. Furthermore, because heterosexual roles are desexualized, public affirmations that one is heterosexual are not construed as a presumption of sexual conduct, including conduct that is prohibited under the Uniform Code of Military Justice (UCMJ), such as oral sex.[2] Homosexual personnel, by contrast, are required to hide their sexual orientation publicly and, if their identity becomes known, they are presumed to have engaged in illegal behavior.

Second, prohibiting gay men and lesbians from disclosing their sexual orientation does not simply mean that they are forbidden from discussing specific private sexual acts. Indeed, discussion of sexual behavior is a relatively minor component of public disclosure of one's sexual orientation. Current military policy has the effect of barring gay male and lesbian personnel from sharing a wide range of personal information with coworkers, friends, and acquaintances — information of the sort that is freely shared among heterosexuals.

Third, the prohibition on self-disclosure by lesbian and gay male personnel has important consequences for homosexuals. By requiring gay men and lesbians to hide significant portions of their lives, the policy imposes serious restrictions on their ability to interact socially. Whether gay people comply with the policy by using discretion, concealment, fabrication, or another strategy, they are disadvantaged — compared to heterosexuals — in establishing interpersonal relationships of the sort that contribute to social cohesion (MacCoun 1996) and opportunities for advancement. Furthermore, the ban on self-disclosure deprives gay men and lesbians of access to social support and may be deleterious to their long-term physical and psychological well being.

Fourth, the policy prevents heterosexual personnel from interacting freely with openly gay men and women in the course of their duties. Ironically, ongoing interpersonal contact would be likely to eliminate the prejudicial attitudes that the DoD currently cites as the reason why its policy is necessary. By allowing homosexuals the same rights of verbal self-disclosure currently permitted to heterosexuals, the military would create many of the conditions specified by social psychological research (e.g., institutional support for intergroup contact, shared goals) as likely to reduce interpersonal hostility and eliminate negative stereotypes.

Taken at face value, the maxim of "Don't ask, don't tell, don't pursue" appears to promote a live-and-let-live atmosphere in which homosexual personnel are tolerated so long as they keep their sexual orientation a private matter. As the foregoing discussion reveals, however, the policy places severe and sweeping strictures on gay people while preventing heterosexual personnel from experiencing the very types of social interactions that are most likely to eliminate antigay sentiment in the military's ranks. In a society in which homosexuality is stigmatized, to refrain from asking recruits about their sexual orientation is, perhaps, a positive step toward respecting the right of gay men and lesbians to retain control over information about their status. But in a society in which all adults are presumed to be heterosexual, to forbid gay people from telling others about their sexual orientation — and all aspects of their lives related to it — is to condemn them to invisibility and to sanction society's prejudice.

Acknowledgment

I wish to thank Steve Franzoi, Rob MacCoun, Jack Dynis, and Jared Jobe for their helpful comments on earlier versions of this paper.

Notes

1. That same-gender relationships lack a desexualized public role comparable to that of husband or wife is evident in the terminology that gay men and lesbians have available for describing the individual with whom they are in a committed relationship. Although *husband* and *wife* are legal terms, they also describe a complex set of relationships that, ideally, encompass the roles of lover, partner, and friend. Lacking legal spousal relationships, gay men and lesbians commonly use terms such as *lover*, *partner*, and *friend*, none of which conveys the complex set of meanings associated with *husband* or *wife*. Nor do those terms unambiguously describe the type of committed relationship signified by husband and wife. One's *partner* may be a business partner. One's *friend* may be simply an old school chum. One's *lover* may be a person with whom one is having a brief extramarital sexual affair. Each of these words creates confusion about the exact nature of the relationship; they describe only one part of it.
2. This assumption persists even though the majority of U.S. heterosexual adults — and, most likely, U.S. military personnel — have engaged in sexual behavior with their spouse that constitutes sodomy under the UCMJ (Laumann et al. 1994 (Laumann et al. 1994).

References

Adam, B. D. 1978. *The Survival of Domination: Inferiorization and Everyday Life.* New York: Elsevier.
Allport, G. 1954. *The Nature of Prejudice.* New York: Addison Wesley.

Altman, I., and D. A. Taylor. 1973. *Social Penetration: The Development of Interpersonal Relationships*. New York: Holt.

Amir, Y. 1976. The role of inter-group contact in change of prejudice and ethnic relations. In P. A. Katz, ed., *Towards the Elimination of Racism*, pp. 245–308. New York: Pergamon.

Anspach, R. R. 1979. From stigma to identity politics: Political activism among the physically disabled and former mental patients. *Social Science and Medicine* 13A:765–73.

Archer, R. L. 1980. Self-disclosure. In D. M. Wegner and R. R. Vallacher, eds., *The Self in Social Psychology*, pp. 183–205. New York: Oxford University Press.

Badgett, M.V.L. 1995. The wage effects of sexual orientation discrimination. *Industrial and Labor Relations Review* 49(4):726–38.

Baxter, L. A. 1987. Self-disclosure and relationship engagement. In V. J. Derlega and J. H. Berg, eds., *Self-Disclosure: Theory, Research, and Therapy*, pp. 155–74. New York: Plenum.

Becker, H. S. 1963. *Outsiders: Studies in the Sociology of Deviance*. New York: Free Press.

Bell, A. P., and M. S. Weinberg. 1978. *Homosexualities: A Study of Diversity Among Men and Women*. New York: Simon and Schuster.

Bellezza, F. S., and G. H. Bower. 1981. Person stereotypes and memory for people. *Journal of Personality and Social Psychology* 41:856–65.

Berg, J. H., and V. J. Derlega. 1987. Themes in the study of self-disclosure. In V. J. Derlega and J. H. Berg, eds., *Self-Disclosure: Theory, Research, and Therapy*, pp. 1–8. New York: Plenum.

Berrill, K. 1992. Anti-gay violence and victimization in the United States: An overview. In G. M. Herek and K. Berrill, eds., *Hate Crimes: Confronting Violence Against Lesbians and Gay Men*, pp. 19–45. Newbury Park, Calif.: Sage.

Blumstein, P., and P. Schwartz. 1983. *American Couples*. New York: Morrow.

Brewer, M. B., and N. Miller. 1984. Beyond the contact hypothesis: Theoretical perspectives on desegregation. In N. Miller and M. B. Brewer, eds., *Groups in Contact: The Psychology of Desegregation*, pp. 281–302. Orlando: Academic Press.

Davies, P. 1992. The role of disclosure in coming out among gay men. In K. Plummer, ed., *Modern Homosexualities: Fragments of Lesbian and Gay Experience*, pp. 75–83. London: Routledge.

Davis, M. H., and S. L. Franzoi. 1986. Adolescent loneliness, self-disclosure, and private self-consciousness: A longitudinal investigation. *Journal of Personality and Social Psychology* 51:595–608.

Derlega, V. J., and J. H. Berg, eds. 1987. *Self-Disclosure: Theory, Research, and Therapy*. New York: Plenum.

Derlega, V. J., M. S. Harris, and A. L. Chaiken. 1973. Self-disclosure reciprocity, liking and the deviant. *Journal of Experimental Social Psychology* 9:277–84.

Devine, P. G., and M. J. Monteith. 1993. The role of discrepancy-associated affect in prejudice reduction. In D. M. Mackie and D. L. Hamilton, eds., *Affect, Cognition, and Stereotyping: Interactive Processes in Group Perception*, pp. 317–44. San Diego: Academic Press.

Doran, A. P., and S. A. Yerkes. 1995. *Attitudes Toward Gay Men and Lesbians in a Naval Hospital Sample*. Paper presented at the annual meeting of the American Psychological Association, August, New York.

Duberman, M. B., M. Vicinus, and G. Chauncey Jr. 1989. *Hidden from History: Reclaiming the Gay and Lesbian Past*. New York: New American Library.

Erikson, E. H. 1963. *Childhood and Society*. 2nd ed. New York: Norton.

Esterling, B. A., M. H. Antoni, M. A. Fletcher, S. Margulies, and N. Schneiderman. 1994. Emotional disclosure through writing or speaking modulates latent Epstein-Barr Virus antibody titers. *Journal of Consulting and Clinical Psychology* 62:130–40.

Fitzpatrick, M. A. 1987. Marriage and verbal intimacy. In V. J. Derlega and J. H. Berg, eds., *Self-Disclosure: Theory, Research, and Therapy*, pp. 131–54. New York: Plenum.

Fowles, D. C. 1980. The three arousal model: Implications of Gray's two-factor theory for heart rate, electrodermal activity, and psychopathy. *Psychophysiology* 17:87–104.

Franzoi, S. L., and M. H. Davis. 1985. Adolescent self-disclosure and loneliness: Private self-consciousness and parental influences. *Journal of Personality and Social Psychology* 48:768–80.

Franzoi, S. L., M. H. Davis, and R. D. Young. 1985. The effects of private self-consciousness and perspective taking on satisfaction in close relationships. *Journal of Personality and Social Psychology* 48:1584–94.

Gentry, C. S. 1987. Social distance regarding male and female homosexuals. *Journal of Social Psychology* 127:199–208.

Gilman, S. L. 1985. *Difference and Pathology: Stereotypes of Sexuality, Race, and Madness*. Ithaca, N.Y.: Cornell University Press.

Goffman, E. 1963. *Stigma: Notes on the Management of Spoiled Identity*. Englewood Cliffs, N.J.: Prentice-Hall.

Gross, A. E., S. K. Green, J. T. Storck, and J. M. Vanyur. 1980. Disclosure of sexual orientation and impressions of male and female homosexuals. *Personality and Social Psychology Bulletin* 6:307–14.

Gross, L. 1993. *Contested Closets: The Politics and Ethics of Outing*. Minneapolis: University of Minnesota Press.

Gurwitz, S. B., and M. Marcus. 1978. Effects of anticipated interaction, sex, and homosexual stereotypes on first impressions. *Journal of Applied Social Psychology* 8:47–56.

Gussow, Z., and G. S. Tracy. 1968. Status, ideology, and adaptation to stigmatized illness: A study of leprosy. *Human Organization* 27:316–25.

Hammersmith, S. K., and M. S. Weinberg. 1973. Homosexual identity: Commitment, adjustment, and significant others. *Sociometry* 36(1):56–79.

Herdt, G. H., ed. 1984. *Ritualized Homosexuality in Melanesia*. Berkeley: University of California Press.

Herdt, G. H. 1989. Gay and lesbian youth, emergent identities, and cultural scenes at home and abroad. *Journal of Homosexuality* 17(1/2):1–42.

Herek, G. M. 1987a. Religion and prejudice: A comparison of racial and sexual attitudes. *Personality and Social Psychology Bulletin* 13(1):56–65.

Herek, G. M. 1987b. Can functions be measured? A new perspective on the functional approach to attitudes. *Social Psychology Quarterly* 50(4):285–303.

Herek, G. M. 1988. Heterosexuals' attitudes toward lesbians and gay men: Correlates and gender differences. *The Journal of Sex Research* 25:451–77.

Herek, G. M. 1990. Illness, stigma, and AIDS. In P. Costa and G. R. VandenBos, eds., *Psychological Aspects of Serious Illness*, pp. 103–50. Washington, D.C.: American Psychological Association.

Herek, G. M. 1992. The social context of hate crimes: Notes on cultural heterosexism. In G. M. Herek and K. T. Berrill, eds., *Hate Crimes; Confronting Violence Against Lesbians and Gay Men*, pp. 89–104. Newbury Park, Calif.: Sage.

Herek, G. M. 1993. Sexual orientation and military service: A social science perspective. *American Psychologist* 48:538–47.

Herek, G. M. 1995. Psychological heterosexism in the United States. In A. R. D'Augelli and C. J. Patterson, eds., *Lesbian, Gay, and Bisexual Identities Across the Life Span: Psychological Perspectives*, pp. 321–46. Oxford University Press.

Herek, G. M. 1997. The HIV epidemic and public attitudes toward lesbians and gay men. In M. P. Levine, P. Nardi, and J. Gagnon, eds., *Changing Times: Gay Men and Lesbians Encounter HIV/AIDS*, pp. 191–218. Chicago: University of Chicago Press.

Herek, G. M., and J. P. Capitanio. 1995. Black heterosexuals' attitudes toward lesbians and gay men in the United States. *The Journal of Sex Research* 32:95–105.

Herek, G. M., and J. P. Capitanio. 1996. "Some of my best friends": Intergroup contact, concealable stigma, and heterosexuals' attitudes toward gay men and lesbians. *Personality and Social Psychology Bulletin* 22:412–24.

Herek, G. M., and E. K. Glunt. 1993. Interpersonal contact and heterosexuals' attitudes toward gay men: Results from a national survey. *The Journal of Sex Research* 30:239–44.

Herek, G. M., and E. K. Glunt. 1995. Identity and community among gay and bisexual men in the AIDS era: Preliminary findings from the Sacramento Men's Health Study. In G. M. Herek and B. Greene, eds., *AIDS, Identity, and Community: The HIV Epidemic and Lesbians and Gay Men*, pp. 55–84. Newbury Park, Calif.: Sage.

Herman, N. J. 1993. Return to sender: Reintegrative stigma management strategies of ex-psychiatric patients. *Journal of Contemporary Ethnography* 22:295–330.

Hooker, E. 1965. An empirical study of some relations between sexual patterns and gender identity in male homosexuals. In J. Money, ed., *Sex Research: New Developments*, pp. 24–52. New York: Holt, Rinehart, and Winston.

Humphreys, L. 1972. *Out of the Closets: The Sociology of Homosexual Liberation*. Englewood Cliffs, N.J.: Prentice-Hall.

Johansson, W., and W. A. Percy. 1994. *Outing: Shattering the Conspiracy of Silence*. New York: Harrington Park.

Jones, E. E., A. Farina, A. H. Hastorf, H. Markus, D. T. Miller, and R. A. Scott. 1984. *Social Stigma: The Psychology of Marked Relationships*. New York: W. H. Freeman.

Jourard, S. M. 1971. *The Transparent Self*. 2nd ed. Princeton, N.J.: Van Nostrand.

Katz, J. N. 1983. *Gay/Lesbian Almanac: A New Documentary*. New York: Harper and Row.

Kite, M. E., and K. Deaux. 1987. Gender belief systems: Homosexuality and the implicit inversion theory. *Psychology of Women Quarterly* 11:83–96.

Kitsuse, J. I. 1980. Coming out all over: Deviants and the politics of social problems. *Social Problems* 28:1–13.

Kurdek, L. A. 1988. Perceived social support in gays and lesbians in cohabiting relationships. *Journal of Personality and Social Psychology* 54:504–9.

Kurdek, L. A. 1994. The nature and correlates of relationship quality in gay, lesbian, and heterosexual cohabiting couples: A test of the individual difference, interdependence, and discrepancy models. In B. Greene and G. M. Herek, eds., *Lesbian and Gay Psychology: Theory, Research, and Clinical Applications*, pp. 133–55. Newbury Park, Calif.: Sage.

Kurdek, L. A., and J. P. Schmitt. 1986. Relationship quality of partners in heterosexual married, heterosexual cohabiting, gay, and lesbian relationships. *Journal of Personality and Social Psychology* 51:711–20.

Larson, D. G., and R. L. Chastain. 1990. Self-concealment: Conceptualization, measurement, and health implications. *Journal of Social and Clinical Psychology* 9:439–55.

Laumann, E. O., J. H. Gagnon, R. T. Michael, and S. Michaels. 1994. *The Social Organization of Sexuality: Sexual Practices in the United States*. Chicago: University of Chicago Press.

Lee, J. A. 1977. Going public: A study in the sociology of homosexual liberation. *Journal of Homosexuality* 3(1):49–78.

Leserman, J., R. DiSantostefano, D. O. Perkins, and D. L. Evans. 1994. Gay identification and psychological health in HIV-positive and HIV-negative gay men. *Journal of Applied Social Psychology* 24:2193–2208.

Levine, M. P. 1979a. Employment discrimination against gay men. *International Review of Modern Sociology* 9(5–7):151–63.

Levine, M. P. 1979b. Gay ghetto. In M. P. Levine, ed., *Gay Men: The Sociology of Male Homosexuality*, pp. 182–204. New York: Harper and Row.

Levine, M. P., and R. Leonard. 1984. Discrimination against lesbians in the work force. *Signs* 9:700–710.

MacCoun, R. J. 1996. Sexual orientation and military cohesion: A critical review of the evidence. In G. M. Herek, J. Jobe, and R. Carney, eds., *Out in Force: Sexual Orientation and the Military*, pp. 157–76. Chicago: University of Chicago Press.

Malyon, A. K. 1982. Psychotherapeutic implications of internalized homophobia in gay men. *Journal of Homosexuality* 7(2/3):59–69.

Martin, A.D. 1982. Learning to hide: The socialization of the gay adolescent. In S. C. Feinstein, J. G. Looney, A. Z. Sohwartzberg, and A.D. Sorosky, eds., *Adolescent Psychiatry: Developmental and Clinical Studies*, vol. 10, pp. 52–65. Chicago: University of Chicago Press.

Mead, G. H. 1934. *Mind, Self, and Society: From the Standpoint of a Social Behaviorist*. Chicago: University of Chicago Press.

Miall, C. E. 1989. Authenticity and the disclosure of the information preserve: The case of adoptive parenthood. *Qualitative Sociology* 12:279–302.

Miller, L. L. 1994. Fighting for a just cause: Soldiers' views on gays in the military. In W. J. Scott and S. C. Stanley, eds., *Gays and Lesbians in the Military: Issues, Concerns, and Contrasts*, pp. 69–85. New York: Aldine de Gruyter.

Millham, J., C. L. San Miguel, and R. Kellogg. 1976. A factor-analytic conceptualization of attitudes toward male and female homosexuals. *Journal of Homosexuality* 2(1):3–10.

Murphy, B.C. 1989. Lesbian couples and their parents: The effects of perceived parental attitudes on the couple. *Journal of Counseling and Development* 68:46–51.

Murray, S. O. 1979. Institutional elaboration of a quasi-ethnic community. *International Review of Modern Sociology* 9:165–78.

National Defense Research Institute. 1993. *Sexual Orientation and U.S. Military Personnel Policy: Options and Assessment*. Santa Monica, Calif.: RAND.

Patterson, C. J. 1992. Children of lesbian and gay parents. *Child Development* 63:1025–42.

Pennebaker, J. W., and C. H. Chew. 1985. Behavioral inhibition and electrodermal activity during deception. *Journal of Personality and Social Psychology* 49:1427–33.

Pennebaker, J. W., J. K. Kiecolt-Glaser, and R. Glaser. 1988. Disclosure of traumas and immune function: Health implications for psychotherapy. *Journal of Consulting and Clinical Psychology* 56:239–45.

Pennebaker, J. W., and R. C. O'Heeron. 1984. Confiding in others and illness rates among spouses of suicides and accidental death victims. *Journal of Abnormal Psychology* 93:473–76.

Pennebaker, J. W., and J. R. Susman. 1988. Disclosure of traumas and psychosomatic processes. *Social Science and Medicine* 26:327–32.

Peplau, L. A. 1991. Lesbian and gay relationships. In J. Gonsiorek and J. Weinrich, eds., *Homosexuality: Research Findings for Public Policy*. Newbury Park, Calif.: Sage.

Peplau, L. A., and S. D. Cochran. 1990. A relationship perspective on homosexuality. In D. P. McWhirter, S. A. Sanders, and J. Reinisch, eds., *Homosexuality/Heterosexuality: Concepts of Sexual Orientation*, pp. 321–49. New York: Oxford University Press.

Plummer, K. 1975. *Sexual Stigma: An Interactionist Account*. London: Routledge and Kegan Paul.

Ponse, B. 1976. Secrecy in the lesbian world. *Urban Life* 5:313–38.

Results of poll. 1989, June 6. *San Francisco Examiner*, p. A-19.

Rothbart, M., and O. P. John. 1985. Social categorization and behavioral episodes: A cognitive analysis of the effects of intergroup contact. *Journal of Social Issues* 41(3):81–104.

Sarbin, T. R. 1996.The deconstruction of stereotypes: Homosexuals and military policy. In G. M. Herek, J. Jobe, and R. Carney, eds., *Out in Force: Sexual Orientation and the Military*, pp. 177–96. Chicago: University of Chicago Press.

Savin-Williams, R. C. 1994. Verbal and physical abuse as stressors in the lives of lesbian, gay male, and bisexual youths: Associations with school problems, running away, substance abuse, prostitution, and suicide. *Journal of Consulting and Clinical Psychology* 62:261–69.

Schneider, J. W., and P. Conrad. 1980. In the closet with illness: Epilepsy, stigma potential, and information control. *Social Problems* 28:32–44.

Schneider, W., and I. A. Lewis. 1984. The straight story on homosexuality and gay rights. *Public Opinion* 7(February/March):16–20, 59–60.

Shilts, R. 1982. *The Mayor of Castro Street: The Life and Times of Harvey Milk*. New York: St. Martin's.

Slater, P. 1963. Social limitations on libidinal withdrawal. *American Sociological Review* 28:339–64.

Snyder, M., and S. W. Uranowitz. 1978. Reconstructing the past: Some cognitive consequences of person perception. *Journal of Personality and Social Psychology* 36:941–50.

Stein, T. S., and C. J. Cohen. 1984. Psychotherapy with gay men and lesbians: An examination of homophobia, coming out, and identity. In E. S. Hetrick and T. S. Stein, eds., *Innovations in Psychotherapy with Homosexuals*, pp. 60–73. Washington, D.C.: American Psychiatric Press.

Stephan, W. G. 1985. Intergroup relations. In G. Lindzey and E. Aronson, eds., *Handbook of Social Psychology*, vol. 2, pp. 599–658. New York: Random House.

Stokes, J. P. 1987. The relation of loneliness and self-disclosure. In V. J. Derlega and J. H. Berg, eds., *Self-Disclosure: Theory, Research, and Therapy*, pp. 175–201. New York: Plenum.

Tversky, A., and D. Kahneman. 1973. Availability: A heuristic for judging frequency and probability. *Cognitive Psychology* 5:207–32.

Warren, C.A.B. 1974. *Identity and Community in the Gay World*. New York: Wiley.

Weis, C. B., and R. N. Dain. 1979. Ego development and sex attitudes in heterosexual and homosexual men and women. *Archives of Sexual Behavior* 8:341–56.

Wells, J. W., and W. B. Kline. 1987. Self-disclosure of homosexual orientation. *Journal of Social Psychology* 127(2):191–97.

Wilder, D. A. 1978. Reduction of intergroup discrimination through individuation of the out-group. *Journal of Personality and Social Psychology* 36:1361–74.

Zerubavel, E. 1982. Personal information and social life. *Symbolic Interaction* 5:97–109.

11 Lesbian, Gay, and Bisexual Youths' Relationships with Their Parents

Ritch C. Savin-Williams

       Much of the popular literature on lesbian, gay, and bisexual youths and their parents focuses on the difficult prospects they face when the child declares her or his same-sex attractions to parents. The youth must decide whether and, if so, when and how to disclose the nature of her or his sexuality to parents. Less popular than the personal "coming out" stories of youths (e.g., Heron 1994) are writings that narrate the reactions of parents once they discover that their child will not be fulfilling their heterosexual expectations (e.g., Borhek 1993; Fairchild and Hayward 1989). The emphasis in these compelling personal accounts and advice-giving tracts centers on the necessary trauma youths encounter if they decide to disclose to parents, or the consequences of not disclosing, and the stages that parents experience in coping with this unsettling news. These youths and their parents are described by therapists, counselors, educators, and others as necessarily facing unique developmental issues not encountered by families in which all immediate members are heterosexual (e.g., Coleman and Remafedi 1989; Strommen 1989).

The popular tracts promote the view that after the self-acknowledgment and self-labeling processes are essentially completed, the most difficult task confronting bisexual, gay, and lesbian youths is disclosing same-sex desires to parents. No task is perceived as more intricate, treacherous, or omnipresent as disclosing to parents (MacDonald 1983). Many youths cite in their personal narratives that they had few expectations that their parents would react in a positive, supportive fashion to the news that they have a lesbian, bisexual, or gay child. Youths fear being disowned, rejected, thrown out of the home, or emotionally or physically harassed.

Once parents become aware of their child's nonheterosexual orientation they often react with emotions and actions that cause considerable fear among the youths. The spectrum of parental reactions has been characterized by a number of writers as similar to those experienced by those undergoing grief and mourning (Anderson 1987; DeVine 1984; Robinson, Walters, and Skeen 1989). In these models parents progress through a series of stages before they are able to accept their child's sexual orientation. As described by Anderson (1987), the initial stages include shock, in which societal-based fears and prejudices surface and the child is in the greatest danger of being disowned, assaulted, or ejected from the home, and denial, in which a parent may refuse to acknowledge that anything is different or may pray for change, send the child to a therapist, or discount the revelation as just an adolescent phase. Then follow anger and guilt, in which a parent feels anger toward the supposed external "causes" of the child's homosexuality or feels guilty that she or he may have caused the "disorder" through bad parenting. Acknowledgment of feelings and concerns, without necessarily accepting the child's condition as moral, normal, or long-lasting, follows the anger and guilt. Finally, integration may come gradually through quiet acceptance followed by increased levels of understanding that eventually lead to the establishment of deep levels of intimacy, a comprehensive understanding of what it means to be gay in our culture, and political activism in gay causes. At the very least, at this point the child's sexual orientation and identity are seldom the focus of attention and conflict within the family.

Some parents never reach the latter stages. Under such circumstances sexual minority youths may regret having ever disclosed to parents; relations with parents become strained and perhaps irreversibly damaged. MacDonald (1983:1) observed that a youth may become a:

> half-member of the family unit: afraid and alienated, unable ever to be totally open and spontaneous, to trust or be trusted, to develop a fully socialized sense of self affirmation. This sad stunting of human potential breeds stress for gay people and their families alike — stress characterized by secrecy, ignorance, helplessness, and distance. . . . Gay people may be, in fact, the only minority in America whose families consistently reject them.

Whether the youth's fears of disclosure are real or imagined and whether parental reactions follow the grieving or mourning stages are difficult to ascertain because relatively few empirical studies have examined the nature of lesbian, gay, and bisexual youths' relations with their parents. Perhaps unwittingly, the personal narratives literature has often contributed to the view that the processes of youth disclosures and parental reactions are nearly identical for most lesbian, gay, and bisexual youths and their parents. Although few writers expressly defend the view that all youths have identical lives and that their parents experience identical symptoms and recoveries, their tracts sometimes make this assumption implicit. Many educators, clinicians, health care providers, and other professionals embrace almost without question these models, which can influence their perspectives and subsequent treatment of bisexual, lesbian, and gay youths and their parents.

Recent reviews assess that which is known regarding whether, when, how, and why youths disclose to parents (Savin-Williams 1998) and the reactions of parents to the disclosure (Savin-Williams and Dube 1998). In this paper the nature of the parent-youth relationship is examined, including that which is known regarding the importance of parents for lesbian, bisexual, and gay youths; reasons not to disclose to parents; whether lesbian, gay, and bisexual youths disclose to parents; and the association between disclosure to parents and the youths' psychological health. Finally, literature is reviewed that examines the overall relations that sexual minority youths have with their parents, with particular attention given to ethnic minority families. It is not my intent to discount the perspectives advanced by the personal stories of bisexual, lesbian, and gay youths and their parents but to present data from empirical research that address issues raised by these narratives.

Importance of Parents

Relations with parents are clearly a source of concern among many gay, bisexual, and lesbian youths. For example, Martin and Hetrick (1988) noted that the second most common presenting problem among those who sought assistance from their New York City social and educational agency for sexual minority youths (Hetrick-Martin Institute) was family relations. These ranged "from feelings of isolation and alienation that result from fear that the family will discover the adolescent's homosexuality, to actual violence and expulsion from the home" (p. 174). Knowing the parents' heterosexual expectations of them and the expressed reality of their homosexuality led many youths to feel a "sense of contradiction and failure" that in turn resulted in "guilt, shame, anger, and a not unfounded fear of rejection" (p. 174).

The limited empirical research conducted thus far has focused on the fact that disclosure to parents is seldom easy because of the significance of parents in the youths' lives. For example, 93 percent of a college sample of gay men (D'Augelli 1991) reported that a "problem" that was "somewhat" to "extremely troubling" to them was telling parents about their sexual orientation. This percentage dropped to 69 percent among gay and 61 percent among lesbian youth group members (D'Augelli and Hershberger 1993), perhaps because a larger percentage of these youths had already disclosed to parents. Although nearly one-quarter of support group youths reported that disclosing to parents was "extremely troubling," ranking second to worries about AIDS, college gay men ranked it first, just ahead of terminating a close relationship. That half the college men characterized disclosing to parents as "*extremely* troubling" supports the view that until this event has occurred it remains a central concern in the lives of gay youths.

From a perspective of parental impact on current aspects of a youth's self-concept, the significance of parents fares poorly compared to the importance of other people and influences in the lives of college youths. Among college gay men, only 15 percent rated their parents as currently the most important people in their life, considerably less than gay male friends (54 percent) and heterosexual friends who were aware of their sexual identity (25 percent) (D'Augelli 1991). In another sample composed primarily of college students, lesbians ranked relationships with parents fifth and gay men ranked them eighth of twelve in a list of items important for one's sense of self-worth, ahead of possessions, frequent sex, having children, and religion (Savin-Williams 1990). Rating as more important for both sexes were same-sex friends, career, academic success, and romantic relationship; gay men also included physical looks and a social life as more important. Despite the seeming irrelevance of relationships with parents, more than half the college students had at least weekly contact with their mother; comparable percentages with father were 33 percent (daughters) and 42 percent (sons).

The mixed findings by research scholars regarding the significance of parents in the lives of sexual minority youths are further illustrated by Hershberger and D'Augelli (1995). They found that high family support and high victimization correlated, suggesting that youths actively sought the support of their family when they experienced victimization, or perhaps the family extended support when the child was injured or distressed. Family support appeared to buffer an adolescent against the harmful effects of victimization on her or his mental health, but only if the family support was high and the victimization that the adolescent faced was low.

Reasons Not to Disclose to Parents

The relationship between the importance of parents and youth disclosing to them has seldom been investigated. Perhaps because parents are of great or of slight importance to them, some youths elect to postpone, possibly indefinitely, telling parents about their sexuality. Youths may not expect them to react positively to the announcement that they have a lesbian, bisexual, or gay child or, in more extreme cases, fear "that they would be rejected, punished, perhaps physically assaulted, or expelled from the family" (Anderson 1987:165). Whether these fears are in danger of being implemented or are merely imagined is difficult to ascertain except on a case-by-case family basis.

Individual life histories, revealed in personal narrative accounts, document many of the most severe reactions that youths receive from parents once they disclose. Empirical research conducted with youths from the Hetrick-Martin Institute supports these reports of dire consequences that some youths encounter after disclosure. Their parents were often unable to move beyond their initial shock and rage, erupting in a barrage of verbal or physical assaults. The majority of violent physical attacks experienced by five hundred primarily African-American and Latino New York City sexual minority youths occurred in the family (Hunter 1990). The range of abuse these youths experienced included ridicule, battering, and rape; as a result, some attempted suicide. A recent review of the literature on the verbal and physical abuse that sexual minority youths, especially male prostitutes, runaways, and homeless youths, suffer confirms the high incidence of violence they receive in the home (Savin-Williams 1994).

These consequences of disclosure were also documented by Pilkington and D'Augelli (1995) in a sample of community support group youths. Slightly over 60 percent had experienced some degree of verbal or physical harassment from a family member, ranging from verbal insults (36 percent) to physical assaults (10 percent). Significantly more girls than boys were physically assaulted. Mothers (22 percent) were the most frequent abusers, followed by brothers (15 percent), fathers (14 percent), and sisters (9 percent). For one-quarter of the youths, fear of verbal and physical abuse reduced the possibility of greater openness about their same-sex attractions.

Another motivation for not disclosing to parents emerges in personal narratives and "coming out" stories, one that is altruistic in intent. Youths desire neither to disappoint nor to hurt parents or place them in an awkward position with relatives and neighbors. They also fear the long-term effects that such disclosure would have on their relationships and status within the immediate and extended family. Yet many youths report that by not telling they feel isolated and alienated from the family and fearful of what parents would do if they were to discover the youth's sexual orientation.

Brown (1988) described tactics that some youths use to survive this "cognitive dissonance" of wanting yet fearing disclosure to family members. One is to maintain an emotional or geographic distance from the family, becoming "independent" with little physical or verbal contact with family members. Another adolescent tactic was suggested by Herdt and Boxer (1993): avoidance of any discussion of personal issues by establishing a "demilitarized zone" of off-limits topics. Parents may respect these boundaries because they fear that they may come to "know" a truth they do not want to hear. A third ploy is to disclose to the parent or sibling who will most likely be supportive and assist in the masquerade of heterosexuality.

The prevalence of these horror stories in the lives of sexual minority youths is difficult to assess because remarkably few empirical studies have examined the relations that lesbian, gay, and bisexual youths have with their parents. More specifically, reasons for not disclosing to parents have seldom been systematically investigated. The greatest deterrents to more openness between youths and their parents appear to be the youths' fear of rejection and verbal or physical abuse. For example, D'Augelli (1991) noted that fear of rejection characterized those in his sample of sixty-one college men who had not yet disclosed to parents. Indeed, youths who lived at home and had disclosed to family members were more likely to be victimized by them than those who had not disclosed (D'Augelli, Hershberger, and Pilkington 1998). Although one-quarter of a sample of urban support group youths reported that they feared verbal abuse from their parents, relatively few (7 percent) expressed fear that they would suffer physical harm from parents if they were to be more open about their sexuality (D'Augelli and Hershberger 1993; Pilkington and D'Augelli 1995). In a similar sample of Chicago youths, seven (3 percent) reported that they had been thrown out of the home and were living in shelters or with friends (Herdt and Boxer 1993). The fear of rejection, especially from the father, haunted many of those who were debating disclosing, although few expected the dire consequences faced by their seven peers or that they would be physically assaulted.

In several studies, however, youths who had not disclosed to parents often expected a more negative parental reaction than that which youths who had disclosed reported receiving. For example, in D'Augelli and Hershberger's (1993) study of 194 youths from various urban support groups, 52 percent of nondisclosers expected their mother to be intolerant or rejecting; 64 percent expected the same reactions from their father. Few (10 percent) of the non-disclosers expected their fathers to be accepting. These percentages contrast markedly from those who had disclosed to their parents: Only 20 percent of mothers and 28 percent of fathers were intolerant or rejecting. In all cases reported thus far, greater fear surrounds youths disclosing to fathers than to mothers, whether the fear is justified or not (Cramer and Roach 1988).

Disclosers and nondisclosers may represent two very different popula-tions. For example, perhaps disclosers have a fairly accurate perception that their parents would respond positively to having a gay child. This could reflect the parents' liberal, accepting nature or the parents' already strong suspicions that they have a gay child. Perhaps disclosers are more sex atypical than nondisclosers (see Pilkington and D'Augelli 1995) and thus less able to hide their same-sex attractions, forcing them out of the closet earlier — by their own inclinations or by being pushed out by peers. Nondisclosers may very well be accurate in their expectations that parental reactions will be harsh and abusive. Unknown are disclosers' expectations before they tell their parents about their same-sex attractions.

Conclusion

Although aware of their same-sex attractions before puberty and disclosing this information to a trusted peer, many adolescents conceal their sexuality from parents until late adolescence or early adulthood, when they are more emotionally and financially independent (Savin-Williams and Diamond 1999). For some youths, parents are among the last to learn about their homoerotic attractions, in large part because the youths want to avoid being verbally or physically assaulted or emotionally rejected by parents, although relatively few believe that they would be as summarily rejected or abused as were the Hetrick-Martin Institute youths. The greatest fear of youths may not be one of rejection but of hurting or disappointing their parents (Cramer and Roach 1988). The possibility that this desire to avoid disappointing parents is the primary motivator not to disclose has not been systematically explored by researchers of sexual minority youths.

The decision to delay disclosure may initially protect youths from feared parental reactions, but it may also create an irreplaceable fissure in the parent-child relationship. As stressful as disclosing their sexuality to parents can be, not disclosing to parents can be an even greater stressor in the lives of lesbian, bisexual, and gay youths (Rotheram-Borus, Rosario, and Koopman 1991). When the physical and emotional danger of disclosing is real, however, the only viable alternative for a youth may be misleading and lying to parents. The other possibility, that the anticipated family crisis may not be as traumatic in reality as it appears in fantasy, must also be seriously considered when debating the consequences of disclosing.

Disclosure to Parents

In recent surveys of more than five thousand readers of *The Advocate*, a national gay and lesbian news magazine for a highly educated, affluent, and politically aware population, two-thirds of bisexual, lesbian, and gay adults reported that they had disclosed their sexual identity to their mother and nearly half had told their father (Lever 1994, 1995). The lesbian or bisexual women (mean age, thirty-four) disclosed to parents at the average age of twenty-four years; for the gay or bisexual men (mean age, thirty-eight), twenty years. Many of the respondents who had not directly disclosed to parents believed that their parents had deduced reality. These results, consistent with previous research with adults reported in the 1970s (e.g., Bell and Weinberg 1978), indicated that more had disclosed to their mother than their father, but these findings are inconsistent with all but the most recent studies in that such a large number of individuals had openly discussed their sexuality with their parents.

One explanation of this recent cultural shift in the percentage of same-sex-oriented individuals who have disclosed to parents is the increased visibility and acceptance of sexual minorities and their communities during the last decade (*USA Today* 1996). For example, lesbian, gay, and bisexual characters are almost routinely included in television shows and in movies (Duin 1996). Even religious conservatives, who emphasize "family values," have dramatically increased the visibility of homosexuality through antigay campaigns. These cultural events have resulted in an openness about same-sex attractions that has likely filtered down to interactions among family members. Thus it is not surprising that current cohorts of bisexual, gay, and lesbian youths, at increasingly earlier ages, are recognizing, acknowledging, and publicly proclaiming their same-sex attractions to friends, family, talk show hosts, the information highway, and anyone else who will listen

(Cohen and Savin-Williams 1996; Savin-Williams 1996; Savin-Williams and Diamond 1999).

Research on sexual minority youths and their struggles in deciding whether they should disclose to family members has been relatively rare until the last five years. One of the first was Anderson's (1987) qualitative study of ninety gay, lesbian, and bisexual Seattle youths between the ages of fifteen and nineteen years who dropped by his "rap group" for gay youth (75 percent male) during a fifteen-month period. "Relatively few" had disclosed to parents, which is consistent with the adult studies of that era.

Recent research with sexual minority youths attending similar urban support groups and college campus groups documents the considerable variability in reports regarding the percentage of youths who have disclosed to at least one parent (see Table 11.1). In most studies, over 60 percent of the youths were white, with the notable exception of the Chicago-based Horizons youth group (Herdt and Boxer 1993). The remaining youths were usually African-Americans, with only single-digit percentages of Latino, Asian, and Native American youths. In most samples the youths were in their late teens or early twenties when completing the questionnaire or interview. All studies included gay or bisexual males but half excluded lesbian or bisexual females. Even in the five inclusive studies, however, the female youths never constituted more than one-third of the total sample. Characteristics other than sex and age, such as physical attributes, cognitive abilities, personality traits, social class, and political ideologies, are seldom provided.

In studies of adolescents who attended support groups serving urban youth, roughly 60 to 80 percent had disclosed to their mothers (Table 11.1). Far fewer, 30 to 60 percent were "out" to their fathers. Percentage of disclosure differed depending, in part, on when data were collected. The first three studies, which registered 20 points lower than the others, were conducted in the 1980s. The youths thus represent a slightly earlier cohort of sexual minority youths, and this may well account for the smaller numbers who had disclosed to parents. In general, the more recent the study, the larger the percentage of youths who had disclosed to parents. Also noteworthy is that sex differences in whether adolescents had disclosed to either parent rarely appear to be large or significant. Finally, if racial variations in disclosure levels existed in the multiethnic sample studies, they were not reported.

A second population source used by investigators to assess developmental milestones of gay, bisexual, and lesbian youths is college campus groups. These youths are, on average, several years older and more highly educated, more likely to have two parents in the home and to come from higher social

TABLE 11.1 Percentage of Youths Who Have Disclosed to Parents

Support Groups	No. of Subjects		Avg. Age	Mother		Father		A Parent	
	Gay	Lesbian		Gay	Lesbian	Gay	Lesbian	Gay	Lesbian
Remafedi (1987)	29	—	18.3	62%		34%			
Sears (1991)	24	12	23					54%	58%
Herdt and Boxer (1993)	141	61	18.3	54%	63%	28%	37%		
D'Augelli and Hershberger (1993)	142	52	18.9					75%	75%
Telljohann and Price (1993)	89	31	19					74%	84%
Savin-Williams and Wright (1995)	51	23	18.3	67%	83%	58%	65%		
College Groups									
Savin-Williams (1990)	214	103	20.3	53%	59%	37%	25%		
D'Augelli (1991)	61	—	21	39%		27%			
Rhoads (1994)	40	—	22.5	61%		48%			
Savin-Williams (1995)	97	—	22.5	65%		47%			

class families, and less likely to be an ethnic minority, as well as many other variables that have not been assessed (e.g., outlook on life, temperament). Table 11.1 indicates that, on average, 20 percent *fewer* college students than support group members reported that they had disclosed their same-sex attractions to parents. Many of the undisclosed college men believed, however, that their parents knew or were suspicious. Similar to the youth group samples, college students of both sexes were less "out" to their fathers than to their mothers. Average age of disclosure to one's mother and father ranged from 16.6 years to 20.1 years, some three months to more than one year after a friend was told (D'Augelli and Hershberger 1993; Savin-Williams 1995; Sears 1991).

Reasons for the lower percentage of disclosure among college students have not been offered, perhaps because investigators have not previously noted this population difference. If they had, the most likely explanations would center on the distinct possibility that the support group and college samples may have been drawn from different populations. Youths who attend support groups may do so because they have told their parents and need peer support, housing, medical services, and counseling; or the youth group may have encouraged them to "come out" fully. College students may feel that they can be out on campus, participate in anonymous research, and remain closeted to their parents who reside in a distant community. Disclosing to parents may be perceived as too risky, including being cut off financially, which they may believe would terminate their career and professional aspirations. Or the population variation may merely be an urban-rural difference. The support groups are located almost exclusively in urban areas where resources are more readily available and visibility of sexual minority communities is higher; by contrast, the college groups investigated draw heavily from small towns and cities in upstate New York, Pennsylvania, Iowa, and Minnesota. D'Augelli and Hart (1987) observed that in rural and small towns youths who dare to question their sexuality often face isolation, anonymity, and few resources or positive role models. Such youths are thus less likely to be out to their family and small-town community where others sometimes take an interest in everyone else's life.

Conclusion

Based on research reviewed in this section, it is not possible to estimate the exact percentage of youths who have disclosed to parents their same-sex attractions. Information regarding when they disclosed this information and how they shared this secret about themselves is even more sparse (Savin-Williams 1998). A parent may be the first to know or the last, told directly, perhaps within the context of a family meeting, or become suspicious because of a son's or daughter's gender role behavior or interests.

Parents are seldom the first person a youth tells about her or his same-sex attractions, and mothers are usually told before fathers. A greater percentage of mothers than fathers know about their child's same-sex attractions. In current research surveys, 40 to 75 percent of sons have disclosed to their mothers and 30 to 55 percent have disclosed to their fathers. Less is known about daughters, but the proportions appear about the same, with perhaps slightly more daughters having openly discussed the issue with their mothers.

The most consistent conclusion that can be drawn from the empirical data is the existence of a cohort effect. Since the beginning of the 1990s a greater percentage of youths are disclosing to their parents; the irreversibility of this trend is not yet certain, given the political climate that many sexual minority youths must now encounter. The effects that either early or late disclosure has on a youth's self-evaluation, however, are considerably less certain than the knowledge that disclosure is occurring earlier.

Disclosure and Youths' Self-Evaluation

One question that several researchers have investigated is how disclosure to parents of one's same-sex attractions affects a young person's mental health. Research has thus far failed to unequivocally demonstrate that disclosure to parents is a healthy decision. Three seemingly contradictory findings regarding the relationship between disclosure and mental health have been supported by research data.

One finding is that those who disclose to parents are *more unhealthy*. For example, in a study of 138 primarily African-American and Hispanic gay and bisexual males seeking assistance from the Hetrick-Martin Institute (mean age, 16.8 years), suicide attempters were more likely than non-attempters to have disclosed to parents or to have been discovered to be gay (Rotheram-Borus, Hunter, and Rosario 1994). Similarly youths from other urban support groups who had previous suicide attempts were more likely to have disclosed to a nonparent family member earlier, to have positive relations with parents, and to have parents aware of their child's sexual orientation (D'Augelli and Hershberger 1993). They did not differ from nonattempters in parental reactions to disclosure or in the distress they faced in discussing their sexual orientation with parents. D'Augelli and Hershberger (1993) suggested that suicide attempters were more out to parents because the youths were aware of same-sex attractions from an early age, which gave them a longer period of time in which to disclose, or because of the youth's past suicide attempts, which sensitized parents to the realization that their child was suffering from issues directly related to his or her sexual identity.

Other research suggests that disclosure to parents is *unrelated* to psychological health. Life satisfaction was unrelated to general openness about being gay in a study of college men (D'Augelli 1991). Similarly, among a younger cohort of youths, self-esteem and all clinical scale scores on the Brief Symptom Inventory were unrelated to whether one was out to parents (D'Augelli and Hershberger 1993). In a third study, consisting of 137 males (82 percent white and 13 percent African-American) recruited through advertisements in gay publications, bars, social support groups, and university groups, gay youths (mean age, 19.6 years) who attempted suicide were no more likely than those who did not to have disclosed to parents (Remafedi, Farrow, and Deisher 1991). Finally, among 103 bisexual and lesbian women ages sixteen to twenty-three years, parental knowledge and acceptance of the daughter's same-sex attractions were unrelated to her self-esteem level (Savin-Williams 1990).

The third alternative, that those who disclose to parents score *better* on psychological functioning measures, is based on the finding that youths use parents, especially mothers for gay boys, as protectors of being victimized by others (Pilkington and D'Augelli 1995). Indeed, college men who were open about their same-sex attractions less often feared verbal and physical harassment or worried about telling their parents (D'Augelli 1991). One of the best predictors of a male youth's self-esteem in another study was the mother's (but not the father's) knowledge of his same-sex attractions (Savin-Williams 1990). Finally, a third indication of greater psychological health is the finding that youths who were least likely to think of suicide were those whose mother and father knew their sexual orientation (D'Augelli and Hershberger 1993).

Conclusion

It has been suggested that if the consequences are affirming and supportive, disclosure to parents enhances a youth's self-esteem (Borhek 1993).

Although parents are often a significant factor in their child's developing sense of self-worth and sexual identity, especially in terms of youths feeling comfortable with their sexuality and disclosing that information to others (Savin-Williams 1990), the effects that disclosure to parents has on the self-evaluations of sexual minority youths have not been systematically or definitively explored.

The three alternatives reviewed above as to whether disclosure and mental health are related are worthy hypotheses for further investigations. Current research findings are generally correlational in nature and thus are not necessarily informative regarding the causal pathway between disclosure and psychological health. For example, if one assumes that disclosure and psychological health are related, one could just as cogently argue that those who are already functioning in a healthy manner are most likely to risk disclosing to family members as to contend that by outing oneself to parents one gains a measure of psychological health. In other words, a satisfying relationship with parents may encourage youths to disclose to them, or, perhaps equally likely, their relationship is satisfying because youths have disclosed to them. Perhaps both are true. A third possibility is that disclosure and mental health are connected through a third variable. Youths may be psychologically healthy because they grew up in a family context that celebrated being true to one's nature, including disclosing one's sexual self to family members.

The three alternatives join a long list of needed items on a research agenda that explores the psychological effects on adolescents who decide to disclose to parents, to postpone telling until a more opportune time in their life, or never to disclose the nature of their sexuality. They also reflect a more basic shortcoming: Relatively little is known regarding the youth-parent relationship in its most general terms.

The Youth-Parent Relationship

Although few researchers have addressed the relationships that sexual minority youths have with their parents other than the initial disclosure reactions or a global rating of how important the parents are to the child, limited empirical evidence suggests that the relationships are positive and satisfying, especially with the mother. This conclusion is incongruent with many of the personal narratives of youths and parents presented in the popular literature.

In general, relationships with the mother, regardless of whether the child has disclosed her or his sexual identity to her, have been reported to be considerably better than with the father. This is apparent in studies of adult children (Ben-Ari 1995; Cramer and Roach 1988) and youths (Herdt and Boxer 1993; Savin-Williams 1990). For example, Cramer and Roach (1988) reported that relationships with fathers were less positive for adult sons than with mothers for those who had disclosed, those who wanted to disclose but had not, and those who did not want to disclose. Almost 60 percent of boys and 50 percent of girls who came to the youth-serving agency Horizons in Chicago had positive or very positive relationships with their mothers, but only 30 percent of boys and 24 percent of girls had similar positive relationships with their fathers (Herdt and Boxer 1993).

Another study supporting the more positive relationship with the mother than the father was reported with a sample of gay, bisexual, and lesbian youths fourteen to twenty-three years of age (Savin-Williams 1989). Satisfaction with the relationship and contact with parents were greater for mothers than for fathers for both sons and daughters. Nearly 40 percent of the youths reported very bad relationships with their fathers; with mothers the number of bad relationships was far less, 15 percent. On a 9-point (low-high) scale, more than half the lesbian and bisexual women (55 percent) and gay and bisexual men (51 percent) rated their maternal relationship as a 7 or better (Savin-Williams 1989). Comparable percentages for the paternal relationship were 35 percent and 29 percent, respectively. The overall mean was on the positive side for mothers but on the slightly negative side for fathers. Another measure of the parental relationship was assessed, contact with parents. Nearly 60 percent of the youths had at least weekly contact by phone, mail, or a visit with their mother. Weekly contact with fathers was reported by 40 percent of the gay men and 33 percent of the lesbian women. The gay and bisexual male youths maintained more contact with both parents than did the lesbian and bisexual women. Thirteen percent of the men and 8 percent of the women had at least daily contact with their mothers; 11 percent of the men and 5 percent of the women had the same frequency of contact with their fathers. Although no comparable data were collected with heterosexual youths, it appears that the vast majority of these 317 youths had positive, satisfying relations with their parents.

Research with youths and their parents has seldom addressed the longitudinal nature of the parent-child relationship, including before disclosure, immediately after disclosure, and during various markers after the youth's announcement. In one study of adult men (Cramer and Roach 1988), one-third felt that disclosure had no negative impact. Based on interviews with 202 youths, Herdt and Boxer (1993) assessed time changes. They were impressed that the overall quality of the mother-child relationship did not appear to be affected, regardless of the mother's initial response to the news of her child's gay or lesbian identity. Father awareness was associated with more *positive* relationships, although whether the changes in their relationship after disclosure would be positive or negative could not be predicted by the data they collected.

Only one investigation has attempted to predict the nature of the youth-parent relationship based on characteristics of the youths, parents, and their relationships (Savin-Williams 1989). Based on anonymous questionnaires from 103 lesbian and bisexual women, the study found that women who reported satisfying relationships with their parents and who had relatively young parents were most likely to have disclosed to them (see also Kahn 1991). Daughters who were most satisfied with their maternal relationships had the most contact with their mothers, a satisfying relationship with their fathers, mothers who knew their same-sex orientation, and high self-esteem. Those most satisfied with their paternal relationships had the most contact with their fathers (although contact did not significantly predict the fathers' knowledge of their daughters' sexual orientation), a satisfying relationship with their mothers, married parents, and fathers who knew their same-sex attractions.

Among the 214 gay and bisexual male youths in the same study (Savin-Williams 1989), sons who were most satisfied with their maternal relationships had young mothers and fathers, considerable contact with their mothers, satisfying paternal relationships, and high self-esteem. Those most satisfied with their paternal relationships had the most contact with their fathers, satisfying maternal relationships, fathers who knew their sexual orientation, and high self-esteem.

As noted earlier, several studies have reported that gay sons had better relations with parents than did lesbian daughters. Muller (1987) found additional support for this. While 72 percent of gay males reported positive relationships with their parents over time, only 46 percent of lesbians achieved this state. The lower level of acceptance experienced by lesbian daughters from their parents was attributed by Muller to the mother's heightened disappointment that the daughter would not be fulfilling the mother's expectations for grandchildren. Another study, however, attributed the lower level of daughter-parent relations to the daughter's relationship with her father (Herdt and Boxer 1993). More daughters than sons reported negative changes in their relationships with their fathers after disclosure. However, the greater negative changes in the daughters' than the sons' relationships with fathers were independent of whether the fathers knew about their daughters' sexual identity; that is, over time relations between father and daughter decreased regardless of disclosure.

An alternative explanation is that although lesbians may be closer than gay men to both parents during childhood and early adolescence, this closeness is jeopardized by disclosure of lesbian status. In contrast, because gay men have worse parental relationships than lesbians before disclosing their homosexuality, they improve relations with their parents after disclosure. In particular, the sex difference may be most apparent in the father-son relationship, which is often so impaired before the revelation that any minor improvement in honesty, communication, and trust would be considered a positive development for the relationship (Cramer and Roach 1988; Herdt and Boxer 1993). Thus over 20 percent of men in one sample (Cramer and Roach 1988) reported an improvement in their relationship with their fathers after disclosure. This was considerably higher than with mothers, which was 7 percent. Additional support for this view comes from the gay and bisexual males interviewed by Savin-Williams (1995), who reported that they never felt particularly close to their fathers because they did not enjoy the activities that their fathers wanted to do, such as playing sports and fixing mechanical things. To them, their fathers appeared embarrassed or disappointed in their sons' atypical behaviors and interests; the gay and bisexual sons more typically enjoyed reading, artistic efforts, and housework. Once they disclosed to their fathers, the relationships improved, perhaps, some speculated, because the fathers felt absolved of any blame for the sons' feminine interests and behaviors (i.e., it now made sense). Herdt and Boxer (1993) noted that "for some fathers it may be a relief to understand their children in a new way; to be aware of an aspect of their lives previously hidden or even confusing to them" (p. 218). It should be noted, however, that despite this improvement, gay and bisexual sons were still more satisfied with maternal than paternal relations (Savin-Williams 1989).

Largely left unexplored, however, is the father-daughter relationship. Perhaps the relationship moves in the opposite direction — toward a deterioration — regardless of the daughter's disclosure of same-sex attractions solely because of her approaching sexual maturity and the dynamics that ensue. In the case of a daughter who does not aspire to loving men, the father may be particularly disappointed in her because he perceives she has rejected wanting men, which he may feel is a rejection of the masculinity he represents. Or if she has engaged in sex atypical behavior (acting like a "tomboy") throughout her life, which probably included playing sports and rough-and-tumble activities with her father, the father may feel guilty that he has "caused" his daughter to become a lesbian. These are matters purely of speculation because few researchers explore the uniqueness of the lesbian daughter-father relationship.

Conclusion

Perhaps the mother's significance in the lives of lesbian, gay, and bisexual youths lies in her unique role as "mother" and the seemingly more distant and less satisfying relationship that such youths have with their fathers. This finding is congruent with adult studies (see review in Bell, Weinberg, and Hammersmith 1981) and for many adolescents in our society regardless of sexual orientation who view mothers as considerably more supportive, warm, and emotional than they do fathers. Apparently this support is most likely to come from a young mother when the issue is her daughter's sexual identity. These daughters were most likely to have disclosed to their young mothers and to have positive self-esteem. A young mother was also important for gay and bisexual sons; those who reported the highest levels of satisfaction with the maternal relationship had young mothers. The significance of the mother's youthfulness may be a cohort effect; she would have had a greater probability of being raised in a culture in which the visibility of homosexuality may have encouraged her to be more knowledgeable, open, and tolerant, if not accepting, of same-sex attractions in her child.

Although Herdt and Boxer (1993) indicated that disclosure had a minimal effect on the youth-parent relationship, which is also contrary to much of the popular literature, the long-term effects of disclosure on the relationships youths have with their parents are unknown. The closer a lesbian, gay, or bisexual youth is to the parent she or he is confiding in, the greater the parent's reaction will impact the youth. This may, in part, be a moot issue, because few youths tell parents at a sufficiently young age to have post-disclosure long-term relations with parents until they are adults. Perhaps indicative of these future relations, the adult men in one study who had disclosed to their parents reported that their relations with their parents initially deteriorated following disclosure (significant for both mother and father) but improved significantly after disclosure (Cramer and Roach 1988).

Ethnic Sexual Minority Youths and Their Families

Morales (1989) observed that most lesbian, bisexual, and gay ethnic minority youths live in three often competing and sometimes mutually exclusive communities — gay, ethnic, and white:

> While each community provides fundamental needs, serious consequences emerge if such communities were to be visibly integrated and merged. . . . It requires a constant effort to maintain oneself in three different worlds, each of which fails to support significant aspects of a person's life. (p. 219)

One major difference that many writers note between white and ethnic family constellations is the greater integration of the extended family within the ethnic support system. The constellation of the traditional, extended family was described by Morales (1983) as a support system that resembles a "tribe" with multiple, often biologically related family groups. For ethnic minority youths, the family often "constitutes a symbol of their basic roots and the focal point of their ethnic identity" (p. 9) and can consequently be a source of great pride and strength. Thus, when youths declare their same-sex attractions to parents, they risk not only intrafamily relationships but also their strong association, identification, and support within their extended community.

Given the emotional centrality of the extended family, youths with same-sex attractions may feel that they must inevitably choose between their familial or ethnic affiliation and their personal sexual identity. Many believe that they can never publicly disclose their same-sex attractions, because they do not want to humiliate or bring shame to their close-knit, multigenerational extended family (Tremble, Schneider, and Appathurai 1989). As a result, "relatively low rates of disclosure to families have been reported among Asian, African-American, and Latino gay men and lesbians" (Garnets and Kimmel 1993:333). If they decide to disclose their sexual orientation, ethnic minority youths risk losing the support of their extended family and hence their ethnic community (Garnets and Kimmel 1993; Greene 1994). Morales (1989) noted that "to live as a minority within a minority leads to heightened feelings of isolation, depression and anger centered around the fear of being separated from all support systems, including the family" (p. 219).

Several authors have noted that Asian-American youths risk disgracing themselves, their immediate family, and all past generations, living and dead, if they publicly declare their same-sex attractions (Carrier, Nguyen, and Su 1992; Chan 1989, 1995). Chan (1989) reported, in her study of Chinese, Japanese, and Korean young adults who had disclosed to most of their friends, that almost 80 percent had told a family member, usually a sister, and only one-quarter had disclosed to parents. To disclose tarnishes the family's honor in the eyes of the ethnic community; it is not the children who have failed but the parents. Thus many remain quietly closeted. Loiacano's (1989) informants also described difficulties finding support, acceptance, and expression within the black community once they disclosed to others. Parents who suspect that their child has same-sex attractions may be co-conspirators in this silence, hesitant to publicly acknowledge their bisexual, lesbian, or gay child to avoid embarrassing relatives and the ethnic community. If a youth progresses to the point of self-recognition of her or his sexual status, familial and cultural proscriptions against disclosing this publicly may block further self-development. Thus a wall of silence is likely to form around a family with a lesbian daughter, gay son, or bisexual child.

This portrait of ethnic families, however, may be too severe. Espin (1987) noted that a Latina lesbian/bisexual youth may face rejection from her ethnic community but seldom from her family:

> Latin families tend to treat their lesbian daughters or sisters with silent tolerance: Their lesbianism will not be openly acknowledged and accepted, but they are not denied a place in the family, either. Very seldom is there overt rejection of their lesbian members on the part of Hispanic families. (p. 40)

This does not imply, however, that a Latina youth is free from anxiety and the psychological burden of keeping her sexual attractions secretive. Pressure to lead a double life and thus protect the family from "embarrassment," and herself from possible stigmatization and rejection from the Hispanic community, places the Latina youth in a compromising position, pitting her needs, family of origin, ethnic community, and lesbian communities against one another.

Conclusion

Regardless of ethnicity, many youths share common dilemmas in deciding whether to disclose their sexual attractions to their family of origin. The
extent of these similarities has often been assumed and seldom investigated
by white researchers. The inverse, that disclosure to parents has singular
attributes unique to ethnic minority youths, has been the predominant assumption in the literature on ethnic minorities. However, data on ethnic
minority youths who are lesbian, bisexual, or gay are primarily based on
reflections of interviewed informants and mental health professionals and
not on empirical research.

One deterrent to sorting through these issues is that relatively few studies
on sexual minority youths have sufficient numbers of ethnic minority individuals to conduct separate analyses. The low numbers may be because
lesbian, gay, and bisexual ethnic minority youths do not feel comfortable
disclosing their sexual orientation to white researchers, or investigators did
not adequately recruit ethnic minorities, either because they were not well
represented in the available population or for reasons unstated or unknown.
Several studies with sufficient numbers of ethnic minority youths with same-
sex attractions did not include ethnicity as a discriminating independent
variable, perhaps because investigators assumed ethnic status did not matter
or they overlooked it. In either case, the net effect has compounded the
silence about ethnicity and sexual orientation among lesbian, gay, and bisexual youths and has perhaps precluded other ethnic minority individuals
from disclosing their sexual orientation and participating in research projects. Thus, because an extremely limited empirical base of support underlies
much of the discourse on ethnicity and sexual orientation, caution must be
emphasized in accepting, without further investigation, any generalizations
about the uniqueness or sameness of ethnic minority gay, lesbian, and bisexual youths and their families.

Another important consideration is that, in describing the experiences of
ethnic minority youths disclosing to parents, issues of variability must not be
ignored. Not all ethnic groups are similar to one another and distinct from
the majority culture in the same way. For example, when contrasted with
white families, both Chinese Americans and Native American families, on
average, place greater value on contact with extended family members and
the wisdom of older generations. However, within each ethnic group, families
have distinct functions and structures because of their "pre-American" histories and their encounter with the American experience. Social class, religious

values, and degree of enculturation (immigration status) may also exert diversifying effects *within* an ethnic group. Unfortunately examples of these effects are quite limited in the literature on sexual minority development.

The dual identities, multiple roles, emotional conflicts, and psychological adjustments that lesbian, bisexual, and gay ethnic minority youths encounter when they disclose to their parents need extensive empirical investigation. The family may not offer them safety from sexual prejudice, which may thus threaten the youths' ethnic identity. In the face of multiple oppressions, lesbian, gay, and bisexual ethnic youths face a difficult task as they attempt to integrate their personal and group identities (Cross 1991). The recent formation of support groups for youths of color give them a reference group for support and validation.

Conclusion

It is difficult to recommend a research agenda when the paucity of research is as significant as it is regarding the relations lesbian, bisexual, and gay youths have with their parents. At this point in the development of research, few issues exist that are not in need of considerable investigation. The published personal narratives and self-help tracts for youths and their parents provide fertile ground for developing testable hypotheses that can guide future research.

Although this literature documents the negative disruptions and sometimes chaos that follow initial disclosure, the crisis mentality of many of these writings may have been overdrawn. Few of the most disruptive, pathological scenarios caricatured by personal chronicles have received widespread confirmation from the empirical research conducted thus far. The personal narratives from both sexual minority youths and their parents do, however, accurately portray the significance of the other in their life. Parents are often figures of authority and respect, and youths desire their support and approval. Most parents still recognize bisexual, gay, and lesbian youths as their children, regardless of their sexual desires and identity.

To maintain their sense of self-integrity and their desire to be honest with parents, many youths are disclosing to their parents at increasingly earlier ages. The age of disclosure may be dependent on the population from which a youth sample is drawn. Those who attend college appear more reluctant than youths from urban support groups to disclose, perhaps because they more often fear the power of parents to sever them from financial and emotional support. Because they frequently live away from home most of the year, college students are often able to lead a new, private life as lesbian, gay, or bisexual persons without disclosing to parents until a "safe" time arrives. Thus many are out on campus and closeted at home. Because they live at home, however, many urban youths may have great difficulty keeping their sexual identity secret.

Mothers are more likely to be told than fathers, in large part because youths have better relations with their mothers and they expect their fathers to react more negatively than their mothers. Few youths, however, expect either parent to respond with outright rejection or a physical assault. Some evidence suggests that more important than fear of rejection as a motivator not to disclose is the desire not to hurt or disappoint parents. Youths do not want to harm their status within the family and the positive relations that most of them have with their parents.

Few investigators have explored the reasons youths choose not to disclose their same-sex orientation to parents. Also obscure from a research point of view is whether parents know their child's sexual proclivities not because the child disclosed to them but because they became suspicious of his or her behavior or mannerisms, friends she or he selected, and/or the absence of heterosexual activities. Worth distinguishing are the families in which the youth's same-sex attractions have been openly disclosed, have not been discussed but everyone knows that everyone else knows, are a source of parental suspicion, and are not known. Family dynamics under these various conditions need to be investigated.

As indicated above, research reviewed in this paper has been largely derived from the perspectives of lesbian, bisexual, and gay youths and not from their parents. Researchers have neglected asking parents their views on having a gay member in the family, largely because few parents are willing to discuss having a gay child and because few youths are willing to volunteer their parents to researchers (see further discussion in Savin-Williams and Dube 1998). To better understand the life-course interactions of sexual minority youths and their parents, prospective, longitudinal studies are needed that assess the relations that youths *and* their parents have before disclosure, shortly after disclosure, and then at regular intervals thereafter. Researchers must recognize, as Herdt and Boxer (1993) argued, that a youth's disclosure takes place within the context of the family and that this act subsequently affects all family members. A longitudinal, interactional research design would allow investigators to study the cause-and-effect relationship of disclosure and family dynamics in a more detailed fashion.

Given the current reality that most data on youth-parent relations originate from the youth, of vital importance to researchers is to clarify the nature of the youth population sampled and to reign in overly dramatized characterizations about "gay youths." Each sample needs to be elaborately described, especially in terms of how youths were recruited and the youths' sociodemographic and psychosocial characteristics, such that other investigators are better able to compare findings among various populations. Similarities across many populations might then warrant generalizations about sexual minority youth; differences could then be attributable to population variations or characteristics. That which is currently believed about the youth-parent relations among sexual minority youths may not reflect the lives of the vast majority of bisexual, gay, and lesbian youths who do not volunteer for research, perhaps because they are not prepared to acknowledge their same-sex orientation to others, such as researchers. Also left untapped by research recruitment strategies are those who vow never to volunteer for political or personal reasons (e.g., those who resent psychologists "studying us"). Until alternative methods with a large number of localized, unique samples of sexual minority youths are implemented or representative samples of lesbian, gay, and bisexual youths can be recruited (currently an impossibility), extreme caution must be observed regarding any attempt to generalize or extrapolate from existing empirical studies.

Finally, researchers have largely ignored the influence of the youths' and parents' ethnicity and family backgrounds. To understand more clearly the unique conditions that sexual minority youths who are also ethnic minorities in North American culture have in relating to their parents, researchers must make special efforts and invent new strategies to recruit the full spectrum of ethnic youths in future research projects. Although ethnic minority youths may face special circumstances when attempting to blend their sexuality and their ethnic identity, they may also have distinctive sources of strength that need to be recognized.

References

Anderson, D. 1987. Family and peer relations of gay adolescents. *Adolescent Psychiatry* 15:163–78.
Bell, A. P., and M. S. Weinberg. 1978. *Homosexualities: A Study of Diversity Among Men and Women.* New York: Simon and Schuster.
Bell, A. P., M. S. Weinberg, and S. K. Hammersmith. 1981. *Sexual Preference: Its Development in Men and Women.* Bloomington: Indiana University Press.

Ben-Ari, A. 1995. The discovery that an offspring is gay: Parents', gay men's, and lesbians' perspectives. *Journal of Homosexuality* 30(1):89–112.

Borhek, M. V. 1993. *Coming Out to Parents: A Two-Way Survival Guide for Lesbians and Gay Men and Their Parents.* 2nd ed. Cleveland: Pilgrim.

Brown, S. 1988. Lesbians, gay men, and their families. *Journal of Gay and Lesbian Psychotherapy* 1:65–77.

Carrier, J. M., B. Nguyen, and S. Su. 1992. Vietnamese American sexual behaviors and HIV infection. *Journal of Sex Research* 29:547–60.

Chan, C. S. 1989. Issues of identity development among Asian-American lesbians and gay men. *Journal of Counseling and Development* 68:16–20.

Chan, C. S. 1995. Issues of sexual identity in an ethnic minority: The case of Chinese American lesbians, gay men, and bisexual people. In A. R. D'Augelli and C. J. Patterson, eds., *Lesbian, Gay, and Bisexual Identities over the Lifespan: Psychological Perspectives*, pp. 87–101. New York: Oxford University Press.

Cohen, K. M., and R. C. Savin-Williams. 1996. Developmental perspectives on coming out to self and others. In R. C. Savin-Williams and K. M. Cohen, eds., *The Lives of Lesbians, Gays, and Bisexuals: Children to Adults*, pp. 113–51. Fort Worth: Harcourt Brace.

Coleman, E., and G. Remafedi. 1989. Gay, lesbian, and bisexual adolescents: A critical challenge to counselors. *Journal of Counseling and Development* 68:36–40.

Cramer, D. W., and A. J. Roach. 1988. Coming out to mom and dad: A study of gay males and their relationships with their parents. *Journal of Homosexuality* 15(3/4):79–91.

Cross, W. E. 1991. *Shades of Black: Diversity in African-American Identity.* Philadelphia: Temple University Press.

D'Augelli, A. R. 1991. Gay men in college: Identity processes and adaptations. *Journal of College Student Development* 32:140–46.

D'Augelli, A. R., and M. M. Hart. 1987. Gay women, men, and families in rural settings: Toward the development of helping communities. *American Journal of Community Psychology* 15:79–93. ·

D'Augelli, A. R., and S. L. Hershberger. 1993. Lesbian, gay, and bisexual youth in community settings: Personal challenges and mental health problems. *American Journal of Community Psychology* 21:421–48.

D'Augelli, A. R., S. L. Hershberger, and N. W. Pilkington. 1998. Lesbian, gay, and bisexual youths and their families: Disclosure of sexual orientation and its consequences. *American Journal of Orthopsychiatry* 68:361–71.

DeVine, J. L. 1984. A systemic inspection of affectional preference orientation and the family of origin. *Journal of Social Work and Human Sexuality* 2:9–17.

Duin, J. 1996. January 25. Homosexuality is "in" on prime time television. *Washington Times*, January 25, p. 1.

Espin, O. M. 1987. Issues of identity in the psychology of Latina lesbians. In Boston Lesbian Psychologies Collective, eds., *Lesbian Psychologies: Explorations and Challenges*, pp. 35–55. Urbana: University of Illinois Press.

Fairchild, B., and N. Hayward. 1989. *Now That You Know: What Every Parent Should Know about Homosexuality*. Updated ed. San Diego, Calif.: Harcourt Brace Jovanovich.

Garnets, L. D., and D.C. Kimmel. 1993. Lesbian and gay male dimensions in the psychological study of human diversity. In L. D. Garnets and D.C. Kimmel, eds., *Psychological Perspectives on Lesbian and Gay Male Experiences*, pp. 1–51. New York: Columbia University Press.

Greene, B. 1994. Ethnic minority lesbians and gay men: Mental health and treatment issues. *Journal of Consulting and Clinical Psychology* 62:243–51.

Herdt, G., and A. Boxer. 1993. *Children of Horizons: How Gay and Lesbian Teens Are Leading a New Way Out of the Closet*. Boston: Beacon Press.

Heron, A., ed. 1994. *Two Teenagers in Twenty: Writings by Gay and Lesbian Youth*. Boston: Alyson.

Hershberger, S. L., and A. R. D'Augelli. 1995. The impact of victimization on the mental health and suicidality of lesbian, gay, and bisexual youths. *Developmental Psychology* 31:65–74.

Hunter, J. 1990. Violence against lesbian and gay male youths. *Journal of Interpersonal Violence* 5:295–300.

Kahn, M. J. 1991. Factors affecting the coming out process for lesbians. *Journal of Homosexuality* 21(3):47–70.

Lever, J. 1994. Sexual revelations. *The Advocate*, August 23, pp. 17–24.

Lever, J. 1995. Lesbian sex survey. *The Advocate*, August 22, pp. 22–30.

Loiacano, D. K. 1989. Gay identity issues among black Americans: Racism, homophobia, and the need for validation. *Journal of Counseling and Development* 68:21–25.

MacDonald, G. B. 1983. December. Exploring sexual identity: Gay people and their families. *Sex Education Coalition News* 5 (December): 1, 4.

Martin, A. D., and E. S. Hetrick. 1988. The stigmatization of gay and lesbian adolescent. *Journal of Homosexuality* 15(1/2):163–83.

Morales, E. S. 1983. Third world gays and lesbians: A process of multiple identities. Paper presented at the Ninety-first Annual Convention of the American Psychological Association, August, Anaheim, California.

Morales, E. S. 1989. Ethnic minority families and minority gays and lesbians. *Marriage and Family Review* 14:217–39.

Muller, A. 1987. *Parents Matter*. New York: Naiad.

Pilkington, N. W., and A. R. D'Augelli. 1995. Victimization of lesbian, gay, and bisexual youths in community settings. *Journal of Community Psychology* 23:33–56.

Remafedi, G. 1987. Male homosexuality: The adolescent's perspective. *Pediatrics* 79:326–30.

Remafedi, G., J. A. Farrow, and R. W. Deisher. 1991. Risk factors for attempted suicide in gay and bisexual youth. *Pediatrics* 87:869–75.

Rhoads, R. A. 1994. *Coming Out in College: The Struggle for a Queer Identity*. Westport, Conn.: Bergin and Garvey.

Robinson, B. E., L. H. Walters, and P. Skeen. 1989. Response of parents to learning that their child is homosexual and concern over AIDS: A national study. *Journal of Homosexuality* 18(1/2):59–80.

Rotheram-Borus, M. J., J. Hunter, and M. Rosario. 1994. Suicidal behavior and gay-related stress among gay and bisexual male adolescents. *Journal of Adolescent Research* 9:498–508.

Rotheram-Borus, M. J., M. Rosario, and C. Koopman. 1991. Minority youths at high risk: Gay males and runaways. In M. E. Colten and S. Gore, eds., *Adolescent Stress: Causes and Consequences*, pp. 181–200. New York: Aldine DeGruyter.

Savin-Williams, R. C. 1989. Coming out to parents and self-esteem among gay and lesbian youths. *Journal of Homosexuality* 18(1/2):1–35.

Savin-Williams, R. C. 1990. *Gay and Lesbian Youth: Expressions of Identity*. New York: Hemisphere.

Savin-Williams, R. C. 1994. Verbal and physical abuse as stressors in the lives of lesbian, gay male, and bisexual youths: Associations with school problems, running away, substance abuse, prostitution, and suicide. *Journal of Consulting and Clinical Psychology* 62:261–69.

Savin-Williams, R. C. 1995. Parents' reactions to the discovery of child's sexual orientation. Paper presented at the Lesbian, Gay, and Bisexual Identities and the Family: Psychological Perspectives Conference, June, Pennsylvania State University, University Park, Pennsylvania.

Savin-Williams, R. C. 1996. Self-labeling and disclosure among gay, lesbian, and bisexual youths. In P. J. Green and J. Laird, eds., *Lesbian and Gay Couple and Family Relationships*. San Francisco: Jossey-Bass.

Savin-Williams, R. C. 1998. The disclosure of same-sex attractions by lesbian, gay, and bisexual youths to their families. *Journal of Research on Adolescence* 8:49–68.

Savin-Williams, R. C., and Diamond L. M. 1999. Sexual orientation as a developmental context for lesbian, gay, and bisexual children and adolescents. In W. K. Silverman and T. H. Ollendick, eds., *Developmental Issues in the Clinical Treatment of Children and Adolescents*, pp. 241–58. Boston: Allyn and Bacon.

Savin-Williams, R. C., and E. M. Dube. 1998. Parental reactions to the disclosure of their child's same-sex attractions. *Family Relations* 47:1–7.

Savin-Williams, R. C., and K. Wright. 1995. A longitudinal study assessing urban sexual minority adolescents for HIV infection and psychological health. Unpublished data, Cornell University and Children's Hospital of Michigan.

Sears, J. T. 1991. *Growing Up Gay in the South: Race, Gender, and Journeys of the Spirit*. New York: Harrington Park.

Strommen, E. F. 1989. "You're a What?": Family Member Reactions to the Disclosure of Homosexuality. *Journal of Homosexuality* 18(1/2):37–58.

Telljohann, S. K., and J. H. Price. 1993. A qualitative examination of adolescent homosexuals' life experiences: Ramifications for secondary school personnel. *Journal of Homosexuality* 26(1):41–56.

Tremble, B., M. Schneider, and C. Appathurai. 1989. Growing up gay or lesbian in a multicultural context. *Journal of Homosexuality* 17(3/4):253–67.

USA Today. 1996. More folks say gay is O.K., March 19, p. 1.

12 Employment and Sexual Orientation: Disclosure and Discrimination in the Workplace

M. V. Lee Badgett

For many years, social scientists have worked to understand how social forces influence individuals in the United States labor market. Economists and sociologists, in particular, have long studied labor market discrimination against women and people of color. In expanding our view to apply similar methods and questions to discrimination because of sexual orientation, however, we must proceed carefully to avoid the overgeneralization that the sources and effects of discrimination are identical for all oppressed groups. When we inquire into the existence of discrimination against lesbians, gay men, and bisexuals, we increase our understanding of forces that influence an individual's labor market position, forces that include race, gender, and class. This paper develops a conceptual framework that shows how a worker's sexual orientation may have independent effects within the workplace and interactive effects with other socially and economically relevant characteristics, mainly race and gender, as well as how the awareness of these effects is relevant to those who work with lesbian, gay, and bisexual individuals.

Extending the scope of labor market research to include the topic of sexual orientation has obvious academic appeal as more widespread interest in lesbian/gay/bisexual studies grows. But this expansion is more than an academic adventure into uncharted territory, as discrimination against gay and bisexual people has become the subject of intense policy and political debate, mainly focusing on whether discrimination against gay people truly exists. In the 1992 elections, opponents of lesbian and gay civil rights forced referenda that would have repealed local gay rights laws in Oregon, Colorado, Tampa, Florida, and Portland, Maine. (At the time of this writing, the Colorado gay rights law was reinstated by the courts.) These campaigns, which were successful statewide in Colorado and citywide in Tampa, shared the argument that such civil rights laws granted gay men and lesbians "special privileges" or "special rights," a claim that clearly challenges the notion that gays and lesbians face discrimination in the labor market. Furthermore, literature published in the Colorado campaign asked:

> Are homosexuals a "disadvantaged" minority? You decide! Records show that even now, not only are gays not economically disadvantaged, they're actually one of the most affluent groups in America! On July 18, 1991, the *Wall Street Journal* reported the results of a nation-wide marketing survey about gay income levels. The survey reported that gays' average income was more than $30,000 over that of the average Americans' [*sic*]. (Colorado for Family Values, 1992)

The basic argument, then, seems to be that lesbians and gay men do not encounter discrimination since they seemed to have achieved unusual economic success without civil rights protections. (The serious flaws in this argument, mainly statistically biased samples and incorrect comparisons, will be discussed further.)

In addition to the academic and policy needs for an understanding of discrimination and its relationship to disclosure, those professionals working with lesbian, gay, and bisexual workers also need to recognize the complex set of influences that shape those workers' work lives and decisions. As gay issues become more prominent in the workplace, supervisors, counselors, and personnel managers must consider new questions: Should we encourage gay workers to come out, i.e., to disclose their sexual orientation within the workplace? Do our employment practices discriminate against gay workers in any way, and is discrimination illegal? How does dealing with sexual orientation fit in with other diversity issues? In seeking answers to these and other questions, human resources professionals must grapple with many of the same conceptual issues as social scientists.

In the next section, this paper offers an overview of the legal situation faced by lesbian, gay, and bisexual workers and shows that most of them have little legal protection against discrimination. Then a conceptual framework of the labor market role of sexual orientation is developed, which will help structure future empirical research and guide helping professionals. The framework connects gay workers' disclosure of their sexual orientation to workplace characteristics, including the workplace social climate and economic incentives, creating the potential for discrimination by employers and coworkers. This framework also reveals points of divergence in the workplace effects of sexual orientation for different race and gender groups. The last section examines existing evidence of discrimination and suggests several other research strategies.

Current Legal Situation

The legal position of lesbian, gay, or bisexual workers differs between public and private employees. Gay and bisexual people have no explicit protection from employment discrimination at the federal level in the private sector. Eight states, as well as the District of Columbia, have civil rights laws that prohibit discrimination by private employers on the basis of sexual orientation: California, Connecticut, Hawaii, Massachusetts, Minnesota, New Jersey, Vermont, and Wisconsin. Many city and/or county laws also provide such legal protection. Estimates vary as to the number of private employers who have a nondiscrimination policy toward lesbians and gay men, but many large companies do have such policies (Martinez 1993).

When not bound by a collective bargaining agreement or by civil rights laws, employers have traditionally been able to hire and fire employees at will. This employment-at-will doctrine has recently come under attack in a variety of contexts as courts increasingly find that implicit contractual limitations allow employers to fire employees only for cause (Editors of *Harvard Law Review* 1991). This notion of an implied contract has been used with mixed results against employers who have fired employees because of their sexual orientation (Editors of *Harvard Law Review*, 1991). In a recent case, a California state judge found that Shell Oil wrongfully discharged an employee because of his homosexuality rather than for job performance, the criterion that Shell claimed guided all dismissal decisions (Shao 1991). But this protection, like that afforded by union contracts, only protects those who are already employed.

Other laws limiting private employers' actions, particularly Title VII of the Civil Rights Act of 1964, have provided little protection against antigay discrimination.[1] The effect of existing local antidiscrimination ordinances in overturning discriminatory acts against lesbians and gay men is still unclear. Such ordinances often face rescission (as evidenced by the referenda noted earlier) and "may be unenforceable when they conflict with federal interests or constitutional rights" (Editors of *Harvard Law Review* 1991).

Public employers operate under additional constraints that private employers do not face. Employees of eighteen states are protected from discrimination by executive orders or state law (*Ten Percent* 1993). Perhaps more important, the government's ability to hire and fire employees is limited by certain constitutional requirements. For federal employees, the Fifth and Fourteenth Amendments guarantee due process and equal protection under the law, respectively. Until recently, these constitutional principles have provided little employment protection for lesbian and gay public employees. Lower-tier due process or equal protection review of a government action based on an employee's sexual orientation would require the government to show a "rational relationship between that person's sexual orientation and the efficiency of governmental operations" (Editors of *Harvard Law Review* 1991). Courts have accepted numerous unsubstantiated rationales in upholding discriminatory actions against military personnel and against those seeking security clearances, but the rational relationship requirement provides some limited protection for civil servants (Editors of *Harvard Law Review* 1991).

Two lower courts have considered sexual orientation as a "suspect" or "quasi-suspect" classification that requires what is known as "heightened equal protection scrutiny." This level of judicial scrutiny requires the government to demonstrate that the classification of people by their sexual orientation serves an "important" interest (if quasi-suspect) or a "compelling" government goal (if suspect) and bears a "substantial" relationship (quasi-suspect) or is "precisely tailored" (suspect) to the issue at hand (Editors of *Harvard Law Review* 1991). The application of heightened scrutiny has not been upheld on appeal, but it has resulted in one case forcing the military to reinstate an openly gay soldier (*Watkins v. U.S. Army*) (ACLU 1991). The Supreme Court has yet to rule on whether sexual orientation is either a suspect classification, as is race, or quasi-suspect, as is sex (Editors of *Harvard Law Review* 1991).

As this section demonstrates, when most lesbian, gay, or bisexual people arrive at their workplaces, they are vulnerable to the kind of discrimination from which heterosexual women and heterosexual people of color are legally protected. And although thirty years of federal antidiscrimination policies have not completely eliminated sex and race discrimination (see, for example, Turner, Fix, and Struyk 1991), those forms of discrimination can be fought through administrative and judicial processes. Professionals who work with gay workers and want to integrate gay workers more fully into their workplaces must recognize this real vulnerability that makes gay workers' situation very different from other protected categories, such as race, gender, and disability status.

Conceptual Framework

Studying labor market discrimination means drawing causal links between an individual's sexual orientation and her or his labor market outcomes — hiring, promotion, wages, employment status, and so on. This requires some understanding of the role of sexuality in the economy, an
understanding that economists, in particular, are only beginning to develop
(see Badgett and Williams 1992; Posner 1992; Matthaei 1993). The approach here is to consider only one dimension of sexuality: the fact that
some individuals' sexual partners are of the same gender. This framework
takes, as a given, the existence of homophobia (the fear of homosexuals and
homosexuality) and heterosexism (the belief that heterosexuality is superior
and should be an enforceable social norm) but acknowledges that these
social attitudes vary in existence and intensity across individuals over time.[2]
In this paper the main question considers how homophobic or heterosexist
attitudes in the workplace affect a lesbian, gay, or bisexual worker.

Identity and Behavior

While the ways that race and gender operate within the economy are
complex, at least those who study these factors (and human resources professionals working with women and people of color) have the empirical
advantage of studying an observable attribute.[3] Because someone's sexuality
is not easily observed or inferred, the option of hiding it in some or all social
contexts is often chosen by lesbian, gay, or bisexual people to avoid the
potential for social ostracism, physical violence, or other sanctions imposed
by an unaccepting society. To complicate the issue of observability further,
the development of a lesbian, gay, or bisexual identity is a process that can
occur at any stage of life and at different rates (Garnets and Kimmel 1991).
This hiddenness, whether from oneself or from others, makes standard research techniques (such as random sampling) extremely difficult and has
impeded social scientific progress on issues of sexuality.

But hiding one's sexuality may also dampen the extent of social or economic sanctions an individual faces, including employment discrimination.
In this framework, the connection between sexuality and labor market outcomes hinges crucially on the issue of *disclosure* of lesbian, gay, or bisexual
behavior and/or identity. And since hiding is associated with avoidance of

sanctions, disclosure is likely to be at least partly determined by workplace factors.

Before further developing the relationship between disclosure and the workplace, at least some discussion of the thorny issue of the relationship between behavior (sexual practices) and identity (considering oneself lesbian, gay, or bisexual) is in order.[4] The assumption in this framework is that both behavior and identity are sufficient to trigger sanctions. For instance, the *act* of sodomy is still prohibited in almost half the states (Editors of *Harvard Law Review* 9), as is the solicitation of "noncommercial, consensual same-sex sexual activity" in many places (Editors of *Harvard Law Review* 1991). Those laws have sometimes been explicitly used to justify employment discrimination against gay people (Rubenstein 1993). And recent political efforts notwithstanding, homosexual acts are still grounds for discharge from the military (Editors of *Harvard Law Review* 1991).

Within the workplace, however, having a gay identity may be more problematic than behavior. Identity suggests the potential for joining other lesbian or gay employees in collective action that challenges existing employment practices and the workplace social environment. For instance, gay employees have formed groups that have pressured employers to provide benefits for domestic partners, presenting a challenge to compensation plans built on the heterosexual bias of the legal institution of marriage (see Building Community at PG&E 1992). Fears of similar action may intensify homophobic attitudes of employers and coworkers toward individual gay-identified workers.

Using sexual orientation broadly also avoids the potential for bias that arises from different cultural relationships between behavior and identity. For example, Alonso and Koreck (1989) point out that in some Mexican and Central American cultures, men who have sex with other men do not necessarily identify themselves as either homosexual or bisexual. Only some of those men, those playing the passive roles, are stigmatized for their sexual practices within their own culture.

Disclosure

Whereas the question of disclosure relates both to behavior and to identity, the issue of voluntary disclosure may relate more to identity, given the general political strategy for the lesbian and gay liberation movement since the 1970s of "coming out." For simplicity, most of the discussion will consider the voluntary disclosure of one's lesbian, gay, or bisexual identity.[5] The framework first posits a relationship between the work environment and disclosure and then shows how disclosure may affect an individual's labor market position. Table 12.1 summarizes five categories of factors in a rough linear approximation of the causal links between sexuality and labor market effects. The relationship among the elements of the categories is complicated, of course, and the individual elements will be woven together in the following discussion.

The Work Environment and Disclosure

Work environments vary along several social dimensions related to sexual orientation. Escoffier (1975) categorizes occupational and job characteristics based on "the stress laid on passing and individual success at passing," where "passing" refers to concealing one's sexual orientation: (1) "Conservative" occupations that allow no deviations from the heterosexual norm, for example, military jobs, elementary school teaching, and certain corporate occupations; (2) "liberal" occupations that are more likely to be tolerant, in which individual productivity is easier to measure; and (3) "ghetto" occupations "that are publicly labeled as predominantly open to gay people or

TABLE 12.1 Elements of Theoretical Framework

Sexuality	Workplace	Disclosure	To Whom	Labor Mkt. Effects
Behavior	Stress on passing	Voluntary	Coworkers	None
		Involuntary	Boss	None
Identity	Sociability			Discrimination: Job loss
	Income			No promotion Harassment
		None/passing		Lower productivity, absenteeism

... employ many gay people." Escoffier suggests that the occupational choices of a lesbian or gay man will depend on the value of passing to that person. In other words, Escoffier focuses on the way that an individual's preferences regarding disclosure determine his or her work environment.

Survey data provide some support for Escoffier's hypothesis. In a national survey conducted by Steve Teichner for the *San Francisco Examiner,* 15 percent of the men and 19 percent of the women said that their sexual orientation played a major role in selecting their job or profession. (The unpublished data from this survey were provided to the author for independent analysis). The small proportions may not be surprising considering that many people develop a lesbian, gay, or bisexual identity after they have already begun a job or career. And Escoffier notes that those who do come out at a younger age have a hard time getting useful input on the differences in work environments at the time they are making decisions regarding education and training.

Schneider (1986) proposed a model to explain the other direction of influence: how the work environment influences a lesbian's propensity to disclose her lesbianism to coworkers. In Schneider's model, workplaces vary according to whether they create "a context conducive to intimacy and self-disclosure." She tested the model using nonrandom survey data from 228 lesbians and allowed sociability and disclosure to be jointly determined in her statistical method. The results revealed that a lesbian's degree of disclosure increased in human service occupations and with a higher percentage of women in the department or workplace. Working with children, having a higher income, and experiencing a previous job loss from disclosure all decreased the degree of disclosure.

Sociability may also be an important factor *within* groups of lesbian, gay, and bisexual workers in the same workplace. Some workplace groups of gay employees have formalized (see Building Community at PG&E 1992; Woods 1993), and even informal groups have developed that may provide enough social and political support for gay employees to come out. As noted earlier, these groups often work for nondiscrimination policies in employment and benefits, and disclosure may be an important part of the intra-company lobbying process.

Income and Disclosure

Putting the two models together provides a more complex understanding of the relationship between a person's management of disclosure and her or his work environment. To add further complexity, economic aspects of the workplace are also likely to be related to disclosure. Schneider's data show a negative relationship between income and disclosure: Higher-income lesbians disclose less (Schneider 1986). The more recent Teichner/*San Francisco Examiner* survey data suggest that this relationship may not be so clear-cut and may even have changed. Table 12.2 shows an inverted V relationship: disclosure increases with income to a point (the 50,000–60,000 range in the national sample and the 30,000–40,000 range in the Bay Area sample) and then declines at higher-income levels.

This relationship might be a result of the lack of controls for age or workplace sociability, but the data in Table 12.2 are provocative. Income could certainly have conflicting influences on disclosure. On the one hand, individuals with higher incomes have more to lose if disclosure results in job loss, motivating a negative relationship between income and disclosure (Schneider 1986). On the other hand, higher incomes may reflect more authority and power in the workplace and therefore a greater ability to overcome or neutralize negative reactions to disclosure. Higher income might then be related to a lower risk of total loss and thus to greater disclosure. Given the figures in Table 12.2, both effects may be at work, with middle-range income acting as a switching point.

Two other economic models generalize the relationship between income and workplace disclosure. If an individual uses a simple cost-benefit approach to make disclosure decisions, she or he will compare the likely bene-

TABLE 12.2 Relationship Between Income and Disclosure to Coworkers

	% out to coworkers	
Annual Income	National	Bay Area
Less than 10,000	42	48
10,000–20,000	48	53
20,000–30,000	51	63
30,000–40,000	58	70
40,000–50,000	64	62
50,000–60,000	78	52
60,000–70,000	40	49
over 70,000	64	57

Source: Unpublished cross-tabulations from the 1989 Teichner/*San Francisco Examiner* survey.

fits, such as enhanced self-esteem or a more accepting and supportive work-place (Woods 1993), to the possible cost of coming out, such as lost income from fewer promotions or job loss. Although the value of these benefits may vary somewhat from person to person, the possible costs will probably vary more since income varies greatly among individuals. A person earning a high income may find that the relative cost of coming out is high compared to the benefits, but a low-income person may find the relative cost of coming out to be lower compared to the benefits (which may be roughly the same as for a high-income worker). Thus, according to this model, gay people earning higher incomes will disclose less than lower-income people.

An investment model of disclosure (a more elaborate cost-benefit ap-proach) provides an approach that more explicitly accounts for risk and for future benefits: Given the risk of economic harm, lesbians and gay men may trade off career advancement or security for a future return when making their disclosure decisions (Woods 1993). Risk depends on the social nature of the workplace and on the lesbian or gay worker's ability to manage any negative reactions. Workers assess risk over time and may do so at the level of the overall workplace as well as the level of the individual co-worker or boss. The future return may again be thought of as psychological or as po-litical. Modeling disclosure as an investment good, then, implies that, all else equal, more may be "purchased" by individuals with higher incomes who "pay" for coming out in terms of income placed at risk.

Describing the disclosure decision process in these ways is intended not to completely represent the process but to highlight the potential importance of income. The income effect will be important in constructing and inter-preting future empirical work on the effects of sexual orientation on income (discussed in the next section), as well as for interpreting how representative members of gay workplace groups are of an employer's entire group of gay workers. The income effect will also influence the distribution of the benefits of any policy changes that require disclosure, such as declaration of domestic partnerships to get employment benefits.

Disclosure and Discrimination

Two important additional points must be made regarding disclosure. First, involuntary disclosure of a gay employee's sexual orientation, some-times known as "outing," can occur in many ways. Inferences of identity or behavior can be made from military and police records, marital status, neighborhood of residence, silences in conversations, and so on. Furthermore, voluntary disclosures to coworkers increase the likelihood of either accidental or deliberate involuntary disclosure to others. The case of Jeffrey Collins, the Shell Oil employee mentioned earlier, illustrates the damaging effects of a series of involuntary disclosures. Collins accidentally left, at the computer printer, a copy of "house rules" for a gay sex party. Another employee found the copy and circulated it, resulting in Collins being fired. Shell later notified headhunters of the reason for Collins's dismissal, reducing his chances for obtaining a new job (Shao 1991).

The second additional point is that a choice not to disclose involves ambiguous economic effects. Escoffier points out that passing may require avoidance of social interactions that contribute to advancement and job satisfaction for other workers (also see Woods 1993). This social isolation could lead to higher absenteeism and job turnover, and the energy devoted to passing might reduce both productivity and incomes. But this costly behavior does not justify discrimination. The behavior is not an intrinsic characteristic of the worker but a result of the work environment and could be thought of as a form of *indirect* discrimination. Alternatively, passing could improve gay workers' productivity if, as Mohr (1988) argues, gay workers "respond to the threat of employment discrimination by becoming workaholics."

Disclosure, whether voluntary or involuntary, can result in sanctions by coworkers, supervisors, or employers. Homophobic or heterosexist reactions by coworkers might reduce the gay worker's income, productivity, and/or advancement. Homophobic supervisors can harass, fire, or refuse to promote lesbian, gay, or bisexual employees. These negative reactions, while at least partly the result of individual attitudes toward gay people, are also likely to be influenced by the work environment. And negative reactions are certain to feed back into a lesbian or gay worker's future disclosure decisions (as Schneider found), many of which are made knowing that legal recourse against discrimination does not exist. Ultimately the overall extent of economic sanctions is an empirical question, as discussed below.

Race and Gender

One advantage of simplifying the disclosure process in this framework is that potential differences in disclosure between race and gender groups are immediately expected. Lesbians of color, white lesbians, and gay men of color must deal with the damaging effects of racism and sexism in the workplace. Would disclosing their sexual orientation add significantly or only slightly to the disadvantage they already may face? Would disclosure of their sexual orientation push them over some threshold of the number of accept- able differences? Table 12.3 presents results from questions about workplace disclosure in two surveys. In both surveys women indicate less workplace disclosure than men. The racial differences are less stark, with black respon- dents indicating different disclosure levels from white and Hispanic workers, but this is not consistent between the Bay Area survey and the national survey. Understanding the reason for these differences is not a simple project, but all three aspects of the relationship between disclosure and the workplace described in this section suggest differences in disclosure by race and gender.

TABLE 12.3 Workplace Disclosure by Gender and Race

Out/Look, 1988: "Are you 'out' at your workplace?"	Men	Women
to no one	8.0	17.2
to anyone	16.4	10.5
to more than two people	18.3	26.0
to the majority of your coworkers	23.0	24.3
to everyone you work with	34.3	22.0
Number of respondents:	213	296

Teichner/San Francisco Examiner:
"Have you told your coworkers about your sexual orientation?"

National percentages (400 respondents)	Men	Women	White	Black	Hispanic
Yes	62	33	57	40	62
No	36	64	42	60	38
Don't Know	2	3	2	—	—

Bay Area percentages (400 respondents)	Men	Women	White	Black	Hispanic
Yes	62	53	61	89	69
No	38	47	39	11	31
Don't Know	—	—	—	—	—

Sources: Unpublished data from both surveys.

The ability of an individual's preferences for disclosure to determine his or her occupation, the first aspect of the work-disclosure relationship, is likely to vary by race and gender. The degree of occupational choice available to an individual has varied significantly in the United States, with race and sex discrimination constraining the choices of women and people of color (for an extensive discussion of occupational segregation by race and gender, see King 1992). Lesbian, gay, and bisexual people of color and white lesbians will thus have more limited occupational options than gay white men for reasons entirely separable from sexual orientation. To the extent that work-place sociability, the second part of the framework, varies by occupation, differences in the occupational distributions of race and gender groups will also lead to differences in the level of disclosure by race and gender.

Within occupations and particular jobs, lesbian and bisexual women may find that their gender is more of a disadvantage than their sexual orientation (Hall 1989). Most economic studies show that married men's incomes are higher than unmarried men's, but married women's incomes are typically *lower* than unmarried women's incomes (e.g., Carlson and Swartz 1988). This suggests that lesbians might actually benefit from the fact that they are (presumably) less likely to marry (i.e., to marry a man). Lesbians disclosing their sexual orientation could conceivably benefit by removing employers' fears or prejudices about their likelihood of marrying and quitting to raise a family (at least until same-sex relationships are allowed the same social and legal status as heterosexual marriages, in which case a lesbian "married" to another woman might be equally suspect in an employer's eyes). While seeing this marriage effect as a lesbian "advantage" may seem far-fetched, it at least suggests that, relative to heterosexual women, disclosure as a lesbian might not make her as vulnerable as a gay man is relative to heterosexual men.

The greater overall economic vulnerability of lesbians as women would certainly affect lesbians' disclosure decisions. This vulnerability is found within the third aspect of the framework concerning the effect of income on disclosure. Persistent inequality in income by race and sex has been well documented (see Blau and Beller 1992) and thus might lead to differences in disclosure by both race and gender. This race-gender wedge occurs both *between* job categories (since white men tend to have higher-paying jobs) and *within* job categories (for evidence of gender pay differentials within detailed occupational categories, see Bergmann 1989).

The influence of income and occupation also suggests important class differences in disclosure. Even sociability within workplace groups of lesbian, gay, and bisexual workers could have important class implications if these organizations are mainly founded by and composed of managerial, professional, and technical employees.

Overall, then, while similar forces may nudge all lesbian, gay, and bisexual workers in the same direction in terms of disclosure, the differences in economic and workplace contexts in which gay workers find themselves because of their race and gender may lead to very different disclosure patterns. And differences in the social treatment of workers within workplaces because of racism and sexism may also influence disclosure of sexual orientation, although the effects of the interaction of these factors are still unclear. Supervisors, personnel managers, and counselors should recognize that sexual orientation must be considered alongside race and gender when working with white lesbians or gay men and lesbians of color.

Implications for Researchers and Workplace Professionals

Starting with a complex conceptual framework encourages comprehensive research strategies while leaving room for more partial and incremental approaches. Important and useful research on employment discrimination against lesbian and gay (and sometimes bisexual) people has been conducted that corroborates many of the assumptions embedded in the framework presented previously. The usefulness of these partial approaches for understanding the complexities discussed in this paper is limited by methodological problems common to much research on sexual orientation, however.

Perhaps the best documented assumption used in the framework is the existence of homophobic and heterosexist attitudes. Herek (1991) reviews public opinion survey data that show persistent and widespread disapproval of homosexual behavior but, in contrast, growing acceptance of the idea that gay people should have equal job opportunities. A survey of 191 Alaskan employers revealed that employers also have homophobic attitudes: 18 percent of those surveyed would fire, 27 percent would not hire, and 26 percent would not promote gay employees (Brause 1989).

Court cases and surveys of self-identified lesbians and gay men demonstrate that attitudes may translate into actual discrimination. Table 12.4 summarizes selected surveys of self-identified lesbians and gay men who were asked about employment discrimination.[6] The proportion of lesbians or gay men who believe that they faced some form of employment discrimination (in hiring, promotion, or firing) during their working lives ranges from 13 percent to 62 percent. Unfortunately these findings come from nonrandom samples,[7] making broader inferences impossible, and even a random sample might not reveal the true incidence of discrimination: Actual discrimination may not be interpreted as such; perceived discrimination may be based on employers' legitimate nondiscriminatory motives; and more discrimination might occur with wider knowledge of individuals' sexual orientation.

Another way economists and sociologists have documented discrimination against women and people of color involves comparing similar individuals to look for the impact of discrimination in lower-income groups. Economic data on lesbians and gay men is difficult to find, not surprisingly. In the nonrandom surveys in which income and other economic data were collected, respondents tended to be disproportionately white, urban, and well-educated, all factors that raise average income, causing what statisticians call "sample selection bias." This bias makes inferences about the incomes of the larger population of lesbian and gay people inaccurate, such as the one cited earlier from the Colorado pamphlet.

Table 12.5 presents income figures from three recent national surveys of lesbian, gay, and bisexual people and compares those figures to national

TABLE 12.4 Summary of Surveys of Employment Discrimination

Survey	Location	Year	Lifetime rate of Discrimination (%)			
Philadelphia Lesbian & Gay Task Force (1988)	Philadelphia	1987	25	(M)	19	(F)
	Pennsylvania	1987	28	(M)	25	(F)
Levine and Leonard (1984)	New York City	1980 1981	—	—	24	(F)
San Francisco Examiner, Teichner	National Bay Area	1989 1989	18 27	(M) (M)	13 36	(F) (F)
National Gay & Lesbian Task Force	National	1991	62	(M)	59	(F)

NOTE: Discrimination rate cross-tabulated by sex where possible.

TABLE 12.5 Income of Lesbian, Gay, or Bisexual People

Survey	Instrument	Sample	Lesbian/ Gay/ Bisexual Income	National Income[a]
Out/Look (1988, n = 510)	Magazine survey, mail-in		(Range for median)	
		Men	25K–29K	27,342
		Women	20K–24K	18,823
Simmons Market Research Bureau (1988)	Gay newspaper inserts		36,900 55,430	(Avg. individual) (Avg. household)
Teichner/ San Francisco Examiner (1989, n = 400)	Phone survey, Random digit dialing		(Median)	
		Men	29,129	28,605
		Women	26,331	19,643
		White[b]	28,266	29,846
		Black[b]	32,503	20,706
		Hisp.[b]	26,666	
		Asian[b]	30,012	

[a]"National income" is median income for full-time, full-year workers.
[b]Medians by race are for men only.
SOURCES: L/G/B incomes from unpublished data from each survey.
National medians from *Economic Report of the President* (1990, 1991).

medians or averages. Without controlling for age or education, comparisons with the national medians may be misleading, especially given the likely sample selection bias. But even the survey with the least biased sampling technique (Teichner/*San Francisco Examiner*) resulted in high median incomes, especially for women and people of color (although small sample sizes probably explain most of the apparent difference for people of color). The crude comparisons of income by sexual orientation are quite different from simple cross-race or cross-gender comparisons, which usually show large differences. The lack of dramatic disparities by sexual orientation does not mean that discrimination does not exist but, rather, that sexual orientation might not have the same labor market effects that race and sex do.

A common statistical approach for capturing the effects of discrimination is to see if people who are similar in all observable and economically relevant ways have similar labor market outcomes.[8] If income varies with nonproductive characteristics such as race or gender among otherwise identical individuals, then researchers infer the existence of discrimination. I recently conducted such a study with data from the General Social Survey, a national random sample, which allows identification of behaviorally lesbian, gay, and bisexual individuals (Badgett 1994). Unlike the studies in Table 12.5, in this sample the behaviorally gay sample has a lower average income even before controlling for education, age, and so on, and the income disadvantage remains after using such controls, although the difference is not statistically significant for lesbians.

Unfortunately the data do not include information about either sexual identity or workplace disclosure, making this finding an imperfect measure — probably an underestimate — of the effects of discrimination. One of the greatest challenges in research on sexual orientation is collecting appropriate data for statistical analysis. The most difficult question for survey design concerns disclosure of a gay or bisexual orientation to the interviewer. What question should a researcher ask? If either behavior or identity can lead to sanctions, then the prudent researcher will ask about both: not all people who engage in same-sex sexual activity consider themselves gay, lesbian, or even bisexual, and not all people who consider themselves gay or lesbian engage in sexual activity at all. A multiquestion approach, including behavior as well as identity, would also avoid the potential cultural bias discussed earlier.

Careful construction of questions and use of both written and verbal response methods, appropriate selection of interviewers, and sensitivity to the concerns of interviewees will increase the reliability of responses. One way of assessing reliability that would also allow some modeling of the disclosure process would be to do in-depth, follow-up interviews on a subsample. Recent advancements in statistical techniques have allowed social science statisticians to remove some of the effects of sample selection bias as well as to analyze longitudinal data[9] and many subtly different decision-making processes.[10] While getting a representative sample will be difficult, given the relative paucity of research on this topic, the usefulness of econometric models requires the information that such an effort could provide.

Two other research strategies, workplace case studies and matched pair testing, offer less costly data collection. Case studies allow greater institutional and personal detail and have an added advantage of allowing an examination of an important assumption, namely, that a lesbian, gay, or bisexual employee's disclosure is perceived correctly by coworkers or employers. And depending on the workplace studied, the researcher may also be able to study the effects of gay employee groups on disclosure and discrimination.

Matched pair testing is most useful in studying the job application process and involves sending out pairs of applicants or applications that are matched in all basic characteristics — age, education, and the like — except for the characteristic being tested (Turner, Fix, and Struyk 1991). This technique has the advantage of controlling for all other relevant variables by construction, including disclosure. (In fact, the testers' actual sexual orientation would be irrelevant in this kind of study.) Adam (1981) used a similar technique to measure discrimination against lesbian and gay Canadian law students who were seeking post-schooling internships: gay-labeled resumes (those with a line "Active in [local] Gay People's Alliance") generated fewer interview offers than identical resumes that were not so labeled. One issue in a larger study is to avoid confounding an employer's bias against lesbians or gay men with an employer's bias against people in political organizations (as the Adams study may have done). Nevertheless, it should be possible to come up with an innocuous sounding organization (Lesbian and Gay Square Dancers, for instance) that keeps the difference between applicants focused on sexual orientation alone.

These suggestions for research show that quantitative studies of sexual orientation and employment discrimination are possible. Combining the results of that research with existing and future qualitative work, such as that done by Woods (1993) and by Hall (1989), will contribute to a more complete understanding of the labor market position of, and discrimination against, lesbian, gay, and bisexual workers. And while we may now know enough about the existence of discrimination to conclude that federal policy should prohibit discrimination because of sexual orientation, a more detailed and sensitive research methodology is necessary to address other policy concerns, such as enforcement, monitoring, and affirmative action.

For lesbian/gay/bisexual workplace groups, results of research on disclosure and discrimination will, first of all, help them to understand the forces working to keep gay people in the closet at work, a situation that can be frustrating to gay workers who are out and are actively seeking changes in the workplace. Second, research will help both gay workers and the helping professionals who work with gay workers to identify potential points of discrimination: Are gay workers more vulnerable during the hiring process? Are they more vulnerable in everyday interactions with supervisors and coworkers, and in promotions? In addition, research can demonstrate to employers that discrimination is costly, whether indirect (from keeping workers in the closet) or direct (from losing productive workers), supporting both personnel managers and gay workers in their efforts to change employment policies.

In direct interactions with individual lesbian, gay, or bisexual workers, personnel managers and counselors must understand the significance of gay workers having no legal protection from discrimination as well as the double or triple jeopardy that lesbians and gay people of color face. Promoting gay workers' psychological and economic health requires a nuanced consideration of the constraints and incentives involved in managing a gay or bisexual identity at work. With that understanding, helping professionals can work to minimize the risk of discrimination while allowing lesbian, gay, and bisexual workers to find a level of disclosure that is both personally comfortable and functional

Acknowledgments

Lisa Moore, Rhonda Williams, Katie King, Richard Cornwall, and Ellen Riggle provided helpful comments and conversations. I also received useful suggestions from participants at the University of Maryland Women's Studies Research Forum and from a panel at the 1992 American Economic Association Meeting, where I presented earlier versions of this paper. Also, I would like to thank Carol Ness of the *San Francisco Examiner*; Steve Teichner, Jeffrey Escoffier, *Out/Look* magazine, and the National Gay and Lesbian Task Force for providing me with unpublished data from their surveys.

Notes

1. Some state courts have interpreted state civil rights codes to include sexual orientation (e.g., *Gay Law Students Associations v. Pacific Telephone and Telegraph Co.*).
2. For instance, Moore (1993) shows that the number of people who believe that homosexuals should have equal job opportunities rose from 56 percent to 80 percent between 1977 and 1993.
3. Although race is considered easily "observable," to say that race is observable by defining it in purely physical terms is an elusive and increasingly mistaken venture. For instance, some light-skinned black people have passed as white in the United States to avoid discrimination (Omi and Winant 1986). A related concept, ethnicity, also involves an important social dimension in its construction. (For further discussion of the social and political nature of racial and ethnic identity, see Omi and Winant 1986.) Gender's connection to the biologically based categories of sex makes its physical observability somewhat less

problematic. In a functional sense, the "observability" of these characteristics refers to an observer's ability to infer the characteristics of race, ethnicity, and gender and an individual's willingness to reveal those characteristics consistently.

4. In its wide range of uses, the term *sexual orientation* refers either to behavior or to identity.

5. Disclosure is not necessarily a binary concept — being either in or out of the closet. Woods's study of how gay men manage their sexual identities in their professional lives reveals three main strategies (Woods 1993). Two of them, "counterfeiting" a heterosexual identity and "avoidance" of topics related to sexual identity, clearly lead to a low degree of disclosure to coworkers. But at least some men using those strategies do reveal their sexual identity to carefully selected coworkers, although under the general assumption of confidentiality. The third strategy, "integration" of a gay identity within the workplace, is a much more disclosive strategy. In the context of this framework, then, "disclosure" could refer to a disclosive strategy involving relative openness about one's sexual identity.

6. Reviews of other similar surveys showing comparable discrimination rates can be found in Badgett, Donnelly, and Kibbe 1992; Levine 1980; Levine and Leonard 1984.

7. The Teichner/*San Francisco Examiner* poll is an exception, using random digit dialing to find lesbian, gay, and bisexual people.

8. Typically researchers use ordinary least squares procedures to determine the relationship between income and the explanatory variables, such as age, education, occupation, race, and gender.

9. Longitudinal data (data collected on the same individuals over time) would allow comparisons of labor market outcomes before and after disclosure for an individual and comparisons with the experience of nondisclosing or straight workers.

10. For instance, the disclosure to come out could be modeled statistically in what is known as a switching regressions model: a lesbian worker chooses between a potentially low-income path (if she discloses her sexual orientation and faces discrimination) and a high-income path (from passing), with her decision based partly on the likely difference in incomes. For a review of this and other techniques, see Maddala 1983.

References

Adam, B. D. 1981. Stigma and employability: Discrimination by sex and sexual orientation in the Ontario legal profession. *Canadian Review of Sociology and Anthropology* 18:216–21.

Alonso, A.M., and M. T. Koreck. 1989. Silences: "Hispanics," AIDS, and sexual practices. *Differences* 1:101–24.

American Civil Liberties Union. 1991. Lesbian and Gay Rights Project.

Badgett, M.V.L. 1995. The wage effect of sexual orientation discrimination. *Industrial and Labor Relations Review* 49(4):726–38.

Badgett, L., C. Donnelly, and J. Kibbe. 1992. Pervasive patterns of discrimination against lesbians and gay men: Evidence from surveys across the United States. National Gay and Lesbian Task Force Policy Institute.

Badgett, M.V.L., and R. M. Williams. 1992. The economics of sexual orientation: Establishing a research agenda. *Feminist Studies* 18:649–57.

Bergmann, B. R. 1989. Does the market for women's labor need fixing? *Journal of Economic Perspectives* 3:43–60.

Blau, F. D., and A. H. Beller. 1992. Black-White earnings over the 1970s and 1980s: Gender differences in trends. *Review of Economics and Statistics* 74:276–86.

Brause, J. 1989. Closed doors: Sexual orientation bias in the Anchorage housing and employment markets. In *Identity Reports: Sexual Orientation Bias in Alaska.* Anchorage, Alaska: Identity Incorporated.

Building Community at PG&E. 1992. *The Gay/Lesbian/Bisexual Corporate Letter* 1:3–6.

Carlson, L. A., and C. Swartz. 1988. The earnings of women and ethnic minorities 1959–1979. *Industrial and Labor Relations Review* 41:530–52.

Colorado for Family Values. 1992. Stop special class status for homosexuality.

Economic report of the president. 1990. Washington, D.C.: U.S. Government Printing Office.

Economic report of the president. 1991. Washington, D.C.: U.S. Government Printing Office.

Editors of *Harvard Law Review.* 1991. *Sexual Orientation and the Law.* Cambridge, Mass.: Harvard University Press.

Escoffier, J. 1975. Stigmas, work environment, and economic discrimination against homosexuals. *Homosexual Counseling Journal* 2:8–17.

Garnets, L. D., and D. Kimmel. 1991. Lesbian and gay male dimensions in the psychological study of human diversity. In J. D. Goodchilds, ed., *Psychological Perspectives on Human Diversity in America.* Washington, D.C.: American Psychological Association.

Hall, M. 1989. Private experiences in the public domain: Lesbians in organizations. In J. Hearn, D. L. Sheppard, P. Tancred-Sherrif, and G. Burrell, eds., *The Sexuality of Organization,* pp. 125–38. London: Sage.

Herek, G. 1991. Stigma, prejudice, and violence against lesbians and gay men. In J. C. Gonsiorek and J. D. Weinrich, eds., *Homosexuality: Research Implications for Public Policy,* pp. 60–80. Newbury Park: Sage.

King, M. 1992. Occupational segregation by race and sex 1940–88. *Monthly Labor Review* 115:30–37.

Levine, M. 1980. Employment discrimination against gay men. In J. Harry and M. S. Das, eds., *Homosexuality in International Perspective*. Vikas.

Levine, M., and R. Leonard. 1984. Discrimination against lesbians in the work force. *Signs* 9:700–710.

Maddala, G. S. 1983. Limited dependent and qualitative variables in econometrics. *Econometric Society Monographs No. 3*. Cambridge: Cambridge University Press.

Martinez, M. N. 1993. Recognizing sexual orientation is fair and not costly. *HR Magazine*, June, 66–72.

Matthaei, J. 1993. The sexual division of labor, sexuality, and lesbian/gay liberation: Towards a Marxist-feminist analysis of sexuality in U.S. capitalism. *Review of Radical Political Economics* 7(2):1–37.

Mohr, R. 1988. *Gays/Justice: A Study of Ethics, Society, and Law*. New York: Columbia University Press.

Moore, D. W. 1993. Public polarized on gay issue. *The Gallup Poll Monthly* 331 (April): 30–34.

Omi, M., and H. Winant. 1986. *Racial Formation in the United States*. New York: Routledge.

Posner, R. 1992. *Sex and Reason*. Cambridge, Mass.: Harvard University Press.

Rubenstein, W. B., ed. 1993. *Lesbians, Gay Men, and the Law*. New York: New Press.

Schneider, B. 1986. Coming out at work: Bridging the private/public gap. *Work and Occupations* 13:463–87.

Shao, M., with H. Dawley. 1991. The right to privacy: A $5.3 million lesson for Shell? *Business Week*, August 26.

Ten Percent. 1993. Why we need a federal civil rights law. Fall, 29.

Turner, M. A., M. Fix, and R. J. Struyk. 1991. *Opportunities Denied, Opportunities Diminished: Racial Discrimination in Hiring*. Washington, D.C.: The Urban Institute Press.

Woods, J. D., with J. H. Lucas. 1993. *The Corporate Closet: The Professional Lives of Gay Men in America*. New York: Free Press.

Part IV

Diversity Among Lesbians, Bisexuals, and Gay Men

To understand experiences of lesbians, bisexuals, and gay men, we must examine the interaction between various forms of diversity and sexual orientation. Before acquiring a gay, bisexual or lesbian identity, one has a racial or ethnic identity and a gender identity, which are part of the core of childhood identity.

Recent attention has focused on cultural diversity among bisexual, gay male, and lesbian individuals and the important role culture plays in shaping and defining the meaning of same-gender sexual and affectional behavior. It is important to recognize the many powerful ways that cultural and historical forces influence the meaning of sexual orientations (Blackwood and Wieringa 1999; Peplau et al. 1999).

Shared sexual orientations by themselves do not guarantee that people have a great deal in common. Moreover, racial and ethnic groups experience prejudice and discrimination based on their minority group status, which may place constraints on various life options. Thus there is a need for a model of sexual orientation based on multiplicity, not sameness, which examines the overlapping identities and statuses of gender, age, race, ethnicity, class, and sexuality.

Diversity within the lesbian, gay, and bisexual community is not limited to gender and ethnic or racial background, however. Greene, in the first selection of part IV, provides an overview of the multiple issues that are important by expanding the discussion to include physically challenged persons, social class, age, and religion in the gay, lesbian, and bisexual community.

Several themes are relevant for understanding cultural influence on lesbian, bisexual, and gay male identity. First are the importance of religion within the culture and the relevance of sexuality to central beliefs in that religion. A second theme focuses on gender roles, especially how the significance of clear distinctions made between male and female roles may serve to increase the difficulty for gay men, bisexuals, and lesbians to carve out a nontraditional or androgynous role. A third theme of cultural diversity is the nature of family structure, including issues regarding the significance and role of family, the way that families are defined, and the ways in which gender roles, sexuality, and sexual orientation are integrated into the concept of family.

The process of developing an identity as a sexual minority appears to be more challenging for bisexuals than for lesbians and gays, because bisexuals are a political and social minority within the gay and lesbian community (Blasingame 1992; Rust 1996). However, there may be a parallel between bisexuality and mixed racial heritage. As a result, some bisexuals who belong to multiple racial or ethnic minorities may feel more comfortable straddling social categories once they develop a positive biracial identity. As one Asian-European woman explained it: "Being multiracial, multicultural has always made me aware of nonbipolar thinking. I have always been outside people's categories, and so it wasn't such a big leap to come out as bi, after spending years explaining my [racial and cultural] identity rather than attaching a single label [to it]" (Rust 1996:71).

Another important dimension of diversity is gender. Gender is used in our culture as a primary organizing principle for the structuring of many aspects of people's lives. Male and female gender roles, which include being heterosexual, comprise a core part of one's identity. Lesbians, gay men, and bisexuals appear to experience the same social pressure to conform to gender norms as do heterosexual men and women.

Gender differences are embedded in a cultural context of social structural and status variables (Blumstein and Schwartz 1989; Nichols 1990; Peplau and Garnets 2000). Likewise, having sex with members of the same gender or sex with both same- and other-gender partners is defined in divergent ways across cultures, reflecting patterns of gender, kinship, and economic structure (Adam 1985; Blackwood and Wieringa 1999; Rust 2000). The interaction of these cultural patterns affects and reflects attitudes, ideologies, sexual division of labor, power relationships, and status differentials between genders, as well as the social organization of sexual opportunities.

In selection 14 Tafoya addresses the concept of a "two-spirited" person among Native Americans. It is an excellent example of the ways in which other cultures can provide models of gender diversity that may be more appropriate for lesbian, gay, and bisexual people than the dominant Western concepts.

Complex sociopolitical factors are linked with gender role and sexual orientation. For this reason, it is important to view lesbian and bisexual women's experience independently and not base it solely on gay or bisexual male models (Garnets and Peplau 2000; Peplau et al. 1998). Moreover, different gender role expectations and status differences between men and women place unequal and different constraints on women and men in sexual expression, same-sex intimacy, gender nonconformity, and the meanings they attach to experiences (Blumstein and Schwartz 1989; Peplau, Spalding et al. 1999). Lesbian and bisexual women experience their attractions in a societal context that devalues women and also devalues homosexuality. Restrictions placed on female sexuality may limit sexual expression of women's diverse potentials (Golden 1987).

In comparison with gay men, lesbians are more likely to define themselves in terms of their total identity and not only their sexual behavior. Likewise, they more frequently define their sexual identity in terms of affectional preferences or political choices than do gay men (Gramick 1984; Peplau and Cochran 1981; Vetere 1983). A predominant pattern for lesbians is to engage in sexual activity as a natural and logical outgrowth of a strong emotional-romantic attachment (Klinkenberg and Rose 1994; Schneider 2001). In general, lesbians report having their first sexual experience in the context of their first relationship (Blumstein and Schwartz 1989). They tend to have few or no sexual experiences with women before defining themselves as lesbians. Realization of being in love with, or in a relationship with, a person of the same gender may serve as a catalyst for solidifying lesbian self-identification (Rose 1996).

These findings fit with data on heterosexual women who are less likely to view sexual acts as a revelation of their true sexual self (Blumstein and Schwartz 1989) and who report sexual fantasies and sexual enjoyment in terms of interest in romantic settings and committed partners (Ellis and Symons 1990; Peplau 2001; Regan and Berscheid 1996; Wilson 1987). Moreover, women, regardless of sexual orientation, value the following more highly than men: emotional expressiveness (Blumstein and Schwartz 1983), sexual exclusivity (Laumann et al. 1994; Oliver and Hyde 1993), and investment in, and commitment to, maintaining relationships (Duffy and Rusbult 1986).

The selection by Blackwood and Wieringa focuses on the varied expres-

sions of same-gender attraction and relationships among women in many
different cultures. It reviews cross-cultural research on lesbian and bisexual
women and reveals the important influence of differing gender systems and
different levels of social stratification on patterns of lesbian and bisexual
experience.

The final selection of part 4 is a brief essay about another form of
diversity — issues facing lesbians, gay men, and bisexuals living in rural areas.
Geographic setting may facilitate or hinder gay, lesbian, or bisexual identity
development. For example, gay men who live in proximity to urban settings
arrive at a gay identity sooner than those living in outlying areas (D'Augelli
1989). In contrast, gay men and lesbians living in rural areas experience
greater isolation and find it more difficult to make enduring friendships and
relationships; rural networks tend to be more inaccessible and exclusionary
than in urban areas (D'Augelli, Collins, and Hart 1987; Hollander 1989).
The article was written for a conference of rural physicians to alert them to
some unique concerns about medical care that is affirmative of lesbians,
bisexuals, and gay men.

Contemporary Issue: Racism in the Gay,
Lesbian, and Bisexual Community

Gay men, bisexuals, and lesbians of color report experiences of racism
within the gay, lesbian, and bisexual community. For example, African-
Americans report being prevented from entering gay bars, clubs, and other
social gatherings by the use of excessive identification, whereas others are
allowed entry without such scrutiny. Likewise, in a study of a lesbian community in America's Southwest, the dominant community norms were found
to be derived from Anglo lesbians. Mexican-American lesbians tended not to
interact with Anglo lesbians but rather to relate primarily with one another;
in addition, Latina lesbians reported experiences of prejudice and discrimination that prevented them from feeling a part of the community (Lockard
1985). Similarly a gay Chinese adolescent commented: "I am a double minority. Caucasian gays don't like gay Chinese, and the Chinese don't like gays.
It would be easier to be White. It would be easier to be straight. It's hard to
be both" (Tremble, Schneider, and Appathurai 1989:263).

Racism may take the form of *sexual racism* in which gender stereotypes
become linked with racial ones. For example, regardless of their gender or
individual characteristics, African-Americans may be assumed to be domi-

nant, aggressive, and masculine; Asian-Americans may be presumed to be passive, shy, and feminine.

Racism may also take the form of being invisible and unconnected with the larger group. It may cause one to feel like a token or someone who is included only because of a need for racial diversity. Frequently racism is so subtle that one may feel a part of the group in public but is not invited home for dinner, as a friend would be.

Lesbians, bisexuals, and gay men of color may not receive the same psychological benefits from the gay, lesbian, and bisexual community that white gay men, bisexuals, and lesbians receive (e.g., social support, visible role models, and simultaneous acceptance for all important aspects of one's identities). Thus their existence is often denied in their own ethnic communities and is also not always reflected in the gay, lesbian, and bisexual community.

During the last decade one of the major ways that gay men, bisexuals, and lesbians of color have gained integration of their multiple identities has been to form groups and organizations specifically focused on their racial or ethnic identity within the gay, lesbian, and bisexual community (Ochs 1996). These networks serve multiple functions. They break down isolation and provide a sense of community by creating new extended families and role models that are more sensitive to their needs. They increase visibility by making their presence known both in the larger ethnic minority and in the gay, lesbian, and bisexual community. The networks help to unify efforts toward reducing oppression and empowering themselves in each of the communities in which they interact.

The hope is that greater appreciation of diversity can result from recognizing the importance of differences and from blending individual, cultural, and gender strengths for mutual support, empowerment, and coping with stigma.

References

Adam, B. D. 1985. Age, structure, and sexuality: Reflections on the anthropological evidence on homosexual relations. *Journal of Homosexuality* 11(3–4):19–33.

Blackwood, E., and S. E. Wieringa. 1999. Female desires: Same-sex relations and transgender practices across cultures. New York: Columbia University Press.

Blasingame, B. M. 1992. The roots of biphobia: Racism and internalized heterosexism. In E. R. Weise, ed., *Closer to Home: Bisexuality and Feminism*, pp. 47–53. Seattle, Wash.: Seal.

Blumstein, P., and P. Schwartz. 1983. *American Couples: Money, Work, Sex.* New York: Morrow.

Blumstein, P., and P. Schwartz. 1989. Intimate relationships and the creation of sexuality. In B. Risman and P. Schwartz, eds., *Gender in Intimate Relationships: A Microstructural Approach*, pp. 120–29. Belmont, Calif.: Wadsworth.

D'Augelli, A. R. 1989. The development of a helping community for lesbians and gay men: A case study in community psychology. *Journal of Community Psychology* 17:18–29.

D'Augelli, A. R., C. Collins, and M. Hart. 1987. Social support patterns of lesbian women in a rural helping network. *Journal of Rural Community Psychology* 8:12–22.

Duffy, S. M., and C. E. Rusbult. 1986. Satisfaction and commitment in homosexual and heterosexual relationships. *Journal of Homosexuality* 12(2):1–24.

Ellis, B. J., and D. Symons. 1990. Sex differences in sexual fantasies. *Journal of Sex Research* 27:527–55.

Garnets, L. D., and L. A. Peplau. 2000. Understanding women's sexualities and sexual orientations: An introduction. *Journal of Social Issues* 56(2):181–92.

Golden, C. 1987. Diversity and variability in women's sexual identities. In Boston Lesbian Psychologies Collective, eds., *Lesbian Psychologies: Explorations and Challenges*, pp. 19–34. Urbana: University of Illinois Press.

Gramick, J. 1984. Developing a lesbian identity. In T. Darty and S. Potter, eds., *Women-Identified Women*, pp. 31–44. Palo Alto, Calif.: Mayfield.

Hollander, J. P. 1989. Restructuring lesbian social networks: Evaluation of an intervention. *Journal of Gay and Lesbian Psychotherapy* 1:63–71.

Klinkenberg, D., and S. Rose. 1994. Dating scripts of gay men and lesbians. *Journal of Homosexuality* 26(4):23–35.

Laumann, E. O., J. H. Gagnon, R. T. Michael, and S. Michaels. 1994. *The Social Organization of Sexuality: Sexual Practices in the United States*. Chicago: University of Chicago Press.

Lockard, D. 1985. The lesbian community: An anthropological approach. *Journal of Homosexuality* 11(3–4):83–95.

Nichols, M. 1990. Lesbian relationships: Implications for the study of sexuality and gender. In D. P. McWhirter, S. A. Sanders, and J. M. Reinisch, eds., *Homosexuality/Heterosexuality: Concepts of Sexual Orientation*, pp. 350–64. New York: Oxford University Press.

Ochs, R. 1996. Biphobia: It goes more than two ways. In B. Firestein, ed., *Bisexuality: The Psychology and Politics of an Invisible Minority*, pp. 217–39. Thousand Oaks, Calif.: Sage.

Oliver, M. B., and J.J.S. Hyde. 1993. Gender differences in sexuality: A meta-analysis. *Psychological Bulletin* 114:29–51.

Peplau, L. A. 2001. Rethinking women's sexual orientation: An interdisciplinary relationship-focused approach. *Personal Relationships* 8:1–19.

Peplau, L. A., and S. D. Cochran. 1981. Value orientations in the intimate relationships of gay men. *Journal of Homosexuality* 6(3):1–19.

Peplau, L. A., and L. D. Garnets. 2000. A new paradigm for understanding women's sexuality and sexual orientation. *Journal of Social Issues* 56(2):329–50.

Peplau, L. A., L. D. Garnets, L. R. Spalding, T. D. Conley, and R. C. Venigas. 1998. A critique of Bem's 'Exotic Becomes Erotic' theory of sexual orientation. *Psychological Review* 105:387–94.

Peplau, L. A., L. R. Spalding, T. D. Conley, and R. C. Venigas. 1999. The development of sexual orientation in women. *Annual Review of Sex Research* 10:70–90.

Regan, P. C., and E. Berscheid. 1996. Beliefs about the state, goals, and objects of sexual desire. *Journal of Sex and Marital Therapy* 22:110–20.

Rose, S. 1996. Lesbian and gay love scripts. In E. D. Rothblum and L. A. Bond, eds., *Preventing Heterosexism and Homophobia*, pp. 151–73. Thousand Oaks, Calif.: Sage.

Rust, P.C.R. 1996. Managing multiple identities: Diversity among bisexual men and women. In B. Firestein, ed., *Bisexuality: The Psychology and Politics of an Invisible Minority*, pp. 53–83. Thousand Oaks, Calif.: Sage.

Rust, P.C.R. 2000. Bisexuality: A contemporary paradox for women. *Journal of Social Issues* 56(2):205–21.

Schneider, M. S. 2001. Toward a reconceptualization of the coming-out process for adolescent females. In A. R. D'Augelli and C. J. Patterson, eds., *Lesbian, Gay, and Bisexual Identities and Youth: Psychological Perspectives*, pp. 71–96. New York: Oxford University Press.

Tremble, B., M. Schneider, and C. Appathurai. 1989. Growing up gay or lesbian in a multicultural context. *Journal of Homosexuality* 17(1–4):253–67.

Vetere, V. A. 1983. The role of friendships in the development and maintenance of lesbian love relationships. *Journal of Homosexuality* 8(2):51–65.

Wilson, G. D. 1987. Male-female differences in sexual activities, enjoyment, and fantasies. *Personality and Individual Differences* 8:125–27.

13 Beyond Heterosexism and Across the Cultural Divide — Developing an Inclusive Lesbian, Gay, and Bisexual Psychology: A Look to the Future

Beverly Greene

Lesbian, gay, and bisexual (LGB) psychology has come a long way since Evelyn Hooker's (1957) pioneering research contradicting the pathology models of homosexuality in mental health. We have witnessed the development of national organizations devoted to the advocacy of fair treatment for LGB people and the development of areas of study within virtually every academic discipline. In psychology, efforts are dedicated toward developing greater scientific and clinical understanding of the lives of lesbians and gay men and the broader meanings of sexual orientation. We have also witnessed more recently the appropriate inclusion of bisexual men and women in the scope of this field of study and in the focus of our concerns for social justice. There has been a veritable explosion of psychological literature that not only explores nontraditional sexual orientations but does so from affirmative perspectives. Despite tenacious, ongoing resistance, this collective work has been instrumental in making public policy changes. These changes in public policy have affected long-standing practices that have previously affected the lives of lesbians, gay men, and bisexual men and women in ways that were, and often continue to be, unequivocally damaging.

This is a far cry from the period when conversion therapy represented the normative and neither the exceptional nor controversial view of how mental health professionals should respond to nontraditional sexual orientations. Douglas Haldeman (2000) has chronicled this long struggle. Despite many significant advances in this discipline in the past several decades, the next century confronts us with many new challenges in the need to explore the more complex nuances and varied meanings of sexual orientation, as well as the many ways that it is interrelated to other aspects of human identity. It is also necessary to conduct similar explorations of heterosexism and its connection to other forms of social oppression.

Conflated Aspects of Heterosexism

Heterosexism is not a singular or isolated experience or event. As such, heterosexism cannot be disconnected from the broader context of an individual's development or existence any more than sexism, for example, can be understood apart from the context of a woman's ethnicity, socioeconomic class, religion, or other significant aspects of her life. I explore a range of aspects of the lives of lesbians and gay men that are conflated by the presence of other identities that transform the experience of heterosexism. The consequence of the invisibility of these individuals in the education and training of clinicians and researchers in mental health are explored, as well as the differentials of privilege and disadvantage that give particular meaning to human differences in the United States.

An exclusive focus on heterosexism as the primary locus of oppression for all lesbians and gay men presumes that it is experienced in the same way for all group members and that it has the same meaning and consequences for them. The core of this assumption is common in the psychological literature as well as in practice. In American psychology, human identity is often understood as something that consists of parts completely separate from one another. Identity is rarely viewed as an integrated whole in which one component can only be understood in relation to and in the context of others. It is assumed that if you split up the parts of an entity and study those parts in isolation you will arrive at a more accurate or, at least, neater description of the reality. Although such practices make it easier to operationalize the study of complex human behaviors, the results of this practice do not necessarily yield a more accurate understanding of behavior or identity. Essed (1996) argues that many varied actual and potential identities come together in every individual and that those multiple identities allow us to be flexible in our dealings with different people and in different situations. Social domination, however, requires that we take physical and psychological characteristics of people that, in reality, exist on a continuum and treat them as if they are dichotomous. Wachtel (1996) explains this as a mechanism needed to create a category of people who are "not me" or "other" and into whom we can project our own unwanted psychic content, behavior, desires, impulses, and feelings. Siegel (1995) observes that fear is an essential ingredient in the maintenance of the distortion and projection Wachtel (1996) describes. In Siegel's (1995) analysis,

> Fear is the glue that maintains existing biases. . . . When people are categorized as *we* or *they*, fear becomes part of the process of projecting onto those whom we see as unlike ourselves all of the attributes that we would like to deny in ourselves. *We* are the good self. *They* are the bad self. All players must be maintained in that position and must deny that this is going on. Socially unacceptable traits can thus remain invisible to the self while we stereotype those whom *we* call *they* or *other* and imbue *them* with negative traits. (p. 297)

The unwanted psychic content, feelings, and behaviors that are projected onto members of societally disadvantaged groups are, in fact, common to all human beings. Despite the common pool of human emotion and desire that, by definition, all human beings share, when the projection process that Wachtel (1996) and Siegel (1995) describe takes place, the exploitation or exclusion of members of disparaged groups from mainstream life is often perceived as if it is not only justified but may even be seen as mandatory. The latter may often be deemed necessary either to protect members of disparaged groups from themselves or to protect "superior" (privileged) group members from them.

An example of the exclusions previously mentioned are found in feminist psychology. Despite worthy attempts to document gender subordination, feminist psychology has been appropriately assailed for its tendency, historically, to put forth an analysis of women's issues that has been created and articulated primarily by privileged, well-educated, predominantly heterosexual, white middle- and upper-class women. Those perspectives certainly are valid for those who articulate them; however, they cannot be automatically generalized to all women. Such an analysis fails to reflect the wide range of diversity among women. In doing so, this analysis cannot seriously consider the interlocking and complex nature of racial, class, heterosexist, and gender oppression for women of color, older women, lesbians, bisexual women, religious women, poor women, and women with disabilities (Hall and Greene 1996). In attempts to address these inequities, studies about gender have been challenged to discern how sexual orientation, ethnicity, other forms of social status, and discrimination transform the meaning or affects the salience of gender oppression for a wider range of women.

Just as feminist psychology has not represented the diverse range of women's concerns, lesbian, gay, and bisexual psychology has often failed to reflect the full spectrum of diversity among lesbians and gay men in an integrated fashion. Doing this leaves us with an incomplete view of the range of challenges that confront this group as whole. We are left without a solid appreciation for how other salient identities transform or color the meaning and experience of heterosexism, or of what it means to be a lesbian, gay man, or bisexual man or woman in a wider range of contexts. Without some discussion of social and cultural context, we are left with a limited view of what is involved in sexual orientation identity development or even whether, in certain cultures or contexts, there is an equivalent to the traditional Western concept. Another consequence of such omissions is that when doing clinical work with diverse populations of lesbians and gay men, practitioners are left ill-equipped to address their clinical needs in ways that are culturally literate and competent.

Psychological Resilience and Vulnerability in Socially Disadvantaged Groups

Just as we have witnessed a significant growth in the psychological literature exploring LGB sexual orientations from affirmative perspectives, there has been a parallel increase in the study of the role of gender, age, socioeconomic class, ethnicity, and membership in other societally disadvantaged groups from affirmative perspectives as well. These perspectives also examine the effects of membership in these groups on the psychological development and coping mechanisms of their members, on the development of psychological theories and paradigms explaining and interpreting human behavior, and on the application of those theoretical paradigms in the practice of psychotherapy and psychological assessment.

Discussion of the relevant effects of membership in institutionally disadvantaged and marginalized groups on the development of what historically has been deemed individual psychopathology and vulnerability have gained increasing prominence. More recently, those discussions have begun to acknowledge that just as social adversity contributes to psychological vulnerability, it can also facilitate the development of psychological resilience and exceptional coping strategies as well, albeit never without a price.

Despite overwhelming social adversity and ill treatment that make them psychologically more vulnerable than heterosexual men and women, lesbians and gay men as a group are not the harbingers of psychopathology that American mental health has historically depicted them to be. Given that they must routinely negotiate a hostile social climate, we might expect to see greater ranges of pathology among lesbians and gay men than their heterosexual counterparts. One might expect similar findings in other groups of disadvantaged people, where they are similarly absent. I suggest that this is no accident. Rather, it is a reflection of a special kind of resilience that may be found among many members of marginalized groups.

Jones (1997) explores the concept of resilience in his review of David Hadju's (1996) biography of the late musical impresario Billy Strayhorn. For more than thirty years Strayhorn was a key collaborator in the work of famed composer Duke Ellington and a major contributor to American jazz music in his own right. His arrangements and compositions bear the indisputable mark of musical genius that was evident early on in what some might consider a potentially difficult and troubled life. Jones (1997), in considering the elements of resilience in Strayhorn's life, observes that "resilience is elusive, difficult to predict and foster . . . it is a complex interaction of individual, constitutional, personality, developmental, and situational variables that, like the images one views through a kaleidoscope, contains intricate individual constellations and subtle colorings that change with every shift in one's viewpoint" (p. 10).

Jones (1997) attempts to grapple with the ostensible paradox of musician Strayhorn's phenomenal musical talent, creativity, and a prevalence of satisfying adult relationships and admirers, in the context of his identity as an African-American gay man who was relatively open about being gay in the social context of the 1940s. Hadju (1996) observes that Strayhorn's relative openness about his sexual orientation was considered extremely rare and potentially dangerous in a social context that was far more overtly and viciously racist and heterosexist than today's climate. In addition to a disadvantageous social climate, Strayhorn had troubled personal beginnings that left him vulnerable to severe psychological difficulties, some of which he did not successfully overcome.

Born physically frail, a victim of rickets early in life, Billy Strayhorn was often the object of his father's abuse and torment. James Strayhorn experienced persistent difficulty finding and keeping jobs, in part because of the racism that diminished opportunities for black men of that era, and in part because of his own progressive alcoholism. Billy was not legally named until he was nearly five years old. Jones (1997) attributed this lapse to both the family's disorganization and to Strayhorn's mother's desire to keep Billy her "baby" for as long as possible, perhaps owing to the death of two children before Billy to childhood illnesses. Prone to depression as an adult, Strayhorn died in 1967 when he was just fifty-one years old. Although esophageal cancer was the official cause of his death, his chronic alcohol consumption and constant cigarette smoking played a significant role in his premature demise.

For all practical purposes Strayhorn faced the challenge of serious family dysfunction and double layers of societal discrimination from his life's earliest days. He was also described as someone who would not have been conventionally regarded as a popular child. Nonetheless, he managed to create and surround himself with what Jones (1997) describes as loyal friends with shared interests, a broader community who saw him as their child prodigy and who ignored differences between Billy and the other children who were his peers, and, as an adult, insulated communities of some of the most talented artists of that period in our history. The precise nature and scope of his family history, his relationship to many communities, and the complexity of his ties to them are beyond the scope of this paper. The reader is referred to Hadju's (1996) book for a more comprehensive analysis of them. This discussion focuses on the nature of certain components of his life that allowed him, as an African-American gay man with troubled personal beginnings, to fortuitously fashion a future from a life that was at risk from its inception. It speaks to the importance of considering the complex nature of understanding someone who has multiple identities, some of which are privileged and others disadvantaged. This understanding also involves integrating the personal familial history and the history of other relationships that develop in the aforementioned context.

Jones (1997) describes a phenomenon that seems most prevalent when individuals like Strayhorn, who have societal and personal challenges (and in his case the resource of his talent), maintain a sense of psychological integrity. He describes it as the ability to maintain a kind of psychological independence in which challenged individuals appear to be able to "mentally remove themselves from destructive people and situations" (p. 10). A severe form of this removal is characterized by the defensive operation of dissociation which can be used adaptively to escape the acute phases of a seriously traumatic event. However, another form of psychological independence can also be characterized by an attitude that allows a person to structure their life so as to "ward off the malevolently controlling intentions of others" (Jones 1997:10). Jones (1997) tells us that this form of psychological independence is nurtured in resilient individuals by loving and effective caregivers. Such caregivers need not be parents or biological relations. However, they are people whose entrance at critical developmental junctures in the course of the resilient individual's life has powerful remedial effects when they occur. In addition to nurturing individuals present at critical junctures, there is also a fortuitous presence of societal opportunities that the individual may use to further develop and strengthen a sense of personal adequacy and effectiveness. The presence and timing of these societal opportunities are often outside the individual's control. Resilience is further enhanced by another element in a blend of personality traits which Jones (1997) sees as characteristic of resilient people, their capacity to evoke affirming reactions from others. In this context, whenever resilient individuals get an affirming response from someone, it reinforces their preexisting appealing personality style and strengthens their capacity for "independent self-construction" (Jones 1997:10).

Jones uses this paradigm to explain the resilience of African-Americans in ways that are applicable to the lives of lesbians, gay men, other people of color, poor people, people who are physically challenged, and other societally disadvantaged individuals. He observes that a detached, independent construction of a serviceable reality characterizes the resilience of members of abused groups. For example, because of American racial apartheid, African-Americans were forced to live and often work in worlds that were wholly separate from white Americans, and were legally denied many opportunities that were built into the structure of American society. Hence they were denied advantages and opportunities that were routinely given only to white Americans. Although living in segregated worlds blocked many opportunities for upward mobility in the mainstream of America, this resulting "structural isolation" (Jones 1979, in Jones 1997:10) fostered the development of distinctive communities in these segregated black communities. A similar kind of structural isolation defined the distinct, often invisible secret subcultures of lesbian and gay communities. Structurally they bear a striking similarity to the segregated communities inhabited by many other people of color, people with physical challenges, as well as other groups rejected by the mainstream.

Despite some of the inequities of segregated communities, they often permit the development of alternative self-images that evolve and even challenge the negative stereotypes and images of victims of discrimination (e.g., African-Americans, lesbians, and gay men). Negative stereotypes of members of disparaged groups often represent fictional creations or exaggerations that the dominant culture designed to justify the exploitation, exclusion, and oppression of members of disadvantaged groups. Jones (1997) points out that in these segregated communities African-Americans, for example, were socialized to mentally challenge white versions of the truth, particularly when those versions of the truth applied to them. This heightened level of suspiciousness observed in African-Americans in their encounters with white Americans has served as an effective coping strategy in their adaptive need to be vigilant about the realistic and often likely potential for exploitation, insult, or injury in such encounters. For African-Americans, this was and continues to be an adaptive mechanism as they cannot conceal their ethnicity and have little choice about being required to negotiate whatever responses they elicit in members of the dominant culture. An important component in the mental health of individuals from societally disadvantaged groups is their ability to rely on their own experiences of themselves and others like them to create self-generated definitions of both themselves and their origins, and to explain their current circumstances. Passively accepting the labels of those who have an obvious stake in defining them by their worst exceptions and believing the worst of them is not a given for members of disadvantaged groups, despite the fact that some group members may do so (internalized racism, homophobia, etc.). The process of independent self-construction allows healthy individuals to materialize the invisible presence of social privilege and correctly understand that their subordinate social position is not the simple result of cultural deficiency, poor or inadequate values, individual or group defect, or mother nature, as they have been told. Rather, social privilege can be recognized as a function of interlocking social systems of selective discrimination and selective patterned advantage that has been deliberately designed to maintain the balance of social power. That balance is reflected in and maintained by the privileging of certain characteristics or identities and the devaluing of others and the different opportunities and rights accorded or denied to individuals on the basis of those identities.

The legacies of discrimination for African-Americans and for lesbians and gay men are not exactly the same, neither in their origins, in the comparison of visible and invisible stigmas, nor in many other ways. Despite this, individuals who are members of either or both groups share the need to negotiate societal discrimination. An analysis of the successful methods that members of either group utilize to cope psychologically is illustrative of the concept of psychological independence and its role in maintaining psychological integrity when the environment is ubiquitously hostile. Furthermore, the successful coping strategies that one group employs in negotiating discrimination may be applicable to the dilemmas other groups face. It may also be useful in therapies with individuals who belong to more than one disparaged

group. Their development of successful strategies in negotiating one devalued identity may be an important source of resilience in the negotiation of
other devalued identities. Overall, the inclusion of these issues, individuals
with multiple identities who face societal disadvantage and their study, is
relevant to a more comprehensive understanding of the effects of societal
discrimination on its victims.

Jones (1997) argues articulately that people who move within carefully
constructed, at times segregated communities, which facilitate the development of self-constructed psychological realities, can develop a high level
of resilience. Pinderhughes (1989) observes that individuals who belong to
groups associated with power and privilege may be so used to negotiating
reality from a position of power that they are ill-prepared to cope with adversity or situations where they are not powerful. Resilience in disadvantaged
individuals can enable them to transform adverse circumstances and even
thrive despite them. However, Jones (1997) warns that people who are forced
to endure "patterned injustice . . . unwarranted and protracted personal
hardship . . . and ongoing oppression" (p. 13), as members of ethnic and
sexual minorities and other victims of abuse are often required to do, are
exposed to chronic stressors and challenges that are always a threat to their
carefully constructed psychological equilibrium. Mental health theoreticians and practitioners must understand that tangible psychological and
physical energies and efforts are required to maintain that equilibrium and
that an emotional and sometimes physical price (expressed in health problems) is always paid for survival, even among those who thrive. It is therefore
important to resist the temptation to use the existence of survivors as a means
of either minimizing the negative effects of the oppressive circumstances
they are forced to endure, to blame those who fail to endure them, or to
suggest that the social system must be working fairly if some of the disadvantaged group's members manage to overcome the barriers and succeed.
It is important to understand the nature of vulnerability and resilience in at-
risk populations if we are to use the therapy process in optimal ways and if
we are to appreciate the complexity of their development as well as the
complexity of their current circumstances.

The degree to which racist, sexist, heterosexist, and other forms of biased
thinking is embedded in theoretical paradigms and research in mental health,
and their subsequent effects on training and practice, has become an appropriate focus of attention in the psychological literature. In this context, relevant
questions have been raised, albeit separately, about the cumulative effects of
negative stereotypes about members of distinct oppressed groups and about

lesbians and gay men on the thinking of practitioners, research scientists, and theoreticians. The subsequent role of such thinking in perpetuating rather than exposing those negative stereotypes for the distortions they really represent has also gained greater prominence. Rarely, however, do these inquiries analyze the complexity of these issues when a person is a member of more than one of these groups. In this context the process of psychological assessment and treatment must begin to explicitly incorporate an understanding of the interactive effects of these combined phenomena and their effects on research and the delivery of psychological services.

Lesbians and gay men of color, members of white ethnic groups, people with disabilities, people who reside in rural parts of the United States or for that matter outside the country altogether, who are poor or homeless, who are old, transgendered, or transsexual individuals (Gainor 2000), and many other lesbians and gay men who are members of more than one group do not generally see themselves fully integrated in the face of American psychology. Moreover, they do not see themselves integrated in the face of American lesbian and gay psychology either. Failing to understand the more complex nature of the life experiences of such individuals not only limits our understanding of sexual orientation but limits our understanding of other aspects of human identity, as well as the phenomenon of heterosexism. Heterosexism, classism, racism, sexism, and other forms of oppression are embedded in the theories of psychology as an academic discipline and are reflected in practice. This systematic oppression is also reflected in the silent agreement to ignore the blatant omission of many diverse groups in the content of our discourse (Wachtel 1996).

Gender, Sexism, and Heterosexism: Making the Connection

In *Engendered Lives* Ellyn Kaschak (1992) writes that the consensual reality of Western culture holds that gender is a given, contained in or identical with the sex of the newborn and that gender and gender-linked attributes are viewed as natural rather than as socially and psychologically constructed. She observes that it is paradoxical that all children must be taught that which is supposed to be natural, and those who do not learn their lessons well are viewed as unnatural (p. 39).

Kaschak's analysis draws our attention to an important but frequently overlooked question. If specific gendered behaviors are natural outgrowths of biological sex and if heterosexual sexual orientation is natural for everyone, why would it be necessary to so assiduously teach that which is supposed to be innate and natural? Furthermore, why would some behavior that is deemed unnatural require such strong prohibitions and stigmatizing to prevent its occurrence? It would seem that natural behavior would just naturally evolve. It is precisely because traditional gender roles, which include heterosexual sexual orientation as the normative sexual orientation, are not ubiquitously natural or normative that they do not naturally evolve in everyone. A natural evolution is not allowed to take place. Gender roles are culturally embedded. As such, a culture's gender roles are socially constructed, assigned, agreed on, and changed over time. It is precisely because of these factors that such roles require enforcing rather than simply allowing them to evolve naturally. In fact, lesbian and gay sexual orientations evolve in individuals in spite of explicit prohibitions, opposition, and punitive responses to them.

Kaschak (1992) observes that it is particularly shameful for people who do not fit neatly into a gender category. This is reflected in the shame and embarrassment people feel when their gender is mistaken or cannot be quickly discerned. It is as if they have done something wrong, are "queer" or peculiar, or as if something is seriously wrong with them. She adds that when methods of enforcing traditional gender roles and categories fail, or as a result of the damage caused by them, the person in question may be deemed ill and in need of psychotherapy. This insistence on viewing gender as dichotomous and fixed and the sexist practices that tend to accompany such thinking are interrelated with heterosexism.

Heterosexist thinking leads to a range of inaccurate assumptions that are commonly held about gay men and lesbians. These beliefs are held by many people and are based on gendered ideas about what men and women are supposed to be and on what constitutes normal behavior for them. One of the most commonly accepted of these false beliefs is that to be gay or lesbian is to want to be a member of the other sex (Bohan 1996; Kite and Deaux 1987), presumably the most damning evidence of one's defect. Men are expected to be sexually attracted to women only and women sexually attracted to men only. Sexual attraction to the other sex and satisfaction with one's biological sex is believed to be an explicit and essential component of being a normal man or woman. In that context, reproductive sexuality is presumed to be the only form that is psychologically healthy and morally correct. Another fallacious assumption that connects heterosexism and gender dichotomies is that there is a direct connection between sexual orientation and a person's conformity or failure to conform to traditional gender stereotypes of roles and physical appearance (Bohan 1996; Kite and Deaux 1987). The erroneous conclusion drawn from this assumption is that men and women who do not conform to traditional gender role stereotypes must be gay or lesbian (Ames 1996; Bohan 1996; Kirk and Madsen 1996). Kirk and Madsen (1996) suggest that one of the seven myths that heterosexual Americans believe about LGB people is that all lesbians and gay men can be easily identified by their outward appearance, that they look like members of the other gender. An equally mistaken assumption is that individuals who conform to traditional gender stereotypes must be heterosexual. These assumptions suggest that to understand the meaning and reality of being a lesbian or gay man requires a careful exploration and understanding of the importance of cultural gender roles, the nature of the culture's traditional gender role stereotypes, the relative fluidity or rigidity of those roles, their range, rewards for conformity, and punishments for failure to conform (Greene 1996, 1997).

At this juncture we are left with a series of questions. If we did not socially construct gender in dichotomous and fixed terms, if there were no assigned gender roles or gender attributes, would the concept of sexual orientation exist? If so, would it be relevant? If deemed relevant, what would it encompass and how would it be defined? Perhaps a more important question is whether anyone would care. The very existence of people with nontraditional sexual orientations challenges traditional assumptions about gender roles and, in turn, challenges the male privileges that adherence to traditional gender roles are used to rationalize and perpetuate (Ames 1996).

Omissions of Diversity in Lesbian and Gay Psychology

Age

There are many lesbians and gay men who are not reflected in contemporary and media images of lesbian and gay communities. In a youth-oriented culture, the lives of older lesbians and gay men do not come under great scrutiny; their underrepresentation in the psychological literature is another indicator of their invisibility. When older people are the focus of such inquiries, the inquiries are usually about the negative aspects of age, such as dependency, decline, deterioration, and disability (Hall and Greene 1996; Schaie 1993). Older people are perceived as if they are always in need of care, rather than as the important caregivers that they often are in many cultures (Schaie 1993). Gatz and Cotten (1994) write that the aged should be included in discussions of nondominant, oppressed groups, as age represents one of the most basic cues by which people are assigned a particular status in the social hierarchy. Negative stereotyping based on age is used to discriminate against people in systematic ways (Gatz and Cotten 1994). Unlike ethnicity and other variables, the aged represent a group with permeable group boundaries to which if we live long enough we will all eventually belong. Unlike people with disabilities, a group to which potentially any of us *could* belong, or specific ethnic groups to which we cannot belong unless we are born into them, all human beings go from not belonging to this group to belonging to it (Gatz and Cotten 1994). As the aged come from all social groups, the degree of their disadvantage because of ageism may vary across the group.

Aging has different meanings across ethnic groups and different implications for men versus women. Ehrenberg (1996) reports that older gay men may be more vulnerable to isolation than older lesbians. Owing to women's longer life span, lesbians may be more likely to have surviving mates and peers and are less biased (than gay men) against older partners. Older gay men were observed to be more concerned about physical appearance than older lesbians, perhaps owing to the preference for younger partners among older gay men (Ehrenberg 1996).

Within many subgroups of people of color, older family members are considered elders who are valued for their life's accumulated wisdom and are accorded respect. In some Asian and East Indian cultural groups, adult children are expected to consult and, in some instances, conform to their parents' wishes regarding career choices, when and who to marry, and in other ways that Western cultures generally do not formally expect. The status of elders in different cultures differs depending on gender as well. In Western or mainstream American cultures, older people are often viewed as if they are no longer as useful as younger people. This perception of older people is confounded if they are no longer producing capital.

Other questions for future research revolve around the invisibility of older lesbians and gay men in a culture where youth and youthful attractiveness are privileged. Older people, like people with disabilities, are frequently regarded as if they are asexual. There may be the assumption that older people do not miss or desire the presence of a romantic partner or companion, are not interested in a date, or do not care about being sexually active. Young, single lesbians and gay men may often find friends matchmaking for them. Older lesbians and gay men may not evoke the same assistance at a time when they may require more help making connections to people. Ehrenberg (1996) reports that finding a partner is an issue for both older lesbians and older gay men. The absence of heterosexual privilege affects older lesbians and gay men as well. As surely as older people are presumed to be asexual, they are also presumed to be heterosexual if they are sexual at all. Many people may find themselves requiring more medical attention when they are older and the disclosure of their sexual orientation may be more relevant than when they were younger. A physician is perhaps more likely to view an older woman who is not married as an old maid rather than a lesbian. This may prompt the greater need for older lesbians and gay men to come out to physicians involved in their care and, when necessary, negotiate the negative consequences that may be associated with disclosure.

Many lesbians and gay men do not necessarily have the family support that their heterosexual counterparts enjoy nor are their relationships accorded similar status, assuming that those relationships are recognized at all. Older lesbians and gay men do not tend to be out to their families to the extent that their younger counterparts are (Ehrenberg 1996). When they are out to families who disapprove of their sexual orientation, they may not have the support of those family members when they are older and in need of care or social contact. Some may be estranged from their families of origin altogether. Furthermore, the inability for LGB people to marry legally has a range of implications for older lesbians and gay men. The absence of marriage licenses results in the absence of any documentation of the existence of a relationship or any legal identity of that relationship. This may contribute to the invisibility of long-term relationships among LGB people. Similarly the absence of older LGB people in research samples may obscure longer relationships as well as their characteristics. Furthermore, the absence of legal status for the relationship may have negative legal implications for older couples. If one member is ill, hospitalized, disabled, or in need of chronic or residential care, the courtesies that would be extended to a married spouse would not be similarly recognized with a same-sex partner. Ehrenberg (1996) observes that institutions have little regard for the partners of lesbians and gay men. They may disregard requests for information and may even actively interfere with the partner's access to the patient. Displays of physical affection in these situations may also elicit disgust both from other patients and staff members, who may seek to prevent that contact wherever possible.

Research on older lesbians and gay men tends to focus on those who are physically healthy, affluent, well-educated, and often connected to the lesbian and gay community. Such findings cannot be generalized to those who are in poor health, impoverished or living poorly, have few lesbian or gay friends, or have few ties to the broader lesbian and gay community, about which we know very little (Ehrenberg 1996). Older LGB people who are in financial need are at greater risk for social isolation and rejection. This is particularly true of lesbians. Their incomes tend not to be commensurate with either their education or their experience (Bradford and Ryan 1987; Ehrenberg 1996). Lesbians are five times as likely as other women to have financial problems.

Older lesbians and gay men are an important source of continuity in the ingredients of lesbian and gay communities. They are a connection to the group's past. Unlike members of ethnic minority groups, lesbians and gay men (as well as people with disabilities) do not receive minority mentoring from their parents or family members, nor do they obtain a sense of history of the struggles of lesbian and gay men from family members. Unfortunately older lesbians and gay men are not visible in the leadership of the LGB community, where their contributions are not always recognized. The presence of tangible links to that history in lesbian and gay communities is an important link to the group's history.

Sexuality

The lesbian and gay community has its own history of dichotomizing sexual orientation in a manner similar to that of gender dichotomies. Group membership is often defined as a function of the dichotomous poles of sexual orientation, reserving a special brand of cynicism, and hostility, for bisexual, transsexual, and transgendered people. Bohan (1996) describes the discomfort people experience about bisexuality or bisexual people as biphobia. A manifestation of biphobia may be reflected in the exclusion of bisexual men and women from social events in some lesbian and gay communities. Bisexuality was, and in some quarters still is, treated as though it were synonymous with promiscuity. The assumption is that if an individual has the capacity to be sexually attracted to men and women, the presence of that capacity alone is deemed synonymous with the uncontrollable need to conduct concurrent and indiscriminate sexual relationships with both men and women. Whereas some bisexual men and women need and desire concurrent relationships with both male and female partners, many heterosexual men and women, lesbians, and gay men also desire and conduct nonmonogamous sexual relationships in a similar manner. It may be a mistake to presume that the desire for nonmonogamy in bisexual men and women is a direct function of their bisexuality. Clinically it is more appropriate to focus on their capacity to experience sexual attraction more broadly rather than on exaggerations or distortions of their actual sexual behavior. The same logic is not used to define heterosexual sexual orientations or behavior but it has been used to depict lesbian and gay sexual orientations negatively. Members of the latter groups are treated as if their lives are defined by distorted depictions of their sexual activity. Lesbians and gay men appropriately protest and reject these reductionist and distorted characterizations when they are applied to them; however, they may have no problem in applying them to bisexual men and women (Fox 2000). Ultimately bisexuality represents an enduring pattern that constitutes a legitimate sexual orientation for many people (Rosenblum and Travis 1996).

Class Privilege, Class Oppression, and Heterosexism

Rarely do we pose questions regarding the effect of socioeconomic class on the development of lesbian and gay identity. We know that class status and income affects variables like physical health, life span, quality of primary education and access to higher education, likelihood of arrest, likelihood of imprisonment if arrested, and the general quality of life of all people. Yet class is ignored in the equations that seek to examine the lives of lesbians and gay men despite the fact that income may have many direct effects on the circumstances that permit, facilitate, or prevent someone from being out. It can similarly affect their ability to purchase books, magazines, and other cultural commodities of lesbian and gay subcultures, as well as the kinds of venues that are available to them for meeting other lesbians and gay men. Fine and Asch (1988) write that class and race influence not only access to decent housing and schooling but access to cultural and recreational opportunities as well. In their work on disability and its effects on women, they observe that class may similarly alleviate or exacerbate the impact of a disability in ways that are not predictable. It would make sense that class status also affects developing identity. We know that gender and race are important variables affecting job status and income, and hence the realities and effects of class would be gender and ethnically coded for lesbians and gay men, as they are for their heterosexual counterparts. Wyche (1996) observes that despite what we know about the salience of class as an important factor in people's lives, it is omitted in analyses of how it affects the treatment process as well as the class beliefs and behaviors of the therapist in that process.

American culture takes a dim view of poor people. Newitz and Wray (1997) write that Americans love to hate the poor and that to be labeled poor does not generally elicit sympathy. Instead, being poor may elicit hostility and disgust from others and trigger a sense of shame in one's self. Economic impoverishment is often associated with negative character traits such as having inadequate or the wrong values, ineptitude, laziness, or outright stupidity (Newitz and Wray 1997; O'Hare 1986). Poor people are also thought of as refusing to work, living in female-headed households, living in inner-city ghettos, and living off welfare (O'Hare 1986). Even if it were not for these direct negative characterizations, our feelings about the poor are reflected in our definitions of lower-and middle-class values and behaviors, and of the word *class* itself. The *Merriam-Webster Collegiate Dictionary* (1996) defines "class" as high social rank, elegance, high quality, and a rating based on grade or quality. Wyche (1996) tells us that when we say that someone has "no class" we do not mean this literally. But what do we mean? We mean that they have lower- or working-class values and are behaving like poor or working-class people. The demeaning implication is that to have lower-class values is the same as having "no class" at all. Consistent with *Webster's* definition, being lower class is to lack elegance, to have no or low quality, or to be of low social rank. Middle-class values are generally deemed to include the presence of upwardly mobile aspirations, valuing an education, possessing the ability to delay gratification, and a willingness to save and work hard. By defining middle-class values in this manner, the implication is that people who are middle class acquired that status because they have the correct values and good moral character. This fails to address, in any significant way, the critical role of class oppression reflected in differential access to opportunities, such as education, at one time, trade union membership, as well as many jobs or careers that were closed to out LGB people, individuals with disabilities, ethnic minority group members, women, and others. These forms of advancement serve as gateways to middle-class status. These gateways are not equally distributed nor are they distributed reliably on the basis of merit in this society. Poor people are blamed for their circumstances with the assumption that they did not work hard enough or take advantage of available opportunities and are exhorted to feel ashamed of themselves and their circumstances. The pervasive and incorrect assumption is that sufficient opportunities are equally available to everyone. Blaming the poor for their plight serves further to obscure the reality of class oppression in this society.

Rothenberg (1988) writes that she grew up with an obliviousness to her race but an acute awareness of her gender and her Jewish, upper-middle-class standing. She recalls being aware that her family was much better off than most people and that she felt sorry for those who were not as well off. Still, she acknowledges believing, with absolute certainty, that poor people must deserve to be poor because they either failed "to work hard enough, study hard enough, or save enough" (Rothenberg 1988:38).

Hartigan (1997) asserts that there is an assumed equation between white-ness and economic social privilege that leaves Americans with "blackness" as the most prevalent image of, and association to, poverty. African-Americans are disproportionately poorer than white Americans (Wyche 1996), and it is commonly believed that most poor people are black and that most black people are poor (O'Hare 1986). The invisibility of poverty among white Americans obscures the reality that the vast majority of America's poor are white. This leads to a range of other problematic assumptions. Poverty and many of the stigmata related to it are not merely associated with being African-American, but some African-Americans come to regard it as if eco-nomic hardship is a part of their ethnic identity. As a result, many people who are members of ethnic minority groups and who are middle class fre-quently experience having their struggles with racism, sexism, and homo-phobia minimized or negated. Members of these groups may be treated as if having middle- or upper-class status diminishes or negates their ethnic identity, minimizes their struggles with racism and other forms of oppression, and calls their ethnic loyalty into question (Ferguson and King 1997). Fer-guson and King (1997) observe a tendency, in some of their African-American female clients, to resist shedding nonfunctional or derogatory identities that may lead to class transformation. There may be a fear that the "better life" will not only invalidate their continuing struggles in the eyes of other group members (as well as their own) but will negate valued aspects of their ethnic identity as well.

There is a perception among many people that most gays (Gates uses the term *gay* throughout his essay to refer to lesbians as well as to gay men) are well educated, socially mobile, and financially comfortable if not well off (Gates 1993). The assumption that most lesbians and gay men are white and that those who are people of color acquired their sexual orientation by assim-ilating into or identifying with the dominant culture has been observed among many people of color (Chan 1992; Greene 1994, 1997). These perceptions reflect both heterosexist and racist beliefs and connect them to each other.

Although many surveys suggest that gay respondents have higher than average educational and income levels, these surveys are rarely done outside major urban areas and may only reflect the responses of younger lesbians and gay men who not only self-identify as lesbian or gay, have the discretionary income to be present in social venues, colleges or universities, or other places where such questionnaires are distributed and are willing to take the time to respond to a questionnaire but are also willing to identify themselves on a questionnaire itself. It is possible that many lesbians and gay men who are not well educated, who are older, and who are poor might be more secretive and perhaps less likely to be out. As such, they might also be less likely to identify themselves, take part in, or even be approached about participating in research. Hence they remain invisible to us (Bradford, Ryan, and Rothblum 1994; Gonsiorek 1991). Their invisibility shapes and perhaps even distorts what we presume to know about lesbians and gay men, and about socioeconomic class issues among this group. There is a connection between the need to racialize America's poor and the perception that most gays are affluent and well educated.

To discern the connection between the coloring of poverty and the notion that gays are affluent, we must first ask why there is a need to render America's white poor invisible. How does it affect the lives of lesbians and gay men, and how can it transform the varied meaning and experience of lesbian and gay identities? Gates (1993) offers that African-Americans perceive most gays as affluent, white, and therefore endowed with greater class and skin color privilege than African-Americans. This makes it difficult for many African-Americans to see how lesbians and gay men are oppressed. It is as if the presence of class privilege eradicates the often severe consequences of heterosexism. Further, this attitude allows many heterosexual African-Americans to minimize the danger of hostile attitudes and physical attacks that are a result of pervasive heterosexism and homophobia, while denying the existence of their own heterosexual privilege. Such thinking contributes to preexisting resentful attitudes toward lesbians and gay men, and prompts what Gates (1993) denotes as a "blacklash," or a view that being lesbian or gay is a chosen identity and a mere inconvenience, whereas being black is to "inherit a legacy of hardship and inequity" (p. 42). African-Americans and members of groups of other people of color often perceive a comparison between heterosexism and racism as oppressions as one that trivializes their history of racial oppression. Gates (1993) warns, however, that the temptation to make these kinds of comparisons should be resisted because there are no simple comparisons.

Hartigan (1997) and Newitz and Wray (1997) write that poor whites in

West Virginia and the Midwest are characterized as "hillbillies" and are stereotyped as "lazy, licentious, sexually promiscuous, prone to violent and indecorous behavior, alcoholic, and stupid." Different names are used to characterize "white trash" that vary depending on the region of the country, but the negative depictions are consistent. Similar characterizations and negative stereotypes are used in America's racist lexicon to define the traits of African-Americans racially. These stereotypes of African-Americans are used to draw clear distinctions between black and white behavior and potential in a racially polarized society and in a social hierarchy designed to justify white skin privilege. When these negative stereotypes, usually reserved for African-Americans, are observed in white Americans, they "disrupt understandings of what it means to be white," and serve as "ruptures of conventions that maintain whiteness as a normative identity" (Hartigan 1997:46). Racial identity and class identity in this context become conflated and overlap rather than appearing clear and distinct (Hartigan 1997:47).

The conflation of race and class identity is an important phenomenon to understand when we attempt to discern the interlocking nature of societal oppressions that include heterosexism. Lesbian and gay sexual orientations challenge traditional definitions of gender, the presumed natural order of male superiority, the gender roles and hierarchies that are based on that presumption, as well as how normal sexual attraction is defined. In doing this, the rationale for male gender privileges based on the presumed natural origins of traditional gender roles is undermined. Similarly the presence of poor whites, who are characterized by all the negative characteristics usually reserved for African-Americans or other people of color, blurs the boundaries of race-based human distinctions. Socially constructed distinctions and distortions based on race/ethnicity exist to create a rationale for white skin privilege that denies it as a structured advantage but, rather, frames it as deserved and fair. If poor white people are more visible, their very existence contradicts and undermines rationales for white skin privilege based on contrived racial and racist distinctions.

In *Queer White Trash* (1997) Jillian Sandell examines the work of Dorothy Allison in an attempt to explore what she considers the difficulty that Americans in both the LGB as well as heterosexual communities have in discussing class privilege and class oppression. Sandell writes that it is easier among LGB people to focus discussions on sexuality and on heterosexism rather than social class and class oppression. She offers an analysis for Allison's embrace of the term *white trash* as an attempt to make class-based discrimination in the United States visible as well as to expose the structural rather than volitional sources of class oppression (Sandell 1997:215). Allison (1994) writes:

> I have known I was a lesbian since I was a teenager and have spent a good twenty years making peace with the effects of incest and physical abuse. . . . but what may be the central fact of my life is that I was born in 1949 in Greenville, SC, the bastard daughter of a white woman from a desperately poor family, just a month past 15 when she had me . . . that fact, the inescapable impact of being born in a condition of poverty that this society finds shameful, contemptible, and somehow deserved has had dominion over me to such an extent that I have spent my life trying to overcome or deny it. I have learned with great difficulty that the vast majority of people believe that poverty is a voluntary condition and that the poor are different, less than fully human, or at least less sensitive to hopelessness, despair and suffering. (pp. 14–15)

Allison, author of *Bastard Out of Carolina* (1992), observes that her status as a lesbian and her class status "fall outside of the normative moral orders of both the middle class and the queer community" (Sandell 1997:216). Like many individuals with multiple identities who experience multiple stigma, Allison (1994) observes that she selectively dropped different aspects of her identity in order to blend in with whatever community she was with at any given time. However, she recounts her sense of alienation as the price she pays for the need to compartmentalize any aspect of her identity. Allison (1994) recollects,

> My people . . . were the *they* everyone talks about, the ungrateful poor . . . By the time I understood that I was queer, the habit of hiding was deeply set in me, so deeply that it was not a choice but an instinct. Hide to survive, I thought. (pp. 13–14)

Allison (1994) goes on to describe the effects of growing up feeling shamed, learning early on to hide, and describing her lack of appropriate entitlement, reflected in her reluctance to pursue jobs, grants, awards, or other things that her lovers and friends felt she deserved and could easily acquire if only she asked.

> Entitlement is a matter of feeling like *we*, not *they* . . . you think you have a right to say things, a place in the world . . . you have a sense of

entitlement, of your own importance that I do not have . . . I have never been able to make clear the degree of my fear, the extent to which I feel myself denied, not only that I am queer in a world that hates queers, but I was born poor in a world that despises the poor . . . the need to make my world believable to people who have never experienced it is why I write fiction . . . I know that some things must be felt to be understood, that despair can never be adequately analyzed, it must be lived. (Allison 1994:14)

Sandell (1997) writes that reviewers of Allison's work tend to occlude certain aspects of her identity reflected in their responses to her writings. Some reviewers focus on her self-proclaimed identity as white trash and ignore issues of gender and sexuality in her stories. Others who concentrate on her essays and short stories focus on her gender and sexuality and neglect race and class issues. In this manner, they further exemplify the need to dichotomize identities as if only one can be important. What is deemed important may be the identity with which the observer most identifies or feels most comfortable or the one that presents the least discomfort.

Sandell (1997) warns that Allison's work reminds us that no single element of identity, be it class, race, gender, or sexual orientation, can truly be understood except in relation to the others. Allison's perspective on her life and stories explores how her willingness to examine her ethnic, class, and sexual selves have contributed to a greater understanding of how poverty shapes and constructs people's lives. When individuals are forced to separate those selves from one another they always experience a sense of alienation.

Ethnicity, Cultural Distinctiveness, and Sexual Orientation: Connecting Racism and Heterosexism

Most of the empirical and clinical research on or with lesbians and gay men is still conducted with overwhelmingly white, middle-class, young, able-bodied participants, most often among urban, college student, or well-educated populations. Those studies conducted with samples recruited in bars are biased toward people who have physical access to bars and clubs (often those who live in urban as opposed to rural communities), consume alcohol, and have sufficient disposable income to spend in those venues (Gonsiorek 1991). Aside from failing to include representative samples of people of color, most studies fail even to mention the ethnicity of their participants as a variable. When ethnicity is mentioned at all, if very few participants are people of color, that fact is mentioned; however, its implications on the validity or limited generalizability of the study findings rarely rates any discussion.

Newitz and Wray (1997) argue that whiteness is a socially constructed identity that serves as an unraced center of a racialized world. Its meaning also varies across the lines of sexual orientation, ethnicity, gender, age, and class, and these constructs vary according to the politics of a geographic region. Although having white skin is a part of a dominant cultural identity, it would be a mistake to assume that it is a monolithic experience or that ethnicity is irrelevant to the identities of all white people. Fygetakis (1997) states that not all white Americans are Anglo-Saxon Protestants, nor do they all espouse those values. Just as much of the current body of lesbian and gay psychological research does not generalize to lesbians or gay men of color, it cannot be assumed to generalize in the same ways to all white lesbians and gay men.

Fygetakis (1997) suggests that subjects who comprise most of the subject pools in LGB research consist of those who are out and, as such, are most likely identified with the dominant culture. She adds that white subjects who are also members of ethnic groups that are less tolerant of lesbian and gay sexual orientations are less likely to be out and therefore less visible. Catholic Italian Americans, particularly those living in concentrated Italian, Portuguese, and Armenian communities, and lesbians and gay men who are Russian, Serbian, Byzantine Orthodox, or Orthodox Jewish are examples of groups of white people in which lesbian and gay members constitute hidden and often very closeted populations (Fygetakis 1997). The factors applied in understanding the role of cultural traditions in lesbians and gay men of color must be similarly understood for white lesbians and gay men whose ethnic identity is very different from the dominant culture, particularly when religion is a part of that ethnic identification (Greene 1997; Fygetakis 1997).

Studies whose focus is on ethnicity, race, gender, religion, the presence of disabilities, socioeconomic class, and other topics rarely if ever acknowledges that not all the members of their group are heterosexual. If anything, the heterosexuality of participants is either presumed or the question about sexual orientation is never asked. Questions about sexual orientation may be deemed particularly irrelevant if the focus of the research is not sexuality per se. We know that sexual orientation is an active component in the development of human identity and, as such, may transform aspects of individual identity and behavior, whether or not the study's focus is on sexual behavior. When the focus of the research is on ethnicity, for example, members of that group are treated as if they experience their ethnicity in the same way. Marginalized members of an ethnic group, lesbian and gay members for example, may experience their ethnicity differently than those who are heterosexual. However, questions about differences and similarities in those experiences may not even arise if no thought is given to the inclusion of sexual orientation as yet another salient variable that cannot be presumed. If the degree to which socioeconomic class, gender, age, sexual orientation, and other variables transforms or "codes" the experience of ethnicity is not explored, the complex interaction between sexual orientation and other major aspects of identity development will remain unexplored as well. As a result, the realistic social tasks and stressors that are a component of gay and lesbian identity formation for people with multiple identities are not well understood nor are they studied. The vicissitudes of racism, cultural similarities, and differences in same-gender couples and the effect of these variables on their relationships will also be harder to discern. The narrow focus on heterosexual couples found in the literature on ethnic minority clients, and the equally narrow focus on predominantly white couples in the gay and lesbian literature, reflects the lack of attention given to these issues.

The aforementioned trends may not only reflect but may in fact reinforce the invisibility of lesbians and gay men of color, distinctions between members of white ethnic groups, and lesbians and gay men who share membership in other disadvantaged or stigmatized groups. It can also facilitate the tendency for families and communities of people of color, as well as some white ethnic and religious groups, to deny the existence of their lesbian, gay, and bisexual members (Greene 1997). Fygetakis (1997) chronicles the invisibility of Greek lesbians among Greeks. "Not only are we invisible in the Greek community, but we also keep ourselves invisible to each other" (p. 155). She adds that "invisibility continues even in language" (p. 171). In a limited study with ten Greek lesbian participants, Fygetakis (1997) asked if any of the women interviewed knew of Greek words that described their sexual orientation. None could name any. She writes that the only Greek words she is aware of that describe lesbian or gay sexual orientations are derogatory words for gay men. She advises that Greek American lesbians are being culturally consistent when they remain closeted in Greek communities, viewing the prospect of coming out in those communities as too risky and difficult, but who are out, active, and visible in the lesbian and gay communities.

The invisibility of Greek lesbians and gay men stands in stark contrast to the myth of tolerance and receptivity of Greek culture to lesbian and gay sexual orientation. If anything, quite the opposite has been observed (Fygetakis 1997). Using Western models of acceptance of lesbian and gay sexual orientation that include being out to family and ethnic community as the yardstick for mental health is ill-advised. The specifics of the culture and competing demands on its lesbian and gay members must be taken into account.

Yaakov Levado (1993) is a closeted gay rabbi and writes about his life in anonymity. Levado holds the privilege of white skin, maleness, and within his culture and religion the respected status of a rabbi. However, he is not simply Jewish; he is an Orthodox Jew (hence more visible) in a culture where Christian identity is presumed among people with white skin and is privileged; he is a gay man in a heterosexist world and a Jew in an anti-Semitic world. Despite the ways that he holds societal privilege, he understands the way that being out would collapse the complexity of his multiple identities into the one that others most despise. He writes of this painful dilemma,

> I am closeted and write in anonymity . . . Were I to come out . . . the controversy would collapse my life, my commitments, my identity as a teacher of Torah into my gayness. . . . Still, the secrecy of my shadowy existence of the closet are morally repugnant and emotionally draining . . . I cannot forever remain in darkness. (p. 60)

Dworkin (1997) writes about the special challenges of being a Jew in a society that presumes Christian-ness, and being lesbian in a society that presumes heterosexuality. The result is a constant need to come out, not only as a lesbian but also as a Jew. She offers,

> Claiming both identities means, among other things, grappling with persuading the heterosexual community that a lesbian identity is more complicated than sexual behavior and simultaneously persuading the lesbian community that a Jewish identity is more complex than mere religious affiliation. . . . invisibility offers some protection and security in a hostile, insecure world, and there are certainly historical reasons for remaining invisible as a lesbian and as a Jew. (Dworkin 1997:65–66)

Lesbians and gay men of color represent other groups with multiple identities who lack both white skin privileges as well as heterosexual privileges.

They may have other salient identities as well. Chan (1989, 1992, 1997), Espin (1987, 1995), Gock (1985), Greene (1994, 1996, 1997), Greene and Boyd-Franklin (1996), Mays, Cochran, and Rhue (1993), Morales (1990, 1992), Potgieter (1997), Smith (1997), Tafoya (1997), Tremble, Schneider, and Appathurai (1989), Trujillo (1991), Weinrich and Williams (1991), and Williams (1986) provide extensive discussions and research on mental health issues confronting African-American, Latino, Mexican, Chicana, Asian-American, black South African, and Native American lesbians and gay men. As a detailed discussion of each group is beyond the scope of this paper, their significant observations and the challenges LGB people of color confront are briefly summarized. Members of these groups face the challenge of integrating more than one major identity that is disparaged and results in societal disadvantage. The presence of multiple oppressions can contribute to the development of special coping strategies and resilience just as their "patterned injustice" can provide challenges that can undermine healthy development.

Many lesbians and gay men of color are taught to challenge the dominant culture's negative ethnic depictions of them and often receive positive cultural mirroring during the course of their development. The psychological independence that Jones (1997) describes is developed in many lesbians and gay men of color before they are aware of their sexual orientation in order to combat the pervasive racism that routinely challenges them. That ability for independent self-construction and a previously developed sense of psychological independence in one aspect of a person's life may be useful in helping that individual develop an affirmative response to other identities such as a lesbian or gay sexual orientation. However, lesbian and gay sexual orientations may also represent yet another source of stress, anxiety, and feeling marginalized. Clearly, in dysfunctional families of origin or those where negative ethnic stereotypes are reinforced rather than negated, individuals are likely to be at greater psychological risk.

Lesbians and gay men of color tend to come from cultures with strong ties to families of origin with the involvement of more extended than nuclear family arrangements in complex networks of interdependence and support. While lesbians and gay men of color may be supported by families and ethnic peers in challenging the validity of negative ethnic stereotypes, family and ethnic group members are often the very same source of negative stereotypes about lesbians and gay men. Because family and community are important buffers against racism and sources of tangible support, the homophobia in these communities often leaves lesbians and gay men of color feeling more vulnerable and less likely to be out in the same ways as their white counterparts. As such, they may be less visible within their communities as well as outside them. This contributes to the tendency of people of color to deny the existence of lesbian and gay members. A common theme in this denial is the suggestion that lesbian and gay sexual orientations are a "white man's disease" or a "Western sickness," acquired as a result of too much assimilation into the dominant culture. It is also viewed among many people of color as incompatible with the identities of people of color. There is also the belief that lesbian and gay sexual orientation is volitional and represents a poor lifestyle choice rather than an integrated aspect of a person's identity. In some cases, clients may be made to feel as if they are supposed to choose one identity over the other. Although coming out is anxiety-provoking for most lesbians and gay men, lesbians and gay men of color may not presume the acceptance or welcome into the dominant lesbian and gay community without continuing confrontations with racism. Hence alienating themselves from their family and ethnic community may carry a different kind of risk than for their white counterparts. Generally their position between what seems to be two contradictory worlds can leave members of these groups at risk for feelings of isolation, alienation, and estrangement, and therefore at risk for greater psychological vulnerability. Another important factor in work with lesbian and gay men of color is the history of the group's ethnic oppression and its impact on social status and available resources and opportunities, as well as a sense of who can be trusted and who cannot.

Sexual orientation must be contextualized if we are to develop accurate and more comprehensive understandings of it. Cultural values and rituals, sex-role socialization, family expectations and obligations, and religions (the more orthodox, the more challenging) are factors that must be considered if we attempt to understand the meaning of sexual orientation and identity development among lesbians and gay men of color as well as members of white ethnic groups. The presence of other variables such as age, disability, class, and so forth, transform these issues and warrant further consideration as well.

These and other exclusions can allow the LGB communities to avoid examining the sexism, ethnocentrism, classism, and other oppressive attitudes that exist within their own ranks by focusing instead solely on their own oppression.

Abilism: LGB People with Disabilities

Another invisible minority of LGB people are those who have disabilities. Research on LGB people who have disabilities are conspicuously absent from the LGB literature. This omission can suggest that sexual orientation is the master identity, that heterosexism is the primary locus of oppression, that there are no lesbians or gay men who have disabilities, which we know is not so, or that the presence of a disability does not have a salient impact on the identity or life of LGB people. Fine and Asch (1988) observe that, in research on disability, sexual orientation, gender, race, and class seem to be regarded as similarly irrelevant, suggesting that having a disability over-shadows all other dimensions of social experience. They suggest that disability (as opposed to the mere presence of physical challenges), like gender, sexual orientation, ethnicity, and so forth, is a social construct. Solomon (1993) writes that it is the interaction between the presence of physical challenges or biological impairments and social, environmental, cultural factors and social prejudice that determines whether the disability becomes a handicap. In their reviews of the literature on disabled women, Fine and Asch (1988) found

> no data on the numbers of lesbians with disabilities or on their accep-
> tance by nondisabled lesbians as partners, but comments made by
> many disabled lesbians indicate that within the community of lesbians,
> the disabled woman is still in search of love. (p. 3)

In their review of published research on women with disabilities, disabled lesbians reported being dismissed, shunned, or relegated to the status of friend and confidante rather than lover, just as heterosexual women with disabilities have been so relegated (Fine and Asch 1988:19). Indeed, when students were interviewed and asked to give their associations to disabled women, their responses included dependent, impaired, crippled, almost life-less, gray, old, an object of pity, lonely, and ugly (Fine and Asch 1988). Lesbians are similar victims of the stereotype of being less attractive and less feminine than heterosexual women. Men with disabilities tend to be stereo-typed as more feminine than nondisabled men (Asch 1988). Yet we have virtually no information about the ways that these identities doubly stigma-tize lesbians and gay men with disabilities. Generally research on disabled women makes it clear that they are not seen as sexual beings. Overall, courses on human sexuality rarely include material on sexual orientation or sexuality relevant to people with disabilities (Linton 1998). Like men with disabilities, women are less likely to fulfill the gender roles traditionally assigned them. It would be important to develop information on the effect that fulfillment of traditional gender roles or its absence has on the relationships of lesbian and gay men and whether there are differences or similarities between that group, heterosexuals, and bisexual men and women. Fine and Asch (1988) question whether these variables facilitate greater freedom, particularly for women, in pursuing nontraditional roles such as lesbian relationships. Fine and Asch (1988) observe, "The thought of a disabled woman as a lover may engender fears of merger, exaggerate lack of boundaries, and spawn fantasies of endless responsibility, of unremitting and unreciprocated care" (p. 19).

These observations generate questions and speculations about the dynamics in lesbian and gay couples when a partner with a disability is involved as well as when both partners are similarly challenged. Whether they conform to the patterns observed in heterosexual relationships is unknown owing, in large measure, to a paucity of data. Of the studies reviewed, some had lesbian-identified participants, albeit in small numbers. Women with disabilities in the studies reported recalled being told by a parent or parents that they would never find a man and should focus on acquiring an education or some kind of skill. Other women reported that their parents actually warned them about sexual relationships with men, with the admonishment that it could be dangerous to them. An example of one direct danger was that they would not be attractive enough to keep a man in their lives. As a result, the parent(s) reasoned, they would be used as sexual objects and then abandoned. Of this group, some women reported that they pursued sexual relationships with women out of the fear that they would be abandoned by men. The data presently available are insufficient to tell us about the ways or to what extent the presence of a disability affects the choices a woman makes about intimate relationships with men or women. Although speculations may emerge from such findings, they should be interpreted with great caution. There is no evidence to warrant assuming that women with disabilities who identify as lesbians do so out of fear of relationships with men or because they feel that they are not sufficiently attractive. The paucity of data on lesbians and gay men with disabilities is such that making any generalizations would be questionable at best. Often we are left with more questions than answers. Lesbians and gay men are often depicted in ways that overly sexualize them. Indeed, folklore and clinical research often focus on the sexuality of lesbians and gay men as if that were all that defines them. What is it like for women and men in these communities who, as a function of their disabilities, are not even seen as sexual beings?

Access to the lesbian and gay community may be difficult to obtain for lesbians and gay men who depend on family members or others for care and mobility. Unlike other characteristics or attributes that people share with family members, sexual orientation is not generally one of them. Lesbians and gay men must largely move beyond the boundaries of family to meet other lesbians and gay men. Their families may not only disapprove of their sexual orientation but may deny their sexuality altogether. Lesbians and gay men with disabilities, particularly those who depend on family members for mobility and care, may encounter obstacles in making contact with the LGB community or with LGB friends. This may be particularly true if their families do not approve of their sexual orientation. Such objections may not prove to be the same kind of obstacle for their heterosexual and able-bodied lesbian and gay counterparts.

Making social contacts with other lesbians and gay men, particularly when one is outside lesbian- and gay-identified establishments, depends on knowing who might be lesbian or gay and who is not. Asch (1988) observes that certain physical impairments (visual, articulation, hand movements) interfere with communication cues. There may be a heightened importance of subtle cues, often based on eye contact, that are not available to lesbians or gay men who are blind or have visual impairments. Furthermore, Asch (1988) reviews studies of the behavior of able-bodied people toward people with disabilities. In those studies, able-bodied people avoided social contact with people with disabilities, reflected in their avoiding eye contact, turning away from the person, or generally ignoring their presence. Although this clearly hinders social interaction for people with disabilities, it may be compounded by obstacles lesbians and gay men already encounter in "finding their own." This is another important area for further research. Fine and Asch (1988) suggest some of the following questions for further inquiry and future research. Do disabled women have less homosexual involvement during adolescence than nondisabled women? Other questions involve exploring the degree to which success or failure in heterosexual relationships during adolescence has any relevance for disabled women who are aware of being lesbian or bisexual. For these women, do parental heterosexual expectations have any effect on their involvement in heterosexual and lesbian activities?

Despite reports from men and women with disabilities that social factors influence their sexual experiences more profoundly than physiological factors, social factors are rarely discussed in the psychological literature (Linton 1998). As in other forms of oppression, Davis (1997) observes that "the problem is not the person with disabilities; the problem is the way that normalcy is socially constructed to create the problem of the disabled. Most people have been acculturated to stigmatize those whose bodies or other aspects of their person are deemed aberrant" (p. 9). Linton (1998) argues that people with disabilities need to be contextualized in contexts of human variation, political category, oppressed minority, and cultural group. Scheer (1994) and Linton (1998) observe that people with disabilities share an important commonality with lesbians and gay men. Both groups share the experience of growing up in families with other members who do not share their minority status. Members of both groups learn about what it means to be a member of their minority group outside their families rather than from their families. This sometimes occurs in the proximity of other peers and mentors, but sometimes not. Scheer (1994) suggests that the isolation that results has demonstrative social consequences and may provide an important driving force for a disability culture. Linton (1998) highlights difficulties in the development of group cohesion, culture, and identity formation when there is no consistent intergenerational transmission of culture as is also true for lesbians, gay men, and people with disabilities (p. 93).

Conducting Inclusive Empirical Research

Gonsiorek (1991) observes that the largest problem in LGB research is in obtaining representative samples. The sampling biases found in the research focusing on lesbian and gay concerns are rarely discussed explicitly either in titles of papers or in statements warning readers of the limited generalizability of their findings. Although there are many realistic obstacles that must be negotiated in obtaining more representative samples in empirical research that should not be minimized, the continued tendency to report the findings of such research as if it generalizes to groups that are not included in samples in representative numbers contributes to the perpetuation of the disturbing trend of invisibility of underrepresented groups. Conducting research with diverse populations is no easy task and may require rethinking the way we approach subject recruitment, selection, and so forth. It also requires considering why members of some groups are reluctant to participate in research endeavors at all. We recognize that personal examination is an important component to advancing more inclusive practice and treatment, but we must remember that such endeavors must be an active component of research efforts as well.

Nikki Gerrard (1995) offers insights about conducting research with members of disadvantaged groups, primarily her own painful experience as a white feminist researcher attempting to do research on women of color. She urges that feelings elicited in the researcher are important to attend to and can enrich the process while at the same time being respectful of the participant. Gerrard writes that she found herself, despite her good intentions, being treated with suspicion, hostility, anger, and resentment by the women of color she attempted to interview for her research. Despite her pain, she offers us an insight into this experience. She writes that when she was left to feel dismissed, powerless, and hopeless by the women of color she wished to interview, women to whom she felt she could offer something, she came to an understanding of how these women must feel all the time. She understood the resistance of her research participants to her well-intentioned inquiries and efforts as a manifestation of their resistance to the racism of a white society of which she just happened to be a member. Croom (2000) elaborates on Gerrard's (1995) dilemma and provides strategies for addressing some of the aforementioned methodological challenges.

Silence and Invisibility: Little Murders and Petty Humiliations

In both the psychology and politics of oppression we acknowledge that those who have the power to define experience also have the power to confer or deny legitimacy to experiences selectively. Exclusive attention to the most explicit, blatant, or outrageous incidents of heterosexism fails to capture the oppressiveness of omission and invisibility for many diverse groups of lesbians, gay men, and bisexual men and women. In his work on the silencing of African-American men, Anderson Franklin (1993) refers to the collective effect of these kinds of phenomena as the *invisibility syndrome*. Franklin (1993) writes,

> All black men, if you ask them, can describe the small social slights that accumulate to create what I call invisibility . . . we are not literally invisible . . . that might sometimes be preferable . . . rather, we are seen as potential criminals, or as servants, but not as ourselves. . . . You are forced to be aware of the negative reactions you elicit . . . and you are forced to develop ways of psychologically and physically surviving those reactions, which always takes their toll. (pp. 33–34)

Maya Angelou (American Broadcasting Company 1989) uses Jules Feiffer's words, "the little murders," with her own expression, "the petty humiliations," to describe what she conceptualizes as the violent and oppressive effect of silencing. The most blatant incidents of oppression, which she calls grand executions, are obvious in their lethality. The petty humiliations, however, have a more insidious, grinding, wearing-down effect. They accumulate over time and are just as oppressive and deadly as the grand executions. Boyd-Franklin (1993) refers to the subtle messages that invalidate people on the basis of race, sexual orientation, gender, and other stigmatized characteristics as microaggressions. She warns that the cumulative effect of these events can be psychologically damaging. Therefore the effects of chronic, lifelong stressors associated with invisibility, multiple identities, and complex challenges to the resulting dilemmas that arise for such people must be more carefully addressed in preventive mental health efforts, clinical practice, and research.

Competing Alliances and Loyalties: Reality or Illusion

The tendency to partition identity into isolated parts and then organize them into hierarchies leads us to assume that we can view the constituents of multiple identities hierarchically as well. The assumption is that different identities or group memberships compete with one another or that one must be considered more important than others across the life span. These assumptions make it more difficult for us to understand more complex experiences as well as the dynamic nature of identity, and the differential importance of different identities across the life span. However, there is a tendency for members of oppressed groups to engage in this practice when they view other oppressed groups, just as members of the majority do. In reality, one aspect of a person's identity may be more salient or prioritized in one setting and less salient or a lower priority in another. One or more aspects of an individual's identity may be more salient to that person than others at certain periods of his or her life.

Gates (1993) observes that if we judge other prejudices only by the ones that personally apply to us, we will fail to recognize other prejudices *as* prejudices. He observes that all oppressions come with different distinctions and histories, and offers the plight of African-Americans, Jews, and lesbians and gay men as examples. Stereotypes and distortions of African-Americans focus on their presumed inferiority on most desired social characteristics. Conversely, homophobic and anti-Semitic rhetoric bear a striking similarity to each other. Both Jews and lesbians and gay men are regarded as sinister and depicted as small, self-interested groups that stick together and favor their own, as cliquish minorities that command disproportionate world influence (Gates 1993; Kirk and Madsen 1996). Kirk and Madsen (1996) also note that what makes lesbians and gay men so suspect is their "conspiratorial invisibility. . . . a secret society whose members can be as collusive as spies. . . . Straights can never be sure whether lesbians and gay men are up to something behind their backs, because they're never entirely sure who might be gay" (p. 410). Certain aspects of homophobia are conflated with racist stereotypes that depict both lesbians and gay men and African-Americans as sexually bestial predators, each "ready to pounce on an unwilling victim with little provocation" (Gates 1993:43). The lesson here is that comparisons between different forms of oppression presume a means of neatly separating and fairly measuring these events; that yardstick does not exist.

Leslie and MacNeill (1995) observe a tendency for members of oppressed groups to cross-blame other oppressed or persecuted communities. They explain that this may be easier on the psyche because it is less daunting than fully acknowledging the potentially overwhelming power of a larger, more powerful, dominant group. Siegel (1995) observes that the best way to avoid being a target of societal discrimination or hostility is to make someone else one.

Summary

Locating Ourselves on the Spectrum of Oppression and Privilege

We all would tend to agree, in principle, that human identity consists of multiple identities and that members of the same group do not necessarily experience the group identity in the same way. This makes the study of human diversity complicated but necessary if we are to develop an inclusive psychology of human behavior and if psychotherapy is to be culturally literate. Despite a sense of intellectual agreement about this among mental health professionals, it frequently fails to make the leap from idea to practice. Although most clinicians agree, in principle, that exploring and understanding the role of culture, sexual orientation, ethnicity, gender, race, class, age, and other variables is important, they may also acknowledge experiencing great discomfort when confronted with the need to discuss these matters. It is important to consider these and other forms of resistance to acquiring the training needed in order competently to address cultural realities more broadly and the comfort or discomfort involved in including these realities routinely in clinical training. For many clinicians, the reluctance or avoidance of addressing this material in practice can certainly be attributed to the fact that its inclusion in the formal and routine training of clinical practitioners has been a relatively recent phenomenon. That phenomenon is still not pervasive. Courses on working with culturally diverse and/or disadvantaged populations are still not a routine feature of graduate training. Despite these realities, other factors may contribute to this resistance.

In considering the nexus of multiple identities, cultural differences, and similarities, we are compelled to ask questions that go beyond our understanding of these variables as mere differences or similarities but speak more directly to their meaning. The need to avoid examining the meaning of differences such as race, ethnicity, class, sexual orientation, and other variables can be attributed at least in part to the discomfort associated with examining the differentials in societal privilege and disadvantage that accompany these human distinctions and give them meaning.

Oliva Espin (1995) defines social privilege as that which provides a person or group with the luxury of not seeing anything that does not have to do directly with them, and the tendency to define whatever it is they do see as if their understanding or interpretation of the phenomenon is the universal truth or the normative experience. Although social privilege and disadvantage stand at opposite ends of the conceptual continuum, in reality they intersect, crisscross, and interact with one another at every moment. Every person operates at the center of these intersections (Wildman 1996). Wildman (1996) and Rothenberg (1988) observe that each of us is embedded in a matrix of categories and contexts, where in some contexts we are privileged and in others we may be disadvantaged, each interacting with the other. A form of privilege can moderate a form of disadvantage simultaneously, just as membership in a disadvantaged group may negatively moderate a locus of privilege. No person fits into only one static category; rather, each of us exists at the nexus of many groups or categories.

Although privilege and social advantage go hand in hand, they are usually invisible to those who hold them. Ignoring the presence of systems of privilege leads to the denial of disadvantage. That denial silences and renders invisible those who are not privileged and further marginalizes them. Laura Brown (1995) comments on the problematic aspects of this phenomenon in psychotherapy. She asserts that when the existence of social privilege is denied, the client's disadvantage goes unacknowledged and becomes a lie of omission. If heterosexual, white skin, middle class, able-bodied, or other forms of privilege are denied, the disadvantages associated with membership in disadvantaged groups is denied as well.

The experiences of oppression and privilege are filtered through the many different lenses and realities that must be incorporated and understood. Hence universalizing human experience should be carefully scrutinized. It increases disempowerment among those who are invisible, silenced, and therefore marginalized. Universalizing may also serve to avoid the difficult tensions that disrupt the false sense of harmony and security that often exists between members of disadvantaged groups. The result is a failure to give voice to the ways that lesbians and gay men may engage in oppressive behavior toward other lesbians, gay men, bisexual men and women, and transsexual and transgendered men and women both personally and institutionally.

There is the potential for oppressive behavior in anyone who holds societal privilege and the power that accompanies it. Because of that potential, it is important in our work as psychologists to determine the nature of our own multiple identities, where along the spectrum of privilege and disadvantage those identities place us, as the research scientist, therapist, supervisor, or teacher, and in what dimensions. It is important to locate and acknowledge our own locus of social advantage and its impact on our perceptions in our professional work. It is equally important to acknowledge the effect of our own membership in groups that may be marginalized on our view of the client, student, research participant, or supervisee. This process often provokes anxiety. Although many people may have ability and may work hard, that is not the most salient ingredient in success. Often, social, familial, and political connections with people in positions of power and influence, good timing, and sometimes just luck is essential. Most people know this on some level and may even articulate it when they feel they have been treated unfairly. However, if they are confronted with the ways that their optimal development is or has been enhanced by factors not based simply on ability, hard work, or fairness but, rather, have been facilitated by social privilege, they may need to avoid acknowledging that reality. To acknowledge this reality may appear synonymous with minimizing their personal ability and effort. Similarly many people will minimize the level at which one form of privilege does not necessarily mitigate a locus of disadvantage. The dimension that makes a locus of privilege or disadvantage salient or relevant is often the context. The need to deny the presence of social privilege, however, creates major obstacles in implementing diversity and, in some settings, even in discussing it. However, in research and in psychotherapy theory and practice, avoiding the acknowledgment and understanding of the broad and divergent role of societal privilege and disadvantage in people's lives is problematic. It will ultimately result in a failure to deliver optimal services whether in treatment to clients or validity of research findings. Therapists, if they are unable to view themselves and their own position fully, will be unable to view the client and the client's position fully.

The Future

The very act of defining the experiences of all lesbians and gay men by the characteristics of the most privileged and powerful members of that group is an oppressive act. It does not ultimately undermine heterosexism because heterosexism has an interlocking relationship to other forms of oppression (Greene and Sanchez-Hucles 1997). To the contrary, it facilitates it. It does so by tolerating the invisibility and thus the silencing of people who are not members of the group that is dominant. The silence and absence of a wider range of lesbians, gay men, and bisexual people, often reflected in the failure to speak about them or their needs, and the tendency to represent the needs of the dominant group as if it represents the full spectrum of lesbians and gay men, permit this sinister evasion. It permits majority lesbians and gay men to identify themselves simply as victims of heterosexism and to use that status as a victim to, at the very least, ignore, and, at the worst, perpetuate racial, gender, or other social class hierarchies of advantage and disadvantage. It also permits them to avoid a realistic confrontation with their own power and locus of privilege and how they use it.

Racism, sexism, classism, ageism, ableism, and heterosexism are all embedded pervasively in our society and are a part of our socialization. These varied types of societal disadvantage assume both personal and institutional designs. Furthermore, the discriminatory practices that accompany them create a unique range of psychological demands and stressors that victims of disadvantage must learn to manage in addition to the routine range of developmental tasks and life stressors that everyone else faces. Clinical training must include an understanding of the salient factors that must be considered in human development in the context of discriminatory systems and institutions, and in ways that are sensitive to the complex psychological and cultural realities of disadvantaged group members. In the context of heterosexism, its varied incarnations and the different ways it is experienced must be explored and better understood for a wider range of lesbians and gay men. Failing to consider these variables in the delivery of mental health services and in the theoretical perspectives underlying practice may only serve to perpetuate our ignorance and ultimately contribute to, rather than mitigate, social ills.

The task of unraveling the conundrum of multiple identities in lesbian, gay, and bisexual psychology theory, research, and practice is no simple task, given that heterosexism is not the primary locus of oppression for all lesbians and gay men. In considering the nexus of LGB psychology on all levels, we are compelled to ask questions that go beyond our understanding of societal disadvantage and privilege as if they exist in isolation. The more we are aware of the diversity of the lives and experiences of LGB men and women, the more cognizant we become of the need to ask how the intensity and effects of forms of disadvantage and privilege vary or interact with other forms of disadvantage and privilege in an individual, particularly in the therapy process. Our inquiry must also include an examination of the ways that LGB psychology itself can be an instrument that facilitates the marginalization of its less visible members. Consequently we are led to consider first the extent to which current LGB psychology reflects or fails to be inclusive of the diversity of LGB experiences and to address those failures. Ultimately we are charged with the task of developing paradigms that assist us in better understanding the ongoing, dynamic, and interactive nature of constituents of human identity, in a context in which any single aspect of identity colors, transforms, and informs the meaning of others in reciprocal ways.

Working through the tension that develops when we are inclusive is necessary in order to achieve authentically both a personal and a professional transformation of the discourse of psychology. When we practice authentic inclusiveness, we enhance LGB psychology and our understanding of heterosexism, as well as other interlocking forms of oppression (Greene 1996, 1997). Fully incorporating the study of many differences that occur simultaneously affords us the multiple perspectives needed to provide for an increasingly comprehensive, representative, accurate, and dynamic knowledge base in psychological theory and practice (Greene and Sanchez-Hucles 1997). Incorporating diverse perspectives and concerns in our paradigms should facilitate an authentic understanding of all human beings. Omitting these diverse perspectives leaves us with a narrow and distorted view of the worlds and realities of LGB men and women. The inclusion of multiple perspectives, however, can transform the discipline of psychology from an instrument of social control to a powerful instrument of advocacy and social change (Greene and Sanchez-Hucles 1997). In this paradigm we will no longer need to see people as the same in order to treat them with fairness. We can make the important leap from equal treatment, which presumes sameness, to fair treatment that acknowledges and even celebrates the richness of human differences.

It seems appropriate to give Audre Lorde (1984) the last words. In *Sister Outsider*, she writes,

Somewhere on the edge of consciousness there is what I call a mythical norm, which each one of us within our hearts knows "that is not me." In America, this norm is usually defined as white, thin, male, young, heterosexual, Christian, and financially secure. It is with this mythical norm that the trappings of power reside in this society. Those of us who stand outside that power often identify one way in which we are different, and we assume that to be the primary cause of all oppression, forgetting other distortions around difference, some of which we ourselves may be practicing. (p. 116)

References

Allison, D. 1992. *Bastard out of Carolina*. New York: Plume.

Allison, D. 1994. A question of class. In D. Allison, ed., *Skin: Talking about Sex, Class, and Literature*. New York: Firebrand.

American Broadcasting Company. 1989. Interview with Maya Angelou and Alice Walker. *The Oprah Winfrey Show*, televised broadcast, June 6. Chicago: Author.

Ames, L. J. 1996. Homo-phobia, homo-ignorance, homo-hate: Heterosexism and AIDS. In E. Rothblum and L. Bond, eds., *Preventing Heterosexism and Homophobia*, pp. 239–56. Thousand Oaks, Calif.: Sage.

Asch, A. 1988. Disability: Its place in the curriculum. In P. A. Bronstein and K. Quina, eds., *Teaching a Psychology of People*, pp. 156–67. Washington, D.C.: American Psychological Association.

Bohan, J. 1996. *Psychology and Sexual Orientation*. New York: Routledge.

Boyd-Franklin, N. 1993. Pulling out the arrows. *Family Therapy Networker* 17(4): 54–56.

Bradford, J., and C. Ryan. 1987. *National Lesbian Health Care Survey: Mental Health Implications for Lesbians*. Rockville, Mo.: National Institute of Mental Health.

Bradford, J., C. Ryan, and E. Rothblum. 1994. National lesbian health care survey: Implications for mental health. *Journal of Consulting and Clinical Psychology* 62:228–42.

Brown, L. S. 1995. Antiracism as an ethical norm in feminist therapy practice. In J. Adleman and G. Enguidanos, eds., *Racism in the Lives of Women: Testimony, Theory, and Guides to Practice*, pp. 137–48. New York: Harrington Park.

Chan, C. 1989. Issues of identity development among Asian-American lesbians and gay men. *Journal of Counseling and Development* 68(1):16–20.

Chan, C. 1992. Cultural considerations in counseling Asian-American lesbians and gay men. In S. Dworkin and F. Gutierrez, eds., *Counseling Gay Men and Lesbians*, pp. 115–24. Alexandria, Va.: American Association for Counseling and Development.

Chan, C. 1997. Don't ask, don't tell, don't know: The formation of a homosexual identity and sexual expression among Asian-American lesbians. In B. Greene, ed., *Ethnic and Cultural Diversity Among Lesbians and Gay Men*, pp. 224–48. Thousand Oaks, Calif.: Sage.

Croom, G. L. 2000. Lesbian, gay, and bisexual adolescent development: Dancing with your feet tied together. In B. Greene and G. L. Croom, eds., *Education, Research, and Practice in Lesbian, Gay, Bisexual, and Transgendered Psychology*, pp. 263–81. Thousand Oaks, Calif.: Sage.

Davis, L. 1997. Constructing normalcy: The Bell Curve, the novel, and the invention of the disabled body in the nineteenth century. In L. Davis, ed., *The Disability Studies Reader*, pp. 9–28. New York: Routledge.

Dworkin, S. 1997. Female, lesbian, and Jewish: Complex and invisible. In B. Greene, ed., *Ethnic and Cultural Diversity Among Lesbians and Gay Men*, pp. 63–87. Thousand Oaks, Calif.: Sage.

Ehrenberg, M. 1996. Aging and mental health: Issues in the gay and lesbian community. In C. Alexander, ed., *Gay and Lesbian Mental Health: A Sourcebook for Practitioners*, pp. 189–209. New York: Harrington Park.

Espin, O. 1987. Issues of identity in the psychology of Latina lesbians. In Boston Lesbian Psychologies Collective, eds., *Lesbian Psychologies: Explorations and Challenges*, pp. 35–51. Urbana: University of Illinois Press.

Espin, O. 1995. On knowing you are the unknown: Women of color constructing psychology. In J. Adleman and G. Enguidanos, eds., *Racism in the Lives of Women: Testimony, Theory, and Guides to Practice*, pp. 127–36. New York: Harrington Park.

Essed, P. 1996. *Diversity: Gender, Color, and Culture*. Amherst: University of Massachusetts Press.

Ferguson, S. A., and T. C. King. 1997. There but for the grace of God: Two black women therapists explore privilege. *Women and Therapy* 20(1):5–14.

Fine, M., and A. Asch, eds. 1988. Beyond pedestals. *Women with Disabilities: Essays in Psychology, Culture, and Politics*, pp. 1–37. Philadelphia: Temple University Press.

Fox, R. 2000. Bisexuality in perspective: A review of theory and research. In B. Greene and G. L. Croom, eds., *Education, Research, and Practice in Lesbian, Gay, Bisexual, and Transgendered Psychology*, pp. 161–206. Thousand Oaks, Calif.: Sage.

Franklin, A. J. 1993. The invisibility syndrome. *The Family Therapy Networker* 17(4):33–39.

Fygetakis, L. 1997. Greek American lesbians: Identity odysseys of honorable good girls. In B. Greene, ed., *Ethnic and Cultural Diversity Among Lesbians and Gay Men*, pp. 152–90. Thousand Oaks, Calif.: Sage.

Gainor, K. A. 2000. Including transgender issues in lesbian, gay, and bisexual psychology: Implications for clinical practice and training. In B. Greene and G. L. Croom, eds., *Education, Research, and Practice in Lesbian, Gay, Bisexual, and Transgendered Psychology*, pp. 131–60. Thousand Oaks, Calif.: Sage.

Gates, H. L., Jr. 1993. May 17. Blacklash. *The New Yorker*, May 17, 69(13):42–44.

Gatz, M., and B. Cotton. 1994. Age as a dimension of diversity: The experience of being old. In E. J. Trickett, R. J. Watts, and D. Birman, eds., *Human Diversity: Perspectives on People in Context*, pp. 334–55. San Francisco: Jossey-Bass.

Gerrard, N. 1995. Some painful experiences of a white feminist therapist doing research with women of color. In J. Adleman and G. Enguidanos, eds., *Racism in the Lives of Women: Testimony, Theory, and Guides to Practice*, pp. 55–63. New York: Harrington Park.

Gock, T. S. 1985. Psychotherapy with Asian Pacific gay men: Psychological issues, treatment approach, and therapeutic guidelines. Paper presented at the annual meeting of the Asian-American Psychological Association, Los Angeles, August.

Gonsiorek, J. 1991. The empirical basis for the demise of the illness model of homosexuality. In J. Gonsiorek and J. Weinrich, eds., *Homosexuality: Research Implications for Public Policy*, pp. 115–36. Thousand Oaks, Calif.: Sage.

Greene, B. 1994. Lesbian women of color. In L. Comas-Diaz and B. Greene, eds., *Women of Color: Integrating Ethnic and Gender Identities in Psychotherapy*, pp. 389–427. New York: Guilford.

Greene, B. 1996. Lesbians and gay men of color: The legacy of ethnosexual mythologies in heterosexism. In E. Rothblum and L. Bond, eds., *Preventing Heterosexism and Homophobia*, pp. 59–70. Thousand Oaks, Calif.: Sage.

Greene, B. 1997. Ethnic minority lesbians and gay men: Mental health and treatment issues. In B. Greene, ed., *Ethnic and Cultural Diversity Among Lesbians and Gay Men*, pp. 216–39. Thousand Oaks, Calif.: Sage.

Greene, B., and N. Boyd-Franklin. 1996. African-American lesbians: Issues in couples therapy. In J. Laird and R. J. Green, eds., *Lesbians and Gay Men in Couples and Families: A Handbook for Therapists*, pp. 251–71. San Francisco: Jossey-Bass.

Greene, B., and J. Sanchez-Hucles. 1997. Diversity: Advancing an inclusive feminist psychology. In J. Worell and N. Johnson, eds., *Shaping the Future of Feminist Psychology: Education, Research, and Practice*, pp. 173–202. Washington, D.C.: American Psychological Association.

Hadju, D. 1996. *Lush Life: The Biography of Billy Strayhorn*. New York: Farrar, Straus, and Giroux.

Haldeman, D.C. 2000. Therapeutic responses to sexual orientation: Psychology's evolution. In B. Greene and G. L. Croom, eds., *Education, Research, and Practice in Lesbian, Gay, Bisexual, and Transgendered Psychology*, pp. 244–62. Thousand Oaks, Calif.: Sage.

Hall, R., and B. Greene. 1996. Sins of omission and commission: Women, psychotherapy, and the psychological literature. *Women and Therapy* 18(1):5–31.

Hartigan, J. 1997. Name calling: Objectifying "poor whites" and "white trash" in Detroit. In M. Wray and A. Newitz, eds., *White Trash: Race and Class in America*, pp. 41–56. New York: Routledge.

Hooker, E. 1957. The adjustment of the male overt homosexual. *Journal of Projective Techniques* 21:18–31.

Jones, F. 1997. Eloquent anonymity. Book review of *Lush Life: A Biography of Billy Strayhorn*. *Readings: A Journal of Reviews and Commentary in Mental Health* 12(1):10–14.

Jones, R. 1979. Structural isolation and the genesis of black nationalism in North America. *Colby Librarian Quarterly* 15:256–66.

Kaschak, E. 1992. *Engendered Lives: A New Psychology of Women's Experience*. New York: Basic Books.

Kirk, M., and H. Madsen. 1996. A field trip to straight America. In K. E. Rosenblum and T-M. C. Travis, eds., *The Meaning of Difference: American Constructions of Race, Class, Sex and Gender, Social Class, and Sexual Orientation*, pp. 400–412. New York: McGraw-Hill.

Kite, M., and K. Deaux. 1987. Gender belief systems: Homosexuality and the implicit inversion theory. *Psychology of Women Quarterly* 11:83–96.

Levado, Rabbi Yaakov, pseudonym. 1993. Gayness and God: Wrestlings of an Orthodox rabbi. *Tikkun: A Bimonthly Jewish Critique of Politics, Culture, and Society* 8(5):54–60.

Leslie, D., and L. MacNeill. 1995. Double positive: Lesbians and race. In J. Adleman and G. Enguidanos, eds., *Racism in the Lives of Women: Theory, Testimony, and Guides to Practice*, pp. 161–69. New York: Harrington Park.

Linton, S. 1998. *Claiming Disability: Knowledge and Identity*. New York: New York University Press.

Lorde, A. 1984. Age, race and class. In A. Lorde, ed., *Sister Outsider: Essays and Speeches*. Freedom, Calif.: Crossing Press.

Mays, V., S. Cochran, and S. Rhue. 1993. The impact of perceived discrimination on the intimate relationships of black lesbians. *Journal of Homosexuality* 25(4):1–14.

Merriam-Webster's Collegiate Dictionary. 1996. 10th ed. Dallas: Merriam-Webster and Zane.

Morales, E. 1990. Ethnic minority families and minority gays and lesbians. In F. W. Bozett and M. B. Sussman, eds., *Homosexuality and Family Relationships*, pp. 217–39. New York: Haworth.

Morales, E. 1992. Counseling Latino gays and Latina lesbians. In S. Dworkin and F. Gutierrez, eds., *Counseling Gay Men and Lesbians: Journey to the End of the Rainbow*, pp. 125–39. Alexandria, Va.: American Association for Counseling and Development.

Newitz, A., and M. Wray. 1997. Introduction. In M. Wray and A. Newitz, eds., *White Trash: Race and Class in America*, pp. 1–12. New York: Routledge.

O'Hare, W. 1986. 8 myths about poverty. *American Demographics* 8(5):22–25.

Pinderhughes, E. 1989. *Understanding Race, Ethnicity, and Power: Keys to Efficacy in Clinical Practice.* New York: Free Press.

Potgieter, C. 1997. From apartheid to Mandela's constitution: Black South African lesbians in the nineties. In B. Greene, ed., *Ethnic and Cultural Diversity Among Lesbians and Gay Men*, pp. 88–116. Thousand Oaks, Calif.: Sage.

Rosenblum, K. E., and T-M. C. Travis. 1996. Experiencing difference: Framework essay. In K. E. Rosenblum and T-M. C. Travis, eds., *The Meaning of Difference*, pp. 137–62. New York: McGraw-Hill.

Rothenberg, P. 1988. Integrating the study of race, gender, and class: Some preliminary observations. *Feminist Teacher* 3(3):37–42.

Sandell, J. 1997. Telling stories of "queer white trash": Race, class, and sexuality in the work of Dorothy Allison. In M. Wray and A. Newitz, eds., *White Trash: Race and Class in America*, pp. 211–30. New York: Routledge.

Schaie, K. W. 1993. Ageist language in psychological research. *American Psychologist* 48:49–51.

Scheer, J. 1994. Culture and disability: An anthropological point of view. In E. J. Trickett, R. J. Watts, and D. Birman, eds., *Human Diversity: Perspectives on People in Context*, pp. 244–60. San Francisco: Jossey-Bass.

Siegel, R. J. 1995. Overcoming bias through awareness, mutual encouragement, and commitment. In J. Adleman and G. Enguidanos, eds., *Racism in the Lives of Women: Testimony, Theory, and Guides to Practice*, pp. 295–301. New York: Haworth.

Smith, A. 1997. Cultural diversity and the coming out process: Implications for clinical practice. In B. Greene, ed., *Ethnic and Cultural Diversity Among Lesbians and Gay Men*, pp. 279–300. Thousand Oaks, Calif.: Sage.

Solomon, S. 1993. Women and physical distinction: A review of the literature and suggestions for intervention. *Women and Therapy* 14(3/4):91–103.

Tafoya, T. 1997. Native gay and lesbian issues: The two spirited. In B. Greene, ed., *Ethnic and Cultural Diversity Among Lesbians and Gay Men*, pp. 1–10. Thousand Oaks, Calif.: Sage.

Tremble, B., M. Schneider, and C. Appathurai. 1989. Growing up gay or lesbian in a multi-cultural context. *Journal of Homosexuality* 17:253–67.

Trujillo, C., ed. 1991. *Chicana Lesbians: The Girls Our Mothers Warned Us About.* Berkeley, Calif.: Third Woman Press.

Wachtel, P. 1996. The inner city and the inner life. Book review of *The Analyst in the Inner City: Race, Class, and Culture Through a Psychoanalytic Lens. Tikkun: A Bimonthly Critique of Politics, Culture, and Society* 11(3):59–61.

Weinrich, J., and W. L. Williams. 1991. Strange customs, familiar lives: Homosexuality in other cultures. In J. Gonsiorek and J. Weinrich, eds., *Homosexuality: Research Findings for Public Policy*, pp. 44–59. Newbury Park, Calif.: Sage.

Wildman, S. 1996. *Privilege Revealed: How Invisible Preference Undermines America.* New York: New York University Press.

Williams, W. L. 1986. *The Spirit and the Flesh: Sexual Diversity in American Indian Culture.* Boston: Beacon.

Wyche, K. F. 1996. Conceptualizations of social class in African-American women: Congruence of client and therapist definitions. *Women and Therapy* 18(3/4):35–43.

14 Native Gay and Lesbian Issues: The Two-Spirited

Terry Tafoya

"Long ago, when the world was young, Coyote was going along . . ." (or perhaps it was Raven, or Wiskijiac, or Dukwebah, or Rabbit . . .) — with these words, a number of the Native stories of the Americas begin to tell of an unbroken connectiveness of past, present, and future.[1] The stories provide a framework for understanding how the world works, how one identifies oneself as a member of a tribe, a clan, a community; what to value and what to avoid. These include issues of sexuality and gender.

Coyote, someone common to many tribes, plays with everything — sexual behavior, gender identity, boundaries, and bodies. This trickster always challenges an audience to think and to deal with concepts of transformation. Often in the stories, when *Evil* (and this term seems inappropriate, but it is a term forced by English usage and convention — *Disharmonic* might be a more accurate term) is encountered, it is not seen as something to be destroyed in some final Armageddon, but as a force or energy that is to be transformed.

For example, in a Pacific Northwest legend, Coyote confronts the Blood Monster Wawa-yai, a giant who kills people by draining them of blood. Offering him baskets full of blood soup, Coyote tempts him into excess, until Wawa-yai has ingested so much blood that he can barely move his enormous bloated body. Coyote then taunts the monster into chasing him, but Wawa-yai's belly is now so huge that he cannot fit through the longhouse door, and he bursts as he runs against the thorn-lined door frame. As Coyote watches, the exploding bits and pieces of the monster turn into mosquitoes. Evil is not eradicated but turned into something that is more in balance with the universe, and, indeed, the universe would not be in balance without Evil. Coyote's action is to stabilize the world by playing with the excess until harmony is restored. If this story is used to form a metaphor for acquired immune deficiency syndrome (HIV/AIDS or substance abuse (contemporary monsters that steal and destroy loved ones in the manner of Wawa-yai), a European worldview of this story (e.g., Hansel and Gretel destroying the witch) would focus on the eradication of the enemy — the dragon is slain, and everyone else lives happily ever after. But just as in substance abuse and real life, where Evil does not disappear when treatment begins, Evil takes on a more manageable form that a person can live with on a daily basis. A mosquito may be a problem but not of the significance of the Blood Monster. There is a place for everything in Creation — a fundamental belief of most Native communities.

Most Native communities tend not to classify the world into the concrete binary categories of the Western world — good/bad, right/wrong, male/female, gay/straight — but rather into categories that range from appropriateness to inappropriateness, depending on the context of a situation.

For example, a Navajo man asked a non-Indian man for food to feed his family, including his wife, who was about to give birth. The non-Indian agreed, but asked why the man's family was going hungry when it was well-known what a good hunter he was. The Navajo replied, "Because it is not appropriate that I, who am about to receive a life, should be taking life at this time." In other words, hunting is not seen as right or wrong but only understandable in the context of a relationship.

This worldview is critical in understanding Native concepts of sexuality and gender, which do not always fit comfortably and neatly into general American concepts of gay/straight or male/female. Indeed, even the discrete categories that exist for social science research will not always make conceptual sense to Native people, who may have a far more sophisticated taxonomy addressing spirituality and function, rather than appearance. For example, how does a Euro-American system of "gay/straight" classify a man who wants to be anally penetrated by a woman wearing a dildo?

When Native American people discovered Columbus five centuries ago, they presented a unique conundrum of identity. Not only did most tribes not organize themselves by kings and queens in European tradition, but the majority classified members as having more than two genders. This radical (for Europeans) way of seeing the world brought swift and tragic responses. The sixteenth-century Spanish explorer Balboa, for example, declared such individuals who were not considered male or female to be "sodomites," and literally had them torn apart by his dogs. Thus, from the very beginning of European contact, Native people learned not to discuss openly matters of sexuality and gender with the newcomers, because they could be killed for being "different." Most U.S. citizens are unaware of Native history and reality. For example, American Indians did not become citizens of the United States until 1924. When the reservations were created by the federal government, the superintendents of the reservations were all appointed Christian missionaries of various denominations, with the mandate to "civilize" American Indians by converting them to Christianity, often by withholding food and starving the Indians into submission. Federal boarding schools were set up for Natives (American Indian and Alaskan). Natives were not permitted to attend public schools until the mid-1930s. There are still a number of Indian boarding schools operating today. Children were forcibly removed from their parents, sometimes at gunpoint, deliberately to prevent them from growing up with the influence of their culture and language.

This forced segregation and isolation had a devastating impact on Native communities as a whole. Critical teachings and attitudes regarding sexuality and gender that would have been provided at the time of puberty, for example, were never passed on in many families and tribes because the young persons were away at boarding school. Such things were not permitted to be discussed. In addition, there was an incredible loss of Native lives through exposure to European diseases to which Native people had no immunity (a situation that has a number of parallels to the AIDS epidemic: Newspaper editorials of the 1880s in the Pacific Northwest condemned Native Americans for having unacceptable sexual behaviors and multiple partners, and declared their deaths by infectious disease to be "God's punishment"). It is estimated that in the Pacific Northwest, 80 percent of the Native population died within two generations of European contact.

It is fascinating in working with the Native "gay and lesbian" community to discover how often even those individuals who were denied access to their tribal histories of alternative gender roles and identities manifest the "duties and responsibilities of office" that were an integral part of being "different" before and after European contact. These traditional roles include teaching, keeping the knowledge of the elders, healing, child care, spiritual leadership and participation, herbal wisdom, interpretation, mediation, and all forms of artistic expression.

Of the 250 or so Native languages still spoken in the United States, at least 168 have been identified as having terms for people who are not considered male or female. In the anthropological literature, the most common word used to describe such an individual is *berdache*. This is an unfortunate historic choice, reflecting as it does an old Persian term for a male sexual slave. The word was picked up in the Middle Ages by Europeans during the Crusades, and its pronunciation and spelling evolved into its contemporary form.

When the French fur traders, explorers, and missionaries encountered Native people in North America who did not fit European standards of gender roles, they used the term *berdache* to describe them. In the seventeenth century, the word in French implied someone who engaged in receptive anal intercourse. It also has a connotation of someone with a biologically male identity, and so tends to exclude Native people who are biologically female. Some modern writers suggest the term *amazon* to discuss biological females who take on an alternative gender role. *Berdache* also indicates a sexual behavior that may or may not be relevant to a particular individual. Neither of these foreign terms is well known to traditional Native people.

In other words, asking a tribal member, "Do you have a *berdache* or *amazon* tradition in your community?" may bring about a confused stare. Asking a Navajo, "Do your people have *Nadle*?" or asking a Lakota, "Do your people have *Winkte*?" may get a very different response, as people recognize their own language's terms for such people. Many contemporary Native people have difficulty being comfortable with identifying themselves as gay, lesbian, or bisexual, feeling as though they are being "herded" into such categories by the power of English. In response to this, the term *two-spirited* or *two-spirited people* seems to be gaining greater acceptance for many of today's Native people in lieu of *berdache*, amazon, or gay/lesbian/bisexual. *Two-spirited* indicates that someone possesses both a male and a female spirit.

A number of non-Native gay, lesbian, and bisexual researchers and writers have suggested the two-spirited tradition as a historic "gay" role model because it often carries with it a sense of positive acceptance or even celebration within many Native communities. For example, a European American gay male nurse reported being surprised and delighted to be visiting a Catholic priest on an Apache Indian reservation when a proud mother came in and told the priest, "My sixteen-year-old son is attracted to other men. We need to arrange for him to be initiated with the medicine men." The nurse was amazed to discover that there was a respected and sanctioned role for such a young person among the Apache, and to note that the mother's response was somehow different from his own mother's when his own sexual orientation became known.

Unfortunately the simplistic reductionism (*berdache* = gay) of many non-Native writers often fails to see that although two-spirited people's and gay/bisexual/lesbian people's experiences and worldviews overlap, they are not the same. The two-spirited position is not one determined primarily by sexual orientation. The role is one of a spiritual/social identity for Native people, as opposed to psychosexual identity. Paula Gunn Allen (1986) (Laguna/Sioux) suggests seeing the *berdache* as a gender role, rather than a sexual identity. Tribal concepts do not stress individuality in the manner of Euro-American concepts, but instead focus on relationships, contexts, and inter-actions. In short, *gay* can be seen as a noun, but *two-spirit* as a verb. (This is meant as a metaphoric statement, meaning that a noun is a person, place, or thing, whereas a verb deals with action and interaction.)

The rigidity of the English language prevents even many self-identified gay/lesbian/bisexual Natives from dealing with fluidity of gender and sexual roles if the only categories that exist in a valued way are "homosexual/heterosexual." Native tradition emphasizes transformation and change, and the idea that an individual is expected to go through many changes in a lifetime. Indeed, many tribes anticipate that someone will change his or her name more than once, since a person at age forty-five is not the same person he or she was at age ten. Hence a name change seems most appropriate.

While hardly identifying as "asexual" (a lesser-used category some researchers employ to indicate a gay or lesbian who is not active with males or females), some two-spirited people will not be involved on a sexual level with a biologically same-gendered partner, although an emotional/affectionate bonding can occur. This may be a matter of personal choice, an individual's *medicine path* (a traditional Native term that indicates one's spiritual behavior and connotes a combination of destiny and free choice), or a result of a specific spiritual vision/perception of his or her appropriate behavior. This should in no way distract from the fact that a number of Native people very strongly identify as members of the gay/lesbian/bisexual community. But to see "gay/straight" as the only possible categories of sexual identity for Native people (and certain other ethnic groups in India, Burma, the Middle East, and so on) is grossly misleading and out of touch with historic and contemporary reality. It is also seen as very reasonable that two-spirited people can be heterosexual, and that their partnering may change over a period of time. In many tribes there is a history of polygamy or polyandry — multiple spouses. This may still have an influence on how Native two-spirited people deal with relationships.

One of the impacts of the gay/lesbian/bisexual movement has actually been to limit the options of younger Native people who are now (in English) informed that they are "gay" or "lesbian" when they begin showing behaviors that in earlier times would indicate that they were *Lamana* or *Bote* or another traditional category. Native concepts of masculinity and femininity are so significantly different from European American concepts of gender that they confuse the issue even more. For example, Jamake Highwater (1990) suggests:

> In hypermasculine societies, machismo is of the utmost importance in both heterosexual and homosexual males. In social systems that place less importance on distinction of sex, like those of many North American Indian tribes, there is a full spectrum of acceptable sexual behavior that makes the dualistic connotation of heterosexuality as opposed to homosexuality meaningless, and which therefore does not place a stigma on women who behave in a masculine manner or on men who behave in a feminine manner. (p. 82)

Interviews and research data that I have obtained with more than two hundred interracial same-sex couples indicate a higher rate of bisexuality (as defined by behavior rather than identity) among Native populations in the United States than in any other ethnic group studied, which may reflect a more fluid concept of gender relations and sexual expression (Allen 1986; Tafoya 1989; Tafoya and Rowell 1988). Indeed, unpublished data from my own work based on interracial same-sex partners show a higher reported rate of heterosexual experience among self-identified gay and lesbian Natives than among other ethnics, even after the Native subjects had entered into long-term (more than a year's duration) same-sex relationships.

Native individuals may be quite comfortable with their presented identity shifting its emphasis on so-called masculine/feminine behavior, depending on social context and the behavior/identity of a partner. In other words, a two-spirited person may become increasingly "masculine" within a specific environment, or when in a relationship with a "feminine" partner, regardless of biological gender. This appears increasingly complex, simply because the English language does not permit this discussion in a useful manner, with its emphasis on gendered pronouns and fundamental categories of male/female. Jay Miller (1992) offers a six-gendered Native model of (a) hypermasculine (warriors and athletes, often reared away from women), (b) ordinary males, (c) *berdaches*, (d) amazons (or biological female *berdaches*), (e) ordinary females, and (f) hyperfeminine. This model would also take into consideration a very strongly femininely identified (e.g., hyperfeminine) individual who would partner an amazon. At issue with risk reduction in HIV prevention, this has significance because, in the two presented examples, the traditional communities would not consider such partnerships to be "homosexual" because they involve individuals classified as different genders. As a result, a commonly asked question, "Are you a man who has sex with other men?" will honestly be answered no by someone who has sex with a *berdache* or, in some cases, with some two-spirited people. (At the risk of being tedious, it should be emphasized that, in HIV transmission, "sex" with any gender is not at issue — rather, certain forms of sexual expression carry risk factors and then only if one or more partners are HIV-positive.)

Yet another alternative would be to see European concepts of gender and sexuality as being polar opposites, or different ends of the same stick. One is either/or male or female, gay or straight. Native American concepts usually prefer circles to lines. If one takes the line of male/female, gay/straight, and bends it into a circle, there are an infinite number of points. Just so, there are theoretically an infinite number of possible points of gender and sexual identity for an individual who can shift and differ over time and location.

Historically the status of the two-spirited person was valued in many Native communities, since an ordinary male sees the world through male eyes and an ordinary female sees the world through female eyes. However, a two-spirited person (who possesses both a male and a female spirit, regardless of the flesh that is worn) will always see further. For this reason, many two-spirited people have become medicine people, leaders, and intermediaries between men and women and between tribal communities and non-Native people. Their greater flexibility provides them with greater possibilities of discovering alternative ways of seeing themselves and the world.

Because of the influence of the federal boarding school system and certain forms of Christianity, some tribal groups may be as homophobic as any other rural community, although Native attitudes tend toward a much greater tolerance and respect for personal choice than found in most Euro-American groups. For some individual Native people, their first contact with the formal category of *berdache* or two-spirited may be in a college course on anthropology or in a gay pride presentation. In those communities where the traditional role of the two-spirited has declined, many younger Native people report seeking partners and experiences off the reservation, believing they are "the only ones" in their communities. As adults, they discover the frequency of same-gender sexual and emotional involvement that had been happening on the reservation all the time.

Finally, the role of the two-spirited person is critical in its relationship to those who are not two-spirited. The alternative behaviors and creative options of the gay and lesbian community inform the entire society of what possibilities exist and, like the Coyote legends, offer guidelines and directions for exploring and living life to its fullest potential. A man or a woman is more clearly and accurately defined by the existence of two-spirited persons, just as a straight person may more fully understand him- or herself in coming to know and understand gays and lesbians.

Appendix: Suggested Reading and Resources

Unfortunately there are simply not many materials available that specifically address Native gay and lesbian issues. Among the most relevant are the following:

Roscoe, Will. 1980. *Living the Spirit: A Gay Native American Anthology.* New York: St. Martin's.
Roscoe, Will. 1991. *The Zuni Man-Woman.* New York: St. Martin's.
Williams, Walter. 1987. *The Spirit and the Flesh: Sexual Diversity in American Indian Culture.* New York: Harper and Row.

Resources

[*Editors' Note:* Those resources marked with an asterisk have been updated in 2002; the others were printed in the original article in 1997.]

Gay American Indian Association
3004 16th Street, Suite 203
San Francisco, CA 94103
(415) 255–7210

WeWah and BarCheAmpe
111 E. 14th Street, Suite 141
New York, NY 10003

American Indian Gays and Lesbians
P.O. Box 10229
Minneapolis, MN 55458

*National Native American AIDS Prevention Center
436 14th Street, Suite 1020
Oakland, CA 94612
(800) 283-AIDS
website: http://www.nnaapc.org

American Indian AIDS Institute
333 Valencia Street, Suite 200
San Francisco, CA 94103

Tahoma Two-Spirits
P.O. Box 4402
Seattle, WA 98104

Vancouver Two-Spirits
P.O. Box 598, Station A
Vancouver, BC
Canada V2S 1V4

*Two-Spirited People of the 1st Nations
45 Charles Street East, Suite 201
Toronto, ON
Canada M4Y 1S2
website: http://www.cdn-domain.colm/tpfn

Nichiwakan N.G.S.
616 Broadway Avenue
Winnipeg, MB
Canada R3C 0W8

Sapphic Shadows: Challenging the
Silence in the Study of Sexuality

Evelyn Blackwood and Saskia E. Wieringa

In this essay we raise a number of methodological issues related to the study of female same-sex relations and transgender practices.[1]
These practices have been less studied and documented than male homosexual practices. Researchers have suggested that the invisibility of emotional
and sexual/erotic associations between women is the result of a paucity of
data on women's same-sex relations, but there are several other reasons, for
example, problems in collection and interpretation as well as the silence of
Western observers and scholars on the topic of female sexuality. In the first
part of this essay we discuss the history of the study of lesbian and female
same-sex practices and investigate the reasons for its invisibility. Then we
provide an overview of the theoretical contributions of lesbian studies to the
study of sexuality.

Documentation of Female Same-Sex Relations

The study of sexuality in general, and female same-sex relations in the
non-Western world in particular, has been neglected by anthropologists and
other social scientists alike. As Vance notes, the study of sexuality is not
viewed as a "legitimate area of study," an attitude that "casts doubts not only
on the research but on the motives and the character of the researcher"
(1991:875). Before the World War II only a handful of anthropologists gathered material on women's same-sex practices. Although some of the most
well-known anthropologists, such as Malinowski, Benedict, and Mead, con-

sidered sexuality as a legitimate field of study, they devoted little attention to same-sex relations.[2] The taboo on homosexuality in the West weighed heavily on them. The rise of structural-functionalism in Great Britain made anthropologists ignore the question of sexuality, while in the United States the culture-and-personality school, founded by Benedict, sustained only a limited interest in the topic of sexuality (Caplan 1987).

In her autobiography published in 1972 Margaret Mead did not mention her female lovers, among whom was Ruth Benedict, whose "remote beauty" (Bateson 1984) enthralled Mead. Mead honored Benedict by writing two biographical books about her, *An Anthropologist at Work: Writings of Ruth Benedict* (1959) and *Ruth Benedict* (1974). In neither of these books is any mention made of their love relationship, although a deep friendship and strong professional cooperation between them is clear. After Mead's death her daughter, Mary Catherine Bateson, felt that in order to understand the work of her mother it was important to uncover this aspect of her life as well. In her biography of Margaret Mead and her father, Gregory Bateson, she maintains that "Margaret continued throughout her life to affirm the possibility of many kinds of love with both men and women, rejecting neither. . . . Through the major parts of her life she sustained an intimate relationship with a man and another with a woman . . . this was . . . satisfying for her . . . but it also created a kind of isolation . . . an isolation of secrecy" (Bateson 1984:118).

The academic stigma associated with anthropological research on women's same-sex relations was also very strong in the Netherlands until well into the 1980s. At a national conference of feminist anthropologists in 1983, Wieringa's proposal to do fieldwork on women engaged in same-sex relations met with disapproval; such women could not be found in the Third World, she was told; besides the major issue for women in those parts of the world was their economic deprivation. Wieringa published her first short stories on her encounters with lesbians in Jakarta and Lima under a pseudonym (Blackwood and Wieringa 1999; Wieringa 1987, 1990). Self-censorship played an important role in this decision. She feared that any publicity about her sexual orientation might jeopardize the research project she was coordinating at the time (Wieringa 1993).

Other anthropologists who observed female same-sex relations decided to publish their findings only after their retirement. Evans-Pritchard published his article on "sexual inversion among the Azande" in 1970, forty years after his fieldwork. Van Lier, who did his fieldwork in Paramaribo, Surinam, in 1947, became interested in the *mati* relations among lower-class Creole women. He stopped his interviews with them after he discovered that this topic was frowned upon. He published his work on the Surinamese *mati* nearly forty years later (Van Lier 1986), calling them "Tropical Tribades."[3]

The bias against research on sexuality was compounded by difficulties that predominantly European and American men researchers faced in getting access to such information. Part of the reason for the invisibility of lesbian or female same-sex practices, Blackwood observed, was "more likely due to the limitations of the observers than to the conditions of women's lives" (1986:9). Some of these limitations included men's reticence or inability to ask questions of women or get answers about women's practices as well as their ignorance of sexual diversity. For many ethnographers, travelers, and colonial authorities, the possibility of married women engaging in non-heterosexual sex practices was unthinkable (Blackwood 1986). They could imagine it only in places where women were "deprived" of access to men. Where there were plenty of men available as sexual partners, it was assumed, as Firth (1936) did for the Tikopia of Melanesia, that lesbianism did not exist. Many also assumed that homosexuality resulted only from sex-segregated conditions (a theory that persists even today). It was indeed predominantly in all-female harems and polygynous households that researchers noted or assumed lesbianism occurred.

The assumption that women engage in same-sex practices because of "heterosexual deprivation" operates in the accounts of travelers who reported on Middle Eastern harems. Homosexual activity was said to be widespread in "harems of Muslim societies around the world" (Carrier 1980:118), although no outsiders ever had access to these areas of royal palaces. Most reports of lesbianism in harems were greatly exaggerated, a product of the imaginations of European travelers and writers who projected their own sexual fantasies of "the Orient" on the forbidden women of the harem (see Blackwood 2000; see also Murray and Roscoe 1997). An example of deprivation theory as an explanation of relations between women comes from the analysis of a "lesbian scandal" at the central Javanese court of Surakarta in 1824. In this case the presumption of deprivation was not from the original reporter, Winter, but the two present-day historians, Carey and Houben (1987), who project onto this incident their disbelief that women could actually enjoy same-sex practices unless forced to by the absence of men. Winter (1902) describes the case of a woman who is discovered playing the masculine role sexually with other royal women in the court of Surakarta during the reign of Pakubuwana V. Carey and Houben locate this "series of lesbian relationships" in the context of "frustrated royal concubines" (1987:20). However, the Dutch translator Winter makes no mention of any frustrations among the women. To the contrary he writes, "Ever since he (Pakubuwana V) had discovered when the women would be lying beside each other in various places, that among their indecencies, by way of a piece of wax which had been shaped in the form of the private parts of men they would be amidst each other, he had it made into law that to prevent this harmful practice, as they might never be interested in love with men any more, he would never allow his permanent servants to sleep at night out of his view, so all of them had to lie in front of the door of his room, in a row, six feet from each other" (Winter 1902:39). According to Winter's account, the issue was not the frustrations of the ladies, but the fear of the ruler that the ladies might like the game with their piece of wax too much. Gayatri's comments on *keputren* (1997) corroborate the suggestion that the court women took pleasure in intimate relations with other women.

Inadequate reporting was another reason sexual relations between women remained invisible. In remarking on a public scandal involving homosexual acts between European men and "native" boys in the Dutch East Indies of the 1930s, Kerkhof states that in Bali "the more enterprising boys [sexually] pursued European men on bicycles" (Kerkhof 1992:203). In a footnote to this sentence Kerkhof adds that "such contacts" were also common between women, but then notes that that subject was beyond the framework of his article. To what does his comment refer? Does he really mean to say that in the 1930s Balinese girls were riding around on bicycles, soliciting older European ladies?

The difficulties involved in getting access to information on women's same-sex relations are not just particular to men, however. On Wieringa's recent field trip to Benin, the former Dahomey, both she and native scholars met with considerable resistance to their questions about women. When Wieringa inquired into the custom of woman-marriages (marriage between two women), everyone denied it had ever existed in Dahomey. Although Herskovits's (1937) work was well known and respected by the historians and lawyers with whom Wieringa spoke on the topic, they insisted that Herskovits must have erred on this issue because of "language problems." At the end of her trip Wieringa met a woman who had done research on the woman warriors of the king of the Fon. This woman had shown great perseverance in her research in the face of her husband's threats to cut her up with his machete if she pursued such an infamous topic. She carried on anyway and is divorced now with four kids, in a society that looks down on divorced women. When asked, she affirmed that she greatly admired Herskovits's work, although she herself did not know of his essay on woman-marriages.

When Wieringa inquired whether she knew anything about this topic, she was silent for a long time. Finally, she looked up and said that her own grandmother had had two wives. Unfortunately she had died before her granddaughter had been able to interview her on the topic.

This case suggests another reason for the difficulties in uncovering lesbian relations. Stories such as those about the warrior women of the king of the Fon, who were called the Amazons of Dahomey, remain in people's memories, but the precise circumstances under which those women lived, loved, and worked are not generally known or have been suppressed as a result of both colonial and postcolonial interventions. The Amazon camp is now being reconstructed on the vast terrain where the palaces of the kings of Abomey are located (it is now a UNESCO site). What is known is that the Amazon army was disbanded after the French conquest of Abomey in 1894 (Garcia 1988). The relatives and descendants of the Fon Amazons have kept the warrior dance alive. This dance is still performed by the girls in a missionary school nearby, accompanied by an all-female percussion band. The girls dress in Amazon costume and move in the same impressive, warriorlike way as their forebears did. They display the same mixture of gender elements that frightened the Amazons' adversaries. The Amazons fought in battle and were renowned for their prowess; it was said that no Amazon ever died with a wound in her back. The most attractive of them seduced enemy chiefs for reconnaissance purposes.[4] Karsch-Haack mentions that these Amazons, who were not allowed to marry and have children, had hetaerae (female attendants or courtesans) at their disposal to serve them sexually (1911:480).

There are many other examples of colonial suppression of lesbian sexuality (Lang 1999; Povinelli 1994). In some cases it was not owing to colonial practices or anthropological neglect. Female same-sex eroticism was nearly erased or rewritten following conquests by patriarchal cultures and religions of earlier indigenous groups (Gayatri 1997; Thadani 1999). Yet despite the apparent silences in the ethnographic record, documentation on women's same-sex relations existed, mainly observations made by early ethnographers, missionaries, and travelers, who noted down customs they witnessed or were told about. These accounts have to be read with great care. The "colonial gaze" of these observers tended to portray the "natives" with whom they came in contact as "primitive" and "pagan." Their emphasis on sexual customs served as proof of how "close to nature" these groups were. The exoticization of colonized peoples was achieved by the eroticization of their lives.[5] Apart from the biases of early observers, informants may have had their own motives in telling tales of certain sexual customs. Hypersexualizing others was not only done by travelers and missionaries but may also have been a way, for instance, in which informants expressed interethnic tensions.[6]

Travelers' accounts and "scientific" reports were often characterized by serious biases about their subjects. In many cases the authors had little direct access to women. Further, many accounts may have been colored by the misogyny of their authors and that of their men informants and interpreters. Yet they do provide invaluable information about aspects of the social and sexual lives of the people they encountered. Based on these accounts Karsch-Haack wrote his monumental compilation on same-sex love in 1911. A "special section" called "Tribadie bei den Naturvölkern" (Tribadism among primitive peoples) contains a wealth of details on female same-sex practices based on accounts by these earlier travelers and observers. Karsch-Haack gives several examples of cross-dressing or transvestite females. He reports, for instance, that in Java the term *wandu* is used for both transgendered males and females, while in Bali cross-dressed women perform temple services (1911:489, 490). Belo later corroborated that finding, noting that the "crossing of the sex roles" for females is "one of the possibilities afforded by" Balinese culture (1949:58).

Deeper into the Silence

In the post-World War II era, men social scientists who investigated sexual practices in other cultures focused on male homosexuality. Their attention to men, they said, was because of the paucity of data on lesbian practices. According to these scholars, lesbianism was cross-culturally less well developed, less common, and less visible than male homosexuality (Ford and Beach 1951; Gebhard 1971), a belief these scholars underwrote by their very silence on the topic. This belief persisted into the 1970s and 1980s as works on homosexuality continued the emphasis on men and men's sexual practices.

An apparent lack of evidence did not stop these researchers from theorizing about female homosexuality, however. Some simply assumed that lesbianism must be the mirror image of male homosexuality; the theories that applied to men were said to apply to women as well (Blackwood 1986). As Mary McIntosh noted in her formative article, "the assumption always is that we can use the same theories and concepts for female homosexuality and that, for simplicity, we can just talk about men and assume it applies to women" (1981:45). According to Blackwood (1986), men scholars mistakenly conflated male and female homosexuality because they assumed that a structurally analogous sexual practice, i.e., sex with a member of one's own sex, somehow meant the same for both men and women. Consequently masculinist theories of female homosexuality were limited and often misplaced attempts to understand practices that were inadequately explored and analyzed.[7]

One of the main problems in the study of homosexuality in countries other than the United States and Europe was that it concentrated primarily on evidence of male-male sex practices. In "Homosexuality in History," a history of male homosexuality in the imagined West from ancient Greece to the Victorian era, Karlen (1980) noted that "some Greek literature and art portrayed sexual relations between two women or two men" (1980:79). Despite the existence of Sappho's love poetry and other well-known stories of love between goddesses and mortal women (Dover 1978; Foster 1958), he did not discuss this material further. The possible implications of women's engagement in same-sex practices for an understanding of Greek sexuality and gender were never considered. Karlen suggested that there might be a relationship between women's "status" and the incidence of Greek male homosexuality, a relationship he thought might be correlated to an increasing improvement in women's social status (Karlen 1980). How ancient Greek sexuality would look, however, if attention were paid to portrayals of women's same-sex love in art and literature (particularly Sappho) was not explored.

In an important attempt to theorize homosexuality cross-culturally Carrier (1980) concluded that there were two significant "sociocultural factors" connected with the expression of homosexual behavior: cultural attitudes and proscriptions (acceptance or disapproval of homosexual behavior) and availability of sex partners. Carrier suggested that the absence of the other sex, owing to the value of virginity (for women), segregation of men in initiatory camps, men's migration, and polygyny (marriage to more than one woman), all increased homosexual behavior. In this scenario, segregation and consequent lack of partners of the other sex was liable to result in homosexual practices for men as well as women.

One of Carrier's contributions to the study of homosexuality was to explain why some cultures accommodate what he called cross-gender behavior (more recently labeled transgender), while others disapprove of it. Although his discussion centered on males rather than females, he asserted that the "same concordance" applied to females.[8] Concerning societies that "disapproved" of cross-gender behavior, Carrier noted that "too little is known" about female homosexuality in these societies to include them in the discussion.

Carrier's conclusion that homosexuality does not always have the same meaning in all cultures stands today as an important insight in lesbian and gay studies. But the lack of attention to female sexuality raises questions about the usefulness of his hypotheses about women. Carrier concluded that "male homosexual behavior generally appears to be more regulated . . . than female homosexual behavior" (1980:118). He suggested that this difference might be because of "the higher status accorded men than women in most societies, and, in particular, to the defense role that men have historically played in protecting women and children" (1980:103). Carrier's assertion that men's higher status and women's subordinate status was the reason for the greater evidence and visibility of male homosexuality has some bearing in patriarchal societies, but it is less plausible as a general theory. His suggestion that "females [are] less likely than males to engage in homosexual activity" (1980:118) raises the possibility of a biological difference between women and men, but there are no data to support such a conclusion. His final suggestion that perhaps there simply was not enough data to provide an adequate explanation made the most sense, given the limited data with which he was familiar.

Masculinist work in the 1980s continued the silence on female same-sex practices. Following on earlier researchers' efforts at cataloging variant sex practices, several typologies of homosexuality were propounded (see Adam 1986; Greenberg 1988; Herdt 1988; Murray 1992). The typologies emphasized genital sexual activity between males as the link among all varieties of male sex and gender practices.[9] Most typologies include three types, transgenderal or gender-differentiated relations (partners occupy different genders), transgenerational or age-differentiated relations (partners belong to different generations), and egalitarian relations (partners occupy the same status category). Greenberg (1988) adds a class-differentiated type to account for relations between members of different classes, and Herdt (1988) adds a role-specialized category, which includes shamans who have spiritual sanction to engage in homosexual acts. Although these typologies are usually said to apply to both men's and women's sexual practices, in actuality they are based on men's homosexual practices. Data on female sexuality rarely enter into the analysis. The standard phrases that females "were also known to" (engage in whatever is being discussed) or "no examples of females are known" are typical of these writings (see, for example, Herdt 1988).

Greenberg's massive work on the construction of (male) homosexuality includes cases of female homosexuality, but his analysis of these cases is hedged with statements about the lack of information on women. Echoing the words of his predecessors, he claims that "we know far less about lesbianism than about male homosexuality" (1988:19) and that it "is less common and less tolerated" (1988:74). As others before him, the few examples he mentions include erotic acts among women in Greek literature, in harems (lumping all the Near East and India together), and between Azande co-wives. Despite the fact that Greenberg pays little attention to women's same-sex relations, he, too, attempts to find some reason for the difference between men's and women's sexual practices. He concludes that in "kinship-based" societies women tend more often than men to have egalitarian lesbian relations "possibly because women are not socialized to compete for status with other women, or to dominate" (1988:73). This hypothesis is interesting but unsupportable since "age-structured relationships" between women of unequal status do occur in kin-based societies, including woman-marriage in Africa, *madivines* in Carriacou, and mummies and babies in Lesotho. Regarding the societies he labeled "early civilizations," he concludes that lack of independence made lesbian relations less possible (1988:183). Although "lack of independence" as a causal explanation hints at the conclusions drawn by feminists doing research on lesbians, this conclusion is speculative at best because of a lack of evidence presented.

Adam's article on "homosexual relations" makes little excuse for not theorizing about female homosexuality. He claims that his category of "age-structured sexuality" is "predominantly a male form of same-sex bonding" (1986:20), citing examples of youthful homosexuality in bachelorhood and that between older and younger men (Melanesia, Greece, Africa). He, too, overlooks similar types of relationships among women. Adam does mention the sexual relations of Azande cowives (1986:24), but he does not assign them to a category, noting only that their relationship does not parallel the "warrior homosexuality" of Azande men. Adam mentions the occurrence of sex between female cross-cousins in Australian groups, but he does so in the context of his discussion of age-graded relations, and this example has no bearing on the larger question at hand. Adam's article carries the study of homosexuality more strongly into the cultural domain without, however, providing the same level of analysis for the cases of female same-sex relations he mentions.

Like women in mainstream anthropology texts before the 1970s, female homosexuality is nearly invisible in the anthropology of homosexuality written by men scholars. So complete is the invisibility of female same-sex practices in these works and in gay studies in general, the editors of *Hidden from History* felt confident in asserting that "the data for women are still far too sketchy to allow for even preliminary generalizations" about lesbians in non-Western societies (Duberman et al. 1989:10). There was, however, a substantial number of works available, as we show in the next section. We now turn to the work on female same-sex practices and transgender relations that developed in the 1980s, work that exploded the myth of invisibility and argued for a feminist analysis of female homosexuality.

Culture and Female Same-Sex Relations

Lesbian feminist work in the 1980s argued for the importance of distinguishing between female and male homosexual practices and experiences. Adrienne Rich was emphatic in her rejection of any correspondences between male and female homosexuality. She argued that "any theory . . . that treats lesbian existence . . . as the mirror image of either heterosexual or male homosexual relations is profoundly weakened thereby, whatever its other contributions" (1980:632). In the introduction to the first anthropological anthology on homosexuality, Blackwood added support to this position. She argued that "because men's and women's roles are structured differently in all cultures, . . . the structure of female homosexuality must be examined as well. A one-sided discourse on homosexuality does not adequately comprehend the complex interplay of factors which shape homosexual behavior, male or female" (1986:6). Further, because sexualities are informed by and embedded in gender hierarchies and gender ideologies that impose different constraints on women and men, sexual roles, behaviors, meanings, and desires are different for women and men. Next to nothing can be gained from collapsing female and male homosexual or transgender practices into one category, because they are not simply sexual practices but practices that have meaning only within particular cultural contexts. As we explain more fully later, we argue that the factors shaping sexualities and identities are appropriated and created differently by females and males because of the way sexed bodies are culturally interpreted and defined.

Cultural accounts of female same-sex relations in the 1980s focused on women's experiences and lives in order to understand the relationship of gender and sexuality to homosexual practices. Despite the silences in other texts, information on female same-sex relations has never been as limited as has been suggested. We have already mentioned several reports of female same-sex relations and transgender practices in early ethnographic and colonial reports, particularly Karsch-Haack's (1911) compilation. In this section we flesh out more fully the extent of research and theory on female same-sex practices.

In a survey of primarily English-language anthropological and historical texts on lesbian relations Blackwood (1984a) found evidence of female transgender and same-sex practices that greatly exceeded previous estimates by American researchers.[10] Ford and Beach's (1951) survey of the Human Relations Area Files placed the number of societies with homosexual behavior at seventy-six, with only seventeen accounts of lesbianism. Blackwood (1948a) located reports of female same-sex practices in ninety-five societies. Given the methodological problems cited earlier, neither of these estimates are definitive, but the number of cases in Blackwood's study raises considerable doubt about the "absence" or rarity of lesbianism. Among the early ethnographic reports by English speakers, the most notable (and rarely cited) are an account of Solomon Islander women's erotic same-sex dances celebrating first menstruation and marriage rites of young women (Blackwood 1935), an intriguing note that lesbian relations among adult women in Malekula and the Big Nambas in Melanesia were commonly practiced (Deacon 1934), and reports of erotic ritual practices and cross-cousin affairs among Australian aboriginal women (Kaberry 1939; Roheim 1933). Although many of the reports were brief, they provided provocative hints of nonheterosexual forms of female sexuality.

The most extensive ethnographic reports by British and American scholars on lesbians, same-sex sexuality, and transgendered practices before 1980 includes Schaeffer's (1965) biography of a Kutenai "female *berdache*," a Native American female two-spirit of the nineteenth century; Hart's (1968) article on "butch-femme" women, *lakin-on* and their partners, in the Negros Islands of the Philippines; and Evans-Pritchard's (1970) report on "sexual inversion among the Azande," intimate friendships between married women. Evans-Pritchard provides the most explicit description of a sexual relationship between women partners. Bond friendships between women were ritualized through a ceremony called *bagburu*. The following story was told to him by Kisanga, one of his most important informants: After two women had concluded the *bagburu* ceremony, they were vigorously making love. One partner was the junior wife of a husband who had agreed to the ceremony but was not happy with their sexual intercourse. When he heard them, he wanted to intervene but was stopped by his senior wife who told him not to meddle in "woman's affairs" (1970:1433).

Early feminist work began with Lorde's (1984) note about African woman-marriage and with Allen's (1981) study of Native American women's sexualities.[11] Her work was the first to question the academic discourse on Native American *berdaches* from a feminist and native perspective. She argued strongly against calling Native American women in same-sex relations *berdaches*, a pejorative colonial term usually applied to males, and claimed "lesbian" as the appropriate term for all Native American women-loving women. Other work on lesbians included a study of "mummy-baby" relations in South Africa, an institutionalized friendship between older and younger adolescent girls (Gay 1986); work on Chinese sisterhoods (Sankar 1986; Topley 1975); a study of wealthy Muslim women in Mombasa, Kenya, who were said to have younger women lovers (Shepherd 1987); an article on Cuban lesbians (Arguelles and Rich 1985); and several works on Native American female two-spirits (previously *berdache*), females who are social men (Blackwood 1984b; Grahn 1986; Medicine 1983; Midnight Sun 1988).

The most well-known Asian example of institutionalized same-sex relations among women are the Chinese sisterhoods. In the southern Chinese province of Guangdon in the nineteenth century a movement existed of thousands of women who entered into relations with other women by forming sisterhoods.[12] The following account refers to the most common form of sisterhood. The hairdressing ritual used to sever the women's association with men resembled the one traditionally performed before a heterosexual marriage. They vowed to the goddess Guan Yin never to marry a man. The women concerned were mostly silk workers whose income allowed them economic independence. They formed sisterhoods with such names as "Golden Orchid Association" or "Association for Mutual Admiration." The sisters lived in cooperative houses and helped one another in cases of illness or death. Some houses were vegetarian halls where the eating of meat and heterosexual contacts were forbidden. In these houses women led a religious life but not as strictly as in a Buddhist nunnery. Sexual relations among the women occurred, just as in the other category, the so-called "spinster halls." These halls were not so strictly religious and vegetarian; however, heterosexual contacts were not allowed either (Honig 1985; Sankar 1986; Smedley 1976; Topley 1975). The sisterhoods were banned as "feudal remnants" after the victory of the Red Army in 1949, and many sisters fled to Malaysia, Singapore, Hong Kong, and Taiwan.

The issue of sexuality and eroticism between women in these sisterhoods has been a matter of controversy for observers describing their relations. Smedley's account (1976) is telling in this respect. The male guide with whom she visited some sisters in the 1930s showed great hostility toward these women who refused to marry, a habit that was caused, he felt, because they earned too much. Smedley herself was more interested in the successful strikes the silk workers had conducted than in their social and erotic bonds.

Honig (1985), in describing Shanghai sisterhoods, focuses on their position as workers as well, stressing the need to band together for protection against hoodlums who might rob or rape them. Only Topley (1975) and Sankar (1986) specifically refer to "lesbian practices," which they relate to a distaste for heterosexual relations as well as the religious advantage (heterosexual) celibacy would have. Sankar noted that "larger sisterhoods may have contained several couples or ménage à trois" (1986:78). Wieringa (1987) conducted interviews with sisters living in a Buddhist temple in Singapore. The abbess and the nuns talked freely of their sexual relations and described their choice to enter a "vegetarian life" as a positive decision.

Following feminist anthropology in the 1980s all these studies underscored the importance of gender ideologies in the construction of women's sexuality. Because women and men are situated differently in all cultures, the factors that may be significant in the construction of male same-sex practices might not pertain to female same-sex practices (Blackwood 1986). It is by now well known that the semen practices of New Guinea have no correlate among women. These practices are explicitly linked to the ritual development of masculinity in young boys. Girls, being viewed as having inherent femininity and reproductive competence, have no such need to be given their femininity ritually (Herdt 1981). Similarly the oppressive conditions of marriage for women in China, which gave rise to marriage resistance and sisterhoods, had no parallel among Chinese men, who were entitled to control wives and family property. Both cases lack a mirror image of the male or female practice because cultural ideals of gender shape sexual practices. In the New Guinea case a cultural practice rooted in an ideology of gender antagonism and the efficacy of fluids legitimates particular sexual behaviors between men and boys. In China the ideology of male dominance and sexual control of women produced public resistance to oppressive marital and economic conditions.

These studies argued that male-dominated gender ideologies controlled and limited the expression of women's sexuality. Rubin argued that in systems where men have greater control over women than vice versa, "homosexuality in women would be subject to more suppression than in men" (1975:183). This statement was echoed by other lesbian feminists who equated the invisibility of lesbianism with the presence of male-dominated societies (societies where women had "low status"). Following that perspective, Blackwood (1986) suggested that it was precisely within societies stratified by class and gender that evidence of women's same-sex practices is lacking or limited to clandestine relations (in harems) or marginalized groups (the Chinese sisterhoods). Nonheterosexual relations for women were neither publicly tolerated nor legitimated. In contrast, Sankar (1986) argued that the Chinese in Kwangtung Province tacitly condoned lesbianism as long as it did not threaten the reproduction of the patrilineage. Her assertion raises the question of whether sisterhoods were the exception in Chinese society, since they were the product of a fairly localized economic system (silk production) in which women earned sufficient income to be independent. Evidence from foraging and horticultural groups, Blackwood (1986) argued, suggests that the absence of oppressive gender ideologies correlated with the presence of institutionalized or culturally sanctioned female same-sex practices, such as among the !Kung of South Africa, the indigenous peoples of Australia, and certain native North American groups. Other works in the 1980s suggested a number of other factors that influence the construction and/or presence of particular sexualities and genders, including marriage and kinship norms, gender polarity, control of fertility and sexuality, social stratification, and economics. Most of these explanations were closely tied to a socialist feminist analysis of women's oppression.

The aim of most of the work in the 1980s was to explore the meaning and cultural construction of women's same-sex relationships. Writers sought to go beyond the psychological and biological explanations of earlier decades, arguing instead that women's relationships were embedded in, and constituted wider social relations of, kinship (indigenous Australians), exchange and trade networks (Azande cowives, mummies and babies, Chinese sisterhoods), and ritual (native North Americans, indigenous Australians). In many cases these relationships coexisted with heterosexual marriage (Blackwood 1986; Gay 1986). Most authors presented rich, local studies of lesbian relations attuned to the nuances of the particular culture but not to larger colonial or postcolonial processes. Based on this evidence, Blackwood (1986) proposed a preliminary typology of women's relations. Contrary to masculinist typologies based on the type of sex partners, Blackwood based her typology on the level of integration of women's relations into larger social processes, distinguishing between relations that pertain only to the immediate social context (informal) and those that are part of a network or social structure extending beyond the relationship (formal) (1986:10). This typology underscored the idea that sexual relations are embedded within social systems and gain their meanings from the social context.

Work in lesbian studies in anthropology in the 1980s brought new material to the analysis of the relationship between gender and sexed bodies. Shepherd (1987) argued that Mombasa lesbians did not change their gender, concluding that biological sex is a much more important determinant of gender than behavior in the Swahili sex/gender system.[13] Men are men and women are women; engaging in same-sex practices does not change that designation. Other work on transgender practices by female-bodied persons, however, helped to unsettle a model that linked sex with gender. Evidence from studies of two-spirit people suggests that, since a person can inhabit the gender not usually assigned to his or her particular body, gender and sex are separable (Blackwood 1984b; Midnight Sun 1988).

This work also helped to illuminate the social construction of categories that were frequently asserted to be "natural," such as the family, the domestic domain, and sexuality. The diversity in forms of women's sexuality underscored the bias of the Euro-American folk model that claimed only one form of "normal" sexuality. More important, the cases of long-term same-sex relations in other cultures, such as that noted by Evans-Pritchard for Azande women, problematized the privileging of heterosexuality as the model and basic grid for family, kinship, and sexuality. Where theories of kinship and family tended to emphasize women's roles as reproducers and mothers, this evidence broadened the view of women's lives to include a range of social relations not defined by domestic caretaking (for example, mummies and babies, Chinese sisterhoods). It even disputed the "naturalness" of male-female domestic coupling and marriage by revealing that female-bodied persons (to use Cromwell's [1997] phrase) created families with women (for example, Native American female two-spirits) and took the father role (woman-marriage in some African societies).

Work in lesbian studies raised questions about the notion of compulsory heterosexuality, which has remained a central tenet in some feminist theories of sexuality. Rich (1980) argued that compulsory heterosexuality was a universal condition for womankind, asserting that all cultures require, and in many cases force, marriage. The debate that took place after publication of her article was not about her idea of compulsory heterosexuality but about her concept of the "lesbian continuum" and lesbianism as an act of resistance. Neither the historicity nor the validity of "compulsory heterosexuality" was adequately challenged. Ferguson criticized Rich for employing a transhistorical discourse but was more concerned that Rich had mistakenly portrayed compulsory heterosexuality as "the key mechanism underlying and perpetuating male dominance" (1981:170). As to Rich's suggestion of the universality of compulsory heterosexuality, Ferguson simply agreed that "lesbian and male-male attractions are indeed suppressed cross-culturally" (1981:170), leaving in place a blanket of compulsory heterosexuality worldwide. Zita's (1981) analysis was more explicit in suggesting that compulsory heterosexuality is connected with patriarchy rather than with all cultures. Yet, more recently, Vicinus noted that "all societies that I know of have denied, controlled, or muted the public expression of active female sexuality," thus suggesting the general suppression of women's sexuality historically and reinforcing the idea of universal compulsory heterosexuality (1993:434).

Compulsory heterosexuality provided a limited vision of sexuality that was always already oppressive. Taken at its baldest, it assumes that women are forced through the dictates of male-imposed culture to be pawns in a sex and marriage system not of their own making and not for their benefit. Having misunderstood the historical production of compulsory heterosexuality, its proponents implied that women were not agents but passive victims or property in the cultural drama of patriarchy. Although little attention was paid to sexuality in societies outside Europe and North America, a feminist view of Third World women primarily as victims (see critique by Mohanty 1984) had as subtext the idea that these women were shackled to their marriage beds, the objects of men's marriage and alliance schemes. Compulsory heterosexuality assumed that because women's sexuality was under men's control women were not participating in the active creation or production of culturally legitimated sexual practices. This view effectively denied any pleasure in heterosexual relations and meant that other forms of sexuality could be seen only as resistance to patriarchy.

In response to the feminist theory of compulsory heterosexuality, work on lesbian or same-sex sexualities in other cultures provided solid evidence of women's sexual agency. Blackwood (1986) challenged the notion of "compulsory heterosexuality" by showing that women did engage in legitimate forms of nonheterosexual practice. These practices were not simply resistant or "deviant" expressions of desire (outside the bounds of proper culture), but within the context of women's social lives and relations. Anthropological accounts of adolescent girls' same-sex play, sex practice in girls' initiation schools, same-sex relations between heterosexually married women, and intimate friendships between older and younger women and cowives in a number of cultures were evidence that women engaged in noncompulsory and nonoppressive forms of sexual practices.[14] That women engaged in sex practices without men underscored women's agency in sexuality, showing that women actively created cultural practices and had the ability to construct and rework sexual meanings and desires of their own making.

This evidence exposed the inaccuracy of the concept of compulsory heterosexuality. Heterosexual marriage may be the norm in all societies, and often constitutes the only avenue to adulthood, but sexuality does not equal marriage nor does marriage deny women's creation of, or participation in, other sexual practices, heterosexual and otherwise. It was not *marriage* or *heterosexuality* that oppressed women or constrained their sexuality. The oppression of women's sexuality was located in particular systems in which masculinity and masculine desire were constructed as more valuable and powerful, whereas women's sexuality was seen as limited or necessarily confined.

The corollary to the concept of compulsory heterosexuality was the idea that lesbianism, where it existed, constituted a form of resistance to heterosexuality, the "breaking of a taboo" (Rich 1980; see also Clarke 1981). In Rich's romantic and eloquent view of lesbian resistance, she argued that

> women in every culture and throughout history *have* undertaken the task of independent, non-heterosexual, woman-connected existence, to the extent made possible by their context. . . . They have undertaken it even though few women have been in an economic position to resist marriage altogether; and even though attacks against unmarried women have ranged from aspersion and mockery to deliberate gynocide. (1980:635)

Like many others of the time, Rich was unaware of the range of women's sexualities and so was unable to imagine women's same-sex erotic practices except as resistance to compulsory heterosexuality. She was quite right, however, that many societies are characterized by a system of compulsory heterosexuality.

Several scholars in lesbian studies echoed the theme of resistance, arguing that in certain cases "lesbianism" was a resistant act. The Chinese women who joined sisterhoods declared publicly their refusal to be exchanged in marriage, rejecting a life dependent on and obligated to husbands and fathers. Their actions were seen as a rejection of men and heterosexuality in favor of strong friendships and erotic bonds with other women (Sankar 1986). Some scholars interpreted the efforts of passing "women" (females who passed as men) to live with women they loved as rejection of their assigned gender and usurpation of men's privileges (Crompton 1981; Katz 1976; Wheelwright 1989). To Shepherd, lesbian relations for wealthy Mombasa women made sense if understood as "the desire to escape the economic conventions of [heterosexual] marriage" (1987:268). Because these women lived in a patriarchal society, she argued that "being a lesbian brings freedom from the extreme constraint normally placed upon high-ranking women in Muslim societies" (1987:257). All these studies fore-grounded resistance as a way to understand women's same-sex relations.

The concept of resistance had the value of attributing agency to women as well as consciousness of the oppressive conditions under which they lived, but it was a negative agency, a reaction to, not a power for. Other lesbian studies in anthropology showed that not all same-sex relations between women were acts of resistance. For adolescent girls in Lesotho who became mummies and babies to each other, it was part of the romantic drama of growing up and learning the pleasures and responsibilities of relationships. Gay argued that "these relationships point to the normality of adolescent homosexuality" (1986:111). For Azande cowives, who solemnized their emotional and erotic relationships through the *bagburu* ritual, those relationships broadened their social and trade networks (Blackwood 1984a; 1986). For many two-spirit females, their lives as social men were understood as legitimate responses to spiritual visions or dreams (Blackwood 1984b; Medicine 1983). These studies suggested that women construct meaningful same-sex liaisons and forms of nonheterosexual pleasure in societies where women's sexuality is not closely tied to reproduction and inheritance. For some, however, the question remains why certain societies have legitimate female same-sex practices and others do not.

In sum, the anthropological evidence from cross-cultural studies of female transgender and same-sex practices has much to offer in understanding sexuality in general and lesbian relations in particular. The evidence bespeaks the plurality of women's sexual practices as well as the constraints of oppressive gender ideologies. "Lesbianism" is not only resistance, deviance, or a means to overthrow the patriarchy; it is also deeply embedded in the social relations of many cultures, expressed in sexual play as well as in intimate friendships. Research on female same-sex practices in the 1980s helped to pinpoint the meaning of sexuality by highlighting the relationship of gender to sexuality. It also underscored women's agency in the construction of sexual meaning. By highlighting women's, as distinct from men's, practices, this work demanded attention to, and analysis of, gender systems and female bodies, while making visible for the first time the extent of female same-sex and transgender practices.

The present volume builds on the insights of these earlier studies. It also contributes to a number of hotly contested issues arising across fields that are imbricated in diverse and contradictory ways: lesbian studies, studies of homosexuality, lesbian and gay studies, and queer theory.

Notes

1. We use the term *female* in reference to anatomical or physical sex of bodies and the term *woman* in reference to the gendered social characteristics and attributes thought to be associated with female bodies in many cultures. Although it is far from a catchy phrase, we use the term *female same-sex relations* rather than the term *lesbian*, which is more familiar to a Western audience, because it is more inclusive of the range of female sexual relations across cultures. Female same-sex relations, then, refers to sexual relations between individuals with female bodies and includes, among others, lesbians, batches, femmes, and transgendered females, as well as women who have sex with other women but who do not identify as lesbians.

2. An interesting note is that the publication in 1967 of Malinowski's field diaries covering his research among the Trobrianders in the 1920s enabled a more open discussion of sexuality in the field than was hitherto common (Kulick 1995).

3. Murray (1997) noted that well-known anthropologists who wrote about homosexual behavior, such as Devereux and Landes, never acquired academic jobs. The French philosopher Foucault, one of the major theorists on male homosexuality, tried to hide his homosexuality from the larger public. For some time after his death in 1984, it was not revealed that he had died of AIDS. As he explained to a friend, the reason for being silent about his homosexuality was that "if he had been labeled a 'gay intellectual' he would not have had the audience that was his here and in the United States" (Miller 1994:25).

4. Their adversaries, not used to fighting against women, were confronted with this dance. The women displayed both their masculine fighting power and weapons and their femininity, swaying their hips and baring their breasts. It was precisely this combination of female bodies and power in an all-male game that scared their enemies most. They associated this with frightening spirits, as the founder of the army, King Gezo (1818–1858), had wisely figured out.

5. An infamous example is the tour through Europe of a South African woman, the so-called Hottentot Venus, to demonstrate aspects of her anatomy and genitalia that were deemed different from European women's (Fausto-Sterling 1995). The so-called difference in genitalia was probably the result of a common initiation practice among girls of lengthening their labia. This practice was thought to enhance their feminine beauty (see Karsch-Haack 1911:455–61, 471–73).

6. See Nina Kammerer 1997 for an account of such a process among the Thai hill tribes.

7. We use the term *masculinist* to identify the theories and perspectives on homosexuality developed by men social scientists, who generally paid little attention to gender issues.

8. Evidence of female cross-gender behavior was available, in particular the Mohave *hwame* (Devereux 1937) and the Philippines *lakin-on* (Hart 1968), but neither of these cases were cited.

9. The focus on sexuality and desire served to distance their theories from other possible cultural interpretations. See Elliston's (1995) critique of the concept of "ritualized homosexuality."

10. Karsch-Haack (1911) was an important German-language source of cross-cultural studies on lesbian practices, but his work was not consulted by American researchers, who based most of their observations on data from the Human Relations Area Files.

11. We are not including here the substantial writings by lesbians of color in the United States because we focus on countries outside Europe and the United States. This division is becoming increasingly arbitrary, however. As Grewal and Kaplan (1994) have noted, divisions between indigenous and diasporic, local and global, are rapidly breaking down in a transnational context. Important early works on lesbians of color in the United States include Hull et al. 1981, Moraga and Anzaldúa 1981, and Smith 1983.

12. See Topley 1975 and Sankar 1986 for a more detailed description of the wide range of social relations included under the term *sisterhood*. These earlier works use the older orthography for Chinese. What is now spelled "Guangdon" was previously "Kwangtung."

13. Porter (1995) questioned Shepherd's assertion of the "utter clarity" of gender in Mombasa, arguing that "some homosexual men and women do transgress gender categories and thus pose a threat to elite male hegemony (1357)."

14. Sources include Blackwood 1984a, Gay 1986, Gregor 1977, Mead 1928, Roheim 1933, and Shostak 1981.

References

Adam, B. 1986. Age, structure, and sexuality: Reflections on the anthropological evidence on homosexual relations. In E. Blackwood, ed., *The Many Faces of Homosexuality: Anthropological Approaches to Homosexual Behavior*, pp. 19–33. New York: Harrington Park.

Allen, P. G. 1981. Beloved women: Lesbians in American Indian cultures. *Conditions* 7:67–87.

Arguelles, L., and R. R. Rich. 1985. Homosexuality, homophobia, and revolution: Notes toward an understanding of the Cuban lesbian and gay male experience. Parts 1 and 2. *Signs: Journal of Women in Culture and Society* 9(4):683–99; 11:120–36.

Bateson, M. C. 1984. *With a Daughter's Eye: A Memoir of Margaret Mead and Gregory Bateson*. New York: Morrow.

Belo, J. 1949. *Bali: Rangda and Barong*. Seattle: University of Washington Press.

Blackwood, B. 1935. *Both Sides of Buka Passage*. Oxford: Clarendon.

Blackwood, E. 1984a. Cross-cultural dimensions of lesbian relations. Master's thesis, San Francisco State University.

Blackwood, E. 1984b. Sexuality and gender in certain Native American tribes: The case of cross-gender females. *Signs: Journal of Women in Culture and Society* 10:27–42.

Blackwood, E. 1986. Breaking the mirror: The construction of lesbianism and the anthropological discourse on homosexuality. In E. Blackwood, ed., *The Many Faces of Homosexuality: Anthropological Approaches to Homosexual Behavior*, pp. 1–17. New York: Harrington Park.

Blackwood, E. 2000. Harems. In B. Zimmerman, ed., *The Encyclopedia of Homosexuality*, vol. 1, 2nd ed., pp. 353–54. *Lesbian Histories and Cultures*. New York: Garland.

Blackwood, E., and S. E. Wieringa, eds. 1999. *Female Desires: Same-Sex Relations and Transgender Practices across Cultures*. New York: Columbia University Press.

Caplan, P., ed. 1987. *The Cultural Construction of Sexuality*. London: Tavistock.

Carey, P., and V. Houben. 1987. Spirited Srikandhis and sly Sumbadras: The social, political, and economic roles of women at the Central Javanese courts in the 18th and early 19th centuries. In E. Locher-Scholten and A. Niehof, eds., *Indonesian Women in Focus*, pp. 12–43. Dordrecht: Foris.

Carrier, J. M. 1980. Homosexual behavior in cross-cultural perspective. In J. Marmor, ed., *Homosexual Behavior: A Modern Reappraisal*, pp. 100–122. New York: Basic Books.

Clarke, C. 1981. Lesbianism: An act of resistance. In C. Moraga and G. Anzaldúa, eds., *This Bridge Called My Back: Writings by Radical Women of Color*, pp. 128–37. Watertown, Mass.: Persephone.

Crompton, L. 1981. The myth of lesbian impunity: Capital laws from 1270 to 1791. *Journal of Homosexuality* 6(1/2):11–25.

Cromwell, J. 1997. Traditions of gender diversity and sexualities: A female-to-male transgendered perspective. In S.-E. Jacobs, W. Thomas, and S. Lang, eds., *Two-Spirit People: Native American Gender Identity, Sexuality, and Spirituality*, pp. 119–42. Urbana: University of Illinois Press.

Deacon, A. B. 1934. *Malekula: A Vanishing People in the New Hebrides*, ed. C. Wedgewood. London: Routledge.

Devereux, G. 1937. Institutionalized homosexuality of the Mohave Indians. *Human Biology* 9:498–527.

Dover, K. J. 1978. *Greek Homosexuality*. Cambridge, Mass.: Harvard University Press.

Duberman, M., M. Vicinus, and G. Chauncey Jr., eds. 1989. *Hidden from History: Reclaiming the Gay and Lesbian Past*. New York: Penguin.

Elliston, D. 1995. Erotic anthropology: "Ritualized homosexuality" in Melanesia and beyond. *American Ethnologist* 22:848–67.

Evans-Pritchard, E. E. 1970. Sexual inversion among the Azande. *American Anthropologist* 72:1428–34.

Fausto-Sterling, A. 1995. Gender, race, and nation: The comparative anatomy of "Hottentot" women in Europe, 1815–17. In J. Terry and J. Urla, eds., *Deviant Bodies: Critical Perspectives on Difference in Science and Popular Culture*, pp. 19–48. Bloomington: Indiana University Press.

Ferguson, A. 1981. Patriarchy, sexual identity, and the sexual revolution. *Signs: Journal of Women in Culture and Society* 7:158–72.

Firth, R. 1936. *We, the Tikopia*. New York: American Book.

Ford, C. S., and F. Beach. 1951. *Patterns of Sexual Behavior*. New York: Harper.

Foster, J. 1958. *Sex Variant Women in Literature*. London: Frederick Muller.

Garcia, L. 1988. *Le Royaume du Dahome: Face a la Penetration Coloniale (1875–1894)*. Paris: Karthala.

Gay, J. 1986. "Mummies and babies" and friends and lovers in Lesotho. In E. Blackwood, ed., *The Many Faces of Homosexuality: Anthropological Approaches to Homosexual Behavior*, pp. 97–116. New York: Harrington Park.

Gayatri, B.J.D. 1997. Outed but remaining invisible: A portrait of lesbians in Jakarta. Unpublished manuscript. Jakarta.

Gebhard, P. 1971. Human sexual behavior: A summary statement. In D. S. Marshall and R. C. Suggs, eds., *Human Sexual Behavior: Variations in the Ethnographic Spectrum*, pp. 206–17. New York: Basic Books.

Grahn, J. 1986. Strange country this: Lesbianism and North American Indian tribes. *Journal of Homosexuality* 12(3/4):43–57.

Greenberg, D. F. 1988. *The Construction of Homosexuality*. Chicago: University of Chicago Press.

Gregor, T. 1977. *Mehinaku: The Drama of Daily Life in a Brazilian Indian Village*. Chicago: University of Chicago Press.

Grewal, I., and C. Kaplan, eds. 1994. *Scattered Hegemonies: Postmodernity and Transnational Feminist Practices*. Minneapolis: University of Minnesota Press.

Hart, D. V. 1968. Homosexuality and transvestism in the Philippines. *Behavior Science Notes* 3:211–48.

Herdt, G. 1981. *Guardians of the Flute*. New York: McGraw-Hill.

Herdt, G. 1988. Cross-cultural forms of homosexuality and the concept "gay." *Psychiatric Annals* 18(1):37–39.

Herskovits, M. J. 1937. A note on "woman marriage" in Dahomey. *Africa* 10:335–41.

Honig, E. 1985. Burning incense, pledging sisterhood: Communities of women workers in the Shanghai cotton mills, 1919–1949. *Signs: Journal of Women in Culture and Society* 10:700–714.

Hull, G., P. B. Scott, and B. Smith, eds. 1981. *All the Women Are White, All the Blacks Are Men, But Some of Us are Brave: Black Women's Studies*. New York: Feminist Press.

Kaberry, P. 1939. *Aboriginal Woman: Sacred and Profane*. London: Routledge.

Kammerer, N. 1997. Hypersexuality: The power of sexual stereotypes in cross-cultural relations. Paper presented at Beyond Boundaries: Sexuality Across Culture, Amsterdam.

Karlen, A. 1980. Homosexuality in history. In Judd Marmor, ed., *Homosexual Behavior: A Modern Reappraisal*, pp. 75–99. New York: Basic Books.

Karsch-Haack, F. 1911. *Das Gleichgeschlechtliche Leben der Naturvölker*. Munich: Reinhardt.

Katz, J. N. 1976. *Gay American History: Lesbians and Gay Men in the U.S.A.* New York: Crowell.

Kerkhof, G. 1992. Het Indiesche Zedenschandaal: een koloniaal incident. In Raymond Feddema, ed., *Wat beweegt de Bamboe? Geschiedenissen uit Zuidoost Azie*, pp. 92–111. Amsterdam: Het Spinhios.

Kulick, D. 1995. Introduction. In D. Kulick and M. Willson, eds., *Taboo: Sex, Identity, and Erotic Subjectivity in Anthropological Fieldwork*, pp. 1–29. London: Routledge.

Lang, S. 1999. Lesbians, men-women, and two-spirits: Homosexuality and gender in Native American cultures. In E. Blackwood and S. E. Wieringa, eds., *Female Desires: Same-Sex Relations and Transgender Practices Across Cultures*, pp. 91–116. New York: Columbia University Press.

Lorde, A. 1984. Scratching the surface: Some notes on barriers to women and loving. In *Sister/Outsider: Essays and Speeches by Audre Lorde*, pp. 45–52. Freedom, Calif.: Crossing Press.

McIntosh, M. 1981. The homosexual role revisited. In K. Plummer, ed., *The Making of the Modern Homosexual*, pp. 30–49. Totowa, N.J.: Barnes and Noble.

Mead, M. 1928. *Coming of Age in Samoa*. New York: Morrow.

Mead, M. 1959. *An Anthropologist at Work: Writings of Ruth Benedict*. Boston: Houghton-Mifflin.

Mead, M. 1972. *Blackberry Winter: My Earlier Years*. New York: Touchstone.

Mead, M. 1974. *Ruth Benedict*. New York: Columbia University Press.

Medicine, B. 1983. "Warrior women": Sex role alternatives for Plains Indian Women. In P. Albers and B. Medicine, eds., *The Hidden Half: Studies of Plains Indian Women*, pp. 267–80. New York: University Press of America.

Midnight Sun. 1988. Sex/gender systems in Native North America. In Gay American Indians and W. Roscoe, eds., *Living the Spirit: A Gay American Indian Anthology*, pp. 32–47. New York: St. Martin's.

Miller, J. 1994. *The Passion of Michel Foucault*. London: Flamingo.

Mohanty, C. 1984. Under Western eyes: Feminist scholarship and colonial discourse. *Boundary* 2/3:333–58.

Moraga, C., and G. Anzaldúa, eds. 1981. *This Bridge Called My Back: Writings by Radical Women of Color*. Watertown, Mass.: Persephone.

Murray, S. O. 1992. *Oceanic Homosexualities*. New York: Garland.

Murray, S. O. 1997. Explaining away same-sex sexualities when they obtrude on anthropologists' notice at all. *Anthropology Today* 13(3):2–5.

Murray, S. O., and W. Roscoe, eds. 1997. *Islamic Homosexualities: Culture, History, and Literature*. New York: New York University Press.

Porter, M. 1995. Talking at the Margins: Kenyan Discourses on Homosexuality. In W. Leap, ed., *Beyond the Lavender Lexicon: Authenticity, Imagination, and Appropriation in Lesbian and Gay Languages*, pp. 133–53. Amsterdam: Gordon and Breach.

Povinelli, E. A. 1994. Sexual Savages/Sexual Sovereignty: Australian Colonial Texts and the Postcolonial Politics of Nationalism. *Diacritics* 24(2–3):122–50.

Rich, A. 1980. Compulsory heterosexuality and lesbian existence. *Signs* 5:631–60.

Roheim, G. 1933. Women and their life in Central Australia. *Journal of the Royal Anthropological Institute of Great Britain and Ireland* 63:207–65.

Rubin, G. 1975. The traffic in women: Notes on the "political economy" of sex. In R. R. Reiter, ed., *Toward an Anthropology of Women*, pp. 157–210. New York: Monthly Review.

Sankar, A. 1986. Sisters and brothers, lovers and enemies: Marriage resistance in Southern Kwangtung. In E. Blackwood, ed., *The Many Faces of Homosexuality: Anthropological Approaches to Homosexual Behavior*, pp. 69–81. New York: Harrington Park.

Schaeffer, C. E. 1965. The Kutenai female berdache: Courier, guide, prophetess, and warrior. *Ethnohistory* 12(3):193–236.

Shepherd, G. 1987. Rank, gender, and homosexuality: Mombasa as a key to understanding sexual options. In P. Caplan, ed., *The Cultural Construction of Sexuality*, pp. 240–70. New York: Tavistock.

Shostak, M. 1981. *Nisa: The Life and Words of a !Kung Woman*. Cambridge, Mass.: Harvard University Press.

Smedley, A. 1976. *Portraits of Chinese Women in Revolution*. Westbury: Feminist Press.

Smith, B., ed. 1983. *Home Girls: A Black Feminist Anthology*. New York: Kitchen Table Women of Color Press.

Thadani, G. 1999. The politics of identities and languages: Lesbian desire in ancient and modern India. In E. Blackwood and S. E. Wieringa, eds., *Female Desires: Same-Sex Relations and Transgender Practices Across Cultures*, pp. 67–90. New York: Columbia University Press.

Topley, M. 1975. Marriage resistance in rural Kwangtung. In M. Wolf and R. Witke, eds., *Women in Chinese Society*, pp. 57–88. Stanford: Stanford University Press.

Van Lier, R. 1986. *Tropische Tribaden: Een Verhandeling over Homoseksualiteit en Homoseksuele Vrouwen in Suriname*. Dordrecht: Foris.

Vance, C. S. 1991. Anthropology rediscovers sexuality: A theoretical comment. *Social Science and Medicine* 33:875–85.

Vicinus, M. 1993. They wonder to which sex I belong: The historical roots of the
    modern lesbian identity. In H. Abelove, M. Barale, and D. M. Halperin, eds.,
    The Lesbian and Gay Studies Reader, pp. 432–52. New York: Routledge.
Wheelwright, J. 1989. *Amazons and Military Maids: Women Who Dressed as Men
    in Pursuit of Life, Liberty, and Happiness.* London: Pandora.
Wieringa, S. 1987. *Uw Toegenegen Dora D.* Amsterdam: Furie.
Wieringa, S. 1990. Een Omgekeerde Parthenogenese: Antropologie en Vrouwelijke
    Homoseksualiteit. *Antropologische Verkenningen* 9(1):1–10.
Wieringa, S. 1993. Feminist anthropology since the mid-seventies: From monocau-
    sality to diversity, a personal view. In M. Krueger, ed., *Was Heisst Hier Eigent-
    lich Feministisch?* Bremen: Donat.
Winter, J. W. 1902. Beknopte Beschrijving van het Hof van Soerakarta in 1824.
    Bijdragen tot de Taal-, Land-, en Volkenkunde 54:15–172.
Zita, J. 1981. Historical amnesia and the lesbian continuum. *Signs: Journal of Women
    in Culture and Society* 7:172–87.

16 Identifying and Addressing Health Issues of Gay, Lesbian, Bisexual, Transgender (GLBT) Populations in Rural Communities: Psychological Perspectives

Douglas C. Kimmel

Two of the most notorious murders of gay men in recent years have occurred in rural states: Matthew Shepard in Laramie, Wyoming, and Charlie Howard in Bangor, Maine. Some good has come from those tragedies, however. For example, Matthew's mother has been active speaking and working to reduce antigay hate crimes and the use of antigay language in schools. Less may be known of Charlie Howard, who was thrown off a bridge by three juvenile males, and, because he could not swim, he drowned. The men were tried as juveniles and given relatively short sentences. However, one of them became proactive in fighting antigay bigotry in the state of Maine.

Laramie and Bangor are relatively large towns compared to the county where I have my practice of psychology. Nonetheless, we have a range of services and programs dealing with issues related to gay, lesbian, bisexual, and transgender (GLBT) persons. There is the Down East AIDS Network in Ellsworth as well as a group known as OutRight—a peer-led support group for GLBT teens that meets weekly with gay and lesbian adult supervision. There is also a chapter of the Parents and Friends of Lesbians and Gays (PFLAG). Some of the members of this group have come to Maine to be with their gay sons during the final period of their lives with AIDS. There is also a local chapter of a group known as GLSEN (Gay, Lesbian, and Straight Education Network) that has been working actively with schools and libraries to enhance positive acceptance of diversity and greater knowledge of GLBT issues. One local high school has two openly gay/lesbian faculty members and an active gay-straight alliance for peer support. There is also a group of volunteers called "Speak Out" who travel to meetings, schools, churches, and community organizations giving first-person accounts of what it is like to be a gay, lesbian, bisexual, or transgender person living in rural Maine. The volunteers cover a span of ages and walks of life; they have been very effective. A recent fund-raiser for the organization featured former senator George Mitchell.

To be sure, much of this proactive education and community support has been the result of three statewide voter referendums regarding extending civil rights legislation to include sexual orientation. The first one resulted in the defeat of an attempt to prohibit such legislation. The second resulted in reversing the legislature's enactment of such legislation. The third was on the ballot this November 2000 and decided that the legislature's enactment of similar legislation again was not accepted by the voters. Naturally the issue of civil rights for minorities should not be subject to public referendum; but it has been educational for the state and has helped to build coalitions and support groups among GLBT persons and their allies.

The other important example from Maine is the decision by the U.S. Supreme Court that a Bangor dentist could not refuse to treat a man because he had AIDS.

From my perspective as a rural psychologist, the most frequent issue to confront is *heterosexist bias*. My partner of more than thirty years and I are still regarded as "the boys" by many in the community. They mean no disrespect, but apparently, "a boy is a boy until he is married and then he is a man!" Similarly an elderly client asked me if "my wife is coming to the conference with me" when I explained why I would be away for a week. Whenever that happens, I have to decide whether to explain why I wear a wedding ring; say "I don't have a wife" or "I'm not married"; or, as in this case, simply answer no.

Less frequent, in my experience, is *homophobia*. One adolescent client, who had come out to his family and minister as gay after a suicide attempt (and so was referred to me), gradually revealed his sexual orientation to his peers. One day he told me how anxious he was because he had heard that word had spread around the local high school and he was afraid of homophobic reactions. The next session he described going to a party with friends from the school and walking into a darkened room. Suddenly, the lights came on and everyone yelled, "Surprise!" They had decided to give him a coming-out party!

While antigay/lesbian language, threats, and violence do happen, current thinking in psychology is to view these in terms of *sexual prejudice*, which is a form of general prejudice that has long been studied by social psychologists. The advantage of this model is that one's motivations for hatred or antipathy are not the issue; that is, it is not the person's fear or *phobia* that is important but rather their prejudice. Generally prejudice tends to be generalized to different types of persons who are perceived to be *different* or *outsiders*. Thus prejudice is often reduced when the person has personal contact with an individual who is the object of prejudice. For that reason, *coming out* is, in general, the most effective strategy for counteracting antigay prejudice. It is especially effective if the person was known before he or she came out.

Thus, although my partner and I are regarded as "the boys," the Town of Hancock voted by a margin of 2–1 in favor of gay rights legislation in the last two referendums. Many people attribute this outcome to our visible presence on boards and committees and in the church.

Gender-related harassment, verbal and physical abuse is often an unusually destructive expression of homophobia and heterosexism. Many observers attribute the violence and killings in schools to the tolerance of bullying and harassment of persons perceived to be deviant by the use of gender-related harassment. Some schools have taken proactive steps to educate faculty and school peer leaders that such language and behavior is unacceptable and will not be tolerated. In addition, some schools have formed peer-led conflict resolution teams. In every survey I have heard of, the use of *faggot* and other gender-related terms of harassment are very common in schools.

Life-Span Issues

It is assumed that blatant homophobia, antigay discrimination, and gender-related harassment would not be appropriate under any circumstances. Heterosexist bias and sexual prejudice do sometimes interfere with meeting the health needs of GLBT persons, however. Let us now turn to a brief review of the health-related issues one might think about in our own rural practice and ways to be proactive in devising prevention as well as treatment. Since I am also a developmental psychologist, a life-span perspective is most useful for me.

Adolescence

School-related issues, coming-out issues, and sexual education issues will be especially important. Here, one should be consciously aware of heterosexist bias. Not all boys date girls or want to. Not all sexually active girls need contraception. School problems may be caused by gender-related harassment. Being withdrawn, depressed, and having a need for privacy may reflect many different issues, including being concerned about gay/lesbian feelings. Suicide risk may be higher for GLBT youth. The presence of an OutRight or similar group for peer support can be helpful. Of course, an adolescent may fear to meet with these groups: Gay people also may have some degree of homophobia or fear of being identified as GLBT.

Family relations may be problematic, especially if the adolescent has come out. Families may be expected to adjust to this information more quickly than is realistic. In some cases homophobia may be manifested, and abuse, harassment, or attempts to coerce change may occur. Some adolescents run away or are pushed out by their families. Services in urban areas where they flee may need a friendly intermediary with the family at home; the family doctor could be such a person or could help to find such a person.

Early Adulthood

For this age group, the health provider should review his or her forms to be sure the routine questions do not contain heterosexist bias. Many people complain about these forms or the questions they are asked, when they first meet with a doctor or clinic. Questions about relationships, sexual behavior, and risk factors, and reactions to being semi-naked during an examination, may differ for GLBT persons than for heterosexual persons. One transgender person described the humiliation of having to repeatedly display her male genitals in an emergency room.

More LBGT persons are having children in their families, so a pediatric practice may have a more diverse waiting room than in the past. Whether a child has two mommies, one gay father, or four co-parents, it is important to note that biological parenthood does not necessarily take precedence over emotional parenthood. The stress of parenting and maintaining relationships in a society with a high degree of sexual prejudice is not to be minimized. There may be a need for support groups, perhaps by using the Internet, as well as proactive education of day care centers, schools, and human service agencies.

Not all GLBT persons have "civil union" relationships, and not all want them. In some cases the partners are of different generations — for example, comfortable being open versus wanting to keep their relationship secret. Gay men typically have different attitudes about relationships compared to lesbians' attitudes. Bisexual persons may have a relationship that appears to be heterosexual or gay/lesbian but is more complex, at least psychologically. Transgender persons may prefer intimate relationships with other transgender persons. In short, there are many areas in which sexual prejudice and heterosexist bias may be a potential threat and should be evaluated carefully. Referral to another professional is often better than inadequate treatment.

Mid-Life

Several of my friends have retired to Maine from urban communities. The adjustment, especially for gay men, may be stressful. Relationship strain, personal adjustment to a less demanding life, and the absence of a visible gay male community seem to be typical causes of the adjustment problems. Often lesbian friends seem to adjust more easily; they find a rural lifestyle comfortable and seem to find their niche more readily than gay men, in my experience.

In addition to generic mid-life concerns (cf. Kooden and Flowers, 2001; Sang, Warshow, and Smith, 1991), lesbians and gay men need to think about financial, legal, and health care planning. A GLBT-friendly lawyer is important. Health care directives, long-term care insurance, and the importance of younger friends in their support system are significant issues.

Old Age

Much of my professional work is in nursing homes. Only one resident told me he was gay. In general, these institutions assume everyone is heterosexual and, further, think that unless one is actively sexual, it doesn't matter anyway. One video entitled Golden Threads showed an activist lesbian in a nursing home (Eaton and Winer, 1999). And conferences on GLBT aging issues have been hosted by SAGE, a thriving social service agency for GLBT persons in New York City; among many other things, they do in-service training in nursing homes (Kimmel and Martin, 2001). In addition, there is growing interest in retirement communities and assisted living facilities for GLBT persons.

One of my aged friends, who died at eighty-one, was cared for at home by home health aids. He made no secret of being gay and had published a multi-volume diary of his life called A Gay Diary. At least one female aide read some of it while she was on duty with him but made no comment. Another came to his memorial service at the Lesbian and Gay Community Center.

The new civil union legislation in Vermont may provide a model for other states. At present, however, let me only point out how difficult it is to plan for health care, death, funerals, and inheritance issues without legal marriage. In a sense it is a valuable exercise to work out all the details without any guidelines, but it is so easy to forget some detail or to lose some benefit.

Practice Issues

Four practice issues need to be considered. First, is your office or clinic accessible and open to GLBT persons? One of my colleagues moved her social work practice to my building because her clients were being harassed in the parking lot of her previous clinic location for their gender non-conformity.

Second, are your schools safe for GLBT youth? Is there something you can do as a role model or ally to make them safer — not just for that group but for everyone who is called "faggot" or "dyke" thirty times a day by bullies while peer leaders and teachers remain silent?

Third, are the hospitals and emergency clinics sensitive to GLBT issues? Can they deal with a "butch" lesbian, "effeminate" gay man, or intact transsexual with the same professional respect that other local civic leaders would receive?

Finally, which of your local skilled nursing facilities, boarding homes, or assisted living houses would be your recommendation for your colleague's lesbian mother or gay father?

References

Eaton, K., and L. Winer, producers, 1999. *Golden Threads*. Independent Television Service and Corporation for Public Broadcasting.

Kimmel, D. C. and Martin, eds. (2001). Midlife and aging in gay America. *Journal of Gay and Lesbian Social Services* 13 (whole no. 4).

Kooden, H., and C. Flowers. 2000. *Golden Men: The Power of Gay Midlife*. New York: Harper-Collins.

Sang, B., J. Warshow, and A. J. Smith, eds. 1991. *Lesbians at Midlife: The Creative Transition*. San Francisco: Spinsters.

Part V

Relationships and Families

This part examines the impact of sexual orientation on two central aspects of human development — intimate relationships and families. Sexual minority relationships develop within a culture that provides virtually no societal legitimization nor institutional support and actively endorses heterosexual bias toward gay male, bisexual, and lesbian relationships (James and Murphy 1998). Not only are same-gender couples generally denied the community recognition, legal protection, and economic benefits accorded to married heterosexual partners but there is also no legal status of same-gender relationships, except in Vermont (under the "civil union" arrangement) and in cases where domestic partnerships can be registered with public authorities. If they are parents, lesbians, bisexuals, and gay men may lose custody of their children as a result of heterosexist assumptions embedded in family law. In addition, most institutional policies (e.g., insurance regulations, inheritance laws, and hospital visitation rules) do not acknowledge same-gender relationships. Moreover, these relationships do not have socially prescribed roles, ceremonies, and rites of passage that typically define and structure heterosexual relationships. In addition, they are often confronted with negative social sanctioning.

Since society does not provide explicit or clear models of interaction, same-gender partners rely more on innovative and idiosyncratic arrangements, expectations, and goals for their relationships instead of adopting or conforming to preexisting culturally defined guidelines for relationships (Peplau and Cochran 1990). This trial-and-success approach to relationship may provide gay men, bisexuals, and lesbians an opportunity for greater creativity in structuring their relationships than is true for heterosexuals. Therefore it is important to define same-gender relationships without using heterosexuality as the model or standard.

Researchers have investigated the experiences of gay men and lesbians by making comparisons among married, cohabiting heterosexual, gay male, and lesbian couples. Comparisons of same-gender and cross-gender couples help in understanding factors that characterize relationships regardless of sexual orientation. Some of the major findings are the following:

1. Many similarities are found between homosexual and heterosexual couples, indicating commonality in dynamics within the relationship and a similar range of diversity among relationships (Eldridge and Gilbert 1990; Kurdek and Schmitt 1987; Murphy 1994).

2. Gender roles appear more powerful than sexual orientation in influencing behaviors in intimate relationships (Kurdek 1987; Schullo and Alperson 1984); for example, gay men and lesbians bring to love relationships many of the same expectations, values, and interests as do heterosexuals of the same gender. Lesbians are more likely than gay men to live with a primary partner, to be in a steady relationship, to prefer having sex only with partners they care about, to view sexuality and love as closely linked, to place higher importance on emotional intimacy, and to value equality (Bell and Weinberg 1978; Bryant and Demian 1994; Duffy and Rusbult 1986; Peplau and Garnets 2000). Gay men are more likely than lesbians to report an interest in sex, sexual variety, and sexual openness in their relationships (Blasband and Peplau 1985; Blumstein and Schwartz 1983; Laumann et al. 1994; Oliver and Hyde 1993).

3. A gender-based division of labor is not necessary for relationships to function well. In general, same-gender couples seldom incorporate elements of husband-wife roles into their relationship; most adopt a peer-friendship model of intimate relationships (Blumstein and Schwartz 1983; Kurdek 1995; Peplau 1991; Schwartz 1994). Partners in same-gender relationships show greater equality, reciprocity, and role flexibility than partners in heterosexual relationships (Howard, Blumstein, and Schwartz 1986; Kurdek 1993; Patterson 1995a; Schreurs and Buunk 1996).

4. Same-gender couples, in comparison with heterosexual couples, perceive greater social support from friends and partners and report less support from their family of origin (Bryant and Demian 1994; Kurdek and Schmitt 1987; Peplau 1991).

Research in this area is very important. New models and theories based on the experiences and patterns of lesbians, bisexuals, and gay men in relationships contribute to general analyses of close relationships (Brown 1989). For example, research examining division of labor in the home suggests a more egalitarian model of family arrangements in gay and lesbian relationships than is found in heterosexual relationships (Chan, Raboy, and Patterson 1998; Kurdek 1995; Patterson 1998); that is, women do the majority of household maintenance and care of children in heterosexual families. In contrast, according to recent research on lesbian families, both parents report sharing household tasks and child care responsibilities, which reflects a pattern of equal sharing among lesbians as the norm (Patterson 1998). Moreover, we need to understand more clearly the diversity in gay male, lesbian, and bisexual relationships by examining variables such as age, cohort, class, ethnicity, openness about sexual orientation, and relationship to the gay, lesbian, or bisexual communities (Demo and Allen 1996; Herdt and Beeler 1998; Peplau, Cochran, and Mays 1997).

Several common issues have been identified that affect long-term lesbian, gay, and bisexual partnerships. Each of these topics deserves further study: (1) external pressures caused by social prejudice, lack of social validation, and social stigma; (2) effects of previous gender role socialization, including expectations about gender roles, especially regarding issues of autonomy and intimacy; (3) differences between the two partners in acceptance of gay identity, stage of coming out, degree of outness, and political activism; (4) maintaining friendships that do not conflict with the lover relationship; and (5) managing the interdependence of each partner's commitment to work and the relationship.

Peplau and Spaulding's article summarizes research on the characteristics of sexual and romantic relationships between lesbian, gay, and bisexual partners. Moreover, the same-gender and cross-gender comparisons in their article highlight similarities and differences between heterosexual and sexual minority relationships.

Research on the experiences of bisexuals in relationships is quite limited. Research has debunked longstanding misconceptions about bisexuals and their relationships, however (Rust 2000; Weinberg, Williams, and Pryor 1994). What has emerged in its place is increased recognition of bisexuality as a uniquely flexible mode of sexual, erotic, and affectional orientation (Firestein 1996). Several concerns have been identified as couples deal with the issue of bisexuality: (1) the perception of sexual attraction as a choice; (2) spousal fear of losing his or her partner to someone of the same sex; (3) issues of nonmonogamy or extramarital sexual relationships; (4) the effect of a parent's bisexual orientation on his or her children; and (5) the effect of coming out as a bisexual on one or both members of the couple (Lourea 1985).

The article by Rust notes that bisexuals form various types of sexual and romantic relationships. As Rust's article describes, making relationship choices can be complicated by prevalent stereotypes about bisexuality. She also challenges the notion that there is only one healthy way to structure relationships — monogamy — which refers to "dependence on one person to fulfill all one's needs" (p. 128). In contrast, she offers the concept of polyamory, which values a variety of possible relational forms.

For a growing number of same-gender couples, parenting is an important part of their lives. Lesbians, gay men, and bisexuals become parents in several ways: by heterosexual contact, often during a marriage; by alternative fertilization, in which the donor may or may not be known; by mutual agreement to rear a child communally, perhaps by a gay male couple and a lesbian couple (parenthood may be known or may be randomly selected); and by foster parenthood and adoption, where allowed, in which case, race or cultural background may be discordant from the parents and other siblings. Since women more often receive custody of children after a divorce, gay and bisexual men are less likely than lesbians and bisexual women to live with their children. Because the relative proportion of bisexuals, closeted gay men, and lesbians in heterosexual marriages, and age at childbearing, vary greatly across ethnic groups, comparisons of these groups are difficult.

Three issues have received considerable attention regarding lesbian, gay male, or bisexual parents. First, research has focused on the question of whether lesbians, bisexuals, and gay men are suitable parents, primarily because of custody and adoption issues. Second, research has focused on evaluating the stereotypical negative effects that homosexual or bisexual parents are presumed to have on children. Third, research has examined the effects of the social stigma that children of gay male or lesbian parents experience. The findings have supported the conclusions that lesbian, gay, and bisexual mothers and fathers are likely to be good parents, to have no ill effects on their children because of their sexual orientation, and that children can cope with this family arrangement satisfactorily (Allen and Burrell 1996; American Psychological Association 1995; Falk 1989). The evidence suggests that home environments provided by gay, lesbian, and bisexual parents are as likely as those provided by heterosexual parents to support and enable children's psychosocial growth (Patterson 1995b). Lesbians, gay men, and bisexuals also have the potential to be positive role models of nontraditional gender roles, interpersonal relationships, and individual diversity (Riddle 1978). These studies and their implications for psychological development are summarized and discussed in the article by Patterson presented in this section.

Lesbians, gay men, and bisexuals are also often concerned about relationships with their own parents — especially at the time they are coming out as a sexual minority. The article by Hom concludes this section with a study of Asian-American mothers who learn that their son is gay or that their daughter is lesbian.

Contemporary Issue: Legal Recognition of Gay, Lesbian, and Bisexual Relationships and Families

There is growing awareness of parenthood in the lesbian, gay male, and bisexual community. Gay male couples who are denied the opportunity to adopt or foster children in most states, lesbians who are choosing to have children, and challenges about visitation and custody of children if a same-gender couple breaks up are issues discussed in the popular media (Patterson and Redding 1996). Clearly there is an important need for more practical attention to the concerns of lesbian, gay, and bisexual parents.

Unlike heterosexual couples, whose parental status is typically assumed by courts, same-gender couples face special legal problems (Cain 1993; Editors of the *Harvard Law Review* 1990; Polikoff 1986). Courts generally treat a nonbiological parent as a legal stranger to the child. In the event of a breakup, a nonbiological parent cannot generally receive custody or visitation rights over the objection of the biological parents. Some courts have noted that couples can avoid such results by having the nonbiological parent adopt the child. This procedure is referred to as *second-parent adoption* and allows the nonbiological parent to adopt children of their partner as co-parents without terminating the partner's parental rights. This arrangement is not permitted in many states, however.

Overall, research has emphasized the similarity of gay male and lesbian parents to heterosexual parents. Dimensions of the uniqueness of lesbian, gay, and bisexual parenting have begun to be explored. This research is important because of the growing number of lesbians, gay men, and bisexuals who are choosing to parent, the complex issues of co-parenting, and parents' continuing concerns regarding custody issues.

Among the topics deserving of research attention are the following:

(1) co-parents: the roles of co-parents, biological versus nonbiological co-parent, and the effects of the legal status of each of the co-parents vis-à-vis the child; (2) children: the impact on children growing up in families where their biological father is not known to them, for example, because of alternative fertilization; strategies used to teach children skills to counter homophobia and the stigma that may be associated with having a nontraditional family; effects of having co-parents who share equal power, including the effects on second-generation gay males, lesbians, and bisexuals of having a gay, lesbian, or bisexual parent; the issue of whether male and female children are reared differently by male or female same-gender parents; and unique issues that become relevant when the child becomes adolescent; and (3) family of origin: issues regarding grandparents and strategies used to counter the heterosexist stigma they may experience. Several of these issues are not unique to lesbian, gay male, and bisexual families; thus studies with well-designed comparison groups may be especially important.

References

Allen, M., and N. Burrell. 1996. Comparing the impact of homosexual and heterosexual parents on children: Meta-analysis of existing research. *Journal of Homosexuality* 32(2):19–35.

American Psychological Association. 1995. *Lesbian and Gay Parenting: A Resource for Psychologists*. Washington, D.C.: American Psychological Association.

Bell, A. P., and M. S. Weinberg. 1978. *Homosexualities: A Study of Diversity Among Men and Women*. New York: Simon.

Blasband, D., and L. A. Peplau. 1988. Sexual exclusivity versus openness in gay male couples. *Archives of Sexual Behavior* 14:395–412.

Blumstein, P., and P. Schwartz. 1983. *American Couples: Money, Work, Sex*. New York: Morrow.

Brown, L. S. 1989. New voices, new visions: Toward a lesbian/gay paradigm for psychology. *Psychology of Women Quarterly* 13:445–58.

Bryant, A. S., and Demian. 1994. Relationship characteristics of American gay and lesbian couples: Findings from a National survey. In L. A. Kurdek, ed., *Social Services for Gay and Lesbian Couples*, pp. 101–17. New York: Haworth.

Cain, P. 1993. Litigating for lesbian and gay rights: A legal history. *Virginia Law Review* 79:1551–1642.

Chan, R. W., B. Raboy, and C. J. Patterson. 1998. Division of labor among lesbian and heterosexual parents: Associations with children's adjustment. *Journal of Family Psychology* 12:402–19.

Demo, D. H., and K. R. Allen. 1996. Diversity within lesbian and gay families: Challenges and implications for family theory and research. *Journal of Social and Personal Relationships* 13:415–34.

Duffy, S. M., and C. E. Rusbult. 1986. Satisfaction and commitment in homosexual and heterosexual relationships. *Journal of Homosexuality* 12(2):1–24.

Editors of the *Harvard Law Review*. 1990. *Sexual Orientation and the Law.* Cambridge, Mass.: Harvard University Press.

Eldridge, N. S., and L. A. Gilbert. 1990. Correlates of relationship satisfaction in relationship satisfaction. *Psychology of Women Quarterly* 14:43–62.

Falk, P. J. 1989. Lesbian mothers: Psychosocial assumptions in family law. *American Psychologist* 44:941–47.

Firestein, B., ed. 1996. *Bisexuality: The Psychology and Politics of an Invisible Minority,* pp. 217–39. Thousand Oaks, Calif.: Sage.

Howard, J. A., P. Blumstein, and P. Schwartz. 1986. Sex, power, and influence tactics in intimate relationships. *Journal of Personality and Social Psychology* 51:102–9.

Herdt, G., and J. Beeler. 1998. Older gay men and lesbians in families. In C. J. Patterson and A. R. D'Augelli, eds., *Lesbian, Gay, and Bisexual Identities in Families: Psychological Perspectives,* pp. 177–96. New York: Oxford University Press.

James, S. E., and B.C. Murphy. 1998. Gay and lesbian relationships in a changing social context. In C. J. Patterson and A. R. D'Augelli, eds., *Lesbian, Gay, and Bisexual Identities in Families: Psychological Perspectives,* pp. 99–121. New York: Oxford University Press.

Kurdek, L. A. 1987. Sex role self-schema and psychological adjustment in coupled homosexual and heterosexual men and women. *Sex Roles* 12(2):85–99.

Kurdek, L. A. 1993. The allocation of household labor in homosexual and heterosexual cohabiting couples. *Journal of Social Issues* 49(3):127–39.

Kurdek, L. A. 1995. Lesbian and gay couples. In C. J. Patterson and A. R. D'Augelli, eds., *Lesbian, Gay, and Bisexual Identities over the Lifespan: Psychological Perspectives,* pp. 243–61. New York: Oxford University Press.

Kurdek, L. A., and J. P. Schmitt. 1987. Perceived emotional support from family and friends in members of homosexual, married, and heterosexual cohabiting couples. *Journal of Homosexuality* 14(3–4):57–68.

Laumann, E. O., J. H. Gagnon, R. T. Michael, and S. Michaels. 1994. *The Social Organization of Sexuality: Sexual Practices in the United States.* Chicago, Ill.: University of Chicago Press.

Lourea, D. N. 1985. Psycho-social issues related to counseling bisexuals. In F. Klein and T. J. Wolf, eds., *Two Lives to Lead: Bisexuality in Men and Women,* pp. 51–62. New York: Harrington Park.

Murphy, B.C. 1994. Difference and diversity: Gay and lesbian couples. *Journal of Gay and Lesbian Social Services* 1(2):5–31.

Oliver, M. B., and J.J.S. Hyde. 1993. Gender differences in sexuality: A meta-analysis. *Psychological Bulletin* 114:29–51.

Patterson, C. J. 1995a. Families of the lesbian baby boom: Parents' division of labor and children's adjustment. *Developmental Psychology* 31:115–23.

Patterson, C. J. 1995b. Lesbian mothers, gay fathers, and their children. In C.J. Patterson and A. R. D'Augelli, eds., *Lesbian, Gay, and Bisexual Identities over the Lifespan: Psychological Perspectives*, pp. 262–89. New York: Oxford University Press.

Patterson, C. J. 1998. The family lives of children born to lesbian mothers. In C.J. Patterson and A. R. D'Augelli, eds., *Lesbian, Gay, and Bisexual Identities in Families: Psychological Perspectives*, pp. 154–76. New York: Oxford University Press.

Patterson, C. J., and R. E. Redding. 1996. Lesbian and gay families with children: Implications of social science research for policy. *Journal of Social Issues* 52(2):29–50.

Peplau, L. A. 1991. Lesbian and gay relationships. In J. C. Gonsiorek and J. D. Weinrich, eds., *Homosexuality: Research Implications for Public Policy*, pp. 177–96. Newbury Park, Calif.: Sage.

Peplau, L. A., and S. D. Cochran. 1990. A relationship perspective on homosexuality. In D. P. McWhirter, S. A. Sanders, and J. M. Reinisch, eds., *Homosexuality/ Heterosexuality: The Kinsey Scale and Current Research*, pp. 321–49. New York: Oxford University Press.

Peplau, L. A., S. D. Cochran, and V. M. Mays. 1997. A national survey of the intimate relationships of African-American lesbians and gay men: A look at commitment, satisfaction, sexual behavior, and HIV disease. In B. Greene, ed., *Ethnic and Cultural Diversity Among Lesbians and Gay Men*, pp. 11–38. Thousand Oaks, Calif.: Sage.

Peplau, L. A., and L. D. Garnets. 2000. A new paradigm for understanding women's sexuality and sexual orientation. *Journal of Social Issues* 56(2):329–50.

Polikoff, N. 1986. Lesbian mothers, lesbian families, legal obstacles, legal challenges. *Review of Law and Social Change* 14:907–14.

Riddle, D. I. 1978. Relating to children: Gays as role models. *Journal of Social Issues* 34(3):38–58.

Rust, P.C.R. 2000. Bisexuality: A contemporary paradox for women. *Journal of Social Issues* 56(2):205–21.

Schreurs, K.M.G., and B. P. Buunk. 1996. Closeness, autonomy, equity, and relationship satisfaction in lesbian couples. *Psychology of Women Quarterly* 20:577–92.

Schullo, S. A., and B. L. Alperson. 1984. Interpersonal phenomenology as a function of sexual orientation, sex, sentiment, and trait categories in long-term dyadic relationships. *Journal of Personality and Social Psychology* 47:983–1002.

Schwartz, P. 1994. *Peer Marriage: How Love Between Equals Really Works*. New York: The Free Press.

Weinberg, M. S., C. J. Williams, and D. W. Pryor. 1994. *Dual Attraction: Understanding Bisexuality*. New York: Oxford University Press.

17   The Close Relationships of Lesbians, Gay Men, and Bisexuals

Letitia Anne Peplau and Leah R. Spalding

During recent years, relationship researchers have slowly widened the scope of their inquiry to include the close relationships of lesbians and gay men. Nonetheless, empirical research on same-sex relationships still is in its infancy. In a review of publications from 1980 to 1993, Allen and Demo (1995) found that only 3 of 312 articles in the *Journal of Social and Personal Relationships* focused on some aspect of sexual orientation, as did only 2 of 1,209 articles in the *Journal of Marriage and the Family*. The past decade has seen a small but noticeable increase in research on same-sex relationships. In this chapter we systematically review the available scientific literature on the relationships of lesbians, gay men, and bisexuals.

Studies of the intimate relationships of lesbians, gay men, and bisexuals suffer from unique problems not faced in studies of heterosexuals. Many homosexual and bisexual individuals are not fully open about their sexual orientation and therefore might be reluctant to volunteer for scientific research projects. Furthermore, lacking information from marriage records and census data, researchers studying same-sex couples are limited in their ability to obtain representative samples or to estimate population characteristics. With few exceptions, the research reported in this chapter is based on convenience samples of younger white adults who currently self-identify as gay or lesbian and are in relationships with same-sex partners. Researchers often provide relatively little information about how they recruited participants or how recruitment strategies influence sample characteristics. In a review of research on gay male relationships published from 1958 to 1992, Deenen, Gijs, and van Naerssen (1995) suggested that there had been a gradual shift away from recruiting gay men in bars and toward the use of ads in gay publications, with a corresponding increase in the average age of participants and length of their relationships. Generalizations about lesbian and gay relationships must be made with caution.

We do not know the percentage of lesbians and gay men who currently are in committed relationships or the percentage who recently have experienced the loss of serious relationships through breakup or the deaths of partners. Many studies find that a majority of participants currently are in romantic relationships, with estimates ranging as high as 60 percent for gay men and 80 percent for lesbians in some samples (Bell and Weinberg 1978; Harry 1983; Peplau and Cochran 1990; Peplau et al. 1978; Raphael and Robinson 1980). Also unavailable are estimates of the typical length of same-sex relationships or the frequency of long-lasting partnerships. Nonetheless, enduring relationships often have been described, especially in studies of older adults. In a recent study, 14 percent of the lesbian couples and 25 percent of the gay male couples had lived together for ten or more years (Bryant and Demian 1994). Today, some lesbians and gay men seek to formalize their relationships through commitment ceremonies. Others are striving to institutionalize same-sex relationships through laws and policies that recognize domestic partnerships or that would legalize same-sex marriages.

In considering the relationships of gay, lesbian, and bisexual people, it is important to recognize the social climate of prejudice and discrimination that sexual minority couples confront (James and Murphy 1998). Although Americans' attitudes about civil rights for homosexuals have become more tolerant during recent years, many people continue to condemn homosexuality and same-sex relationships (Savin-Williams 1996). In a recent study, Jones (1996) found that hotels were significantly less likely to make a room reservation for a same-sex couple than for an opposite-sex couple. Walters and Curran (1996) reported biased service by clerks in a shopping mall; compared to heterosexual couples, same-sex couples received slower service and experienced more incidents of staring and rude treatment. We know relatively little about how such experiences affect the daily lives of gay and lesbian couples or about the strategies that same-sex couples use to cope with homophobia.

Research on gay and lesbian relationships serves three important purposes. First, empirical research provides more accurate descriptions of the relationships of lesbians and gay men. These findings often challenge negative cultural stereotypes about same-sex couples. Second, comparisons of same-sex and heterosexual couples provide insights about the way that relationships are influenced by gender and social roles. Third, studies of gay and lesbian samples provide valuable information about the generalizability of relationship theories, most of which have been developed and tested on heterosexual samples.

In the following sections, we consider a range of relationship issues including the initiation of same-sex relationships, satisfaction, power, the division of labor, sexuality, conflict, commitment, and the ending of relationships. We briefly review the limited research available on the relationships of bisexuals and then offer general conclusions.

Beginning a Relationship

Research has begun to investigate how lesbians and gay men meet new relationship partners, how they initiate romantic relationships, and the qualities they seek in romantic partners. In a recent national survey of 1,266 same-sex couples, lesbians and gay men reported that they were most likely to meet potential dates through friends, at work, at bars, or at social events (Bryant and Demian 1994). In general, opportunities to meet potential partners might be greater for those who live in urban areas with gay and lesbian communities (Laumann et al. 1994). In their efforts to meet new partners, lesbian and gay individuals might face unique challenges including societal pressures to conceal their sexual orientation, a small pool of potential partners, and limited ways in which to meet people. These factors might make it difficult to meet others with similar interests, and there is some evidence that gay male couples might have larger partner differences in age, education, and employment compared to lesbians and heterosexuals (Bell and Weinberg 1978; Blumstein and Schwartz 1983; Kurdek and Schmitt 1987). Note, however, that a recent study of African-Americans found considerable partner similarity among both gay men and lesbians (Peplau, Cochran, and Mays 1997).

Negotiating the initiation of a new relationship can be awkward for anyone, but lesbian and gay male individuals might have to contend with some additional issues. For example, Rose, Zand, and Cini (1993) found that many lesbian relationships followed a "friendship script" whereby two women first became friends, then fell in love, and later initiated a sexual relationship. Some women reported difficulties with this pattern of relationship development such as problems in knowing whether a relationship was shifting from friendship to romance and problems gauging the friend's possible sexual interest.

When gay men and lesbians go on dates, they might rely on fairly conventional scripts that depict a typical sequence of events for a first date (Rose et al. 1993). For example, Klinkenberg and Rose (1994) coded 95 gay men's and lesbians' accounts of typical and actual first dates. They found many common events for both gay men and lesbians (e.g., discuss plans, dress, get to know date, go to a movie, eat or drink, initiate physical contact). Men's and women's dating scripts differed in some ways, with gay men more likely than lesbians to include sexual intimacy as part of a first date (e.g., made out, had sex) and lesbians more likely than gay men to emphasize emotions associated with the date (e.g., evaluate feelings postdate). In many ways, the scripts reported by lesbians and gay men were similar to those reported by young heterosexual adults (Rose and Frieze 1989).

What attributes do gay males and lesbians desire in potential partners? Researchers have used two methods to answer this question: analyses of personal advertisements placed in newspapers or other media and responses to confidential questionnaires. Many studies have compared the preferences of heterosexuals, lesbians, and gay men. In general, homosexuals want many of the same qualities in partners as do heterosexuals. Regardless of sexual orientation, individuals seek partners who are affectionate, dependable, and similar in interests and religious beliefs (Engel and Saracino 1986). Gender often has a stronger influence on partner preferences than does sexual orientation (Davidson 1991; Hatala and Prehodka 1996; Laner 1978). In personal ads, gay and heterosexual men are more likely to request physically attractive partners than are lesbian and heterosexual women (Bailey et al. 1997; Feingold 1990; Koestner and Wheeler 1988). The ads of lesbian and heterosexual women describe in greater detail the personality characteristics they seek in partners compared to the partners' physical characteristics (Deaux and Hanna 1984; Hatala and Prehodka 1996).

Several researchers have investigated whether gay men and lesbians prefer masculine or feminine partners, perhaps because of the stereotype that same-sex couples typically include a masculine or "butch" partner and a feminine or "femme" partner. To test this idea, researchers have coded descriptions of desired partners as "masculine" (e.g., seeks a partner who is physically strong or independent) or "feminine" (e.g., seeks a partner with long hair or who is submissive). Research generally has not supported the butch-femme stereotype. More often, gay men prefer men who are physically masculine and have traditionally masculine traits (Bailey et al. 1997; Davidson 1991; Laner 1978; Laner and Kamel 1977). Research on lesbians' preferences has produced mixed results that do not clearly show strong preferences for "masculine" or "feminine" partners (Bailey et al. 1997; Gonzales and Meyers 1993; Laner 1978; Laner and Kamel 1977).

Finally, the AIDS epidemic has prompted gay men to emphasize health in their personal advertisements. Compared to ads from the late 1970s, ads placed by gay males during the late 1980s were more likely to mention HIV status and to request sexual exclusivity (Davidson 1991). One study found that HIV-negative men were more likely to mention the desired physical characteristics of partners, whereas HIV-positive men were more likely to mention their own physical health (Hatala, Baack, and Parmenter 1998). Both HIV-positive and HIV-negative men preferred partners with similar HIV status.

Relationship Quality

Stereotypes depict gay and lesbian relationships as unhappy. In one study, heterosexual college students described gay and lesbian relationships as less satisfying, more prone to discord, and "less in love" than heterosexual relationships (Testa, Kinder, and Ironson 1987). By contrast, empirical research has found striking similarities in the reports of love and satisfaction among contemporary lesbian, gay, and heterosexual couples.

Comparing Satisfaction Among Lesbian, Gay, and Heterosexual Couples

Several studies have compared gay male, lesbian, and heterosexual couples to investigate differences in the partners' love for each other and their satisfaction with their relationships. These studies either have matched homosexual and heterosexual couples on age, income, and other background characteristics that might bias the results or have controlled for these factors in statistical analyses. In an early study, Peplau and Cochran (1980) compared matched samples of lesbians, gay men, and heterosexuals, all of whom currently were in romantic/sexual relationships. Among this sample of young adults, about 60 percent said that they were in love with their partners, and most of the rest said that they were "uncertain" about whether they were in love. On standardized love and liking scales, the lesbians and gay men generally reported very positive feelings for their partners and rated their current relationships as highly satisfying and close. No significant differences were found among lesbians, gay men, and heterosexuals on any measure of relationship quality. In a recent longitudinal study of married heterosexual and cohabiting homosexual couples, Kurdek (1998b) found similar results. Controlling for age, education, income, and years cohabiting, the three types of couples did not differ in relationship satisfaction at initial testing. Over the five years of this study, all types of couples tended to decrease in relationship satisfaction, but no differences were found among gay, lesbian, or heterosexual couples in the rate of change in satisfaction. Several studies have replicated the finding that gay men and lesbians report as much satisfaction with their relationships as do heterosexuals (Duffy and Rusbult 1986; Kurdek and Schmitt 1986a, 1986b, 1987; Peplau, Padesky, and Hamilton 1982).

Unfortunately virtually all studies of satisfaction in gay and lesbian relationships have been based on predominantly white samples. One exception is a survey of 398 African-American lesbians and 325 African-American gay men in committed relationships (Peplau et al. 1997). On average, participants had been in their relationships for more than two years. The majority (74 percent of women and 61 percent of men) indicated that they were in love with their partners. Only about 10 percent indicated that they were not in love, and the rest were unsure. In general, respondents reported high levels of closeness in their relationships, with mean scores approaching 6 on a 7-point scale. In this sample, the partners' race was unrelated to relationship satisfaction; interracial couples were no more or less satisfied, on average, than same-race couples.

Recently researchers have begun to investigate other facets of the quality of same-sex relationships. Kurdek (1998b) predicted that gay and lesbian partners would differ from heterosexual partners in their experiences of intimacy and autonomy in their relationship. He reasoned, "If women are socialized to define themselves in terms of their relationships, then, relative to partners in married couples, those in lesbian couples should report greater intimacy" (p. 554). He assessed intimacy by self-reports of the partners' spending time together, engaging in joint activities, building identities as couples, and thinking in terms of "we" instead of "me." Analyses controlled for demographic variables. Lesbians reported significantly greater intimacy than did heterosexuals and gay men, although the effect size was small. Kurdek further predicted that if men are socialized to value independence, then gay couples should report greater autonomy than do heterosexuals. He assessed autonomy by self-reports of the partners' having major interests and friends outside the relationships, maintaining a sense of being individuals, and making decisions on their own. Contrary to expectation, both lesbians and gay partners reported higher autonomy than did heterosexual partners.

Correlates of Relationship Satisfaction Among Same-Sex Couples

Researchers have begun to identify factors that enhance or detract from satisfaction in same-sex relationships. Like their heterosexual counterparts, gay and lesbian couples appear to benefit from similarity between partners (Kurdek and Schmitt 1987). Consistent with social exchange theory, perceived rewards and costs also are significant predictors of happiness in same-sex relationships (Duffy and Rusbult 1986; Kurdek 1991a, 1994c). A study of lesbian relationships found support for another exchange theory prediction, that satisfaction is higher when partners are equally involved in or committed to a relationship (Peplau et al. 1982). For lesbian couples, greater satisfaction also has been linked to perceptions of greater equity or fairness in the relationship (Schreurs and Buunk 1996). There also might be links between the balance of power in a relationship and partners' satisfaction. Several studies of lesbians and gay men have found that satisfaction is higher when partners believe that they share relatively equally in power and decision making (Eldridge and Gilbert 1990; Harry 1984; Kurdek 1989, 1998b; Kurdek and Schmitt 1986b; Peplau et al. 1982).

Individual differences in values also are associated with satisfaction in gay and lesbian relationships. For example, individuals vary in the degree to which they value dyadic attachment (Peplau et al. 1978). A person is high in attachment to the extent that he or she emphasizes the importance of shared activities, spending time together, long-term commitment, and sexual exclusivity in a relationship. Lesbians and gay men who strongly value dyadic attachment in a relationship report significantly higher satisfaction, closeness, and love for their partners than do individuals who score lower on attachment values (Eldridge and Gilbert 1990; Peplau and Cochran 1981; Peplau et al. 1978). Individuals also can differ in the degree to which they value personal autonomy, defined as wanting to have separate friends and activities apart from one's primary relationship. Some studies have found that lesbians and gay men who place strong emphasis on autonomy report significantly lower love and satisfaction than do individuals who score lower on autonomy values (Eldridge and Gilbert 1990; Kurdek 1989), but other studies have not (Peplau and Cochran 1981; Peplau et al. 1978).

Personality also can affect same-sex relationships. In a recent investigation, Kurdek (1997b) assessed links between the "Big Five" personality traits and relationship quality among lesbian, gay, and heterosexual couples. Neuroticism emerged as a significant predictor for all types of couples. Compared to less neurotic individuals, highly neurotic partners rated their relationships as more costly and as diverging more from their ideal relationship standards. In another new line of work, Greenfield and Thelen (1997) showed that high scores on a measure of fear of intimacy were associated with lower relationship satisfaction among lesbians and gay men.

Recently researchers have begun to consider how the social stigma of homosexuality might affect the relationships of lesbians and gay men. It has been suggested that the stress associated with concealing one's homosexuality can be harmful to relationship satisfaction. Three studies have provided some evidence that being known as gay to significant others such as parents, friends, and employers is associated with greater relationship satisfaction among gay men (Berger 1990b) and lesbians (Berger 1990b; Caron and Ulin 1997; Murphy 1989). By contrast, a recent analysis of a sample of 784 lesbian couples found no association between extent of disclosure of sexual orientation and relationship satisfaction (Beals and Peplau 1999). A better understanding of this issue is needed.

Power

Many Americans endorse power equality as an ideal for love relationships. For example, Peplau and Cochran (1980) investigated the relationship values of matched samples of young lesbians, gay men, and heterosexuals. All groups rated "having an egalitarian [equal power] relationship" as quite important. When asked what the ideal balance of power should be in their current relationships, 92 percent of gay men and 97 percent of lesbians said it should be "exactly equal." In a more recent study (Kurdek 1995a), partners in gay and lesbian couples responded to multi-item measures assessing various facets of equality in an ideal relationship. Both lesbians and gay men rated equality as quite important, on average, although lesbians scored significantly higher on the value of equality than did gay men.

Not all couples who strive for equality achieve this ideal. In the Peplau and Cochran (1980) study, only 38 percent of gay men and 59 percent of lesbians reported that their current relationships were "exactly equal." The percentages describing their same-sex relationships as equal in power have varied across studies. For example, equal power was reported by 60 percent of the gay men studied by Harry and De Vall (1978) and by 59 percent of the lesbians studied by Reilly and Lynch (1990).

Social exchange theory predicts that greater power accrues to the partner who has relatively greater personal resources, such as education, money, and social standing. Several studies have provided empirical support for this hypothesis among gay men. Harry and colleagues found that gay men who were older and wealthier than their partners tended to have more power (Harry 1984; Harry and De Vall 1978). Similarly, in their large-scale study of couples, Blumstein and Schwartz (1983) concluded, "In gay male couples, income is an extremely important force in determining which partner will be dominant" (p. 59). For lesbians, research findings on personal resources and power are less clear-cut. In two studies, partner differences in income were significantly related to power (Caldwell and Peplau 1984; Reilly and Lynch 1990). By contrast, Blumstein and Schwartz (1983) concluded from their research, "Lesbians do not use income to establish dominance in their relationship[s]. They use it to avoid having one woman dependent on the other" (p. 60). Further research on the balance of power among lesbian couples is needed to clarify these inconsistent results.

A second prediction from social exchange theory is that when one person in a relationship is relatively more dependent or involved than the other, the dependent person will be at a power disadvantage. This has been called the "principle of least interest" because the less interested person tends to have more power. Studies of heterosexuals have demonstrated clearly that lopsided dependencies are linked to imbalances of power (Peplau and Campbell 1989). To date, only one study has tested this hypothesis with same-sex couples. Among the young lesbians studied by Caldwell and Peplau (1984), there was a strong association between unequal involvement and unequal power, with the less involved person having more power.

A further aspect of power concerns the specific tactics that partners use to influence each other. Falbo and Peplau (1980) asked lesbians, gay men, and heterosexuals to describe how they influence their romantic partners to do what they want. These open-ended descriptions were reliably categorized into several influence strategies. The results led to two major conclusions. First, gender affected power tactics but only among heterosexuals. Whereas heterosexual women were more likely to withdraw or express negative emotions, heterosexual men were more likely to use bargaining or reasoning. This sex difference did *not* emerge in comparisons of lesbians and gay men influencing their same-sex partners. Second, regardless of gender or sexual orientation, individuals who perceived themselves as relatively more powerful in their relationships tended to use persuasion and bargaining. By contrast, partners low in power tended to use withdrawal and negative emotions.

Another study comparing the intimate relationships of lesbians, gay men, and heterosexuals also found that an individual's use of influence tactics depended on his or her relative power in the relationship (Howard, Blumstein, and Schwartz 1986). Regardless of sexual orientation, partners with relatively less power tended to use "weak" strategies such as supplication and manipulation. Those in positions of strength were more likely to use autocratic and bullying tactics, both "strong" strategies. Furthermore, individuals with male partners (i.e., heterosexual women and gay men) were more likely to use supplication and manipulation. Similarly Kollock, Blumstein, and Schwartz (1985) found that signs of conversational dominance, such as interrupting a partner in the middle of a sentence, were linked to the balance of power. Although interruption sometimes has been viewed as a male behavior, it actually was used more often by the dominant person in the relationship, regardless of that person's gender or sexual orientation. Taken together, the results suggest that although some influence strategies have been stereotyped as "masculine" or "feminine," they may more correctly be seen as a reflection of power rather than gender.

The Division of Labor

How do gay and lesbian couples organize their lives together? Tripp (1975) noted, "When people who are not familiar with homosexual relationships try to picture one, they almost invariably resort to a heterosexual frame of reference, raising questions about which partner is 'the man' and which 'the woman' " (p. 152). Today most lesbians and gay men reject traditional husband-wife or masculine-feminine roles as a model for enduring relationships (Blumstein and Schwartz 1983; Harry 1983, 1984; McWhirter and Mattison 1984). Most lesbians and gay men are in dual-worker relationships, so that neither partner is the exclusive breadwinner and each partner has some measure of economic independence. The most common division of labor involves flexibility, with partners sharing domestic activities or dividing tasks according to personal preferences. When Bell and Weinberg (1978) asked lesbians and gay men which partner in their relationship does the "housework," nearly 60 percent of lesbians and gay men said that housework was shared equally. Asked whether one partner consistently did all the "feminine tasks" or all the "masculine tasks," about 90 percent of lesbians and gay men said no.

In a more recent study Kurdek (1993) compared the allocation of household labor (e.g., cooking, shopping, cleaning) in cohabiting gay and lesbian couples and in heterosexual married couples. None of the couples had children. Replicating other research on married couples, the wives in this study typically did the bulk of the housework. By contrast, gay and lesbian couples were likely to split tasks so that each partner performed an equal number of different activities. Gay partners tended to arrive at equality by each partner specializing in certain tasks, whereas lesbian partners were more likely to share tasks. A study of lesbian couples raising young children found a similar pattern (Patterson 1995). Both the biological and nonbiological mothers reported that household and decision-making activities were shared equally. There also was substantial sharing of child care activities, although the biological mothers were seen as doing somewhat more child care. In summary, although the equal sharing of household labor is not inevitable in same-sex couples, it is much more common than among heterosexuals.

Sexuality

Sexuality is an important part of many romantic relationships. One research goal has been to describe the frequency of sexual activity in homosexual couples and to compare same-sex and heterosexual couples. Some researchers have reported that, on average, gay male couples have sex more often than do heterosexual couples, who, in turn, have sex more often than lesbian couples do (Rosenzweig and Lebow 1992). In one study, for example, 46 percent of gay male couples reported having "sexual relations" at least three times a week, compared to 35 percent of married or cohabiting heterosexual couples and 20 percent of lesbian couples (Blumstein and Schwartz 1983). By contrast, a study of African-Americans found no difference in reported frequencies of "having sex" among gay male and lesbian couples (Peplau, Cochran, and Mays 1997).

These mixed results might be the result of the unrepresentativeness of samples or to differences linked to ethnic background. It also is possible, however, that they reflect more fundamental problems about how to conceptualize and measure sexuality in relationships. McCormick (1994) observed that "most scientific and popular writers define sex as what people do with their genitals" (p. 34) and consider penile-vaginal intercourse to be the "gold standard" for human sexuality. For example, in a recent survey of nearly six hundred college undergraduates, 59 percent did not consider oral-genital contact to be "having sex" with a partner (Sanders and Reinisch 1999), and 19 percent thought that penile-anal contact was not "having sex." These conceptions of sexuality might be poorly suited for understanding same-sex couples and, in particular, lesbian relationships. For example, lesbians who accept common cultural definitions of terms such as *having sex* and *sexual relations* might be less likely to interpret or describe their behavior with female partners as fitting these categories. Equally important, preconceptions based on heterosexual models of sexuality might lead researchers to ignore important erotic components of same-sex relationships. New approaches to understanding sexuality in same-sex relationships are needed.

Sexual monogamy versus openness is an issue for all intimate couples. In contrast to heterosexual and lesbian couples, gay male couples are distinctive in their likelihood of having nonmonogamous relationships. For example, 82 percent of the gay male couples who participated in Blumstein and Schwartz's (1983) study reported being nonmonogamous, compared to 28 percent of lesbian couples, 23 percent of heterosexual married couples; and 31 percent of heterosexual cohabiting couples. Other studies conducted during the 1970s and 1980s found similar patterns (Bell and Weinberg 1978; Blasband and Peplau 1985; McWhirter and Mattison 1984; Peplau 1991; Peplau and Cochran 1981). There is some evidence that the AIDS epidemic has reduced the rates of nonmonogamy among gay men (Berger 1990a; Deenen et al. 1995; Siegel and Glassman 1989). In contrast to gay men, most lesbians characterize their relationships as monogamous. Estimates are that 70 percent to 80 percent of lesbian couples are monogamous (Blumstein and Schwartz 1983). Most lesbians report that they prefer sexually exclusive relationships (Bell and Weinberg 1978; Peplau and Amaro 1982).

The impact of nonmonogamy may differ for lesbians and gay male couples. For example, Blumstein and Schwartz (1983) found that, among lesbian couples, nonmonogamy was associated with less satisfaction with sex with their partners and less commitment to the relationships, whereas among gay men, outside sex was unrelated to satisfaction or commitment to the relationships. Other studies also have documented this lack of association between sexual exclusivity and relationship satisfaction among gay male couples (Blasband and Peplau 1985; Kurdek 1988, 1991a; Silverstein 1981). One reason for this difference is that gay male couples are more likely than lesbians to have agreements that outside sex is permissible (Blasband and Peplau 1985).

Conflict and Violence

Problems and disagreements are inevitable in close relationships. Research indicates that lesbian, gay male, and heterosexual couples are similar in how often and how intensely they report arguing (Metz, Rosser, and Strapko 1994). Comparative studies of homosexual and heterosexual relationships suggest that similar types of conflict are likely to arise. In a study of 234 gay male, lesbian, and heterosexual couples, Kurdek (1994a) found that all three types of couples had very similar ratings of which topics they most frequently fought about, with intimacy and power issues ranked at the top and distrust ranked at the bottom. Some differences have been found between same-sex and heterosexual couples. For example, gay and lesbian couples report fighting less about money management than do heterosexual couples, perhaps because same-sex couples are less likely to merge their funds and more likely to have two incomes (Blumstein and Schwartz 1983).

Some have suggested that same-sex couples might experience unique problems based on their shared gender role socialization (for a review, see Patterson and Schwartz 1994). For lesbians, intimacy issues might be particularly important because women are socialized to place a strong value on closeness and intimacy. As one example, clinicians have described partners who become so close that personal boundaries are blurred and a healthy sense of individuality is threatened (Burch 1986; Falco 1991). This emphasis on closeness might be reflected in survey data showing that lesbians are more likely than gay men to report conflicts about work cutting into relationship time (Blumstein and Schwartz 1983).

For gay men, gender role socialization can foster competition with intimate partners (Hawkins 1992; Shannon and Woods 1991; but see also McWhirter and Mattison 1984). For example, although partners in heterosexual, lesbian, and gay male couples all feel successful when they earn high incomes, only gay men feel even more successful when they earn more than their partners do (Blumstein and Schwartz 1983). Gay men are more likely than lesbians to report relationship conflicts over income differences or partners' unemployment (Blumstein and Schwartz 1983; Harry 1984).

How well do lesbians and gay men solve problems that arise in their relationships? In a recent study of 353 homosexual and heterosexual couples, Kurdek (1998b) found no differences in the likelihood of using positive problem-solving styles such as focusing on the problem and negotiating or compromising. Nor were differences found in the use of poor strategies such as launching personal attacks and refusing to talk to the partner (Kurdek 1994b, 1998b). As with heterosexual couples, happy lesbian and gay male couples are more likely to use constructive problem-solving approaches than are unhappy lesbian and gay male couples (Kurdek 1991b; Metz et al. 1994).

Recently researchers have begun to investigate violence in same-sex relationships. Given problems of sampling and social desirability, it is impossible to estimate accurately the frequency of such violence. In recent studies, 48 percent of lesbian respondents and 30 percent to 40 percent of gay male respondents (Landolt and Dutton 1997; Waldner-Haugrud, Gratch, and Magruder 1997) reported having been victims of relationship violence. To date, most studies of same-sex violence have focused on lesbians, but violence actually may be very similar in lesbians' and gay men's relationships. For example, lesbians and gay men report experiencing similar types of abuse, with threats, slapping, pushing, and punching being the most common (Landolt and Dutton 1997; Waldner-Haugrud et al. 1997). Risk factors for violence in gay male, lesbian, and heterosexual relationships also may be similar, and interviews with abused individuals suggest that battering occurs in a cycle of violence for all three types of relationships (Renzetti 1992; Schilit, Lie, and Montagne 1990).

Lesbians and gay men face unique difficulties in seeking professional help for relationship violence. Reluctance to reveal their sexual orientation might deter battered individuals from contacting the police or seeking therapy (Hammond 1989). Many professionals and social service organizations are not trained to deal effectively with same-sex couples and might underestimate the severity of abuse when it occurs in same-sex relationships (Hammond 1989; Harris and Cook 1994). For example, counseling students who read similar scenarios depicting abuse in either a lesbian or a heterosexual couple thought that the abuse was more violent in the heterosexual relationship (Wise and Bowman 1997). In sum, research suggests that gay men and lesbians may face rates of relationship violence similar to those of heterosexual couples but might experience greater difficulties in getting professional help.

Maintaining and Ending a Relationship

How successful are lesbians and gay men in maintaining enduring intimate relationships? One of the few large-scale studies of lesbian, gay, and heterosexual couples (Blumstein and Schwartz 1983) assessed the stability of relationships over an eighteen-month period. For couples who already had been together for at least ten years, the breakup rate was quite low — less than 6 percent. For couples who had been together for only two years or less, some differences in the breakup rates were found — 22 percent for lesbian couples, 16 percent for gay male couples, 17 percent for heterosexual cohabiting couples, and 4 percent for married couples. Note that the biggest difference among these short-term couples was not between heterosexual and homosexual couples but between legally married couples and other couples, both heterosexual and homosexual, who were not married. In a recent five-year prospective study, Kurdek (1998b) reported breakup rates of 7 percent for married heterosexual couples, 14 percent for cohabiting gay male couples, and 16 percent for cohabiting lesbian couples. Controlling for demographic variables, both cohabiting gay and cohabiting lesbian couples were significantly more likely than married heterosexuals to break up.

Relationship Commitment

Several factors affect commitment and stability. A first factor concerns positive attraction forces that make a person want to stay with a partner, such as love and satisfaction with the relationship. As noted earlier, research shows that same-sex and male-female couples typically report comparable levels of happiness in their relationships.

Second, commitment is affected by barriers that make it difficult for a person to leave a relationship (Kurdek 1998b). Barriers include anything that increases the psychological, emotional, or financial costs of ending a relationship. Heterosexual marriage can create many barriers such as the cost of divorce, investments in joint property, concerns about children, and the wife's financial dependence on her husband. These obstacles can encourage married couples to work toward improving declining relationships rather than ending them. By contrast, gay and lesbian couples are less likely to experience comparable barriers; they cannot marry legally, are less likely to own property jointly, are less likely to have children in common, might lack support from their families of origin, and so on.

Kurdek and Schmitt (1986b) systematically compared the attractions and barriers experienced by partners in gay, lesbian, and heterosexual cohabiting couples as well as married couples. All groups reported comparable feelings of love and satisfaction. But barriers, assessed by statements such as "Many things would prevent me from leaving my partner even if I were unhappy," did differ. Married couples reported significantly more barriers than did either gays or lesbians, and cohabiting heterosexual couples reported the fewest barriers of all. In a more recent longitudinal study, Kurdek (1998b) also found that lesbians and gay men reported fewer barriers than did heterosexuals, and he further demonstrated that barriers to leaving the relationships were a significant predictor of relationship stability over a five-year period (see also Blumstein and Schwartz 1983; Kurdek 1992).

A third factor affecting the longevity of a relationship is the availability of alternatives. The lack of desirable alternatives typically represents a major obstacle to ending a relationship. Two studies have compared the perception of available alternatives among gay, lesbian, and heterosexual couples, and these studies differ in their findings. One study found that lesbians and married couples reported significantly fewer alternatives than did gay men and heterosexual cohabitors (Kurdek and Schmitt 1986b). By contrast, a second study found no significant differences among lesbians, gay men, and heterosexuals, all of whom reported having moderately poor alternatives (Duffy and Rusbult 1986).

In summary, research suggests that gay and lesbian couples can and do have committed enduring relationships. Heterosexual and homosexual couples, on average, report similar high levels of attraction toward their partners and satisfaction with their relationships. Where couples differ, however, is in the obstacles that make it difficult to end relationships. Here, the legal and social context of marriage creates barriers to breaking up that do not typically exist for same-sex partners or for cohabiting heterosexuals. The relative lack of barriers might make it less likely that lesbians and gay men will be trapped in hopelessly miserable and deteriorating relationships. But weaker barriers also might allow partners to end relationships that could have improved if given more time and effort. As lesbians and gay men gain greater recognition as "domestic partners," the barriers for gay and lesbian relationships might become more similar to those for heterosexuals. The impact of such trends on the stability of same-sex relationships is an important topic for further investigation.

Reactions to Ending a Relationship

The dissolution of an intimate relationship can be difficult and upsetting for anyone. The limited data currently available suggest that partners' reactions to the ending of same-sex and heterosexual relationships might be similar (Kurdek 1997a). Kurdek (1991b) asked former partners from twenty-six gay male and lesbian couples about the specific emotional reactions and problems they encountered after the breakups of their relationships. The three most frequent emotional reactions were personal growth, loneliness, and relief from conflict (in that order). The three most frequently reported problems were the continuing relationship with the ex-partner, financial stress, and difficulties in getting involved with someone else. Anecdotal accounts suggest that because gay male and lesbian communities often are small, there might be pressure for ex-lovers to handle breakups tactfully and remain friends (Weinstock and Rothblum 1996).

The death of a loved partner is devastating for anyone regardless of sexual orientation, but gay men and lesbians might face unique challenges. Some researchers have speculated that the stress of bereavement might be increased if the surviving partner has concealed his or her sexual orientation and/or the true nature of their relationship so that open grieving is not possible (McDonald and Steinhorn 1990). Inheritance laws and employment policies about bereavement leave designed for married couples can add to the burdens faced by gay men and lesbians. An emerging area of research concerns the experiences of gay men who have lost friends and partners to AIDS (Goodkin et al. 1996; Martin and Dean 1993). In the only study to focus exclusively on the loss of a romantic partner, Kemeny et al. (1995) found that recent bereavement was associated with impaired immune functioning in a sample of HIV-positive gay men. Much remains to be learned about the bereavement experiences of lesbian and gay individuals.

The Relationships of Bisexual Women and Men

What are relationships like for individuals who report romantic interest in both men and women? Research on this topic is severely limited. A further complication is that the term *bisexual* has been defined in widely differing ways (for a discussion, see Fox 1996). Some scholars use the term to refer to a presumed innate human capacity to respond to partners of both sexes, whereas others characterize a person as bisexual if his or her life-time history of sexual attractions or behavior includes partners of both sexes. Here we focus on individuals who self-identify as bisexual, as we did in reviewing research on the relationships of men and women who self-identify as lesbian or gay.

Bisexuals are stereotyped as having poor intimate relationships. In a recent study by Spalding and Peplau (1997), heterosexual college students read vignettes that systematically varied the gender and sexual orientation of the partners in a dating relationship. Participants perceived the bisexuals as more likely than heterosexuals to be sexually unfaithful. Bisexuals also were seen as more likely than either heterosexuals or homosexuals to give sexually transmitted diseases to partners. Lesbians and gay men also might have negative stereotypes of bisexuals, for example, believing that bisexuals are denying their "true" sexual orientation or that bisexuals are likely to desert same-sex partners for heterosexual partners (Hutchins and Ka'ahumanu 1991; Rust 1992, 1995).

Currently the main source of information about bisexuals' relationships is provided by Weinberg, Williams, and Pryor (1994). Beginning during the early 1980s they interviewed ninety-six male and female bisexuals who attended social functions at a San Francisco center for bisexuals and later used a mailed questionnaire to collect additional data. These participants were predominantly white, well educated, nonreligious, and sexually adventurous. Their experiences probably do not represent "typical" bisexuals. A majority (84 percent) of the bisexual respondents in this San Francisco sample were in couple relationships, most commonly with partners of the other sex, and 19 percent were in heterosexual marriages. More than 80 percent indicated that their longest relationships had been with partners of the other sex. These bisexuals reported that they usually met other-sex partners through friends, work, or school. By contrast, they were more likely to meet same-sex partners through what the researchers termed the "sexual underground" — bars, bathhouses, sex parties, and the like.

Available evidence suggests wide differences among bisexuals in the patterning of their intimate relationships (Blumstein and Schwartz 1977; Engel and Saracino 1986; Weinberg et al. 1994). In the San Francisco study, 80 percent of bisexuals characterized their current relationships as sexually open; this most often meant that the people had relatively casual sexual liaisons with other partners in addition to their primary relationships. It is likely, however, that other bisexuals prefer to have monogamous relationships. A study of 19 bisexuals, 78 gay men and lesbians, and 148 heterosexuals found no differences in the extent to which respondents believed that the ideal relationship is sexually exclusive (Engel and Saracino 1986).

Research on the relationships of bisexuals has barely begun, and there are many possible directions for future research. For example, how does the gender of a bisexual's partner affect the couple's relationship? Does the relationship of a bisexual woman differ on dimensions such as power, the division of labor, sexuality, and commitment if her partner is a woman as opposed to a man? A second research direction is to identify issues that might be unique to the relationships of bisexuals. As one illustration, research suggests that heterosexuals perceive bisexuals as particularly likely to be sexually unfaithful to their partners (Spalding and Peplau 1997). How does this belief affect relationships between bisexual and heterosexual partners? Similarly, if lesbians and gay men endorse the stereotype that bisexuals are likely to abandon their same-sex lovers, then are jealousy and concerns about commitment problems present in the same-sex relationships of bisexuals? Future research on the relationships of bisexual men and women can take many promising directions.

Final Comments

The growing body of research on same-sex relationships leaves many questions unanswered. We know little about the experiences of lesbians, gay men, and bisexuals from ethnic minority and/or working-class backgrounds. Similarly a reliance on young adults as research participants means that we know little about the dating experiences of sexual minority adolescents or the relationship issues confronting middle-aged and older adults. The widely differing patterns of same-sex relationships found in non-Western cultures has received little attention from American researchers (Peplau et al. 1999).

All close relationships are influenced by historical events. Several social trends affecting same-sex couples are noteworthy. First, the impact of the AIDS epidemic on the relationships of gay men, lesbians, and bisexuals is poorly understood. Second, many of today's middle-aged lesbians were strongly influenced by the modern feminist movement. By contrast, the relationship attitudes of younger adults, especially those in college, might be more strongly influenced by the development of "queer theory" and by lesbian, gay, and bisexual programs on campus. Third, the efforts of gay and lesbian civil rights activists to bring about the formal recognition of same-sex domestic partnerships are changing the legal and economic conditions of gay and lesbian couples. The impact of these changes has not been studied. Fourth, the increased visibility of same-sex couples raising children suggests that researchers will need to expand their focus beyond couples to include the families created by lesbians, gay men, and bisexuals. Finally, the prejudice and discrimination faced by lesbians and gay men has been well documented. Yet little is known about how same-sex couples and families cope with social hostility and create supportive social networks.

Despite these limitations, several consistent themes emerge from the available research on gay and lesbian relationships (Kurdek 1995b). Many lesbians and gay men are involved in satisfying close relationships. Contemporary same-sex couples in the United States often prize equality in their relationships and reject the model of traditional male-female marriage in favor of a model of best friendship. Comparisons of heterosexual and same-sex couples find many similarities in relationship quality and in the factors associated with satisfaction, commitment, and stability over time. Finally, efforts to apply basic relationship theories to same-sex couples have been largely successful. There is much commonality among the issues facing all close relationships, regardless of the sexual orientation of the partners.

References

Allen, K. R., and D. H. Demo. 1995. The families of lesbians and gay men: A new frontier in family research. *Journal of Marriage and the Family* 57:111–27.

Bailey, J. M., P. Y. Kim, A. Hills, and J.A.W. Linsenmeier. 1997. Butch, femme, or straight acting? Partner preferences of gay men and lesbians. *Journal of Personality and Social Psychology* 73:960–73.

Beals, K., and L. A. Peplau. 1999. The quality of lesbian relationships: Effects of disclosure and community involvement. Unpublished manuscript, University of California, Los Angeles.

Bell, A. P., and M. A. Weinberg. 1978. *Homosexualities: A Study of Diversity Among Men and Women*. New York: Simon and Schuster.

Berger, R. M. 1990a. Passing: Impact on the quality of same-sex couple relationships. *Social Work* 35(4):328–32.

Berger, R. M. 1990b. Men together: Understanding the gay couple. *Journal of Homosexuality* 19(3):31–49.

Blasband, D., and L. A. Peplau. 1985. Sexual exclusivity versus openness in gay male couples. *Archives of Sexual Behavior* 14:395–412.

Blumstein, P., and P. Schwartz. 1977. Bisexuality: Some social psychological issues. *Journal of Social Issues* 33(2):30–45.

Blumstein, P., and P. Schwartz. 1983. *American Couples: Money, Work, Sex*. New York: Morrow.

Bryant, A. S. and Demian. 1994. Relationship characteristics of American gay and lesbian couples: Findings from a national survey. In L. A. Kurdek, ed., *Social Services for Gay and Lesbian Couples*, pp. 101–17. New York: Haworth.

Burch, B. 1986. Psychotherapy and the dynamics of merger in lesbian couples. In T. S. Stein and C. J. Cohen, eds., *Contemporary Perspectives on Psychotherapy with Lesbians and Gay Men*, pp. 57–72. New York: Plenum Medical Books.

Caldwell, M. A., and L. A. Peplau. 1984. The balance of power in lesbian relationships. *Sex Roles* 10:587–600.

Caron, S. L., and J. Ulin. 1997. Closeting and the quality of lesbian relationships. *Families in Society* 78:413–19.

Daniluk, J. C. 1998. *Women's Sexuality Across the Life Span: Challenging Myths, Creating Meanings*. New York: Guilford.

Davidson, A. G. 1991. Looking for love in the age of AIDS: The language of gay personals 1978–1988. *Journal of Sex Research* 28:125–37.

Deaux, K., and R. Hanna. 1984. Courtship in the personals column: The influence of gender and sexual orientation. *Sex Roles* 11:363–75.

Deenen, A. A., L. Gijs, and L. X. van Naerssen. 1995. Thirty-five years of research into gay relationships. *Journal of Psychology and Human Sexuality* 7(4):19–39.

Duffy, S. M., and C. E. Rusbult. 1986. Satisfaction and commitment in homosexual and heterosexual relationships. *Journal of Homosexuality* 12(2):1–24.

Eldridge, N. S., and L. A. Gilbert. 1990. Correlates of relationship satisfaction in lesbian couples. *Psychology of Women Quarterly* 14:43–62.

Engel, J. W., and M. Saracino. 1986. Love preferences and ideals: A comparison of homosexual, bisexual, and heterosexual groups. *Contemporary Family Therapy* 8:241–50.

Evans, N. J., and A. R. D'Augelli. 1996. Lesbians, gay men, and bisexual people in college. In R. C. Savin-Williams and K. M. Cohen, eds., *The Lives of Lesbians, Gays, and Bisexuals*, pp. 201–26. Orlando, Fla.: Harcourt Brace.

Falbo, T., and L. A. Peplau. 1980. Power strategies in intimate relationships. *Journal of Personality and Social Psychology* 38:618–28.

Falco, K. L. 1991. *Psychotherapy with Lesbian Clients*. New York: Brunner/Mazel.

Feingold, A. 1990. Gender differences in effects of physical attractiveness on romantic attraction: A comparison across five research paradigms. *Journal of Personality and Social Psychology* 59:981–93.

Fox, R. C. 1996. Bisexuality in perspective: A review of theory and research. In B. A. Firestein, ed., *Bisexuality: The Psychology and Politics of an Invisible Minority*, pp. 3–50. Thousand Oaks, Calif.: Sage.

Gonzales, M. H., and S. A. Meyers. 1993. "Your mother would like me": Self-presentation in the personal ads of heterosexual and homosexual men and women. *Personality and Social Psychology Bulletin* 19:131–42.

Goodkin, K., N. T. Blaney, R. S. Tuttle, and R. H. Nelson. 1996. Bereavement and HIV infection. *International Review of Psychiatry* 8:201–16.

Greenfield, S., and M. Thelen. 1997. Validation of the fear of intimacy scale with a lesbian and gay male population. *Journal of Social and Personal Relationships* 14:707–16.

Hammond, N. 1989. Lesbian victims of relationship violence. *Women and Therapy* 8(1/2):89–105.

Harris, R. J., and C. A. Cook. 1994. Attributions about spouse abuse: It matters who the batterers and victims are. *Sex Roles* 30:553–65.

Harry, J. 1982. Decision making and age differences among gay male couples. *Journal of Homosexuality* 8(2):9–22.

Harry, J. 1983. Gay male and lesbian relationships. In E. Macklin and R. Rubin, eds., *Contemporary Families and Alternative Life Styles*, pp. 216–34. Thousand Oaks, Calif.: Sage.

Harry, J. 1984. *Gay Couples*. New York: Praeger.

Harry, J., and W. B. DeVall. 1978. *The Social Organization of Gay Males*. New York: Praeger.

Hatala, M. N., D. W. Baack, and R. Parmenter. 1998. Dating with HIV: A content analysis of gay male HIV-positive and HIV-negative personal advertisements. *Journal of Social and Personal Relationships* 15:268–76.

Hatala, M. N., and J. Prehodka. 1996. A content analysis of gay male and lesbian personal advertisements. *Psychological Reports* 78:371–74.

Hawkins, R. L. 1992. Therapy with male couples. In S. Dworkin and F. Gutierrez, eds., *Counseling Gay Men and Lesbians*, pp. 81–94. Alexandria, Va.: American Association for Counseling and Development.

Howard, J. A., P. Blumstein, and P. Schwartz. 1986. Sex, power, and influence tactics in intimate relationships. *Journal of Personality and Social Psychology* 51:102–9.

Hutchins, L., and L. Ka'ahumanu, eds. 1991. *Bi Any Other Name: Bisexual People Speak Out*. Boston: Alyson.

Jacobson, S., and A. H. Grossman. 1996. Older lesbians and gay men. In R. C. Savin-Williams and K. M. Cohen, eds., *The Lives of Lesbians, Gays, and Bisexuals*, pp. 345–74. Orlando, Fla.: Harcourt Brace.

James, S. E., and B.C. Murphy. 1998. Gay and lesbian relationships in a changing context. In C. J. Patterson and A. R. D'Augelli, eds., *Lesbian, Gay, and Bisexual Identities in Families*, pp. 99–121. New York: Oxford University Press.

Jones, D. A. 1996. Discrimination against same-sex couples in hotel reservation policies. *Journal of Homosexuality* 31(1/2):153–59.

Kemeny, M. E., H. Weiner, R. Duran, and S. E. Taylor. 1995. Immune system changes after the death of a partner in HIV-positive gay men. *Psychosomatic Medicine* 57:547–54.

Klinkenberg, D., and S. Rose. 1994. Dating scripts of gay men and lesbians. *Journal of Homosexuality* 26(4):23–35.

Koestner, R., and L. Wheeler. 1988. Self-presentation in personal advertisements: The influence of implicit notions of attractiveness and role expectations. *Journal of Social and Personal Relationships* 5:149–60.

Kollock, P., P. Blumstein, and P. Schwartz. 1985. Sex and power in interaction: Conversational privileges and duties. *American Sociological Review* 50:34–46.

Kurdek, L. A. 1998. Relationship outcomes and their predictors: Longitudinal evidence from heterosexual married, gay cohabiting, and lesbian cohabiting couples. *Journal of Marriage and the Family* 60:553–68.

Kurdek, L. A. 1997a. Relation between neuroticism and dimensions of relationship commitment: Evidence from gay, lesbian, and heterosexual couples. *Journal of Family Psychology* 11:109–24.

Kurdek, L. A. 1997b. Adjustment to relationship dissolution in gay, lesbian, and heterosexual partners. *Personal Relationships* 4:145–61.

Kurdek, L. A. 1996. The deterioration of relationship quality for gay and lesbian cohabiting couples: A five-year prospective longitudinal study. *Personal Relationships* 3:417–42.

Kurdek, L. A. 1995a. Developmental changes in relationship quality in gay and lesbian cohabiting couples. *Developmental Psychology* 31:86–94.

Kurdek, L. A. 1995b. Lesbian and gay couples. In A. R. D'Augelli and C. J. Patterson, eds., *Lesbian, Gay, and Bisexual Identities over the Lifespan*, pp. 243–61. New York: Oxford.

Kurdek, L. A. 1994a. The nature and correlates of relationship quality in gay, lesbian, and heterosexual cohabiting couples. In B. Greene and G. M. Herek, eds., *Lesbian and Gay Psychology*, vol 1, pp. 113–55. Thousand Oaks, Calif.: Sage.

Kurdek, L. A. 1994b. Areas of conflict for gay, lesbian, and heterosexual couples: What couples argue about influences relationship satisfaction. *Journal of Marriage and the Family* 56:923–34.

Kurdek, L. A. 1994c. Conflict resolution styles in gay, lesbian, heterosexual nonparent, and heterosexual parent couples. *Journal of Marriage and the Family* 56:705–722.

Kurdek, L. A. 1993. The allocation of household labor in gay, lesbian, and heterosexual married couples. *Journal of Social Issues* 49(3):127–39.

Kurdek, L. A. 1992. Relationship stability and relationship satisfaction in cohabiting gay and lesbian couples: A prospective longitudinal test of the contextual and interdependence models. *Journal of Social and Personal Relationship* 9:125–42.

Kurdek, L. A. 1991a. Correlates of relationship satisfaction in cohabiting gay and lesbian couples. *Journal of Personality and Social Psychology* 61:910–22.

Kurdek, L. A. 1991b. The dissolution of gay and lesbian couples. *Journal of Social and Personal Relationships* 8:265–78.

Kurdek, L. A. 1989. Relationship quality in gay and lesbian cohabiting couples: A 1-year follow-up study. *Journal of Social and Personal Relationships* 6:39–59.

Kurdek, L. A. 1988. Relationship quality of gay and lesbian cohabiting couples. *Journal of Homosexuality* 15(3/4):93–118.

Kurdek, L. A., and J. P. Schmitt. 1987. Partner homogamy in married, heterosexual cohabiting, gay, and lesbian couples. *Journal of Sex Research* 23:212–32.

Kurdek, L. A., and J. P. Schmitt. 1986a. Relationship quality of partners in heterosexual married, heterosexual cohabiting, and gay and lesbian relationships. *Journal of Personality and Social Psychology* 51:711–20.

Kurdek, L. A., and J. P. Schmitt. 1986b. Early development of relationship quality in heterosexual married, heterosexual cohabiting, gay, and lesbian couples. *Developmental Psychology* 22:305–9.

Landolt, M. A., and D. G. Dutton. 1997. Power and personality: An analysis of gay male intimate abuse. *Sex Roles* 37:335–59.

Laner, M. R. 1978. Media mating II: "Personals" advertisements of lesbian women. *Journal of Homosexuality* 4(1):41–61.

Laner, M. R., and G.W.L. Kamel. 1977. Media mating I: Newspaper "personals" ads of homosexual men. *Journal of Homosexuality* 3(2):149–62.

Laumann, E. O., J. H. Gagnon, R. T. Michael, and S. Michaels. 1994. *The Social Organization of Sexuality*. Chicago: University of Chicago Press.

Leigh, B.C. 1989. Reasons for having and avoiding sex: Gender, sexual orientation, and relationship to sexual behavior. *Journal of Sex Research* 26(2):199–209.

Lynch, J. M., and M. E. Reilly. 1986. Role relationships: Lesbian perspectives. *Journal of Homosexuality* 12(2):53–69.

Marecek, J., S. E. Finn, and M. Cardell. 1982. Gender roles in the relationships of lesbians and gay men. *Journal of Homosexuality* 8(2):45–50.

Martin, J. L., and L. Dean. 1993. Bereavement following death from AIDS: Unique problems, reactions, and special needs. In M. S. Stroebe, W. Stroebe, and R. O. Hansson, eds., *Handbook of Bereavement*, pp. 317–30. Cambridge: Cambridge University Press.

McCormick, N. B. 1994. *Sexual Salvation: Affirming Women's Sexual Rights and Pleasures*. Westport, Conn.: Praeger.

McDonald, H. B., and A. I. Steinhorn. 1990. *Homosexuality: A Practical Guide to Counseling Lesbians, Gay Men, and Their Families*. New York: Continuum.

McWhirter, D. P., and A.M. Mattison. 1982. *The Male Couple*. Englewood Cliffs, N.J.: Prentice-Hall.

Metz, M. E., B.R.S. Rosser, and N. Strapko. 1994. Differences in conflict-resolution styles among heterosexual, gay, and lesbian couples. *Journal of Sex Research* 31:1–16.

Murphy, B.C. 1989. Lesbian couples and their parents: The effects of perceived parental attitudes on the couple. *Journal of Counseling and Development* 68:46–51.

Patterson, C. J. 1995. Families of the lesbian baby boom: Parents' division of labor and children's adjustment. *Development Psychology* 31:115–23.

Patterson, D. G., and P. Schwartz. 1994. The social construction of conflict in intimate same-sex couples. In D. D. Cahn, ed., *Conflict in Personal Relationships*, pp. 3–26. Mahwah, N.J.: Erlbaum.

Peplau, L. A. 1991. Lesbian and gay relationships. In J. C. Gonsiorek and J. D. Weinrich, eds., *Homosexuality: Research Findings for Public Policy*, pp. 177–96. Thousand Oaks, Calif.: Sage.

Peplau, L. A., and H. Amaro. 1982. Understanding lesbian relationships. In W. Paul,

J. D., Weinrich, J. D. Gonsiorek, and M. E. Hotvedt, eds., *Homosexuality: Social Psychological and Biological Issues*, pp. 233–48. Newbury Park, Calif.: Sage.

Peplau, L. A., and S. M. Campbell. 1989. The balance of power in dating and marriage. In J. Freeman, ed., *Women: A Feminist Perspective*, 4th ed., pp. 121–37. Mountain View, Calif.: Mayfield.

Peplau, L. A., and S. D. Cochran. 1981. Value orientations in the intimate relationships of gay men. *Journal of Homosexuality* 6(3):1–19.

Peplau, L. A., and S. D. Cochran. 1980. September. *Sex Differences in Values Concerning Love Relationships*. Paper presented at the annual meeting of the American Psychological Association, September, Montreal, Canada.

Peplau, L. A., S. D. Cochran, and V. M. Mays. 1997. A national survey of the intimate relationships of African-American lesbians and gay men: A look at commitment, satisfaction, sexual behavior, and HIV disease. In B. Greene, ed., *Ethnic and Cultural Diversity Among Lesbians and Gay Men*, pp. 11–38. Thousand Oaks, Calif.: Sage.

Peplau, L. A., S. D. Cochran, K. Rook, and C. Padesky. 1978. Women in love: Attachment and autonomy in lesbian relationships. *Journal of Social Issues* 34(3):7–27.

Peplau, L. A., and S. L. Gordon. 1983. The intimate relationships of lesbians and gay men. In E. R. Allgeier and N. B. McCormick, eds., *The Changing Boundaries: Gender Roles and Sexual Behavior*, pp. 226–44. Mountain View, Calif.: Mayfield.

Peplau, L. A., C. Padesky, and M. Hamilton. 1982. Satisfaction in lesbian relationships. *Journal of Homosexuality* 8(2):23–35.

Peplau, L. A., L. R. Spalding, T. D. Conley, and R. C. Veniegas. 1999. The development of sexual orientation in women. *Annual Review of Sex Research* 10:70–99.

Raphael, S. M., and M. K. Robinson. 1980. The older lesbian: Love relationships and friendship patterns. *Alternative Lifestyles* 3:207–30.

Reilly, M. E., and J. M. Lynch. 1990. Power-sharing in lesbian partnerships. *Journal of Homosexuality* 19(3):1–30.

Renzetti, C. M. 1992. *Violent Betrayal: Partner Abuse in Lesbian Relationships*. Newbury Park, Calif.: Sage.

Rose, S., and I. Frieze. 1989. Young singles' scripts for a first date. *Gender and Society* 3:258–68.

Rose, S., and D. Zand. 2000. Lesbian dating and courtship from young adulthood to midlife. *Journal of Gay and Lesbian Social Services* 11(2/3):77–104.

Rose, S., D. Zand, and M. Cini. 1993. Lesbian courtship scripts. In E. D. Rothblum and K. A. Brehony, eds., *Boston Marriages: Romantic but Asexual Relationships Among Contemporary Lesbians*, pp. 70–85. Amherst, Mass.: University of Massachusetts Press.

Rosenzweig, J. M., and W. C. Lebow. 1992. Femme on the streets, butch in the sheets? Lesbian sex roles, dyadic adjustment, and sexual satisfaction. *Journal of Homosexuality* 23(3):1–20.

Rust, P. C. 1992. The politics of sexual identity: Sexual attraction and behavior among lesbian and bisexual women. *Social Problems* 39:366–86.

Rust, P. C. 1995. *Bisexuality and the Challenge to Lesbian Politics: Sex, Loyalty, and Revolution*. New York: New York University Press.

Sanders, S. A., and J. M. Reinisch. 1999. Would you say you "had sex" if . . .? *Journal of the American Medical Association* 281:275–77.

Savin-Williams, R. C. 1996. Dating and romantic relationships among gay, lesbian, and bisexual youths. In R. C. Savin-Williams and K. M. Cohen, eds., *The Lives of Lesbians, Gays, and Bisexuals*, pp. 166–80. Orlando, Fla.; Harcourt Brace.

Schilit, R., G. Lie, and M. Montagne. 1990. Substance use as a correlate of violence in intimate lesbian relationships. *Journal of Homosexuality* 19(3):51–65.

Schreurs, K.M.G., and B. P. Buunk. 1996. Closeness, autonomy, equity, and relationship satisfaction in lesbian couples. *Psychology of Women Quarterly* 20:577–92.

Shannon, J. W., and W. J. Woods. 1991. Affirmative psychotherapy for gay men. *Counseling Psychologist* 19:197–215.

Siegel, K., and M. Glassman. 1989. Individual and aggregate level change in sexual behavior among gay men at risk for AIDS. *Archives of Sexual Behavior* 18:335–48.

Silverstein, C. 1981. *Man to Man: Gay Couples in America*. New York: Morrow.

Smith, R. B., and R. A. Brown. 1997. The impact of social support on gay male couples. *Journal of Homosexuality* 33(2):39–61.

Spalding, L. R., and L. A. Peplau. 1997. The inconstant lover: Heterosexuals' perceptions of bisexuals. *Psychology of Women Quarterly* 21:611–25.

Testa, R. J., B. N. Kinder, and G. Ironson. 1987. Heterosexual bias in the perception of loving relationships of gay males and lesbians. *Journal of Sex Research* 23:163–72.

Tripp, C. A. 1975. *The Homosexual Matrix*. New York: Signet.

Waldner-Haugrud, L. K., L. V. Gratch, and B. Magruder. 1997. Victimization and perpetration rates of violence in gay and lesbian relationships: Gender issues explored. *Violence and Victims* 12:173–84.

Walters, A. S., and M. Curran. 1996. "Excuse me, sir? May I help you and your boyfriend?": Salespersons' differential treatment of homosexual and straight customers. *Journal of Homosexuality* 31(1/2):135–52.

Weinberg, M. S., C. J. Williams, and D. W. Pryor. 1994. *Dual Attraction: Understanding Bisexuality*. New York: Oxford University Press.

Weinstock, J. S., and E. D. Rothblum, eds. 1996. *Lesbian Friendships: For Ourselves and Each Other*. New York: New York University Press.

Wise, A. J., and S. L. Bowman. 1997. Comparison of beginning counselors' responses to lesbian vs. heterosexual partner abuse. *Violence and Victims* 12:127–35.

18 Monogamy and Polyamory: Relationship Issues for Bisexuals

Paula C. Rust

Bisexuals, like lesbians, gay men, and heterosexuals, form many different types of sexual and romantic relationships with other people and sometimes seek help in making healthy choices about their relationships.[1] But for bisexuals, making relationship choices can be complicated by prevalent stereotypes about bisexuality. Counselors who wish to help bisexuals make these choices must confront their own stereotypes about bisexuals, understand the cultural assumptions about sexuality and relationships that underlie these stereotypes, recognize the impact that stereotypes can have on bisexual clients, and develop a realistic and nonjudgmental awareness of the issues that arise in the various types of relationships bisexual clients choose.

One common stereotype is that bisexuals are promiscuous because of an inability to commit themselves to long-term monogamous relationships (see Blumstein and Schwartz 1974; MacDonald 1981; Rust 1993, for information about bisexual stereotypes). This stereotype arises out of the Western dualistic conception of sexuality, in which heterosexuality and homosexuality are constructed as the two basic forms of sexuality. Within this view, bisexuality can be conceptualized only as a hybrid form of sexuality, in which heterosexuality is mixed with homosexuality. The bisexual person is therefore not holistically bisexual but dualistically half heterosexual and half homosexual. Because heterosexuality and homosexuality are often conceptualized as conflicting or opposing forms of sexuality, bisexuals are believed to experience conflict between their "heterosexual desires" and their "homosexual desires." This conflict allegedly surfaces in bisexuals' attempts to form stable relationships with others;

for example, when a bisexual is with someone of the same sex, she[2] is thought to experience an unsatisfied desire for someone of the other sex that will threaten the stability and longevity of her same-sex relationship, and conversely when she is with someone of the other sex. Her relationship with a single person of a particular gender is perceived as an expression and fulfillment of her "heterosexual side" or her "homosexual side" rather than her *bisexuality*. Thus the bisexual's ability to form relationships with members of both sexes is interpreted as a need for relationships with members of both sexes, a need that cannot be fulfilled by any one relationship and that therefore dooms the bisexual to a life of promiscuity or, at best, serial monogamy in an effort to satisfy both sides of her conflicted self. To recognize the absurdity of such a leap in logic, imagine concluding that a person who finds both blue and brown eyes attractive would require two lovers, one with each eye color, instead of concluding that this person would be happy with *either* a blue-eyed or a brown-eyed lover.

The stereotype of the bisexual who has concurrent female and male lovers or who alternates female and male lovers in an effort to satisfy both sides of her desire is supported by another common stereotype — that is, that bisexuality is a phase or a temporary form of sexuality adopted by people who are either coming out as lesbian or gay or returning to heterosexuality. Because bisexuality is perceived as temporary or transitional, others are rarely willing to accept the bisexual's claim to bisexuality at face value. Instead, they watch for clues that will reveal the bisexual's "real" orientation. Often the clue is found when the bisexual chooses a single partner. Because that one partner usually has a particular gender, the gender of that partner is used as evidence that the bisexual has "come out as gay" if the partner is same-sex or that she has "returned to heterosexuality" if the partner is other-sex. Thus, as soon as a bisexual chooses a single partner, she is no longer perceived as bisexual, thereby tautologically proving the point that bisexuals cannot be monogamous. In this way, the stereotype that bisexuality is a phase serves to bolster the stereotype that bisexuals are promiscuous and nonmonogamous.

Bisexual stereotypes are also reinforced by the popular tendency to see bisexuality strictly as a sexual and behavioral phenomenon rather than as a social or political identity. When bisexuality is defined strictly in terms of sexual behavior, a bisexual is, by definition, a person who is simultaneously involved with both a woman and a man and therefore necessarily nonmonogamous. But this is a narrow definition that does not correspond to the way most bisexuals define their bisexuality and is therefore of limited practical or therapeutic value. Most people who consider themselves bisexual do so because they feel attracted to both women and men, because they believe they could potentially become involved with either women or men, or because they have had relationships with both women and men in the past and do not wish to adopt either a lesbian/gay or heterosexual identity that would effectively deny the reality of part of their sexual feelings or experiences. Heterosexuals and lesbians/gay men also tend to define their sexuality in terms of their feelings of attraction and past sexual experience rather than solely in terms of their current behavior, and these definitions are generally accepted by others. For example, heterosexuals are generally thought to be no less heterosexual during periods when they are not involved with someone of the other sex. Why, then, should one's bisexuality be questioned during periods when one is either single or involved with people or a person of only one gender?

Finally, the stereotypes of bisexuals as promiscuous and nonmonogamous are perpetuated by media images of bisexuality. In the mid-1980s popular magazines seized on the "bisexual" as the gateway through which HIV would spread from the gay population to the heterosexual population (Hutchins 1996; Ochs 1996; Rila 1996; Stokes et al. 1996). Wives were warned that their husbands might be "bisexual," that is, that they might be having sex with men on the side, in articles such as "The Secret Life of Bisexual Husbands" in *Redbook* (Davidowitz 1993) and "The Hidden Fear: Black Women, Bisexuals, and the AIDS Risk" in *Ebony* (Randolph 1988; see also Gelman 1987; Gerrard and Halpin 1989; Heller 1987). More recently TV talk shows have discovered that bisexuality is a sexy topic. Despite bisexual political activists' admonitions that there are many ways to be bisexual, talk show staff are routinely interested in the most sensational images of bisexuality — the married man with a male lover, the ménage à trois, swingers who swing both ways, and so on. Far from educating the public about bisexuality, these shows reinforce stereotypical images of bisexuality.

Stereotypes tend to be self-fulfilling for bisexuals who lack role models for other ways of being bisexual. The individual who feels attracted to both women and men and is beginning to wonder if she is bisexual might fear that coming out as bisexual will doom her to a life of promiscuity and shallow, short-lived relationships. She receives no assurance that she can maintain a bisexual identity in the context of a committed long-term relationship, much less any role models for doing so or any alternative models for healthy relationships. If she chooses to identify herself as bisexual, thinking that romantic stability will therefore be impossible for her, then she might abandon a relationship at the first sign of discord, taking that discord as a sign that the inevitable breakup is imminent, thus fulfilling the prophecy. Or she might feel that to be bisexual she must have sexual experiences with both women and men and therefore set out to acquire these experiences to validate her bisexual identity. Alternatively, and perhaps more frequently, she might choose not to identify as bisexual in the hope of being able to maintain the type of committed relationship that she has learned to associate with relational maturity. For example, if she becomes involved with a single individual of her own sex, then she might concur with her friends that she has indeed come out as a lesbian. She might be able to suppress or rationalize feelings of attraction for men that threaten her lesbian identity, as subcultural ideology encourages her to do (Blumstein and Schwartz 1977; Ponse 1978; Udis-Kessler 1990, 1991). Or she might find it difficult to maintain her lesbian identity in the face of her continued feelings of attraction for men. But the fear that giving up her lesbian identity would foreclose her chance at monogamous happiness keeps her laboring to maintain the lesbian identity that by now has become the bedrock of her relationship with her partner.

Stereotypes also affect bisexuals by affecting their partners' or potential partners' expectations of them. Bisexuals often find that nonbisexuals are reluctant to become involved with them (Rust 1995) and that nonbisexuals who do become involved expect them to be less faithful or committed by virtue of their bisexuality. To avoid having to educate partners who have stereotypical expectations of bisexuals, many bisexuals prefer partners who also identify as bisexual, believing that other bisexuals are more likely to understand that bisexuality does not imply nonmonogamy and more likely to be understanding if the bisexual partner does, in fact, desire additional lovers. Unfortunately, because many individuals with bisexual feelings or behaviors identify as gay, lesbian, or heterosexual (see Fox 1996), a bisexual-identified partner might be difficult to find. Moreover, because of internalized biphobia, many bisexuals hold the same stereotypical views that nonbisexuals do (Rust 1995).

Bisexuals are affected not only by stereotypes themselves but also by the cultural assumptions that underlie these stereotypes. Underlying the stereotype of bisexuals as promiscuous and nonmonogamous is a cultural idealization of monogamy. Whereas the stereotypes tend to be self-fulfilling, thereby inhibiting bisexuals from forming monogamous relationships, the idealization of monogamy prevents bisexuals from conceptualizing and positively valuing other relational forms. To clear the way for a realistic assessment of bisexuals' relational options, it is therefore necessary not only to reject the overt stereotypes but also to challenge the cultural idealization of monogamy that underlies these stereotypes.

The modern concept of monogamy is based on the assumption that the monogamous relationship should fulfill all the partners' sexual and romantic needs and the greater part of their emotional needs. This type of relationship is a peculiarly modern invention called *companionate marriage* (Burgess and Locke 1953). At other times and in other cultures, marriage was and is not expected to fulfill so many of the partners' needs; sexual fidelity was sometimes prescribed for one or both partners, but partners were not also expected to seek primary fulfillment of their emotional needs within marriage. In contrast, the partners in today's companionate marriage are not supposed to need outside sexual or romantic liaisons. If either partner does feel a need for outside liaisons, this is taken as a sign that the relationship is not working properly. In other words, sexual and romantic monogamy — institutionalized in the legally recognized marriage — becomes the hallmark of the successful modern romantic partnership.

Of course, as a culture we acknowledge that many relationships fail to meet these standards, and the prescription in such cases is to "fix" the relationship through honest communication between the partners, including, if necessary, couple counseling. If efforts are not made, or if they are unsuccessful, the result will be either unhappiness for the partners, "cheating" as one or both partners seek to have their needs fulfilled elsewhere, or, ultimately, the breakup of the relationship. Thus relationships that do not conform to the traditional monogamous model are constructed as "failed" relationships; by constructing them this way, we protect the institution of monogamy itself from challenge.

The cultural model of the monogamous relationship does work for many people, including many bisexuals, who find it possible to have their sexual, romantic, and emotional needs met by a single other person and who find a person who can meet these needs. Other people find that no one person could meet all their relational needs, not necessarily because they have greater needs than others but because they have needs that cannot be met within a monogamous relationship. For example, some people need or want diversity in sexual, romantic, or emotional input. Others need a level of emotional independence that they cannot experience in a monogamous relationship. Still others who have bisexual attractions feel the need to explore their feelings for lovers of both genders. Whatever the reason, some people are happier and more secure receiving sexual, emotional, and romantic support from a variety of people instead of only one person.

If we take off our cultural blinders, we can see that this is, in fact, a very reasonable approach to needs fulfillment that provides greater security than monogamy; dependence on one person for all one's needs is a shaky premise indeed, compared to multiple sustaining relationships that can provide greater support in a wider variety of circumstances. Once this has been recognized, it should be clear that monogamists do not have a monopoly on either maturity or stability. Both monogamous and nonmonogamous forms of relating can reflect emotional maturity, and neither one guarantees it.

Once we have rejected the cultural idealization of monogamy in favor of an approach that values a variety of relational forms, the term *nonmonogamy* no longer seems appropriate because of the negative connotations implicit in defining something in terms of what it is not rather than what it is. In recent years, the term *polyamory* has begun to replace nonmonogamy among individuals who wish to symbolize linguistically their rejection of monogamy as the only ideal form of relating.

Rejecting the stereotypes of bisexuals as promiscuous and nonmonogamous, as well as the idealization of monogamy, leaves an intellectual void to be filled with positive information about the variety of monogamous and polyamorous relationships that are possible for bisexual individuals. Counselors who wish to help bisexual clients make healthy relationship choices must not only avoid making value judgments based on stereotypes and unquestioned cultural morality, they must also be able to offer their clients alternatives, validate polyamorous as well as monogamous relational styles, and deal realistically and nonjudgmentally with the problems that arise in various types of relationships. Toward this end, the remainder of this paper is devoted to exploring the various types of relationships bisexual individuals form and the therapeutic issues that arise for individuals who choose alternatives to monogamy.

Methods and Sample

The following discussion of bisexuals' relational forms is based primarily on the findings of an ongoing international study entitled "Sexual/Bisexual Identities, Communities, and Politics." The overall purpose of the study is to explore how individuals who are attracted to both genders or have had sexual contact with members of both genders arrange their psychological and social worlds in the context of a society that is organized to facilitate either exclusive heterosexuality or exclusive lesbianism/gayness. It is the second large-scale study conducted in the United States to include an examination of the variety in bisexuals' relational forms, as opposed to issues that arise for bisexuals in traditional heterosexual relationships; the first study was conducted by Weinberg, Williams, and Pryor (1994). Data are being collected for the current study via in-depth interviews, participant observation, and a self-administered questionnaire that is distributed with postage-paid envelopes in the United States and with postal coupons in several other countries, including the United Kingdom, France, Germany, Belgium, Canada, Australia, and New Zealand.

The questionnaire was designed to be self-explanatory and anonymous to encourage a wide range of people to participate, including those who are secretive about their sexual and social practices. Because it is impossible to draw a representative sample of any population that is defined by its sexual and social practices, sampling is focused instead on drawing a diverse sample. Toward this end, the questionnaire is being distributed by multiple means, including distribution at conferences on sexuality, through social networks, at meetings of bisexual and LesBiGay social and political organizations, and via advertisements in bisexual newsletters, mainstream "alternative" newspapers, and the Internet. Particular efforts are being made to maximize the respondents' racial-ethnic, sexual, age, gender, and geographic diversity.

The remainder of this article is based on the first 577 completed questionnaires received from respondents living in the United States. Of these respondents, 65 percent are women and slightly less than 4 percent are transgendered individuals, including postoperative male to female transsexuals, nontranssexual transgenderists, and male cross-dressers. The age range of respondents is fifteen to eighty-two, with 39 percent in their twenties, 31 percent in their thirties, 18 percent in their forties, and 9 percent fifty years or older. Twenty-seven percent are students, half of whom are also employed full- or part-time. Among respondents who are not students, the median income is in the range $20,000 to $29,999 with 13 percent earning less than $10,000 and 25 percent earning $50,000 or more. In general, the respondents are highly educated; nearly three-quarters have finished four years of college, and most of these have had some graduate-level education. Eleven percent are people of color, including African-Americans, Asian-Americans, Indigenous Peoples, and Latinas/Latinos. Further details about the racial and ethnic identities of respondents in this study are provided in Rust 1996.

Early in the questionnaire, respondents were asked, "When you think about your sexual orientation today, what term do you use most often to describe yourself?" They were given a list of twenty-three response options, including "bisexual," "gay," "bisexual lesbian," "polyfidelitous," "queer," "I am not sure," "I prefer not to label myself," and "other." Respondents were invited to choose more than one response option but were asked to indicate which identity they use "most often." Of the 577 respondents described above, 277 identified themselves solely or primarily as bisexual, 83 identified themselves solely or primarily as lesbian or gay, and 27 identified themselves as heterosexual. Most of the remainder identified themselves as bisexual in combination with other identities, for example, as a "lesbian bisexual," a "gay-identified bisexual," or a "bisexual queer," or preferred alternative terms such as "pansensual." Recall that all respondents in this study have either felt attracted to or have been romantically or sexually involved with both women and men. That substantial numbers nevertheless identified themselves as heterosexual, lesbian, or gay is consistent with previous findings that many people with "bisexual" feelings or experiences choose not to identify themselves as bisexual (e.g., Blumstein and Schwartz 1974, 1976; Chapman and Brannock 1987; Earl 1990; Hedblom 1973; Humphreys 1970; Klein, Sepek-off, and Wolf 1985; Lever et al. 1992; Loewenstein 1984/ 1985; Nichols 1988; Rust 1992; Saghir and Robins 1973).

Later in the questionnaire, respondents were asked a series of questions about their sexual and romantic relationships. The first such question was very open-ended and provided the richest description of respondents' relational styles:

> Describe your current relationship status by describing all the sexual or romantic relationships you are involved in now, if any. For each relationship, describe what kind of relationship it is, how long you have been in the relationship, the sex of your partner, and the sexual orientation or sexual identity of your partner. Finally, do you and your partner(s) have any agreements regarding romantic or sexual relationships with other people, and are you sexually or romantically active with people other than your partner(s)?

Respondents were also asked whether they are currently looking for, hoping for, or open to having (additional) encounters, dates, or relationships and what their ideal relationship status would be. After each question, respondents were presented with a number of detailed response options and invited to choose a response or to write their own answer.

The Prevalence of Monogamy Among Bisexuals

One way to put bisexuals' relationship choices into perspective is to compare them with the relationship choices of heterosexuals, gay men, and lesbians. In an earlier study of self-identified lesbians and bisexual women conducted in 1986, I found that lesbians and bisexual women were equally likely to be uninvolved romantically; 23.5 percent of lesbians and 21.4 percent of bisexual women in that study were single. Furthermore, only one out of six (16.7 percent) bisexual women was simultaneously involved with members of both genders; the remainder were involved with one or more people of only one gender, usually in serious or marriagelike relationships (Rust 1992). These findings indicate that the stereotype that bisexuals require sexual partners of both sexes is untrue.

Similar findings are obtained from the current study, in which fully one-third of bisexual respondents (33.7 percent), 40.7 percent of lesbians and gay men, and 33.3 percent of heterosexuals are not involved with anyone. Further patterns are revealed when these findings are broken down by gender;[3] 36.4 percent of bisexual women compared to 37.5 percent of lesbians, and 30.1 percent of bisexual men compared to 43.3 percent of gay men are not involved with anyone. Thus it appears that women are equally likely to be single regardless of lesbian or bisexual identity and that both lesbians and bisexual women are more likely to be single in the 1990s than they were in the 1980s, whereas gay men are more likely than bisexual men to be single.

Among respondents in the current study who are sexually or romantically involved, there are differences in the rates of monogamy among bisexuals compared to lesbians and gay men. When asked if they are looking or hoping for new sexual or romantic encounters, lesbians and gay men were more likely than bisexual women and men to respond that they are involved in monogamous relationships and therefore are not looking for additional sexual or romantic partners. Of lesbians and gay men, 28 percent, compared to 16.4 percent of bisexuals, said they are in monogamous relationships either by agreement or by default. Conversely, bisexuals were twice as likely (33.0 percent) as lesbians and gay men (16.0 percent) to say that they are dating or casually or seriously involved with one or more people and that they are also open to additional sexual encounters or relationships. Thus it appears that bisexuals are less likely than lesbians and gay men to form monogamous relationships, a finding also reported by Weinberg et al. (1994). This finding must not be allowed to overshadow the fact that 16.4 percent of bisexuals in the current study are involved in monogamous relationships from which they do not desire to stray. Monogamy might be less popular among bisexuals than among lesbians and gay men, but it is certainly a realistic option.

The different rates of monogamy among bisexuals compared to lesbians and gay men showed up even more dramatically when respondents were asked to describe their ideal relationship status. Asked "if you could have any combination of any types of sexual and romantic relationships you wanted, what would this be?" only 29.5 percent of bisexual women and 15.4 percent of bisexual men replied that they would like to have a lifetime committed monogamous relationship with one partner. In comparison, 46.7 percent of lesbians and 75.9 percent of gay men indicated that they want a lifetime monogamous relationship. The extremely high rate of desire for monogamy among gay men might be a response to the fear of AIDS.

In summary, it appears that bisexuals generally do not idealize monogamy nor are they generally involved in monogamous relationships. Many desire some form of polyamorous relationship. It is therefore important to examine the types of relationships that bisexuals who reject monogamy desire. It is also important to keep in mind that bisexuals are not the only individuals who sometimes desire polyamorous relationships. Although the following discussion focuses on the polyamorous relational forms of bisexuals, the discussion is equally applicable to lesbians, gay men, and heterosexuals who reject the cultural idealization of monogamy.

Alternatives to the All-Encompassing Relationship

Whereas monogamy is based on the concept of an all-encompassing relationship, in which the partners attempt to fulfill all of each other's sexual and romantic needs and most of their emotional needs, polyamorous relationships tend to be based on less all-encompassing forms of relating, in which individuals only partially fulfill their partner's needs. Before moving on to a discussion of the various ways in which bisexuals organize their relationships with others, therefore, it is necessary to examine the kinds of relationships within which different bisexual individuals find their needs fulfilled.

Respondents in the current study described a number of different types of relationships that fulfill particular needs for them. Some respondents like the idea of a partner who fulfills multiple needs, including sexual, emotional, and romantic needs but who does not have to carry the sole responsibility for fulfilling their needs in each of these areas. Other respondents choose to separate their sexual, emotional, and romantic needs and find satisfaction for these various needs in different people. For example, some respondents find satisfaction in romantic relationships that do not involve sexual activity. Some refer to their partners in these relationships as "nonsexual lovers" to indicate that this is a relationship whose nature is romantic but not sexual.

Others maintain "sexual friendships" in which they have sex with people whom they regard as friends but with whom they would not consider entering a romantic relationship. Two types of sexual friendships are "cuddle buddies" (or "cuddle bunnies") and "fuck buddies." Cuddle buddies are people who share warmth and companionship in bed; they might engage in various degrees of sex with each other and have varying degrees of emotional involvement. Fuck buddies, on the other hand, are more narrowly focused on fulfilling each other's sexual needs. Some respondents reported being part of a "circle of friends," the members of which have sex with each other. For individuals involved in sexual friendships, this type of relationship combines some of the best elements of traditional monogamy and the purely sexual encounter; it provides sex without strings that is nevertheless enhanced by a personal relationship and avoids the risks of sexual encounters with strangers. Sometimes, sexual friendships develop out of previous romantic relationships; some respondents explained that they broke up with their partners but decided to maintain sexual relationships until either they or their partners found new partners.

Finally, many respondents feel that their sexual needs are best fulfilled through purely sexual encounters with acquaintances or strangers. Some of these individuals simultaneously maintain intense emotional or romantic relationships, demonstrating that their desire for sex outside the context of emotional or romantic relationships is not merely a symptom of an inability to form close emotional bonds. Our cultural proscription of purely sexual activity and our concern for sexually transmitted diseases might cause us to label this behavior immature or irresponsible. But I assert that this reaction is conditioned by a sex-negative and monogamy-positive culture and that purely sexual encounters are no more inherently immature or irresponsible than sexual behavior within the context of a relationship. The danger we attribute to purely sexual encounters stems not from the nature of these encounters themselves but from the circumstances in which these encounters tend to occur in a culture that devalues them. Individuals who maturely assess that they obtain maximum sexual gratification from sex outside the context of emotional or romantic relationships and who are aware of dangers such as sexually transmitted diseases, might be, in fact, more likely to take the necessary precautions than individuals who are lulled into a false sense of security because their sex is taking place within the context of a relationship. In counseling these individuals, counselors should be aware that, whereas the concept of "sexual addiction," popularized in the wake of AIDS, accurately describes the experiences of some clients, it also tends to reinforce traditional sexual morality by pathologizing behavior that offends traditional sensibilities (Levine and Troiden 1988; Pincu 1989; cf. Quadland 1985, 1987; Schneider and Schneider 1990). Clients who desire sex outside the context of emotional and romantic relationships should be encouraged to examine their motivations — as should any other clients making decisions about sexual activity — but they should not a priori be assumed to be avoiding commitment or incapable of commitment or to have self-destructive motivations.

Many respondents who divide their sexual, emotional, and romantic needs among multiple relationships explained that at least some of their lovers live in other cities, states, or countries. Typically they see these lovers only occasionally, a circumstance that both creates and facilitates the desire to have multiple relationships. For example, many respondents have sexual relationships with people whom they see only once or twice a year, as well as local partners with whom they can be sexual on a more regular basis. Such arrangements seem particularly well adapted to today's society in which both women and men move in response to the dictates of their careers, and many people are unwilling or unable to uproot themselves to be geographically close to a romantic-sexual partner.

Polyamorous Relational Forms

When bisexuals choose to meet their needs with multiple partners instead of a single monogamous partner, what are some of the ways in which these multiple relationships can be organized? Among bisexual women and men in the current study, the most common preference is for a primary relationship or marriage with one person and secondary sexual encounters or romantic relationships with other people. In such cases, the primary relationship is an "open" relationship, in which the partners have agreed that each may form secondary sexual, romantic, or emotional (or any combination thereof) relationships with other people. Women tend to prefer secondary romantic relationships (17.4 percent) over sexual encounters (14.5 percent), whereas men tend to prefer secondary sexual encounters (28.2 percent) over romantic relationships (19.2 percent). The open primary relationship is not only the most frequently preferred type of polyamorous relationship, it is also the most common type among respondents in the current study. Many respondents' open primary relationships resulted when they and their partners decided to open previously monogamous relationships, whereas other respondents' relationships were open by mutual agreement from the beginning. Many respondents reported having two primary relationships, one with a man and one with a woman. In some cases, these two relationships are separate from each other, and, in other cases, the three people form a single triadic relationship. These findings agree with the findings of Weinberg et at. (1994), who reported that dual primary and simultaneous primary and secondary relationships were the most popular ideal relational forms among the respondents they interviewed in 1983.

The next most common preference for bisexual women is serial monogamy (11.0 percent) followed by lifetime polyfidelity (7.5 percent), whereas bisexual men are more likely to prefer lifetime polyfidelity (14.1 percent) or multiple relationships in which none are primary (9.0 percent). A polyfidelitous relationship, sometimes called a "group marriage" even though such relationships do not enjoy the legal recognition of marriage, is one in which three or more people agree that sexual, emotional, and romantic relationships may be formed among individuals within the group but place limits on the types of relationships that may be formed with individuals who are not members of the group. Members are, in short, fidelitous to a group of people rather than to a single individual as in monogamy. For example, one respondent who is married to a bisexual woman and who identifies as bisexual himself said that he and his spouse would like to form a polyfidelitous family with another other-sex couple in which both partners are bisexual.

Very few respondents want a "swinging" type relationship in which two or more primary couples exchange partners; some have tried swinging but gave it up, either because it was emotionally stressful or because one partner — usually the woman in an other-sex couple — did not enjoy it. This lack of popularity is a notable finding, as swinging is one of the few forms of polyamory that has achieved any degree of publicity in the mainstream media. According to research by Dixon (1984, 1985), swinging is one of the contexts in which women become aware of their ability to feel sexually attracted to other women. Dixon also reviewed earlier research findings that 60–92 percent of women involved in swinging exhibit bisexual behavior (including Bartell 1971; Gilmartin 1978; O'Neill and O'Neill 1970; see also Blumstein and Schwartz 1974, 1977). If bisexuality is common among swinging women, the fact that few bisexuals in the current study are into swinging might reflect the primarily heterosexual nature of swinging culture; those women who discovered their bisexuality through swinging might have since left swinging in search of cultural environments more conducive to their newfound sexual interests in women. Alternatively, it is possible that bisexuality is more common than swinging, such that bisexual swingers comprise a large proportion of swingers but a small proportion of bisexuals.[4]

Because open primary relationships are the most common and most desired form of polyamorous relationship among respondents in the current study, and because the issues that arise in these relationships are similar to the issues that arise in other forms of polyamory, the last section of this paper focuses in detail on these relationships and their therapeutic implications.

Counseling Primary Partners in an Open Relationship

Any individual who is contemplating becoming involved in an open primary relationship, or opening up a monogamous relationship, must take care to discuss the parameters of the new open relationship with their primary partner. Whereas people entering monogamous relationships can and often do fail to discuss explicitly the parameters of their monogamy, because they have a cultural model available to them that they (sometimes erroneously) assume they share, people entering open relationships have no cultural model to fall back on. Therefore the openness of the primary relationship must refer not only to the fact that the partners are open to having relationships with individuals other than each other but also to the fact that the partners are open and honest with each other about their feelings and needs with regard to these secondary relationships. Without the latter form of openness, the former becomes little more than permission to "cheat."

Respondents in the current study who are involved in open relationships stressed the importance of establishing ground rules for the conduct of sexual or romantic relationships outside the primary relationship. Ground rules serve to protect the primary relationship from the potential threat of outside relationships, to ease feelings of jealousy, and to promote honesty within the primary relationship. Weinberg et al. (1994) also discussed the importance of ground rules in open primary relationships and provided examples of the various ground rules suggested by respondents. Establishing ground rules requires intensive and honest communication between the partners, which the counselor can facilitate by making sure that each partner hears and responds to the other and by ensuring that no important aspect of the relationship is overlooked. One way to avoid oversights is to organize the discussion in terms of *issues*.

The first issue to discuss, once the partners have agreed that they do not want a traditional monogamous relationship, is what kinds of outside activity are permissible. Are outside sexual liaisons allowed? With or without romantic involvement? What about romantic involvements or intense emotional involvements that do not involve sex? Some couples agree that outside sexual relationships are permissible, as long as they do not develop into emotional or romantic relationships; others agree to be romantically polyamorous but sexually monogamous. One respondent in the current study agreed with her primary partner that both outside sexual and romantic relationships are permissible but that all such relationships must remain of secondary importance. If either partner found someone else with whom they wanted to establish a relationship of equal importance, then they agreed that that person would have to become a third equal partner in their primary relationship. One way to minimize the chance that an outside relationship will compete with the primary relationship is for the partners to find outside lovers who are themselves involved in open primary relationships. Such lovers are most likely to understand and respect the nature of the partners' primary bond and least likely to make demands that would strain that bond.

If sexual activity is permissible, then what kinds of sex are allowed and how frequently? How comfortable would each partner feel if the other established a second ongoing sexual relationship, as opposed to having several different sex partners, having one-night stands, or going to sex parties? Rules about permissible sexual activity often grow out of concern about HIV and limit the partners to "safer sex" practices. Partners who decide that all outside sex must be safer sex should discuss in detail what each partner considers safer and come to an agreement about exactly which activities are permitted and which are forbidden. For example, one male respondent explained that he has agreed not to have heterosexual intercourse, even with his primary partner. Rules about sexual activity also grow out of the partners' regard for each other's feelings. For example, one respondent who was about to move into a house with her primary partner hoped to establish a rule that no outside sexual activity would take place within the house so that neither primary partner would have to listen to the other having sex with someone else. Weinberg et al. (1994) described couples that developed rules pertaining to the timing or frequency of outside sexual and romantic activity; a certain day of the week might be designated for outside activity or certain days might be reserved for the primary couple to spend together.

During the discussion of which types of outside activity are permissible, the counselor should point out that agreeing that certain activities may take place does not mean that they must or will take place. Many couples who have agreed to open relationships are monogamous in practice, simply because neither partner has found an outside person with whom they wish to become involved. The partners should be reassured that, if they do not find outside lovers, their attempt at an open relationship has not failed and that they should not feel compelled to find outside lovers just because they have agreed that it is permissible. This might also be an opportune moment to ask the partners how each would feel if one partner found one or more outside lovers and the other found none. If the partners imagine that feelings of jealousy would arise, these feelings need to be examined to make sure that each partner is truly comfortable with the established parameters of the open relationship and that partners' decisions about their own outside involvements will not be influenced by feelings of competitiveness with the other partner.

The second issue to discuss is with whom outside liaisons may take place. While discussing this issue, the partners should take care to envision the various types of people with whom either partner might have outside sexual or romantic liaisons, examining and sharing their feelings about each scenario. Of particular importance is the gender of the third party; often one's feelings about a partner's outside sexual or romantic liaisons depend on the gender of the partner's other lover. Some people feel more threatened by other lovers who are the same sex as they are, because they perceive such lovers as direct competition. Other people feel more threatened by lovers who are of the other sex, because they feel they cannot offer their partners the same types of experiences that people of the other sex can. This exercise will also uncover assumptions either partner might be making about the gender of their partner's potential lovers. For example, the partner of a self-identified lesbian might assume that her lesbian partner's outside lovers will be women; she might be surprised to learn that her partner considers a male lover to be a possibility.

On the topic of what kinds of people are permissible, the partners should also take care to discuss the possibility of outside liaisons with people who are already known to either or both partners. Is it permissible for one partner to have a sexual encounter or begin a romantic relationship with a person who is a mutual friend of both partners? A person who is a good friend of the other partner? An ex-primary lover of one's own? A total stranger? Some people would feel very threatened if their partners became sexually involved with a mutual friend, because they feel that would undermine the basis of the friendship; others might feel more threatened by involvements with strangers, because strangers are unknown, unpredictable, and therefore, potentially dangerous. One respondent agreed with his partner that neither partner would become involved with anyone they would not want the other to meet. This rule serves as a screening device that forces each partner to take the feelings of the other into account at the moment of decision. If the partners agree that they prefer outside liaisons with persons known to both of them, then, at a minimum, each partner should be given an opportunity to meet and get to know any prospective outsiders who are not already friends of the couple.

The third issue is disclosure, that is, how much the partners should tell each other about their outside involvements. Among polyamorous respondents in the current study, disclosure is generally considered the minimum necessary requirement for a successful open relationship. Virtually all had agreed with their partners that each would inform the other whenever they became sexually or romantically involved with an outside person. Those respondents who had not agreed to disclose were usually individuals who were behaving nonmonogamously within the context of a default monogamous relationship that they expected to end soon. But the issue of disclosure is not closed once the partners agree on the importance of disclosure; it is also important to discuss the kinds of involvements that require disclosure. For example, assuming that one-night stands have been designated permissible, does one need to tell their partner about a one-night stand? An intense emotional friendship? Unrequited feelings of erotic attraction for another individual? Some respondents agreed with their partners that they are free to have nonromantic sexual encounters without telling each other about every incident but that, if any of these sexual encounters appear likely to become ongoing sexual relationships or romantic involvements, disclosure becomes necessary. Some partners feel that anything less than full disclosure is a form of dishonesty, whereas others feel that it is better if they do not know or that it is none of their business. Although the former attitude might seem healthier from certain therapeutic perspectives, any decision partners make regarding the extent of disclosure should be respected, as long as it is made within the context of an explicit and clear agreement that outside liaisons may take place.

The partners should also discuss the timing of disclosure. When disclosure is required, is it required before becoming involved, or is disclosure after the fact sufficient? Several couples agreed that they had to inform each other before becoming sexually involved with an outsider; others were content to inform each other after the fact. Among those who agreed to inform each other beforehand, many agreed that outside relationships were completely subject to the approval of the primary partner. A combination of requirements about disclosure is also possible; partners might decide that some types of outside involvements need not be disclosed, whereas others merit disclosure after the fact, and still others require disclosure before the involvement begins and are subject to the approval of the other partner.

Even when partners have the best intentions and have discussed the parameters of their relationship in detail, jealousies can arise at the moment of disclosure. Feelings of jealousy might take the partners in an open relationship by surprise, because they might think of jealousy as an irrational or primitive emotion or as an emotion culturally induced by a monogamous society, one that they have overcome. This attitude might lead the partners to suppress their feelings of jealousy instead of talking about them, thus preventing the ongoing communication that is important in a working relationship. The counselor can help prevent such breakdowns in communication by discussing with the partners the possibility that, despite all precautions, jealousies might arise and by helping them envision and examine their reactions to these jealousies. By imagining the circumstances under which they might become jealous, clients can reassess their comfort with the ground rules they have established and discuss what each partner would need from the other, if, in fact, jealousies were to arise. Often these needs will involve reassurance about their partner's love and commitment to the relationship and its ground rules.

A fourth issue to discuss is the presentation of the primary relationship to others, such as family and friends. Given the cultural idealization of monogamy, disclosing the open nature of the relationship to others will undoubtedly generate disapproval and demands for explanations, especially from family. How does each partner feel about their family knowing the open nature of their relationship? If a partner does not want their family to know, can the other partner accept this and feel comfortable "passing" as a monogamous couple? If a partner does want their family to know, can both partners withstand the questions and misunderstandings that will probably follow? If friends are to be told, do the partners think that these friends will still be able to respect the primacy of their relationship with each other, or will friends interpret the openness of their relationship as a sign that the relationship is ending and that each partner is "fair game"? If friends are not told, how will outside liaisons be handled so that they are not observed — and misinterpreted as cheating — by friends?

Finally, the partners should discuss the possibility that they will have to revise their rules as their relationship develops. At least they should agree that, if either partner becomes dissatisfied with the rules, then that partner should communicate dissatisfaction to the other. Rules are conservative in the sense that they do not change unless they are intentionally changed; relationships, on the other hand, grow and change seemingly without any conscious intent on anyone's part. It is important that the lines of communication be kept open to allow this growth and change to take place and to permit adjustment of the rules as the relationship changes. For example, as partners become more and more invested in a relationship, they might begin to experience feelings of jealousy in circumstances that they previously found unthreatening. Or one partner might begin to feel stifled by the requirement that the relationship remain primary and might want to reconsider this primacy. Whatever changes take place in the relationship, the rules need to be subject to renegotiation to accommodate these changes and maximize each partner's comfort and satisfaction with the relationship.

Conclusion

Whatever relational forms bisexuals choose, they often need special support from mental health professionals because of the lack of support they receive elsewhere. If they desire monogamy, their efforts to build monogamous relationships are often frustrated by partners or potential partners who equate bisexuality with promiscuity and nonmonogamy, and by their own internalization of the same stereotypes. If they desire polyamorous relationships, they find little social and no legal support for establishing and maintaining such relationships. This lack of support comes from others who perceive polyamory as failed monogamy and as evidence that the stereotypes of bisexuals are true. It also exists in the lack of cultural models for polyamorous relationships and in the lack of legal recognition for polyamorous and same-sex relationships in the United States.

It is therefore vital that mental health professionals examine their own stereotypes about bisexuality, question cultural beliefs about relational maturity and morality, and familiarize themselves with the issues that arise in polyamorous relationships so that they can provide bisexuals with the kinds of support and guidance that they are unlikely to find elsewhere. They can also help bisexual clients locate the few resources that do exist; for example, bisexual clients who are polyamorous can be encouraged to read Deborah Anapol's (1992) *Love Without Limits* or Arno Karlen's (1988) *Threesomes*.

Notes

1. The research on which this article is based was supported by funding from Hamilton College and a grant from the Society for the Psychological Study of Social Issues.
2. I use *their* and *her* or *she* as generic pronouns. I use *their* preferentially, reserving *her* or *she* for cases in which the use of *their* would require inappropriate use of a pluralized verb.
3. Findings for heterosexuals are not presented separately for men and women because the small number of respondents who identified themselves primarily as heterosexual renders these findings subject to high levels of statistical uncertainty. Furthermore, these few heterosexual-identified individuals are hardly representative of all heterosexuals, most of whom do not acknowledge feelings of attraction for people of their own gender.
4. Sampling bias is another possible explanation. If heterosexual swinging subculture and bisexual subculture are distinct, albeit overlapping subcultures, swingers might perceive their same-sex activity as an aspect of swinging rather than evidence of bisexuality. Such people would probably not have self-selected into the current study.

References

Anapol, D. 1992. *Love Without Limits: Responsible Nonmonogamy and the Quest for Sustainable Intimate Relationships*. San Rafael, Calif.: Intinet Resource Center.

Bartell, G. D. 1971. *Group Sex*. New York: Peter H. Wyden.

Blumstein, P. W., and P. Schwartz. 1974. Lesbianism and bisexuality. In E. Goode, ed., *Sexual Deviance and Sexual Deviants*, pp. 278–95. New York: Morrow.

Blumstein, P. W., and P. Schwartz. 1976. Bisexuality in men. *Urban Life* 5:339–58.

Blumstein, P. W., and P. Schwartz. 1977. Bisexuality: Some social psychological issues. *Journal of Social Issues* 33(2):30–45.

Burgess, E. W., and H. J. Locke. 1953. *The Family: From Institution to Companionship*. New York: American Book.

Chapman, B. E., and J. C. Brannock. 1987. Proposed model of lesbian identity development: An empirical examination. *Journal of Homosexuality* 14(3/4):69–80.

Davidowitz, E. 1993. The secret life of bisexual husbands. *Redbook* 181(September):114–17, 135.

Dixon, J. K. 1984. The commencement of bisexual activity in swinging married women over age thirty. *Journal of Sex Research* 20:71–90.

Dixon, J. K. 1985. Sexuality and relationship changes in married females following the commencement of bisexual activity. In F. Klein and T. J. Wolf, eds., *Two Lives to Lead: Bisexuality in Men and Women*, pp. 115–33. New York: Harrington Park.

Earl, W. L. 1990. Married men and same-sex activity: A field study on HIV risk among men who do not identify as gay or bisexual. *Journal of Sex and Marital Therapy* 16(4):251–57.

Fox, R. C. 1996. Bisexuality in perspective: A review of theory and research. In B. A. Firestein, ed., *Bisexuality: The Psychology and Politics of an Invisible Minority*, pp. 3–50. Thousand Oaks, Calif.: Sage.

Gelman, D. 1987. A perilous double love life. *Newsweek* (July 13) 110:13, 44–47.

Gerrard, S., and J. Halpin. 1989. The risky business of bisexual love. *Cosmopolitan* (October) 207:203–5.

Gilmartin, B. G. 1978. *The Gilmartin Report*. Secaucus, N.J.: Citadel.

Hedblom, J. H. 1973. Dimensions of lesbian sexual experience. *Archives of Sexual Behavior* 2:329–41.

Heller, A. C. 1987. Is there a man in your man's life? What every girl should know about the bisexual guy. *Mademoiselle* (July) 93:134–35, 153–54.

Humphreys, L. 1970. *Tearoom Trade: Impersonal Sex in Public Restrooms*. Chicago: Aldine.

Hutchins, L. 1996. Bisexuality: Politics and community. In B. A. Firestein, ed., *Bisexuality: The Psychology and Politics of an Invisible Minority*, pp. 240–59. Thousand Oaks, Calif.: Sage.

Hutchins, L., and L. Ka'ahumanu, eds. 1991. *Bi Any Other Name: Bisexual People Speak Out*. Boston: Alyson.

Karlen, A. 1988. *Threesomes: Studies in Sex, Power, and Intimacy*. New York: Morrow.

Klein, F., B. Sepekoff, and T. J. Wolf. 1985. Sexual orientation: A multi-variable dynamic process. In F. Klein and T. J. Wolf, eds., *Two Lives to Lead: Bisexuality in Men and Women*, pp. 35–49. New York: Harrington Park.

Lever, J., D. E. Kanouse, W. H. Rogers, S. Carson, and R. Hertz. 1992. Behavior patterns and sexual identity of bisexual males. *Journal of Sex Research* 29:141–67.

Levine, M. P., and R. R. Troiden. 1988. The myth of sexual compulsivity. *Journal of Sex Research* 25:347–63.

Loewenstein, S. F. 1984/1985. On the diversity of love object orientations among women. *Journal of Social Work and Human Sexuality* 3(2–3):7–24.

MacDonald, A. P., Jr. 1981. Bisexuality: Some comments on research and theory. *Journal of Homosexuality* 6:21–35.

Nichols, M. 1988. Bisexuality in women: Myths, realities, and implications for therapy. *Women and Therapy* 7(2–3):235–52.

Ochs, R. 1996. Biphobia: It goes more than two ways. In B. A. Firestein, ed., *Bisexuality: The Psychology and Politics of an Invisible Minority*, pp. 217–39. Thousand Oaks, Calif.: Sage.

O'Neill, G. C., and N. O'Neill. 1970. Patterns in group sexual activity. *Journal of Sex Research* 6:101–12.

Pincu, L. 1989. Sexual compulsivity in gay men: Controversy and treatment. *Journal of Counseling and Development* 68:63–68.

Ponse, B. 1978. *Identities in the Lesbian World: The Social Construction of Self.* Westport, Conn.: Greenwood.

Quadland, M. C. 1985. Compulsive sexual behavior: Definition of a problem and an approach to treatment. *Journal of Sex and Marital Therapy* 11:121–32.

Quadland, M. C. 1987. AIDS, sexuality, and sexual control. *Journal of Homosexuality* 14(1–2):277–98.

Randolph, L. B. 1988. The hidden fear: Black women, bisexuals, and the AIDS risk. *Ebony* (January).

Rila, M. 1996. Bisexual women and the AIDS crisis. In B. A. Firestein, ed., *Bisexuality: The Psychology and Politics of an Invisible Minority*, pp. 169–84. Thousand Oaks, Calif.: Sage.

Rust, P. C. 1992. The politics of sexual identity: Sexual attraction and behavior among lesbian and bisexual women. *Social Problems* 39:366–86.

Rust, P. C. 1993. Neutralizing the political threat of the marginal woman: Lesbians' beliefs about bisexual women. *Journal of Sex Research* 30:214–28.

Rust, P. C. 1995. *The Challenge of Bisexuality to Lesbian Politics: Sex, Loyalty, and Revolution.* New York: New York University Press.

Saghir, M. T., and E. Robins. 1973. *Male and Female Homosexuality.* Baltimore, Md.: Williams and Wilkins.

Schneider, J. P., and B. H. Schneider. 1990. Marital satisfaction during recovery from self-identified sexual addiction among bisexual men and their wives. *Journal of Sex and Marital Therapy* 16:230–50.

Stokes, J. P., K. Taywaditep, P. Vanable, and D. J. McKirnan. 1996. Bisexual men, sexual behavior, and HIV/AIDS. In B. A. Firestein, ed., *Bisexuality: The Psychology and Politics of an Invisible Minority*, pp. 149–68. Thousand Oaks, Calif.: Sage.

Udis-Kessler, A. 1990. Bisexuality in an essentialist world. In *Bisexuality: A Reader and Sourcebook*, pp. 51–63. Novato, Calif.: Times Change.

Udis-Kessler, A. 1991. Present tense: Biphobia as a crisis of meaning. In L. Hutchins and L. Ka'ahumanu, eds., *Bi Any Other Name: Bisexual People Speak Out*, pp. 350–58. Boston: Alyson.

Weinberg, M. S., C. J. Williams, and D. W. Pryor. 1994. *Dual Attraction: Understanding Bisexuality.* New York: Oxford University Press.

19 Children of Lesbian and Gay Parents

Charlotte J. Patterson

What kinds of home environments are best able to support children's psychological adjustment and growth? This question has long held a central place in the field of research on child development. Researchers in the United States have often assumed that the most favorable home environments are provided by white, middle-class, two-parent families, in which the father is paid to work outside the home but the mother is not. Although rarely stated explicitly, it has most often been assumed that both parents in such families are heterosexual.

Given that smaller numbers of American families fit the traditionally normative pattern (Hernandez 1988; Laosa 1988) today than in earlier years, it is not surprising that researchers have increasingly challenged implicit or explicit criticism of home environments that differ from it by virtue of race, ethnicity, income, household composition, or maternal employment (Harrison et al. 1990; Hetherington and Arasteh 1998; Hoffman 1984; McLoyd 1990; Spencer, Brookins, and Allen 1985). Together with the authors of cross-cultural and historical studies (Cole 1988; Elder 1986; Rogoff 1990), these researchers have emphasized the variety of pathways through which healthy psychological development can take place, and the diversity of home environments that can support such development.

In this chapter, I describe recent research from the social sciences on the personal and social development of children with lesbian and gay parents. Beginning with estimates of the numbers of such children, I then outline sociocultural, theoretical, and legal reasons that justify attention to their development. With this material as background, I then review research evidence on sexual identity, personal development, and social relationships among children of lesbian and gay parents. I first describe research on children of divorced lesbian and gay parents; I then examine research on children born to or adopted by lesbian mothers, describing in some detail the findings from my own Bay Area Families Study. In the final section, I draw a number of conclusions from the results of research to date and offer suggestions for future work.

Perspectives on Lesbian and Gay Parents and Their Children

Interest in children of lesbian and gay parents has emerged from a number of directions (Allen and Demo 1995; Laird 1993; Patterson 1992). For lesbians and gay men, especially those who may be parents themselves or who may be considering parenthood, it is valuable to learn about issues and challenges that are common to lesbian and gay parents and their children. Information about the psychosocial development of children with gay or lesbian parents may also be of interest to clinical psychologists and others who are concerned with processes of coping with prejudice, discrimination, and oppression.

In addition to those just mentioned, there are at least three other perspectives from which interest in children of lesbians or gay men has emerged. First, the phenomenon of openly gay or lesbian parents bearing and/or raising children represents a sociocultural innovation that is unique to the present historical era; as such, it raises questions about the impact of cultural change on children. Second, from the standpoint of psychological theory, children of lesbian or gay parents pose a number of significant questions for existing theories of psychosocial development. Finally, both in adjudication of child-custody disputes and in administration of adoption and foster-care policies, the legal system in the United States has frequently operated under strong assumptions about difficulties that children of lesbians and gay men face, and there are important questions about the veridicality of such assumptions. Before reviewing the results of empirical research, I briefly discuss key issues from each of these three perspectives.

Social and Cultural Issues

Although same-sex attractions and sexual activities have undoubtedly existed throughout history, the emergence of large numbers of openly self-identified gay men and lesbians is a recent phenomenon. Although the beginnings of homophile organizations date to the 1950s and even earlier (D'Emilio 1983; Faderman 1991), the beginnings of contemporary gay liberation movements are generally dated to police raids on the Stonewall Inn Bar in the Greenwich Village neighborhood of New York City in 1969 and to resistance shown by members of the gay community to these raids (Adam 1987; D'Emilio 1983). In the years since these events at the Stonewall, more and more lesbians and gay men have abandoned secrecy, come out of the closet, and joined the movement for gay and lesbian rights (Blumenfeld and Raymond 1988).

With greater openness among lesbian and gay adults, a number of family forms have emerged in which one or more of a child's parents identify themselves as lesbian or gay (Allen and Demo 1995; Baptiste 1987; Martin 1993; Weston 1991). Most are families in which children were born in the context of a heterosexual relationship between the biological parents (Falk 1989). These include families in which the parents divorce when one or both parents come out as lesbian or gay, and families in which one or both of the parents come out as lesbian or gay and the parents decide not to divorce. The gay or lesbian parent may be either the residential or the non-residential parent, or children may live part of the time in both homes. Gay or lesbian parents may be single, or they may have same-sex partners who may or may not take up stepparenting relationships with the children.

In addition to children born in the context of heterosexual relationships between parents, both single and coupled lesbians are believed increasingly to be giving birth to children (Benkov 1994; Laird 1993; Lewin 1993; Martin 1989, 1993; Patterson 1994b; Pies 1985, 1990; Steckel 1985). The majority of such children are believed to be conceived through donor insemination (DI). Although DI techniques have been known for many years, it is only in recent years that they have become widely available to unmarried heterosexual women and to lesbians (Martin 1989, 1993; Pies 1985, 1990). Lesbians who seek to become mothers may also do so by becoming foster or adoptive parents (Laird 1993; Martin 1993; Patterson 1994b, 1995c).

A number of gay men have also sought to become parents after coming out (Bigner and Bozett 1990; Bozett 1989; Patterson and Chan 1996; Ricketts 1991; Ricketts and Achtenberg 1990). Options pursued by such gay men include adoption and foster care of children to whom the men are not biologically related (Patterson 1995c). Through DI or through sexual intercourse, gay men may also become biological fathers of children whom they intend to coparent with a single woman (whether lesbian or heterosexual), with a lesbian couple, or with a gay male partner (Martin 1993; Patterson 1994b).

Thus many children today are being brought up in a diverse array of lesbian and gay families, most of which did not exist as recently as fifty years ago (Allen and Demo 1995; Benkov 1994; Laird 1993; Lewin 1993; Patterson 1995a; Weston 1991). Of the different types of families, those of divorced lesbian mothers living with their children and those of nonresidential gay fathers are probably the largest groups. In addition, the numbers of families in which children are now being conceived by lesbian mothers using DI are unprecedented. The birth and upbringing of children in such families provides a unique opportunity to observe the formation, growth, and impact of new family forms.

Although it is widely believed that family environments exert significant influences on children who grow up in them, authoritative scholarly treatments of such influences have rarely considered children growing up in families with lesbian or gay parents (e.g., Jacob 1987; Parke 1984). Even treatments of nontraditional family forms (e.g., Lamb 1982) have generally failed to consider lesbian and gay parents and their children. Given the many new family forms among lesbian and gay parents, and in view of their apparent vitality, the experiences of children with gay or lesbian parents would seem, however, to be a topic deserving of study. Indeed, newer treatments of parenting and of parent-child relationships are beginning to recognize the existence of lesbian and gay parents and their children (Bornstein 1995; Gottfried and Gottfried 1994; Lamb 1996).

To the extent that parental influences are seen as critical in psychosocial development, and to the extent that lesbians or gay men may provide different kinds of influences than heterosexual parents, then the children of gay men and lesbians can be expected to develop in ways that are different from children of heterosexual parents. Whether any such differences are expected to be beneficial, detrimental, or nonexistent depends, of course, on the viewpoint from which the phenomena are observed. For instance, some feminist theorists have imagined benefits that might accrue to children growing up in an all-female world (e.g., Gilman 1979 [1915]). Expectations based on many psychological theories are, however, more negative.

Theoretical Issues

Theories of psychological development have traditionally emphasized distinctive contributions of both mothers and fathers to the healthy personal and social development of their children. As a result, many theories predict negative outcomes for children who are raised in environments that do not provide these two kinds of input (Nungesser 1980). Thus an important theoretical question concerns the extent to which such predictions are sustained by results of research on children of gay or lesbian parents.

For instance, psychoanalytic theory places heavy weight on the Oedipal drama, in which children experience very different reactions to their mothers and fathers (Bronfenbrenner 1960). From the psychoanalytic perspective, healthy psychological development is believed to require the child's eventual resolution of Oedipal issues. Factors that inhibit or distort this process are therefore thought to be detrimental to the child's development. Recent writers in the psychoanalytic tradition (e.g., Chodorow 1978; Dinnerstein 1976) also emphasize different influences of male and female parents in the socialization of children. From psychoanalytic perspectives, then, when one or both parents are either absent or homosexually oriented, disruptions of personality development for their children could be anticipated.

From the point of view of social learning approaches to personality development (e.g., Huston 1983), children are seen as learning distinctive lessons from the examples and rewards offered by both male and female parents. For example, fathers are thought to model and reward masculine behavior among sons, and mothers to model and reward feminine behavior among daughters. Predictions based on social learning suggest negative outcomes for children brought up in families that do not provide conventional models or rewards for the acquisition of sexual identities.

There have been significant challenges to these theoretical positions, especially from cognitive developmental theory (Kohlberg 1966) and from gender schema theory (Bem 1983), neither of which requires, in principle, that a child's home environment include both heterosexual male and heterosexual female parents in order to support favorable development. Advocates of cognitive developmental and gender schema theory have not, however, discussed the assumption that children's development is best fostered in families that contain both male and female parents nor have they challenged the premise that development is optimal in families where the parents are heterosexual.

In short, psychoanalytic and social learning theories of personal and social development during childhood emphasize the importance of children having both heterosexual male and heterosexual female parents, and they predict generally negative outcomes for children whose parents do not exemplify these qualities. Although cognitive developmental theory and gender schema theory do not require such assumptions, proponents of these views have not challenged them. As a result, these perspectives on individual differences in personal and social development are commonly believed to predict difficulties in development among children of lesbian and gay parents. Empirical research with such children thus provides an opportunity to evaluate anew these theoretical assumptions.

Legal and Public Policy Issues

The legal system in the United States has long been hostile to gay men and lesbians who are parents or who wish to become parents (Brantner 1992; Cain 1993; Editors of the *Harvard Law Review* 1990; Falk 1989, 1994; Hitchens 1979/1980; Kleber, Howell, and Tibbets-Kleber 1986; Patterson and Redding 1996; Polikoff 1990; Ricketts and Achtenberg 1990; Rivera 1991). Because of judicial and legislative assumptions about adverse effects of parental homosexuality on children, lesbian mothers and gay fathers have often been denied custody or visitation with their children following divorce (Editors of the *Harvard Law Review* 1990; Falk 1989, 1994; Patterson and Redding 1996; Rivera 1991). Although some states now have laws stipulating that sexual orientation is not relevant to determinations of parental fitness in custody disputes, in other states parents who admit a gay or lesbian sexual orientation are presumed to be unfit as parents (Brantner 1992; Editors of the *Harvard Law Review* 1990). In addition, regulations governing foster care and adoption in many states have made it difficult for lesbians or gay men to adopt children or to serve as foster parents (Patterson 1995c; Ricketts 1991; Ricketts and Achtenberg 1990).

One issue underlying both judicial decision making in custody litigation and public policies governing foster care and adoption has been questions concerning the fitness of lesbians and gay men to be parents (Falk 1989, 1994). In particular, courts have sometimes assumed that gay men and lesbians are mentally ill and hence not fit to be parents, that lesbians are less maternal than heterosexual women and hence do not make good mothers, and that lesbians' and gay men's relationships with sexual partners leave little time for ongoing parent-child interaction (Patterson and Redding, in press).

Although systematic empirical study of these issues is just beginning, results of research to date have failed to confirm any of these fears. The idea that homosexuality constitutes a mental illness or disorder has long been repudiated both by the American Psychological Association and by the American Psychiatric Association (Blumenfeld and Raymond 1988). Lesbians and heterosexual women have been found not to differ markedly either in their overall mental health or in their approaches to child rearing nor have lesbians' romantic and sexual relationships with other women been found to detract from their ability to care for their children (Falk 1989, 1994; Patterson 1995d). Research on gay fathers has been similarly unable to unearth any reasons to believe that they are unfit as parents (Barret and Robinson 1990; Bozett 1980, 1989; Patterson and Chan 1996). Studies in this area are still rather scarce, and more information would be helpful. On the basis of research to date, though, negative assumptions about lesbian and gay adults' fitness as parents appear to be without foundation (Cramer 1986; Crawford 1987; Falk 1989, 1994; Gibbs 1988; Patterson 1995a, 1995d).

In addition to judicial concerns about gay and lesbian parents themselves, there are three major kinds of fears about the impact of lesbian or gay parents on children that are reflected in judicial decision making about child custody and in public policies such as regulations governing foster care and adoption policies. I outline each of the areas of concern here; in the review of empirical literature which follows, I describe research findings relevant to each of these issues. (For further discussion of these issues, see Patterson 1995c and Patterson and Redding 1996.)

The first area of judicial concern is that development of sexual identity will be impaired among children of lesbian or gay parents (Falk 1989, 1994; Patterson 1992, 1995a). For instance, it is feared that children brought up by gay fathers or lesbian mothers will show disturbances in gender identity or in gender-role behavior. It is also feared that children brought up by lesbian mothers or gay fathers will themselves become gay or lesbian, an outcome the courts view as undesirable.

A second category of judicial concern about the influences of lesbian or gay parents on their children involves aspects of personal development other than sexual identity. For example, courts have expressed fears that children in the custody of gay or lesbian parents will be more vulnerable to mental breakdown or that they will exhibit more adjustment difficulties and behavioral problems. It is also feared that these children will be less psychologically healthy or less well adjusted than children growing up in homes with heterosexual parents.

A third category of specific fears expressed by the courts is that children of lesbian and gay parents may experience difficulties in social relationships. For example, judges have repeatedly expressed concern that children living with lesbian mothers may be stigmatized, teased, or otherwise traumatized by peers. Another common fear is that children living with gay or lesbian parents may be more likely to be sexually abused by the parent or by the parent's friends or acquaintances.

Because such negative assumptions have often been explicit in judicial determinations when child custody has been denied to lesbian and gay parents or when visitation with gay or lesbian parents has been curtailed (Falk 1989, 1994; Patterson and Redding, in press), and because such assumptions are open to empirical testing, they provide an important impetus for research. Given the enormous significance of custody determinations in the lives of lesbian mothers, gay fathers, and their children, it is essential that evidence regarding oft-expressed judicial assumptions be examined with care.

Summary

There are thus a number of perspectives from which interest in lesbian and gay parents and their children has emerged. In the next sections, I review the available research findings on children of lesbian and gay parents. I first describe research on children who were born in the context of heterosexual relationships between parents. In the majority of these families, the parents were married at the time of the children's birth or adoption, then divorced after one or both parents came out, and, for this reason, I refer to them as divorced lesbian and gay parents and their children. A review of research on children of divorced lesbian and gay parents is followed by a description of work on children born to or adopted early in life by parents who had already identified as lesbian or gay.

Children of Divorced Lesbian and Gay Parents

Much of the impetus for early research on children of lesbian and gay parents has been generated by judicial concerns about the psychosocial development of children residing with gay or lesbian parents. Research in each of three main areas of judicial concern, namely, children's sexual identity, other aspects of children's personal development, and children's social relationships, will be summarized here. (For other recent reviews of this material, see Cramer 1986; Crawford 1987; Falk 1989, 1994; Gibbs 1988; Green and Bozett 1991; Patterson 1992, 1995a; and Tasker and Golombok 1991.)

Reflecting issues relevant in the largest number of custody disputes, most of the research compares development of children with custodial lesbian mothers to that of children with custodial heterosexual mothers. Since many children living in lesbian mother-headed households have undergone the experience of parental divorce and separation, it has been widely believed that children living in families headed by divorced but heterosexual mothers provide the best comparison group. Although some studies focus exclusively on children of gay men or lesbians (Green 1978; Paul 1986), most compare children in divorced lesbian mother-headed families with children in divorced heterosexual mother-headed families.

Sexual Identity

Following Money and Ehrhardt (1972), I considered research on three aspects of sexual identity here; gender identity, gender-role behavior, and sexual orientation. Gender identity concerns a person's self-identification as male or female. Gender-role behavior concerns the extent to which a person's activities, occupations, and the like are regarded by the culture as masculine, feminine, or both. Sexual orientation refers to a person's attraction to and choice of sexual partners (e.g., heterosexual, homosexual, or bisexual). To examine the possibility that children in the custody of divorced lesbian mothers or gay fathers experience disruptions of sexual identity, I describe research findings relevant to each of these three major areas of concern.

Research on gender identity has failed to reveal any differences in the development of children as a function of their parents' sexual orientation. In one of the earliest studies, Kirkpatrick, Smith, and Roy (1981) compared the development of twenty elementary-school-aged children of lesbian mothers to that of twenty children of the same age of heterosexual mothers. In projective testing, as expected, most children in both groups drew a same-sex figure first. Of those who drew an opposite-sex figure first, only three (one with a lesbian mother and two with heterosexual mothers) showed concern about gender issues in clinical interviews. Similar findings have been reported in projective testing by other investigators (Green 1978; Green et al. 1986). Studies using more direct methods of assessment (e.g., Golombok, Spencer, and Rutter 1983) have yielded similar results. No evidence for difficulties in gender identity among children of lesbian mothers has been reported.

Research on gender-role behavior has also failed to reveal difficulties in the development of children with lesbian or gay parents. Green (1978) reported that twenty of twenty-one children of lesbian mothers in his sample named a favorite toy consistent with conventional sex-typed toy preferences and that all twenty-one children reported vocational choices within typical limits for conventional sex roles. Results consistent with those described by Green have also been reported for children by Golombok et al. (1983), Hoeffer (1981), and Kirkpatrick et al. (1981); and for adult daughters of lesbian mothers, by Gottman (1990). In interviews with fifty-six children of lesbians and forty-eight children of heterosexual mothers, Green et al. (1986) found no differences with respect to favorite television programs, television characters, games, or toys. These investigators did, however, report that daughters of lesbian mothers were more likely to be described as taking part in rough-and-tumble play or as playing with "masculine" toys such as trucks or guns but found no comparable differences for sons. In all these studies, the behavior and preferences of children in unconventional families were seen as falling within conventional limits.

Rees (1979) administered the Bem Sex-Role Inventory to a group of young adolescent offspring of lesbian mothers and a group of youngsters of the same age with heterosexual mothers. Although children of lesbian and heterosexual mothers did not differ on masculinity or on androgyny, adolescent offspring of lesbian mothers reported greater psychological femininity than did their same-aged peers with heterosexual mothers. This result would seem to run counter to expectations based on stereotypes of lesbians as lacking in femininity. Overall, research has failed to reveal any notable difficulties in the development of sex-role behavior among children of lesbian mothers.

A number of investigators have also studied sexual orientation, the third component of sexual identity. For instance, Huggins (1989) interviewed thirty-six youngsters who were between thirteen and nineteen years of age; half were the offspring of lesbian mothers and half had mothers who were heterosexual in their orientation. No child of a lesbian mother identified as lesbian or gay, but one child of a heterosexual mother did; this difference was not statistically significant. Similar results have been reported by Golombok and her colleagues (1983), Gottman (1990), Green (1978), Paul (1986), and Rees (1979), and by Tasker and Golombok (1995); some children of lesbian mothers have identified themselves as gay, lesbian, or bisexual, but their numbers did not exceed expectations based on presumed population base rates. Studies of the offspring of gay fathers have yielded similar results (Bozett 1980, 1982, 1987, 1989; Miller 1979; Patterson and Chan 1996).

Despite the consistency of the findings, this research can be criticized on a variety of grounds. For instance, many lesbians do not self-identify as such until adulthood (Brown 1995; Kitzinger and Wilkinson 1995); for this reason, studies of sexual orientation among adolescents may count as heterosexual some individuals who will come out as lesbian later in life. Concern has also been voiced that in many studies comparing children of divorced heterosexual mothers with children of divorced lesbian mothers, lesbian mothers were more likely to be living with a romantic partner; in these cases, maternal sexual orientation and household composition variables have been confounded. Although these and other methodological issues still await resolution, it remains true that no significant problems in the development of sexual identity among children of lesbian mothers have yet been identified.

Other Aspects of Personal Development

Studies of other aspects of personal development among children of gay and lesbian parents have assessed psychiatric and behavioral problems (Golombok et al. 1983; Kirkpatrick et al. 1981), personality (Gottman 1990), self-concept (Huggins 1989; Puryear 1983), locus of control (Puryear 1983; Rees 1979), moral judgment (Rees 1979), and intelligence (Green et al. 1986). As was true for sexual identity, studies of other aspects of personal development have revealed no significant differences between children of lesbian or gay parents and children of heterosexual parents.

Social Relationships

Studies assessing potential differences between children of lesbian and gay versus heterosexual parents have sometimes included assessments of children's social relationships. Because of concerns voiced by the courts that children of lesbian and gay parents might encounter difficulties among their peers, the most common focus of attention has been on peer relations. Studies in this area have consistently found that school-aged children of lesbian mothers report a predominantly same-sex peer group, and that the quality of their peer relations is described by their mothers and by the investigators as good (Golombok et al. 1983; Green 1978; Green et al. 1986). Anecdotal and first-person accounts describe children's worries about being stigmatized as a result of their parents' sexual orientation (Pollack and Vaughn 1987; Rafkin 1990), but available research provides no evidence for the proposition that the development of children of lesbian mothers is compromised by difficulties in peer relations. In fact, a recent study of adult children of divorced lesbian mothers found that they recalled no more teasing by peers during childhood than did adult children of divorced heterosexual parents (Tasker and Golombok 1995).

Research has also been directed toward description of children's relationships with adults, especially fathers. For instance, Golombok et al. (1983) found that children of lesbian mothers were more likely than children of heterosexual mothers to have contact with their fathers. Most children of lesbian mothers had some contact with their father during the year preceding the study, but most children of heterosexual mothers had not; indeed, almost a third of the children of lesbian mothers reported at least weekly contact with their fathers, whereas only one in twenty of the children of heterosexual mothers reported this. Kirkpatrick and her colleagues (1981) also reported that lesbian mothers in their sample were more concerned than heterosexual mothers that their children have opportunities for good relationships with adult men, including fathers. Lesbian mothers' own social networks have been found to include both men and women, and their offspring as a result have contact with adults of both sexes. Hare and Richards (1993) reported that the great majority (90 percent) of children living with divorced lesbian mothers in their sample also had contact with their fathers. Overall, results of the meager research to date suggest that children of lesbian parents have satisfactory relationships with adults of both sexes.

Concerns that children of lesbian or gay parents are more likely than children of heterosexual parents to be sexually abused have also been voiced by judges in the context of child-custody disputes. Results of research in this area show that the great majority of adults who perpetrate sexual abuse are male; sexual abuse of children by adult women is very rare (Finkelhor and Russell 1984; Jones and MacFarlane 1980). Lesbian mothers are thus extremely unlikely to expose their children to sexual abuse. Moreover, the overwhelming majority of child sexual abuse cases involve an adult male abusing a young female (Jenny, Roesler, and Poyer 1994; Jones and MacFarlane 1980). Gay men are no more likely than heterosexual men to perpetrate child sexual abuse (Groth and Birnbaum 1978; Jenny et al. 1994). Fears that children in custody of gay or lesbian parents might be at heightened risk for sexual abuse are thus without empirical foundation.

In summary, then, results of research to date suggest that children of divorced lesbian and gay parents have normal relationships with peers and that their contacts with adults of both sexes are satisfactory. Thus the picture

of children with divorced lesbian and gay parents emerging from this research is one of general engagement in social life with peers, with parents,
and with adult relatives and friends of both genders.

Diversity Among Children with Divorced Lesbian or Gay Parents

Despite the tremendous diversity of gay and lesbian communities
(Blumenfeld and Raymond 1988), research on individual differences among
children of divorced lesbian and gay parents is still very limited. Here I focus
on the impact of parental psychological and relationship status, as well as
on the influence of other stresses and supports.

One important dimension of variability among gay and lesbian families
concerns whether the custodial parent is involved in a romantic relationship
and, if so, what implications this may have for children. Pagelow (1980),
Kirkpatrick et al. (1981), and Golombok et al. (1983) all reported that divorced lesbian mothers were more likely than divorced heterosexual mothers
to be living with a romantic partner. Huggins (1989) reported that self-
esteem among daughters of lesbian mothers whose lesbian partners lived
with them was higher than that among daughters of lesbian mothers who
did not live with a partner. This finding might be interpreted to mean that
mothers who are high in self-esteem are more likely to be involved in romantic relationships and to have daughters who are also high in self-esteem,
but many other interpretations are also possible. In view of the small sample
size and absence of conventional statistical tests, Huggins's finding should
be interpreted with caution. In view of the judicial attention that lesbian
mothers' romantic relationships have received during custody proceedings
(Falk 1989; Hitchens 1979/1980; Kirkpatrick 1987), however, it is surprising
that more research has not examined the impact of this variable on children.

Rand, Graham, and Rawlings (1982) found that divorced lesbian mothers'
sense of psychological well-being was related to the extent to which they
were open about their lesbian identity with employers, ex-husbands, and
children. In this sample, a mother who felt more able to disclose her lesbian
identity was also more likely to express a greater sense of well-being. In light
of the consistent finding that children's adjustment in heterosexual families
is often related to maternal mental health (Rutter, Izard, and Read 1986;
Sameroff and Chandler 1975), one might expect factors that enhance mental health among lesbian mothers also to benefit these women's children.

Another area of great diversity among families with a gay or lesbian parent concerns the degree to which a parent's sexual identity is accepted by other significant people in children's lives (Casper, Schultz, and Wickens 1992). Huggins (1989) found a tendency for children whose fathers were rejecting of maternal lesbianism to report lower self-esteem than those whose fathers were neutral or positive. Because of the small sample size and absence of conventional statistical tests, however, this finding should be seen as suggestive rather than definitive. Huggins's results raise questions about the extent to which reactions of important adults in a child's environment can influence responses to discovery of a parent's gay or lesbian identity.

Effects of the age at which children learn of parents' gay or lesbian identities have also been a topic of study. Paul (1986) reported that those who were told either in childhood or in late adolescence found the news easier to cope with than those who first learned of it during early to middle adolescence. Huggins (1989) reported that those who learned of maternal lesbianism in childhood had higher self-esteem than those who were not informed until adolescence. Some writers have suggested that early adolescence is a particularly difficult time for children to learn of their parents' lesbian or gay identities (Baptiste 1987; Lewis 1980).

As this brief review reveals, research on diversity among families with gay and lesbian parents is just beginning (Freiberg 1990; Martin 1989, 1993; Patterson 1995a). Existing data favor early disclosure of identity to children, positive maternal mental health, and a supportive milieu, but the available data are still limited. No information is yet available on differences stemming from race or ethnicity, family economic circumstances, cultural environments, or related variables. Because none of the published work has employed observational measures or longitudinal designs, little is known about behavior within these families or about any changes over time. Clearly much remains to be learned about differences among gay and lesbian families and about the impact these differences have on children growing up in these homes.

Children Born to or Adopted by Lesbian Mothers: The Bay Area Families Study

Although many writers have recently noted an increase in childbearing among lesbians, research with these families is still very new (Patterson 1992, 1994a, 1994b, 1995a, 1995e; Polikoff 1990; Pollack and Vaughn 1987; Riley 1988; Weston 1991). In this section I summarize the research to date on children born to or adopted by lesbian mothers. Although some gay men are also undertaking parenthood after coming out (Patterson and Chan 1996), no research has yet been reported on their children.

In one of the first systematic studies of children born to lesbians, Steckel (1985, 1987) compared the progress of separation-individuation among eleven preschool children born via DI to lesbian couples to that among eleven preschool children of heterosexual couples. Using parent interviews, parent and teacher Q-sorts, and structured doll-play techniques, Steckel compared independence, ego functions, and object relations among children in the two types of families. Her main results documented impressive similarity in development among children in the two groups. Similar findings, based on extensive interviews with five lesbian-mother families were also reported by McCandlish (1987).

Steckel (1985, 1987) did, however, report some suggestive differences between groups. Children of heterosexual parents saw themselves as somewhat more aggressive than did children of lesbians, and they were seen by both parents and teachers as more bossy, domineering, and negativistic. Children of lesbian parents, on the other hand, saw themselves as more lovable and were seen by parents and teachers as more affectionate, more responsive, and more protective toward younger children. In view of the small sample size and the large number of statistical tests performed, these results must be considered suggestive rather than definitive. Steckel's work is, however, the first to make systematic comparisons of development among children born to lesbian and to heterosexual couples.

More recently Flaks et al. (1995) compared social and personal development among fifteen three- to nine-year-old children born to lesbian couples via DI with that among fifteen children from matched, two-parent heterosexual families. Across a wide array of assessments of cognitive and behavioral functioning, there were notable similarities between the children of lesbian and heterosexual parents. The only significant difference between the two groups was in the area of parenting skills and practices; lesbian couples revealed more parenting skills than did heterosexual couples.

In this context, I designed the Bay Area Families Study to contribute to understanding children born to lesbian mothers. In this section I describe the study itself and its principal results to date; they fall into four major areas. First, I describe demographic and other characteristics of the participating families. Next, I describe assessments of the adjustment of both mothers and children, relative to normative expectations based on large comparison samples drawn from the population at large. In families that were headed by lesbian couples, the study also examined key facets of couple functioning (e.g., relationship satisfaction, division of labor), and I report normative findings in this area. The study also explored individual differences in children's adjustment, and their correlates, and I present these findings next. Finally, the study examined the degree to which children in participating families have contact with grandparents and other members of the extended family, and I present these findings as well. Although I do not provide statistical details here, all findings described as statistically significant were at the $p = .05$ level. The methods and findings are summarized briefly, but additional details and commentary are available elsewhere (see Patterson 1994a, 1995b, 1995f; Patterson and Kosmitzki 1995). There were no significant sex differences in the data presented here, so my presentation does not consider this variable.

Description of Participating Families

Families were eligible to participate in the Bay Area Families Study if they met each of three criteria. First, at least one child between four and nine years of age had to be present in the home. Second, the child had to have been born to or adopted by a lesbian mother or mothers. Third, only families who lived within the greater San Francisco Bay Area (e.g., San Francisco, Oakland, and San Jose) were eligible.

Recruitment began when I contacted friends, acquaintances, and colleagues who might be likely to know eligible lesbian-mother families. I described the proposed research and solicited help in locating families. From names gathered in this way, I telephoned each family to describe the study and ask for their participation. In all, I made contact with thirty-nine eligible families, of whom thirty-seven participated in the study. Thus approximately 95 percent of the eligible families who were contacted did take part. Participation involved a single home visit during which all the data reported here were collected.

Twenty-six of the thirty-seven participating families (70 percent) were headed by a lesbian couple. Seven families (19 percent) were headed by a single mother living with her child. In four families (11 percent), the child had been born to a lesbian couple who had since separated, and the child was in de facto joint custody (i.e., living part of the time with one mother and part of the time with the other mother). In this last group of families, one mother was out of town during the period of testing and so did not participate.

Sixty-six lesbian mothers took part in the study. Their ages ranged from twenty-eight to fifty-three years, with a mean age of 39.6 years of age. Sixty-one (92 percent) described themselves as white or non-Hispanic Caucasian, two (3 percent) as Afro-American or black, and three (4 percent) as coming from other racial/ethnic backgrounds. Most were well educated; 74 percent had received college degrees, and 48 percent had received graduate degrees.

The great majority of mothers (94 percent) were employed on a regular basis outside the home, and about half said that they worked forty hours or more per week. Most (62 percent) of the women were in professional oc-cupations (e.g., law, nursing), but others were in technical or mechanical occupations such as car repair (9 percent), business or sales such as real estate (9 percent), or in other occupations such as artist (14 percent). Only four mothers were not employed outside the home. Thirty-four families reported family incomes of more than $30,000 per year, and seventeen fam-ilies reported incomes of more than $60,000 per year.

In each family the focal child was between four and nine years of age (mean age, six years, two months); there were nineteen girls and eighteen boys. Thirty-four of the children were born to lesbian mothers, and three had been adopted. Thirty of the children were described by their mothers as white or non-Hispanic Caucasian, three as Hispanic, and four as some other racial/ethnic heritage.

Some additional descriptive information was also collected. Mothers were asked to explain the circumstances surrounding the child's conception, birth, or adoption. Mothers were also asked about the child's biological father or sperm donor, the degree to which the mothers had knowledge of his identity or contact with him, and the degree to which the focal child had such knowledge or contact. In addition, mothers were asked to give the child's last name and to explain how the child had been given that name.

The mothers' accounts of the conception, birth, or adoption of their chil-dren made clear that, in general, the focal children were very much wanted. The average amount of time that it took for biological mothers to conceive focal children after they began to attempt to become pregnant was ten months. Adoptive mothers reported that, on average, the adoption process took approximately twelve months. In the great majority of cases, these les-bian mothers had devoted considerable time and effort to making the birth or adoption of their children possible.

There was tremendous variability in the amount of information that fam-ilies had about the donor or biological father of the focal child. In seventeen families (46 percent), the child had been conceived via DI with sperm from an anonymous donor (e.g., sperm that had been provided by a sperm bank or clinic). In these cases families had only very limited information (e.g., race, height, weight, hair color) about the donor, and none knew the donor's name. In ten families (27 percent), the child was conceived via DI, with sperm provided by a known donor (e.g., a family friend). In four families (11 percent), children were conceived when the biological mother had intercourse with a man. In three families (8 percent), the child was adopted. In the three remaining families, some other set of circumstances applied, or the parents acknowledged that the child had been born to one of the mothers but preferred not to disclose any additional information about their child's conception.

Mothers reported relatively little contact with biological fathers or donors. Most of the families (62 percent) reported no contact at all with the biological father or donor during the previous year. Only ten families (27 percent) had had two or more contacts with the biological father or sperm donor during the previous year.

Given that many families did not know the identity of the child's sperm donor or biological father, and that most currently had little or no contact with him, it is not surprising that the donor or biological father's role with the child was described by mothers as being quite limited. In the majority of families (60 percent), mothers reported that the donor or biological father had no special role vis-à-vis the child; this figure includes the families in which the sperm donor had been anonymous. In a minority of families (35 percent), the biological father's identity was known to parents and children, but he took the role of a family friend rather than that of a father. There were only two families in which the biological father was acknowledged as such and in which he was described as assuming a father's role.

Questions about selection of the child's last name are of particular interest in families headed by lesbian couples. In this sample, the majority of children — twenty-six, or 70 percent — bore the last names of their biological or adoptive mothers; this figure includes children in four families in which *all* family members (i.e., both mothers and all children) shared the same last name. In seven families, children had been given hyphenated last names, created from the two mothers' last names. Finally, in four families, children had some other last name.

Thus the families who participated in the Bay Area Families Study were mostly white, well educated, and relatively affluent. Almost every mother was employed, and many were in professions. Most children had been conceived via donor insemination, and most had little or no contact with the sperm donor or biological father.

Mental Health of Mothers and Their Children

For purposes of presentation, I will refer to the biological or legal adoptive mother in each family as the "biological mother," and the other mother, if any, as the "nonbiological mother." In what follows I describe first the assessment procedures and results for mothers and then turn to those for children (for details, see Patterson 1994a and Patterson and Kosmitzki 1995).

Assessment of Maternal Self-Esteem and Adjustment   Maternal self-esteem was assessed using the Rosenberg Self-Esteem Scale (Rosenberg 1979). This scale consists of ten statements, with four response alternatives, indicating the respondent's degree of agreement with each statement. Results were tabulated to obtain total scores, based on the recommendations contained in Rosenberg (1979).

Maternal adjustment was assessed using the Derogatis Symptom Checklist — Revised (SCL-90-R; Derogatis 1983), which consists of ninety items addressing a variety of psychological and somatic symptoms. Each respondent rated the extent to which she had been distressed by each symptom during the past week (0 = Not at all; 4 = Extremely). Nine subscales (i.e., anger/hostility, anxiety, depression, interpersonal sensitivity, obsessive-compulsiveness, paranoid ideation, phobic anxiety, psychoticism, and somatization) were scored, as well as a global severity index (GSI), which summarized the respondent's overall level of distress.

Results for Maternal Self-Esteem and Adjustment   Total scores on the Rosenberg Self-Esteem Scale were calculated for each mother, following the method described by Rosenberg (1979). The means for both biological and nonbiological mothers were almost identical, and both were well within the range of normal functioning. These results (see Table 19.1) indicate that lesbian mothers who took part in this research reported generally positive views about themselves.

For the Derogatis SCL-90, nine subscale scores and one GSI for each mother were computed, and then average scores on each measure both for biological and nonbiological mothers were calculated (Derogatis 1983). Mean scores for biological and nonbiological mothers were virtually identical for most subscales as well as for the GSI, and they were all well within a normal range (see Table 19.1). None of the scores deviated substantially from the expected mean, indicating that lesbian mothers' reports of symptoms are no greater and no smaller than those expected for any other group

TABLE 19.1 Means and T-Scores of SCL-90-R Subscales and Rosenberg Self-Esteem Scale for Biological and Nonbiological Mothers

	Biological mothers		Nonbiological mothers	
	Mean	T-score[a]	Mean	T-Score
Anger/hostility	.36	55	.31	52
Anxiety	.29	52	.24	51
Depression	.40	53	.43	53
Interpersonal sensitivity	.33	53	.36	54
Obsessive-compulsiveness	.31	50	.51	54
Paranoid ideation	.32	52	.25	52
Phobic anxiety	.01	44	.12	53
Psychoticism	.11	53	.11	53
Somatization	.29	50	.32	50
Global severity index (GSI)	.34	53	.38	55
Rosenberg Self-Esteem	16.00		16.10	

[a]T-scores based on norms of nonpatient group according to Derogatis (1983); T-scores for Rosenberg scale were not available. Reprinted from Patterson and Kosmitzki 1995.

of women of the same age. Thus the results for maternal adjustment revealed that lesbian mothers who took part in the Bay Area Families Study reported few symptoms and good self-esteem.

Assessment of Children's Adjustment   To assess levels of child social competence and of child behavior problems, the Child Behavior Checklist (CBCL) (Achenbach and Edelbrock 1983) was administered (Patterson 1994a). The CBCL was selected because of its ability to discriminate children in the clinical versus normative range of functioning for both internalizing (e.g., inhibited, overcontrolled behavior) and externalizing (e.g., aggressive, antisocial, or undercontrolled behavior) problems, as well as in social competence. It is designed to be completed by parents. In the present study, all participating mothers completed this instrument.

Norms for the CBCL (Achenbach and Edelbrock 1983) were obtained from heterogeneous normal samples of two hundred four- to five year olds and six hundred six- to eleven year olds, as well as from equivalent numbers of children at each age who were drawn from clinical populations (e.g., those receiving services from community mental health centers, private psychological and psychiatric clinics or practices, etc.). For purposes of the present research, mean scores reported by Achenbach and Edelbrock (1983:210–14) were averaged across four- to five- and six- to eleven-year-old age levels to provide estimates of average scores for social competence, internalizing, externalizing, and total behavioral problems among normative and clinical populations at the ages studied here. To assess the extent of their resemblance to normal and clinical populations, then, scores for children in the current sample were compared to these figures.

Assessment of children's self-concepts was accomplished using five scales from Eder's Children's Self-View Questionnaire (CSVQ) (Eder 1990). These scales, designed especially to assess psychological concepts of self among three- to eight-year-old children, assess five different dimensions of children's views of themselves. The Aggression scale assessed the degree to which children saw themselves as likely to hurt or frighten others. The Social Closeness scale assessed the degree to which children enjoyed being with people and preferred to be around others. The Social Potency scale assessed the degree to which children liked to stand out or be the center of attention or both. The Stress Reaction scale assessed the extent to which children said they often felt scared, upset, and/or angry. Finally, the Well-Being scale assessed the degree to which children felt joyful, content, and comfortable with themselves. Using hand puppets, the CSVQ was administered individually to participating children, and their answers were tape-recorded for later scoring.

Children's sex-role behavior preferences were assessed in a standard, open-ended interview format, such as that employed in earlier research on children of divorced lesbian mothers (e.g., Golombok et al. 1983; Green 1978; Green et al. 1986). The interviewer explained to each child that she was interested in learning more about the friends and other children that he or she liked to play with, and about his or her favorite toys and other things. She then asked each child to name the friends and other children he or she liked to play with. Following this, each child was asked to name his or her favorite toys, favorite games, and favorite characters on television, in movies, or in books. The interviewer wrote down each of the children's responses. Children's responses were also tape-recorded, and the interviewer's notes were later checked for accuracy against the audiotapes.

After testing had been completed, each child's answers for each of four topics (peer friendships, favorite toys, favorite games, and favorite characters) were coded into one of four categories with regard to their sex-role relevant qualities. The four categories were "Mainly same-sex" (e.g., a boy reports having mostly or entirely male friends), "Mixed sexes" (e.g., an even or almost even mix of sexes in the friends mentioned by a child), "Opposite sex" (e.g., a girl reports having mostly or entirely male friends), and "Can't tell" (e.g., an answer was unscorable, or not clearly sex-typed — for instance, children saying that playing Chutes and Ladders was one of their favorite games). Because children's play groups are known to be highly sex-segregated at this age, children were expected to give mainly "Same sex" answers to these questions.

Results for Children's Adjustment   As expected, social competence among children with lesbian mothers was rated as normal (see Figure 19.1). Scores for children of lesbian mothers were significantly higher than those for Achenbach and Edelbrock's (1983) clinical sample but were not different from those for the normal sample. This was true for reports given by both mothers in the lesbian-mother families (Patterson 1994a).

Results for behavioral problems revealed the same pattern. For internalizing (see Figure 19.2), externalizing (see Figure 19.3), and total behavioral problems, scores for children of lesbian mothers were significantly lower than those for children in the clinical sample but did not differ from those in the normal sample. This was true of reports given by both mothers in the lesbian mother families. Overall, then, the behavioral problems of lesbian mothers' children were rated as significantly smaller in magnitude than those of children in the clinical sample and as no greater than those of children in the normal sample.

On three scales of the Eder CSVQ, there were no significant differences between the self-reports of children of lesbian mothers compared to those of Eder's (1990) heterosexual mothers. Specifically, there were no significant differences between children of lesbian and heterosexual mothers on self-concepts relevant to aggression, social closeness, and social potency. Children of lesbian mothers in the present sample saw themselves as neither more or less aggressive, sociable, or likely to enjoy being the center of attention than did children of heterosexual mothers in Eder's sample.

On two scales, however, differences did emerge between children of lesbian and heterosexual mothers (see Figure 19.4). Specifically, children of lesbian mothers reported greater reactions to stress than did children of het-

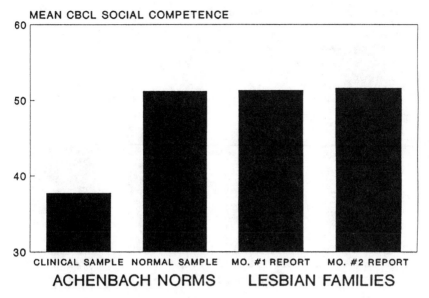

FIGURE 19.1 Mean Child Behavior Checklist Social Competence Scores *(data from Patterson 1994a).*

erosexual mothers, and they also reported a greater overall sense of well-being than did children of heterosexual mothers. In other words, children of lesbian mothers said that they more often felt angry, scared, or upset but also said that they more often felt joyful, content, and comfortable with themselves than did children of heterosexual mothers.

The aspect of children's sexual identity studied here was that of preferences for sex-role behavior. As expected (Green 1978), most children reported preferences for sex-role behaviors that are considered to be normative at this age (see Table 19.2). For instance, every child reported that his or her group of friends was mainly or entirely made up of same-sex children. The great majority of children also reported favorite toys and favorite characters (e.g., from books, movies, or television) that were of the same sex. In the case of favorite games, a number of children mentioned games that were not clearly sex-typed (e.g., board games such as Chutes and Ladders) and hence were not categorizable; however, the great majority mentioned games that are generally associated with their own rather than with the opposite sex. In short, preferences for sex-role behavior among the children of lesbian mothers studied here appeared to be quite typical for children of these ages.

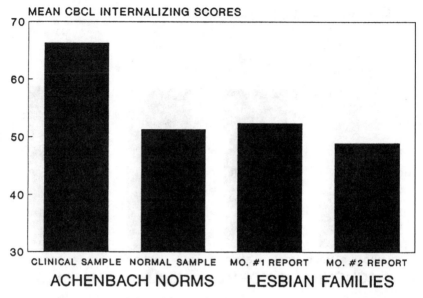

FIGURE 19.2 Mean Child Behavior Checklist Internalizing Behavior Problem Scores *(data from Patterson 1994a)*.

Couple Functioning

Couple functioning was assessed among the twenty-six participating families that were headed by a lesbian couple (Patterson 1995b). In this section the assessment instruments are described first, followed by results for the couples who took part in the study.

Assessment of Couple Functioning   To assess division of labor as well as satisfaction with role arrangements in each family, an adapted form of the "Who Does What?" for parents of five-year-olds (Cowan and Cowan 1990, 1992) was administered to each adult respondent (Patterson 1995b).

The instrument began with thirteen items concerning the division of household labor (e.g., planning and preparing meals, cleaning up after meals). Respondents were asked to decide for each item "How it is now" and "How I would like it to be" on a scale of 1 to 9, in which 1 meant "She does it all" and 9 meant "I do it all." These are referred to as the "real" and "ideal" divisions of labor, respectively. At the bottom of that page, each

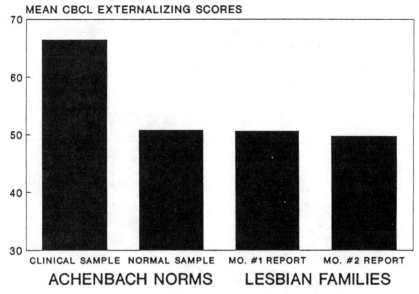

FIGURE 19.3 Mean Child Behavior Checklist Externalizing Behavior Problem Scores *(data from Patterson 1994a).*

respondent was asked to indicate how satisfied overall she was with "the way you and your partner divide family tasks," and with "the way you and your partner divide work outside the family"; in each of these two cases, scores ranged from 1 ("Very dissatisfied") to 5 ("Very satisfied").

The next page contained twelve items about family decision making (e.g., decisions about major expenses, deciding which friends and family to see). Respondents were again asked to indicate the real and ideal division of labor. At the bottom of this second page, each respondent was asked to indicate on a 5-point scale how satisfied she was overall with "the way you and your partner divide family decisions."

The third page contained twenty items about child-care responsibilities (e.g., playing with our child, disciplining our child, picking up after our child). Respondents were again asked to indicate the real and ideal divisions of labor for each item.

The fourth page contained four questions about overall evaluations of child-care responsibilities. Respondents were asked to rate their own and their partner's overall involvement with their child on a scale running from

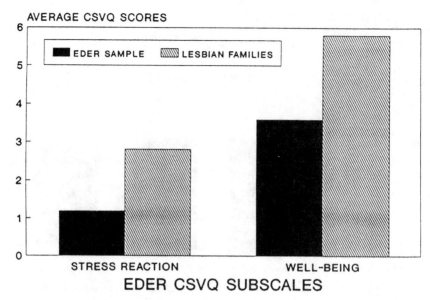

FIGURE 19.4 Mean Child Self-View Questionnaire Stress Reaction and Well-Being Scores *(data from Patterson 1994a)*.

TABLE 19.2 Children's Sex Role Behavior[a]

	Peer friendships	*Favorite toys*	*Favorite games*	*Favorite characters*
Mainly same sex	35	31	12	24
Mixed sexes	1	0	1	9
Mainly opposite sex	0	1	1	2
Not clearly sex typed	0	4	22	1

[a]Reprinted with permission from Patterson 1994a.

"No involvement" to "Shared involvement" to "Sole responsibility." Respondents also were asked to rate their satisfaction with their own and with their partner's involvement in child-care responsibilities, from "Very dissatisfied" to "Very satisfied."

To assess satisfaction with couple relationships, the Marital Adjustment

Test (Locke and Wallace 1959) was administered to all adult respondents. The Marital Adjustment Test is a sixteen-item instrument designed to record in a standardized format the overall satisfaction of spouses with their hetero-sexual marriages. A handful of small changes in wording (e.g., substituting the word *partner* for the word *spouse*) made the instrument more suitable for use with lesbian couples. Scoring was accomplished using the methods described by the authors.

Results for Couple Functioning   The actual and ideal reported participation of biological and nonbiological mothers in each of three domains of family work was compared (Patterson 1995b) (see Table 19.3). Results showed that biological and nonbiological mothers did not differ in their

TABLE 19.3 Parental Reports of Actual and Ideal Division of Family Labor

Division of labor		Report of biological mother	Report of nonbiological mother	t(25) =
Actual				
Household tasks	M	5.33	4.80	2.52
	SD	.59	.66	
Child-care tasks	M	5.70	4.35	3.92**
	SD	.90	.92	
Decision making	M	5.14	4.94	1.05
	SD	.65	.42	
Ideal				
Household tasks	M	5.10	4.86	1.55
	SD	.56	.52	
Child-care tasks	M	5.20	4.75	2.42
	SD	.63	.42	
Decision making	M	5.02	4.97	<1
	SD	.25	.23	

Note: Scores of 1 indicate that "She does it all," scores of 5 indicate that "We both do this about equally," and scores of 9 indicate that "I do it all." To protect alpha levels against inflation because of multiple comparisons, the Bonferroni correction has been applied to all t-tests. Reprinted with permission from Patterson 1995b.

** $p < = .01$.

evaluations of ideal distributions of labor in the three domains; most believed that tasks should be shared relatively evenly in all domains. In terms of the actual division of labor, biological and nonbiological mothers did not differ in their reported participation in household labor or family decision making. In the area of child care, however, biological mothers reported themselves as responsible for more of the work than nonbiological mothers. Thus, although lesbian mothers agreed that ideally child care should be evenly shared, they reported that in their families, the biological mother was actually more responsible than the nonbiological mother for child care.

To assess satisfaction with division of labor, comparisons between actual and ideal divisions of labor were made (see Figure 19.5). Results showed that biological mothers reported that ideally they would do fewer household tasks and less child care. Nonbiological mothers did not report feeling that they should be significantly more involved in household tasks but did agree that an ideal allocation of labor would result in them doing more child care. There were no effects for family decision making. Thus the main result was that both mothers felt that an ideal allocation of labor would involve a more equal sharing of child-care tasks between them.

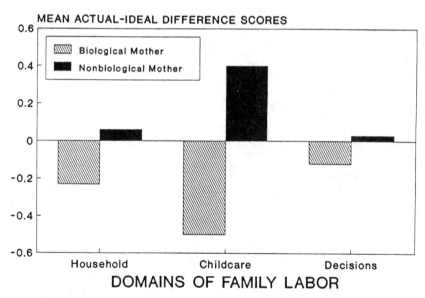

FIGURE 19.5 Mean Differences Between Parent Reports of Actual versus Ideal Division of Labor *(reprinted with permission from Patterson 1995b).*

Each respondent also had been asked to provide a global rating of each mother's overall involvement in child-care activities. On this measure, biological mothers reported that they were more involved than nonbiological mothers. Reports of the nonbiological mothers were in the same direction but did not reach statistical significance. Global judgments thus confirmed the more detailed reports described earlier in showing that, if anyone takes more responsibility for child care, it is the biological mother.

In interviews, parents were asked to estimate the average number of hours both biological and nonbiological mothers spent in paid employment each week. Results showed that biological mothers were less likely than nonbiological mothers to be working forty hours per week or more in paid employment (see Figure 19.6). Thus whereas biological mothers reported greater responsibility for child care, nonbiological mothers reported spending more time in paid employment.

There were no differences between relationship satisfaction reported by biological and nonbiological mothers (see Table 19.4). Consistent with expectations based on earlier findings with lesbian mothers (Koepke, Hare,

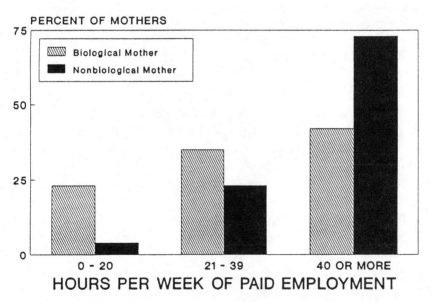

FIGURE 19.6 Percent of Biological and Nonbiological Mothers Spending 0–20, 21–39, and 40 or More Hours per Week in Paid Employment *(reprinted with permission from Patterson 1995b).*

TABLE 19.4 Parental Reports of Satisfaction with Division of Family Labor
and with Couple Relationships

Satisfaction with		Report of biological mother	Report of nonbiological mother	t(25) =
Division of household tasks	M	3.96	3.88	<1
	SD	.72	.86	
Division of work outside family	M	3.69	3.88	<1
	SD	1.05	.91	
Division of family decisions	M	4.15	4.12	<1
	SD	.78	.71	
Own involvement with child	M	4.38	4.08	1.28
	SD	.98	1.06	
Partner's involvement with child	M	4.58	4.38	1.22
	SD	.50	.85	
Locke-Wallace Relationship	M	118.46	117.42	<1
Satisfaction score	SD	15.70	15.18	

Note: Except for the Locke-Wallace Relationship Satisfaction score, all scores are on a 5-point scale, with higher scores indicating greater satisfaction. None of the comparisons between satisfaction among biological versus nonbiological mothers were significant. Reprinted with permission from Patterson 1995b.

and Moran 1992), lesbian mothers reported feeling very satisfied in their couple relationships. Overall satisfaction with the division of family labor was also high, and there were no significant differences between biological and nonbiological mothers in this regard.

Parental Division of Labor, Satisfaction, and Children's Adjustment

The study also assessed the strength of overall association between the three measures of child adjustment, on the one hand, and the four measures of parents' division of labor and satisfaction with division of labor, on the other (Patterson 1995b). Results of multivariate analysis showed a significant association between the two sets of variables. Parents' reports of division of labor, satisfaction with division of labor, and measures of a child's adjustment were significantly associated with one another. When biological mothers did less child care and when nonbiological mothers did more and were more satisfied, children's adjustment was rated as being more favorable.

In this study, then, both children and mothers reported more positive adjustment in families in which the nonbiological mother was described as a relatively equal participant in child care and in which the biological mother was not described as bearing an unequal burden of child-care duties. In other words, the most positive outcomes for children occurred in families that reported sharing child-care tasks relatively evenly between parents.

Contacts with Members of the Extended Family

One common stereotype about lesbian mothers and their children is that they are isolated from extended family networks. In particular, because it is sometimes assumed that lesbian women who are open with parents or siblings about their sexual identities will be disowned or rejected by — and therefore estranged from — their relatives, it is sometimes expected that children of lesbian mothers will have little or no contact with their grandparents, aunts, or uncles. One concern that is sometimes expressed about children growing up in the custody of lesbian mothers, then, is that they may be isolated in a single-sex home, without access to heterosexual adults, both male and female, who might serve as role models for them.

To evaluate these possibilities, lesbian mothers were asked to provide information about their children's contacts with grandparents and with any other adults outside the immediate household who were seen by the mothers as being important to their children (Patterson et al. 1995). For each person named, mothers were asked to give the person's relationship to the focal child and an estimate of the person's frequency of contact with the focal child, including visits, telephone calls, cards, and letters.

Results showed that, contrary to the stereotypes, most children were in relatively active contact with grandparents and with other members of their extended families. For instance, mothers reported that more than 60 percent of children had contact with at least one grandmother, and more than 50 percent of children had contact with at least one grandfather, once a month or more often. Similarly mothers reported that many children had such contact with at least one additional adult relative (usually an aunt or an uncle) and most had such contact with parents' adult friends, both male and female. Clearly, then, the results suggested that children were in active contact with both male and female grandparents and other relatives.

Summary and Discussion of Bay Area Families Study

The Bay Area Families Study was designed to examine child development and family functioning among families in which children were born or adopted after their mothers had acknowledged lesbian identities. Although findings from this study should be regarded as preliminary in a number of respects, four principal results have emerged to date. The first major finding was that, according to the standardized assessment techniques used here, both mothers' and children's adjustment fell clearly within the normative range. Considering that this result is consistent with the findings of other research on lesbian women in general (Gonsiorek 1991), lesbian mothers in particular (Falk 1989, 1994; Patterson 1992, 1995d), children of divorced lesbian and gay parents (Patterson 1992), and children born to lesbian mothers (Flaks et al. 1995; McCandlish 1987; Steckel 1985, 1987), this outcome was not surprising. Particularly in light of judicial and popular prejudices against lesbian and gay families that still exist in many parts of the country, however, the result is worthy of attention. The present study found not only that lesbian mothers' adjustment and self-esteem were within the normative range but also that social and personal development among their children were proceeding quite normally.

Although psychosocial development among children of lesbian versus heterosexual parents was generally quite similar, there were nevertheless also some differences among children in the two groups, most notably in the area of self-concept. Even though their answers were well within the normal range, children of lesbian mothers reported that they experienced more reactions to stress (e.g., feeling angry, scared, or upset) and also a greater sense of well-being (e.g., feeling joyful, content, and comfortable with themselves) than did the children of heterosexual parents studied by Eder (1990).

The best interpretation of this difference is not yet clear. One possibility is that children of lesbian mothers report greater reactions to stress because they actually experience more stress than other children do. In other words, children of lesbian mothers may actually encounter more stressful events and conditions than children with heterosexual parents do (Casper, Schultz, and Wickens 1992; Lott-Whitehead and Tully 1993; O'Connell 1993). If so, then their more frequent reports of emotional responses to stress might simply reflect the more stressful nature of their experience. From this view-point, however, it is difficult to account for the greater sense of well-being reported by children of lesbian mothers.

Another possibility is that, regardless of actual stress levels, children of lesbian mothers may be more conscious of their affective states in general or more willing to report their experiences of negative emotional states. If, as some have suggested (e.g., Pollack and Vaughn 1987; Rafkin 1990), children in lesbian homes may have more experience with the naming and verbal discussion of feelings in general, then they might exhibit increased openness to the expression of negative as well as positive feelings. In this view, the greater tendency of lesbian mothers' children to admit feeling angry, upset, or scared might be attributed not as much to differences in experiences of stress as to a greater openness to emotional experience and expression of all kinds.

Consistent with this latter interpretation, children of lesbian mothers in the present study reported greater feelings of joy, contentedness, and comfort with themselves than did children of heterosexual mothers in Eder's (1990) sample. Although these findings do not rule out the possibility that children of lesbian women do indeed experience greater stress, they do suggest that these children may be more willing than other children to report a variety of intense emotional experiences, whether positive or negative. Because this study was not designed to evaluate alternative interpretations of these differences, however, clarification of these issues must await the results of future research.

A second main finding was that lesbian couples who took part in this study reported that they divide various aspects of the labor involved in household upkeep and child care in a relatively even manner. That lesbian mothers in this sample reported sharing many household and family tasks is consistent with, and expands on, earlier findings on the division of household labor among lesbian and gay couples. For instance, Kurdek's (1993) study of lesbian, gay, and heterosexual couples without children found that lesbian couples were the most likely to share household responsibilities such as cooking, cleaning, and doing laundry. In the present study, results showed that lesbian couples with children not only reported sharing such household tasks but also reported enjoying equal influence in family decision making. Thus, even under pressure of child-rearing responsibilities, lesbian couples seem to maintain relatively egalitarian divisions of household responsibilities. In this way, lesbian couples with children resembled lesbian couples without children.

On the other hand, there were also some indications of specialization in the allocation of labor among lesbian couples who participated in this study. Consistent with patterns of specialization in heterosexual families (Cowan and Cowan 1992), biological mothers reported greater involvement with child care, and nonbiological mothers reported spending more time in paid employment. In accommodating to the demands of child rearing, it would appear that lesbian couples who took part in this research specialized to some degree with regard to their engagement in child care versus paid work. In this way, lesbian couples with children resembled heterosexual couples with children.

It is important, however, not to overemphasize the similarities between division of labor in lesbian and heterosexual families. In an unpublished dissertation, Hand (1991) compared division of labor among lesbian and heterosexual couples with children under two years of age. Consistent with the present findings, she found that household tasks and decision making were shared evenly by both lesbian and heterosexual couples with children, and that biological lesbian mothers reported greater involvement in child care than nonbiological mothers did. She also found, however, that both biological and nonbiological lesbian mothers were more involved in child care than were heterosexual fathers. Thus, even though differences between biological and nonbiological lesbian mothers were significant, both in the present study and in the study by Hand (1991), they were much less pronounced than the differences between husbands and wives in the matched group of heterosexual families studied by Hand (1991). These results are depicted in Figure 19.7. As can be seen in the figure, the division of labor involved in child care was more pronounced among heterosexual couples than among lesbian couples.

The third major result documented significant associations between division of labor among lesbian couples and psychosocial outcomes for mothers and their children. When lesbian couples shared child care more evenly, mothers were more satisfied and children were more well adjusted. Thus, even within the context of largely egalitarian arrangements, more equal sharing of child care was associated with more positive outcomes among both lesbian mothers and their children.

Mothers' ratings of their children's behavior problems were significantly associated with assessment of the parents' division of labor as well as with nonbiological mother's satisfaction with the allocation of tasks. Especially striking was the extent to which the nonbiological mother's satisfaction with child-care arrangements was associated with children's self-reports of well-

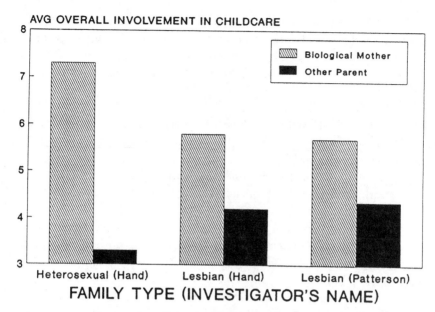

FIGURE 19.7 Average Overall Involvement in Child Care of Biological Mother and of Other Parent *(reprinted with permission from Patterson 1995b).*

being. Even within this well-adjusted nonclinical sample, children with mothers who shared child-care tasks evenly, and who expressed satisfaction with this arrangement, appeared to enjoy the most favorable adjustment.

That equal sharing of child care was associated with favorable adjustment among children is a result very much in concert with ideas proposed by Okin and other scholars working from a feminist perspective (e.g., Hochschild 1989; Okin 1989). These writers have suggested that models of fairness in the division of labor at home are important influences on children's development and that children who observe equal division of responsibilities between their parents may enjoy developmental advantages. Although this is by no means the only possible interpretation of the present findings, these results are certainly consistent with such a view.

One possible pathway through which benefits of equality in parents' division of labor might accrue to children involves parental satisfaction with their couple relationships. Given the egalitarian ideals expressed so clearly by lesbian couples who took part in this research, higher relationship satisfaction was expected among those who succeeded — by equal division of labor — in putting these ideals into action. Whether by its association with the relative absence of conflict between parents or with other aspects of parenting behavior (Belsky 1984), satisfaction was expected to mediate connections between division of labor and child adjustment. Contrary to expectations, however, no consistent association emerged among relationship satisfaction and the other study variables. In retrospect, this may have been because of the global nature of the assessments of relationship satisfaction used here. Ruble et al. (1988) have reported that some aspects of marital satisfaction are more tied to division of labor than others. Future research employing more detailed measures of potential mediators will, it is hoped, more clearly explicate pathways that link parental division of labor and child adjustment.

Although questions about causal linkages are of great interest, one should keep in mind that the present data are correlational in nature and therefore cannot support causal inferences. Are happy, well-adjusted lesbian families more likely to divide labor evenly? Or does the equal division of labor among lesbian couples with children lead to better adjustment and satisfaction with domestic arrangements? Or both? The present study was not designed to examine such possibilities, and the present data do not allow for their evaluation. Future work employing other kinds of research designs will be needed to disentangle causes and consequences in these domains.

The fourth major finding concerned children's contact with grandparents and other adult members of their extended families. Common stereotypes suggest that lesbian mothers who disclose their sexual identities to family members may be rejected for that reason, and hence that they and their children may be estranged to some extent from members of their extended families. In contrast to such expectations, results from the Bay Area Families Study suggested that most children were in relatively active contact with at least some of their grandparents, aunts, and uncles. Far from being isolated from lesbian mothers' families of origin, then, the results suggested that children were actively engaged in relationships with grandparents and other relatives of both sexes.

A number of limitations of this research should be acknowledged. This research relied on mothers' and children's reports as sources of data. The study included no observational assessments, and so the correspondence between parental reports about division of labor and the actual division of labor cannot be determined. Likewise, assessments of children's adjustment completed by independent observers would have been a valuable addition to the study. On the other hand, the use of well-known and widely used instruments such as the Locke-Wallace Marital Adjustment Test and the Achenbach and Edelbrock Child Behavior Checklist enhances the degree to which the present results may be compared to those of other researchers.

Some concerns relevant to sampling issues should also be acknowledged. Most of the families who took part in the Bay Area Families Study were headed by lesbian mothers who were white, well educated, relatively affluent, and living in the greater San Francisco Bay Area. For these reasons, no claims about representativeness of the present sample can be made. The reliability and generalizability of findings would likely be enhanced by the participation of more diverse samples of lesbian families over longer periods of time.

In summary, the Bay Area Families Study was designed to study child development, maternal mental health, and family functioning among the families of the lesbian baby boom. Results to date suggest that maternal mental health is good and that child development is proceeding normally. Lesbian couples described equal sharing of many household and decision-making tasks involved in their lives together, but they also reported that child care and paid employment were specialized to some degree. The more evenly they shared child care, the more satisfied mothers reported feeling, and the better adjusted their children were. In addition, children were reported to be in relatively active contact with their grandparents and with other adult members of their extended families.

Conclusions

Overall, results of research on children of lesbian and gay parents suggest that such children develop in a normal fashion. Despite strong legal presumptions against lesbian and gay parents in a number of jurisdictions, despite negative expectations about such children's development drawn from well-known psychological theories, and despite the accumulation of a substantial amount of research in this area, no evidence for significant difficulties in development among children of lesbian or gay parents has been produced. Indeed, the results of research to date are exceptionally clear, and they suggest that home environments provided by lesbian and gay parents are as likely as those supplied by heterosexual parents to support and enable children's psychosocial growth.

Without denying the clarity of the research findings, it is also important to emphasize that this is a relatively new area of study. As the present review of the literature reveals, systematic research on lesbian and gay parents and their children is a phenomenon of the past twenty years, and most of the studies have been published within the last ten years. Some issues have been studied by many investigators, whereas others have as yet received little attention. Most studies have involved relatively small samples, and the range of methodological approaches has been limited. Questions can be raised about the degree to which various methodological challenges of research in this area have been met, and few studies would be entirely invincible to all criticism. Much remains for future research to accomplish. Despite limitations, however, results of work to date are quite clear, and they merit attention from a number of perspectives.

First, inasmuch as they serve to counter ignorance and prejudice, results of research on children of lesbian and gay parents contribute to ongoing processes of social change. Fears of new or unfamiliar ways of living can characterize lesbian and gay as well as heterosexual individuals and can lead to negative expectations about the impact of novel arrangements. Just as questions about the impact on children of other kinds of recent social innovations, such as maternal employment (Hoffman 1984), have often arisen at least in part from lack of information, it is also the case that lack of familiarity with lesbian and gay parents and their children may lead to unrealistic concerns. Research in this area has already been helpful in addressing many misconceptions that exist about children of lesbian and gay parents.

Evidence from research on children of lesbian and gay parents also has important implications for theoretical accounts of human development. Results of research on children of divorced lesbian mothers or divorced gay fathers reveal that parents' sexual orientation has not proven to be an important determinant of development during childhood or adolescence among the offspring of such parents. Because parents in these studies typically lived together during children's earliest years, however, there is still the possibility that children's normal development should be attributed to this fact. Thus studies of divorced lesbian and gay parents and their children, although suggestive from a theoretical point of view, are not likely to be definitive with regard to the theoretical significance of parental sexual orientation on human development.

More likely to have definitive theoretical implications are studies of children born to (or adopted early in life by) lesbian or gay parents. In the Bay Area Families Study, for example, most children had little or no contact with the sperm donor or biological father who had made their conception possible;

about half the children did not even know this man's identity (Patterson 1994a). In these families, then, children have lived their entire lives in custody of lesbian mothers; no heterosexual parent has ever lived in the child's household. To the extent that normal development can be observed within this group of children, then, it cannot be attributed to any social influences from heterosexual parents.

To the extent that the findings from initial studies of children born to lesbian parents (e.g., Flaks et al. 1995; McCandlish 1987; Patterson 1994a, 1995b, 1995f; Patterson and Kosmitzki 1995; Steckel 1985, 1987) replicate in future research and are extended into adolescent and adult development, they will suggest that important revisions of well-known theories of psychological development may be necessary. If development of children born into lesbian-mother homes is normal, then traditional emphases on contributions of a heterosexual male parent to socialization may need to be reconsidered. If contributions of heterosexual male and female parents are not essential to satisfactory psychosocial development, then it will be necessary to consider alternative formulations.

A number of different approaches might be examined. For example, it might be argued that certain kinds of family interactions, processes, and relationships are beneficial for children's development but that parents need not be heterosexual to provide them. In other words, variables related to family processes (e.g., qualities of relationships) may be more important predictors of child adjustment than variables related to family structure (e.g., sexual orientation, number of parents in the home).

A possible analogy in this regard is provided by research on the impact of parental divorce on children. Although early studies of children's reactions to divorce focused on variables related to household composition and family structure (e.g., divorced versus nondivorced families), more recent research has highlighted the important contributions of variables related to family processes and interactions (e.g., conflict, warmth). For instance, a number of investigators (e.g., Emery 1982; O'Leary and Emery 1984) have argued that child behavioral problems associated with parental divorce are best understood as the result of interparental conflict rather than changes in household composition or structure as such. Research on divorcing families has thus suggested the preeminence of process over structure in mediating outcomes for children.

Applied to the present concerns, this perspective suggests the hypothesis that structural variables such as parental sexual orientation may be less important in mediating child outcomes in lesbian and gay families than qualities of family interactions, relationships, and processes. Many theoretical perspectives are compatible with an emphasis on function. For instance, attachment theory (Ainsworth 1985a, 1985b; Bowlby 1988) emphasizes the functional significance of sensitive parenting in creating secure relationships but does not require any particular family constellation or structure. Similarly self psychology (Kohut 1971, 1977, 1984) describes the significance of mirroring and idealizing processes in human development but does not require that they occur in the context of any specific family structure. Theoretical perspectives such as attachment theory and self psychology would seem to be compatible with an emphasis on functional rather than structural aspects of family life and hence to provide promising interpretive frameworks within which to conceptualize further research in these directions.

To evaluate the impact of both process and structural variables on child outcomes in lesbian, gay, and heterosexual families, research would need to assess variables of both types. Research with other kinds of nontraditional families (Eiduson and Weisner 1978; Weisner and Wilson-Mitchell 1990) has demonstrated the potential utility of this approach. Most research on lesbian and gay families, however, has focused on structural rather than process variables (e.g., on comparisons between children of lesbian and heterosexual mothers rather than on the qualities of interactions and relationships within these families). An adequate evaluation of the significance of process versus structure in lesbian and gay families therefore awaits the results of future research.

An alternative theoretical response might be to shift the focus of attention away from parental influences on children's development. As Maccoby (1990) has proposed, important forms of learning (e.g., about behavior considered appropriate for members of each sex) may be less dependent on parental input than traditionally believed. Other social influences, such as those of peers, should also be considered. It will also be important to identify and acknowledge contributions of genetic influences (Dunn and Plomin 1990). By investigating the impact of new family forms on the development of children who are growing up in these families, it seems likely that research on children of lesbian and gay parents will provide opportunities to broaden understanding of human development.

Results of research on children of lesbian and gay parents also have significant implications for public policies governing child custody, foster care, and adoption in the United States (Falk 1989, 1994; Patterson 1995c; Patterson and Redding 1996; Polikoff 1986, 1990). Unless and until the weight of evidence can be shown to have shifted, there is no empirically verifiable reason under the prevailing "best interests of the child" standard (Reppucci 1984; Rivera 1991) to deny or curtail parental rights of lesbian or gay parents on the basis of their sexual orientation, nor is there any empirically verifiable reason to believe that lesbians or gay men are less fit than heterosexuals to serve as adoptive or foster parents (Editors of the *Harvard Law Review* 1990; Patterson 1995c; Ricketts 1991; Ricketts and Achtenberg 1990). Existing research evidence provides no justification for denial of parental rights and responsibilities to lesbians and gay men on the basis of their sexual orientation.

Indeed, protection of the best interests of children in lesbian and gay families increasingly demands that courts and legislative bodies acknowledge realities of life in nontraditional families (Falk 1994; Patterson 1995c; Patterson and Redding 1996; Polikoff 1990). Consider, for example, a family created by a lesbian couple who undertake the conception, birth, and upbringing of their child together. Should this couple separate, it is reasonable to expect that the best interests of the child will be served by preserving the continuity and stability of the child's relationships with both parents. In law, however, it is generally only the biological mother who is recognized as having parental rights and responsibilities. From a legal standpoint, the nonbiological mother is generally considered a stranger, with no legal rights or responsibilities with respect to the child. When courts and legislatures fail to acknowledge facts of children's lives in nontraditional families, they experience great difficulty in serving the best interests of children in these families (Polikoff 1990).

A number of approaches to rectifying this situation have been proposed. For instance, a small number of families have obtained second-parent adoptions (Patterson 1995c; Ricketts and Achtenberg 1990), in which a nonbiological parent legally adopts a child without the biological parent giving up his or her legal rights and responsibilities; this avenue is not, however, available in most states. Others (e.g., Polikoff 1990) have advocated legislative reform, including changes in the standards for legal designation as a parent. As the number of lesbian and gay families with children increase, pressures for legal and judicial reform seem likely to increase.

As this review has revealed, most of the existing research has focused primarily on comparisons between children of gay or lesbian parents and those of heterosexual parents. It has taken this approach in order to address what can be considered heterosexist or homophobic questions (Herek 1995). Heterosexism reflects the belief that everyone is or ought to be heterosexual. Homophobic questions are those that are based on prejudice against lesbians and gay men, and are designed to raise the expectation that various negative outcomes will befall children of gay or lesbian parents compared to children of heterosexual parents. Examples of such questions that were considered earlier include the following: Won't the children of lesbians and gay men have difficulty with sexual identity? Won't they be more vulnerable to psychiatric problems? Won't they be sexually abused? Now that research has begun to provide negative answers to such heterosexist or homophobic questions or both, the time has come for child developmental researchers to address a broader range of issues in this area (Allen and Demo 1995; Laird 1993; Patterson 1995a, 1995d).

Many important research questions can stem from a more positive approach to the concerns of gay and lesbian communities. Such questions may raise the possibility of various desirable outcomes for children of gay and lesbian parents. For instance, won't these children grow up with increased tolerance for viewpoints other than their own? Won't they be more at home in the multicultural environments that almost all people increasingly inhabit? A number of children of lesbian mothers have reported that they see increased tolerance for divergent viewpoints as a benefit of growing up in lesbian-mother families (Rafkin 1990), but systematic research in this area is still lacking. Alternatively, these approaches may suggest study of the great diversity among gay and lesbian families. For example, how does growing up with multiple gay and lesbian parents differ from the experience of growing up with a single parent or with two parents who are a gay or lesbian couple? It will be helpful in future research to explore ways in which family processes are related to child outcomes in different kinds of lesbian and gay families (Allen and Demo 1995; Laird 1993; Patterson 1995a, 1995d).

A few studies that provide information relevant to issues of diversity among children of gay and lesbian parents have already been reported. Results of work with families headed by divorced lesbian mothers suggest that children are better off when their mothers have high self-esteem and are currently living with a lesbian partner (Huggins 1989; Kirkpatrick 1987). Research and clinical reports suggest that children in such families also appear to show more favorable adjustment when their fathers or other important adults accept their mothers' lesbian identities, and perhaps also when they have contact with other children of lesbians and gay men (Huggins 1989; Lewis 1980). In addition, there are indications that those who learn as children that they have a gay or lesbian parent experience less difficulty in adapting to this reality than those who are not told until adolescence (Paul 1986). In one study, young children whose lesbian parents shared child care relatively evenly were better adjusted than those whose parents reported less egalitarian arrangements (Patterson 1995b). Such findings are best regarded as preliminary glimpses of a territory in need of further exploration.

As a number of writers have pointed out (Martin 1993; Patterson 1995a, 1995d), much remains to be done to understand differences between and among gay and lesbian families, and to comprehend the impact of such differences on children and youths. It would be valuable to know more about the economic, religious, racial, ethnic, and cultural diversity in gay and lesbian families, and about the ways in which parents and children in such families manage the multiple identities available to them. It would be helpful to learn more about different kinds of parenting experiences — such as noncustodial parenting, nonbiological parenting, coparenting, multiple parenting, adoption, and foster care — and about their likely influences on the children involved. Studies are also needed to explore the nature of stresses and supports encountered by children of lesbian and gay parents — in the parents' families of origin (e.g., with grandparents and other relatives), among parents' and children's friends, and in their larger communities. Research is needed about the ways in which effects of heterosexism and homophobia are felt by parents and children in lesbian and gay families, and about the way they cope with the ignorance and prejudice they encounter.

To address these issues most effectively, future research should be conducted from an ecological perspective and should, where possible, employ longitudinal designs. Studies of development over time, especially during middle and later childhood and adolescence, are badly needed. Research should seek to assess not only child adjustment over time but also the family processes, relationships, and interactions to which child adjustment may be linked. Family processes, in turn, should be viewed in the context of the prevailing ecological conditions of family life.

In conclusion, it would seem that research on children of gay and lesbian parents, although still quite new, is well under way. Having begun to address heterosexist and homophobic concerns represented in psychological theory, judicial opinion, and popular prejudice, researchers are now in a position also to explore a broader range of issues raised by the emergence of and increased openness among lesbian and gay parents and their children. Research in this area has the potential to contribute to knowledge about nontraditional family forms and about their impact on children, encourage innovative approaches to the conceptualization of human development, and inform legal rulings and public policies relevant to children of gay and lesbian parents.

Acknowledgments

Grateful acknowledgment is due to the Society for Psychological Study of Social Issues for its support of the Bay Area Families Study. I thank especially Mitch Chyette, Deborah Cohn, Carolyn Cowan, Philip Cowan, Charlene Depner, Ellie Schindelman, and all the families who participated in the Bay Area Families Study for their support and assistance. I also wish to thank Alicia Eddy, David Koppelman, Meg Michel, and Scott Spence for their efficient work in coding the data for this study, and Sally Hand for her generosity in granting permission to present results from her research.

References

Achenbach, T. M., and C. Edelbrock. 1983. *Manual for the Child Behavior Checklist and Revised Child Behavior Profile*. Burlington: University of Vermont, Department of Psychiatry.

Adam, B. D. 1987. *The Rise of a Gay and Lesbian Movement*. Boston: Twayne.

Ainsworth, M.D.S. 1985a. Patterns of infant-mother attachments: Antecedents and effects on development. *Bulletin of the New York Academy of Medicine* 61:771–91.

Ainsworth, M.D.S. 1985b. Attachments across the life span. *Bulletin of the New York Academy of Medicine* 61:792–812.

Allen, K. R., and D. H. Demo. 1995. The families of lesbians and gay men: A new frontier in family research. *Journal of Marriage and the Family* 57:111–27.

Baptiste, D. A. 1987. Psychotherapy with gay/lesbian couples and their children in "step-families": A challenge for marriage and family therapists. In E. Coleman, ed., *Integrated Identity for Gay Men and Lesbians: Psychotherapeutic Approaches for Emotional Well-being*, pp. 223–38. New: York: Harrington Park.

Barret, R. L., and B. E. Robinson. 1990. *Gay Fathers*. Lexington, Mass.: Lexington Books.

Belsky, J. 1984. The determinants of parenting: A process model. *Child Development* 55:83–96.

Bem, S. L. 1983. Gender schema theory and its implications for child development: Raising gender-schematic children in a gender-schematic society. *Signs: Journal of Women in Culture and Society* 8:598–616.

Benkov, L. 1994. *Reinventing the Family*. New York: Crown.

Bigner, J. J., and F. W. Bozett. 1990. Parenting by gay fathers. In F. W. Bozett and M. B. Sussman, eds., *Homosexuality and Family Relations*, pp. 155–76. New York: Harrington Park.

Blumenfeld, W. J., and D. Raymond. 1988. *Looking at Gay and Lesbian Life*. Boston: Beacon.

Bornstein, M. H., ed. 1995. *Handbook of Parenting*. Hillsdale, N.J.: Erlbaum.

Bowlby, J. 1988. *A Secure Base: Parent — Child Attachment and Healthy Human Development*. New York: Basic Books.

Bozett, E. W. 1980. Gay fathers: How and why they disclose their homosexuality to their children. *Family Relations* 29:173–79.

Bozett, F. W. 1982. Heterogeneous couples in heterosexual marriages: Gay men and straight women. *Journal of Marital and Family Therapy* 8:81–89.

Bozett, F. W. 1987. Children of gay fathers. In F. W. Bozett ed., *Gay and Lesbian Parents*, pp. 39–57. New York: Praeger.

Bozett, F. W. 1989. Gay fathers: A review of the literature. In F. W. Bozett ed., *Homosexuality and the Family*, pp. 137–62. New York: Harrington Park.

Brantner, P. A. 1992. When mommy or daddy is gay: Developing constitutional standards for custody decisions. *Hastings Women's Law Journal* 3:97–121.

Bronfenbrenner, U. 1960. Freudian theories of identification and their derivatives. *Child Development* 31:15–40.

Brown, L. S. 1995. Lesbian identities: Concepts and issues. In A. R. D'Augelli and C. J. Patterson, eds., *Lesbian, Gay, and Bisexual Identities over the Lifespan*, pp. 3–23. New York: Oxford University Press.

Cain,-P. 1993. Litigating for lesbian and gay rights: A legal history. *Virginia Law Review* 79:1551–1642.

Casper, V., S. Schultz, and E. Wickens. 1992. Breaking the silences: Lesbian and gay parents and the schools. *Teachers College Record* 94:109–37.

Chodorow, N. 1978. *The Reproduction of Mothering: Psychoanalysis and the Sociology of Gender*. Berkeley: University of California Press.

Cole, M. 1988. Cross-cultural research in the sociohistorical tradition. *Human Development* 31:137–57.

Cowan, C. P., and P. A. Cowan. 1990. Who does what? In J. Touliatos, B. F. Perlmutter, and M. A. Straus, eds., *Handbook of Family Measurement Techniques*, pp. 447–48. Newbury Park, Calif.: Sage.

Cowan, C. P., and P. A. Cowan. 1992. *When Partners Become Parents: The Big Life Change for Couples*. New York: Basic Books.

Cramer, D. 1986. Gay parents and their children: A review of research and practical implications. *Journal of Counseling and Development* 64:504–7.

Crawford, S. 1987. Lesbian families: Psychosocial stress and the family-building process. In Boston Lesbian Psychologies Collective, *Lesbian Psychologies: Explorations and Challenges*, pp. 195–214. Urbana: University of Illinois Press.

D'Emilio, J. 1983. *Sexual Politics, Sexual Communities: The Makings of a Homosexual Minority in the United States 1940–1970*. Chicago: University of Chicago Press.

Derogatis, L. R. 1983. *SCL-90-R Administration, Scoring, and Procedures Manual*. Towson, Md.: Clinical Psychometric Research.

Dinnerstein, D. 1976. *The Mermaid and the Minotaur: Sexual Arrangements and Human Malaise*. New York: Harper and Row.

Dunn, J., and R. Plomin. 1990. *Separate Lives: Why Siblings Are So Different*. New York: Basic Books.

Eder, R. A. 1990. Uncovering young children's psychological selves: Individual and developmental differences. *Child Development* 61:849–63.

Editors of the *Harvard Law Review*. 1990. *Sexual Orientation and the Law*. Cambridge, Mass.: Harvard University Press.

Eiduson, B. T., and T. S. Weisner. 1978. Alternative family styles: Effects on young children. In J. H. Stevens and M. Mathews, eds., *Mother/Child Father/Child Relationships*, pp. 197–221. Washington, D.C.: National Association for the Education of Young Children.

Elder, G. H., Jr. 1986. Military timing and turning points in men's lives. *Developmental Psychology* 22:233–45.

Emery, R. E. 1982. Interparental conflict and the children of discord and divorce. *Psychological Bulletin* 92:310–30.

Faderman, L. 1991. *Odd Girls and Twilight Lovers: A History of Lesbian Life in Twentieth-Century America*. New York: Columbia University Press.

Falk, P. J. 1989. Lesbian mothers: Psychosocial assumptions in family law. *American Psychologist* 44:941–47.

Falk, P. J. 1994. The gap between psychosocial assumptions and empirical research in lesbian-mother child custody cases. In A. E. Gottfried and A. W. Gottfried, eds., *Redefining Families: Implications for Children's Development*, pp. 131–56. New York: Plenum.

Finkelhor, D., and D. Russell. 1984. Women as perpetrators: Review of the evidence. In D. Finkelhor, ed., *Child Sexual Abuse: New Theory and Research*, pp. 171–87. New York: Free Press.

Flaks, D., I. Ficher, F. Masterpasqua, and G. Joseph. 1995. Lesbians choosing motherhood: A comparative study of lesbian and heterosexual parents and their children. *Developmental Psychology* 31:104–14.

Freiberg, P. 1990. Lesbian moms can give kids empowering role models. *APA Monitor* 21:33.

Gibbs, E. D. 1988. Psychosocial development of children raised by lesbian mothers: A review of research. *Women and Therapy* 8:55–75.

Gilman, C. P. 1979 [1915]. *Herland*. New York: Pantheon.

Golombok, S., A. Spencer, and M. Rutter. 1983. Children in lesbian and single-parent households: Psychosexual and psychiatric appraisal. *Journal of Child Psychology and Psychiatry* 24:551–72.

Gonsiorek, J. 1991. The empirical basis for the demise of the illness model of homosexuality. In J. C. Gonsiorek and J. D. Weinrich, eds., *Homosexuality: Research Implications for Public Policy*, pp. 115–36. Newbury Park, Calif.: Sage.

Gottfried, A. E., and A. W. Gottfried, eds. 1994. *Redefining Families: Implications for Children's Development*. New York: Plenum.

Gottman, J. S. 1990. Children of gay and lesbian parents. In F. W. Bozett and M. B.

Sussman, eds., *Homosexuality and Family Relations*, pp. 177–96. New York: Harrington Park.

Green, G. D., and F. W. Bozett. 1991. Lesbian mothers and gay fathers. In J. C. Gonsiorek and J. D. Weinrich, eds., *Homosexuality: Research Implications for Public Policy*, pp. 197–214. Beverly Hills, Calif.: Sage.

Green, R. 1978. Sexual identity of 37 children raised by homosexual or transsexual parents. *American Journal of Psychiatry* 135:692–97.

Green, R., J. B. Mandel, M. E. Hotvedt, J. Gray, and L. Smith. 1986. Lesbian mothers and their children: A comparison with solo parent heterosexual mothers and their children. *Archives of Sexual Behavior* 15:167–84.

Groth, A. N., and H. J. Birnbaum. 1978. Adult sexual orientation and attraction to underage persons. *Archives of Sexual Behavior* 7:175–81.

Hand, S. I. 1991. *The Lesbian Parenting Couple*. Unpublished doctoral dissertation, Professional School of Psychology, San Francisco, California.

Hare, J., and L. Richards. 1993. Children raised by lesbian couples: Does the context of birth affect father and partner involvement? *Family Relations* 42:249–55.

Harrison, A. O., M. N. Wilson, C. J. Pine, S. Q. Chan, and R. Buriel. 1990. Family ecologies of 15 ethnic minority children. *Child Development* 61:347–62.

Herek, G. M. 1995. Psychological heterosexism in the United States. In A. R. D'Augelli and C. J. Patterson, eds., *Lesbian, Gay, and Bisexual Identities over the Lifespan: Psychological Perspectives*, pp. 321–46. New York: Oxford University Press.

Hernandez, D. J. 1988. Demographic trends and the living arrangements of children. In E. M. Hetherington and J. D. Arasteh, eds., *Impact of Divorce, Single Parenting, and Stepparenting on Children*, pp. 3–22. Hillsdale, N.J.: Erlbaum.

Hetherington, E. M., and J. D. Arasteh, eds. 1988. *Impact of Divorce, Single Parenting, and Stepparenting on Children*. Hillsdale, N.J.: Erlbaum.

Hitchens, D. J. 1979/1980. Social attitudes, legal standards, and personal trauma in child custody cases. *Journal of Homosexuality* 5:1–20, 89–95.

Hochschild, A. R. 1989. *The Second Shift: Working Parents and the Revolution at Home*. New York: Viking Penguin.

Hoeffer, B. 1981. Children's acquisition of sex-role behavior in lesbian-mother families. *American Journal of Orthopsychiatry* 5:536–44.

Hoffman, L. W. 1984. Work, family, and socialization of the child. In R. D. Parke, ed., *Review of Child Development Research*. Vol. 7: *The Family*, pp. 223–82. Chicago: University of Chicago Press.

Huggins, S. L. 1989. A comparative study of self-esteem of adolescent children of divorced lesbian mothers and divorced heterosexual mothers. In F. W. Bozett, ed., *Homosexuality and the Family*, pp. 123–35. New York: Harrington Park.

Huston, A. 1983. Sex typing. In E. M. Hetherington, ed., P. H. Mussen series, *Handbook of Child Psychology*. Vol. 4: *Socialization, Personality, and Social Development*, pp. 387–487. New York: Wiley.

Jacob, T., ed. 1987. *Family Interaction and Psychopathology: Theories, Methods, and Findings.* New York: Plenum.

Jenny, C., T. A. Roesler, and K. L. Poyer. 1994. Are children at risk for sexual abuse by homosexuals? *Pediatrics* 94:41–44.

Jones, B. M., and K. McFarlane, eds. 1980. *Sexual Abuse of Children: Selected Readings.* Washington, D.C.: National Center on Child Abuse and Neglect.

Kirkpatrick, M. 1987. Clinical implications of lesbian mother studies. *Journal of Homosexuality* 14(1/2):201–11.

Kirkpatrick, M., C. Smith, and R. Roy. 1981. Lesbian mothers and their children: A comparative survey. *American Journal of Orthopsychiatry* 51:545–51.

Kitzinger, C., and S. Wilkinson. 1995. Transitions from heterosexuality to lesbianism: The discursive production of lesbian identities. *Developmental Psychology* 31:95–104.

Kleber, D. J., R. J. Howell, and A. L. Tibbits-Kleber. 1986. The impact of parental homosexuality in child custody cases: A review of the literature. *Bulletin of the American Academy of Psychiatry and Law* 14:81–87.

Koepke, L., J. Hare, and P. B. Moran. 1992. Relationship quality in a sample of lesbian couples with children and child-free lesbian couples. *Family Relations* 41:224–29.

Kohlberg, L. 1966. A cognitive-developmental analysis of children's sex-role concepts and attitudes. In E. E. Maccoby, ed., *The Development of Sex Differences,* pp. 82–173. Stanford, Calif.: Stanford University Press.

Kohut, H. 1971. *The Analysis of the Self.* Madison, Conn.: International Universities Press.

Kohut, H. 1977. *The Restoration of the Self.* Madison, Conn.: International Universities Press.

Kohut, H. 1984. *How Does Analysis Cure?* Chicago: University of Chicago Press.

Kurdek, L. 1993. The allocation of household labor in gay, lesbian, and heterosexual married couples. *Journal of Social Issues* 49(3):127–39.

Laird, J. 1993. Lesbian and gay families. In F. Walsh, ed., *Normal Family Processes,* 2nd ed., pp. 282–328. New York: Guilford.

Lamb, M. E., ed. 1982. *Nontraditional Families: Parenting and Child Development.* Hillsdale, N.J.: Erlbaum.

Lamb, M. E., ed. 1996. *The Role of the Father in Child Development,* 3rd ed. New York: Wiley.

Laosa, L. M. 1988. Ethnicity and single parenting in the United States. In E. M. Hetherington and J. D. Arasteh, eds., *Impact of Divorce, Single Parenting, and Stepparenting on Children,* pp. 23–49. Hillsdale, N.J.: Erlbaum.

Lewin, E. 1993. *Lesbian Mothers: Accounts of Gender in American Culture.* Ithaca, N.Y.: Cornell University Press.

Lewis, K. G. 1980. Children of lesbians: Their point of view. *Social Work* 25: 198–203.

Locke, H., and K. Wallace. 1959. Short marital adjustment and prediction tests: Their reliability and validity. *Marriage and Family Living* 21:251–55.

Lott-Whitehead, L., and C. T. Tully. 1993. The family lives of lesbian mothers. *Smith College Studies in Social Work* 63:265–80.

Maccoby, E. E. 1990. Gender and relationships: A developmental account. *American Psychologist* 45:513–20.

Martin, A. 1989. The planned lesbian and gay family: Parenthood and children. *Newsletter of the Society for the Psychological Study of Lesbian and Gay Issues* 5/6:16–17.

Martin, A. 1993. *The Lesbian and Gay Parenting Handbook: Creating and Raising Our Families.* New York: Harper Collins.

McCandlish, B. 1987. Against all odds: Lesbian mother family dynamics. In F. Bozett, ed., *Gay and Lesbian Parents*, pp. 23–38. New York: Praeger.

McLoyd, V. 1990. The impact of economic hardship on black families and children: Psychological distress, parenting, and socioemotional development. *Child Development* 61:311–46.

Miller, B. 1979. Gay fathers and their children. *Family Coordinator* 28:544–52.

Money, J., and A. A. Ehrhardt. 1972. *Man and Woman, Boy and Girl: The Differentiation and Dimorphism of Gender Identity from Conception to Maturity.* Baltimore, Md.: The Johns Hopkins University Press.

Nungesser, L. G. 1980. Theoretical bases for research on the acquisition of social sex roles by children of lesbian mothers. *Journal of Homosexuality* 5(3):177–87.

O'Connell, A. 1993. Voices from the heart: The developmental impact of a mother's lesbianism on her adolescent children. *Smith College Studies in Social Work* 63:281–99.

Okin, S. M. 1989. *Justice, Gender, and the Family.* New York: Basic Books.

O'Leary, K. D., and R. E. Emery. 1984. Marital discord and child behavior problems. In M. D. Levine and P. Satz, eds., *Middle Childhood: Development and Dysfunction*, pp. 345–64. Baltimore, Md.: University Park Press.

Pagelow, M. D. 1980. Heterosexual and lesbian single mothers: A comparison of problems, coping, and solutions. *Journal of Homosexuality* 5(3):189–204.

Parke, R. D., ed. 1984. *Review of Child Development Research.* Vol. 7: *The Family.* Chicago: University of Chicago Press.

Patterson, C. J. 1992. Children of lesbian and gay parents. *Child Development* 63:1025–42.

Patterson, C. J. 1994a. Children of the lesbian baby boom: Behavioral adjustment, self-concepts, and sex-role identity. In B. Greene and G. Herek, eds., *Contemporary Perspectives on Lesbian and Gay Psychology: Theory, Research, and Applications*, pp. 156–75. Newbury Park, Calif.: Sage.

Patterson, C. J. 1994b. Lesbian and gay couples considering parenthood: An agenda for research, service, and advocacy. *Journal of Lesbian and Gay Social Services* 1(2):33–55.

Patterson, C. J. 1995a. Lesbian mothers, gay fathers, and their children. In A. R. D'Augelli and C. J. Patterson, eds., *Lesbian, Gay, and Bisexual Identities over the Lifespan: Psychological Perspectives*, pp. 262–90. New York: Oxford University Press.

Patterson, C. J. 1995b. Families of the lesbian baby boom: Parents' division of labor and children's adjustment. *Developmental Psychology* 31:115–23.

Patterson, C. J. 1995c. Adoption of minor children by lesbian and gay adults: A social science perspective. *Duke Journal of Gender Law and Policy* 2:191–205.

Patterson, C. J. 1995d. Lesbian and gay parenthood. In M. H. Bornstein,, ed., *Handbook of Parenting*. Vol. 3: *Status and Social Conditions of Parenting*, pp. 255–74. Hillsdale, N.J.: Erlbaum.

Patterson, C. J. 1995e. Sexual orientation and human development: An overview. *Developmental Psychology* 31:3–11.

Patterson, C. J., and R. W. Chan. 1996. Gay fathers and their children. In R. P. Cabaj and T. S. Stein, eds., *Homosexuality and Mental Health: A Comprehensive Textbook*, pp. 371–93. Washington, D.C.: American Psychiatric Press.

Patterson, C. J., S. Hurt, and C. Mason. 1995. Families of the lesbian baby boom: Children's contacts with grandparents and other adults outside their households. Unpublished manuscript, Department of Psychology, University of Virginia, Charlottesville.

Patterson, C. J., and C. Kosmitzki. 1995. Families of the lesbian baby boom: Maternal mental health, household composition, and child adjustment. Unpublished manuscript, Department of Psychology, University of Virginia, Charlottesville.

Patterson, C. J., and R. Redding. 1996. Lesbian and gay families with children: Public policy implications of social science research. *Journal of Social Issues* 52:29–50.

Paul, J. P. 1986. *Growing Up with a Gay, Lesbian, or Bisexual Parent: An Exploratory Study of Experiences and Perceptions*. Unpublished doctoral dissertation, University of California at Berkeley.

Pies, C. 1985. *Considering Parenthood*. San Francisco: Spinsters/Aunt Lute.

Pies, C. 1990. Lesbians and the choice to parent. In F. W. Bozett and M. B. Sussman, eds., *Homosexuality and Family Relations*, pp. 137–54. New York: Harrington Park.

Polikoff, N. 1986. Lesbian mothers, lesbian families, legal obstacles, legal challenges. *Review of Law and Social Change* 14:907–14.

Polikoff, N. 1990. This child does have two mothers: Redefining parenthood to meet the needs of children in lesbian mother and other nontraditional families. *Georgetown Law Review* 78:459–575.

Pollack, S., and J. Vaughn. 1987. *Politics of the Heart: A Lesbian Parenting Anthology*. Ithaca, N.Y.: Firebrand.

Puryear, D. 1983. *A Comparison Between the Children of Lesbian Mothers and the Children of Heterosexual Mothers*. Unpublished doctoral dissertation, California School of Professional Psychology, Berkeley.

Rafkin, L. 1990. *Different Mothers: Sons and Daughters of Lesbians Talk about Their Lives*. Pittsburgh: Cleis.

Rand, C., D. L. Graham, and E. I. Rawlings. 1982. Psychological health and factors the court seeks to control in lesbian mother custody trials. *Journal of Homosexuality* 8(1):27–39.

Rees, R. L. 1979. *A Comparison of Children of Lesbian and Single Heterosexual Mothers on Three Measures of Socialization*. Berkeley: California School of Professional Psychology.

Reppucci, N. D. 1984. The wisdom of Solomon: Issues in child custody determination. In N. D. Reppucci, L. A. Weithorn, E. P. Mulvey, and J. Monahan, eds., *Children, Mental Health, and the Law*, pp. 59–78. Beverly Hills, Calif.: Sage.

Ricketts, W. 1991. *Lesbians and Gay Men as Foster Parents*. Portland: National Child Welfare Resource Center, University of Southern Main.

Ricketts, W., and R. Achtenberg. 1990. Adoption and foster parenting for lesbians and gay men: Creating new traditions in family. In F. W. Bozett and M. B. Sussman, eds., *Homosexuality and Family Relations*, pp. 83–118. New York: Harrington Park.

Riley, C. 1988. American kinship: A lesbian account. *Feminist Issues* 8:75–94.

Rivera, R. 1991. Sexual orientation and the law. In J. C. Gonsiorek and J. D. Weinrich, eds., *Homosexuality: Research Implications for Public Policy*, pp. 81–100. Newbury Park, Calif.: Sage.

Rogoff, B. 1990. *Apprenticeship in Thinking*. New York: Oxford University Press.

Rosenberg, M. 1979. *Conceiving the Self*. New York: Basic Books.

Ruble, D. N., A. S. Fleming, L. S. Hackel, and C. Stangor. 1988. Changes in the marital relationship during the transition to first time motherhood: Effects of violated expectations concerning division of household labor. *Journal of Personality and Social Psychology* 55:78–87.

Rutter, M., C. E. Izard, and P. B. Read, eds. 1986. *Depression in Young People: Developmental and Clinical Perspective*. New York: Guilford.

Sameroff, A. J., and M. Chandler. 1975. Reproductive risk and the continuum of caretaking casualty. In F. D. Horowitz, ed., *Review of Child Development Research*, Vol. 4., pp. 187–244. Chicago: University of Chicago Press.

Spencer, M. B., G. K. Brookins, and W. R. Allen, eds. 1985. *Beginnings: The Social and Affective Development of Black Children*. Hillsdale, N.J.: Erlbaum.

Steckel, A. 1985. *Separation-Individuation in Children of Lesbian and Heterosexual Couples*. Unpublished doctoral dissertation, Wright Institute Graduate School, Berkeley, California.

Steckel, A. 1987. Psychosocial development of children of lesbian mothers. In F. W. Bozett, ed., *Gay and Lesbian Parents*, pp. 75–85. New York: Praeger.

Tasker, F. L., and S. Golombok. 1991. Children raised by lesbian mothers: The empirical evidence. *Family Law* 21:184–87.

Tasker, F., and S. Golombok. 1995. Adults raised as children in lesbian families. *American Journal of Orthopsychiatry* 65:203–15.

Weisner, T. S., and J. E. Wilson-Mitchell. 1990. Nonconventional family lifestyles and sex typing in six year olds. *Child Development* 61:1915–33.

Weston, K. 1991. *Families We Choose: Lesbians, Gays, Kinship.* New York: Columbia University Press.

20 Stories from the Homefront: Perspectives of Asian-American Parents with Lesbian Daughters and Gay Sons

Alice Y. Hom

> Having been a classroom teacher since 1963, I have new knowledge that 10 percent of all the students who came through my classroom have grown up and are gay and lesbian. . . . Because I cannot undo the past, I want to teach people the truth about homosexuality so people will not abandon these children.[1]

These are stories from the homefront; the emotions, responses, and attitudes of Asian-American parents about their lesbian daughters or gay sons.[2] The stories attempt to shed light on parents' attitudes and to inform lesbians and gay men about various ways parents may react and respond to their coming out.

I focus on four themes that illustrate important concepts surrounding the understanding of Asian-American parents and their views on homosexuality. These themes emerged from interviews investigating the following: (1) parents' attitudes before disclosure/discovery; (2) parents' attitudes and reactions after disclosure/discovery; (3) responses following disclosure to friends and their communities; and (4) advice for other parents.

Sexuality is an issue rarely, if ever, discussed among Asian families, yet it remains a vital aspect of one's life. What are the implications of alternative sexualities in family situations? Coming-out stories and experiences of Asian-American lesbians and gay men have had some exposure and relevant publications,[3] but the voices of the parents are rarely presented or known.

I found the majority of interviewees through personal contacts with individuals in organizations such as Asian Pacifica Sisters in San Francisco, Mahu Sisters and Brothers Alliance at the University of California, Los Angeles, and Gay Asian Pacific Alliance Community HIV Project in San Francisco. I met one set of parents through the Parents and Friends of Lesbians and Gays group in Los Angeles. Obviously this select group of people, who were willing to talk about their children, might represent only certain perspectives. Nonetheless, I managed to pool a diverse set of parents despite the small size in terms of disclosing time and the time lapse — some parents have known for years and a few only recently found out. I did receive some "no" answers to my request. I also offered complete anonymity in the interviews; most preferred pseudonyms. Names with an asterisk denote pseudonyms.

I interviewed thirteen parents altogether, all mothers except for two fathers.[4] The interviewee pool consisted of four single mothers by divorce, a widower, two couples, and four married mothers. The ethnicities included four Chinese, four Japanese, three Pilippinas, one Vietnamese, and one Korean. Most live in California, with one living in Portland and another in Hawaii. All the interviews were conducted in English, with the exception of one, which was conducted in Japanese with the lesbian daughter as translator. Ten of thirteen interviewees are first-generation immigrants. The other three are third-generation Japanese American. I interviewed four mothers of gay sons, including one mother with two gay sons. The rest had lesbian daughters, including one mother with two lesbian daughters. Six were told and seven inadvertently discovered about their children's sexual orientation.[5]

Most books on the topic of parents of lesbian and gay children report mainly on white middle-class families.[6] *Beyond Acceptance: Parents of Lesbians and Gays Talk about Their Experiences*, by Carolyn W. Griffin, Marian J. Wirth and Arthur G. Wirth, discusses the experiences of twenty-three white middle-class parents from a Midwestern metropolitan city involved with Parents and Friends of Lesbians and Gays (PFLAG).[7] Another book, entitled *Parents Matter: Parents' Relationships with Lesbian Daughters and Gay Sons*, by Ann Muller, relates the perspectives of lesbian and gay children with a few stories by the parents. Seventeen percent of the seventy-one people interviewed were black.[8] These examples present mainly an Anglo picture and fail to account for the diversity of lesbian and gay communities as well as different experiences of parents of color.

Attitudes of Parents Toward Gays and Lesbians Predisclosure

The knowledge of lesbians and gay men in their native countries and in their communities in the United States serves as an important factor in dismantling the oft-used phrase that a son or daughter is gay or lesbian because of assimilation and acculturation in a Western context. The parents interviewed did not utter, "It's a white disease" — a phrase often heard and used when discussing coming out in an Asian-American community and context. Connie S. Chan, in her essay, "Issues of Identity Development among Asian-American Lesbians and Gay Men," found in her study that nine out of ninety-five respondents were out to their parents. Chan suggested that this low number might be related to, "specific cultural values defining the traditional roles, which help to explain the reluctance of Asian-American lesbians and gay men to 'come out' to their parents and families."[9]

Nonetheless, the parents interviewed recounted incidents of being aware of lesbians and gays while they were growing up and did not blame assimilation and Anglo-American culture for their children's sexual orientation. One quote by Lucy Nguyen*, a fifty-three-year-old Vietnamese immigrant who has two gay sons, does, however, imply that the environment and attitudes of the United States allowed her sons to express their gay identity. She stated:

I think all the gay activities and if I live at this time, environment like this, I think I'm lesbian. You know, be honest. When I was young, the society in Vietnam is so strict — I have a really close friend, I love her, but just a friendship nothing else. In my mind, I say, well in this country it's free. They have no restraint, so that's why I accept it, whatever they are.[10]

This revealing remark assumes that an open environment allows for freedom of sexual expression. Nevertheless, it does not necessarily suggest lesbians and gay men exist solely because of a nurturing environment. Rather, lesbians and gay men must live and survive in different ways and make choices depending on the climate of the society at the time.

Midori Asakura*, a sixty-three-year-old Japanese immigrant with a lesbian daughter, related an example of lesbianism in Japan. She remembered, while studying to be a nurse, talk in the dorm rooms about "S," which denotes women who had really close friendships with one another.[11] She recalled,

One day you'd see one woman with a certain blouse and the next day, you'd see the other woman with the same blouse. They would always sit together, they went everywhere together. There was talk that they were having sex, but I didn't think they were. . . . People used to say they felt each other out. I thought, 'Nah, they're not having sex, why would they?' Everyone thought it was strange, but no one really got into it.[12]

When asked what she thought of the "S" women, Midori replied, "I didn't think much of it, although I thought one was manlike, Kato-san, and the other, Fukuchi-san, who was very beautiful and sharp-minded, was the woman."[13]

Another parent, George Tanaka*, a fifty-three-year-old Japanese-American who grew up in Hawaii and has a lesbian daughter, remembers a particular person known as *mahu*.[14] Toni Barraquiel, a fifty-four-year-old Pilippina single mother with a gay son, commented on gay men in Manila because of their effeminacy and admission of being gay. Toni asserted that these men would be in certain careers, such as manicurists and hairdressers. When asked of the people's attitudes toward them, she replied,

that they look down on those gays and lesbians, they make fun of them. . . . It seems as if it is an abnormal thing. The lesbian is not as prominent as the gays. They call her a tomboy because she's very athletic and well built.[15]

Maria Santos*, a fifty-four-year-old Pilippina immigrant with two lesbian daughters, spoke of gays and lesbians in Luzon. She said, "There were negative attitudes about them. 'Bakla' and 'Tomboy' — it was gay-bashing in words not in physical terms. There was name-calling that I did not participate in."[16]

Lucy Nguyen* had lesbian classmates in her all-girls high school. She said, "They were looked down upon, because this isn't normal. They were called 'homo.' "[17] A common thread throughout the observations of the parents about gays and lesbians lies in stereotypical gender role associations. For example, Margaret Tsang*, a sixty-year-old Chinese single parent who has a gay son, recalled a family member who might possibly be gay, although there was not a name for it. She observed, "He was slanted toward nail polish and make-up and all kinds of things. And he liked Chinese opera. He behaved in a very feminine fashion."[18]

Similarly Liz Lee, a forty-two-year-old Korean single parent with a lesbian daughter, clearly remembered lesbians in Seoul. "My mother's friend was always dressed like man in suit. She always had mousse or grease on her hair, and she dressed like a man. She had five or six girlfriends always come over."[19] Liz related that she did not think anything about it and said they were respected.[20] When asked of people's attitudes toward these women, Liz responded, "They say nature made a mistake. They didn't think it was any-body's choice or anybody's preference."[21]

For the most part the interviewees, aware of gays and lesbians during their growing-up years, associated gender role reversals with gays and lesbians. The men were feminine and the women looked male or tomboy with the women couples in a butch-femme type relationship. The belief and expe-riences with lesbians and gay men who dress and act in opposite gender roles serve as the backdrop of what to compare their children to when faced with their coming out. Most of what these parents see is a part of homosex-uality, the dress or behavior. They have not seen the whole range of affec-tional, emotional, intellectual, and sexual components of a person. Although I asked the interviewees if they had any thoughts or attitudes about lesbians or gay men, most said they did not think about them and did not participate in the name calling or bashing. This might not be necessarily true because they were able to relate quite a few incidents of homophobic opinions that might have been internalized. Moreover, once they know they have a lesbian or gay child, that distance or nonjudgmental attitude radically changes. As one mother remarked, "The fire is on the other side of the river bank. The matter is taking place somewhere else; it's not your problem."[22]

Disclosure or Discovery

For the most part, parents experience a wide range of emotions, feelings, and attitudes when they find out they have a lesbian daughter or gay son. Parents find out through a variety of ways, ranging from a direct disclosure by the child themselves, discovering the fact from a journal, confronting the child because of suspicions, or by walking in on them.

For example, Liz Lee, who walked in on her daughter, Sandy, said, "[It was] the end of the world. Still today I can't relate to anything that's going on with my daughter, but I'm accepting."[23] She found out in 1990 and said,

I was hoping it was a stage she's going through and that she could change. I didn't accept for a long time. I didn't think she would come out in the open like this. I thought she would just keep it and later on get married. That's what I thought but she's really out and open. . . . I said to myself I accept it because she is going to live that way.[24]

Because Sandy serves as the co-chair of the Gay, Lesbian, and Bisexual Association at school, her mother sees Sandy as happy and politically fulfilled in this position, which assists her mother's process in accepting Sandy's sexual orientation. However, like many of the parents interviewed, she initially thought she had done something wrong. "I didn't lead a normal life at the time either. But Sandy always accept me as I was, and she was always happy when I was happy, and I think that's love. As long as Sandy's happy."[25]

Toni Barraquiel responded differently when Joel told her at an early age of thirteen or fourteen that he was gay back in the mid-1980s. She plainly asked him if he felt happy, to which he replied affirmatively. Thus her response, "Well, if you're happy I'll support you, I'll be happy for you."[26] Their relationship as a single mother and only child has always been one of closeness and open communication, so problems did not arise in terms of disclosing his sexual orientation. Toni Barraquiel experienced confusion because at the time he had girlfriends, and she did not think of him as a typical feminine gay man, since he looked macho. She also wondered if her single-mother role had anything to do with Joel's gay orientation:

Maybe because I raised him by myself, it was a matriarchal thing. I have read now that these gays, there is something in the anatomy of their bodies that affect the way they are. So it is not because I raised him alone, maybe it's in the anatomy of the body. Even if I think that because I raised him alone as a mother, even if he came out to be gay, he was raised as a good person. No matter what I would say I'm still lucky he came out to be like that.[27]

In the end she accepted Joel no matter what caused his sexual orientation.

Katherine Tanaka*, a fifty-three-year-old Japanese-American from Hawaii, found out about Melissa's lesbianism through an indirect family conversation. George Tanaka* brought up the issue of sexuality and asked Melissa* if she was a lesbian. He suspected that she was after reading her work on the computer. Katherine* remembered her own response:

I was in a state of shock. I didn't expect it, so I didn't know how to react. It was the thing of disbelief, horror, and shame and the whole thing. I guess I felt the Asian values I was taught surface in the sense that something was wrong. That she didn't turn out the way we had raised her to be.[28]

George Tanaka* recalled, "After we hugged, she went off to her bedroom. As she was walking away from us, all of a sudden I felt like she was a stranger. I thought I knew [her]. Here was a very important part of her and I didn't know anything about it."[29] The idea of not knowing one's children anymore after discovering their sexual orientation remains a common initial response from the interviewees. Because of this one aspect, parents believe that their child has changed and is no longer the person they thought they knew. For example, one parent said:

The grieving process took a long time. Especially the thing about not being a bride. Not having her be a bride was a very devastating change of plans for her life. I thought I was in her life and it made me feel when she said she was a lesbian that there was no place for me in her life. I didn't know how I could fit into her life because I didn't know how to be the mother of a lesbian.[30]

On finding out, the parents interviewed spoke of common responses and questions they had. What did I do wrong? Was I responsible for my child's lesbian or gay identity? What will others think? How do I relate to my child? What role do I have now that I know my child is a lesbian or gay man? A parent's emotions range from the loss of a dream they had for their child to a fear of what is in store for them as a gay or lesbian person in this society. Nancy Shigekawa*, a third-generation Japanese-American born and residing in Hawaii, recalled her reaction:

I had come home one night and they were in the bedroom. Then I knew it wasn't just being in the room. My reaction was outrage, to say the least. I was so angry. I told them to come out . . . and I said [to her girlfriend] "I'm going to kill you if you ever come back." That's how I was feeling. I look back now and think I must have been like a crazy lady.[31]

Maria Santos* remembered her discovery.

I found out through a phone call from the parents of [her] best friend. They [Cecilia* and her friend] were trying to sneak out and they had a relationship. I thought it would go away. Let her see a psychiatrist. But she fooled me. In her second year at college she told me she was a lesbian. It broke my heart. That was the first time I heard the word lesbian, but I knew what it meant. Like a tomboy.[32]

She also had a feeling about her youngest daughter, Paulette*:

At Cecilia's graduation I saw them talking secretly and I saw the pink triangle on her backpack. I can't explain it. It's a mother's instinct. I prayed that it would not be so [starts to cry]. Paulette told me in a letter that she was a lesbian and that Cecilia had nothing to do with it. I wanted it to change. I had the dream, that kids go to college, get married, and have kids.[33]

Maria Santos* did not talk to anyone about her daughters. She grew up having to face the world on her own without talking to others. However, she said, "I read books, articles all about gays and lesbians as members of the community. They are normal people. I did not read negative things about them."[34]

In this sense, parents also have a coming-out process that they go through. They must deal with internalized homophobia and reevaluate their beliefs and feelings about lesbians and gay men. One method in this process in- cludes reading about and listening to gay men and lesbians talk about their lives. Having personal contact or at least information on lesbian and gay life takes the mystery out of the stereotypes and misconceptions that parents might have of lesbian and gay people. What helped some women was their personal interaction with, and reading about, lesbian and gay men's lives. They had more information with which to contrast, contradict, and support their previous notions of lesbians and gay men.

Yet sometimes some parents interviewed have not yet read on the subject nor sought outside help or information. Some of the parents did not talk to others and have remained alone in their thinking. This does not necessarily have negative effects. Liz Lee said, "Still today I don't think I can discuss with her in this matter because I can't relate. . . . I can't handle it. I wouldn't know how to talk to her about this subject. I just let her be happy."[35]

MG Espiritu*, a sixty-year-old Pilippina immigrant, believes her daugh- ter's lesbianism stems from environmental causes such as being with other lesbians. Nonetheless, less than a couple of years after finding out about her daughter, Michelle, she went with her daughter to an Asian-Pacific lesbian

Lunar New Year banquet. MG* did so because her daughter wanted it, and she wanted to please her. When asked how she felt at the event, MG* replied, "Oh, it's normal. It's just like my little girls' parties that they go to."[36] She speaks of gradually trying to accept Michelle's lesbianism.

Parents, Friends, and Their Ethnic Communities

For some parents, having a lesbian or gay child brings up the issue of their status and reputation in the community and family network. Questions such as: What is society going to think of me? Will the neighbors know and what will it reflect on us? Did we raise a bad child?

> I told her we would have to move away from this house. I felt strongly neighbors and friends in the community would not want to associate with us if they knew we had a child who had chosen to be homosexual.[37]

The above quote reflected one parent's original reaction. Now she feels differently but is still not quite out to her family in Hawaii.

Some parents have told their siblings or friends. Others do not talk to relatives or friends at all because they fear they will not understand.

The following quote highlighted parents' typical anxiety:

> I was ashamed. I felt I had a lot to do with it, too. In my mind I'm not stupid, I'm telling myself, I know I didn't do it to her. I don't know if it's only because I'm Japanese . . . that's the way I saw it. I felt a sense of shame, that something was wrong with my family. I would look at Debbie* and just feel so guilty that I have these thoughts that something's wrong with her. But mostly I was selfish. I felt more for myself, what I am going to say? How am I going to react to people when they find out?[38]

Despite her apprehension in the beginning, she did disclose Debbie's lesbianism to a close friend:

> I have a dear friend who I finally told because she was telling me about these different friends who had gay children. I couldn't stand it, I said, "You know, Bea, I have to tell you my daughter is gay." She was dum-

founded. I'm starting to cheer her up and all that. That was a big step for me to come out.

Nancy Shigekawa's* quote emphasizes the complexity of feelings parents have when adjusting to their children's sexual orientation.

If parents are not close to their immediate family, they might not have told them. Others have not spoken because they do not care whether their family knows. Some parents do not disclose the fact of their gay son or lesbian daughter to protect them from facing unnecessary problems.

When asked how their respective ethnic communities feel about lesbians and gay men, some parents responded with firm conviction. Liz Lee, who spoke about the Korean community, said, "As long as they're not in their house, not in their life, they accept it perfectly."[39] She mentioned her daughter's lesbianism to a nephew but not to others in her family. "I'm sure in the future I have to tell them, but right now nobody has asked me and I don't particularly like to volunteer."[40] Jack Chan*, a sixty-one-year-old Chinese immigrant claimed, "Shame, that's a big factor. Shame brought on the family. You have to remember the Chinese, the name, the face of the family is everything. I don't know how to overcome that."[41]

Lucy Nguyen* gave this answer about the Vietnamese community, "They won't accept it. Because for a long, long time they say they [gays and lesbians] are not good people, that's why."[42] Lucy felt that talking about it would help to teach the community to open their minds. The frankness and openness of speaking out about gay and lesbians will inform people of our existence and force the issue in the open. In this way, having parents come out will make others understand their experiences and also allow for their validation and affirmation.

Although most of these parents have negative views about the acceptance level of friends, particularly in ethnic communities, some have taken steps to confide in people. One must also realize that their opinion reflects their current situation and may change over time. Three of the parents have participated in panels and discussions on Asian-American parents with lesbian and gay kids.

Advice to Other Parents

In many ways, the mere fact that these parents agreed to the interview has much to say about their feelings or attitudes toward lesbian and gay sexuality and their kids. Although some parents might feel some unease and reservations, they had enough courage to speak to me and voice their opinions. Many of the parents did so out of love and concern for their children. A few thought they had nothing to say but agreed to talk to me. In the process of these interviews, some parents expressed appreciation and comfort in talking to someone about their experiences. Their struggle to come to terms with their lesbian daughters and gay sons merits notice.

One of my last questions related to helping other parents. While some did not have an answer to the question, "What advice do you have for other parents with lesbian and gay kids?" a few responded with suggestions:

> Love them like a normal individual. Give all the compassion and understanding. Don't treat your child differently because the person is gay, because this is an individual. . . . I cannot understand why it is so hard for these parents to accept their child is gay. What makes them so different, because they are gay? The more you should support your kid, because as it is in society, it has not been accepted one hundred percent.[43]

> I cannot throw them out. I love them so much. Even more now because they are more of a minority. They are American Asian women and lesbian. Triple minority. I have to help fight for them. . . . Accept them as they are. Love them more. They will encounter problems. It will take years and years to overcome homophobia. Make them ambitious, well-educated, better than others so they can succeed.[44]

Tina Chan*, a fifty-eight-year-old Chinese immigrant, offers similar advice, with which other parents concurred:

> My advice is to accept them. They haven't changed at all. They're still the same person. The only thing different is their sexual orientation. They should really have the support from the family, so they would not have this battle like they're not even being accepted in the family. They should look at them like they have not changed. Parents can't do it. They think the whole person has changed and I think that's terrible because they haven't. I mean it's so stupid.[45]

Jack Chan* also leaves us with heartfelt advice:

> Don't feel depressed that their parent [is] coming around so slow or not coming around at all. Remember when you come out to them, the parent generally go[es] into the closet themselves. However long

it take you to come out, it'll probably take them longer to accept. It's a slow process. Don't give up.[46]

Concluding Remarks

George Tanaka* relates an incident where he and his wife told their coming-out process in front of ten Asian-American gay men and in the end found some of the men were crying. "The tears surprised me. . . . We were representing the sadness that there could not be loving parents. Representing some hope their parents would likewise be able to become loving about it."[47] The belief that parents can change and go through a process resulting in eventual acceptance and support appears to have a basis in reality, although a happy ending may not always be the case.

From these interviews one can sense some of the thoughts, actions, and experiences of Asian-American parents. These stories are not the last word but signal the beginning of a more informed dialogue.

What would the stories of their daughters and sons look like against their parents' perceptions? It would be helpful to have the stories side by side to evaluate the differences. Moreover, gay and lesbian children might have perspectives that inform parents. Other issues, such as socialization processes, religion, language, and culture need further exploration, as does the issue of spouses' opinions. I did not include a discussion on the origins of lesbian and gay sexual identity. I hope these stories from the homefront can serve as an initial mapping of a complex sexual territory that is part of Asian-American family dynamics.

Acknowledgments

Grateful acknowledgments go to the Rockefeller Humanities Asian Pacific American Generations program for funding this project during 1992–93 and to the parents who courageously shared their stories. Thanks to Russell Leong for his lenient soul on deadlines and fine eye for editing.

Notes

1. Interview with Katherine Tanaka*, Los Angeles, California, February 21, 1993.
2. The desire to work on this project came after listening to two Japanese-American parents, George and Katherine Tanaka*, talk about their lesbian daughter. They revealed a painful process of going through their own coming out while

grappling with their daughter's sexual identity and their own values and beliefs. As members of Parents and Friends of Lesbians and Gays (PFLAG), they mentioned they were the only Asian-Americans, the only parents of color, for that matter, in this organization. Despite being the Asian-American contact, Katherine* has received fewer than ten calls during a two-year period, and not one Asian-American parent has ever come to PFLAG. She recounted her feelings and belief of being the only Asian parent with a gay child. That feeling of loneliness and alienation struck me deeply because, as an Asian-American lesbian, I could identify with her feelings.

3. See Kitty Tsui, *The Words of a Woman Who Breathes Fire* (San Francisco: Spinsters Ink, 1983); C. Chung, Alison Kim, and A. K. Lemshewsky, eds., *Between the Lines: An Anthology by Pacific/Asian Lesbians* (Santa Cruz: Dancing Bird Press, 1987); Rakesh Ratti, ed., *A Lotus of Another Color: The Unfolding of the South Asian Gay and Lesbian Experience* (Boston: Alyson, 1993); Silvera Makeda, ed., *A Piece of My Heart: A Lesbian of Colour Anthology* (Toronto: Sister Vision, 1993).

4. Mothers comprise the majority of the parents interviewed. Perhaps mothers are more apt to talk about their feelings and emotions about having a gay son or lesbian daughter than fathers are. Mothers may be more understanding and willing to discuss their emotions and experiences than fathers are.

5. I did not interview parents who had a bisexual child. I believe a son or daughter who comes out as bisexual might encounter a different set of questions and reactions. Especially since the parent might hope and persuade the daughter or son to "choose" heterosexuality instead of homosexuality.

6. See Carolyn W. Griffin, Marian J. Wirth, and Arthur G. Wirth, *Beyond Acceptance: Parents of Lesbians and Gays Talk about Their Experiences* (New York: St. Martin's, 1986).

7. Parents and Friends of Lesbians and Gays (PFLAG) has chapters throughout the United States. One couple and a father interviewed are involved with PFLAG in their respective locales.

8. Ann Muller, *Parents Matter: Parents' Relationships with Lesbian Daughters and Gay Sons* (Tallahassee: Naiad, 1987), p. 197.

9. Connie S. Chan, "Issues of Identity Development among Asian-American Lesbians and Gay Men," *Journal of Counseling and Development* 68 (September/October 1989):19.

10. Interview with Lucy Nguyen*, Los Angeles, California, February 20, 1993.

11. Interview with Midori Asakura*, Los Angeles, California, April 18, 1993.

12. Midori Asakura*.

13. Ibid.

14. *Mahu* does not necessarily mean gay but defines a man who dresses and acts feminine. However, its common usage does denote a gay man.

15. Interview with Toni Barraquiel, Los Angeles, California, April 18, 1993.

16. Telephone interview with Maria Santos*, Portland, Oregon, May 9, 1993.
17. Lucy Nguyen*.
18. Interview with Margaret Tsang*, San Francisco, California, February 5, 1993.
19. Interview with Liz Lee, Los Angeles, California, May 11, 1993.
20. Liz based this respect on this particular woman's election to something similar to a city council and her standing in the community.
21. Liz Lee.
22. Midori Asakura*.
23. Liz Lee.
24. Ibid.
25. Ibid.
26. Toni Barraquiel.
27. Ibid.
28. Katherine Tanaka*.
29. Interview with George Tanaka, Los Angeles, California, February 21, 1993.
30. Katherine Tanaka.
31. Telephone interview with Nancy Shigekawa, Kaneohe, Hawaii, March 20, 1993.
32. Maria Santos.
33. Ibid.
34. Ibid.
35. Liz Lee.
36. Interview with MG Espiritu, northern California, July 20, 1993.
37. Katherine Tanaka.
38. Nancy Shigekawa.
39. Liz Lee.
40. Ibid.
41. Interview with Jack Chan, northern California, July 18, 1993.
42. Lucy Nguyen.
43. Toni Barraquiel.
44. Maria Santos.
45. Interview with Tina Chan, northern California, July 18, 1993.
46. Jack Chan.
47. George Tanaka.

Part VI

Adolescence, Midlife, and Aging

One useful way of viewing sexual orientation issues is to use the lifespan developmental perspective — from the first awareness of sexual and affectional feelings through adolescence, adulthood, and old age. Research on gay men, bisexuals, and lesbians has made a contribution to lifespan developmental psychology by challenging and stretching the existing models to include the diversity that results from sexual orientation (Kimmel 1978).

Many adult lesbians and gay men report that they had sexual feelings and experiences during late childhood and early adolescence that provided the first cues about their sexual orientation (Bell, Weinberg, and Hammersmith 1981; Savin-Williams 1998). Thus, about the time some adolescents are beginning to date and explore heterosexual feelings and behaviors, others are sensing that they are different or that they are attracted to same-gender friends and have crushes. There is great variation in the ways lesbians, gay men, and bisexuals handle this discovery. Even if one does not feel shame or guilt because of cultural or religious influences, the unpredictability of other's response — both positive and negative — tends to discourage being open about one's minority sexual orientation (Rotheram-Borus, Rosario, and Koopman 1991).

In contrast to most gay and bisexual men, for whom the first clues are usually explicitly sexual, for many lesbian and bisexual women sexual orientation development is not solely about sexual attractions but more broadly about personal relationships (Peplau and Garnets 2000). In general, love and intimacy are more important for understanding the development of female sexuality than for understanding male sexuality (Baldwin and Baldwin 1997;

DeLamater 1987; Schneider 2001). For example, adolescent girls generally achieve higher levels of intimacy, sensitivity, and empathy in their close relationships than do adolescent boys, regardless of sexual orientation (Diamond and Savin-Williams, this volume; Dube, Savin-Williams, and Diamond 2001; Peplau 2001). As a result, sexual identity development and explorations of same-gender experiences may follow different developmental patterns for adolescent boys and girls. "For women, who often come out in the context of a relationship, identity and intimacy as developmental tasks may become interwoven, whereas men's socialization toward autonomy and sexual freedom may lead to the resolution of identity tasks prior to negotiation of intimacy" (Fassinger 1991:168).

Moreover, research has indicated that important variations exist among lesbian, bisexual, and gay male youth in their experience of acquiring a sexual identity based on social class (Greene, this volume), race or ethnicity (Dube and Savin-Williams 1999; Rotheram-Borus, Rosario, and Koopman 1991; Savin-Williams and Rodriguez 1993), and community size (D'Augelli 1991; Sears 1991). The pattern may also differ for bisexual adolescents compared to lesbian or gay male adolescents (Diamond and Savin-Williams, this volume; Savin-Williams and Diamond 2000; Rust 2000).

A number of adolescents may be stigmatized by their behavior, mannerisms, or preferences that others interpret as lesbian or gay. Likewise some precocious adolescents identify as gay, bisexual, or lesbian, and this may become known or may be openly acknowledged. Often they experience considerable harassment from peers and seldom have family support (Rivers and D'Augelli 2001). If not counteracted by peers or teachers, the resulting stigma can lead to continued harassment and even violence, severe pressure in school, and the need for special educational resources. These kinds of problems in school settings led to the creation of specific high schools dedicated to serving lesbian, gay, and bisexual youth such as the Harvey Milk High School in New York City and the EAGLES Center in California (Battey 1995). Some schools are providing space for student-led support groups (often called a "gay straight alliance"). The Gay, Lesbian, and Straight Education Network (GLSEN) is an important resource for students, teachers, administrators, and parents (www.glsen.org).

In recent years there has been a substantial increase in community-based youth programs. The majority of these programs combine social and recreational opportunities with support and informal counseling (Rivers and D'Augelli 2001). A greater range of services specifically directed to bisexual, lesbian, and gay youth are still needed, however. These services have been difficult to establish, especially in suburban and rural areas where young people usually rely on their parents to provide transportation.

Homeless lesbian and gay teenagers, many of whom have run away from abusive homes to urban areas, are among the most highly at-risk populations of young people today (Kruks 1991). Several model programs now exist including Project 10 in Los Angeles and the Hetrick-Martin Institute for the Protection of Lesbian and Gay Youth in New York City (Rivers and D'Augelli 2001).

Resources on the Internet can provide support for gay, lesbian, and bisexual youth, but there is no quality control on the information provided and some sites may be restricted by software designed to protect children from sexually oriented sites. Books written for gay, lesbian, and bisexual adolescents also are providing useful information (e.g. Marcus 2000).

The article by Anhalt and Morris in this section reviews the research on gay, lesbian, and bisexual adolescents. They describe typical developmental issues such as coming out and dating, potentially stressful aspects such as victimization and high-risk sexual behavior, studies on suicide, behavioral problems, substance use, and academic problems; they also identify some risk and protective factors for gay, lesbian, and bisexual adolescents.

Midlife and aging among lesbians, bisexuals, and gay men has also begun to emerge from the shadows of heterosexist views of normal human development. This dimension of development is especially important because few lesbian, bisexual, and gay adolescents have family role models for their future life course who can suggest answers to life-span issues. How do middle-aged and older lesbians, bisexuals, and gay men resolve developmental needs for occupational success, sexual and emotional intimacy, and spiritual growth? If they do not have children, what provides them with a sense of fulfillment and promise? What dimensions differ for them in the course of their development from adolescence to late adulthood? Studies have only begun to examine these questions (e.g., Kimmel and Martin 2001; Weinberg, Williams, and Pryor 2001).

The selection by Kimmel and Sang is a review of research and theory on midlife issues for lesbians and gay men. These studies are based on a cohort of pioneers whose lives spanned a unique period of history; many were among the creators and activists of the emerging gay, lesbian, and bisexual communities. Other published resources on midlife include studies and personal descriptions of lesbian experiences (Sang, Warshow, and Smith 1991), issues for gay men (Lee 1991), and a self-help book written for men by one of the pioneers in gay psychology (Kooden and Flowers 2000).

Older lesbians, bisexuals, and gay men today grew up in a different historical period than younger people have experienced. Their lives were shaped by puritanical views of sexuality; economic hardship during the Depression that reinforced gender roles that had relaxed somewhat during the 1920s; and World War II, which brought many lesbians and gay men together with their own kind for the first time in the armed forces and in urban centers. When homosexuals began to be excluded from the armed forces near the end of the war, and later were linked with Communists as threats to national security in the 1950s, witch hunts and legal suppression forced many into hiding their homosexuality. Gay and lesbian bars were raided repeatedly, and patrons were arrested; sometimes a list of those arrested was published in the daily newspaper, with many victims of arrest losing their employment, family, and friends as a result. Even in New York City and Chicago this practice continued into the 1960s. By 1969, when the Stonewall Inn Bar was raided, patrons were not routinely arrested and exposed in the newspapers, but lesbian and gay life was still a twilight world of illegal bars existing through police bribery and underworld connections. One book on older gay men quoted a respondent born in 1926: "I've been gay longer than it's been popular. . . . Talk about harassment! They backed a paddy wagon up to the back door of one of those bars and emptied everyone right into the wagon. In those days we used to get a lot of heat and there was no such thing as entrapment. They'd just come in and bust everyone there. And get away with it!" (Vacha 1985:69).

In the past, negative stereotypes of lonely, depressed, ostracized old "dykes" and "queens" leading lives of quiet desperation were common, adding to the burden of fear and stigma younger lesbians, bisexuals, and gay men had to face. Today we are viewing the elder generation as pioneers, as well as survivors, who can provide a link with the history of sexual minorities.

One important finding from the emerging field of lesbian, bisexual, and gay gerontology is that the population is very diverse. For example, one finds older lesbians, bisexuals, and gay men who have lived openly, often as a same-sex couple, for many years. Others have spent the majority of their adult years hiding their homosexuality. Some had a heterosexual marriage and may have children and grandchildren. The research also indicates that there can be advantages to aging as a gay man, bisexual, or lesbian. Potential benefits include the possibility of creating one's family and social roles to suit one's individual needs. In addition, some develop a kind of *crisis competence* that may reflect resilience as a result of successful coping with heterosexist bias and sexual prejudice (Kimmel 1978, 1995).

A variety of social service agencies, programs, and organizations have emerged for older lesbians, bisexuals, and gay men, including Senior Action in a Gay Environment (SAGE) in New York City (*www.sageusa.org*), Gay and Lesbian Outreach to Elders (GLOE) in San Francisco, and many others. Development of these organizations represents the empowerment of the lesbian, bisexual, and gay communities. Not only do these services meet important needs of vulnerable members of the community, but they also provide intergenerational role models and resources for successful aging to persons of all ages. One elderly lesbian expressed this well:

> Just because I'm old and sick and eighty-five doesn't mean I didn't have quite a gay life. You see I've loved a lot of women and a lot of women have loved me. In fact, if I weren't sick, that would still be the case. . . .
>
> I need somebody most every day of the week. I have some people from GLOE, and a woman from Catholic Charities comes in once a week for $5.50 an hour. She does a good job. She cleans the house. . . .
>
> I have friends who come by and cook me dinner every now and then, and I have friends who take me to my doctors' appointments. These are new and younger gay friends.
>
> At one point, I thought gay people were no good. But now all these gay people are helping me. It's not my family that is taking care of me; it's my gay friends. They have been wonderful to me. (Adelman 1986:207–9)

The selection by Grossman, D'Augelli and O'Connell reports on a large national study of older lesbians, gay men, and bisexuals; it focuses on psychosexual and health characteristics, support networks, stress, resilience, and distress in their lives. This paper was first presented at a national conference hosted by SAGE (Kimmel and Martin 2001). Other resources on aging issues are available from the Lesbian and Gay Aging Issues Network of the American Society on Aging (*www.asaging.org*) and from the National Gay and Lesbian Task Force (see Cahill, South, and Spade 2000).

Contemporary Issue: The Impact of AIDS on Adolescents and Older Persons

The impact of acquired immune deficiency syndrome (AIDS) on adolescents and young adults is a high priority. Young people often feel they are immune from dangers, so they are more likely to take risks. Young people also tend to be more sexually active and may be uninformed about AIDS prevention because of social taboos regarding education about sexuality, safer sex, and contraception. In addition, the belief that medical treatment can prevent the effects of HIV infection may gave false hopes to those who choose to risk infection.

With regard to AIDS and aging, we may optimistically assume that medical advances will allow many persons infected with HIV/AIDS to live for extended periods of time. However, the physical and psychosocial effects of growing older with the disease are unknown. Therefore a critical issue for research is the impact of AIDS on older gay men, bisexuals, and lesbians (Allers 1990). For example, SAGE in New York City has expanded its services to include specialized training for hospital and nursing-home staff, and programs for persons with HIV/AIDS, including support groups for seniors with AIDS, their care partners, and friendly visitors.

Lesbians, although much less frequently infected with HIV/AIDS than gay men, have carried a major burden of coordinating and providing services to people infected with the virus, so their community has also been deeply affected. In addition, a large number of gay men died in young adulthood and middle age, leaving an underpopulated male cohort in the aging process. Many lesbians have helped to fill this gap by taking on leadership positions in lesbian, gay, and bisexual communities.

A remark attributed to Margaret Mead noted that communities could be defined by the fact that they care for their vulnerable members. Since the mid-1970s the lesbian, gay, and bisexual communities have established services to care for their most vulnerable members: adolescents, persons with AIDS, and elders. In many ways the building of a community has taken place within our lifetime. Now we can be empowered by it and nurture its growth for future generations.

References

Adelman, M., ed. 1986. *Long Time Passing: Lives of Older Lesbians*. Boston, Mass.: Alyson.

Allers, C. T. 1990. AIDS and the older adult. *The Gerontologist* 30:405–7.

Baldwin, J. D., and J. I. Baldwin. 1997. Gender differences in sexual interest. *Archives of Sexual Behavior* 26:181–21.

Bell, A. P., M. S. Weinberg, and S. K. Hammersmith. 1981. *Sexual Preference: Its Development in Men and Women*. Bloomington: Indiana University Press.

Cahill, S., K. South, and H. Spade. 2000. *Outing Age: Public Policy Issues Affecting*

Gay, Lesbian, Bisexual, and Transgender Elders. Washington, D.C.: National Gay and Lesbian Task Force.

D'Augelli, A. R. 1991. Lesbians and gay men on campus: Visibility, empowerment, and educational leadership. *Peabody Journal of Education* 66:124–42.

DeLamater, J. 1987. Gender differences in sexual scenarios. In K. Kelley, ed., *Females, Males, and Sexuality: Theories and Research*, pp. 127–29. Albany: State University of New York Press.

Dube, E. M., and R. C. Savin-Williams. 1999. Sexual identity development among ethnic sexual-minority male youths. *Developmental Psychology* 35:1389–99.

Dube, E. M., R. C. Savin-Williams, L. M. and Diamond. 2001. Intimacy development, gender, and ethnicity among sexual-minority youth. In A. R. D'Augelli and C. J. Patterson, eds., *Lesbian, Gay, and Bisexual Identities and Youth*, pp. 129–52. New York: Oxford University Press.

Fassinger, R. E. 1991. The hidden minority: Issues and challenges in working with lesbian women and gay men. *The Counseling Psychologist* 19:157–76.

Kimmel, D.C. 1978. Adult development and aging: A gay perspective. *The Journal of Social Issues* 34(3):113–30.

Kimmel, D.C. 1995. Lesbians and gay men also grow old. In L. A. Bond, S. J. Cutler, and A. Grams, eds., *Promoting Successful and Productive Aging*, pp. 289–303. Thousand Oaks, Calif.: Sage.

Kimmel, D.C., and D. L. Martin, eds. 2001. Midlife and aging in gay America. *Journal of Gay and Lesbian Social Services* 13 (whole no. 4).

Kooden, H., and C. Flowers. 2000. *Golden Men: The Power of Gay Midlife*. New York: Harper-Collins.

Kruks, G. 1991. Gay and lesbian homeless/street youth: Special issues and concerns. *Journal of Adolescent Health* 12:51–518.

Lee, J. A., ed. 1991. Gay midlife and maturity. *Journal of Homosexuality* 20, nos. 3/4.

Marcus, E. 2000. *What If Someone I Know Is Gay? Answers to Questions about Gay and Lesbian People*. New York: Price Stern Sloan.

Peplau, L. A. 2001. Rethinking women's sexual orientation: An interdisciplinary, relationship-focused approach. *Personal Relationships* 8:1–19.

Peplau, L. A., and L. D. Garnets. 2000. A new paradigm for understanding women's sexuality and sexual orientation. *Journal of Social Issues* 56(2):329–50.

Rivers, I., and A. R. D'Augelli. 2001. The victimization of lesbian, gay, and bisexual youths. In A. R. D'Augelli and C. J. Patterson, eds. *Lesbian, Gay, and Bisexual Identities and Youth*, pp. 199–223. New York: Oxford University Press.

Rotheram-Borus, M. J., M. Rosario, and C. Koopman. 1991. Minority youth at risk: Gay males and runaways. In M. E. Colten and S. Gore, eds., *Adolescent Stress: Causes and Consequences*, pp. 181–200. New York: Aldine de Gruyter.

Rust, P.C.R. 2000. Bisexuality: A contemporary paradox for women. *Journal of Social Issues* 56(2):205–21.

Sang, B., J. Warshow, and A. J. Smith, eds. 1991. *Lesbians at Midlife: The Creative Transition*. San Francisco: Spinsters.

Savin-Williams, R. C. 1998. " . . . *and Then I Became Gay": Young Men's Stories*. New York: Routledge.

Savin-Williams, R. C., and L. M. Diamond. 2000. Sexual identity trajectories among sexual-minority youths: Gender comparisons. *Archives of Sexual Behavior* 29:419–40.

Savin-Williams, R. C., and R. G. Rodriguez. 1993. A developmental, clinical perspective on lesbian, gay male, and bisexual youth. In T. P. Gullotta, G. R. Adams, and R. Montemayor, eds., *Adolescent Sexuality: Advances in Adolescent Development*, vol. 5, pp. 77–101. Newbury Park, Calif.: Sage.

Schneider, M. S. 2001. Toward a reconceptualization of the coming-out process for adolescent females. In A. R. D'Augelli and C. J. Patterson, eds. *Lesbian, Gay, and Bisexual Identities and Youth*, pp. 71–96. New York: Oxford University Press.

Sears, J. T. 1991. *Growing up Gay in the South: Race, Gender, and Journeys of the Spirit*. Bimingham, N.Y.: Harrington Park.

Vacha, K. 1985. *Quiet Fire: Memoirs of Older Gay Men*. Trumansburg, N.Y.: Crossing.

Weinberg, M. S., C. J. Williams, and D. W. Pryor. 2001. Bisexuals at midlife: Commitment, salience, and identity. *Journal of Contemporary Ethnography* 30:180–208.

21   Developmental and Adjustment Issues of Gay, Lesbian, and Bisexual Adolescents: A Review of the Empirical Literature

Karla Anhalt and Tracy L. Morris

Various adjustment problems experienced by gay, lesbian, and bisexual (GLB) adolescents have been reported in the empirical literature. Difficulties that have been studied include past suicide attempts, substance use and abuse, conduct problems, and academic concerns. Some of these difficulties have been related to stress regarding acceptance and disclosure of a GLB sexual orientation. For example, a considerable number of GLB youth report a history of suicide attempts, with prevalence rates ranging from 11 to 42 percent (e.g., D'Augelli and Hershberger 1993; Remafedi 1987; Roesler and Deisher 1972; Rotheram-Borus et al. 1995). Those percentages can be contrasted with a 7.1 percent lifetime prevalence rate of suicide attempts in a representative community sample of adolescents (Lewinsohn, Rohde, and Seeley 1996). In addition, several investigators have reported "problematic" rates of substance use and abuse, conduct problems, and academic difficulties in young gay and bisexual men (e.g., Remafedi 1987; Rotheram-Borus et al. 1994, 1995).

The empirical literature on the adjustment difficulties of GLB adolescents is replete with methodological problems (Savin-Williams 1994). Thus, although data suggest that GLB youth have particular adjustment problems related to the acceptance and disclosure of their sexual orientation, the methodological flaws in most published studies limit conclusive findings in this area. To date, the authors are not aware of a published critical review of empirical studies on adjustment issues of GLB adolescents who have lived in the United States. A primary purpose of this paper is to critically review this literature as it pertains to U.S. samples. In the first sections we describe characteristics of development that are particular to GLB adolescents. The review of studies on adjustment issues follows. We conclude with a proposal of risk and protective factors particular to GLB youth and offer suggestions for future research in this area.

It is important to note that published empirical studies regarding the life experiences of GLB youth were scarce before the 1980s; however, there has been an increase in the last decade. The paucity of research on GLB adolescents before the 1980s may be understood best against a historical background. During most of the twentieth century, people who have identified as GLB typically have refrained from disclosing their sexual orientation as a result of religious, legal, and cultural repression (Patterson 1995). Further, until the year 1969, people who identified as GLB generally could not be both open about their sexual orientation and publicly respected (Rothblum 1994).

In June 1969 an uprising took place at the Stonewall Inn Bar in Greenwich Village in New York City. During this uprising (hereafter referred to as "Stonewall"), GLB individuals publicly demanded an end to oppression and discrimination on the basis of sexual orientation (Newton 1994). Stonewall marked the beginning of the U.S. modern GLB liberation movement, and it greatly impacted the lives of GLB people in the country. To illustrate, before Stonewall, fewer than fifty formal organizations were available in the United States for GLB individuals to meet socially and actively fight discrimination on the basis of sexual orientation. In contrast, five years after Stonewall, more than three thousand of these groups had been established (Strickland 1995). In addition, only in the last twenty-five years have large numbers of individuals publicly identified themselves as GLB (Patterson 1995). Thus, as would be expected, the post-Stonewall era has opened more doors for GLB adolescents to accept and disclose their sexual orientation (Herdt 1989).

It should be noted that adolescents who identified as GLB during the first part of the twentieth century were visible in the gay male and lesbian communities of their time. For example, during World War II, the formation of gay male and lesbian relationships within the military was common, and youth often acknowledged their romantic feelings for people of the same gender within the context of the military (Faderman 1991; Kennedy and Davis 1993). Other contexts that facilitated the immersion of young people into gay male and lesbian culture included sports teams, bars, and colleges (Faderman 1991; Kennedy and Davis 1993).

Definition of Sexual Orientation During Adolescence

Same-gender sexual behavior has existed throughout history; however, until about 1850 the labels "heterosexual," "lesbian," and "gay male" did not exist in Western societies (D'Emilio 1983). Further, to this day, many non-Western societies do not conceive of sexual behavior along the homosexual and heterosexual continuum (e.g., Weinrich and Williams 1991). Therefore the process of defining sexual orientation in adults has been debated since the term's inception. For example, social scientists have argued whether fantasies and attractions, as well as sexual behavior, are components of sexual orientation (see Gonsiorek, Sell, and Weinrich 1995, or Gonsiorek and Weinrich 1991, for a discussion of these issues). Further, some authors have encouraged models of sexual orientation that focus on identity (e.g., self-labeling as a gay man), sexual behavior (e.g., engaging in sexual activity with same-gender partners), and community participation (e.g., belonging to a lesbian political organization; Golden 1987).

There are certain issues that present difficulties in defining and measuring sexual orientation during adolescence. Many adolescents are likely to experience sexual interests and behaviors for the first time in their lives during puberty (Petersen, Leffert, and Graham 1995). Further, exploration of the sexual self is an important developmental milestone for many adolescents (Petersen et al. 1995). As such, many adolescents may engage in same-gender sexual behavior or experience same-gender sexual attraction but not self-label as lesbian or gay male. In addition, some youths who self-label as GLB may identify as heterosexual in adulthood. As becomes clear throughout this paper, research on GLB youths has taken place with participants who readily identify in that manner. Thus psychological research about adolescents who experience same-gender behavior, fantasies, or attractions but who do not self-label as GLB is scarce.

Because of their breadth, the following definitions have been chosen for this paper. A gay or lesbian sexual orientation is defined here as a self-label that implies "a preponderance of sexual or erotic feelings, thoughts, fantasies, and behaviors desired with members of the same sex" (Savin-Williams 1990:3). A bisexual sexual orientation is defined here as a self-label that implies sexual or erotic feelings, thoughts, fantasies, and behaviors that are desired with men and women.

Characteristics of Development Particular to GLB Youths

The areas discussed in this paper, including developmental characteristics, stressors, and maladaptive behaviors of GLB adolescents need to be studied in the context of typical adolescent development. However, a description of developmental processes related to adolescence is beyond the scope of this paper (for reviews in this area, see Adams, Gullota, and Markstrom-Adams 1994; Petersen et al. 1995). Still, some aspects of typical adolescent development are highlighted throughout the paper as they pertain to the discussion on GLB adolescents.

In this paper, the words *youth* and *adolescence* are used interchangeably. Adolescence is conceptualized here to contain three subphases: (a) early adolescence (ages ten to fourteen); (b) middle adolescence (ages fifteen to seventeen); and late adolescence (eighteen to twenty; e.g., Elliot and Feldman 1990). In general, early adolescence marks the period of transition from childhood to adolescence. An important milestone of this subphase is puberty (Petersen et al. 1995). During middle adolescence, contact with peers becomes a crucial activity for development. Finally, late adolescence is characterized by the transition into adulthood, when the young person begins to take on the roles of adult life (Petersen et al. 1995).

Most studies of GLB adolescents discussed here have varied in the age ranges of their participants. Studies have included adolescents ages fourteen to twenty-four years old. Generally, however, participants in studies of GLB youths fall within the subphases of middle and late adolescence. Several of the most important aspects of development relevant to GLB adolescents are described in the following section. These areas include (a) gender role nonconformity; (b) prevalence of same-gender sexual behavior and identification as GLB during adolescence; (c) *coming out* (defined below) to self, peers, family, and other individuals; and (d) dating and love relationships among GLB youths.

Gender Role Nonconformity

Bailey and Zucker (1995) reviewed forty-one retrospective studies that examined the association between atypical gender role behavior (before puberty) and sexual orientation (in adulthood) of a total of 27,724 heterosexual, gay male, and lesbian participants. Examples of areas measured in studies to evaluate cross-gender behavior include fantasy roles (e.g., pretending to be a girl during play), interest in rough-and-tumble play, toy interests, and gender of playmates (Zucker 1985). Bailey and Zucker (1995) found that both gay men and lesbians recalled significantly more cross-sex-typed behavior in childhood than heterosexual participants. Further, the effect sizes on these findings were among the largest reported in the area of gender differences (Bailey and Zucker 1995). Cross-gender behavior was a stronger predictor of sexual orientation for men than for women.

The few prospective studies that have been published also report a strong association between cross-gender behavior and sexual orientation. Such studies typically have identified boys who displayed extreme patterns of sex-typed behavior and assessed their sexual orientation in late adolescence or young adulthood. To illustrate, Green (1987) examined the sexual orientation outcome of sixty-six feminine boys and fifty-six controls. The author found that up to 80 percent of the "feminine" group self-labeled as gay or bisexual, in contrast to about 4 percent of the "control" group. It is important to consider that prospective studies in this area have mainly used boys who were clinic-referred because of their gender role preferences and thus may not be representative of boys who prefer cross-gender behavior. Further, reports of girls who have been followed prospectively to evaluate sex-typed behavior and sexual orientation are scarce (Bailey and Zucker 1995).

Prevalence of Adolescents Who Identify as GLB

Only a few studies since the 1970s have reported prevalence rates of adolescents who self-label as GLB or engage in same-gender sexual behavior. Further, such studies have tended to focus on only one variable of interest (e.g., same-gender sexual behavior), thus neglecting others that would provide more information relevant to sexual orientation (e.g., prevalence of adolescents who self-label as GLB, prevalence of same-gender attraction). For example, Sorenson (1973) noted that 17 percent of male adolescents and 6 percent of female adolescents in his study reported at least one same-gender sexual experience. Also, in their National Survey of Adolescent Males, Sonenstein, Pleck, and Ku (1989) found that 3 percent of adolescent males between fifteen and nineteen years of age had engaged in same-gender sexual behavior.

The study published by Remafedi et al. (1992) is an exception to the above-mentioned shortcomings, as the authors addressed multiple sexual orientation variables in their questionnaire. Specifically Remafedi and colleagues surveyed 34,706 junior and senior high school Minnesota residents from diverse living settings (e.g., urban, rural) and socioeconomic backgrounds. Most participants were Caucasian. Findings revealed that 4.5 percent of the sample reported experiencing primarily same-gender attractions. In addition, 2.6 percent of students endorsed a history of same-gender sexual fantasies. However, less than one-third of all participants with predominantly same-gender attractions, fantasies, or behaviors self-labeled as GLB (Remafedi et al. 1992).

With regard to sexual orientation, 88.2 percent of adolescents defined themselves as predominantly heterosexual, 10.7 percent of students were "unsure" of their sexual orientation, and 1.1 percent defined themselves as GLB. Students who reported being unsure of their sexual orientation were more likely to report same-gender fantasies and attractions and less likely to have had other-gender sexual experiences. However, such students also may not have known the meaning of sexual orientation. Finally, older adolescents were more likely than younger adolescents to report a GLB sexual orientation (Remafedi et al. 1992).

Currently it is estimated that 4 to 17 percent of the U.S. population identifies as GLB (Gonsiorek et al. 1995). Therefore it appears that adolescents are less likely to self-label as GLB than are older individuals. Still, in order to draw conclusions about the prevalence of youths who self-label as GLB or experience other behaviors relevant to sexual orientation (e.g., same-gender attractions), more studies with representative samples from the U.S. population are needed.

Coming Out to Self, Peers, Family, and Others

Definition of Coming Out   Coming out to oneself is defined as "a process during which a number of milestone events occur whereby an individual moves from nonrecognition of his or her homosexuality [sic], with perhaps a degree of sensitization of being somehow different from others, to self-recognition that he or she is indeed a homosexual [sic] person" (Savin-Williams 1990:30). Coming out to others involves an individual's disclosure of a GLB sexual orientation to people in his or her life (e.g., peers, family, coworkers). Although many people may experience coming out as a steplike progression (e.g., first awareness of same-gender attractions, acceptance of a GLB sexual orientation, disclosure to others), little empirical attention has been given to potential stages of coming out (Savin-Williams 1990). Even less empirical attention has been given to the process of coming out in adolescence, as most discussions of acceptance and disclosure of a GLB sexual orientation are based on retrospective data from adults or adult-based models (Savin-Williams 1995).

Sexual Orientation Milestones of GLB Adolescents   The following summarizes findings from recent studies about coming out variables of GLB adolescents (for an extensive review of this topic, see Cohen and Savin-Williams 1996). Note that only average ages of different milestones are reported, and they do not reflect the variability that exists within and between samples. With regard to the experiences of young lesbian and bisexual women, the average age of first awareness of same-gender attraction has been between the ages of ten and eleven across several samples (e.g., D'Augelli and Hershberger 1993; Herdt and Boxer 1993; Sears 1991). Further, first same-gender sexual experiences have been reported to happen (on average) between fifteen and seventeen years of age (Herdt and Boxer 1993; Sears 1991). In general, young lesbian and bisexual women have tended to self-label as such between fourteen and seventeen years of age (D'Augelli and Hershberger 1993; Sears 1991). Finally, the age of first disclosure about sexual orientation to another person appears to take place about two years following the self-labeling experience (D'Augelli and Hershberger 1993; Sears 1991). With regard to the experiences of gay and bisexual young men, first same-gender attractions have been reported to occur (on average) between the ages of nine and thirteen (D'Augelli 1991; D'Augelli and Hershberger 1993; Herdt and Boxer 1993; Newman and Muzzonigro 1993; Sears 1991). First same-gender sexual experiences reportedly follow about four years after initial same-gender attractions are acknowledged, between thirteen and sixteen years of age (D'Augelli 1991; Herdt and Boxer 1993; Sears 1991). In addition, self-labeling as gay or bisexual tends to occur between the ages of twelve and seventeen (D'Augelli 1991; D'Augelli and Hershberger 1993; Newman and Muzzonigro 1993; Sears 1991). Finally, on average, gay and bisexual male adolescents report first disclosing their sexual orientation to another person when they are between sixteen and twenty years of age (D'Augelli 1991; D'Augelli and Hershberger 1993; Herdt and Boxer 1993; Newman and Muzzonigro 1993; Sears 1991).

Consequences of Coming Out to Self and Others   A positive correlation has been reported in the empirical literature between accepting a GLB sexual orientation and self-esteem. To illustrate, individuals who positively accept their GLB sexual orientation report higher levels of self-esteem (e.g., based on the Rosenberg self-esteem scale) than individuals who have difficulties accepting their sexual orientation (Savin-Williams 1995). The process of affirming and disclosing a GLB sexual orientation has also been examined as a potential stressor for GLB youth. This aspect of coming out is discussed in the following section.

Dating and Love Relationships Among Gay Male and Lesbian Youth

It is important to note that most research on adolescent sexuality and love relationships has not addressed the variables of same-gender attractions, fantasies, or sexual behavior among their participants (see Savin-Williams and Rodriguez 1993, for a discussion of this issue). Thus scientific research regarding same-gender dating and love relationships is scarce (Savin-Williams 1995). Further, the authors are not aware of any empirical study that has examined dating and love relationships among bisexual adolescents.

The data presented in this section are based on Savin-Williams's (1990) study of 317 young gay men and lesbian women, as his study is one of few empirical investigations on dating and love relationships among this group. However, information presented in the following paragraphs should be interpreted with caution because (a) participants may not be representative of the U.S. GLB adolescent population (e.g., few geographic areas were included; most participants were in college); (b) adequate psychometric properties were not reported for the instruments administered to participants; and (c) results are based on single-item questions to a self-report measure.

Dating and Love Relationships Among Gay Male Youth   Savin-Williams (1990) surveyed 214 gay men, a majority (75 percent) of whom were college students. The gay men ranged in age from 14 to 23 years of age. Male participants were from diverse religions and living settings (e.g., rural areas, small towns, large metropolitan areas), and 90 percent were Caucasian. On average, youth reported having experienced between one and two relationships. In general, love relationships had begun when male participants were 17.2 years old and lasted less than a year (their length ranged from several days to seven years). Of interest, 58 percent of love affairs were with other men, and participants were more likely to have their first love affair with another man than with another woman. Further, men who had their first sexual encounter with a man were more likely to have continued relationships with men. In addition, men were more likely to have long-term love relationships when their first affairs were at an early age.

Dating and Love Relationships Among Lesbian Youth Savin-Williams (1990) surveyed 103 lesbian women, a majority (86 percent) of whom were college students. The young lesbian women were within the age range of 16 to 23 years of age. The female participants' demographic characteristics were similar to male participants in this study. On average, young lesbian women reported having experienced between two and three love relationships. These relationships reportedly lasted an average of fifteen months and ranged from a few days to just less that ten years. In general, women reported that their first love relationship was equally likely to be with another woman than with a man, and began, on average, at the age of 16.6 years of age.

Commentary on Other-Gender Sexual Experiences As noted above, and as stated in other reports (e.g., Savin-Williams 1995), a large percentage of adolescents who self-label as gay and lesbian have engaged in other-gender sexual behaviors. Some youths have reported that they could not really know that they were lesbian women or gay men without having other-gender sexual experiences. In addition, some gay male youths have reported engaging in other-gender sexual behaviors to deny homoerotic attractions, and some lesbian youths have reported that other-gender sexual behaviors resulted from peer pressure and coercion (Savin-Williams 1995). Therefore other-gender sexual behaviors and dating may allow gay and lesbian youths to better understand their affectionate feelings and to be included in a heterosexual peer group.

Similarities in Patterns of Dating Between Gay, Lesbian, and Heterosexual Youth Although further research is necessary to obtain conclusive findings in this area, it appears that gay male and lesbian adolescents progress through dating in a pattern similar to heterosexual adolescents. For example, research suggests that heterosexual adolescents (a) progress through dating in a continuum characterized, on one end, by casual acquaintances and, on the other end, by having a committed relationship; and (b) are more likely to become involved in steady relationships and to engage in sexual behavior the earlier they begin to date (Miller, Christopherson, and King 1993). Gay male and lesbian adolescents also seem to progress through a continuum of low and high levels of commitment in their dating behaviors. In addition, lesbian and gay male adolescents are likely to become involved in steady relationships and sexual behaviors if they begin the dating process early.

Potentially Stressful Aspects of Identifying as GLB

Stressors related to sexual orientation in GLB youth include (a) victimization related to sexual orientation; (b) fear and negative consequences of coming out to others; and (c) high-risk sexual behaviors. The term *potential stress* was chosen because some GLB adolescents may not experience events described in this section, and some individuals that do experience such events may not interpret them as stressful.

Victimization Related to Sexual Orientation

Several authors have examined victimization of GLB youth related to sexual orientation issues (e.g., Hunter and Schaecher 1990; Martin and Hetrick 1988). However, most studies have either been qualitative in their methodology or have used samples from clinic settings (Savin-Williams 1994). Still, victimization based on known or presumed GLB sexual orientation is a common form of bias-related violence (Pilkington and D'Augelli 1995), and youths who are coming out are at particular risk for victimization among their family and peers (Savin-Williams 1994).

Pilkington and D'Augelli (1995) overcame some of the methodological flaws of previous research on victimization of GLB youth. First, the authors contacted gay and lesbian community centers throughout the country that had activities for youths, and fourteen centers from diverse urban areas agreed to distribute the authors' survey. Second, a relatively high participation rate (i.e., 44 percent) was reported. Third, the authors reported an adequate age distribution of adolescent participants, ranging from ages fifteen through twenty-one. Finally, participants were from diverse ethnic backgrounds.

Overall, respondents reported that they had experienced a mean of 2.7 instances of victimization ($SD = 2.5$) that they attributed to their sexual orientation. Participants from ethnic minorities reported significantly fewer forms of victimization than did Caucasian participants. The following frequencies of different types of victimization related to sexual orientation were reported by participants: (a) 80 percent reported experiencing verbal insults;

(b) 44 percent reported one or more threats of physical violence; (c) 33 percent reported having objects thrown at them; (d) 31 percent reported being chased or followed; (e) 22 percent reported experiencing sexual assault; (f) nearly 20 percent reported that they had been physically assaulted (e.g., hit, kicked, punched); and (g) 13 percent reported being spat on (Pilkington and D'Augelli 1995).

Total victimization scores for participants were significantly correlated with fear for safety in the community and at school. Clearly GLB youths suffer specific and sometimes dangerous forms of verbal and physical abuse that they perceive to be because of sexual orientation-related issues. However, little is known about how these experiences impact their lives. Still, victimization related to sexual orientation has been reported by GLB adolescents as a negative consequence of coming out to others. A detailed description of this issue follows.

Fear and Negative Consequences of Coming Out to Others

Many GLB adolescents fear disclosing their sexual orientation to heterosexual friends, family members, and other individuals in their life (e.g., coworkers, peers at school) because of fears of being rejected or harassed by these individuals (Pilkington and D'Augelli 1995). In the following paragraphs, issues regarding disclosure of a GLB sexual orientation are briefly discussed as they pertain to coming out to family members and friends. For more in-depth discussion of these issues, see Pilkington and D'Augelli (1995) and Rotheram-Borus and Fernandez (1995).

Coming Out to Family Members   In one sample of GLB youths, approximately 67 percent rated the prospect of disclosure to their family members between *somewhat troubling* and *extremely troubling* (Pilkington and D'Augelli 1995). In addition, 22 percent of youths in this sample feared verbal abuse at home and reported that this fear reduced the likelihood that they would disclose their sexual orientation. Prevalence of abuse related to sexual orientation was reported by Pilkington and D'Augelli (1995). The authors noted that 36 percent of youths in their sample had been verbally insulted at least once by an immediate family member. In addition, 10 percent of youths reported having experienced physical harm from a family member that was related to a sexual orientation issue. The stress of disclosing a GLB sexual orientation may be compounded by changes in the parent-child interaction that take place for typical adolescents. Changes in this relationship include an increase of parent-adolescent conflict during early adolescence (Petersen et al. 1995), and greater expectations of the adolescent's responsibility for behavior from parents (Ebata, Petersen, and Conger 1990). Also, some GLB youth who may have experienced close relationships with certain family members until adolescence may lose these sources of social support on disclosure of their sexual orientation.

Coming Out to Friends   Pilkington and D'Augelli (1995) reported that 36 percent of young men and 27 percent of young women in their study expressed that fears of losing friends limit their disclosure of sexual orientation. In fact, 43 percent of young men and 54 percent of young women in their sample reported losing at least one friend as a result of disclosure of a GLB sexual orientation. Fear of rejection from peers and actual loss of friendships may be interpreted as particularly stressful, as peer relationships become increasingly important to youths when they progress through adolescence. During adolescence, young people typically spend more time with peers than in previous years (Crockett and Petersen 1993), and any loss of social support during this period may have more negative consequences for them than at other times in their development.

High-Risk Sexual Behaviors Among GLB Youth

Some research has suggested that there are high rates of unprotected sexual acts among certain groups of GLB youth (e.g., American Medical Association [AMA] 1994; Lemp et al. 1994; Rotheram-Borus and Koopman 1991). These sexual behaviors may place certain GLB adolescents at risk of becoming infected with sexually transmitted diseases, including HIV. In fact, high-risk sexual behavior between men accounts for the largest proportion of AIDS cases among adolescents between the ages of thirteen and twenty-one (Remafedi 1994). Further, AIDS is the sixth leading cause of death among adolescents between the ages of fifteen and twenty-four in the United States (Hunter and Haymes 1998). Therefore high-risk sexual behaviors are conceptualized here as potential stressors for some GLB adolescents. A summary of findings from major studies in this area follows.

Most research on HIV status and high-risk sexual behaviors of GLB youth has focused on the experiences of gay and bisexual young men (Hunter and Haymes 1998; Rotheram-Borus, Hunter, and Rosario 1995). For example,

Rotheram-Borus and Koopman (1991) studied safe-sex practices among mostly Hispanic and African-American gay and bisexual male adolescents (age range of fourteen to eighteen years old) who sought services from the Hetrick-Martin Institute (HMI), a social service agency in New York City. Findings revealed that 37 percent of participants reported sometimes having protected sex and 33 percent of youth reported never having protected sex. High-risk sexual practices were therefore common among this sample.

Lemp et al. (1994) also investigated the prevalence and consequences of sexual and other risk behaviors among young gay and bisexual men. Their sample was from the San Francisco and Berkeley areas and was formed by approaching young men in public venues (e.g., parks, dance clubs, and street corners). Lemp et al. found that 32.7 percent of participants reported having unprotected anal intercourse in the previous six months. In addition, 17 percent of participants reported intravenous drug use at some point in their lives. Further, prevalence of HIV infection among this sample was 9.4 percent; the seroprevalence of Hepatitis B markers was 19.8 percent; and syphilis prevalence was 1 percent (Lemp et al. 1994).

Finally, Remafedi (1994) investigated the reported high-risk sexual practices of young gay and bisexual men from mostly urban areas in Minnesota. The author attempted to target a representative sample of this area (i.e., by recruiting from social groups, gay publications, and referrals from the community). Of the participants, 63 percent reported having engaged in unprotected anal intercourse or intravenous drug use; 47 percent of participants reported inconsistent use of condoms during anal sex; and 94 percent reported inconsistent use of condoms during oral sex (Remafedi 1994). Thus certain populations of gay and bisexual male adolescents appear to be particularly at risk of contracting sexually transmitted diseases (STDs), including HIV.

The above mentioned figures may be compared to a report from the Centers for Disease Control (1996) stating that 54.4 percent of adolescents from a large representative U.S. sample endorsed having used a condom during their last sexual intercourse. Further, Friedman et al. (1997) noted that only 19 percent of youths surveyed reported that they always used condoms while engaging in sexual activity. Adolescents in this study were recruited from a neighborhood with a high prevalence of drug injection.

With regard to studies on high-risk sexual behavior of lesbian and bisexual women, the American Medical Association (1994) published a report based on a sample of 711 women from low-income backgrounds in San Francisco. Findings revealed that lesbian and bisexual women were more likely (a) to report having anal sex with men; and (b) to be infected with HIV than heterosexual women. In addition, Lemp et al. (1995) interviewed lesbian and bisexual women (ages seventeen to forty) in public venues of San Francisco and Berkeley. The authors found that 40 percent of participants reported having experienced unprotected vaginal or anal sex with men in the past. Still, transmission of HIV from woman to woman was rare (Lemp et al. 1995).

In conclusion, some groups of lesbian and bisexual women also appear to be at high risk of contracting STDs, including HIV. However, empirical reports about high-risk sexual behavior of lesbian and bisexual young women are scarce and needed to expand on the clinical reports that are available (e.g., Hetrick and Martin 1987; Hunter and Haymes 1998; Rotheram-Borus, Hunter, and Rosario 1995). Finally, it is also possible that young women who only have sexual experiences with other women are at *decreased* risk of contracting HIV and other STDs, although this remains to be investigated.

Review of Studies on Adjustment Issues of GLB Youth

Adjustment issues of GLB adolescents that have been associated with sexual orientation factors are exemplified here in five different areas: (a) history of suicide attempts; (b) risk factors for suicide attempts; (c) history of conduct problems; (d) past substance use and abuse; and (e) academic difficulties. These areas are not comprehensive of adjustment problems that may pertain to GLB youth; however, they comprise difficulties that have been examined across studies. Research included in this review was quantitative in its methodology and systematically studied the variables of interest. Therefore discussion articles and qualitative studies regarding adjustment issues of GLB adolescents are not contained in this report. Further, only research focusing on youths (i.e., cutoff age of twenty-four) was incorporated into the review.

History of Suicide Attempts

Most studies that have explored adjustment issues of GLB adolescents have assessed the youths' history of suicide attempts. In the next paragraphs findings from individual studies are presented, followed by a summary and critique of the group of studies. The earliest investigation in this area was made by Roesler and Deisher (1972), who interviewed sixty young gay and bisexual men. Participants were recruited through acquaintances of the researchers, from the selective service, and in social settings (e.g., bars). Participants were interviewed, and the authors found that 31 percent of participants reported having made at least one suicide attempt. In addition, 8.6 percent of participants had a past history of multiple suicide attempts (Roesler and Deisher 1972).

The next systematic assessment of suicide attempts was made by Remafedi (1987). The investigator interviewed 29 young gay and bisexual men who were recruited through advertisements in gay newspapers, gay radio shows, and a health department clinic. Participants were interviewed by the author regarding a variety of areas. Remafedi found that 34 percent of participants reported attempting suicide at some time in their lives and 7 percent had made multiple attempts. In a later study, Remafedi, Farrow, and Deisher (1991) interviewed 137 gay and bisexual male adolescents who were recruited from advertisements in gay publications, bars, social and counseling groups, and peer referral. The authors used a structured interview to gather information in different areas of the adolescents' lives. In addition, participants completed self-report measures regarding suicide attempts and ideation. Findings revealed that 30 percent of participants reported at least one suicide attempt, and 44 percent of these participants reported more than one attempt. Studies by Remafedi and colleagues were composed primarily of Caucasian participants.

Schneider, Farberow, and Kruks (1989) also assessed the past suicidal behavior and other characteristics of 108 young bisexual and gay men. Participants were recruited from gay and lesbian student organizations from fourteen colleges in Los Angeles and "rap" groups conducted by a local gay and lesbian community center. Among other areas assessed, participants responded to questions regarding past suicide attempts. Schneider et al. found that 20 percent of participants reported past suicide attempts.

Rotheram-Borus et al. (1995) reported findings from their longitudinal study of 136 mostly Hispanic and African-American adolescent gay and bisexual men who attended the Hetrick Martin Institute (HMI). The authors assessed the frequency of suicide attempts through a single interview item administered. Investigators in this study reported that at baseline, and during subsequent six-month time frames, 11 percent of youth reported attempting suicide. In a previous study, Rotheram-Borus, Hunter, and Rosario (1994) administered items from a suicide-related scale and found that 39 percent of the adolescents reported a past suicide attempt. Of those who had attempted suicide, 52 percent reported making more than one attempt.

The following two studies made some improvements to the methodology of previously mentioned studies by (a) including women as participants; and (b) gathering descriptive data from multiple geographic areas. First, Proctor and Groze (1994) administered self-report questionnaires to 221 GLB youths who were recruited from ethnically diverse youth groups in the United States and Canada. The authors found that 40 percent of participants reported past suicide attempts and 26 percent reported seriously thinking about suicide at least once. Second, D'Augelli and Hershberger (1993) administered self-report measures to 194 GLB adolescents from fourteen community centers across the United States. Among other areas assessed, participants were asked questions regarding past suicide attempts. Forty-two percent of the sample reported a past suicide attempt. The number of attempts made by participants who reported this behavior ranged from one to fifteen ($M = 3.1$, $SD = 3.2$).

Finally, Remafedi et al. (1998) compared reports of suicide attempts from GLB adolescents as well as gender-matched heterosexual participants who lived in Minnesota. Remafedi et al. found that suicide attempts were endorsed by (a) 28.1 percent of bisexual and gay male adolescents; (b) 20.5 percent of bisexual and lesbian adolescents; (c) 14.5 percent of heterosexual young women; and (d) 4.2 percent of heterosexual young men in their sample. In addition, Garofalo et al. (1998) also found that GLB youths were more likely than their school peers to have engaged in suicide ideation and attempts.

Summary and Critique of Findings   Based on the studies reviewed, the prevalence rates for reported past suicide attempts among GLB youths have ranged from 11 to 42 percent, although rates from most studies fall between 30 and 42 percent (e.g., D'Augelli and Hershberger 1993; Remafedi 1987; Remafedi et al. 1991; Roesler and Deisher 1972; Rotheram-Borus et al. 1995). Furthermore, 8.6 to 52 percent of attempters have reported repeated suicidal behaviors (Remafedi et al. 1991; Roesler and Deisher 1972; Rotheram-Borus, Hunter, and Rosario 1994). The variability in rates across studies may be attributed to differences in (a) the number of participants; (b) the demographic characteristics of participants; (c) the definitions used to assess past history of suicide attempts; and (d) the methodology used for assessment (e.g., interview vs. paper-and-pencil scales).

Methodological limitations of studies were similar across reports. They include (a) selective recruitment strategies, for example, bars, counseling groups, and social service agencies); (b) reliance on retrospective data and self-report to obtain information; (c) lack of reported psychometric properties for measures used; and (d) exclusion of female participants from studies (with the exception of two studies described above). Such methodological flaws limit the conclusions that can be made for findings regarding suicide attempts among GLB youth.

Note that most of the studies reviewed in this section did not assess suicide attempts in a heterosexual comparison group. However, prevalence rates reported among GLB adolescents appear to be higher than those reported for the general adolescent population. To illustrate, Lewinsohn et al. (1996) found that 7.1 percent of their representative adolescent community sample had reported a past history of suicide attempts. Rates reported by Lewinsohn and colleagues were higher for girls than for boys. This finding is interesting to note, as most studies on GLB youths have not included young women as participants.

Risk Factors for Suicide Attempts

A series of suicide risk factors have been reported for typical community and clinical adolescent samples. One study reported the following risk factors for an adolescent community sample: (a) past history of suicide attempts; (b) current episode of major depression and other internalizing behaviors; (c) current externalizing behaviors; (d) female gender; (e) past diagnoses of psychopathology; (f) interpersonal difficulties; and (g) poor academic performance; among others (Lewinsohn et al. 1996). In another report, suicide risk factors for adolescents included (a) chronic and debilitating illness; (b) failure in school; (c) family discord; (d) lack of peer social network; (e) recent and frequent attempts; (f) depression; and (g) other psychopathology; among others (Fremouw, de Perczel, and Ellis 1990).

Studies of GLB adolescents generally have not assessed suicide risk factors based on empirical findings for typical adolescents. Still, several studies have assessed these risk factors in GLB youth. For example, Rotheram-Borus, Hunter, and Rosario (1994) reported that suicide attempters were more likely to (a) have dropped out of school; (b) live outside their home; (c) have family or friends who attempted suicide; and (d) have disclosed their sexual orientation to parents and siblings in contrast to nonattempters. As expected, Hershberger, Pilkington, and D'Augelli (1997) noted that youth with greater mental health problems and suicide ideation were more likely to have had a history of suicide attempts.

Also, Remafedi and colleagues (1991) reported that participants noted the following reasons for attempting suicide: (a) family problems (e.g., conflict with family members, parents' marital discord, divorce, or alcoholism); (b) turmoil about sexuality; (c) depression; (d) conflict with peers; (e) problems in romantic relationships; and (f) dysphoria associated with substance abuse. In contrast, when GLB youths have reported low rates of victimization, high levels of family support and self-acceptance have been associated with fewer mental health difficulties (Hershberger et al. 1997).

Some studies of GLB adolescents have compared reports of participants who have and have not attempted suicide with regard to sexual orientation variables. For example, attempters have been found to self-label as GLB and disclose their sexual orientation to others at younger ages than nonattempters (D'Augelli and Hershberger 1993; Remafedi et al. 1991; Schneider et al. 1989). In addition, attempters have reported a greater loss of friends as a result of disclosure of sexual orientation than nonattempters (D'Augelli and Hershberger 1993; Hershberger et al. 1997). Finally, suicide attempters have reported greater instances of victimization owing to their sexual orientation and lower self-esteem than nonattempters (Hershberger et al. 1997).

Of interest, among men, attempters have been found to report a more feminine or undifferentiated gender role than nonattempters (Remafedi et al. 1991). Also, male attempters appear to be more likely to have disclosed their sexual orientation to parents or siblings than nonattempters (Rotheram-Borus, Hunter, and Rosario 1994).

History of Conduct Problems

Few studies have assessed conduct problems in GLB adolescents (e.g., Remafedi 1987; Rotheram-Borus et al. 1995). In his sample of young gay and bisexual men, Remafedi (1987) found that (a) 48 percent of participants had run away from home at least once in their lifetime; (b) 43 percent of youth who ran away at least once reported doing so for sexuality-related conflicts; and (c) the remaining 57 percent reported running away because of family conflict in general. Further, approximately 50 percent of all subjects had been arrested, had been in juvenile detention, or had been arraigned in juvenile court at least once (Remafedi 1987).

Rotheram-Borus et al. (1995) assessed delinquency and other conduct problems in their sample of gay and bisexual adolescent men. When delinquent acts were assessed, 85 percent of their sample reported that they never had contact with the criminal justice system. Also, participants reported a mean of 3.2 conduct problems at baseline. Problems assessed included truancy from work or school, destroying property, and lying. Although these behaviors were labeled problematic by the authors, their deviance when compared to norms, as well as functional impairment, were not assessed. Methodological limitations discussed in the section on history of suicide attempts also apply to the studies reviewed in this section.

Past Substance Use and Abuse

Remafedi (1987) assessed substance abuse in gay and bisexual male adolescents based on the definition in the *Diagnostic and Statistical Manual of Mental Disorders*, 3rd ed. (*DSM-III*) (American Psychiatric Association [APA] 1980) and found that 58 percent of participants met criteria for this disorder. However, the method for assessing substance abuse was not specified, and the specific substances abused were also not reported. Of interest, the Centers for Disease Control (1996) reported that 32.6 percent of their large adolescent sample indicated that they had consumed five or more drinks of alcohol at least once in the previous thirty days. Further, 2 to 42 percent of this sample endorsed consuming another substance (e.g., marijuana, cocaine) in their lifetime.

Several articles have also reported "high" or "problematic" rates of substance use among mostly Hispanic and African-American gay and bisexual male adolescents (Rotheram-Borus et al. 1994, 1995), but clear rationales for the labeling of substance use as high or problematic were not provided. In a more thorough and comprehensive study, Rosario, Hunter, and Gwadz (1997) interviewed 154 ethnically diverse GLB youths from various sites in New York City (e.g., college campuses, community centers, and social service agencies) about their past history of substance use. The authors found that the majority of young women and men reported a history of frequent multiple substance use. Further, symptoms of substance abuse were common among this sample (Rosario et al. 1997).

Substance use rates of GLB youth in the above-mentioned studies were not compared to heterosexual peers. Such comparisons are necessary in order to assess whether behaviors are normative for other youth with similar demographic characteristics but a different sexual orientation. Interestingly, Garofalo et al. (1998) found that GLB youth from high schools in Massachusetts were more likely than heterosexual peers to report engaging in multiple substance use. In addition, GLB youths in this study were more likely to have initiated this behavior earlier in their lifetime than were heterosexual peers (Garofalo et al. 1998).

Academic Difficulties Associated with Sexual Orientation Variables

The assessment of academic difficulties in GLB youths has received little attention in the empirical literature. Findings from the few studies that have examined this adjustment issue are reported here. For example, Remafedi (1987) found that 69 percent of participants reported school concerns related to sexual orientation-related issues (e.g., verbal abuse from peers); 28 percent of participants left high school before graduating; and 39 percent of participants reported frequent truancy. The exact nature of the association between academic problems and difficulties related to sexual orientation, as well as the clinical significance of the behaviors, cannot be determined from these findings. Another study that assessed school issues found that 28 percent of gay and bisexual men and 19 percent of lesbian and bisexual women feared being physically hurt at school because of prejudice related to their sexual orientation (Pilkington and D'Augelli 1995). Of concern, 22 percent reported actually being physically hurt at school for this reason (Pilkington and D'Augelli 1995).

Risk and Protective Factors for Typical and GLB Adolescents

The following discussion is based on concepts from the field of developmental psychopathology. This area of study focuses on understanding childhood and adolescent psychopathology within the context of antecedent and consequent events, and relating behaviors that deviate from the norm to typical development (Wenar 1994). Risk factors are defined here as "factors that increase the probability that development will be diverted from its normal path, resulting either in clinically significant problem behavior or psychopathology" (p. 511). In contrast, protective factors are "factors that promote healthy development and counteract the negative effects of risks" (p. 510).

In this section, general factors that have been related to psychopathology in adolescence are described first. It is assumed that an understanding of these factors can facilitate a conceptualization of risk and protective factors for GLB youths. Following that, potential risk and protective factors that may be related to maladaptive behaviors (e.g., suicide attempts) of GLB adolescents are proposed. Factors proposed in this section have not been established in the research literature as having a causal association with maladaptive behaviors or psychopathology. Therefore future research will need to explore their relevance to GLB youths.

Risk and Protective Factors for Typical Adolescents

Ebata et al. (1990) proposed a model of risk and protective factors related to the development of psychopathology during adolescence. Their model is briefly presented here. Ebata et al. identified (a) individual characteristics that may be risks or protective factors in coping with stressful events; (b) factors related to the social context; and (c) particular challenges of development in adolescence. These areas are discussed in the following paragraphs.

Individual Characteristics as Risk or Protective Factors   One component that merits consideration in assessing any form of psychopathology for an adolescent is the biological disposition she or he may have to particular disorders. This can be explored, in part, by determining the adolescent's family history of mental illness. Another area to examine is the adolescent's past history of internalizing and externalizing behavioral problems (Ebata et al. 1990). Both family history and individual history of mental health problems are risk factors for the development of psychopathology in all stages of life (e.g., Kovaks and Paulaustkas 1984). In addition, the adolescent's gender should be considered, as the forms in which maladaptive behavior are manifested have different gender ratios. For example, externalizing behavioral problems (e.g., attention-deficit hyperactivity disorder, conduct disorder) are more prevalent in boys than in girls, and internalizing behavioral problems (e.g., depression, anxiety) are more prevalent in girls than in boys, particularly during adolescence (Ebata et al. 1990). Garmezy (1985) identified different individual variables that can serve as risk or protective factors for the development of psychopathology. Protective factors include high levels of self-esteem, feelings of control, a view of the environment as predictable, a view of life as basically a positive experience, an ability to evoke positive responses from the environment (e.g., through good temperament, sociability), and high intellectual abilities. Opposite aspects of the above-mentioned variables may place an individual at risk for mental health concerns (e.g., low levels of self-esteem, a view of the environment as unpredictable, low intellectual abilities). In addition, children who have experienced high levels of distress (e.g., resulting from extreme poverty or debilitating physical illness) have greater difficulties in attaining psychologically healthy states, although some children may be resilient to their adverse circumstances and have quite adaptive outcomes (Garmezy 1985).

Factors Related to the Social Context   Garmezy (1985) also identified environmental circumstances that may be risk and protective factors to the development of psychopathology. Risk factors resulting from the individual's social context include (a) severe marital discord within the family; (b) low socioeconomic status; (c) large family size; (d) a history of criminal behavior on the part of the parent or adolescent; (e) psychiatric disorder of a family member, particularly the mother; and (f) care of the child by government authorities at any particular time. In contrast, social factors that play protective roles include a close personal bond with at least one relative, preferably an adult relative, and a supportive school environment (Garmezy 1985).

Challenges Particular to Adolescence   Timing of developmental changes that is generally different from peers, as well as multiple, simultaneous changes, have been associated with negative behavioral outcomes for adolescents (Ebata et al. 1990). For example, poor outcomes have been reported for girls who have an early physical development during adolescence (e.g., Petersen and Taylor 1980). Special features of adolescence make it likely to be more challenging than other age periods, because this phase is characterized by multiple changes with regard to the adolescent's individual development and social context (Petersen 1987). Particular situations that may be interpreted as stressors during adolescence include (a) increased expectations and demands on the part of parents and teachers, who may attempt to encourage greater individual responsibility for behavior; (b) stress related to the timing of puberty; and (c) first experiences of dating and the development of love relationships (Ebata et al. 1990). However, the situations mentioned above, as well as other challenging events during adolescence, may also afford opportunities for growth and positive outcomes. Further, attainment or maintenance of psychological well-being, as well as adaptation to new demands and environments, may be facilitated by the youth's capacity to draw on individual and environmental resources (Ebata et al. 1990).

Risk and Protective Factors Particular to GLB Youths

One aspect of development that may be added to the individual-historical factors in the model of Ebata et al. (1990) is the greater likelihood of experience of childhood gender-role nonconformity among GLB individuals (Bailey and Zucker 1995). An individual's past experience of these behaviors could result in potential risk for being punished by peers and family if the behaviors are unacceptable in those social contexts. However, gender role nonconforming behaviors also may function as strengths for the individual. For example, a girl with a history of involvement in many sports activities (a behavior that may be more expected or common for boys) may develop better spatial and motor abilities than girls without such experience.

Some developmental challenges that may be experienced by GLB adolescents could pose specific risks for maladaptive behavior (e.g., suicide ideation, suicide attempt, substance use). These pertain to their social context. Specifically, negative consequences of coming out to family members and friends, and victimization owing to sexual orientation are among potentially harmful events. Clearly the interpretation and occurrence of these events will vary across individuals. Also, as discussed previously, factors pertaining to the disclosure of a GLB sexual orientation have been related to attempting suicide. Specifically, greater loss of friends after disclosure and younger self-labeling have been associated with suicide attempts (D'Augelli and Hershberger 1993; Remafedi et al. 1991).

Conversely, a GLB adolescent's disclosure of his or her sexual orientation to someone in the environment actually may be positive. In fact, many family members, friends, and other individuals in a GLB adolescent's life could respond to this information with acceptance and support. Supportive and accepting individuals in a GLB youth's life may protect the adolescent from harmful effects of other risk factors. As noted earlier, Hershberger and D'Augelli (1995) found that family support was associated with GLB adolescents' greater self-acceptance, which, in turn, was associated with fewer mental health difficulties reported by youth.

Suggestions for Future Research

Issues Regarding Sampling

As is evident from this review, most of the studies about GLB youths have been performed with participants recruited from the following settings:

(a) centers that offered specific programs for GLB adolescents (e.g., HIV prevention, social events); (b) universities; and (c) agencies that required youths to travel to the site in order to participate in the study. The authors' efforts in recruiting such samples are commendable, as GLB youths are a difficult population to access, regardless of the setting or region. In addition, many adolescents who have participated in research studies may have been at a vulnerable stage in their coming-out process, and the information gathered about them remains invaluable. However, this research only can be generalizable to youths who make use of such facilities.

As such, the nature of past research has excluded the experiences of other adolescents in community settings that may be at different stages of coming out. In future studies targeting adolescents dealing with sexual orientation issues, it is important to evaluate the experiences of youths who (a) have predominantly same-gender sexual attractions and behavior but do not self-label as GLB; (b) self-label as GLB but are not public about it; and (c) have come out to themselves and others but do not frequent formal activities for GLB adolescents, among other groups.

In an ideal situation, a large number of participants would be recruited from school and other community settings in order to obtain representative samples from the geographic areas studied (Working Groups 1995). Such sampling strategies would allow the recruitment of heterosexual comparison groups. A heterosexual comparison group would be a group of adolescents matched by age and other demographic characteristics (except for sexual orientation) to GLB adolescents. This addition to future studies should prove beneficial for several reasons. First, data obtained from this group would assist with controlling for findings related to demographic characteristics other than sexual orientation. Second, if differences in the prevalence of psychopathology do exist for variables related to sexual orientation, then the study will have more power to detect them. Finally, it is crucial that bisexual and lesbian women be included in future studies, particularly when justifications for having all male participants in past studies have been weak.

Future researchers in this area should be particularly invested in ensuring the privacy and confidentiality of participants (Working Groups 1995). In fact, whenever possible, a waiver of parental/guardian involvement should be obtained (Working Groups 1995). Such measures are not only in line with ethical standards but may increase the likelihood that participants are honest in responding to sensitive questions. Still, some adolescents, such as members of certain ethnic minority groups, may be more hesitant to acknowledge struggles with sexual orientation, because that may place them at higher risk of discrimination (Greene 1994).

Issues Related to Methodology

Future studies evaluating the prevalence and factors related to mental health concerns and suicidality may be more methodologically sound if the following characteristics are considered. To obtain a wide spectrum of experiences, studies may include participants from clinical settings, but these should be balanced with samples from community and school settings. Second, if mental health variables are of interest, then diagnostic criteria should be used to evaluate the clinical significance of behavioral concerns. Third, hypotheses should be based on conceptual models that are empirically based (e.g., suicide risk factors already reported in the literature for adolescents should be evaluated in future studies of suicidality). Finally, whenever possible, information should be obtained through several methods (e.g., clinical interviews, self-report measures) with adequate psychometric properties. Assessments with valid and reliable measures increase the internal validity of a study, the conclusiveness of findings, and the potential to replicate a study. A detailed example of such an investigation follows.

A comprehensive study of mental health concerns would involve screening participants to evaluate whether they meet criteria for psychiatric categories that often apply to adolescents (e.g., depression, anxiety disorders, substance abuse or dependence). Such categories should be drawn from the latest edition of the *Diagnostic and Statistical Manual of Mental Disorders* (*DSM-IV*; APA 1994), as this manual is the most widely accepted among mental health professionals in the United States. Further, criteria for diagnoses are empirically based.

To arrive at different diagnoses, it is recommended that participants undergo a structured clinical interview. The Diagnostic Interview for Children and Adolescents-IV (Reich, Welner, and Herjanic 1998) and the Anxiety Disorders Interview Schedule for *DSM-IV*: Child Version (Albano and Silverman 1996) are both based on *DSM-IV* categories. Further, participants should be asked to complete self-report measures developed to evaluate the clinical significance of emotional concerns. For example, the Children's Depression Inventory (Kovacs 1992) and the Reynolds Adolescent Depression Scale (Reynolds 1986) are commonly used, psychometrically sound measures of depressive symptoms.

If a researcher is interested in evaluating the relation between the development of psychopathology and sexual orientation variables, a very large participant pool is needed. The study should begin a few years before the variables are expected to peak. For example, before significant levels of alcohol consumption are expected to occur, before the person is likely to recognize same-gender sexual attractions, or before cross-sex-typed behavior may be evident. This would allow the researcher to evaluate what proportion of individuals develop a GLB identification, the history of atypical gender-role behavior in the sample, and how these factors are related to psychosocial stress, anxiety, depression, and so forth.

In sum, there are specific experiences that are unique to GLB adolescents (e.g., coming out). Future investigations into these processes will facilitate a broader understanding of the impact of gender role and sexual orientation development on adolescents' lives. The literature points to a strong possibility that GLB youths are at particular risk for developing psychopathology and maladaptive behaviors. However, conclusive findings in this area cannot be achieved until methodologically sound research is performed. Such research may reveal that GLB adolescents are, indeed, an at-risk group with regard to the development of psychopathology. Conversely, findings may reveal that most GLB youths are resilient during a particularly challenging period of their lives, while a subgroup of these youths may require increased community and family support.

Acknowledgments

The authors acknowledge and thank Kimberly Kalish, Staci Robyn, and Rosemary Srebalus for their helpful suggestions, editorial comments, and support during the preparation of this manuscript.

References

Adams, G. R., T. P. Gullota, and C. Markstrom-Adams. 1994. *Adolescent Life Experiences*. 3rd ed. Pacific Grove, Calif.: Brooks/Cole.
Albano, A.M., and W. Silverman. 1996. *Anxiety Disorders Interview Schedule for DSM-IV: Child Version*. San Antonio, Tex.: Psychological Corp.
American Medical Association. 1994. Health care needs of gay men and lesbians in the U.S.A. Report presented by the Council on Scientific Affairs to the AMA House of Delegates Interim Meeting.
American Psychiatric Association. 1980. *Diagnostic and Statistical Manual of Mental Disorders*. 3rd ed.. Washington, D.C.: Author.
American Psychiatric Association. 1994. *Diagnostic and Statistical Manual of Mental Disorders*. 4th ed. Washington, D.C.: Author.
Bailey, J. M., and K. J. Zucker. 1995. Childhood sex-typed behavior and sexual orientation: A conceptual analysis and quantitative review. *Developmental Psychology* 31:43–55.

Centers for Disease Control. 1996. Youth risk behavior surveillance system: United States. *Morbidity and Mortality Weekly Report* 45:1–86.

Cohen, K. M., and R. C. Savin-Williams. 1996. Developmental perspectives on coming out to self and others. In R. C. Savin-Williams and K. M. Cohen, eds., *The Lives of Lesbians, Gays, and Bisexuals: Children to Adults*, pp. 113–44. Fort Worth, Tex.: Harcourt Brace.

Crockett, L. J., and A. C. Petersen. 1993. Adolescent development: Health risks and opportunities for health promotion. In S. G. Millstein, A. C. Petersen, and E. O. Nightingale, eds., *Promoting the Health of Adolescents: New Directions for the Twenty-first Century*, pp. 13–37. New York: Oxford University Press.

D'Augelli, A. R. 1991. Gay men in college: Identity processes and adaptations. *Journal of College Student Development* 32:140–46.

D'Augelli, A. R., and S. L. Hershberger. 1993. Lesbian, gay, and bisexual youth in community settings: Personal challenges and mental health problems. *American Journal of Community Psychology* 21:421–48.

D'Emilio, J. 1983. *Sexual Politics, Sexual Communities: The Making of a Homosexual Minority in the United States, 1940–1970*. Chicago: University of Chicago Press.

Ebata, A. T., A. C. Petersen, and J. J. Conger. 1990. The development of psychopathology in adolescence. In J. Rolf, A. S. Masten, D. Cicchetti, K. H. Nuechterlein, and S. Weintraub, eds., *Risk and Protective Factors in the Development of Psychopathology*, pp. 308–33. New York: Cambridge University Press.

Elliott, G. R., and S. S. Feldman. 1990. Capturing the adolescent experience. In S. S. Feldman and G. R. Elliott, eds., *At the Threshold: The Developing Adolescent*, pp. 1–14. Cambridge, Mass.: Harvard University Press.

Faderman, L. 1991. *Odd Girls and Twilight Lovers: A History of Lesbian Life in Twentieth-century America*. New York: Penguin.

Fremouw, W. J., M. de Perczel, and T. E. Ellis. 1990. *Suicide Risk: Assessment and Response Guidelines*. New York: Pergamon.

Friedman, S. R., R. Curtis, B. Jose, A. Neaigus, J. Zenilman, J. Culpepper-Morgan, L. Borg, J. Kreek, D. Paone, and D.C. Des Jarlais. 1997. Sex, drugs, and infections among youth: Parenterally and sexually transmitted diseases in a high-risk neighborhood. *Sexually Transmitted Diseases* 24:322–26.

Garmezy, M. 1985. Stress-resistant children: The search for protective factors. In J. E. Stevenson, ed., *Recent Research in Developmental Psychopathology*, pp. 213–33. Oxford: Pergamon.

Garofalo, R., R. C. Wolf, S. Kessel, S. J. Palfrey, and R. H. DuRant. 1998. The association between health-risk behaviors and sexual orientation among a school-based sample of adolescents. *Pediatrics* 101:895–902.

Golden, C. 1987. Diversity and variability in women's sexual identities. In The Boston Lesbian Psychologies Collective, eds., *Lesbian Psychologies: Explorations and Challenges*, pp. 18–34. Urbana: University of Illinois Press.

Gonsiorek, J. C., R. L. Sell, and J. D. Weinrich. 1995. Definition and measurement of sexual orientation. *Suicide and Life-Threatening Behavior* 25 (Suppl. 1):40–51.

Gonsiorek, J. C., and J. D. Weinrich. 1991. The definition and scope of sexual orientation. In J. C. Gonsiorek and J. D. Weinrich, eds., *Homosexuality: Research Implications for Public Policy*, pp. 1–12. Newbury Park, Calif.: Sage.

Green, R. 1987. *The "Sissy Boy Syndrome" and the Development of Homosexuality*. New Haven, Conn.: Yale University Press.

Greene, B. 1994. Ethnic-minority lesbians and gay men: Mental health and treatment issues. *Journal of Consulting and Clinical Psychology* 62:243–51.

Herdt, G. 1989. Introduction: Gay and lesbian youth, emergent identities, and cultural scenes at home and abroad. In G. Herdt, ed., *Gay and Lesbian Youth*, pp. 315–55. Binghamton, N.Y.: Harrington Park.

Herdt, G., and A.M. Boxer. 1993. *Children of Horizons: How Gay and Lesbian Teens Are Leading a New Way Out of the Closet*. Boston: Beacon.

Hershberger, S. L., and A. R. D'Augelli. 1995. The impact of victimization on the mental health and suicidality of lesbian, gay, and bisexual youths. *Developmental Psychology* 31:65–74.

Hershberger, S. L., N. W. Pilkington, and A. R. D'Augelli. 1997. Predictors of suicide attempts among gay, lesbian, and bisexual youth. *Journal of Adolescent Research* 12:477–97.

Hetrick, E. S., A.D. and Martin. 1987. Developmental issues and their resolution for gay and lesbian adolescents. *Journal of Homosexuality* 14:25–44.

Hunter, J., and R. Haymes. 1998. It's beginning to rain: Gay/lesbian/bisexual adolescents and AIDS. In M. S. Schneider, ed., *Pride and Prejudice: Working with Lesbian, Gay, and Bisexual Youth*, pp. 137–63. Toronto: Central Toronto Youth Services.

Hunter, J., and R. Schaecher. 1990. Stresses on lesbian and gay adolescents in schools. *Social Work in Education* 9:180–89.

Kennedy, E. L., and M. D. Davis. 1993. *Boots of Leather, Slippers of Gold: The History of a Lesbian Community*. New York: Routledge.

Kovacs, M. 1992. *Children's Depression Inventory*. North Tonawanda, N.Y.: Multi-Health Systems.

Kovacs, M., and S. L. Paulaustkas. 1984. Developmental stage and the expression of depressive disorders in children. In D. Cichetti and K. Schneider-Rosen, eds., *Childhood Depression*, pp. 59–80. San Francisco: Jossey-Bass.

Lemp, G. F., A.M. Hirozawa, D. Givertz, G. N. Nieri, L. Anderson, M. L. Lindegren, R. S. Janssen, and M. Katz. 1994. Seroprevalence of HIV and risk behaviors among young homosexual and bisexual men: The San Francisco/Berkeley young men's survey. *Journal of the American Medical Association* 272:449–54.

Lemp, G. F., M. Jones, T. A. Kellogg, G. N. Nieri, L. Anderson, D. Withum, and M. Katz. 1995. HIV seroprevalence and risk behaviors among lesbians and bisexual women in San Francisco and Berkeley, California. *American Journal of Public Health* 85:1549–52.

Lewinsohn, P.M., P. Rohde, J. R. and Seeley. 1996. Adolescent suicidal ideation and attempts: Prevalence, risk factors, and clinical implications. *Clinical Psychology: Science and Practice* 3:25–46.

Martin, A.D., and E. S. Hetrick. 1988. The stigmatization of the gay and lesbian adolescent. *Journal of Homosexuality* 15:(1/2)163–83.

Miller, B.C., C. R. Christopherson, and P. K. King. 1993. Sexual behavior in adolescence. In T. P. Gullots, G. R. Adams, and R. Montemayor, eds., *Adolescent Sexuality*, pp. 57–76. Newbury Park, Calif.: Sage.

Newman, B. S., and P. G. Muzzonigro. 1993. The effects of traditional family values on the coming-out process of gay male adolescents. *Adolescence* 28:213–26.

Newton, D. E. 1994. *Gay and Lesbian Rights: A Reference Handbook*. Santa Barbara, Calif.: ABC-CLIO.

Patterson, C. J. 1995. Sexual orientation and human development: An overview. *Developmental Psychology* 31:3–11.

Petersen, A. C. 1987. The nature of biological-psychosocial interactions: The sample case of early adolescence. In R. M. Lerner and T. T. Foch, eds., *Biological-Psychological Interactions in Early Adolescence: A Life-Span Perspective*, pp. 35–61. Hillsdale, N.J.: Erlbaum.

Petersen, A. C., N. Leffert, and B. L. Graham. 1995. Adolescent development and the emergence of sexuality. *Suicide and Life-Threatening Behavior* 25(Suppl. 1):4–17.

Petersen, A. C., and B. Taylor. 1980. The biological approach to adolescence. In J. Adelson, ed., *Handbook of Adolescent Psychology*, pp. 117–55. New York: Wiley.

Pilkington, N. W., and A. R. D'Augelli. 1995. Victimization of lesbian, gay, and bisexual youth in community settings. *Journal of Community Psychology* 23:34–57.

Proctor, C. D., and V. K. Groze. 1994. Risk factors for suicide among gay, lesbian, and bisexual youths. *Social Work* 39:504–12.

Reich, W., Z. Welner, and B. Herjanic. 1998. *Diagnostic Interview for Children and Adolescents-IV*. North Tonawanda, N.Y.: Multi-Health Systems.

Remafedi, G. 1987. Adolescent homosexuality: Psychosocial and medical implications. *Pediatrics* 79:331–37.

Remafedi, G. 1994. Predictors of unprotected intercourse among gay and bisexual youth: Knowledge, beliefs, and behavior. *Pediatrics* 94:163–68.

Remafedi, G., J. A. Farrow, and R. W. Deisher. 1991. Risk factors for attempted suicide in gay and bisexual youth. *Pediatrics* 87:869–75.

Remafedi, G., S. French, M. Story, M. D. Resnick, and R. Blum. 1998. The relationship between suicide risk and sexual orientation: Results of a population-based study. *American Journal of Public Health* 88:57–60.

Remafedi, G., M. Resnick, R. Blum, and L. Harris. 1992. Demography of sexual orientation in adolescents. *Pediatrics* 89:714–21.

Reynolds, W. M. 1986. *Reynolds Adolescent Depression Scale.* Odessa, Fla.: Psychological Assessment Resources.

Roesler, T., and R. W. Deisher. 1972. Youthful male homosexuality: Homosexual experience and the process of developing homosexual identity in males aged 16 to 22 years. *Journal of the American Medical Association* 219:1018–23.

Rosario, M., J. Hunter, and M. Gwadz. 1997. Exploration of substance use among lesbian, gay, and bisexual youth: Prevalence and correlates. *Journal of Adolescent Research* 12:454–76.

Rothblum, E. D. 1994. "I only read about myself on bathroom walls": The need for research on the mental health of lesbians and gay men. *Journal of Consulting and Clinical Psychology* 62:213–20.

Rotheram-Borus, M. J., and M. I. Fernandez. 1995. Sexual orientation and developmental challenges experienced by gay and lesbian youth. *Suicide and Life-Threatening Behavior* 25(Suppl. 1):26–34.

Rotheram-Borus, M. J., J. Hunter, and M. Rosario. 1994. Suicidal behavior and gay-related stress among gay and bisexual male adolescents. *Journal of Adolescent Research* 9:498–508.

Rotheram-Borus, M. J., J. Hunter, and M. Rosario. 1995. Coming out as lesbian or gay in the era of AIDS. In G. M. Herek and B. Greene, eds., *AIDS, Identity, and Community: The HIV Epidemic and Lesbians and Gay Men*, pp. 150–68. Thousand Oaks, Calif.: Sage.

Rotheram-Borus, M. J., and C. Koopman. 1991. Sexual risk behavior, AIDS knowledge, and beliefs about AIDS among predominantly minority gay and bisexual male adolescents. *AIDS Education and Prevention* 3:305–12.

Rotheram-Borus, M. J., M. Rosario, H.F.L. Meyer-Bahlburg, C. Koopman, S. C. Dopkins, and M. Davis. 1994. Sexual and substance use acts of gay and bisexual male adolescents in New York City. *Journal of Sex Research* 31:47–57.

Rotheram-Borus, M. J., M. Rosario, R. Van Rossem, H. Reid, and R. Gillis. 1995. Prevalence, course, and predictors of multiple problem behaviors among gay and bisexual male adolescents. *Developmental Psychology* 31:75–85.

Savin-Williams, R. C. 1990. *Gay and Lesbian Youth: Expressions of Identity.* New York: Hemisphere.

Savin-Williams, R. C. 1994. Verbal and physical abuse as stressors in the lives of lesbian, gay male, and bisexual youths: Associations with school problems, running away, substance abuse, prostitution, and suicide. *Journal of Consulting and Clinical Psychology* 62:261–69.

Savin-Williams, R. C. 1995. Lesbian, gay male, and bisexual adolescents. In A. R. D'Augelli, and C. J. Patterson, eds., *Lesbian, Gay, and Bisexual Identities over the Lifespan: Psychological Perspectives*, pp. 165–89. Oxford: Oxford University Press.

Savin-Williams, R. C., and R. C. Rodriguez. 1993. A developmental, clinical perspective on lesbian, gay male, and bisexual youths. In T. P. Gullota, G. R. Adams, and R. Montemayor, eds., *Adolescent Sexuality*, pp. 77–101. Newbury Park, Calif.: Sage.

Schneider, S. G., N. L. Farberow, and G. N. Kruks. 1989. Suicidal behavior in adolescent and young adult gay men. *Suicide and Life-Threatening Behavior* 19:381–94.

Sears, J. T. 1991. *Growing Up Gay in the South: Race, Gender, and Journeys of the Spirit*. Binghamton, N.Y.: Haworth.

Sonenstein, F. L., J. H. Pleck, and L. C. Ku. 1989. Sexual activity, condom use, and AIDS awareness among adolescent males. *Family Planning Perspectives* 21:152–58.

Sorenson, R. C. 1973. *Adolescent Sexuality in Contemporary America*. New York: World.

Strickland, B. R. 1995. Research on sexual orientation and human development: A commentary. *Developmental Psychology* 31:137–40.

Wenar, C. 1994. *Developmental Psychopathology: From Infancy Through Adolescence*. 3rd ed. New York: McGraw-Hill.

Weinrich, J. D., and W. L. Williams. 1991. Strange customs, familiar lives: Homosexualities in other cultures. In J. C. Gonsiorek and J. D. Weinrich, eds., *Homosexuality: Research Implications for Public Policy*, pp. 44–59. Newbury Park, Calif.: Sage.

Working Groups, Workshop on Suicide and Sexual Orientation. 1995. Recommendations for a research agenda in suicide and sexual orientation. *Suicide and Life Threatening Behavior* 25(Suppl. 1):82–88.

Zucker, K. J. 1985. Cross-gender-identified children. In B. W. Steiner, ed., *Gender Dysphoria: Development, Research, Management*, pp. 75–174. New York: Plenum.

22   Lesbians and Gay Men in Midlife

Douglas C. Kimmel and Barbara E. Sang

Research on middle-aged gay men and lesbians today is best understood when viewed in its cultural and historical context. First, persons who are between the ages of forty and sixty today reached sexual maturity before the impact of the 1969 protest demonstrations following a police raid on the Stonewall Inn Bar in Greenwich Village, New York City. That event began to change the social construction of homosexuality from a personal pathology to minority-group membership. Some middle-aged persons were active participants in the historical events that brought about those changes. Second, middle-aged lesbians and gay men were in the prime of middle adulthood when the AIDS epidemic emerged. Many have been personally touched by the AIDS epidemic. Survivors of this cohort will enter old age and be followed by a cohort of middle-aged lesbians and gay men with different historical and cultural experiences. Therefore, to review characteristics of midlife today, we must recall the context in which this cohort of gay men and lesbians constructed their identity and the beliefs they held about their lives as a result. It is difficult to delimit the precise age range for these cohort effects, however, because of individual variation, socioeconomic status, geographical location, able-bodiedness, gender, race, and ethnicity.

Historical Background

In general, middle-aged lesbians and gay men today were isolated from one another in their youth. There were few books or magazines, especially for lesbians. As the baby boom followed World War II, the roles of housewife and mother with several children were emphasized, and education for women was discouraged. For gay men and lesbians, the climate was one of secrecy, very few positive role models, and great fear of exposure (D'Emilio 1983). However, in the 1950s, organizations such as the Daughters of Bilitis and the Mattachine Society emerged despite the "witch hunts" of homosexuals and Communists led by Senator Joseph McCarthy. Research studies and occasional books began to question the pathology model of homosexuality, but most portrayed it negatively. A few novels, such as Radcliffe Hall's *The Well of Loneliness* and James Baldwin's *Another Country*, were available and provided a sense of identification. Some gay men found ways to meet sexually, but lesbians often remained isolated. Many living in rural areas moved to brighter prospects in urban areas, where social networks could be found, at least for gay men. The view of the future was not positive: relationships were thought to be short-lived, exposure and arrest were feared, and aging was seen as lonely. Nonetheless, many ignored these stereotypes and coped with whatever difficulties came along, formed long-term relationships, and led lives of quiet nonconformity.

The historical changes of the 1970s had effects on all cohorts of lesbians and gay men and demonstrated the effects a younger generation can have on older ones. As a pioneer in the homophile movement noted, what had once been a personal identity for gay men and lesbians became a collective identity, and the stigma of homosexuality as mental illness dissolved into the possibility of an open and proud minority status (Hay 1990). Other historical influences have also had significant effects on this group of midlife lesbians and gay men. For example, the feminist movement had such profound effects on some women that Faderman (1984) coined the term *new gay lesbians* to describe those women who came out after the feminist emergence in contrast to those who came out before. Likewise, Kitzinger (1987) has argued that, for some women, the radical lesbian movement redefined the nature of sexual orientation from a psychological characteristic to a political ideology.

The AIDS epidemic of the 1980s also brought profound changes to gay men and lesbians. With the AIDS crisis now in its second decade, most midlife gay men have been confronted with the premature deaths of friends their age or younger. Some, of course, are infected with the virus thought to cause AIDS, a status that can result in unusual awareness of mortality. Many middle-aged gay men have partners who are experiencing AIDS-related illnesses or who have died. Unlike many other fatal diseases, AIDS can be transmitted to the sexual partner, so caring for a lover who is ill may be a rehearsal for one's own dying. The direct impact of the AIDS epidemic has been greater among gay men than among lesbians. Thus historical events have affected the psychology of middle age in markedly different ways for lesbians and gay men today.

Overview of Midlife Theories

Development during adulthood, especially during the midlife years, has been described in three different ways (Kimmel 1990). Although often seen as contradictory, these perspectives are complementary: (1) adult development is a relatively continuous process of maturation or unfolding of personality themes that were laid down early in life; (2) adult development consists of a series of predictable stages or periods when significant change or crisis may occur; and (3) social age norms, historical effects, and idiosyncratic transitions combine to provide the pattern of adult lives.

Research on adult development has been almost exclusively heterosexual in its focus. Women have typically been viewed in terms of their biological time clocks and traditional family or relationship roles such as caregiving. Men have been assumed to be highly involved in work. With few exceptions (Fertitta 1984; Kimmel 1978; Lee 1989; Sang, Warshow, and Smith 1991), lesbian and gay midlife development has not been included in theories of adult development (Cornett and Hudson 1987). One implication of this omission is that gays and lesbians have had few developmental models for conceptualizing their own life course or interpreting normative crises they may experience. This may enhance the opportunity for creating individual norms and roles (Brown 1989).

One contribution of research on lesbian and gay male midlife has been to add the dimension of sexual orientation to these models of adult development. Several new variables are added in this way: coming out as a lesbian or gay man as a developmental event; integrating one's sexual orientation into broader developmental themes; creating self-relevant norms and expectations for the order and timing of developmental events or periods; and fitting one's relatively unique life into the progression of developmental events of significant others, such as one's parents, children, and lovers. Moreover, adult development overlaps for many people with the development of long-term relationships, which sometimes follow a developmental sequence of their own (Kurdek 1995). Further, for some gay men and lesbians, parenting is a major theme in adult development (Patterson 1995).

Our task in this chapter is to integrate these various themes into an overview of the diversity of midlife experiences among gay men and lesbians. We begin with a focus on central aspects for lesbians: changes in the self, working life, relationships, menopause, and sexuality. In the following section we focus on gay men. We conclude with a discussion of what we know and what we hope to learn about lesbians and gay men in midlife.

Lesbians at Midlife

Sense of Self

Children leaving home is frequently cited as the central event that marks the beginning of midlife changes for traditional heterosexual women. At this time many women return to the work force, if they are not already working. Women whose lives have been oriented around caretaking and performing the role of the "other" have begun to search for their own identity, separate from children and husbands (Junge and Maya 1985; Rubin 1979). In contrast, a study by Fertitta (1984) of sixty-eight white, child-free lesbian women, never legally married, forty to fifty-five years of age, highly educated, all from the West Coast reported that finding an identity separate from others and proving themselves as independent persons were not central issues for these women. Many lesbians have spent a lifetime learning to define themselves independent of other people's reactions. Some midlife lesbians reported that in fighting their oppression as lesbians they have developed a stronger sense of self (Sang 1991). Moreover, there is reason to believe that lesbians place less emphasis on youth and traditional standards of beauty than heterosexual women and are therefore less threatened by the aging process (Kirkpatrick 1989; Posin 1991).

Another characteristic that distinguishes lesbians and nonconventional women from traditional middle- and upper-middle-class midlife women is the continuity of their work lives (Fertitta 1984; Sang 1991). Although their careers or the nature of their work may change in midlife, most lesbians work out of economic necessity, for stimulation, and as part of their identity throughout adult life (Hall and Gregory 1991; Fertitta 1984; Sang 1991). The observation that women's employment histories seem to be more fluid and less linear than men's employment histories (Baruch and Brooks-Gunn 1984) may thus not apply to most lesbians. A major theme that emerged for midlife lesbians in a questionnaire study by Sang (1991) of 110 self-identified lesbians, age forty to fifty-nine, who were generally well-educated and white, was the desire to have more fun and to be less achievement oriented. Many reported not wanting to push or strive as much as they did when younger. Work was described as easier, less stressful, and consequently more enjoyable and satisfying. There was a new sense of freedom; women described themselves as more open, playful, and spontaneous. Thus midlife appears to be a particularly creative time for lesbians (Sang 1996).

Affluent college-educated heterosexual women in their early fifties whose children had just left home have been reported to be in their "prime" (Mitchell and Helson 1990). These women describe their lives in very positive terms at this time. Midlife lesbians also appear to be in their "prime" despite the fact that, in the Sang study, about half (46 percent) the respondents reported that they had or were going through a "midlife crisis" (Sang 1991, 1996). These midlife lesbians felt this to be the best time in their life (76 percent) and felt more self-directed and self-confident than they remembered having felt at younger ages. One respondent wrote, "Each year seems to get better despite some of the seemingly endless struggles. Generally I feel better about myself and my life than I ever have . . . more focused yet more diverse in my interests and activities." Lesbians in the Fertitta (1984) study also reported a variety of positive internal changes such as gaining perspective, resolution of conflicts, self-acceptance, and wisdom when asked what the meaning of middle age was for them. Specific questions about worries and stressors, however, elicited concerns about finances and time pressures in other studies on midlife lesbians (Bradford and Ryan 1991; Woodman 1990). If there are times that are better than others, they do not appear to be triggered by such predictable markers as children leaving the home. The qualities that Mitchell and Helson (1990) posit for enhancing the quality of life for midlife women, autonomy and intimacy, appear to be characteristic of lesbians throughout their adult development.

In Sang's (1991) study it is not clear to what extent children leaving home affected the lives of midlife lesbians with children. In the accounts of midlife children, there was no spontaneous mention of this issue. It is conceivable that children leaving the home is not as great a change in the lives of lesbian mothers as it is for traditional heterosexual women because of the existence and continuity of many other significant roles and interests. Because their identities may be derived from many other sources as well, the meaning and significance of motherhood may also be different for lesbians than for heterosexual women. Further research is needed in this area.

One factor that may contribute to midlife being viewed as such a positive time among lesbians studied by Sang (1991) is the feeling that they have attained greater wisdom, power, and freedom. As a result of the gay and women's movements, more midlife lesbians and feminists are coming into contact with each other for the first time and are feeling a need to find new rituals and new ways of expressing their "midlife passage" (Downing 1987; Gauding 1991; Walker 1985). In our culture the wisdom and maturity that comes with aging has traditionally been attributed to midlife men. Gentry and Seifert (1991) describe the "Croning Celebration," a special birthday party, typically for a woman who is fifty or older or who is postmenopausal. This celebration is a public rite of passage that recognizes the wisdom that comes to women from life experience. For the past seven years lesbians in the Washington, D.C., area have also been holding a yearly weekend conference entitled "Passages," which is a multicultural, multiracial conference on aging and ageism for all lesbians. Events such as these emphasize positive aspects of aging for lesbians.

Work and Income

Midlife lesbians have been found to derive meaning and identity from both work and relationships throughout their adult lives (Fertitta 1984; Sang 1990, 1991). Midlife lesbians also reported a significant number of personal interests — an average of ten each, in addition to political and spiritual activities (Sang 1991). A major midlife issue for these lesbians is the striving for balance and wholeness. Each woman, in her own way, described her efforts to accommodate relationships, work, and personal interests. Because of perceived pressure to spend long hours at work, finding a balance between work life and home life was difficult for many lesbians. This issue also emerged as a major theme for lesbians in other studies and is further discussed in the next section.

Fertitta (1984) and Turner (1987) suggested that it is never-married lesbians who are most comparable to men in terms of commitment to careers. Men in our society know from childhood that they are expected to be self-supporting. Some lesbians are also aware from an early age that they will have to support themselves. Lesbians who are in midlife today, however, grew up at a time when girls were discouraged from having careers and taking an active part in the world. Lesbians who came out in their teens and twenties were more likely to report having had career expectations as teenagers (79 percent) compared to lesbians who came out in their thirties (59 percent) or older (over forty; 44 percent) (Sang 1990, 1991). Of the women who did have career aspirations, somewhat more than half (64 percent) were of a nontraditional nature, for example, scientist, doctor, professor, business owner, and athlete. It was the women who came out in their teens, twenties, and thirties who were more likely to envision themselves in nontraditional careers (74 percent) compared to women who identified themselves as lesbians at midlife (44 percent). The majority of lesbians who came out at midlife had been married heterosexually (96 percent). It is significant that lesbians in this sample became self-supporting, on average, at twenty-six years of age. Lesbians who came out earlier, however, were self-supporting in their early twenties (Sang 1991). In summary, evidence suggests that work has greater salience and is a more significant part of the midlife lesbian's identity than is reported for traditional midlife heterosexual women (Fertitta 1984; Sang 1991).

The career achievements of lesbians, like those of other women, are limited by sex discrimination in hiring, promotion, pay, and access to informal networks (Riddle and Sang 1978). Data from the *National Lesbian Health Care Survey* (Bradford and Ryan 1991) revealed that the earned income of middle-aged lesbians in this sample was not commensurate with their educational preparation and professional experience. Reasons for this discrepancy between training and income are not clear. It is possible that to feel comfortable, lesbians may work outside the mainstream in jobs that do not pay well. Further study of this issue is clearly in order.

With few exceptions, lesbians in the Sang (1991) study did not express anguish over their career achievements the way traditional midlife men are reported to do. Other studies also found no such concerns. Although it is possible that these studies failed to inquire about such issues, lesbians also may not be as concerned with making it to the "top." Lesbians may even avoid prestigious, high-level positions because, to survive in them, they must keep home and work lives separate and hide more than they would like to (Woodman 1990; Woods and Harbeck 1991). It is also likely that, because lesbians find meaning and self-esteem from many other areas, work does not assume such all-consuming importance. Eighty-six percent of the sample described their work as satisfactory or very good. These findings may not apply to working-class women; more research is needed in this area.

Relationships

Are lesbian relationships different at midlife from those at earlier ages? There are no longitudinal studies that make such comparisons; however, a few studies on midlife lesbians' relationships suggest developmental differences. Hall and Gregory (1991) interviewed nine mostly white midlife professional lesbian couples from the San Francisco Bay area who were between thirty-five and fifty and who had been in their relationships, on average, for six years. All interviewees had previous significant relationships and most had more than one. Because of separations, infidelity, illness, and so on, the original expectation that they would find one partner with whom they would live "forever after" had been tempered among these women. These midlife lesbians tended to see romance, if not relationships, as transitory.

A number of midlife lesbians were found to be single, that is, not in a committed couple relationship (Bradford and Ryan 1991, 40 percent; Fertitta 1984, 43 percent; Sang 1991, 33 percent). Based on the available data, reasons for being single or not cannot be determined, nor can one tell how relationship status affected women's quality of life. Midlife lesbians, who do not define themselves as part of a couple relationship, may be seeing one woman, many, or none. Raphael and Robinson (1984) found single midlife lesbians to have more lesbian friends than coupled lesbians of the same age. They also reported that a few single midlife lesbians were experimenting with alternative forms of bonding and intimacy that might or might not have sexual components, such as communal living.

Midlife lesbians were reported (Bradford and Ryan 1991) to be nearly twice as likely to be living alone (27 percent vs. 17 percent) as women in the general population, even if they were in a relationship. By the time one arrives at midlife, it may not be economically feasible to move in with a new lover, especially if one has done this several times in the past. Another possible reason that midlife lesbians are more likely to live alone is suggested by a small study conducted by Coss (1991). Based on intensive interviews with eight women between twenty-four and sixty-one, she found that women who grew up in the 1950s never considered living openly as lesbians the way younger lesbians do today. In addition, a few of these single midlife lesbians said that they would welcome a relationship but only if it "fit" in and was not disruptive to the satisfying balance they had achieved in their work and social lives.

One of the biggest problems midlife lesbian couples report is finding sufficient time for each other and for friends, that is, finding a balance between work and intimacy (Fertitta 1984; Sang 1991; Woodman 1990). Problems also arise when one member of a couple is less busy than the other. Not only do lesbians provide support for one another's work, but work itself seems to affect the couples' experience of intimacy; partners report spending more time together conferring about career projects, problem solving, arguing about and debriefing from their jobs than in any other activity.

Midlife lesbians, whether in couples or single, tended to derive support and a sense of connection from friends, family, and the lesbian community (Bradford and Ryan 1991; Fertitta 1984; Sang 1991; Woodman 1990). One of their greatest sources of support they reported, however, was lesbian women friends around the same age. Fertitta (1984) found that 81 percent of her midlife sample of lesbians were more likely to get support from their "new family" — that is, lovers, ex-lovers, and friends — than from their family of origin. She also reported that twice as many lesbians (50 percent) as heterosexual women (25 percent) in her sample reported being close to ex-lovers. Tully (1989) reported that the majority of midlife lesbians (89 percent) in her sample turned to their women friends for caregiving rather than their biological family or community health institutions. A large percentage of middle-aged lesbians were found to be hiding their lesbianism from most or all their family members (Bradford and Ryan 1991), and this might be one reason why midlife lesbians are less involved with their family of origin. Raphael and Robinson (1984) found that midlife lesbians with high self-esteem tended to have weak sibling ties and strong friendship ties.

The extent of a midlife lesbian's connection to the lesbian community is related to many variables, some of which are the age at which she came out, her need for secrecy, and her geographical area (Bradford and Ryan 1991; Woodman 1990). All sixty-eight of the mostly professional midlife lesbians in Fertitta's study (1984) were actively involved in the lesbian community. This affiliation played an important role in their self-acceptance and in their maintenance of a positive gay identity. In contrast, fewer than half (34 percent) of the midlife lesbians in Woodman's study (1990) were affiliated with lesbian and gay organizations. Fear of disclosure was the primary reason given among those who were not affiliated. One of the primary concerns for this socially isolated group of midlife lesbians was finding other lesbians their own age with whom to socialize. This sample of midlife lesbians differs from other samples of professional midlife women in terms of geographical region (64 percent are from the Southwest, South, and Midwest), relationship status (all were in couple relationships), and age when they came out (thirties and forties).

In addition to lovers, ex-lovers, and friends, midlife lesbians may also have significant relationships with their own children and grandchildren and those of their partners. Kirkpatrick (1989), Rothschild (1991), and Sang (1992) describe some of the dynamics of midlife lesbian mothers dealing with adolescent children. Such relationships can be particularly difficult if the mother is first coming out as a lesbian at midlife.

Another significant role for many midlife lesbians is that of caregiver to aging parents. Warshow (1991) pointed out that 75 percent of caregivers are women, and the "unmarried" daughter has historically been considered the best candidate for this position. Her career and relationships have often been considered expendable. It is not known what percentage of midlife lesbians are caregivers, nor is there much information about the impact of such caregiving on the lives of lesbian caregivers.

Menopause and Sexuality

Cole and Rothblum (1990, 1991) conducted the first systematic survey of sexual attitudes and behaviors of lesbian women at menopause. Their sample consisted of forty-one women (thirty-eight self-identified lesbians, one bisexual, and two who did not indicate their sexual orientation). The average age of this entirely white nonclinical sample was 51.5 years. The majority of respondents (56 percent) were postmenopausal, that is, had ceased to menstruate for at least one year. An additional 16 percent had a hysterectomy. In contrast to menopausal heterosexual women who expressed a great deal of worry about their changing sexuality (e.g., were concerned about being able to please their partner, arousal time, dry vaginas, and loss of clitoral sensitivity) (Cole 1988; Leiblum 1990; Morokoff 1988), 75 percent of lesbians reported that their sex lives were as good as or better than ever. For lesbians, the emphasis was firmly on the quality of their *relationships* instead of on their sexual functioning (Cole and Rothblum 1991).

Sang (1993)[1] reported similar findings for her sample of midlife women (average age of forty-seven), 22 percent of whom were postmenopausal or had hysterectomies (15 percent). Half (50 percent) of these midlife respondents reported that their sex life was more open and exciting than in the past. Better sex was attributed to being able to be more open and vulnerable, to enhanced communication, and to less pressure about orgasms as well as to the greater importance of touching, loving, and sharing. Many of the women who came out as lesbians at midlife reported being sexual for the first time. The majority of midlife lesbians reported being sexually active with a partner (71 percent in the Cole and Rothblum study and 74 percent in the Sang study). There was little change since the onset of menopause in the types of sexual activities lesbians enjoyed (Cole and Rothblum 1991).

The reasons for the differences reported in sexual satisfaction between lesbians and heterosexual women during menopause are not clear and deserve additional research. Cole and Rothblum suggested that one reason is that lesbian women are not as focused on intercourse or penetration as heterosexual women, and therefore the physiological changes of menopause might not be so disruptive. A variety of other factors including a dependence on male sexual performance, interest, and attraction may interfere with sexual satisfaction for midlife heterosexual women.

Menopause may not have the same psychological significance for lesbians and nontraditional women as it does for women whose main role and identity has been connected to child rearing. For some midlife lesbians, however, the approach of menopause can be a time of loss and conflict. Lesbians who grew up in the 1950s and 1960s did not have the options of parenting in the same way some lesbians do today. At midlife, lesbians who do want children are faced with the decision of whether to have them. Lesser (1991) explains that choosing whether to become a mother today is an often grueling process of sifting through contradictory personal feelings and cultural beliefs in an effort to identify one's own preferences and desires. Lesser interviewed fifteen mostly white professional women between the ages of thirty-six and forty-seven who were childless to explore their experiences. A third of the women reported a clear sense that having children was not something they wanted to do and that they experienced no regrets. At the other extreme, a few women reported wanting children but changing their minds when they considered the difficulties that children of lesbians would encounter. The rest of the sample were ambivalent about wanting children.

A significant midlife change reported by 25 percent of the women in the Sang (1991) sample was identifying themselves as "lesbians" for the first time, that is, "coming out." Of these women, 39 percent had their first same-sex sexual experience before midlife but had not labeled themselves lesbian until midlife. Some of these respondents reported being aware of same-sex sexual feelings in childhood (26 percent) and adolescence (37 percent). Charbonneau and Lander (1991) reported on another sample of midlife women (thirty women ranging in age from the mid-thirties to the mid-fifties) who, with few exceptions, never considered the possibility that they could be lesbians and were initially quite surprised to find that they had fallen in love with a woman. Lesbians who came out at midlife also sometimes reported feeling sexual for the first time. These findings attest to the fact that sexual development does not necessarily proceed according to one defined path.

Summary

Midlife lesbians who have been studied to date have been mainly white, professional, able-bodied middle- and upper-middle-class women. The majority of midlife lesbians were found to feel good about themselves and to report that midlife was the best period in their life. Both work and relationships were integral parts of the midlife lesbians' sense of identity. They also reported numerous personal interests in addition to political and spiritual involvement. Financial worry was a source of stress for many midlife lesbians; there was often considerable discrepancy between their level of education and their income.

Unlike traditional heterosexual women, who at midlife are returning to work or are working for the first time after children leave home, midlife lesbians were found to have been self-supporting since early adulthood. Midlife lesbians reported changes at work such as not striving as hard as they did when younger and the feeling of being knowledgeable and at "maximum capacity" in their field.

The majority of midlife lesbians studied reported being in a "couple" relationship. Close women friends were also reported to be important sources of support and intimacy. Some midlife lesbians were involved in the lesbian and gay community, but others from this generation remained closeted for fear of losing their jobs. The majority of midlife lesbians reported being active sexually and enjoyed sex more at this time because of better interpersonal communication. Midlife was also a time for some women to come out as lesbians.

Based on the studies that have been done on midlife lesbians, it appears possible that the lives of midlife lesbians are in some ways more diverse and complex than those reported for other midlife adults. Midlife lesbians certainly have many roles to integrate and balance. It may be that the complexity of their lives contributes to the sense of life satisfaction expressed by many lesbians at midlife.

Gay Men at Midlife

No research similar to the studies just described on lesbians at midlife has been reported for gay men. Before the 1970s the study of gay men was largely confined to research on psychopathology (Morin 1977). Life-span developmental psychologists and gerontologists did not focus on gay men growing older until a few pioneering studies emerged (Francher and Henkin 1973; Kelly 1977; Kimmel 1977, 1978, 1979; Weinberg 1969; Weinberg and Williams 1974). Despite continued research attention since 1980 on older gay men (e.g., Berger 1980, 1982, 1984; Gray and Dressel 1985; Lee 1987; Quam and Whitford 1992), little research has focused specifically on middle-aged men. It was not uncommon in these studies to include persons over age forty or forty-five in the "aging" group; for example, 26 percent of Berger's (1982) sample of 112 "older homosexual men" were between the ages of forty and forty-nine, and 44 percent were between the ages of fifty and fifty-nine. Others compared younger and "older" groups (over forty-five or fifty), with no specific attention to the middle-aged respondents (Gray and Dressel 1985; Weinberg and Williams 1974).

One study did focus on the age at which middle age is thought to begin (Bennett and Thompson 1990). It found that gay men perceived their middle age as beginning at forty-one and old age as beginning at sixty-three, on average, which was consistent with Minnigerode's (1976) finding for gay men and similar to findings from studies based on general samples (e.g., Neugarten, Moore, and Lowe 1965). However, the study also found that gay male respondents perceived middle age and old age as beginning earlier for gay men in general (ages thirty-nine and fifty-four, respectively) than for themselves — a phenomenon described as "accelerated aging" that is consistent with ageist stereotypes within the gay male community. Kooden (unpublished), in a discussion of middle-aged gay men, has given a useful definition of ageism: "The man is measured by how much of his youth he has retained, which devalues his present age."

Thus, in the absence of specific research, we have few road maps of adult development for gay men; those maps that do exist are based primarily on the interplay of heterosexual family models, work trajectories, and personal maturation. In the next section we seek to identify a few themes that may be unique for gay men.

Themes of Midlife

It is clear that there is great diversity in patterns of adult development among gay men. For example, those men who do not come out as gay until midlife experience these years as a prolonged search for identity, especially in terms of sexuality. Guilt, secrecy, heterosexual marriage, conflicted relationships with both women and men, and tentative forays into gay social life

often characterize this struggle. The result can be delayed social development, traumatic family crises, and a dramatic change in life when one comes
out. In contrast, a second pattern is the gay man who recognizes that he is
gay early in life and takes advantage of the benefits this identity offers, such
as an opportunity to cross social boundaries of race, class, and age. Others
use opportunities for education and travel as steppingstones out of rural areas
into urban centers with extensive gay communities.

Within this perspective of diversity, we focus on four aspects of midlife
that are important for many gay men: education, work, and retirement; intimate relationships; social networks; and sexuality. For many gay men, this
phase of development is similar to the phase described by Vaillant (1977)
in his longitudinal study of adult development among men: *intimacy and
career consolidation*. One strives to focus on occupational development and
to establish loving relationships with friends and, in many cases, with a
special companion.

Education, Work, and Retirement

Several questions about the interaction of gay identity, socioeconomic
status, occupational choice, and work need further investigation. For example, most samples of gay men studied in empirical research tend to be
more affluent and better educated than average men of the same age (Adams
and Kimmel 1997; Berger 1982; Lee 1987; Quam and Whitford 1992;
Weinberg and Williams 1974). However, it is clear that this finding could
be a sampling artifact, since there is evidence of a hidden gay male population. Harry (1990) reported on the characteristics of a nationwide telephone survey by the American Broadcasting Company — Washington Post
poll in 1985 that included a question about sexual orientation. The characteristics of gay males in this sample (3.7 percent of all men surveyed)
contrast sharply with those of samples studied in research to date: 42 percent
of the self-identified homosexual or bisexual group were currently married;
they were underrepresented in the highest-income groups and overrepresented in the lower-income groups; more than half lived in small towns; and
a sizable minority were African- or Hispanic-American. Harry concluded
that there is a substantial married homosexual or bisexual population that is
disproportionately minority and low in educational status. This group is difficult to locate and is undoubtedly overlooked in most studies of urban gay
white males that have been reported to date.

Several research questions are raised by the usual studies that find relatively high levels of education and income in samples of gay men compared to the general male population. Is it that freedom from family responsibilities and expenses allows greater educational and financial opportunities for these gay men who are not married or are open? Perhaps success at work and the stimulation, income, and power it can provide is a significant aspect of identity and feelings of success for some gay men because other traditional sources of male success, such as family roles, are often unavailable. It might also be that some gay men strive to compensate for feelings of inadequacy or inferiority or to create positions of relative invulnerability by means of their achievements. For example, based on his four-year longitudinal study of forty-seven gay male respondents over age fifty, Lee (1987) observed that the level of life satisfaction was associated with the respondent's social class and perception that he was above the average standard of living for his age. Moreover, Lee concluded that the gay men who were aging most successfully were also those who remained "in the closet." This finding contrasts sharply with the idea that being open about one's sexuality or active in the gay community is associated with satisfaction in aging (Quam and Whitford 1992). It also contradicts the idea that an individual's experience in coping competently with an earlier crisis, such as coming out, is associated with satisfaction later in life (Kimmel 1978). Whether this result will replicate among younger cohorts of gay men is a question that cannot be resolved without further research.

Another line of research is suggested by the report that gay men experience a "glass ceiling" to job promotion within many companies that prevents gay workers from advancing to the highest ranks (Stewart 1991). A dissertation by Woods (cited in Stewart 1991) reported that a typical response for lesbians and gay men is to "cap their ambitions and watch the clock, or find a ghetto in the company." One respondent in this study who was blatantly harassed changed jobs at Pacific Gas and Electric and retreated to the closet: "I just sit very quietly in my office and do my job. I am not interested in advancing. It's just not worth it" (p. 46). Another reported changing jobs so that he would not have to relocate, since he had to consider his long-term partner but believed his employer would not understand. For this reason, some gay men in midlife opt out of the corporate world into business for themselves, a style Woods termed *entrepreneurial flight*. Thus the "career ladder" may differ for gay men as a result of discrimination, some of which may be based on marital status or social networks instead of sexual orientation per se. Today, of course, some gay men are also retiring early or going on disability leave because of AIDS-related health problems.

The importance of self-employment for gay men was suggested in earlier studies of "aging" gays. Weinberg and Williams (1974) and Berger (1982) reported that self-employed gay men were less concerned than those who worked for others with concealment and were more integrated into the gay community, respectively: "It is the self-employed who stand out the most. As a group, they anticipate the least discrimination, and . . . are the least concerned with passing" (Weinberg and Williams 1974:228). Russo (1982) likewise found that gay leaders were typically self-employed. Recent changes by a few major employers (such as Levi-Strauss and Lotus) to respond openly to the concerns of their lesbian and gay employees might reduce the need for midlife gays to seek self-employment in the future.

Finally, patterns of retirement and activities in the early years of retirement deserve study. It may be that gay men express creativity in this sphere also (Brown 1989). Conversely, in the absence of biological children and other traditional contributions to future generations, work may take on added importance for many gay men and they may choose not to retire as early as they might otherwise. Work may also be one sphere where gay men have meaningful contact with older and younger generations — an important theme for some older gay men (Kimmel 1978). Research has also begun examining the retirement housing preferences of gay men and lesbians, finding that a large majority do have an interest in living arrangements that are sensitive to their needs (Lucco 1987; Quam and Whitford 1992).

In summary, our understanding of midlife gay men would benefit greatly from research that focuses on the importance, development, and patterns of education, career or occupation, and retirement for gay men. Useful comparisons could be made with lesbians and with general samples. Variations by socioeconomic status, ethnicity, and race would be expected.

Intimate Relationships

Although some research has focused on gay male relationships (see Kurdek 1995), little attention has been given to special issues for long-term or middle-aged couples. For example, studies of aging have reported lovers who have been together for thirty to forty or more years. It would be useful to examine the issues and strengths these couples identify. Also, age differences between partners have rarely been examined (Lee 1987; Steinman 1990). Another issue that has been described primarily in response to the AIDS epidemic is the impact of bereavement on gay male partners (Geis, Fuller, and Rush 1986; Klein and Fletcher 1986).

A particular concern for some couples is relations with each partner's family, especially if the care of aged parents or other relatives falls on either partner's shoulders. For example, coming out to one's family and extended relatives may become moot after a certain number of years as a couple. How do gay couples manage these relationships, especially as caregiving becomes more intense? Likewise, what roles do gay men seek with members of younger generations in the family of origin, including nieces and nephews? Ethnic and racial differences are likely to be especially important for studies of these family relationships (Adams and Kimmel 1997).

Another important dimension that deserves research attention is the way gay male couples negotiate career decisions and balance each other's occupational development, as well as retirement choices. It is likely that some parallel patterns exist to those identified for heterosexual couples or lesbian couples. However, Blumstein and Schwartz (1983), in their sample of couples, noted that 51 percent of the gay men (average age of thirty-five years) and 61 percent of the lesbians (average age of thirty-two years) were predominately relationship-centered — a higher level than among heterosexual groups of the same gender and comparable ages; conversely, 16 and 18 percent, respectively, were predominately work-centered — lower than among the heterosexual groups, especially for men. Thus gay males may opt out of the career competition ladder not only because of discrimination but also because of a desire to balance career and a relationship more equally.

In addition, little is known about the ways that two male partners maintain commitment to each other and to two separate career ladders. For example, is the decision to relocate made on a "your turn, my turn" pattern or on the basis of relative income or power in the relationship? Blumstein and Schwartz (1983) found that one partner tends to be work-centered and the other tends to be the caretaker in the relationship, regardless of sexual orientation or gender. They also found that couples in which both are relationship-centered were the happiest, and those in which both were career-centered were the least happy. Age differences, and developmental differences based on the length of the relationship, may also be relevant.

Social Networks

Various studies of aging gay men have noted the importance of self-created friendship networks that replace or supplement the biological family (Friend 1987). An important aspect of the friendship network is that younger friends need to be found and maintained, since the family does not necessarily provide contact with younger generations for gay men (Kimmel 1979).

It is especially important to note the significance of long-term friends, for it becomes impossible to replace relationships spanning several decades later in life. Thus the diabolical impact of AIDS has robbed many middle-aged gay men of their compatriots who experienced with them the persecution of the 1960s, the struggle and sexual freedom of the 1970s, and the AIDS epidemic of the 1980s. In many parts of the country, the depletion of surviving midlife gay men's social networks because of losses to AIDS is extreme.

Research on gay male social networks also needs to consider their volunteer roles both in the gay and lesbian community and outside it. Many middle-aged gay men were involved and some played leading roles in creating the services and supports that presently exist. Religious, social service, social, and AIDS-related organizations provide significant social networks and contacts for some gay men (see D'Augelli and Garnets 1995). Others have little interest but may have benefited indirectly and applaud their existence (Adams and Kimmel 1997).

Sexuality

Patterns of aging male sexual response are well known (Friend 1987; Kimmel 1990). For example, slower and less firm erections result from a variety of factors, both psychosocial and physical; the sense of impending ejaculation tends to disappear; and the need for ejaculation at each sexual occasion is reduced. Some gay men report that these changes are associated with an increase in sexual pleasure, since they focus less on orgasm and more on generalized sexual pleasure (Kimmel 1979). It may also be that reduced sexual activity, which is expected based on studies of general samples of aging men, may increase the perception of pleasure as the act becomes less frequent. A study by Pope and Schulz (1990) reported that nearly all the eighty-seven gay males (aged forty to seventy) in the sample said that they were sexually active (91 percent); most reported no change in sexual enjoyment (69 percent) and 13 percent reported an increase in enjoyment. Gray and Dressel (1985) reported that there was no significant difference by age group (sixteen to twenty-nine years, thirty to forty-nine years, fifty years and older) in number of sexual partners or in the amount of sexual activities for the sample studied by Jay and Young (1979). Berger (1982) reported that over 60 percent of his respondents (aged forty to seventy-nine) had engaged in sex once a week or more often during the six months before the study; moreover, 73 percent reported that they were "somewhat or very satisfied" with their sex lives. However, Weinberg and Williams (1974) found that older homosexuals (aged forty-five years or older) reported less frequent sex than the younger respondents. Blumstein and Schwartz (1983) noted that the length of the relationship was associated with a decrease in sexual activity for gay men and lesbians greater than the effect of age alone, although the latter was important also.

It is likely that gay men place great importance on sexual activity, including masturbation, since homosexuality (and, to a large extent, masculinity) may be seen as socially constructed and based on sexuality. Therefore gay males in midlife are likely to be more sexually active than heterosexuals or lesbians of the same age; Blumstein and Schwartz (1983) reported similar findings for a younger sample of gay men, lesbians, and heterosexuals. We would expect that the AIDS epidemic, use of VCRs for pornography, and norms about safe sex would each have important effects on the frequency of, satisfaction with, and role of sex in the lives of middle-aged gay men today. All these areas deserve empirical study.

Summary

A great deal of attention has been given to the midlife crisis or transition (Kimmel 1990). One could argue that gay men are likely to experience a midlife crisis for two reasons. First, Livson (1981) found that well-adjusted men and women at age fifty who had been nontraditional earlier in life were more likely than traditional men and women to have experienced a period of change and reassessment in midlife. Second, several studies and theories of the midlife crisis have suggested that certain factors might intensify a midlife crisis for gay men, regardless of their traditional or nontraditional personality: concerns about issues of mortality and a search for meaning and wholeness in life within a heterosexist society, fear of physical illness, occupation-related stress or being passed over for a promotion, family issues including care of aging parents, concerns about one's family lineage, and a feeling that one has lost some masculine prowess with advancing age. The literature on "accelerated aging" and the feared loss of sexual attractiveness noted earlier might also intensify the threat of a midlife crisis. In addition, Kooden (unpublished) suggested that the tasks of midlife gay men involve other specific issues, including shedding internalized negative and ageist attitudes. He suggests that this process requires confronting the fact that one's physical persona has changed so that one cannot be loved for physical attributes alone, taking responsibility for the choices one has made so far, and finding one's own voice. This latter concept refers to the idea that gay men often hide part of themselves from others and develop a guarded stance toward the world associated with hiding their gayness from significant others. In contrast, middle-aged gay men have the opportunity to begin "writing the book of one's life while being its central character"—taking authorship of one's past and future goals. Also, given the concurrent development of the gay community, middle-aged gay men have the opportunity to choose whether and how to connect themselves with circles of influence and power, whereas before they felt it was important to remain secretive and unconnected with others. Potentially, according to Kooden, this prospect allows them to recognize individual diversity among their peers and also to acknowledge the family they may have created over the years.

On the other hand, gay men could be less likely than others to experience a midlife crisis, because they tend to be socially outside the mainstream of normative developmental events. Thus they would be expected to experience midlife in a way that is similar to other periods of their lives; that is, determined more by previous patterns of coping with individualized cultural, social, and personal influences than by any of the generalized patterns described here. Those who developed competence in coping with crises earlier in life and who are in a position to take advantage of a creative stance toward midlife may find that it yields high levels of developmental potential.

Conclusions

This discussion of midlife has been an exploration of the experiences of a pioneer generation. Many have been positive role models and were among the creators and activists of the emerging gay and lesbian community. They were substantially less closeted than older generations. Some are actively challenging ageism (Copper 1988; Macdonald and Rich 1983). Thus this generation will have an impact on patterns of aging for gays and lesbians in the future. It is important that this generation be studied now, because their lives have spanned a unique period of history.

It is also important to examine gay and lesbian midlife samples to expand our understanding of, and theories about, midlife. For example, are the issues associated with intimacy and generativity (Erikson 1968) different for gay men and lesbians? How do the coping skills that enable the transitions of middle age differ by socioeconomic status, race, ethnicity, gender, and marital status for lesbians and gay men? What are the differences between early and late midlife (the forties versus age fifty-five and older)? Since aging is generally occurring later because of improved physical health and age norms are becoming less salient in many areas of life (Brooks-Gunn and Kirsch 1984; Kimmel 1990), what effect is this having on the experience of middle age for gays and lesbians? Finally, what questions are important to ask differently for lesbians and gay men in order to understand this period of the lifespan?

Our review here has suggested four overarching themes that are relevant for lesbians and gay men at midlife. Each of these points is also a call for additional research, because very little relevant data exist with which to evaluate these tentative conclusions.

First, there are several examples of greater diversity and more fluidity in developmental patterns for gay men and lesbians in comparison with heterosexual samples.

Second, parallels may be noted in work and career issues for lesbians and gay men, including limitations placed on promotions by the "glass ceiling," reactions to discrimination on the job such as withdrawing from competition or the choice of self-employment, and attitudes toward retirement.

Third, lesbians and gay men seem to be similar in their styles of more equal balance of career and relationship commitments, especially compared to heterosexual men. Choosing a partner whose focus on the relationship or on the career is complementary to one's own may also be a characteristic shared by many lesbians and gay men.

Fourth, differences in ethnicity and race, as well as in socioeconomic status, prior and current heterosexual experiences, and marital status, may be expected to influence patterns of midlife for lesbians and gay men. Almost no data exist on these variations, but there are emerging signs that such data may soon become available, as telephone surveys and studies of ethnic and racial groups become more frequent.

Virtually all research approaches in this area have been limited to interviews and questionnaires with cross-sectional samples. More longitudinal and observational forms of research need to be undertaken. For a variety of reasons, longitudinal studies are problematic, including issues of confidentiality, funding, and continued accessibility over time. However, a study that compared over time, for example, lesbians and gay men who came out pre-Stonewall with post-Stonewall cohorts would be a welcome advance in the field. Several alternative approaches also might be suggested. Observation of selected behavior variables at a social gathering sponsored by a lesbian and gay aging program could be used to compare age groups. Reactions of coworkers to middle aged versus younger and older gay and lesbian workers could be assessed. A dating service type of questionnaire could be used to compare respondents by age group; also, ratings by young and older raters of the questionnaire responses could be compared. A variety of attitude studies related to age discrimination by gender would be of interest. For example, videotaped interactions of lesbians and gay men in prearranged situations could be studied by age group according to selected variables related to concepts such as ageism. Measures of social distance in seating arrangements between college-age research subjects and confederates who differ by age and gender could be assessed. An innovative type of study would be to employ a beeper signal to alert the participant several times each day to enter into a log book the type of activity currently under way and related variables such as affect and involvement in the activity; age, gender, and sexual orientation might be relevant independent variables (cf. Csikszentmihalyi and Larson 1984). It is important to study this midlife population now since the pre-Stonewall cohort of lesbians and gay men will soon be chronologically in old age, making only retrospective studies of middle age possible. Attention also needs to be given to issues of able-bodiedness, socioeconomic status, ethnicity, and race in this population.

One underlying theme of this review is that middle age is more complex than either adolescence or aging: It involves more roles, greater diversity in daily tasks and commitments, and few general themes or markers. Perhaps, for this reason, midlife has often been overlooked in empirical research. But, for the same reason, it offers a rich variety of relevant opportunities for studies on a remarkable population of lesbians and gay men.

Notes

1. The specific question on menopause was introduced later in the study, and therefore only 75 women were asked this question instead of 110.

References

Adams, C. L., and D. C. Kimmel. 1997. Exploring the lives of older African American gay men. In B. Greene, ed., *Ethnic and Cultural Diversity among Lesbians and Gay Men*, pp. 132–51. Thousand Oaks, Calif.: Sage.

Baruch, G., and J. Brooks-Gunn. 1984. The study of women in midlife. In G. Baruch and J. Brooks-Gunn, eds., *Women in Midlife*, pp. 1–8. New York: Plenum.

Bennett, K. C., and N. L. Thompson. 1990. Accelerated aging and male homosexuality: Australian evidence in a continuing debate. *Journal of Homosexuality* 20(3/4):65–75.

Berger, R. M. 1980. Psychological adaptation of the older homosexual male. *Journal of Homosexuality* 5(3):161–75.

Berger, R. M. 1982. *Gay and Gray: The Older Homosexual Man.* Urbana: University of Illinois Press.

Berger, R. M. 1984. Realities of gay and lesbian aging. *Social Work* 29(1):57–62.

Blumstein, P., and P. Schwartz. 1983. *American Couples: Money, Work, Sex.* New York: Morrow.

Bradford, J., and C. Ryan. 1991. Who we are: Health concerns of middle-aged lesbians. In B. Sang, J. Warshow, and A. Smith, eds., *Lesbians at Midlife: The Creative Transition*, pp. 147–63. San Francisco: Spinsters.

Brooks-Gunn, J., and B. Kirsch. 1984. Life events and the boundaries of midlife for women. In G. Baruch and J. Brooks-Gunn, eds., *Women in Midlife*, pp. 11–30. New York: Plenum.

Brown, L. S. 1989. New voices, new visions: Toward a lesbian/gay paradigm for psychology. *Psychology of Women Quarterly* 13:445–58.

Charbonneau, C., and P. Lander. 1991. Redefining sexuality: Women becoming lesbian in midlife. In B. Sang, J. Warshow, and A. Smith, eds., *Lesbians at Midlife: The Creative Transition*, pp. 35–43. San Francisco: Spinsters.

Csikszentmihalyi, M., and R. Larson. 1984. *Being Adolescent: Conflict and Growth in the Teenage Years.* New York: Basic Books.

Cole, E. 1988. Sex at menopause: Each in her own way. In E. Cole and E. Rothblum, eds., *Women and Sex Therapy*, pp. 159–68. New York: Harrington Park.

Cole, E., and E. Rothblum. 1990. Commentary on "Sexuality and the Midlife Woman." *Psychology of Women Quarterly* 14:509–12.

Cole, E., and E. Rothblum. 1991. Lesbian sex after menopause: As good or better than ever. In B. Sang, J. Warshow, and A. Smith, eds., *Lesbians at Midlife: The Creative Transition*, pp. 184–93. San Francisco: Spinsters.

Copper, B. 1988. *Over the Hill: Reflections on Ageism Between Women.* Freedom, Calif.: Crossing.

Cornett, C. W., and R. A. Hudson. 1987. Middle adulthood in the theories of Erikson, Gould, and Vaillant: Where does the gay man fit? *Journal of Gerontological Social Work* 10(3/4):61–73.

Coss, C. 1991. Single lesbians speak out. In B. Sang, J. Warshow, and A. Smith, eds., *Lesbians at Midlife: The Creative Transition*, pp. 132–40. San Francisco: Spinsters.

D'Augelli, A. R., and L. D. Garnets. 1995. Lesbian, gay, and bisexual communities. In A. R. D'Augelli and C. J. Patterson, eds., *Lesbian, Gay, and Bisexual Identities over the Lifespan*, pp. 293–320. New York: Oxford University Press.

D'Emilio, J. 1983. *Sexual Politics, Sexual Communities.* Chicago: University of Chicago Press.

Downing, C. 1987. *Journey Through Menopause: A Personal Rite of Passage.* New York: Crossroad.

Erikson, E. H. 1968. *Identity: Youth and Crisis.* New York: Norton.

Faderman, L. 1984. The "new gay" lesbians. *Journal of Homosexuality* 10(3/4):85–95.

Fertitta, S. 1984. Never married women in the middle years: A comparison of lesbians and heterosexuals. Unpublished doctoral dissertation. Wright University, Los Angeles.

Francher, J. S., and J. Henkin. 1973. The menopausal queen: Adjustment to aging and the male homosexual. *American Journal of Orthopsychiatry* 43:670–74.

Friend, R. A. 1987. The individual and social psychology of aging: Clinical implications for lesbians and gay men. *Journal of Homosexuality* 14(1/2):307–31.

Gauding, M. 1991. Meditation on the goddess Kali. In B. Sang, J. Warshow, and A. Smith, eds., *Lesbians at Midlife: The Creative Transition*, pp. 215–22. San Francisco: Spinsters.

Geis, S. B., R. L. Fuller, and J. Rush. 1986. Lovers of AIDS victims: Psychosocial stresses and counseling needs. *Death Studies* 10(1):43–53.

Gentry, J., and F. Seifert. 1991. A joyous passage: Becoming a crone. In B. Sang, J. Warshow, and A. Smith, eds., *Lesbians at Midlife: The Creative Transition*, pp. 225–33. San Francisco: Spinsters.

Gray, H., and P. Dressel. 1985. Alternative interpretations of aging among gay males. *The Gerontologist* 25:83–87.

Hall, M., and A. Gregory. 1991. Subtle balances: Love and work in lesbian relationships. In B. Sang, J. Warshow, and A. Smith, eds., *Lesbians at Midlife: The Creative Transition*, pp. 122–33. San Francisco: Spinsters.

Harry, J. 1990. A probability sample of gay males. *Journal of Homosexuality* 19(1): 89–104.

Hay, H. 1990. Identifying as gay: There's the key. *Gay Community News*, April 22–28, p. 5.

Jay, K., and A. Young. 1979. *The Gay Report: Lesbians and Gay Men Speak About Sexual Experiences and Lifestyles.* New York: Summit.

Junge, M., and V. Maya. 1985. Women in their forties: A group portrait and implications for psychotherapy. *Women and Therapy* 4:3–19.

Kelly, J. 1977. The aging male homosexual: Myth and reality. *The Gerontologist* 17:328–32.

Kimmel, D.C. 1977. Psychotherapy and the older gay man. *Psychotherapy: Theory, Research, and Practice* 14:386–93.

Kimmel, D.C. 1978. Adult development and aging: A gay perspective. *Journal of Social Issues* 34(3):113–30.

Kimmel, D.C. 1979. Life-history interviews of aging gay men. *International Journal of Aging and Human Development* 10:239–48.

Kimmel, D.C. 1990. *Adulthood and Aging: An Interdisciplinary, Developmental View.* 3rd ed. New York: Wiley.

Kirkpatrick, M. 1989. Lesbians: A different middle-age? In J. Oldham and R. Liebert, eds., *New Psychoanalytic Perspectives: The Middle Years*, pp. 135–48. New Haven, Conn.: Yale University Press.

Kitzinger, C. 1987. *The Social Construction of Lesbianism*. London: Sage.

Klein, S. J., and W. Fletcher. 1986. Gay grief: An examination of its uniqueness brought to light by the AIDS crisis. *Journal of Psychosocial Oncology* 4(3):15–25.

Kooden, H. 1994. The excitement of being a middle-aged gay man. Unpublished manuscript.

Kurdek, L. A. 1995. Lesbian and gay couples. In A. R. D'Augelli and C. J. Patterson, eds., *Lesbian, Gay, and Bisexual Identities over the Lifespan*, pp. 243–61. New York: Oxford University Press.

Lee, J. A. 1987. What can homosexual aging studies contribute to theories of aging? *Journal of Homosexuality* 13(4):43–71.

Lee, J. A. 1989. Invisible men: Canada's aging homosexuals. Can they be assimilated into Canada's "liberated" gay communities? *Canadian Journal on Aging* 8(1):79–97.

Leiblum, S. 1990. Sexuality and the midlife woman. *Psychology of Women Quarterly* 14:495–508.

Lesser, R. 1991. Deciding not to become a mother. In B. Sang, J. Warshow, and A. Smith, eds., *Lesbians at Midlife: The Creative Transition*, pp. 84–90. San Francisco: Spinsters.

Livson, F. B. 1981. Paths to psychological health in the middle years: Sex differences. In D. H. Eichorn, J. A. Clausen, N. Haan, M. P. Honzik, and P. H. Mussen, eds., *Present and Past in Middle Life*, pp. 195–221. New York: Academic Press.

Lucco, A. J. 1987. Planned retirement housing preferences of older homosexuals. *Journal of Homosexuality* 14(3/4):35–56.

Macdonald, B., C. and Rich. 1983. *Look Me in the Eye: Old Women, Aging, and Ageism*. San Francisco: Spinsters.

Minnigerode, F. A. 1976. Age-status labeling in homosexual men. *Journal of Homosexuality* 1:273–76.

Mitchell, V., and R. Helson. 1990. Women's prime of life: Is it the 50s? *Psychology of Women Quarterly* 14:451–70.

Morin, S. 1977. Heterosexual bias in psychological research on lesbianism and male homosexuality. *American Psychologist* 32:629–37.

Morokoff, P. 1988. Sexuality in premenopausal and postmenopausal women. *Psychology of Women Quarterly* 12:489–511.

Neugarten, B. L., J. W. Moore, and L. C. Lowe. 1965. Age norms, age constraints, and adult socialization. *American Journal of Sociology* 70:710–17.

Patterson, C. J. 1995. Lesbian mothers, gay fathers, and their children. In A. R. D'Augelli and C. J. Patterson, eds., *Lesbian, Gay, and Bisexual Identities over the Lifespan*, pp. 262–90. New York: Oxford University Press.

Pope, M., and R. Schulz. 1990. Sexual attitudes and behavior in midlife and aging homosexual males. *Journal of Homosexuality* 20(3/4):169–77.

Posin, R. 1991. Ripening. In B. Sang, J. Warshow, and A. Smith, eds., *Lesbians at Midlife: The Creative Transition*, pp. 143–46. San Francisco: Spinsters.

Quam, J. K., and G. S. Whitford. 1992. Adaptation and age-related expectations of older gay and lesbian adults. *The Gerontologist* 32:367–74.

Raphael, S., and M. Robinson. 1984. The older lesbian: Love relationships and friendship patterns. In T. Darty and S. Potter, eds., *Women-Identified Women*, pp. 67–82. Palo Alto: Mayfield.

Riddle, D., and B. Sang. 1978. Psychotherapy with lesbians. *Journal of Social Issues* 34(3):84–100.

Rothschild, M. 1991. Life as improvisation. In B. Sang, J. Warshow, and A. Smith, eds., *Lesbians at Midlife: The Creative Transition*, pp. 91–98. San Francisco: Spinsters.

Rubin, L. 1979. *Women of a Certain Age: The Midlife Search for Self*. New York: Harper and Row.

Russo, A. J. 1982. Power and influence in the homosexual community: A study of three California cities. *Dissertation Abstracts International* 43 561B (University Microfilms No. DA8215211).

Sang, B. 1990. Reflections of midlife lesbians on their adolescence. In E. Rosenthal, ed., *Women, Aging, and Ageism*, pp. 111–17. New York: Haworth.

Sang, B. 1991. Moving towards balance and integration. In B. Snag, J. Warshow, and A. Smith, eds., *Lesbians at Midlife: The Creative Transition*, pp. 206–14. San Francisco: Spinsters.

Sang, B. 1992. Counseling and psychotherapy with midlife and older lesbians. In S. Dwolkin and F. Gutierrez, eds., *Counseling Gay Men and Lesbians: Journey to the End of the Rainbow*, pp. 35–48. Alexandria, Va.: American Association for Counseling and Development.

Sang, B. 1993. Some existential issues of midlife lesbians. In L. D. Garnets and D.C. Kimmel, eds., *Psychological Perspectives on Lesbian and Gay Male Experiences*, pp. 500–516. New York: Columbia University Press.

Sang, B. 1996. Midlife as a creative time for lesbians. In G. Vida, ed., *The New Our Right to Love: A Lesbian Resource Book*. New York: Touchstone.

Sang, B., J. Warshow, and A. Smith, eds. 1991. *Lesbians at Midlife: The Creative Transition*. San Francisco: Spinsters.

Steinman, R. 1990. Social exchanges between older and younger gay male partners. *Journal of Homosexuality* 20(3/4):179–206.

Stewart, T. A. 1991. Gay in corporate America. *Fortune*, December 16, 42–56.

Tully, C. 1989. Caregiving: What do midlife lesbians view as important? *Journal of Gay and Lesbian Psychotherapy* 1:87–103.

Turner, B. 1987. Developmental perspectives on issues for lesbians at midlife. Paper presented at the meeting of the American Psychological Association, August, Atlanta, Georgia.

Vaillant, G. 1977. *Adaptation to Life*. Boston: Little, Brown.

Walker, B. 1985. *The Crone: Women of Age, Wisdom, and Power.* San Francisco: Harper and Row.

Warshow, J. 1991. Eldercare as a feminist issue. In B. Sang, J. Warshow, and A. Smith, eds., *Lesbians at Midlife: The Creative Transition,* pp. 65–72. San Francisco: Spinsters.

Weinberg, M. S. 1969. The aging male homosexual. *Medical Aspects of Human Sexuality* (December): 66–67, 71–72.

Weinberg, M. S., and C. J. Williams. 1974. *Male Homosexuals: Their Problems and Adaptations.* New York: Oxford University Press.

Woodman, N. 1990. Twenty-five women: Their perspectives on oppression and the relationships which sustain them. Unpublished paper.

Woods, S. E., and K. M. Harbeck. 1991. Living in two worlds: Identity management strategies used by lesbian physical educators. *Journal of Homosexuality* 22(3/4):141–66.

23 Being Lesbian, Gay, Bisexual, and Sixty or Older in North America

Arnold H. Grossman, Anthony R. D'Augelli, and Timothy S. O'Connell

Most people have opinions about aging, and many people have thoughts about homosexuality. But few individuals have considered them simultaneously. In fact, many scholars, advocates for older adults, and other individuals consider the terms *gay* and *aging* to be incompatible. Consequently there have been comparatively few studies about the lives of older lesbian, gay, and bisexual people. As a result, not only have the members of this segment of the aging population remained invisible, but myths and stereotypes have been created about them and have persisted. We decided to ask older lesbian, gay, and bisexual individuals across the country about their lives and to learn from their telling. Specifically we designed this study to meet the following needs: (a) to give visibility to the experiences of older lesbians, gay men, and bisexual people in the gay and lesbian, aging, and academic communities; (b) to combat the myths and stereotypes about older lesbians and gay men; and (c) to expand our knowledge about older lesbians, gay men, and bisexual people so as to enhance resources and programs to meet their needs.

The linking of ages to the stages of human life has been valuable in studying and learning about the experiences of various groups of people, that is, children, adolescents, adults, and older adults. At the same time, it is important to acknowledge that there are many individual variations in developmental pathways and that the linkage of life stage and chronological age may be imprecise.

Although all stages of development present challenges for all people, those individuals who are not part of society's mainstream tend to face additional hurdles. While we have a growing body of knowledge that says this is true for gay and lesbian adolescents and adults, we have comparatively limited information about the lives of older lesbian, gay, and bisexual adults (see D'Augelli and Patterson 1995; Duberman 1997; Garnets and Kimmel 1993; Patterson and D'Augelli 1998; Savin-Williams and Cohen 1996).

The study had these purposes: (a) to describe the psychosocial and health characteristics of a national sample of older lesbians, gay men, and bisexual women and men; (b) to describe the nature of the perceived support networks of older lesbians, gay men, and bisexuals; and (c) to investigate whether older lesbians, gay men, and bisexuals were more satisfied with the support they received from people who are aware of their sexual orientation and from people who are similar to them in terms of sexual orientation, gender, and age.

Method

A survey research design using a self-administered questionnaire was employed. Participants evaluated their mental emotional health, physical health, overall loneliness, responsibility for their loneliness, alcohol use, drug abuse, self-esteem, and perceived social support.

Procedures

To obtain a national sample for the study, we identified agencies and groups providing social, recreational, and support services to older lesbians, gay men, and bisexuals through agency networks and by community leaders. We identified a contact person for the study at each of the nineteen sites (eighteen in the United States and one in Canada) who agreed to recruit participants. The contact person distributed and collected the study's questionnaires from those lesbians, gay men, and bisexual people sixty years and older who volunteered for the study. Each person who volunteered was asked to complete the questionnaire anonymously, and the questionnaire was returned to the contact person in a sealed envelope. In an effort to increase the diversity of the sample, a snowball sampling approach was used. Members of the sites who agreed to participate were asked to recruit other older people who were not affiliated with their group and who were not their partners or their roommates. Data collection occurred in 1997–98. Each person who completed the questionnaire was given $10.00. We report results for a final sample of 416 older lesbian, gay, and bisexual adults. A response rate cannot be calculated because the number of older adults available at each site to complete the questionnaire could not be determined.

Instrument

The questionnaire contained several standard measures and additional questions designed for this study. We assessed self-esteem using the ten-item scale developed by Rosenberg (1965); the coefficient alpha for this scale was .86 in this study. We measured internalized homophobia, or negative views of one's sexual orientation, with the Revised Homosexuality Attitude Inventory (RHAI) (Shidlo 1994); the coefficient alpha was .82. We used three scales to assess dimensions of loneliness and its management. Overall loneliness was determined with an eight-item version of the UCLA Loneliness Scale (Hays and DiMatteo 1987). The two other dimensions of loneliness — perceived responsibility for loneliness (or the attribution of the causes of loneliness to one's own efforts or to others) and the personal control over loneliness — were each assessed by four-item, 4-point scales (Moore and Schultz 1987). In this study, coefficient alphas for the three scales were .86, .86, and .57, respectively. We measured alcohol abuse with the ten-item Alcohol Use Disorders Identification Test (AUDIT), which was developed by the World Health Organization to identify people whose alcohol consumption could jeopardize their health (Bohn, Babor, and Kranzler 1995). Coefficient alpha for the AUDIT in this study was .77. We assessed drug abuse with the ten-item version of the Drug Abuse Screening Test (DAST-10; Skinner 1982). Coefficient alpha for the DAST-10 was .62. To measure mental and physical health, we used several questions from a survey instrument designed to assess health and mental health problems in the elderly (Ahern and Gold 1991; Hancock et al. 1991), which were answered on 5-point scales. (A sample question was, "How would you describe your mental and emotional health at the present time?" answered from "Excellent" to "Very Poor.")

We used a modified version of the Support Network Survey (SNS) (Berger 1992; Berger and Mallon 1993) to measure perceived social support. The SNS instructs the respondent to (a) list up to ten members of his or her support network; (b) designate the gender, age, and sexual orientation of each person and his or her relationship to the participant; (c) indicate the types of support the person gives; (d) rate his or her level of satisfaction with the person's support (on a 5-point scale, "not at all satisfied" to "extremely satisfied"); and (e) indicate the extent to which the person is aware of the respondent's sexual orientation (a three-item scale: 1 = "definitely knows"; 2 = "definitely or probably suspects"; and 3 = "does not seem to know or suspect"). The instrument also included demographic questions and items designed to assess the participants' experiences related to HIV/AIDS.

Finally, several questions concerned participants' lifelong experience of victimization based on their sexual orientation. They were asked how often the following types of victimization had occurred: verbal insults, threats of physical violence, assaults, objects thrown, assaults with weapons, threats to have one's sexual orientation exposed, discrimination at work, and discrimination in housing. Response choices were in four categories, "never," "once," "twice," or "three or more." A total victimization score was computed by adding the scores of all types of victimization.

Participants

The sample consisted of 416 older lesbians, gay, and bisexual adults — 297, or 71 percent, males; and 119, or 29 percent, females. They ranged in age from sixty to ninety-one years, with an average age of 68.5. Most (92 percent) identified as lesbian or gay, and 8 percent identified as bisexual. More than three-fourths (327, or 79 percent) were members of the gay-identified agencies or groups; and the remaining 89, or 21 percent, were social contacts of those who were affiliated with the groups. About half (51 percent) of the respondents said they belonged to one or two gay or lesbian organizations; some reported belonging to no groups, while others reported belonging to up to twenty groups. Additionally, most participants (66 percent) said they regularly attended one or two groups on a regular basis. Some indicated attending no groups regularly, while others attended up to eight groups on a regular basis. Twenty-one percent of the participants were high school graduates, 14 percent had obtained associate degrees or various types of certificates, and 65 percent received a bachelor's or higher degrees. Most participants were European/Caucasian/white, with 3 percent describing themselves as African-American/black, and 2 percent as Hispanic/Latino or Latina. One-third (34 percent) lived in a major metropolitan area, and approximately another third (35 percent) lived in a small city; with the remainder living in a suburb (10 percent), a small town or rural area (13 percent), or another type of community (7 percent). Approximately half (47 percent of males and 50 percent of females) stated that they had a current partner. Couples averaged 15.25 years together, with no difference between males and females in the longevity of their relationships. Almost two-thirds (63 percent) of the participants lived alone, 29 percent lived with their partners, 2 percent lived with friends, 2 percent lived with relatives, and 3 percent said they were homeless. Three-quarters (74 percent) were retired, 18 percent were working, 3 percent were receiving disability payments, and 5 percent continued to work despite retirement from other work. Participants reported being retired for an average of at least nine years ($M = 9.32$), with some participants having recently retired (three months) and others having retired more than forty-five years ago. With regard to personal yearly income, 15 percent earned less than $15,000, 44 percent earned from $15,000 to $35,000, and 41 percent earned more than $35,000.

Limitations of the Study

The participants in this study are not a representative sample of older lesbian, gay, and bisexual adults. This points to the difficulty in recruiting a representative sample of older lesbian, gay, and bisexual people for health-related research. Although the sample is geographically diverse, it is biased in favor of those who participated in a gay-identified group or knew people who did. The study also used self-identification in terms of sexual identity; therefore older adults who have had same-sex experiences but do not identify as gay, lesbian, or bisexual were not included. Consequently the findings cannot be generalized to all older lesbian, gay, and bisexual individuals.

Findings

The results of the study will be presented in five sections: mental health characteristics, selected physical health characteristics, substance use and abuse, support networks, and experiences with HIV/AIDS. Gender differences are reported as appropriate. Results for group differences on major study variables are shown in Table 23.1.

TABLE 23.1 Group Differences on Major Study Variables

| | Gender | | | | | Sexual Orientation | | | | | Living Arrangements | | | | | Total | |
| | Male | | Female | | | Gay/Lesbian | | Bisexual | | | Alone | | Domestic Partner | | | | |
Variable	M	SD	M	SD	F	M	SD	M	SD	F	M	SD	M	SD	F	M	SD
Mental Health	4.14	.83	4.20	.75	.52	4.18	.78	4.18	.68	<.001	4.10	.83	4.36	.58	9.13**	4.18	.77
Self-Esteem	34.69	4.50	35.25	4.56	1.29	34.80	4.60	35.21	3.74	.25	34.45	4.74	35.80	3.84	7.78**	34.85	4.52
Loneliness	14.15	4.14	13.83	4.71	.46	14.07	4.35	13.84	3.92	.09	14.65	4.47	12.65	3.56	19.19***	14.06	4.31
Responsibility for Loneliness	10.47	2.63	9.79	2.73	5.58*	10.33	2.73	9.59	1.92	2.42	10.15	2.65	10.56	2.71	1.99	10.28	2.67
Internalized Homophobia	24.27	6.50	22.13	5.06	10.31**	23.40	6.23	25.98	5.46	2.42	24.29	6.49	22.14	5.21	10.44**	23.66	6.21
Suicidality	3.95	1.96	3.44	1.28	6.77***	3.80	1.84	3.79	1.41	<.001	3.84	1.81	3.71	1.82	.42	3.80	1.81
Physical Health	3.92	.79	4.00	.81	.76	3.93	.80	4.12	.74	1.75	3.88	.82	4.11	.70	7.21**	3.95	.79
Alcohol Use (AUDIT)	3.36	3.46	2.32	2.47	8.89***	3.05	3.21	3.47	3.74	.53	2.98	3.10	3.29	3.57	.78	3.71	4.37
Drug Use (DAST)	10.24	.66	10.19	.57	.52	10.24	.65	10.18	.46	.29	10.23	.64	10.24	.65	.03	10.23	.64
Victimization	4.12	4.58	2.68	3.60	8.91**	3.69	4.36	3.94	4.48	.09	3.91	4.56	3.25	3.87	1.87	3.71	4.37

*p < .05, **p < .01, ***p < .001

Mental Health Characteristics

Data were collected for six areas including overall mental health, self-esteem, loneliness, responsibility for loneliness, internalized homophobia, and suicidality.

Mental Health   Eighty-four percent of the participants reported that their mental health was good to excellent, 14 percent said fair, and 2 percent said poor ($M = 4.18; SD = .77$). Regarding changes in mental health status over the past five years, 33 percent said that their mental health was better currently than it was five years ago, 54 percent reported that it stayed the same, and 13 percent said it became worse ($M = 3.35; SD = .91$). Additionally, current mental health was significantly positively related ($r = .22; p < .001$) to household income, indicating that those participants reporting better mental health had higher income. There was a significant negative relationship between victimization and mental health ($r = -.14; p < .01$), indicating that those participants reporting more victimization had lower levels of mental health. There was no relationship between reported mental health and the amount of time spent with other gay men or lesbians, or with the number of gay/lesbian organizations to which participants belonged. We used analyses of variance to examine differences in reported mental health between men and women, gay men/lesbians, and bisexuals, and whether or not a participant lived with a domestic partner. No differences were found between men and women ($F(1, 406) = .52, ns$) or between gay men/lesbians and bisexuals ($F(1, 405) = .001, ns$). However, those participants living with a domestic partner rated their mental health significantly more positively than whose who lived alone ($F(1, 405) = 9.13; p < .01$).

Self-Esteem   Most of the participants reported fairly high levels of self-esteem ($M = 34.85, SD = 4.52, range = 17.5 - 40$). Those living with domestic partners ($M = 35.8, SD = 3.84$) reported significantly higher levels of self-esteem ($F(1, 411) = 7.78, p < .01$) than those living alone ($M = 34.45; SD = 4.74$). However, an Analysis of Variance (ANOVA) showed that self-esteem did not differ by gender ($F(1, 413) = 1.29, ns$), or by sexual orientation (i.e., gay/lesbian vs. bisexual) ($F(1, 409) = .25, ns$). Those participants with higher levels of self-esteem had greater household income ($r = .22, p < .001$) and more people in their support networks ($r = .15, p < .01$). There was also a positive relationship between self-esteem and victimization, with those with fewer instances of victimization reporting higher self-esteem ($r = -.15$; $p < .01$). However, self-esteem was lower among older participants ($r = -.10$, $p < .05$). As with mental health, self-esteem was not affected by spending time with other gay men or lesbians or by involvement with gay or lesbian organizations.

Loneliness   Loneliness was experienced by many participants. More than one-quarter (27 percent) said they lacked companionship, and 13 percent reported feeling isolated. There was no relationship between age and loneliness ($r = .05$, *ns*). Also, the amount of time spent with other gays or lesbians and involvement in gay or lesbian organizations were not related to loneliness. There was a significant positive correlation between loneliness and household income; those reporting more income were less lonely ($r = -.18$; $p < .001$). As would be expected, participants were less lonely when they had more people in their support network ($r = -.23$; $p < .001$). There was also a significant relationship between loneliness and victimization; those who were more lonely experienced more victimization ($r = .18$, $p < .001$). An ANOVA was used to examine differences in loneliness between those living with domestic partners and those living alone; participants living with domestic partners were significantly less lonely ($F(1, 410) = 19.19$; $p < .0001$). However, the ANOVA yielded no significant differences in reported loneliness between gay men/lesbians and bisexuals, or between men and women.

Responsibility for Loneliness   Slightly more than half (52 percent) of the respondents agreed or strongly agreed that loneliness is a person's own fault. Men ($M = 10.47$; $SD = 2.63$) were more likely to feel responsible for their loneliness ($F(1, 408) = 5.58$, $p < .05$) than women ($M = 9.79$; $SD = 2.73$). There were no differences in feeling responsible for loneliness between gay men/lesbians and bisexuals ($F(1, 405) = 2.42$, *ns*) or those living with a domestic partner or living alone ($F(1, 407) = 1.99$, *ns*). Unlike feelings of loneliness, there was a significant positive relationship between age and responsibility for loneliness; older respondents felt more responsible for feeling lonely ($r = .15$, $p < .01$). Feeling responsible for loneliness was not related to household income, number of people in a person's support network, time spent with other gay men or lesbians, or involvement in gay and lesbian organizations.

Internalized Homophobia   Most of the participants reported low levels of internalized homophobia ($M = 23.66$; $SD = 6.21$), with men ($M = 24.27$;

$SD = 6.50$) reporting significantly more negative attitudes toward homosexuality than women ($M = 22.13$; $SD = 5.06$; $F(1, 411) = 10.31$; $p < .01$). Additionally, those respondents living alone reported more internalized homophobia than those living with a domestic partner ($F(1, 409) = 10.44$; $p < .01$). There was no difference in internalized homophobia between gay men/ lesbians and bisexuals. Internalized homophobia was related to age; older respondents reported more homophobia ($r = .13$; $p < .05$). Those respondents with more household income reported less internalized homophobia ($r = < .11$; $p < .05$). Contact with more people appears to be related to internalized homophobia. Respondents who were members of more gay or lesbian organizations and who had greater levels of involvement in these organizations had less internalized homophobia. Additionally, those with more people in their support networks reported less internalized homophobia. Victimization was not related to internalized homophobia ($r = .04$; $p = ns$).

Suicidality   Related to internalized homophobia, 8 percent of all participants reported being depressed about their sexual orientation, and 9 percent had been to counseling to stop their same-sex feelings; however, 17 percent of all participants stated that they would prefer being heterosexual. Of all the respondents, 10 percent sometimes or often considered suicide. Of these, 29 percent said that their suicidal thoughts related to their sexual orientation, with men reporting significantly more suicidality related to their sexual orientation than women ($F(1, 406) = 6.77$; $p < .01$). Thirteen percent (52 people) reported a suicide attempt at some point in their lives, with most doing so between the ages of twenty-two and fifty-nine. We found no differences in suicidal thoughts between those who lived with a domestic partner and those living alone ($F(1, 404) = .42$, ns), or between gay men/lesbians and bisexual people ($F(1, 402) < .001$, ns). Additionally, there were no significant relationships between suicidal thoughts and age, household income, network size, or involvement in gay or lesbian organizations.

Selected Physical Health Characteristics

Three-fourths of the participants (75 percent) reported that their physical health was good to excellent, 21 percent said fair, and 4 percent said poor. Regarding changes in their physical health status over the past five years, 11 percent said that their health was better; 50 percent reported that it stayed the same; and 30 percent said that it became worse. Eleven percent described their health status as interfering with activities they wanted to do. More than half (57 percent) indicated that they exercised regularly; 27 percent, sometimes; 12 percent, seldom; and only 4 percent, never. There was no apparent difference in reported physical health between men and women or between gay men/lesbians and bisexuals. Individuals living with a domestic partner ($M = 4.11$; $SD = .70$) reported significantly better physical health than those living alone ($M = 3.88$; $SD = .82$), $F(1, 406) = 7.21$; $p < .01$). Physical health was related to household income; those reporting better physical health had higher incomes ($r = .24$; $p < .001$). Additionally, individuals experiencing less lifetime victimization reported better physical health ($r = -.14$, $p < .01$). Although not significant, physical health status was related to the number of people in the respondents' support networks; participants who had more people in their networks reported better physical health.

Substance Use and Abuse

Only 9 percent of the sample (thirty-eight people) could be classified as "problem drinkers" on the AUDIT. Eleven participants added comments indicating that they were "recovering alcoholics." Men ($M = 3.36$; $SD = 3.46$) reported significantly more alcohol use than women ($M = 2.32$; $SD = 2.47$), $F(1, 412) = 8.89$; $p < .01$), and significantly more men could be classified as "problem drinkers." For this sample, it appears that contact with other people does not affect alcohol use. There was no difference between those living with a domestic partner and those living alone ($F(1, 410) = .78$, ns). Further, there was no relationship between alcohol use and number of people in support networks or involvement with gay or lesbian organizations, nor was alcohol use related to age. There was no relationship between alcohol use and household income, or with victimization experiences.

Eighty-three percent reported no evidence of drug abuse in the past year on the DAST, with thirty-six participants emphasizing abstinence from drug use by writing unsolicited comments on their questionnaires such as, "I don't do drugs," and "No drugs ever!" There were no gender differences with regard to drug abuse.

Support Networks

The 416 participants listed a total of 2,612 people in their support networks, so the respondents' networks averaged 6.3 people. Participants' sexual orientation was not related to the size of their networks. The most frequently reported category was "close friends," listed by 90 percent of the participants. The second most frequently reported category was "partners" (listed by 44 percent), followed by "other relatives" (listed by 39 percent), "siblings" (listed by 33 percent), and "social acquaintances" (listed by 32 percent). Coworkers were listed only by 15 percent of the participants, parents by 4 percent, and husbands/wives by 3 percent. Half (49 percent) of the people in the networks were younger than sixty years of age, and half were sixty or older. The range of networks members' ages was from fifteen to ninety-four (average age = 58). Respondents were significantly older than their network members ($t[387] = 23.56$; $p < .001$), on average by about ten years, a finding that held for both women and men.

Women listed significantly more people in their networks ($t[414] = 2.94$; $p < .01$) than men did, and had more women (75 percent) in their networks (both lesbian and heterosexual) than men did (26 percent). Men's networks contained more gay/bisexual males (54 percent) than women's networks (10 percent). Heterosexual men were equally represented in men's and women's networks. Bisexual women and men reported having significantly more heterosexual people in their networks compared to lesbian and gay respondents ($F(2, 390) = 6.07$; $p < .01$). An average of six people in the networks "definitely knew" the participants' sexual orientation, an average of about two persons "definitely or probably suspected," and an average of 2.5 persons "did not know or suspect." Participants were more satisfied with the support they received from those who definitely knew of their sexual orientation than from those who suspected or were unaware of it. They were most satisfied with the support provided by their lovers/partners, and they were very satisfied with the support from close friends or coworkers. An ANOVA showed significant differences among the most frequently reported category of people offering support (i.e., partners/lovers, close friends, spouse, coworkers, other relatives, and social acquaintances) ($F(8, 2819) = 22.51$; $p < .0001$). Post hoc tests (Tukey Honestly Significant Difference) revealed significant ($p < .05$) differences between (a) parents and: social acquaintances, close friends, and partners/lovers; (b) siblings and: social acquaintances, close friends, and partners/lovers; (c) coworkers and: social acquaintances, close friends, and partners/lovers; and (d) other relatives and: social acquaintances, close friends, and partners/lovers. Participants were not more satisfied with the support they received from people of the same sexual orientation ($F(3, 2689) = 1.2$, ns) or who were close to them in age ($F(2, 2827) = 1.91$, ns). The more satisfied participants felt with support received, the less lonely they felt ($r = -.32$; $p < .01$). Regarding the types of support received, 62 percent indicated that they received emotional support from their networks; 54 percent, practical support; 13 percent, financial support; 41 percent, advice and guidance; and 72 percent, general social support (Grossman, D'Augelli, and Hershberger 2000).

Victimization Based on Sexual Orientation

Sixty-three percent of the participants reported experiencing verbal abuse based on their sexual orientation over their lifetimes, 29 percent were victims of threats of violence, 16 percent experienced assault, 11 percent had objects thrown at them, and 12 percent were assaulted with a weapon. Twenty percent reported employment discrimination based on their sexual orientation, and 7 percent experienced housing discrimination. Being victimized by someone who threatened to disclose their sexual orientation was reported by 29 percent of participants. Victimization was related to gender ($F(1, 398)$ = 8.91; $p < .01$), with men ($M = 4.12$; $SD = 4.58$) reporting more victimization than women ($M = 2.68$; $SD = 3.60$). Additionally, increased victimization was related to visibility: Those participants who had memberships in more lesbian, gay, or bisexual organizations ($r = .19$, $p < .001$) or attended them regularly ($r = .16$; $p < .01$) reported more victimization. However, the size of an individual's support network was not related to victimization ($r = .007$), ns. Reported levels of victimization were related to household income; as income increased, levels of victimization decreased ($r = -.19$, $p < .001$). Although not significant, older individuals reported less victimization than their younger counterparts ($r = -.09$; $p < .10$). There was no difference in victimization reported by those individuals living with a domestic partner or those living alone ($F(1, 397) = 1.87$, ns). Further, there was no reported difference between gay men/lesbians and bisexuals ($F(1, 398) = .09$, ns).

Experiences with HIV/AIDS

Ninety-three percent of the participants knew people diagnosed with HIV/AIDS, and 90 percent knew someone who died from HIV/AIDS. Further, 47 percent indicated that they knew three or more people who had died from HIV/AIDS. Ninety percent said that they are very unlikely or unlikely to be infected with HIV, 6 percent did not know, 2 percent said they were likely or very likely, and 2 percent reported being infected. Of the 2 percent who reported being HIV infected, eight were men and one was a woman. Participants were asked about whether they had been tested for HIV/AIDS, and, if not, whether they planned to be tested in the next year. Forty percent indicated that they had two or more HIV/AIDS tests, 18 percent had only one test, and 2 percent expected to be tested in the next year. The remaining 40 percent reported that they did not expect to take an HIV/AIDS test.

Discussion

Today's older lesbian, gay, and bisexual people grew up when heterosexism and homophobia remained largely unchallenged. Furthermore, the culture and institutions of the time reflected pathologizing models of homosexuality. Lesbians and gay men were classified as mentally ill, and they were thereby stigmatized and assigned to a low status. Therefore, in addition to the negative events related to society's homophobia, lesbians, gay men, and bisexuals experienced social stress and stigmatization as members of a sexual minority group in a dominant heterosexual society. At the center of this experience was (is) the incongruence between their culture, needs, and experiences and societal structures (DiPlacido 1998; Meyer 1995). This incompatibility has led lesbians, gay men, and bisexuals to experience negative life events (e.g., loss of custody of children, antigay violence), as well as more chronic daily hassles (e.g., hearing antigay jokes, always being on guard). Some studies and reports have linked minority stress to greater mental health problems, emotional distress, and depressive mood among gay men, and excessive cigarette smoking, heavy alcohol consumption, excessive weight, and high-risk sexual behaviors among lesbians and bisexual women. However, there is evidence to suggest that some gay men, lesbians, and bisexuals deal successfully with minority stress, so that it does not lead to negative health outcomes. Social support and certain personality characteristics, such as hardiness and self-esteem, have been found to moderate the negative effects of stress (DiPlacido 1998).

The older lesbians, gays, and bisexuals in this study experienced much of their development at a time when many stress-buffering factors were not available. On average, they were born in 1929 and were forty years of age at the time of the 1969 Stonewall riots in New York City, which marked the beginning of the modern lesbian, gay, bisexual, and transgender civil rights movement. They averaged forty-four years of age when homosexuality was removed from the American Psychiatric Association's list of mental illnesses in 1973, fifty-two when the first cases of AIDS were reported in 1981, and sixty-nine when the television character "Ellen" disclosed her sexual orientation to a national audience in 1997. Although older lesbians, gay men, and bisexuals constitute a diverse group, these life-course markers indicate that they experienced many years of stress before these sociopolitical events influenced their lives. In addition to altering the perceived status of lesbians, gay men, and bisexuals in American society, these events empowered many older people to disclose their sexual orientation for the first time (Herdt and Beeler 1998) and have encouraged others to attend support and social groups designed to meet their needs. As a result, the experiences resulting from these events have enabled many older lesbians and gays to construct positive identities (Friend 1989, 1990).

The older lesbians, gay men, and bisexuals who participated in this study experienced their early identity development at a time when homosexuality was synonymous with abnormality, inferiority, and shame. As a result, many feared that identifying their sexual orientation would lead to humiliation, dishonor, and rejection, and they remained invisible. They tended to internalize society's negative stereotypes about them, developing feelings of unworthiness and self-hate (Friend 1990; Grossman 1997). However, it appears that most of the study's participants have mastered their sexual identity challenges leading to identity acceptance, identity pride, or identity synthesis (Cass 1979), which have led them to become members of social groups of older lesbians, gay men, and bisexuals.

Their overall mastery of sexual identity development is apparent in many of the study's findings, which is consistent with the findings of Berger (1996) and Kehoe (1989). The large majority of the participants reported fairly high levels of self-esteem, low levels of internalized homophobia, and a good or excellent mental health status. The large majority of the participants also reported no evidence of drug use in the past year, and relatively few could be classified as "problem drinkers." The large majority of the participants described support networks that consisted mainly of close friends, thereby creating "families of choice"; however, almost half (44 percent) also listed partners among their network members. Although the participants were most satisfied with the support that they received from partners, they were very satisfied with the support received from close friends and coworkers. The most important factor in determining support satisfaction was the knowledge of their sexual orientation by the support group member, which is a prime example of their identity acceptance and pride.

Although a majority of the participants appear to have developed some resilience to the stress related to their minority status, evidence of distress remains. Most striking is the victimization based on sexual orientation, with almost two-thirds (63 percent) of the participants having experienced verbal abuse and more than one-quarter (29 percent) having experienced threats of physical violence. A similar percentage of people (29 percent) reported being victimized by someone who threatened to disclose their sexual orientation to others. As indicated by Herek, Gillis, and Cogan (1999), stigma-based personal attacks on lesbian, gay, and bisexual adults are more deleterious to their mental health than other types of attacks.

Other evidence of ongoing distress was reported by participants in this study. For example, more than one-quarter (27 percent) reported feeling lonely, and more than half (52 percent) reported that responsibility for loneliness was a person's own fault. Other indexes of continuing distress were the following: 10 percent of participants reported that they sometimes or often considered suicide, and 17 percent indicated that they wished they were heterosexual and that increased visibility led to greater victimization experiences. If Lee's (1987) conclusion, based on his four-year longitudinal study of older gay men in Canada, is correct, that is, successful aging involves being fortunate and/or skilled enough to avoid stressors (including the stress of coming out), then these participants are engaged in such a process. Lee found that health, wealth, and lack of loneliness were associated with high life satisfaction among the study's participants. Another distress related to their sexual orientation was knowing large numbers of people diagnosed with HIV/AIDS (93 percent) and knowing who had died as a result of HIV/AIDS (93 percent). The impact of these experiences was not assessed, and it is recommended that future research include the implications of living as an older lesbian, gay, or bisexual person through the HIV/AIDS epidemic.

Using a snowball sampling approach, we asked older lesbian, gay, and bisexual people who belonged to social and recreational agencies and groups to tell us about themselves. There were 416 responses, producing a larger and more geographically diverse sample than has been gathered in other studies. They completed structured questionnaires to inform us about some of their experiences and current lives. We learned that our findings are consistent with a recent development in social gerontology: socioemotional selectivity theory, which posits that older adults engage in motivated processes to regulate their social interactions with the primary purpose of controlling their emotionality (Carstensen 1992; Carstensen, Gross, and Fung 1998). Using this approach, the findings of the current study support the idea that older lesbian, gay, and bisexual people engage in processes to reduce the stress associated with their minority status, thereby reducing their internalized homophobia, enhancing their identity acceptance and pride, and creating supportive social networks. Future research is needed to understand these processes, not only for the implications of providing programs and services but to help older lesbian, gay, and bisexual people who are not able to engage in these programs and services on their own.

Acknowledgment

The authors gratefully acknowledge initial funding from New York University's School of Education's Research Challenge Fund.

References

Ahern, F. M., and C. Gold. 1991. Risk due to use of alcohol and alcohol-interactive drugs among the elderly. Paper presented at the meetings of the Gerontological Society, November, Boston.

Berger, R. M. 1992. Passing and social support among gay men. *Journal of Homosexuality* 23(3):85–97.

Berger, R. M., and D. Mallon. 1993. Social support networks of gay men. *Journal of Sociology and Social Welfare* 20:155–74.

Berger, R. M. 1996. *Gay and Gray: The Older Homosexual Man.* 2nd ed. New York: Harrington Park.

Bohn, M. J., T. F. Babor, and H. R. Kranzler. 1995. The Alcohol Use Disorders Identification Test (AUDIT); Validation of a screening instrument for use in medical settings. *Journal of Studies in Alcohol* 56:423–32.

Carstensen, L. L. 1992. Social and emotional patterns in adulthood: Support for socioemotional selectivity theory. *Psychology and Aging* 7:331–38.

Carstensen, L. L., J. J. Gross, and H. H. Fung. 1998. The social context of emotional experience. In K. W. Schaie and M. P. Lawton, eds., *Annual Review of Gerontology and Geriatrics,* Vol. 17, pp. 325–52. New York: Springer.

Cass, V. C. 1979. Homosexual identity formation: A theoretical model. *Journal of Homosexuality* 4(3):219–35.

D'Augelli, A. R., and C. J. Patterson, eds. 1995. *Lesbian, Gay, and Bisexual Identities over the Lifespan: Psychological Perspectives.* New York: Oxford University Press.

DiPlacido, J. 1998. Minority stress among lesbians, gay men, and bisexuals: A consequence of heterosexism, homophobia, and stigmatization. In G.M. Herek, ed., *Stigma and Sexual Orientation: Understanding Prejudice Against Lesbians, Gay Men, and Bisexuals,* pp. 138–59. Thousand Oaks, Calif.: Sage.

Duberman, M., ed. 1997. *A Queer World: The Center for Lesbian and Gay Studies Reader.* New York: New York University Press.

Friend, R. A. 1989. Gay aging: Adjustment and the older gay male. *Alternative Lifestyles* 3:231–48.

Friend, R. A. 1990. Older lesbian and gay people: A theory of successful aging. *Journal of Homosexuality* 20(3/4):99–118.

Garnets, L. D., and D.C. Kimmel. 1993. *Psychological Perspectives on Lesbian and Gay Male Experiences*. New York: Columbia University Press.

Grossman, A. H. 1997. The virtual and actual identities of older lesbians and gay men. In M. Duberman, ed., *A Queer World: The Center for Lesbian and Gay Studies Reader*, pp. 615–26. New York: New York University Press.

Grossman, A. H., A. R. D'Augelli, and S. L. Hershberger. 2000. Social support networks of lesbian, gay, and bisexual adults 60 years of age and older. *Journal of Gerontology: Psychological Sciences* 55B:P171–79.

Hancock Gold, C. H., F. Ahern, and D. Heller. 1991. Health outcomes associated with use of alcohol and alcohol-interactive prescription drugs by the elderly. Paper presented at the meetings of the American Public Health Association, November, Atlanta.

Hays, R. D., and M. R. DiMatteo. 1987. A short-form measure of loneliness. *Journal of Personality Assessment* 51:69–81.

Herek, G. M., J. R. Gillis, and J. C. Cogan. 1999. Psychological sequelae of hate crime victimization among lesbian, gay, and bisexual adults. *Journal of Consulting and Clinical Psychology* 67:945–51.

Herdt, G., and J. Beeler. 1998. Older gay men and lesbians in families. In C. J. Patterson and A. R. D'Augelli, eds., *Lesbian, Gay, and Bisexual Identities in Families: Psychological Perspectives*, pp. 177–96. New York: Oxford University Press.

Kehoe, M. 1989. *Lesbians over Sixty Speak for Themselves*. New York: Haworth.

Lee, J. A. 1987. What can homosexual aging studies contribute to theories of aging? *Journal of Homosexuality* 13(4):43–71.

Meyer, I. H. 1995. Minority stress and mental health in gay men. *Journal of Health and Social Behavior* 36:38–56.

Moore, D., and N. R. Schultz Jr. 1987. Loneliness among the elderly: The role of perceived responsibility and control. *Journal of Social Behavior and Personality* 2 (part 2): 215–24.

Patterson, C. J., and A. R. D' Augelli, eds. 1998. *Lesbian, Gay, and Bisexual Identities in Families: Psychological Perspectives*. New York: Oxford University Press.

Rosenberg, M. 1965. *Society and the Adolescent Self-Image*. Princeton, N.J.: Princeton University Press.

Savin-Williams, R. C., and K. M. Cohen. 1996. *The Lives of Lesbians, Gays, and Bisexuals: Children to Adults*. Fort Worth: Harcourt Brace College Publishers.

Shidlo, A. 1994. Internalized homophobia: Conceptual and empirical issues in measurement. In B. Greene and G. Herek, eds., *Lesbian and Gay Psychology: Theory, Research, and Clinical Applications*, pp. 176–205. Thousand Oaks, Calif.: Sage.

Skinner, H. 1982. *The Drug Abuse Screening Test (DAST): Guidelines for Administration and Scoring*. Toronto, Canada: Addiction Research Foundation.

Part VII

Mental Health

For many years, a bisexual, lesbian, or gay sexual orientation was not considered a reflection of human diversity but of pathology. The conceptualizations about gay, lesbian, and bisexual people have shifted over the past four decades from an illness model — "Nonheterosexual people are sick; being gay, lesbian, or bisexual is the problem" — to an affirmative model: "Nonheterosexual people are normatively different; heterosexism is the problem."

The *illness model* makes a sharp distinction that heterosexuals are normal and mentally healthy but that homosexuals and bisexuals are abnormal and impaired in their psychological functioning (Bullough and Bullough 1997). This model views homosexuality per se as a form of psychopathology, developmental arrest, or other psychological disorder. Homosexuals are seen as a group of people with definite characteristics — one can generalize about "the homosexual." The aims of treatment and research are to ferret out the causes of homosexuality and bisexuality, to eliminate the illness, and to discourage people from adopting or maintaining a homosexual or bisexual identity. The bottom line is that everyone should be heterosexual.

A growing body of empirical research has refuted the illness model. Based on scientific evidence, the consensus is that homosexuality is not a form of pathology nor is it associated with mental illness or poor psychological functioning. On standardized measures of personal adjustment and psychological well-being, gay and lesbian individuals (Gonsiorek 1991), couples (Peplau and Spalding 2000), and parents (Patterson and Redding 1996) are comparable to their heterosexual counterparts. Although research about bisexuals is limited, Fox (1996) found no evidence of psychopathology in non-clinical samples of bisexual women and men.

Rothblum's article in this section provides a rich historical view of the evolving perspectives on lesbian, gay, and bisexual mental health during the 1900s.

In the past, therapists focused on "reorienting" lesbian, gay, and bisexual patients to encourage them to become heterosexual or at least to function as if they were heterosexuals in marriage and family life. Sexual orientation "reparative" or "conversion" therapies have supported and reinforced the social stigmatization of homosexuality and bisexuality. Haldeman's article in this section reviews the literature on scientific data that indicated that reorientation or conversion therapy is ineffective; it led to the American Psychological Association adopting a resolution condemning the unethical use of such treatments (DeLeon 1998).

The *affirmative model* that developed during the 1970s holds a very different perspective about sexual minorities and their mental health. This model focuses on the ability of gay men, lesbians, and bisexuals to cope adaptively with the impact of stigma, minority status, and difference from the heterosexual mainstream. From this viewpoint, psychologically healthy homosexual and bisexual people are those who come to terms with their sexual orientation and integrate it into their lives.

The affirmative model opens up new vistas regarding mental health issues among this population. While lesbians, gay men, and bisexuals appear to be as well adjusted as heterosexuals, they can have adjustment problems. Both internal characteristics and social factors facilitate general life adjustment. Many of the problems of living associated with lesbian, gay, or bisexual sexual orientations are thought to result from societal prejudice and negative social attitudes about homosexuality and bisexuality. The affirmative model views the cause of distress as rooted in social norms, others' attitudes, and pressure from family, peers, and institutions — not in homosexuality or bisexuality per se.

Unfortunately many bisexuals, lesbians, and gay men internalize these negative social attitudes. The result is often *internalized homophobia*, defined as "a set of negative attitudes and affects toward homosexuality in other persons and toward homosexual features in oneself" (Shildo 1994). Internalized homophobia has been found to be related to depression (Placido 1998; Shildo 1994), lower self-esteem and self-hatred (Gonsiorek 1993; Placido 1998), substance abuse (Glaus 1988), and relationship instability (Meyer and Dean 1998).

The question then is, can gay men, lesbians, and bisexuals as stigmatized minorities cope with oppression without also harming their own mental health? Clearly, if one recognizes the link between social oppression and mental health, then our psychological perspective must attend to a broad range of social and personal mental health issues. A *minority stress* model has emerged in recent years; it posits that lesbians, gay men, and bisexuals may be at increased risk for mental distress because of exposure to both external stressors from the social environment and internal stressors from within the individual. Likely sources of stress result from social oppression and discrimination, guilt and shame from internalized homophobia, and pressure from others to fulfill family roles including propagation and heterosexual marriage.

The article by Meyer provides empirical support for the minority stress model. In his research, three minority stressors have been found to independently predict psychological distress for gay men: internalized homophobia, perceived stigma, and actual prejudice events. Placido (1998) pointed out that almost no research has addressed minority stress among lesbian and bisexual women. She has begun to examine sexual minority stress in lesbian and bisexual women and has found that negative lesbian-related events and internal stress of self-concealment, emotional inhibition, and internalized homophobia are positively associated with physical and psychological problems.

In addition to overtly stressful events, lesbians, bisexuals, and gay men may be hassled, ignored, and denied relevant privileges such as spouse benefits or recognition. They may be denied conjugal visits in a hospital or nursing home, have their care or their partner's care taken over, against their wishes, by biological families, or lose control over the funeral and inheritance to legal "next of kin." Moreover, disabled gays, bisexuals, and lesbians face stigma because of their disability and their sexual orientation; alternatively their sexuality may be ignored completely.

Sexual prejudice compounded by AIDS-related stigma may compromise health care and mental health care for gay and bisexual men and for bisexual women and lesbians who are HIV-positive. Lesbians, bisexuals, and gay men of color, those with low income, and adolescents who have left home are often unable to access the full range of health and mental health care because of a lack of health insurance, discrimination, or other reasons.

In spite of greater vulnerability to these forms of oppression, gay men, lesbians, and bisexuals generally have demonstrated resilience (D'Augelli and Garnets 1995; Frable, Wortman, and Joseph 1997; Miranda and Storms

1989). Through the support of a variety of personal resources and the lesbian, gay, bisexual communities, they have turned crises into competent adaptations. Nonetheless, including sexual orientation in civil rights protections, widely available domestic partner health benefits, reduced heterosexist discrimination, full access to mental health care, and an end to sexual and gender prejudice as well as to anti-gay/lesbian/bisexual violence would be very good medicine indeed — for everyone, including lesbians, gay men, and bisexuals.

Contemporary Issue: Effects of State and National Legislation and Popular Votes Regarding Sexual Orientation Issues on the Psychological Well-Being of Gay Men, Lesbians, and Bisexuals

A number of local, state, and national popular votes regarding sexual orientation have brought the civil rights struggles of gay men, lesbians, and bisexuals into national prominence. What have been the psychological consequences of these civil rights struggles on the well-being of gay men, lesbians, and bisexuals?

On the one hand, antigay legislation and voter referendums have helped to foster a group identity as members of a minority group and as part of a broader political movement (D'Augelli and Garnets 1995). The psychological impact for these people is a sense of empowerment and a desire to mobilize to fight the oppression (Russell 2000). This, in turn, has helped lesbians, gay men, and bisexuals to resist the negative consequences of sexual prejudice. This sense of belonging to a larger collective also decreases a sense of isolation and enhances one's sense of efficacy as a sexual minority. Gay, lesbian, and bisexual people who may have considered their struggle as either private or an issue of sexual freedom are now aware of being part of a broader civil rights movement. Moreover, there has been an increase in the number of men and women who are living openly as gay, lesbian, or bisexual. On the other hand, national and state public debates on these civil rights issues have exposed gay and bisexual people to the hatred and ignorance that still exists. The greater visibility of gay, lesbian, and bisexual people has increased the vocalization of institutional and personal hostility toward them. For some gay, lesbian, and bisexual individuals, this has led to increased psychological distress, resulting from minority stress. For example, in 1992 the citizens of Colorado ratified Amendment 2, which stripped lesbians, gay men, and bisexuals of protection from discrimination under the state's constitution. The psychological impact of this antigay legislation on some members of the gay community included depression, anger, and anxiety (Russell 2000). It is important to understand the value of this national public discourse in spite of the possible increase in minority stress. Rather than keeping these antigay views hidden and insidious, they are open to public scrutiny. This exposure is allowing gay affirmative views to be overtly expressed and legitimized as well. In addition, heterosexual Americans have had more contact with openly gay people, and the inaccuracy of stereotypes about sexual minorities has become more evident (Herek and Capitanio 1996). As a result, public opinion polls reflect a trend toward greater tolerance and acceptance of homosexuality and support of the right not to be discriminated against, particularly in the workplace (Berke 1998). An example of the value of this public discourse is the same-gender marriage battle. First, this struggle has given gay men, lesbians, and bisexuals an opportunity to educate the nation about the reality and diversity of lesbian, bisexual, and gay lives and family relationships. This increased visibility has shifted the public discourse from an exclusive focus on sexual behavior to discussions about the recognition and legitimization of personal relationships and commitments. Second, it has helped to raise the nation's consciousness about the ways that sexual minorities are discriminated against and experience unequal treatment in marriage, child custody, adoption, and foster care.

The gay, lesbian, and bisexual civil rights movement has helped to identify sources of bias against sexual minorities and has worked to change social institutions that maintain the marginality of lesbians, gay men, and bisexuals. In addition to actual civil rights gains, the involvement of members of the lesbian, gay male, and bisexual community has facilitated decreased stigma and increased empowerment and self-esteem. On balance, the struggle for nondiscrimination laws and against right-wing views of so-called traditional marriage and family values has been positive in terms of mental health and personal growth of lesbians, gay men, and bisexuals. The movement has identified the problem — it is not sexual orientation; it is bigotry, hatred, and prejudice.

References

Berke, R. L. 1998. Chasing the polls on gay rights. *New York Times*, August 2, WK3.
Bullough, V. L., and B. Bullough. 1997. The history of the science of sexual orientation, 1880–1980. *Journal of Psychology and Human Sexuality* 9(2):1–16.

D'Augelli, A. R., and L. D. Garnets. 1995. Lesbian, gay, and bisexual communities. In A. D'Augelli and C. Patterson, eds., *Lesbian, Gay, and Bisexual Identities over the Lifespan*, pp. 293–320. New York: Oxford University Press.

DeLeon, P. H. 1998. Proceedings of the American Psychological Association, Incorporated, for the year 1997: Minutes of the Annual Meeting of the Council of Representatives. *American Psychologist* 53:882–939.

Fox, R. 1996. Bisexuality in perspective: A review of theory and research. In B. Firestein, ed., *Bisexuality: The Psychology and Politics of an Invisible Minority*, pp. 3–50. Thousand Oaks, Calif.: Sage.

Frable, D. E., C. Wortman, and J. Joseph. 1997. Predicting self-esteem, well-being, and distress in a cohort of gay men: The importance of cultural stigma, personal visibility, community networks, and positive identity. *Journal of Personality* 65:559–624.

Glaus, O. K. 1988. Alcoholism, chemical dependency, and the lesbian client. *Women and Therapy* 8:131–44.

Gonsiorek, J. 1991. The empirical basis for the demise of the illness model of homosexuality. In J. Gonsiorek and J. Weinrich, eds., *Homosexuality: Research Implications for Public Policy*, pp. 115–36. Newbury Park, Calif.: Sage.

Gonsiorek, J. 1993. Mental health issues of lesbian and gay adolescents. *Journal of Adolescent Health Care* 9:114–22.

Herek, G. M. and J. P. Capitanio. 1996. "Some of my best friends": Intergroup contact, concealable stigma, and heterosexuals' attitudes toward gay men and lesbians. *Personality and Social Psychology Bulletin* 22:412–24.

Meyer, I., and L. Dean. 1998. Internalized homophobia, intimacy, and sexual behavior among gay and bisexual men. In G. M. Herek, ed., *Stigma and Sexual Orientation: Understanding Prejudice against Lesbians, Gay Men, and Bisexuals*, pp.160–86. Thousand Oaks, Calif.: Sage.

Miranda, J., and M. Storms. 1989. Psychological adjustment of lesbians and gay men. *Journal of Counseling and Development* 68:41–45.

Patterson, C. J., and R. E. Redding. 1996. Lesbian and gay parents and their children: Legal and public policy implications of social science research. *Journal of Social Issues* 52(2):29–50.

Peplau, L. A., and L. R. Spalding. 2000. The close relationships of lesbians, gay men, and bisexuals. In C. Hendrick and S. S. Hendrick, eds., *Close Relationships: A Sourcebook*, pp. 111–24. Thousand Oaks, Calif.: Sage.

Placido, J. 1998. Minority stress among lesbians, gay men, and bisexuals: A consequence of heterosexism, homophobia, and stigmatization. In G. M. Herek, ed., *Stigma and Sexual Orientation: Understanding Prejudice against Lesbians, Gay Men, and Bisexuals*, pp.138–59. Thousand Oaks, Calif.: Sage.

Russell, G. M. 2000. *Voted Out: The Psychological Consequences of Antigay Politics*. New York: New York University Press.

Shildo, A. 1994. Internalized homophobia: Conceptual and empirical issues in measurement. In B. Greene and G. M. Herek, eds., *Lesbian and Gay Psychology: Theory, Research, and Clinical Applications*, pp. 176–205. Thousand Oaks, Calif.: Sage.

24   "Somewhere in Des Moines or San Antonio": Historical Perspectives on Lesbian, Gay, and Bisexual Mental Health

Esther D. Rothblum

What is gay history? Is it just when we discover that someone from the past had a long-term intimate relationship with someone of the same sex? Or is gay history simply the history of self-identified homosexuals? What do we make of Native American cultures that did not have concepts of homosexuality vs. heterosexuality? . . . Unlike other minorities, for whom finding oneself in history is simply a matter of finding out a person's race or religion, gay people have to put together the pieces of a complex puzzle, often using suspicion and loose associations to discover the hidden lineage that is part of our history.

–L. Witt, S. Thomas, and E. Marcus, *Out in All Directions: The Almanac of Gay and Lesbian America*

So many events have influenced the current status of lesbian, gay, and bisexual (LGB) mental health that a whole book could be devoted to this topic alone. In fact, it could be argued that any past legal, political, social, religious, or educational issue related to lesbians, bisexual women, gay men, or bisexual men has affected the status and knowledge of LGB mental health. After describing the history of the language of sexual orientation, this paper focuses on three historical phenomena that have been important for the current understanding of LGB mental health. The first factor consists of changing social roles — specifically concerning the economy, education, and the military — that allowed some women and men to discover LGB identities in the United States. Second, I briefly review the

Harlem Renaissance, Greenwich Village, and the Stonewall uprisings — three phenomena in New York City that profoundly influenced modern-day LGB communities. Third, I review LGB newsletters and organizations that created a national awareness of LGB issues.

Also reviewed are events and issues specific to LGB mental health and counseling today. These are (a) psychoanalysis and "reorientation" therapy; (b) sex surveys such as Kinsey's; (c) psychological research concerning LGB issues; and (d) the changing versions of the *Diagnostic and Statistical Manual of Mental Disorders* (DSM) of the American Psychiatric Association.

The purpose here is to present highlights in LGB history that have influenced LGB-affirmative psychology as it is practiced today. LGB terminology and communities were necessary to the development and practice of a lesbian, gay, and bisexual psychology. In the mental health field itself, research and clinical practice have often had a conflicting past, with research indicating that LGB individuals were similar to heterosexuals in adjustment and mental health whereas psychotherapists continued to try to "reorient" their LGB clients to become heterosexual. The removal of the diagnosis of "homosexuality" from the *DSM* and the affirmative stance of the U.S. mental health professions toward LGB issues today are the end result of social and economic changes.

The History of Language and Terminology

The Language of Sexual Orientation

What language is used, in earlier centuries and across geographical regions, to describe women who had sex with women or men who loved men? How is sexual orientation understood when gender itself has had different meanings across time and culture? There have been many books, articles, and posters featuring women and men from the past who were lesbian, gay, or bisexual (or are now believed to have been). How did these people view their own sexuality before the advent of present-day LGB communities? This paper begins with a historical review of the language that refers to sexual orientation and gender.

Historians generally agree that some form of specialized language is necessary for the development of a group identity. LGB individuals had to view themselves — and be viewed as — different from heterosexuals.

According to Neil Miller (1995), the word *homosexuality* first appeared in print in 1869 in Germany in an anonymous pamphlet urging an end to that country's sodomy law. Regarding early use of the word *gay*, Miller cited Donald Webster Cory's (1960) book *The Homosexual in America*:

> How, when, and where this word originated, I am unable to say. I have been told by experts that it came from the French, and that in France as early as the sixteenth century the homosexual was called gaie; significantly enough, the feminine form was used to describe the male. The word made its way to England and America, and was used in print in some of the more pornographic literature soon after the First World War. Psychoanalysts have informed me that their homosexual patients were calling themselves gay in the nineteen-twenties, and certainly by the nineteen-thirties it was the most common word in use among homosexuals themselves. (pp. 358–59)

In contrast, Emma Donoghue (1993) argued that there has been knowledge of same-sex love for centuries. In her book *Passions Between Women: British Lesbian Culture, 1668–1801*, she wrote the following:

> The Oxford English Dictionary . . . traces "lesbianism" back to 1870, "lesbic" to 1892, and lesbian, as an adjective to 1890 and as a noun to 1925. Similarly, the entries for "Sapphism" start in 1890, with 1902 given as the first date for "Sapphist." These entries give the impression that only after the publications of late nineteenth-century male sexologists such as Havelock Ellis did words for eroticism between women enter the English language. . . . *Passions Between Women* is urgently committed to dispelling the myth that seventeenth- and eighteenth-century lesbian culture was rarely registered in language and that women who fell in love with women had no words to describe themselves. (pp. 2–3)

Donoghue gives examples of the phrases "lesbian loves," "a lover of her sex," "Sapphic lovers," "woman-lover," and "she loved women in the same manner as men love them" being used in print in the seventeenth and eighteenth centuries (1993:3–5).

Gert Hekma (1998) found the first use of the word *bisexual* in Dutch in 1877, although it was used in a different context from its current use:

> Bisexual referred in this case to a hermaphrodite who started her sexual career as a heterosexual woman in Germany and who continued his

career as a heterosexual man in America. In this first case, it is not
clear in which sense the adjective was used, but most likely it referred
to passing through both sexes: to being a woman with her menses and
later being a man with ejaculation, and not to having both sexual
object-choices. It was still a time when the attribution of gender could
be done on the basis of sexual object-choice: loving a man meant being
a woman. (pp. 113–14)

Minton and Mattson (1998) cited the lyrics of a 1940 Broadway musical:
"I don't like a deep contralto, or a man whose voice is alto, Zip, I'm a
heterosexual" (p. 44). It is interesting that there has been practically no
research performed or theories proposed about heterosexuality itself. Although psychological research often compares a sample of LGB individuals
to a "control group" of heterosexuals, little is known about heterosexuality.
In 1993 Sue Wilkinson and Celia Kitzinger (two lesbian psychologists) edited a volume devoted to heterosexuality among women. They stated in their
introduction:

Heterosexuality has been largely untheorized within both feminism
and psychology. . . . The set of questions we asked in our "Call for
Contributions" was a deliberate reversal of those which psychology has
traditionally addressed to the topic of lesbianism: What is heterosexuality and why is it so common? Why is it so hard for heterosexuals
to change their "sexual orientation"? What is the nature of heterosexual sex? How does heterosexual activity affect the whole of a woman's
life, her sense of herself, her relationships with other women, and her
political engagements? (p. 1)

Their volume is only the barest introduction to an enormous field, and I
encourage researchers and theorists to explore heterosexuality in more depth.

The Language of Gender and Its Relation to Sexual Orientation

Gender is necessary for definitions of sexual orientation. When one conceptualizes gay men as men who love men, or lesbians as women who have
sex with women, one has fixed ideas of the terms men and women. The
Western concepts of lesbian, gay, and bisexual assume constancy of gender.
It is only in the 1990s that the social sciences are beginning to grapple with

ideas of gender as fluid and continuous, but these ideas have a long history in non-European cultures.

Recently a number of books have appeared on "two-spirit people," a term coined by Native Americans for individuals in their cultures who are gay or lesbian, are transgendered, or have multiple gender identities (see Brown 1998; Jacobs, Thomas, and Lang 1997; Roscoe 1998). Carrie House (1997), of Navajo-Oneida descent, wrote:

> Our oral traditions acknowledge that the he-shes and she-hes (those who hold in balance the male and female, female and male aspects of themselves and the universe) were among the greatest contributors to the well-being and advancement of their communities. They were (and we are) the greatest probers into the ways of the future, and they quickly assimilated the lessons of changing times and people. Recent studies into the lives of she-hes and he-shes have recovered models or near models of this rich, inventive, reverential, and highly productive approach to keeping balance within a society viewed as an extension of nature. (p. 225)

The term *two-spirit* reflects an attempt by Native American communities to redefine their past, in contrast to the way it was depicted by white male anthropologists, and also to distinguish Native American concepts of gender and sexuality from those of the Western gay and lesbian communities. In the late nineteenth century white male anthropologists "discovered" the *berdache*, a French word for Native American men whose gender roles did not match their anatomical sex. Neil Miller (1995) described the way that berdaches did not fit the categorical Western concepts of sex and gender of the time.

Gloria Wekker (1997) described identity among working-class women of West African origin in Suriname as follows:

> Most Western European languages have only one way to refer to the self—with the personal pronoun "I," "je," "ich," or "ik." This suggests a monolithic, static, unique conception of personhood. In contrast, in Sranan Tongo, the Surinamese creole, there are a wide variety of ways to make statements about the self. In Sranan Tongo it is possible to talk about the self in singular or plural terms, in masculine or feminine forms, and even in third-person constructions, irrespective of one's gender. (p. 331)

Gender intersects with sexuality as Afro-Surinamese women engage in *mati-ism*, or sexual relations with women while also being in relationships with men (Wekker 1993).

Paula Rust (1996), one of the leading researchers of bisexuality in the United States today, stated the following:

> First of all, in some cultures, sexuality is not perceived to be a source of identity, and a lack of sexual identity in individuals from such cultures is not an indication of psychosexual immaturity or unresolved sexual issues. . . . Second, even among cultures in which sexuality does serve as a source of identity, the concepts used to understand and organize sexuality often differ from those in European-American culture. (p. 56)

Nevertheless, many people in the United States who identified as lesbian, gay, or bisexual generally followed rigid gender roles until the women's movement of the 1970s provided more alternative gender roles for people in general. Lillian Faderman (1991) and Kennedy and Davis (1993) described the strictly mandated butch versus femme roles, behaviors, and dress codes for women, particularly working-class women who went to gay bars (gay men had the choice of being nelly or butch). There was hostility and suspicion when a woman was "kiki" (neither butch nor femme). Audre Lorde wrote in her autobiography, "I wasn't cute or passive enough to be 'femme' and I wasn't mean or tough enough to be 'butch' " (quoted in Miller 1995:319). Faderman (1991) stated the following:

> A Columbus, Ohio, woman recalls walking into a lesbian bar in the 1950s and finding that no one would speak to her. After some hours the waitress told her it was because of the way she was dressed — no one could tell what her sexual identity was, butch or femme, and they were afraid that if she did not know enough to dress right it was because she was a policewoman. (pp. 164–65)

Middle-class and wealthy lesbians tended to avoid a butch or femme appearance and were more likely to "pass" as heterosexual. They often condemned butch and femme roles as increasing society's negative attitudes about lesbians. The organization Daughters of Bilitis urged its middle-class readership to adopt "a mode of behavior and dress acceptable to society" (Faderman 1991:180). Middle-class lesbians were encouraged to wear feminine, professional clothing and not to appear lesbian. Faderman (1991) pointed out that the same message to blend in reemerged in the late 1980s with the publication of the book *After the Ball* (Kirk 1989). Consequently it was poor and working-class lesbians who communicated through their appearance to the dominant culture that lesbians existed, who were portrayed in the media, and who paid for this by frequent police raids in bars and arrests.

In summary, anatomical sex and gender roles (including the appearance of being male or female) intersect with sexual orientation. Only at the end of the twentieth century are members of LGB communities beginning to realize the complexities of gender. Not only have bisexual politics emphasized that sexual orientation is fluid, but transgender politics are also focusing on gender as fluid. Just as it took language — the terms *gay*, *lesbian*, *bisexual*, and *heterosexual* — to form an awareness of identity in the middle of the twentieth century, so, too, does language allow a continuing expansion of awareness at the end of the millennium. "Transgender" politics have replaced the more binary concept of "transsexualism"; the younger LGB communities often use the word *queer* as a self-descriptor; and cultural and regional variations are affecting language and identity.

Historical and Economic Factors

It takes more than language to form a sense of LGB identity. This section reviews some of the societal institutions — urbanization, education, and the military — that allowed some individuals greater freedom of sexual expression and to move away from traditional family roles.

Changing Roles in a Changing Economy

Lillian Faderman (1991) described education as the pathway for women to become lesbians. Education gave women choices other than marriage and motherhood. It also brought women together in all-female colleges and professions. College-educated women were much less likely to marry than those without such education:

> Even worse, some writers eventually came to fear (not without cause) a problem they hardly dared to express: that higher education for females, especially in all-women's colleges, not only "masculinized"

women but also made men dispensable to them and rendered women more attractive to one another. (Faderman 1991:14)

Even today, surveys of lesbians indicate that they are more highly educated than are women represented in the general census data. In the National Lesbian Health Care Survey (Bradford, Ryan, and Rothblum 1994), 85 percent of the sample had at least some college education, and more than 30 percent had an advanced degree. In a more recent survey of nearly twenty-four hundred lesbians (Morris and Rothblum 1999), about three-quarters had at least a college degree, and 33 percent had a graduate or professional degree. Although such "convenience samples" have been criticized for focusing on young, highly educated lesbians who live in urban areas and have access to lesbian newsletters, bars, churches, and so on, it is likely that education continues to be important in allowing women to come out as lesbian or bisexual.

For working-class people who did not have access to higher education, the military served as a vehicle for LGB individuals to come out (Berube 1990; Faderman 1991). Faderman (1991) described World War II as a "government-sponsored subculture" (p. 125) where women became aware of their lesbianism:

> Less than a third of a million women served in the military during the war, but many of them were lovers of other women. For those who already identified themselves as lesbians, military service, with its opportunities to meet other women and to engage in work and adventure that were ordinarily denied them, was especially appealing. For many others who had not identified themselves as lesbians before the war, the all female environment of the women's branches of the armed services, offering as it did the novel emotional excitement of working with competent, independent women, made lesbianism an attractive option. The "firm public impression" during the war years that a women's corps was "the ideal breeding ground for lesbians" had considerable basis in fact. (p. 120)

Moreover, World War II created civilian jobs for women that were previously available only to men, and these work settings had predominantly female employees while men were at war. Heterosexuals in the military were exposed to gay men, lesbians, and bisexuals in ways they never would have been in their hometowns. When the war ended, military personnel were shipped back to the large port cities of New York, San Francisco, Boston, and Los Angeles, and many stayed there, creating large LGB communities in these cities (Faderman 1991).

In contrast to historians who view social institutions (e.g., higher education, the military) as vehicles to becoming LGB, British sociologist Gill Dunne (1997) examined how being out as a lesbian results in more nontraditional jobs and education for women.

> For working-class women who don't have access to higher education, it is hard to imagine having a life that is financially independent of men. Coming out young presents women with an economic problem which cannot be solved by following their peers into dead-end low-paid women's work. Hence the appeal of traditionally male-dominated occupations, like the trades or the military. Having a job in the trades, like being a mechanic, gives women a hell of a lot more financial freedom than working behind a cash register. Women who aren't economically privileged, but who have an early sense of not wanting to be dependent on men, more often try to enter jobs that men have traditionally held. Not because they want to become men, but because they want to earn a living wage. (Dunne, personal communication, January 1998)

John D'Emilio (1992) and Neil Miller (1995) pointed to the role of the changing economy in influencing the birth of the present-day LGB movement. Urbanization and industrialization gave rise to a sense of personal identity and choice outside the structure of the extended family. Individuals could move to cities where they had more anonymity and where they could find a gay subculture. They could choose not to marry, a choice that would have been difficult in agrarian societies. More recently the National Lesbian Health Care Survey of more than nineteen hundred lesbians conducted in the mid-1980s (Bradford et al. 1994) asked respondents about geographic moves. Only 10 percent of the sample were still residing in the town or city where they had been born. The vast majority resided in large metropolitan areas, with more than half living in cities of more than 1 million residents. There was a general movement away from the Northeast, where 31 percent of the sample had been born, to the Pacific states. One has only to read the obituaries in the San Francisco Bay Times to see how many men moved there from Midwestern or Southern communities. But it is increasingly common to find LGB communities in most towns, no matter how rural or small.

Nevertheless, the extended family is still an important issue for LGB individuals who are members of ethnic minority groups (Greene 1994; Rust 1996). These authors have reported that members of oppressed groups value the support of their families in a way that members of more privileged groups do not. African-American, Latino, Asian-American, and Native American communities often value kinship, whereas European American cultures emphasize individuation and separation from families.

When LGB individuals were feeling isolated, they could move to or visit urban centers or take solace in the knowledge that such communities existed. New York City became a leading center of LGB communities in the 1920s and 1930s, even while police raids were quite extensive. Miller (1995) stated the following:

> Artistic and bohemian enclaves were among the places where a modern sense of gay and lesbian community first began to emerge. Whether they be New York's Greenwich Village or Jazz Age Harlem or Left Bank Paris, bohemias were self-enclosed geographical and spiritual worlds where unconventionality was prized and new ideas venerated; where women experienced an enhanced degree of freedom; where the power of religion and family to enforce cultural, political, and sexual conformity was limited. (p. 137)

The Harlem Renaissance was important not only in African-American history but also in the history of LGB communities. After thousands of African-Americans moved from the rural South to the urban North, Harlem became the center for black music, literature, and politics. Gay parties, balls, and other entertainment flourished in Harlem in the 1920s and 1930s. African-American lesbians and gay men were creating a gay subculture that attracted white LGB individuals as well (see Faderman 1991, and Garber 1990, for reviews).

The uprisings at the Stonewall Inn Bar at 53 Christopher Street in Greenwich Village in late June and early July 1969 are usually seen as the events that created the modern-day LGB movement. For example, Grube (1990) used 1969, the year of Stonewall, to distinguish men who came out early ("natives") from those who came out more recently ("settlers"). The gay pride marches in most U.S. cities are on or near the date of June 29, to commemorate the time of the Stonewall uprisings.

On that day, the people who were inside the Stonewall Inn Bar in Greenwich Village fought the police who had arrived to raid the bar. Police raids were a normal part of gay life, but this was the first time that bar patrons fought back. The Stonewall riots continued for several days. Martin Duberman (1993) described the events of that night in his book *Stonewall*. When Duberman interviewed people who had witnessed the Stonewall riots, some remembered a lesbian dressed in men's clothing. Others noticed drag queens locked in a paddy wagon, kicking out with their high heels at the cops.

One of the people who was living in New York City at that time was Ray Rivera. According to Eric Marcus's (1992) oral history, Ray was born in 1951 in the South Bronx. When he was seven, he asked his grandmother to teach him how to sew so he could dress in drag. When he was ten, he tried to kill himself because he thought he was the only faggot in the world. When he was thirteen, he left home to sell his body on New York City's streets. When he was eighteen, in the summer, Ray was invited to a birthday party but decided not to go because Judy Garland had just died, and he was feeling depressed. So Ray was home when a friend called and asked him to come along to a bar that Ray had never been to. And that's how Ray Rivera happened to be at the Stonewall Inn Bar at 2:00 A.M. on June 28. Only a small number of "drag queens" were allowed into the Stonewall. Ray, who is Latino, was allowed in because he was dressed as a White woman.

Ray Rivera described that night as follows:

> I don't know if it was the customers or if it was the police, but that night everything just clicked. . . . When they ushered us out, they very nicely put us out the door. Then we were standing across the street in Sheridan Square Park. But why? Everybody's looking at each other. "Why do we have to keep putting up with this?" Suddenly the nickels, dimes, pennies, and quarters started flying. I threw quarters and pennies and whatnot. . . . To be there was so beautiful. It was so exciting. I said: "Well, great, now it's my time. I'm out there being a revolutionary for everybody else, and now it's time to do my thing for my own people." . . . The police thought that they could come in and say, "Get out," and nothing was going to happen. . . . This is what we learned to live with at that time. Until that day. (Marcus 1992:191)

Not all gays in New York participated in or were aware of the Stonewall uprisings. The more conservative gays, in chinos and sweaters, watched cautiously from the sidelines, and some disapproved of the action. The wealthier gay men and lesbians were not at the scene of the Stonewall riots. Some ignored the action when it was reported in the media; others did not hear about it (Duberman 1993). Nevertheless, Stonewall is considered today to have been the start of the modern LGB movement.

Early Newsletters and Organizations

Not everyone lived in a metropolis. Many people did not know a single other person who was LGB like themselves, but they stayed current with the rising LGB movement through newsletters and books.

In Marcus's (1992) oral history, he used the pseudonym "Lisa Ben" for the woman who, in 1945, produced one of the first lesbian newsletters, *Vice Versa*. A secretary in Los Angeles, Lisa typed each issue on her office type-writer, making nine carbon copies. These copies were distributed from friend to friend and had quite a distribution. Lisa said,

> I wrote *Vice Versa* mainly to keep myself company. I called it *Vice Versa* because in those days our kind of life was considered a vice. . . . There was never anything in the magazine that was sexy or suggestive. I purposely kept it that way in case I got caught. They couldn't say that *Vice Versa* was dirty or naughty or against the law. . . . I typed the magazine at work. I had a boss who said, "You won't have a heck of a lot to do here, but I don't want you to knit or read a book. I want you to always look busy." (Marcus 1992:8–9)

A more widely known lesbian publication was *The Ladder*, which was published from 1956 to 1972 by the organization Daughters of Bilitis (see Soares 1998, for a review). *The Ladder* did not use the word *lesbian* until 1967; before that time it referred to its readers as "variants." To maintain confidentiality, only two copies of *The Ladder*'s mailing list existed, and, like *Vice Versa*, *The Ladder* was distributed from friend to friend. One woman interviewed by Soares (1998) said,

> After I finished reading it, I would put it in a darkroom bag and put it in the darkroom and I would let other women know where it was or we would pass it on to other women, like we were passing film back and forth because that's the environment we were working in. (p. 29)

The Ladder had an "integrationist" stance, affirming the right of lesbians to assimilate into mainstream culture. This stance later led to conflicts within the organization Daughters of Bilitis, when the emerging lesbian feminist movement had a more separatist approach, and ultimately to the magazine's demise.

The Mattachine Society existed from 1950 to 1953, a strong foundation of the present-day gay rights movement. The founders of this organization, among them Harry Hay and Chuck Rowland, had been involved in communist organizations and had visions of a society that would give gays the same minority-group status as other oppressed groups in the United States. Miller (1995) stated the following:

> According to Hay, the name Mattachine derived from a medieval French society of unmarried townsmen who conducted dances and rituals in the countryside during the Feast of Fools at the vernal equinox. The original Mattachines always performed wearing masks; their dance rituals sometimes turned into peasant protests against the aristocracy. Hay chose this name for his new society because he saw the homosexuals of the 1950s as a "masked people, unknown and anonymous, who might become engaged in morale building and helping ourselves and others." (p. 334)

The Mattachine Society began the magazine *One* at a time when sending homosexual material through the U.S. mail was still illegal.

According to Jay Paul (1998), the first bisexual organization in the United States was the Bisexual Forum in New York City. However, the Bisexual Center of San Francisco, which spanned the period from 1976 to 1985, had an important role, according to Paul:

> In that span of time, it had a profound impact; it created a sense of a bisexual community, educated the general public and professionals about bisexuality, confronted the gay and lesbian communities about the tendency to render the bisexual invisible, spawned several organizations (including political action groups), and changed the lives of many women and men who had felt marginalized by both the heterosexual and homosexual communities. (p. 130)

Along with newsletters and magazines, alternative bookstores and publishing companies proliferated in the 1970s, giving rise to the large market in LGB books, publishing companies with LGB book series, and "mainstream" bookstores with LGB sections today. In fact, it was precisely the ease with which mainstream publishers and bookstores accepted LGB books that led to the end of many small, alternative, feminist and lesbian presses and women's bookstores. On the other hand, feminist bookstores often survived long after other feminist and lesbian centers ceased to exist, and some continue today. In her review of lesbian and feminist publishing, Kate Adams (1998) stated the following:

> And to sell and distribute the steadily growing stream of lesbian and feminist books, newspapers, and magazines, a new kind of capitalist enterprise was popping up as well in neighborhoods across the nation: the women's bookstore. In 1973, there were 9 such stores; in 1976, the number had grown to 44; in 1978, 60 bookstores were surviving. Each one served as meeting place, cultural center, and information clearinghouse for its community, and most survived through the 1970s and into the 1980s, long after other kinds of community space — women's centers and buildings, for example — had disappeared. (p. 126)

It is no coincidence, then, that the characters in Alison Bechdel's popular comic strip "Dykes to Watch Out For" are employed in a women's bookstore.

Today there are hundreds of national, state, and local periodicals about LGB (and transgender) issues. Both university presses and trade publishers routinely publish books about aspects of the LGB experience. Not only LGB but heterosexual people also hear about LGB issues through the printed word as well as radio, television, and films.

The Mental Health Field

Psychoanalysis and "Reorientation" Therapy

The practice of psychology was heavily influenced by Freud and subsequent psychoanalytically oriented therapy. Psychotherapists focused on "reorienting" the sexual orientation of LGB individuals to allow them to become heterosexual and engage in "normal sex," that is, heterosexual intercourse.

As in most of his work on mental health, Freud's writings on homosexuality profoundly influenced the attitudes and practices of mental health professionals. Most mental health professionals who work with LGB clients are familiar with Freud's quote about homosexuality:

Homosexuality is assuredly no advantage, but it is nothing to be ashamed of, no vice, degradation; it cannot be classified as an illness; we consider it to be a variation of the sexual function, produced by a certain arrest of sexual development. (Freud, Letter to an American mother 1935, cited in Drescher 1998:19)

Drescher (1998) stated the following:

Although he never dedicated a major work solely to the subject of homosexuality, Freud's contributions on the subject range across a period of almost twenty years (1905, 1908, 1909, 1910, 1911, 1914, 1920, 1923). The contradictions in his voluminous works make Freud's position opaque to the casual, modern reader. Attempts to find "the real Freud" are too often motivated by those who seek his agreement with their own point of view. . . . Taken out of the historical context in which he wrote, and depending upon the author's selective citations, Freud can be portrayed as either virulently antihomosexual . . . or as a closeted friend of gays. (p. 21)

Drescher (1998) described Freud as having an affirmative attitude about homosexuality for the time in which he lived. For example, in the 1930s he signed a statement for the decriminalization of homosexuality in Germany and Austria. Freud also believed that everyone had homosexual as well as heterosexual feelings, which he referred to as *psychological bisexuality*, although he believed that the homosexual part should be sublimated. He also thought that homosexuality was difficult to treat. In his "Psychogenesis of a Case of Homosexuality in a Woman" (1920, cited in Drescher 1998), he portrayed the woman as a man hater and as suffering from penis envy.

Many of the "reorientation" therapies that existed until the late 1960s were based on psychoanalytic theory. However, their developers differed from Freud in that they did not believe in people's innate bisexuality and instead viewed heterosexual intercourse as the only normal end result of human sexual development (Drescher 1998). Parental psychopathology was scrutinized, particularly the mother-son relationship.

One of the most poignant accounts of such therapy is Martin Duberman's (1991) book, *Cures: A Gay Man's Odyssey*. Duberman was a prize-winning professor of history at Princeton University who had an offer of an endowed chair at Oxford University. Nevertheless, he was given stereotyped diagnoses by therapists, including having a weak will, psychopathic tendencies, and a tendency to "act out." In 1959 he tried hard to become attracted to a woman but found himself unable to do so; Duberman (1991) described his therapy session:

> Dr. Igen kept the focus steady. He encouraged me to speculate about the source of my "unconscious resistance" to physical love with a woman. Though rarely theoretical, he made reference to a possible "breast complex" and asked me if I had reacted violently to being weaned. When I laughed and said I couldn't remember as far back as yesterday's movie, let alone my experiences in the crib, he replied, with a pained expression, that that too was part of the resistance. . . . Alarmed at how sulky he looked (would he tell me I was hopeless? would he give up on me?), I offered in quick substitution a lengthy speculation about how unlikely it was that a mother as devoted as mine would have weaned me prematurely and thus provoked my rage. His expression lightened a bit, and he took up the theme of my mother's devotion. "Yes," he said, "devotion embedded in control, devotion as a mask for seduction. Is it any wonder you have had difficulty ever since in entrusting yourself to a female? You're chronically angry at women and refuse to get it up for them. To enter a vagina is for you to risk being swallowed alive." (pp. 58–59)

Despite societal changes and scientific data indicating that reorientation therapy is ineffective (see Haldeman 1994, for a review of this literature), such therapy continues to be offered today. At a time when U.S. society is more affirmative of LGB cultures and also of changing gender roles for heterosexuals, reparative therapists are increasingly coming from a religious rather than scientific perspective (Drescher 1998). The National Association for Research and Therapy of Homosexuality (NARTH) was founded by reparative therapists. Drescher (1998) stated the following:

> In the current political climate, NARTH's dogmatic views have been marginalized in professional and scientific organizations. . . . For the present, however, reparative therapists have demonstrated their willingness to ally themselves with religious denominations that condemn homosexuality. Because they are unable to find reputable scientific support for their positions, these antihomosexual religious organizations have turned to reparative therapists to treat their flocks and to provide a veneer of modern respectability. . . . Anti-homosexual poli-

tics make strange bedfellows and Freud, the devoutest of atheists . . .
would find this wedding of psychoanalysis and fundamentalism astonishing." (p. 38)

Given the homophobic history of psychotherapy, it would not be surprising if LGB individuals avoided traditional psychotherapy. Recent research has provided some evidence to the contrary: Lesbians are more likely
to seek therapy than heterosexual women (and the same phenomenon may
be true for gay men and bisexuals). Kris Morgan (1992) distributed flyers at
a women's basketball game inviting spectators to participate in a survey (a
creative setting for finding both lesbians and heterosexual women). In this
sample, 77.5 percent of the lesbians and 28.9 percent of the heterosexual
women had been in therapy, an enormous difference. On the Attitudes
Toward Seeking Professional Psychological Help Scale, lesbians scored
higher than heterosexual women on the subscales Recognition of Personal
Need, Tolerance of Stigma, Confidence in the Mental Health Profession,
and Counseling as Growth. In a later study, Kris Morgan and Michele
Eliason (1992) interviewed twenty-three lesbians who had been in therapy
and seventeen lesbians who never had been in therapy and found that both
groups viewed lesbians to be introspective and saw the lesbian communities
as valuing personal growth.

Celia Kitzinger and Rachel Perkins (1993) critiqued the increasing tendency of lesbians to seek therapy in their book, *Changing Our Minds*. They
argued that psychological terminology (e.g., the "inner child") has replaced
political activism in the lesbian communities and that therapy privatizes and
individualizes lesbians' lives. At the same time, there are few resources for
lesbians with serious, long-term mental health problems, and these authors
urge lesbian communities to organize around sharing resources for long-
term caregiving.

Charles Silverstein (1991) made sense of this shift from mistrust to advocacy of therapy in his book, *Gays, Lesbians, and Their Therapists*. He
described three generations of gay therapists. The first, trained and practicing
before Stonewall (pre-1969), did not have degrees and practiced as coun-
terculture therapists. They were the only alternative to reorientation therapy
at the time. The second generation practiced in the 1970s, at a time when
gay liberation led to the first gay counseling centers, staffed by peer counselors. Silverstein recalled this period: "While gays flocked to our services,
established professionals, who earned their living by 'curing' gay men and
women, saw us as a cabal of reckless incompetents who, when successful,

doomed our clients to a life of misery" (p. 5). The third generation, trained in the 1980s, were the first who could be both out as LGB people and admitted to mainstream mental health degree programs.

Sexologists and Sex Surveys

Neil Miller (1995) argued that a crucial factor leading to the formation of present-day LGB identity was medical labeling and terminology at the end of the nineteenth century:

> One crucial factor was biomedical conceptualization of homosexuality in an age that increasingly classified people by their sexual inclinations — the heterosexual and the homosexual; the fetishist, the sadist, the masochist. This new way of looking at homosexuality tended to stigmatize it, set it apart from the rest of society, and represent it as a medical condition or a symptom of degeneracy. This view, at least early on, insisted that homosexuals possessed characteristics and attributes of the opposite gender. (p. xxiii)

Nineteenth-century sexologists such as Krafft-Ebing and Havelock Ellis published hundreds of case histories of homosexuals. Such research was often conducted among "sexual inverts" (Faderman 1991) in prisons and psychiatric institutions. Poor and working-class parents were blamed for inappropriate child rearing and a weak genetic pool.

The most influential sexologist of the twentieth century was Alfred Kinsey. After decades as a zoologist, studying and labeling insects, Kinsey applied his scientific skills to interviewing thousands of American men and women about their sexual behaviors. Kinsey managed to portray himself as a family man who just happened to become interested in sex as the result of teaching a course on the subject; in fact, recent revelations have shown that Kinsey himself was bisexual and engaged in sex with his interviewees and members of his research team (Jones 1997). Furthermore, Kinsey's sampling biases have been critiqued as overrepresenting college students, prisoners, and members of urban gay communities. Nevertheless, Kinsey's reports had a major influence on sexology. They gave rise to the "Kinsey scale," which measured sexual orientation on a continuum and thus included bisexuality; they focused on the prevalence of same-gender behavior even among people who were married or otherwise "conventional"; and they viewed homosexuality and bisexuality as normative. The *Kinsey Reports* were followed by a number of other "reports" that included data on lesbians, gay men, and bisexuals — by Shere Hite (1976) and Masters and Johnson (1979); one was even called *The Gay Report* (Jay 1979).

The Role of Psychological Research

It has been only in the past twenty-five years that psychological researchers have conducted studies of LGB individuals from an affirmative perspective. Before that time, a few studies focused on prisoners or psychotherapy clients who wanted to change their sexual orientation. The focus was often on the pathology of homosexuality.

A landmark study by Evelyn Hooker changed the direction of LGB research. In the 1940s Hooker was teaching a psychology course through the extension services at the University of California, Los Angeles. Through the friendship and encouragement of a gay male student in her class, she conducted the first study of gay men. In 1953, at the height of McCarthyism, she applied to the new National Institute of Mental Health for a grant to study "normal homosexual men" and compare them to matched heterosexual men. Unlike those described in prior published case studies, these men were not psychiatric patients or prisoners. Each participant was given the Rorschach Test, the Thematic Apperception Test, and the Make a Picture Story Test; the results were judged by a panel of nationally known psychological experts who did not know the sexual orientation of the participants. At that time psychologists were convinced that projective test responses would indicate a participant's sexual orientation. When Hooker presented her results — that homosexual men were as well adjusted as heterosexuals — at the American Psychological Association convention in 1955, the ballroom was packed. The study received widespread publicity (for reviews, see Boxer and Carrier 1998; Marcus 1992).

Hooker stated the following (in Marcus 1992):

But what means the most to me, I think, is . . . excuse me while I cry . . . if I went to a gay gathering of some kind, I was sure to have at least one person come up to me and say, "I wanted to meet you because I wanted to tell you what you saved me from." . . . I know that wherever

I go, there are men and women for whom my little bit of work and my caring enough to do it has made an enormous difference in their lives. (p. 25)

In 1992, one of Evelyn Hooker's original study participants, Wayne Placek, died and left her a considerable sum of money in his will. He had long since left Los Angeles and was a farmer in Nebraska, but he always remembered how significant his participation in Hooker's study had been to his life. This money, the Wayne Placek Fund, is now available for LGB research through the American Psychological Foundation.

Hooker's landmark study set the stage for other research that used her method of matching lesbians and gay men with heterosexuals who were demographically similar. In 1969 Hopkins matched twenty-four lesbians and twenty-four heterosexual women on age, intelligence, and professional-educational background. Using Cattell's Personality Factor Questionnaire, she found the lesbian sample to be more independent, resilient, reserved, dominant, "bohemian," self-sufficient, and composed. In another early study using a larger sample (Thompson, McCandless, and Strickland 1971), lesbians and gay men were matched with heterosexual women and men, respectively, on age and education. Gay men were less defensive and less self-confident than heterosexual men; lesbians were more self-confident than heterosexual women. There were no significant differences between the matched groups on personal adjustment. Given the extremely negative attitudes held by the public and by mental health professionals at the time, it is remarkable that lesbians and gay men were so well adjusted.

Research today need not show comparability to heterosexuals in order to be published in academic journals; some academic journals are even dedicated to LGB issues. It is no longer necessary to demonstrate that LGB individuals are well adjusted. Nevertheless, relatively little research has been done on lesbian and gay mental health issues (compared to the amount of research on lesbian and gay relationships, identity development, coming out, and aging) and practically no research has been done on the mental health of bisexual women and men (see Bieschke 2000).

The Changing DSM and the Mental Health Professions

Mental health professionals began to play a significant role when "homosexuality" changed from being a sin to a sickness (Morin and Rothblum

1991). As described earlier, therapists, especially psychoanalysts, maintained the "normalcy" of heterosexuality in the politically conservative postwar years and interpreted male and female "homosexuality" as deviant. The second edition of the *Diagnostic and Statistical Manual of Mental Disorders (DSM-II)* (American Psychiatric Association 1968) included "homosexuality" as a mental illness. This diagnosis was placed in the section on "sociopathy," described as "crimes against society," along with substance abuse and sexual disorders.

By the 1960s the civil rights movement, the women's movement, and the new gay rights movement that followed in the wake of the Stonewall uprisings all served to put pressure on mental health professionals to affirm LGB rights. Much of the LGB advocacy in the mental health professions focused on removing "homosexuality" from the *DSM* list of mental disorders. On December 15, 1973, the American Psychiatric Association removed this diagnosis from its official list of mental disorders (Adam 1987). However, a residual category of "ego-dystonic homosexuality" was retained to categorize distress experienced by individuals who wished to change their sexual orientation. In 1987 the American Psychological Association urged its members not to use this diagnosis (Fox 1988) and joined a coalition that eventually succeeded in having this diagnosis dropped from the *DSM-III* (American Psychiatric Association 1987). These actions helped to counteract the previous association of same-gender sexual orientation with mental illness.

A survey of twenty-five hundred members of the American Psychiatric Association, conducted soon after the removal of "homosexuality" as a diagnostic category from the *DSM* (*Time* 1978, in Marmor 1980), found that a majority considered homosexuality pathological and also perceived homosexuals to be less happy and less capable of mature and loving relationships than heterosexuals. More recently the APA *Task Force Report on Heterosexual Bias in Psychotherapy* (Garnets et al. 1991) surveyed more than twenty-five hundred members of the American Psychological Association and found that psychologists differed in their use of gay-affirmative practice. Biased, inappropriate, or inadequate practice was found in the understanding, assessment, and intervention concerning a wide range of topics such as identity development, lesbian and gay relationships, and parenting.

Changing the *DSM* resulted in more affirmative stances by mental health professions. In 1975 the American Psychological Association adopted the official policy statement that "homosexuality per se implies no impairment in judgment, stability, reliability, or general social or vocational capabilities" (Conger 1975:633). Similar resolutions supporting the removal of "homo-

sexuality" from the official list of mental disorders and deploring discrimination based on sexual orientation had been passed before that time by the
American Sociological Association, the National Association for Mental
Health, the National Association of Social Workers, and the American Psychiatric Association (Adam 1987). However, the American Psychological
Association resolution went further than most earlier resolutions by urging
psychologists and all mental health professionals to "take the lead in removing the stigma of mental illness that has long been associated with homosexual orientation" (Conger 1975:633).

Lesbian and gay activism in the American Psychological Association became organized in 1973 with the formation of the Association of Lesbian
and Gay Psychologists, which formed the basis for the current Division 44
(Society for the Psychological Study of Lesbian, Gay, and Bisexual Issues)
of the American Psychological Association (for a history of APA's Division
44, see Kimmel and Browning 1999). The Task Force on the Status of
Lesbian and Gay Psychologists was formed to address a number of fundamental issues facing lesbian and gay members of the association. This group
was succeeded by the Committee on Lesbian, Gay, and Bisexual Concerns,
which continues to monitor the association's involvement in the broader
agenda of advancing the civil rights of lesbians and gay men.

Conclusion

A number of historical events came together to influence modern-day
views of LGB mental health. A sense of identity and a language for discussing
lesbian, gay, and bisexual issues had to be developed. Through education,
the military, and other vehicles for socioeconomic change, some individuals
were able to escape traditional pathways to heterosexuality. Large urban areas
such as New York City served as a magnet for LGB individuals to allow them
to see other people like themselves or to experiment with new gender and
sexual orientation roles. Local and national media spread the word about
emerging LGB communities.

In the mental health arena, Freud's often contradictory views on homosexuality were translated into a pathology-based psychodynamic model for
LGB individuals who sought mental health care. At the same time, sex
surveys and psychological research began to demonstrate that there were
more LGB people than the general public assumed and that LGB people
were as well adjusted as heterosexuals. The DSM removed homosexuality

from its list of mental disorders, and the mental health professions established divisions that specialized in LGB issues.

The history of lesbians, gay men, and bisexuals is a history of increasing visibility. Following is a quote from Harvey Milk, the openly gay supervisor of San Francisco who was assassinated in 1978 by a homophobic coworker. It sums up the fight for acceptance and equal rights that LGB individuals have been waging over the course of this century and that is far from over despite extraordinary progress. It points out the ways that LGB issues have moved from being pathologized to being accepted, paving the way for the LGB-affirmative psychology that exists today:

> Somewhere in Des Moines or San Antonio, there's a young person who all of a sudden realizes that she or he is gay, knows that if the parents find out they'll be tossed out of the house, the classmates will taunt the child, and the Anita Bryants and John Briggs are doing their bit on TV.
>
> And the child has two options: staying in the closet or suicide. Then one day that child might open a paper that says "Homosexual elected in San Francisco." And now the child has two new options: go to California or stay in San Antonio and fight. (*The Times of Harvey Milk* [Film] 1982)

References

Adam, B. D. 1987. *The Rise of the Gay and Lesbian Movement*. Boston: Twayne.

Adams, K. 1998. Built out of books: Lesbian energy and feminist ideology in alternative publishing. *Journal of Homosexuality* 34(3/4):113–41.

American Psychiatric Association. 1968. *Diagnostic and Statistical Manual of Mental Disorders*. 2nd ed. Washington, D.C.: Author.

American Psychiatric Association. 1987. *Diagnostic and Statistical Manual of Mental Disorders*. 3rd ed., rev. Washington, D.C.: Author.

Berube, A. 1990. *Coming Out under Fire*. New York: Free Press.

Bieschke, K. J., M. McClanahan, E. Tozer, J. L. Grzegorek, and J. Park. 2000. Programmatic research on the treatment of lesbian, gay, and bisexual clients: The past, the present, and the course for the future. In R. M. Perez, K. A. Debord, and K. J. Bieschke, eds., *Handbook of Counseling and Psychotherapy with Lesbian, Gay, and Bisexual Clients*, pp. 309–35. Washington, D.C.: American Psychological Association.

Boxer, A.M., and J. M. Carrier. 1998. Evelyn Hooker: A life remembered. *Journal of Homosexuality* 36(1):1–17.

Bradford, J., C. Ryan, and E. D. Rothblum. 1994. National Lesbian Health Care Survey: Implications for mental health. *Journal of Consulting and Clinical Psychology* 62:228–42.

Brown, L. 1998. *Two-Spirit People.* New York: Haworth.

Cogan, J., and J. Erickson. 1999. *Lesbians, Levis, and Lipstick: The Meaning of Beauty in Our Lives.* New York: Haworth.

Conger, J. 1975. Proceedings of the American Psychological Association, Incorporated, for the year 1974: Minutes of the annual meeting of Council of Representatives. *American Psychologist* 30:620–51.

Cory, D. W. 1960. *The Homosexual in America.* New York: Castle.

D'Emilio, J. 1992. *Making Trouble.* New York: Routledge.

Donoghue, E. 1993. *Passions Between Women: British Lesbian Culture, 1668–1801.* New York: HarperCollins.

Drescher, J. 1998. I'm your handyman: A history of reparative therapies. *Journal of Homosexuality* 36(1):19–42.

Duberman, M. 1991. *Cures: A Gay Man's Odyssey.* New York: Penguin.

Duberman, M. 1993. *Stonewall.* New York: Penguin.

Dunne, G. A. 1997. *Lesbian Lifestyles: Women's Work and the Politics of Sexuality.* Toronto, Canada: University of Toronto Press.

Faderman, L. 1981. *Surpassing the Love of Men.* New York: Morrow.

Faderman, L. 1991. *Odd Girls and Twilight Lovers: A History of Lesbian Life in Twentieth-century America.* New York: Columbia University Press.

Fox, R. E. 1988. Proceedings of the American Psychological Association, Incorporated, for the year 1987: Minutes of the annual meeting of Council of Representatives. *American Psychologist* 43:527–28.

Garber, E. 1990. A spectacle in color: The lesbian and gay subculture of Jazz Age Harlem. In M. Duberman, M. Vicinus, and G. Chauncey, eds., *Hidden from History: Reclaiming the Gay and Lesbian Past*, pp. 318–31. New York: Penguin.

Garnets, L. D., K. A. Hancock, S. D. Cochran, J. Goodchilds, and L. A. Peplau. 1991. Issues in psychotherapy with lesbians and gay men: A survey of psychologists. *American Psychologist* 46:964–72.

Greene, B. 1994. Ethnic-minority lesbians and gay men: Mental health and treatment issues. *Journal of Consulting and Clinical Psychology* 62:243–51.

Grube, J. 1990. Natives and settlers: An ethnographic note on early interaction of older homosexual men with younger gay liberationists. *Journal of Homosexuality* 20(3/4):119–35.

Haldeman, D.C. 1994. The practice and ethics of sexual orientation conversion therapy. *Journal of Consulting and Clinical Psychology* 62:221–27.

Hekma, G. 1998. Bisexuality: Historical perspectives. In E. J. Haeberle and R. Gindolf, eds., *Bisexualities: The Ideology and Practice of Sexual Contact with Both Men and Women*, pp. 113–17. New York: Continuum.

Hite, S. 1976. *The Hite Report: A Nationwide Survey of Female Sexuality.* New York: Macmillan.

Hopkins, J. H. 1969. The lesbian personality. *British Journal of Psychiatry* 115: 1433–36.

House, C. 1997. Navajo woman warrior: An ancient tradition in a modern world. In S. Jacobs, W. Thomas, and S. Lang, eds., *Two-Spirit People: Native American Gender Identity, Sexuality, and Spirituality*, pp. 223–27. Urbana: University of Illinois Press.

Jacobs, S., W. Thomas, and S. Lang. 1997. *Two-Spirit People: Native American Gender Identity, Sexuality, and Spirituality.* Urbana: University of Illinois Press.

Jay, K. 1979. *The Gay Report: Lesbians and Gay Men Speak Out about Sexual Experiences and Lifestyles.* New York: Summit.

Jones, J. H. 1997. *Alfred C. Kinsey: A Public/Private Life.* New York: Norton.

Kennedy, E. L., and M. D. Davis. 1993. *Boots of Leather, Slippers of Gold.* New York: Routledge.

Kimmel, D.C., and C. Browning. 1999. A history of Division 44 (society for the psychological study of lesbian, gay, and bisexual issues). In D. A. Dewsbury, ed., *Unification through Division: Histories of Divisions of the American Psychological Association.* Washington, D.C.: American Psychological Association.

Kirk, M. 1989. *After the Ball: How America Will Conquer Its Hatred and Fears of Gays in the 90s.* New York: Doubleday.

Kitzinger, C., and R. Perkins. 1993. *Changing Our Minds: Lesbian Feminism and Psychology.* New York: New York University Press.

Marcus, E. 1995. *Making History: The Struggle for Gay and Lesbian Equal Rights 1945–1990. An Oral History.* New York: HarperCollins.

Marmor, J. 1980. Epilogue: Homosexuality and the issue of mental illness. In J. Marmor, ed., *Homosexual Behavior*, pp. 391–402. New York: Basic Books.

Masters, W., and V. Johnson. 1979. *Homosexuality in Perspective.* Boston: Little, Brown.

Miller, N. 1995. *Out of the Past: Gay and Lesbian History from 1869 to the Present.* New York: Vintage.

Minton, H. L., and S. R. Mattson. 1998. Deconstructing heterosexuality: Life stories from Gay New York. *Journal of Homosexuality* 36(1):43–61.

Morgan, K. S. 1992. Caucasian lesbians' use of psychotherapy. *Psychology of Women Quarterly* 16:127–30.

Morgan, K. S., and M. J. Eliason. 1992. The role of psychotherapy in Caucasian lesbians' lives. *Women and Therapy* 13(1):27–52.

Morin, S. F., and E. D. Rothblum. 1991. Removing the stigma: Fifteen years of progress. *American Psychologist* 46:947–49.

Morris, J. F., and E. D. Rothblum. 1999. Who fills out a "lesbian" questionnaire? The interrelationship of sexual orientation, years out, disclosure of sexual orientation, sexual experience with women, and participation in the lesbian community. *Psychology of Women Quarterly* 23:11–38.

Paul, J. 1998. San Francisco's Bisexual Center and the emergence of a bisexual movement. In E. J. Haeberle and R. Gindorf, eds., *Bisexualities: The Ideology and Practice of Sexual Contact with Both Men and Women*, pp. 130–39. New York: Continuum.

Roscoe, W. 1998. *Changing Ones: Third and Fourth Genders in Native North America*. New York: St. Martin's.

Rust, P. 1995. *Bisexuality and the Challenge to Lesbian Politics: Sex, Loyalty, and Revolution*. New York: Columbia University Press.

Rust, P. 1996. Managing multiple identities: Diversity among bisexual women and men. In B. A. Firestein, ed., *Bisexuality: The Psychology and Politics of an Invisible Minority*, pp. 53–83. Newbury Park, Calif.: Sage.

Schmeichen, R. (producer), and R. Epstein (producer/director). 1982. *The Times of Harvey Milk* [Film]. Beverly Hills, Calif.: Pacific Arts Video.

Silverstein, C. 1991. *Gays, Lesbians, and Their Therapists*. New York: Norton.

Soares, M. 1998. The purloined ladder: Its place in lesbian history. *Journal of Homosexuality* 34(3/4):27–49.

Thompson, N. L., B. R. McCandless, and B. R. Strickland. 1971. Personal adjustment of male and female homosexuals and heterosexuals. *Journal of Abnormal Psychology* 78:237–40.

Wekker, G. 1993. Mati-ism and black lesbianism: Two idealtypical expressions of female homosexuality in black communities of the diaspora. *Journal of Homosexuality* 24(3/4):145–58.

Wekker, G. 1997. One finger does not drink okra soup: AfroSurinamese women and critical agency. In J. Alexander and C. T. Mohanty, eds., *Feminist Genealogies, Colonial Legacies, Democratic Futures*, pp. 330–32. New York: Routledge.

Wilkinson, S., and C. Kitzinger. 1993. *Heterosexuality: A Feminism and Psychology Reader*. London: Sage.

Witt, L., S. Thomas, and E. Marcus. 1995. *Out in All Directions: The Almanac of Gay and Lesbian America*. New York: Warner.

25 The Practice and Ethics of Sexual Orientation Conversion Therapy

Douglas C. Haldeman

The question of how to change sexual orientation has been discussed as long as homoeroticism itself has been described in the literature. For more than a century, medical, psychotherapeutic, and religious practitioners have sought to reverse unwanted homosexual orientation through various methods: These include psychoanalytic therapy, prayer and spiritual interventions, electric shock, nausea-inducing drugs, hormone therapy, surgery, and various adjunctive behavioral treatments, including masturbatory reconditioning, rest, visits to prostitutes, and excessive bicycle riding (Murphy 1992). Early attempts to reverse sexual orientation were founded on the unquestioned assumption that homosexuality is an unwanted, unhealthy condition. Although homosexuality has long been absent from the taxonomy of mental disorders, efforts to reorient gay men and lesbians persist. Recently, for example, a coalition of mental health practitioners formed an organization dedicated to the "rehabilitation" of gay men and lesbians. Many practitioners still adhere to the officially debunked "illness" model of homosexuality, and many base their treatments on religious proscriptions against homosexual behavior. Still others defend sexual reorientation therapy as a matter of free choice for the unhappy client, claiming that their treatments do not imply a negative judgment on homosexuality per se. They seek to provide what they describe as a treatment alternative for men and women whose homosexuality is somehow incongruent with their values, life goals, or psychological structures.

Of the articles to be examined in this review, few have addressed the question of how sexual orientation is defined. Such a definition seems necessary before one can describe how sexual orientation is changed. However, most research in this area offers a dichotomous view of human sexuality in which undesired homoerotic impulses can be eradicated through a program that replaces them with heterosexual competence. Few studies even rely on the relatively simplistic Kinsey scale (Kinsey, Pomeroy, and Martin 1948) to make an attempt at assessing a subject's sexual orientation. Although a comprehensive discussion is well beyond the scope of this article, I begin with a passing reference to what is meant by the terms *homosexuality* and *heterosexuality*.

The data of Kinsey et al. (1948) suggested that as many as 10 percent of American men considered themselves to be primarily or exclusively homosexual for at least three years of their adult lives. His assessment was based on the subject's actual behavior as well as the content of the subject's fantasy life. Subsequent efforts to quantify sexual orientation have incorporated gender-based, social, and affectional variables (Coleman 1987). Several complex questions involved in the defining of sexual orientation have been either reduced or overlooked in the literature on conversion therapy. For instance, those conversion therapy programs that claim the greatest success included more subjects whose behavioral histories and fantasy lives appeared to have significant heteroerotic components (Haldeman 1991). Instructing a "homosexual" subject with a priori heteroerotic responsiveness in heterosexual behavior appears to be easier than replacing the cognitive sociosexual schema and redirecting the behavior of the "homosexual" subject with no reported heteroerotic inclinations. Nevertheless, both types of "homosexual" subjects are often included in the same treatment group.

Any definition of sexuality based solely on behavior is bound to be deficient and misleading. Sense of identity, internalized sociocultural expectations, and importance of social and political affiliations all help to define an individual's sexual orientation, and these variables may change over time. The content of an individual's fantasy life may provide information that is not influenced by the individual's need for social acceptance, but even these are subject, in some women and men, to variations in gender of object choice, based on environmental or political factors. Social demand variables also figure in describing sexual orientation, given the frequency with which gay men and lesbians marry (Bell and Weinberg 1978). Writer Darrell Yates Rist examined the lives of gay men in rural America with respect to how sexual orientation is constructed (1992). He described "Sven," a heterosexually married father of two:

It occurred to me that there were men — perhaps most men — whom sexual labels failed. Rudy seemed to think of Sven as a gay man stuck with a wife. Others might describe him as "bisexual," yet a third sexual breed. But those terms, like "straight," signify a way of life in which sex is deemed the core of identity, the single Freudian need or act that controls the psyche and determines the scope of a human being . . . such a way of looking at sex was beginning to seem exotic to me, a precious myth. One might as sensibly concoct natural categories out of the sports men choose to play or the foods they eat, religious dogmas or politics — any multitude of the changeable preferences to which men and women devote themselves. (1992:141)

The categories homosexual, heterosexual, and bisexual, conceived by many researchers as fixed and dichotomous, are in reality very fluid for many. Therefore, in addition to how sexual orientation is defined, one must also consider how it is experienced by the individual. For many gay men, the process of coming out may be likened to an internal evolution of sorts, a conscious recognition of what has always been. On the other hand, many lesbians describe coming out as a process tied to choices or social and political constructions. In this regard, many lesbians may have more in common with heterosexual women than with gay men, suggesting a gender-based distinction relative to the development of homosexual identity.

Questions about the complex nature of sexual orientation and its development in the individual must be addressed before change in sexual orientation is assessed. Many previously heterosexually identified individuals "come out" as lesbian or gay later in life, and some people who identify themselves as gay or lesbian engage in heterosexual behavior and relationships for a variety of personal and social reasons. How, then, are spontaneously occurring shifts in sexual orientation over the life span to be differentiated from behavior resulting from the interventions of a conversion therapist? Essentially the fixed, behavior-based model of sexual orientation assumed by almost all conversion therapists may be invalid. For many individuals, sexual orientation is a variable construct subject to changes in erotic and affectional preference, as well as changes in social values and political philosophy that may ebb and flow throughout life. For some, coming out may be a process with no true end point. Practitioners assessing change in sexual orientation have ignored the complex variations in an individual's erotic responses and shifts in the sociocultural landscape.

Psychological Conversion Programs

The case for conversion therapy rests on its ability to understand who is being converted and its ability to describe the nature of the conversion taking place. Acknowledging the theoretical complexities and ambiguities left unaddressed by most conversion therapists, the first question is, "Are these treatments effective?" In assessing the efficacy of conversion therapy, psychotherapeutic and religious programs will be reviewed. Those interested in reviews of medical therapies (drug or hormonal and surgical interventions) are referred to Silverstein (1991) and Murphy (1992).

Psychotherapeutic approaches to sexual reorientation have been based on the a priori assumption that homoeroticism is an undesirable condition. Two basic hypotheses serve as the foundation for most therapies designed to reverse sexual orientation. The first is that homosexuality results from an arrest in normal development or from pathological attachment patterns in early life. The second is that homosexuality stems from faulty learning. Therapies most closely associated with the first perspective are of the psychoanalytic and neo-analytic orientations.

Psychoanalytic tradition posited that homosexual orientation represented an arrest in normal psychosexual development, most often in the context of a particular dysfunctional family constellation. Such a family typically featured a close-binding mother and an absent or distant father. Despite the relative renown of this theory, it is based solely on clinical speculation and has never been empirically validated. Subsequent studies have indicated that etiologic factors in the development of sexual orientation are unclear but that the traditional psychoanalytic formulations concerning family dynamics are not viable (Bell, Weinberg, and Hammersmith 1981).

Psychoanalytic treatment of homosexuality is exemplified by the work of Bieber et al. (1962), who advocate intensive, long-term therapy aimed at resolving the unconscious anxiety stemming from childhood conflicts that supposedly cause homosexuality. Bieber et al. saw homosexuality as always pathological and incompatible with a happy life. Their methodology has been criticized for using an entirely clinical sample and for basing outcomes on subjective therapist impression, not externally validated data or even self-report. Follow-up data have been poorly presented and not empirical in nature. Bieber et al. (1962) reported a 27 percent success rate in heterosexual shift after long-term therapy; of these, however, only 18 percent were exclusively homosexual in the first place. Fifty percent of the successfully treated subjects were more appropriately labeled bisexual. This blending of "apples and oranges" returns us to the original question: Who is being converted, and what is the nature of the conversion?

Another analytically based study reported virtually no increase in heterosexual behavior in a group of homosexual men (Curran and Parr 1957). Other studies report greater success rates: For instance, Mayerson and Lief (1965) indicate that, of nineteen subjects, half reported engaging in exclusive heterosexual behavior 4.5 years post-treatment. However, as in Bieber et al.'s study, those subjects had heteroerotic traits to begin with; exclusively homosexual subjects reported little change, and outcomes were based on patient self-report. As in other studies, an expansion of the sexual repertoire toward heterosexual behavior is viewed as equivalent to a shift of sexual orientation.

California psychologist Joseph Nicolosi has developed a program of reparative therapy for "non-gay" homosexuals, individuals who reported being uncomfortable with their same-sex orientation. Nicolosi stated, "I do not believe that the gay life-style can ever be healthy, nor that the homosexual identity can ever be completely ego-syntonic" (1991:13). This belief erroneously presupposes a unitary gay lifestyle, a concept more reductionist than that of sexual orientation. It also prejudicially and without empirical justification assumes that homosexually oriented people can never be normal or happy, a point refuted numerous times in the literature. Nonetheless, this statement is the foundation for his theoretical approach, which cites numerous studies that suggest that gay men have greater frequencies of disrupted bonds with their fathers, as well as a host of psychological concerns, such as assertion problems. These observations are used to justify a pathological assessment of homosexuality. The error in such reasoning is that the conclusion has preceded the data. There may be cause to examine the potentially harmful impact of a detached father and his effect on the individual's self-concept or capacity for intimacy, but why should a detached father be selected as the key player in causing homosexuality, unless an a priori decision about the pathological nature of homosexuality has been made and unless the father is being investigated as the cause? This perspective is not consistent with available data, nor does it explain the millions of heterosexual men who come from backgrounds similar to those of gay men, or, for that matter, those gay men with strong father-son relationships. Nicolosi does not support his hypothesis or his treatment methods with any empirical data.

Group treatments have also been used in sexual reorientation. One study of thirty-two subjects reports a 37 percent shift to heterosexuality (Hadden

1966), but the results must be viewed with some skepticism because of the entirely self-reporting nature of the outcome measures. Individuals involved in such group treatments are especially susceptible to the influence of social demand in their own reporting of treatment success. Similarly a study of ten gay men resulted in the therapist's impressionistic claims that homosexual patients were able to "increase contact" with heterosexuals (Mintz 1966). Birk (1980) described a combination insight-oriented-social-learning-group format for treating homosexuality. He claimed that, overall, 38 percent of his patients achieved "solid heterosexual shifts." Nonetheless, he acknowledges that these shifts represent "an adaptation to life, not a metamorphosis" and that homosexual fantasies and activity are ongoing, even for the "happily married" individual (Birk 1980:387). If a solid heterosexual shift is defined as one in which a happily married person may engage in more than occasional homosexual encounters, perhaps this method is best described as a laboratory for heterosexual behavior rather than a change of sexual orientation. A minority of subjects, likely with preexisting heteroerotic tendencies, may be taught proficiency in heterosexual activities. Eager to equate heterosexual competence with orientation change, these researchers have ignored the complex questions associated with the assessment of sexual orientation. Behavior alone is a misleading barometer of sexual orientation, which includes biological, gender-based, social, and affectional variables. No researchers who conducted conversion studies have displayed any such thoughtfulness in their assessment or categorization of subjects.

Behavioral programs designed to reverse homosexual orientation are based on the premise that homoerotic impulses arise from faulty learning. These studies seek to countercondition the "learned" homoerotic response with aversive stimuli, replacing it with the reinforced, desired heteroerotic response. The aversive stimulus, typically consisting of electric shock or convulsion- or nausea-inducing drugs, is administered during presentation of same-sex erotic visual material. The cessation of the aversive stimulus is accompanied by the presentation of heteroerotic visual material, supposedly to replace homoeroticism in the sexual response hierarchy. These methods have been reviewed by Sansweet (1975). Some programs attempted to augment aversive conditioning techniques with a social learning component (assertiveness training, how to ask women out on dates, etc.; Feldman and McCullogh 1965). Later, the same investigators modified their approach, calling it "anticipatory avoidance conditioning," which enabled subjects to avoid electrical shock when viewing slides of same-sex nudes (Feldman 1966). Such a stressful situation could likely inhibit feelings of sexual responsiveness in any direction; nevertheless, a 58 percent cure rate was claimed, with outcome criteria defined as the suppression of homoerotic response. Cautela (1967) reported on single subjects who were taught to imagine such aversive stimuli rather than undergo them directly. His later work focuses on structured aversive fantasy, in which subjects are asked to visualize repulsive homoerotic encounters in stressful circumstances (Cautela and Kearney 1986). The investigators deny a homophobic bias to this therapeutic approach.

Other studies suggest that aversive interventions may extinguish homosexual responsiveness but do little to promote alternative orientation. One investigator suggests that conversion treatments have poor outcomes because they "disregard the complex learned repertoire and topography of homosexual behavior" (Faustman 1976). Other studies echo the finding that aversive therapies in homosexuality do not alter subjects' sexual orientation (McConaghy 1981). Another study similarly suggests that behavioral conditioning decreases homosexual orientation but does not elevate heterosexual interest (Rangaswami 1982). Methodologically the near-exclusive use of self-reporting outcome measures is problematic, particularly in an area where social demand factors may strongly influence subjects' reports. The few studies that do attempt to externally validate sexual reorientation through behavioral measures show no change after treatment (Conrad and Wincze 1976).

Masters and Johnson (1979) reported on the treatment of fifty-four "dissatisfied" homosexual men. This was unprecedented for the authors, as their previous works on heterosexual dysfunction did not include treatment for dissatisfied heterosexual people. The authors hypothesized homosexuality to be the result of failed or ridiculed attempts at heterosexuality, neglecting the obvious: that heterosexual "failures" among homosexual people are to be expected because the behavior in question is outside the individual's normal sexual response pattern. Despite their comments to the contrary, the study is founded on heterosexist bias. Gonsiorek (1981) raises a variety of concerns with the Masters and Johnson study. Of the numerous methodological problems with this study, perhaps most significant is the composition of the sample itself. Of fifty-four subjects, only nine (17 percent) identified themselves as Kinsey 5 or 6 (exclusively homosexual). The other forty-five subjects (83 percent) ranged from 2 to 4 on the Kinsey scale (predominantly heterosexual to bisexual). Furthermore, because 30 percent of the sample was lost to follow-up, it is conceivable that the outcome sample does not include any homosexual men. Perhaps this is why such a high success rate is reported after two weeks of treatment. It is likely that, rather than converting or reverting homosexual people to heterosexuality, this program enhances heterosexual responsiveness in people with already established heteroerotic sexual maps.

Evidence for the efficacy of sexual conversion programs is less than compelling. All research in this area has evolved from unproven hypothetical formulations about the pathological nature of homosexuality. The illness model has never been empirically validated; to the contrary, a broad literature validates the nonpathological view of homosexuality, leading to its declassification as a mental disorder (Gonsiorek 1991). Thus treatments in both analytic and behavioral modes are designed to cure something that has never been demonstrated to be an illness. From a methodological standpoint, the studies reviewed here reveal inadequacies in the selection criteria and the classification of subjects and poorly designed and administered outcome measures. In short, no consistency emerges from the extant database, which suggests that sexual orientation is amenable to redirection or significant influence from psychological intervention.

Religion-Based Conversion Programs

In a recent symposium on Christian approaches to the treatment of lesbians and gay men, one panelist said of his numerous unsuccessful attempts at sexual reorientation: "I felt it was what I had to do in order to gain a right to live on the planet." Such is the experience of many gay men and lesbians, who experience severe conflict between their homoerotic feelings and their need for acceptance by a homophobic religious community. This conflict causes such individuals to seek the guidance of pastoral care providers or Christian support groups whose aim is to reorient gay men and lesbians. Such programs seek to divest the individual of his or her "sinful" feelings or at least to make the pursuit of a heterosexual or celibate lifestyle possible. Their theoretical base is founded on interpretations of scripture that condemn homosexual behavior, their often unspecified treatment methods rely on prayer, and their outcomes are generally limited to testimonials. Nonetheless, these programs bear some passing examination because of the tremendous psychological impact they have on the many unhappy gay men and lesbians who seek their services and because of some psychologists' willingness to refer to them. Lastly, many such programs have been associated with significant ethical problems.

Gay men who are most likely to be inclined toward doctrinaire religious practice are also likely to have lower self-concepts, to see homosexuality as more sinful, to feel a greater sense of apprehension about negative responses from others, and to be more depressed in general (Weinberg and Williams 1974). Such individuals are vulnerable targets for the "ex-gay" ministries, as they are known. Fundamentalist Christian groups, such as Homosexuals Anonymous, Metanoia Ministries, Love In Action, Exodus International, and EXIT of Melodyland are the most visible purveyors of conversion therapy. The workings of these groups are well documented by Blair (1982), who states that, although many of these practitioners publicly promise change, they privately acknowledge that celibacy is the realistic goal to which gay men and lesbians must aspire. He further characterizes many religious conversionists as individuals deeply troubled about their own sexual orientation or whose own sexual conversion is incomplete. Blair reports a host of problems with such counselors, including the sexual abuse of clients.

The most notable of such ministers is Colin Cook. Cook's counseling program, Quest, led to the development of Homosexuals Anonymous, the largest antigay fundamentalist counseling organization in the world. The work of Cook, his ultimate demise, and the subsequent cover-up by the Seventh Day Adventist Church, are described by sociologist Ronald Lawson (1987). Over the course of seven years, approximately two hundred people received reorientation counseling from Cook, his wife, and an associate. From this ministry sprang Homosexuals Anonymous, a 14-step program modeled after Alcoholics Anonymous, which has become the largest fundamentalist organization in the world with a unitary antigay focus. Lawson, in attempting to research the efficacy of Cook's program, was denied access to counselees on the basis of confidentiality. Nonetheless, he managed to interview fourteen clients, none of whom reported any change in sexual orientation. All but two reported that Cook had had sex with them during treatment. According to Blair, another homosexual pastor who used his ministry to gain sexual access to vulnerable gay people was Guy Charles, founder of Liberation in Jesus Christ. Charles was a homosexual man who had claimed a heterosexual conversion subsequent to his acceptance of Christ. Like Cook, Charles was ultimately disavowed by the Christian organization that sponsored him after charges of sexual misconduct were raised.

To date, the only spiritually based sexual orientation conversion program to appear in the literature has been a study by Pattison and Pattison (1980). These authors describe a supernatural healing approach in treating thirty individuals culled from a group of three hundred who sought sexual reorientation counseling at EXIT of Melodyland, a charismatic ex-gay ministry affiliated with a Christian amusement park. The Pattisons do not explain their sampling criteria, nor do they explain why nineteen of their thirty subjects refused follow-up interviews. Their data indicate that only three subjects of the eleven (from the group of three hundred) report no current homosexual desires, fantasies, or impulses, and that one of the three subjects is listed as still being "incidentally homosexual." Of the other eight subjects, several indicated ongoing neurotic conflict about their homosexual impulses. Although six of these men have married heterosexually, two admit to more than incidental homosexual ideation as an ongoing issue.

Recently, founders of another prominent ex-gay ministry, Exodus International, denounced their conversion therapy procedures as ineffective. Michael Busse and Gary Cooper, co-founders of Exodus and lovers for thirteen years, were involved with the organization from 1976 to 1979. The program was described by these men as "ineffective . . . not one person was healed." They stated that the program often exacerbated already prominent feelings of guilt and personal failure among the counselees; many were driven to suicidal thoughts as a result of the failed reparative therapy (Newsbriefs 1990:43).

The fundamentalist Christian conversion programs hold enormous symbolic power over many people. Possibly exacerbating the harm to naive, shame-ridden counselees, these programs operate under the formidable auspices of the Christian Church, and outside the jurisdiction of any professional organizations that may impose ethical standards of practice and accountability on them. A closer look at such programs is warranted, given the frequency with which spiritual conversion programs seek to legitimize themselves with psychologists as affiliates.

An examination of psychotherapeutic and spiritual approaches to conversion therapy reveal a wide range of scientific concerns, from theoretical weaknesses to methodological problems and poor outcomes. This literature does not suggest a bright future in studying ways to reorient people sexually. Individuals undergoing conversion treatment are not likely to emerge as heterosexually inclined, but they often do become shamed, conflicted, and fearful about their homoerotic feelings. It is not uncommon for gay men and lesbians who have undergone aversion treatments to notice a temporary sharp decline in their sexual responsiveness, with some subjects reporting long-term sexual dysfunction. Similarly subjects who have undergone failed attempts at conversion therapy often report increased guilt, anxiety, and low self-esteem. Some flee into heterosexual marriages that are doomed to problems inevitably involving spouses, and often children as well. Not one investigator has ever raised the possibility that conversion treatments may harm some participants, even in a field where a 30 percent success rate is seen as high. The research question, "What is being accomplished by conversion treatments?" may well be replaced by, "What harm has been done in the name of sexual reorientation?" At present, no data are extant.

Ethical Considerations

We have considered the question of whether sexual orientations are amenable to change or modification by means of therapeutic interventions. Of equal, if not greater, import is the question of whether psychology should provide or endorse such "cures." Ethicists object to conversion therapy on two grounds: first, that it constitutes a cure for a condition that has been judged not to be an illness and, second, that it reinforces a prejudicial and unjustified devaluation of homosexuality.

The American Psychiatric Association's 1973 decision to remove homosexuality from its *Diagnostic and Statistical Manual of Mental Disorders* marked the official passing of the illness model of homosexuality. The American Psychological Association (APA) followed suit with a resolution affirming this anti-illness perspective, stating, in part, that "the APA urges all mental health professionals to take the lead in removing the stigma of mental illness that has long been associated with homosexual orientations" (APA 1975). Homosexuality was replaced with the confusing "ego-dystonic homosexuality" diagnosis, which was dropped altogether in 1987.

It is beyond the scope of this article to provide a comprehensive review of the literature on the depathologizing of homosexuality. Briefly, recent scholarship in the area suggests that human homosexuality, despite being nonreproductive in nature, is as biologically natural as heterosexuality.

> Biological arguments cannot be used to distinguish morally between homosexuality and heterosexuality. Like left- and right-handedness, the two are expressions of a single human nature that can be expressed differently in different individuals. If homosexuality is therefore part of a range of behavior that has molded *Homo sapiens*, then it is clear that homosexuality is not a disease, and certainly the general object should not be to "cure" it. (Kirsch and Weinrich 1991:30)

Homosexual behavior and identity exist in many cultures, and its relative normalcy seems to be more a function of subjective social attribution than of intrinsic properties.

Our society has taken a natural kind of sexuality and made it taboo, in a way that is completely unnecessary for its stability or its values. It is time for us to learn from other cultures that uniform sameness is not a desirable goal for society. (Weinrich and Williams 1991:59)

Proponents of conversion therapy continue to insist, in the absence of any evidence, that homosexuality is pathological. This model was rejected because of a lack of such evidence, and its demise has been described by Gonsiorek (1991). This review underscores the faulty logic inherent in classic psychoanalytic theories of family dysfunction as etiologic of homosexuality. Researcher bias, as well as methodological inadequacies, characterize studies supporting the illness model. Psychological test data, from Hooker's (1957) study to present-day studies, have been reviewed and show no substantive differences between homosexual and heterosexual subjects.

Were there properties intrinsic to homosexuality that make it a pathological condition, we would be able to observe and measure them directly. In reality, however, there exists a wide literature indicating just the opposite: that gay men and lesbians do not differ significantly from heterosexual men and women on measures of psychological stability, social or vocational adjustment, or capacity for decision making. In fact, psychological adjustment among gay men and lesbians seems to be directly correlated to the degree to which they have accepted their sexual orientation (Weinberg and Williams 1974). In light of such evidence, the number of studies examining the pathogenesis of homosexuality has diminished in recent years.

Davison (1976, 1978, 1991) has detailed many of the ethical objections to conversion therapies. A behavioral therapist once well known for his program to change sexual orientation, Davison believes that a disservice is done to the gay or lesbian individual by offering sexual orientation change as a therapeutic option. In Davison's view, conversion therapy reinforces antigay prejudice. He asks, "How can therapists honestly speak of nonprejudice when they participate in therapy regimens that by their very existence — and regardless of their efficacy — would seem to condone the current societal prejudice and perhaps also impede social change?" (1991:141).

In his paraphrase of Halleck (1971), Davison states that therapeutic neutrality is a myth and that therapists, by the nature of their role, cannot help but influence patients with respect to values. Davison suggests that the question of whether sexual orientation can be changed is secondary to the consideration that it should not be changed, because of the devaluation and pathologizing of homosexuality implicit in offering a "cure" for it. Because

therapists operate from positions of power, to affirm the viability of homosexuality and then engage in therapeutic efforts to change it sends a mixed message: If a cure is offered, then there must be an illness. This point is echoed
by Begelman, who stated that "[conversion therapies] by their very existence,
constitute a significant causal element in reinforcing the social doctrine that
homosexuality is bad; therapists . . . further strengthen the prejudice that homosexuality is a 'problem behavior,' since treatment may be offered for it"
(1975:180). Charles Silverstein (1977) points to social factors (e.g., rejecting
families, hostile peer interactions, and disapproving society) as being responsible for people seeking sexual orientation change. These authors indicate that
what were historically viewed as "ego-dystonic" responses to homosexuality
are really internalized reactions to a hostile society.

Proponents of conversion therapy often deny any coercive intent, claiming
that theirs is a valuable service for distressed lesbians and gay men who freely
seek their services. However, the concept that individuals seek sexual orientation change of their own free will may be fallacious. Martin (1984) stated
that "a clinician's implicit acceptance of the homosexual orientation as the
cause of ego-dystonic reactions, and the concomitant agreement to attempt
sexual orientation change, exacerbates the ego-dystonic reactions and reinforces and confirms the internalized homophobia that lies at their root" (p.
46).

State psychological associations have started to address the issue of conversion therapy in order to provide reasonable guidelines to consumer and practitioner. In 1991 the Washington State Psychological Association adopted an
advisory policy on sexual orientation conversion therapy. An excerpt follows:

> Psychologists do not provide or sanction cures for that which has been
> judged not to be an illness. Individuals seeking to change their sexual
> orientation do so as the result of internalized stigma and homophobia,
> given the consistent scientific demonstration that there is nothing
> about homosexuality per se that undermines psychological adjust-
> ment. It is therefore our objective as psychologists to educate and
> change the intolerant social context, not the individual who is victim-
> ized by it. Conversion treatments, by their very existence, exacerbate
> the homophobia which psychology seeks to combat. (Washington
> State Psychological Association 1991)

Discussion

Our understanding of human sexuality is entering a new era, one in which formerly sacrosanct assumptions and classifications are no longer applicable. A new generation of individuals, no longer self-identified as gay or lesbian but as "queer," is developing a perspective of sexual orientation more complex and fluid than what has historically been viewed along rigid lines. This new construction of sexuality, combined with the antiquated, unscientific hypotheses on which conversion therapy has been based, render traditional reorientation therapy anachronistic.

The lack of empirical support for conversion therapy calls into question the judgment of clinicians who practice or endorse it. The APA "Fact Sheet on Reparative Therapy" opens with the following statement: "No scientific evidence exists to support the effectiveness of any of the conversion therapies that try to change sexual orientation." A review of the literature makes it obvious why this statement is made. Psychologists are obliged to use methods that have some empirically demonstrable efficacy, and there is a paucity of such evidence relative to conversion therapy. Moreover, there is a need to understand fully the potentially damaging effects of a failed conversion treatment.

A next logical question, then, involves standards of practice for the treatment of lesbians and gay men that *are* compatible with scientific data. In 1991 the APA's Committee on Lesbian and Gay Concerns published the results of a survey on bias in psychotherapeutic treatment of lesbians and gay men. This survey is an initial step in providing the clinician with guidelines that are consistent with science and that promote the welfare and dignity of the gay or lesbian individual. More research is needed to refine these recommendations for the myriad of issues that gay people bring to therapy. It is the responsibility of psychologists to provide accurate scientific information, particularly since so much misinformation is currently being used to further stigmatize and justify, even legislate, discrimination against gay people. The current wave of antigay political activity is founded on the mistaken assumptions that homosexuality is a chosen way of life and an abnormal one at that. It may be impossible to understand why so many people would believe that lesbians and gay men would deliberately choose a way of life that puts them at risk for discrimination and violence. It is, however, well within psychology's purview to disseminate accurate information from our considerable database about homosexuality.

Even more significant than the practical considerations of conversion therapy are the ethical concerns. Psychologists are obliged to use methods that promote the dignity and welfare of humankind. Conversion therapies fail in this regard, because they are necessarily predicated on a devaluation of homosexual identity and behavior. Some contemporary conversionists would claim a value-neutral stance, insisting that conversion therapy is simply a matter of the client's right to choose treatment, but what is the purpose of attempting to change sexual orientation if it is not negatively valued? How many dissatisfied heterosexual men and women seek a similar conversion to homosexuality? What message does psychology send to society when it affirms the normalcy of homosexuality yet continues to give tacit approval to efforts to change it? Murphy, summarizing his review of the conversion therapy literature, addressed this:

> There would be no reorientation techniques where there was no interpretation that homoeroticism is an inferior state, an interpretation that in many ways continues to be medically defined, criminally enforced, socially sanctioned, and religiously justified. And it is in this moral interpretation, more than in the reigning medical theory of the day, that all programs of sexual reorientation have their common origins and justifications. (1992:520)

This morality is at work in all aspects of homophobic activity, from the alarming increase in violent hate crimes against gay men and lesbians to the political and legislative agendas of antigay organizations. Perpetrators of violence and antigay political groups justify their actions with the same devaluation of homosexuality that conversion therapists use.

Given the extensive societal devaluation of homosexuality and lack of positive role models for gay men and lesbians, it is not surprising that many gay people seek to become heterosexual. Homophobic attitudes have been institutionalized in nearly every aspect of our social structure, from the government and the military to our educational systems and organized religions. For gay men and lesbians who have identified with the dominant group, the desire to be like others and to be accepted socially is so strong that heterosexual relating becomes more than an act of sex or love. It becomes a symbol of freedom from prejudice and social devaluation. Psychology cannot free people from stigma by continuing to promote or tacitly endorse conversion therapy. Psychology can only combat stigma with a vigorous avowal of empirical truth. The appropriate focus of the profession is what reverses prejudice, not what reverses sexual orientation.

References

American Psychological Association. 1975. Minutes of the Council of Representatives. *American Psychologist* 30:633.

Begelman, D. A. 1975. Ethical and legal issues of behavior modification. In M. Hersen, R. Eisler, and P.M. Miller, eds., *Progress in Behavior Modification*, pp. 175–88. San Diego, Calif.: Academic Press.

Bell, A., and M. Weinberg. 1978. *Homosexuality: A Study of Diversity Among Men and Women*. New York: Simon and Schuster.

Bell, A., M. Weinberg, and S. Hammersmith. 1981. *Sexual Preference: Its Development in Men and Women*. Bloomington: Indiana University Press.

Bieber, I., H. Dain, P. Dince, M. Drellich, H. Grand, R. Gundlach, M. Kremer, A. Rifkin, C. Wilbur, and T. Bieber (Society of Medical Psychoanalysts). 1962. *Homosexuality: A Psychoanalytic Study*. New York: Basic Books.

Birk, L. 1980. The myth of classical homosexuality: Views of a behavioral psychotherapist. In J. Marmor, ed., *Homosexual Behavior: A Modern Reappraisal*, pp. 376–90. New York: Basic Books.

Blair, R. 1982. *Ex-Gay*. New York: Homosexual Counseling Center.

Cautela, J. 1967. Covert sensitization. *Psychological Reports* 2:459–68.

Cautela, J., A. Kearney. 1986. *The Covert Conditioning Handbook*. New York: Springer.

Coleman, E. 1987. The assessment of sexual orientation. *Journal of Homosexuality* 14(1/2):9–24.

Conrad, S., and J. Wincze. 1976. Orgasmic reconditioning: A controlled study of its effects upon the sexual arousal and behavior of male homosexuals. *Behavior Therapy* 7:155–66.

Curran, D., D. and Parr. 1957. Homosexuality: An analysis of 100 male cases. *British Medical Journal* 1:797–801.

Davison, G. 1976. Homosexuality: The ethical challenge. *Journal of Consulting and Clinical Psychology* 44:157–62.

Davison, G. 1978. Not can but ought: The treatment of homosexuality. *Journal of Consulting and Clinical Psychology* 46:170–72.

Davison, G. 1991. Constructionism and morality in therapy for homosexuality. In J. Gonsiorek and J. Weinrich, eds., *Homosexuality: Research Implications for Public Policy*, pp. 137–48. Newbury Park, Calif.: Sage.

Faustman, W. 1976. Aversive control of maladaptive sexual behavior: Past developments and future trends. *Psychology* 13:53–60.

Feldman, M. 1966. Aversion therapy for sexual deviation: A critical review. *Psychological Bulletin* 65:65–69.

Feldman, M., and M. McCullogh. 1965. The application of anticipatory avoidance learning to the treatment of homosexuality: Theory, technique, and preliminary results. *Behavior Research and Therapy* 2:165–83.

Gonsiorek, J. 1981. Review of *Homosexuality in Perspective*, by Masters and Johnson. *Journal of Homosexuality* 6(3):81–88.

Gonsiorek, J. 1991. The empirical basis for the demise of the illness model of homosexuality. In J. Gonsiorek and J. Weinrich, eds., *Homosexuality: Research Implications for Public Policy*, pp. 115–36. Newbury Park, Calif.: Sage.

Hadden, S. 1966. Treatment of male homosexuals in groups. *International Journal of Group Psychotherapy* 16:13–22.

Haldeman, D. 1991. Sexual orientation conversion therapy: A scientific examination. In J. Gonsiorek and J. Weinrich, eds., *Homosexuality: Research Implications for Public Policy*, pp. 149–60. Newbury Park, Calif.: Sage.

Halleck, S. 1971. *The Politics of Therapy*. New York: Science House.

Hooker, E. 1957. The adjustment of the male overt homosexual. *Journal of Projective Techniques* 21:17–31.

Kinsey, A. C., W. B. Pomeroy, and C. E. Martin. 1948. *Sexual Behavior in the Human Male*. Philadelphia: Saunders.

Kirsch, J., and J. Weinrich. 1991. Homosexuality, nature, and biology: Is homosexuality natural? Does it matter? In J. Gonsiorek and J. Weinrich, eds., *Homosexuality: Research Implications for Public Policy*. pp. 13–31. Newbury Park. Calif.: Sage.

Lawson, R. 1987. Scandal in the Adventist-funded program to "heal" homosexuals: Failure, sexual exploitation, official silence, and attempts to rehabilitate the exploiter and his methods. Paper presented at the annual convention of the American Sociological Association, June, Chicago, Illinois.

Martin, A. 1984. The emperor's new clothes: Modern attempts to change sexual orientation. In E. S. Hetrick and T. S. Stein, eds., *Innovations in Psychotherapy with Homosexuals*, pp. 24–57. Washington, D.C.: American Psychiatric Association.

Masters, W., and V. Johnson. 1979. *Homosexuality in Perspective*. Boston: Little, Brown.

Mayerson, P., and H. Lief. 1965. Psychotherapy of homosexuals: A follow-up study of nineteen cases. In J. Marmor, ed., *Sexual Inversion*, pp. 302–44. New York: Basic Books.

McConaghy, N. 1981. Controlled comparison of aversive therapy and covert sensitization in compulsive homosexuality. *Behavior Research and Therapy* 19:425–34.

Mintz, E. 1966. Overt male homosexuals in combined group and individual treatment. *Journal of Consulting Psychology* 20:193–98.

Murphy, T. 1992. Redirecting sexual orientation: Techniques and justifications. *Journal of Sex Research* 29:501–23.

Newswatch briefs. 1990. *Gay Chicago Magazine* (February 22) 8:43.

Nicolosi, J. 1991. *Reparative Therapy of Male Homosexuality*. Northvale, N.J.: Jason Aronson.

Pattison, E., and M. Pattison. 1980. "Ex-gays": religiously mediated change in homosexuals. *American Journal of Psychiatry* 137:1553–62.

Rangaswami, K. 1982. Difficulties in arousing and increasing heterosexual responsiveness in a homosexual: A case report. *Indian Journal of Clinical Psychology* 9:147–51.

Rist, D. Y. 1992. *Heartlands: A Gay Man's Odyssey Across America*. New York: Dutton.

Sansweet, R. J. 1975. *The Punishment Cure*. New York: Mason/Charter.

Silverstein, C. 1977. Homosexuality and the ethics of behavioral intervention. *Journal of Homosexuality* 2(3):205–11.

Silverstein, C. 1991. Psychological and medical treatments of homosexuality. In J. Gonsiorek and J. Weinrich, eds., *Homosexuality: Research Implications for Public Policy*, pp. 101–14. Newbury Park, Calif.: Sage.

Washington State Psychological Association. 1991. March. Policy statement on sexual orientation conversion therapy. Unpublished document, March.

Weinberg, M., and C. Williams. 1974. *Male Homosexuals: Their Problems and Adaptations*. New York: Penguin.

Weinrich, J., and W. Williams. 1991. Strange customs, familiar lives: Homosexualities in other cultures. In J. Gonsiorek and J. Weinrich, eds., *Homosexuality: Research Implications for Public Policy*. Newbury Park, Calif.: Sage.

26 Minority Stress and Mental Health in Gay Men

Ilan H. Meyer

Four years before he killed himself, sixteen-year-old Bobby Griffith wrote in his diary: "I can't let anyone find out that I'm not straight. It would be so humiliating. My friends would hate me, I just know it. They might even want to beat me up. . . . I guess I'm no good to anyone . . . not even God. Life is so cruel and unfair. Sometimes I feel like disappearing from the face of this earth" (Miller 1992:88–89). Since he had realized he was homosexual, Bobby Griffith struggled to accept himself and find some comfort in his California suburban community and family. But to his family, friends, and religion, being gay was evil and perverted. At the end, societal attitudes and stigma proved too powerful: Lacking all hope, Bobby envisioned a life of loneliness and condemnation. In the predawn hours of August 27, 1983, two months after his twentieth birthday, Bobby Griffith killed himself by jumping off a freeway overpass into the path of a passing truck (Miller 1992).

The cause of Bobby Griffith's suicide was a homophobic social environment that he could no longer tolerate. Bobby Griffith is not alone. Like members of other stigmatized minority groups, gay men and lesbians must contend with negative societal attitudes and stigma. The purpose of this paper is to discuss the effects of this social environment within a stress discourse. I describe the concept *minority stress* as psychosocial stress derived from minority status (Brooks 1981). This concept is based on the premise that gay people, like members of other minority groups, are subjected to chronic stress related to their stigmatization. Consistent with a social stress discourse (Mirowsky and Ross 1989; Pearlin 1989) and the evidence for social causality of distress (Dohrenwend et al. 1992), it is proposed that such stress leads to adverse mental health outcomes.

The concept of minority stress is not based on one congruous theory, but is inferred from several social and psychological theoretical orientations. In general, minority stress can be described as being related to the juxtaposition of minority and dominant values and the resultant conflict with the social environment experienced by minority group members (Mirowsky and Ross 1989; Pearlin 1989). Lazarus and Folkman (1984) describe such a conflict between individuals and their experience of society as the essence of all social stress. Several theories describe alienation and incongruence between individual needs and social structures (Durkheim 1951; Merton [1957] 1968: Moss 1973). Certainly, when the individual is a minority person in a stigmatizing and discriminating society, the conflict between him or her and the dominant culture can be onerous, and the resultant minority stress significant. Symbolic interaction and social comparison theories give a different perspective. These theories view the social environment as providing people with meaning to their world and organization to their experiences (Pettigrew 1967; Stryker and Statham 1985). Negative regard from others therefore leads to negative self-regard (Rosenberg 1979) and adverse mental health outcomes (Crocker and Major 1989; Jones et al. 1984).

Societal reaction theory directly addresses the effects of stigma and negative social attitudes on stigmatized individuals. According to societal reaction, deviance may lead to labeling and negative societal reaction. Consequently stigmatized individuals develop adaptive and maladaptive responses that may include mental health symptoms, and this is termed *secondary deviance* (Lemert 1967: Link and Cullen 1990; Schur 1971). Similarly Allport (1954) describes "traits due to victimization" as the defensive reaction of stigmatized individuals. These may be caused by introverted mechanisms, including self-hate and ingroup aggression, and/or extroverted mechanisms, including shyness, obsessive concern with the stigmatizing characteristic, and rebellion.

Minority group members are also exposed to negative life events related to their stigmatization and discrimination (Brooks 1981; Dohrenwend and Dohrenwend 1969). However, minority stress arises not only from negative events, but from the totality of the minority person's experience in dominant society. At the center of this experience is the incongruence between the minority person's culture, needs, and experience, and societal structures.

Many studies have attempted to study the effects of minority status (especially ethnicity) on mental health. The most widely used approach compares rates of psychopathology and distress between minority and nonminority groups. It has been predicted that, if minority position is stressful, and if this stress is related to psychological distress, then minority groups must have higher rates of distress than nonminority groups. But studies that compared rates of distress and disorder between blacks and whites, women and men, and homosexuals and heterosexuals did not confirm such predictions, leading some researchers to refute minority stress conceptualizations (see Hirschfeld and Cross 1983; McCarthy and Yancey 1971; Neighbors 1984; Robins and Regier 1991; Thomas and Sillen [1972] 1991; Warheit, Holzer, and Arey 1975; and Williams 1986, on black-white differences; see Dohrenwend and Dohrenwend 1976; Schwartz 1991; and Robins and Regier 1991, on men-women differences; see Gonsiorek 1991; Hart et al. 1978; Marmor 1980; Martin 1990; Pillard 1988; Reiss 1980; Saghir and Robins 1973; Tross et al. 1987; and Williams et al. 1991, on gay-straight differences). For example, Mirowsky and Ross (1989) conclude that economic conditions, rather than stigmatization and prejudice, are related to adverse mental health outcomes (among ethnic minorities). Their conclusion challenges minority stress conceptualizations as described here, as it posits socioeconomic status (SES) — whether related to minority status or not — as the cause of distress. This suggests that at higher SES, minority status should have no deleterious mental health effects. The present study disputes this conclusion.

I suggest that we must reexamine our reliance on evidence from intergroup comparisons of rates of distress. Despite the intuitive appeal of this approach, numerous methodological problems lead to bias, making it difficult to interpret the evidence from studies using this approach (Hirschfeld and Cross 1983; Kessler, Price, and Wortman 1985; Meyer 1993). A central problem, pertinent to the study of gay-straight differences, is selection bias in sampling. For example, individuals who do not accept themselves, and who have not successfully "come out," are less likely to participate in studies of gay men than individuals who accept themselves (Joseph 1986; Meyer 1993). Since self-acceptance is related to better psychological adjustment and less distress (e.g., Bell and Weinberg 1978), this selection bias leads to overrepresentation of healthier members of the minority group, thus underestimating rates of distress in that group (Meyer 1993). Black-white differences are similarly affected by selection bias. This is because African-Americans in the United States are disproportionately more frequently institutionalized, and institutionalized individuals are likely to have higher rates of distress and disorder. Other methodological problems that often plague research on minority stress include bias as a result of cultural (or gender) differences in response to stan-

dardized measures of distress that present strong competing explanations for
intergroup differences (e.g., Dohrenwend and Dohrenwend 1969; Mirowsky
and Ross 1980; Sowa and Lustman 1984).

Support for minority stress formulations is provided by some research. For
example, a review of studies of differences between gay and straight men in
psychological tests suggests that, although gay men are not more distressed
overall, when they do become distressed it is usually in areas that are consistent with minority stress conceptualizations, such as self-acceptance, alienation, and paranoid symptoms (Meyer 1993). Support for minority stress
conceptualizations in studies of black-white differences is provided by
Kessler and Neighbors (1986), who reanalyzed eight epidemiological surveys
that had concluded that race differences in distress are entirely explained by
social class. The reanalysis showed that, although overall higher levels of
distress for African-Americans are explained by SES, the hypothesized direct
minority stress effect is at work at low SES. The authors called on researchers
not to accept the premature conclusion that minority status is unrelated to
distress and to reinvest themselves in studying the issue. They suggested that
understanding the mechanisms through which minority position affects distress will help to clarify findings on rate differences.

The present study takes such an approach. This approach specifies causal
relationships based on theoretical conceptualizations and formulates hypotheses that directly test these relationships. Using this approach we avoid
the methodological difficulties in comparing rates between groups. Instead,
we study ingroup variability and examine the differential effect of minority
stress on minority members. For this purpose, the general conceptualizations
of minority stress discussed above must be transformed into concrete stress
processes. I discuss such processes as they apply to gay men, but the general
approach is suited for studying other stigmatized groups as well. I posit three
processes of minority stress: internalized homophobia, perceived stigma (expectations of rejection and discrimination), and actual prejudice events.

Internalized Homophobia

Internalized homophobia refers to the direction of societal negative attitudes toward the self. Long before they begin to realize their own homosexuality, homosexually oriented people internalize societal antihomosexual attitudes. When, as adolescents or young adults, they recognize same-sex
attraction, they begin to question their presumed heterosexuality and apply

the label "homosexual" or "gay" to themselves. Such self-labeling occurs before any public disclosure of their homosexuality. But as self-labeling begins, individuals also begin to apply negative attitudes to themselves, and the psychologically injurious effects of societal homophobia take effect. Thoits (1985:222) describes such a process and explains that "role-taking abilities enable individuals to view themselves from the imagined perspective of others." Link (1987:97) describes a similar process in individuals who become labeled as mental patients and notes that societal negative attitudes that "once seemed to be an innocuous array of beliefs . . . now become applicable personally and [are] no longer innocuous."

Thus, along with the recognition of same-sex attraction, a deviant identity (Goffman 1963) begins to emerge that threatens the psychological well-being of the homosexually oriented person (Hetrick and Martin 1984: Stein and Cohen 1984). Although internalized homophobia is likely to be most acute early in the coming-out process, it is unlikely that internalized homophobia completely abates even when the person accepts his or her homosexuality (Cass 1984; Coleman 1982; Troiden 1989). Because of the strength of early socialization experiences and continued exposure to antihomosexual attitudes, internalized homophobia remains an important factor in the gay person's psychological adjustment throughout life (Hetrick and Martin 1984; Gonsiorek 1988; Malyon 1982; Nungesser 1983).

Perceived Stigma

The negative effects of stigma and labeling have been discussed in psychological and sociological literature (e.g., Goffman 1963; Jones et al. 1984; Link and Cullen 1990; Warren 1980). For example, stigmatization is related to adverse effects in self-esteem, employment, and social acceptance among the mentally ill (Link 1987; Link and Cullen 1990; Link et al. 1987). Goffman (1963:7) discusses the anxiety with which the stigmatized individual approaches interactions in society. Such an individual "may perceive, usually quite correctly, that whatever others profess, they do not really 'accept' him and are not ready to make contact with him on 'equal grounds.' " Goffman (1963:13) cites Sullivan (in Perry, Gawell, and Gibbon 1956:145) to explain that "the fear that others can disrespect a person because of something he shows means that he is always insecure in his contact with other people; and this insecurity arises . . . from something which he knows he cannot fix."

Similarly Allport (1954) describes vigilance as one of the "traits" that targets of prejudice might develop in defensive coping with their minority status. This concept helps to explain the stressful effect of stigma. A high level of perceived stigma would lead minority group members to maintain a high degree of vigilance — expectations of rejection, discrimination, and violence — regarding the minority components of their identity in interactions with dominant group members. By definition, such vigilance is chronic in that it is repeatedly and continually evoked in the everyday life of the minority person. This vigilance is stressful in that it requires the exertion of considerable energy and resources in adapting to it (Allport 1954). Hetrick and Martin (1987:35) describe "learning to hide" as the most common coping strategy of gay and lesbian adolescents, and note that "individuals in such a position must constantly monitor their behavior in all circumstances: how one dresses, speaks, walks, and talks become constant sources of possible discovery."

The stress experienced by the vigilant person leads to a general experience of fear and mistrust in interactions with the dominant culture, and a sense of disharmony and alienation with general society. Warren (1980:130) notes that the struggle to reconcile one's gay identity with societal stigma "involve[s] a considerable investment of emotional energy, and . . . a considerable psychic toll." This hypervigilance may also lead to taxing "costs of coping" (Cohen et al. 1986) and to coping fatigue. High levels of perceived stigma, then, will lead gay men to to experience stress chronically as they feel that they must remain vigilant to avoid being harmed.

Discrimination and Violence (Prejudice Events)

In the United States homosexuality is still criminalized in twenty-four states, and in most states gay people have no protection under the law. Gay people are therefore legally discriminated against in housing, employment, entitlements, and basic civil rights. As gay men and lesbians become more visible, they increasingly become targets of antigay violence, prejudice, and discrimination (American Psychological Association 1986; Dean, Wu, and Martin 1992; Herek and Berrill 1992; Herek and Glunt 1988; National Gay and Lesbian Task Force 1991; Wilson 1992).

The most explicit sources of minority stress are rejection, discrimination, and violence that minority persons experience because of their stigmatized minority position (Garnets, Herek, and Levy 1990). Garnets and colleagues describe the mechanisms for the effect of victimization on psychological distress. They note that victimization interferes with perception of the world as meaningful and orderly, and leads people to self-devaluation (Garnets et al. 1990). Perhaps the most critical aspect of antigay violence and discrimination is its meaning within the context of societal heterosexism and minority oppression. Prejudice events have a powerful impact more because of the deep cultural meaning they activate than because of the ramifications of the events themselves (Brooks 1981). A seemingly minor event, such as a slur directed at a gay man, may evoke deep feelings of rejection and fears of violence disproportionate to the event that precipitated them.

Hypotheses

Together these three stressors represent a matrix that defines the different dimensions of minority stress in gay men for the present investigation. The effects of these stressors will be tested on five measures of psychological distress — demoralization, guilt, suicide ideation and behavior, AIDS-related traumatic stress response, and sex problems. The different distress domains have either a general or more specific relationship to the three minority stress constructs. Demoralization is a generalized distress measure, analogous to body temperature in somatic illness (Dohrenwend et al. 1980). Guilt might be more directly related to minority stress in that a man who feels that his sexual orientation is condemnable (indicated by high internalized homophobia) or that it is, in fact, condemned and debased (indicated by high stigma and prejudice or both), may be especially vulnerable to guilt feelings. Similarly sex problems, which are directly related to the expression of intimacy with other men, might be closely related to internalized homophobia, as internalized homophobia will evoke conflict and anxiety that could inhibit achievement of satisfying intimate relationships (Coleman, Rosser, and Strapko 1992; Friedman 1991).

(H1) It is predicted that each minority stressor will have an independent effect on each distress domain.

(H2) It is further predicted that, when the effects of the stressors are combined, each will maintain an independent effect on distress, so that their combined effect will be greater than their individual effects.

In addition, I will examine interactions among the three minority stressors to describe more complex associations. In particular, it has been suggested that self-blame attributions lead to more deleterious mental health effects than attributions of blame to external agents (Brewin 1985; Jones et al. 1984).

(H3) Because internalized homophobia predisposes one to self-blame attributions, it is predicted that the effects of stigma and prejudice events on distress will be exacerbated at higher levels of internalized homophobia.

In all analyses, the effects of gay identity and involvement with the gay community will be considered. This paper will examine an alternative hypothesis, namely, that the minority stressors affect distress indirectly by diminishing social networks and affiliations in the gay community. If minority stress were found to affect distress only through its effect on social networks, it could be argued that it is social support, rather than minority stress per se, that is related to distress. In a similar vein, the effect of minority stress on African-Americans has been "explained away" by attributing it wholly to lower SES, even though lower SES may be conceived as an intervening variable in the causal association between minority status and distress (Mirowsky and Ross 1989). The inclusion of these "gay identity" variables represents a conservative approach in detecting the associations of minority stress. A less conservative approach would claim that, even if these variables add to the association of minority stress and distress, they are not extraneous to this association, and their "contribution" should therefore not be extracted. But while both direct and indirect factors may be considered minority stress effects, I set out to test the direct effects of minority stress and therefore include these variables as potential confounders. Controlling for the effects of gay identity variables makes it possible to attribute distress effects directly to minority stress processes.

Sample

Gay men who lived in New York City and did not have a diagnosis of AIDS in 1985 were eligible for a longitudinal study about the psychological and behavioral impact of the AIDS epidemic. The sample was assembled from a wide variety of sources in the gay community. Thirty-nine percent of the men were recruited from a stratified random sample of one hundred gay organizations and groups, and 61 percent were recruited using a snowball technique to include unaffiliated gay men. This approach was taken to reach a diversity of sampling sources that reflect the community of urban gay men in New York City (Martin and Dean 1990). The recruitment method and characteristics of the original sample have been described in detail elsewhere (Martin 1987; Martin 1988; Martin and Dean 1990; Martin et al. 1989). Data were collected by trained interviewers in face-to-face interviews.

The present analysis used a sample of 741 men who were interviewed in 1987, the first year that internalized homophobia was measured. This sample reflects an attrition of 13 percent from the 851 men recruited in 1985. The respondents were twenty-one to seventy-six years old in 1987, and their mean age was thirty-eight (s.d. = 8.4). They had a mean education of sixteen years (s.d. = 1.7), and their median income was $35,000. Eleven percent were non-white. Men in the sample were strongly connected to the gay community: Most (85 percent) considered themselves to be completely or mostly "out of the closet," most (59 percent) belonged to at least one gay organization, and many (48 percent) read gay newspapers regularly. About half (45 percent) the men were coupled.

It is impossible to assess the degree to which the present sample represents the population of gay men, because this population has not been described or enumerated. The similarity of the sample to two independent samples obtained by random probability sampling in San Francisco (Research and Decision Corporation 1984; Winkelstein, Lyman, and Padian 1987; Martin and Dean 1990) suggests that the samples represent a cohesive group of gay-identified urban gay men who are often referred to as the "gay community." It is important to note, however, that the representativeness of the sample is not a major limitation here, because this investigation does not attempt to describe population parameters. By contrast, because this sample represents a section of gay men who are self-accepting, and who cope with their minority status more effectively than those men whose representation in the sample is lacking, the sample may present a bias for internal validity. This is a bias of the "healthy worker" type (Kelsey, Thompson, and Evans 1986) *against* finding the hypothesized associations between minority stress and mental health.

Measures

Independent Variables   Internalized Homophobia (IHP) is a 9-item scale (alpha = .79) that inquires about the extent to which gay men are uneasy about their homosexuality and seek to avoid homosexual feelings. Items include the following: "How often have you wished you weren't gay?"; "Have you thought that being gay was a personal shortcoming?"; and "How often have you tried to become more sexually attracted to women in general?" Respondents rated the frequency with which they experienced such thoughts in the year before the interview on a 4-point Likert scale ranging from "often" to "never" (Martin and Dean 1987). As expected for this community sample of gay men, the distribution of internalized homophobia was positively skewed, indicating that most men had low scores of internalized homophobia. Nevertheless, about 70 percent reported some self-directed homophobic attitudes.

Stigma is an 11-item scale (alpha = .86) that inquires about expectations of rejection and discrimination regarding homosexuality. The scale was originally designed by Link (1987) to tap expectations of rejection and discrimination with regard to being a psychiatric patient, and was adapted by Martin and Dean (1987). Items include the following: "Most people would willingly accept a gay man as a close friend." "Most people feel that homosexuality is a sign of personal failure," and "Most employers will pass over the application of a gay man in favor of another applicant." Respondents rated their responses on a 6-point Likert scale ranging from "strongly agree" to "strongly disagree." The distribution of stigma was close to normal.

Prejudice is scored 1 for respondents who experienced any event of antigay violence or discrimination or both in the year before the interview. Antigay violence was measured by asking: "In the past year, have you been the victim of antigay violence? That is, was an attempt made to harm you or were you harmed because you were gay?" Antigay (or AIDS-related) discrimination was assessed by asking: "In the past year, have you been discriminated against in any way because of being gay or because of fear of AIDS?" AIDS-related discrimination was included because perpetrators of antigay violence and discrimination often associate being gay with having AIDS. Ninety-one (12 percent) of the men reported at least one event of antigay violence in the year before the interview, and 116 (16 percent) of the men reported at least one event of discrimination related to being gay or to AIDS in that same time period. There was little overlap in the reporting of violence and discrimination events (only 20 men reported both); overall, 187 (25 percent) of the sample reported an event of discrimination or violence (Dean et al. 1992). This combined measure is what is termed *prejudice events*.

Interrelationships of minority stress measures. The associations among the three minority stress measures were weak. Internalized homophobia was somewhat related to stigma ($r = .09$; $p = .01$), but reporting of actual prejudice events was not associated with either internalized homophobia or stigma ($r = -.03, p = .20; r = .05, p = .10$, respectively). These findings support the validity of this objective measure; significant associations with stigma or internalized homophobia would have raised our suspicion of a reporting bias because of subjective expectations of rejection and discrimination. The association between internalized homophobia and stigma suggests some overlap, but there were important divergences in the validation of these scales that indicated that these are indeed different constructs. Internalized homophobia, being directed toward the self, was associated with a wide range of functions of gay men within the gay community and with their partners: Men who had higher levels of internalized homophobia were less likely to be open about their homosexuality, to read gay newspapers, to be members of gay organizations, and to be coupled with a partner. Among coupled men, internalized homophobia was related to less stable relationships. By contrast, stigma, which concerns external nongay sources of homophobia, was associated with the extent to which gay men disclose their homosexuality to others but not with their relationships within the gay community (Meyer 1993).

Dependent Variables   Psychological distress measures referred to distress during the year before the interview. Scales from the Psychiatric Epidemiology Research Instrument (PERI; Dohrenwend et al. 1980) were used. Demoralization is a 27-item scale (alpha = .92) consisting of eight highly intercorrelated subscales that tap dread, anxiety, sadness, helplessness, hopelessness, psychophysiological symptoms, perceived physical health problems, poor self-esteem, and confused thinking. Other PERI distress measures are guilt, a measure of rational or irrational feelings of guilt (4 items, alpha = .79); sex problems, a measure of problems related to inhibited sexual desire, excitement, or orgasm (4 items, alpha = .72); and suicide, a measure of suicidal ideation and behavior or both (4 items, alpha = .52). AIDS-Related Traumatic Stress Response (AIDS-TSR) is a 17-item scale (alpha = .89) that measures symptoms of psychological distress related to the effects of the AIDS epidemic, such as preoccupation, avoidance, nightmares, problems in daily functioning, and panic attacks. Many AIDS-TSR items were adapted from Horowitz's Impact of Events Scale (Horowitz, Wilner, and Alvarez 1979).

Potential Confounding Variables   *Demographic characteristics.* Included were age, ethnicity, education, income, and religious affiliation. "Age" is age in years; "ethnicity" is coded 1 for white men, 0 for non-white men; "edu-

PART VII: MENTAL HEALTH

cation" is a scale of highest grade completed; "income" is a scale of annual income clusters in varying-sized increments ranging from 1 (less than $3,000) to 19 (more than $150,000); "religious" is coded 1 = yes, 0 = not religious, or religious but in a gay church. (Because gay religious groups are distinct from nongay religious groups in their positive attitudes toward homosexuality, men who were religious but who practiced in a gay church or synagogue were grouped together with nonreligious men.)

Gay identity/involvement with the community. Gay identity was measured as the degree to which a man defines himself as in or out of the "closet." "Being in or out of the closet" is an item ranging from 0 (definitely in the closet) to 4 (completely out of the closet). "Involvement in the gay community" was measured as (a) whether men participated in gay groups and organizations (gay organization: 1 = yes, 0 = no); (b) whether men regularly read gay newspapers (read gay: 1 = yes, 0 = no); and (c) the proportion of gay men or lesbians in their social network (gay network).

Intimate relationships. Men were defined as being coupled based on three self-reported criteria: (a) "duration" — relationship lasts at least six months: (b) "reciprocity" — each man sees the other as his partner: and (c) "social recognition" — others consider the men a couple (coupled: 1 = yes, 0 = no).

AIDS status. AIDS-Related Complex (ARC) and AIDS status were reported by respondents who independently tested for HIV or who were diagnosed by a physician after AIDS-related symptoms appeared (ARC/AIDS: 1 = yes. 0 = no).[1]

Statistical Analysis

I begin by assessing the individual effects of each minority stressor on the five psychological distress measures considered in a multivariate test and then on each distress measure in separate multiple regressions. The multivariate procedure differs from ordinary multiple regression in that it provides a test of the effect of the independent variable on several dependent variables considered simultaneously while holding constant potential confounding variables (Bray and Maxwell 1985: Norusis/SPSS 1990:chap. 3). In all analyses, potential confounders are considered and their effect partialed out. Once the associations of each minority stressor are examined, the interactions among the minority stressors, and their combined effect on distress, are assessed. Cases with missing data were excluded listwise within each analysis, leading to variation in the number of cases as indicated in the tables. Data were analyzed using the SPSS statistical package for personal computers.

Results

Minority Stress Effects Tables 29.1–29.3 show results of the regression of each minority stressor on the five psychological distress measures. In each table, the last column presents the multivariate regression of the effect of minority stress on psychological distress. As predicted, these results show that each minority stressor — internalized homophobia (Table 29.1), stigma (Table 29.2), and prejudice events (Table 29.3) — significantly predicts the five psychological distress outcomes when they are considered simultaneously.

The tables also show results of the multiple regression analyses testing the relationship of each minority stressor with each of the five distress measures considered separately. In the tables, for each distress measure, the first column shows standardized betas for the bivariate association of the minority stressor and distress, and the second column shows betas of the multiple regression, with the minority stressor and control variables included in the equation. Table 29.1 shows that the bivariate associations demonstrate a significant association of internalized homophobia with all the distress measures. The multiple regressions confirm these associations for all the distress measures, and show that internalized homophobia retained its association with distress after control for possible confounders. Table 29.2 shows that the bivariate associations demonstrate a significant association of stigma with four of the five distress measures (sex problems were not associated with stigma). The multiple regressions demonstrate that for all the significant bivariate associations, stigma remained a significant predictor when the associations of possible confounders were partialed out. Similarly the bivariate associations of prejudice events and distress (Table 29.3) demonstrate a significant association of prejudice events and four of the distress measures (prejudice events were not related to sex problems), and the multiple regressions demonstrate that for all the significant bivariate associations, prejudice remained a significant predictor when the associations of possible confounders were partialed out.

The findings that stigma and prejudice events were not associated with sex problems were not predicted but are not surprising. It appears that stigma and prejudice — both of which relate to discrimination and rejection by external nongay sources — have little to do with gay men's relations with other gay men, and thus with their sex problems. By contrast, as others (Coleman et al. 1992; Friedman 1991) have suggested, internalized homophobia, which is concerned with internal processes, showed a direct effect on gay men's intimate relations.

In summary, the findings support the hypothesized prediction about the

TABLE 29.1 Distress Measures Predicted by Internalized Homophobia Alone and by Internalized Homophobia and Possible Confounding Variables

Dependent→ Independent Variables	Demoralization		Guilt		Suicide		AIDS-TSR		Sex Problems		All Distress Outcomes Multivariate Test with Confounders†
	IHP Alone	With Confounders	IHP Alone	With Confounders	IHP Alone	With Confounders	IHP Alone	With Confounders	IHP Alone	With Confounders	
N	731	665	737	671	719	655	734	669	736	670	642
R^2	.06	.11	.10	.11	.02	.06	.06	.16	.01	.06	n/a
Internalized Homophobia (IHP)	.25***	.27***	.31***	.31***	.15***	.21***	.24***	.33***	.12**	.16***	21.83***
Age		−.04		−.08*		−.05		−.12***		.13***	5.07***
Ethnicity		.03		.03		.07		.09**		.03	2.46*
Education		−.11**		−.02		−.003		−.08*		.03	2.83**
Income		−.06		.02		−.04		.09*		.04	3.71**

Religious	.01	.04	−.03	−.002	−.04	.89
Closet	.03	−.007	.09*	.11**	.04	3.86**
Gay Organization	.08*	.09*	.07	.11**	−.04	3.08**
Gay Network	.09*	.05	.07	.10**	.06	1.42
Read Gay	.04	−.006	−.02	.04	.02	.34
Coupled	−.02	.05	−.03	.11**	−.05	4.88***
ARC/AIDS	.09*	.009	.06	.10**	.11**	3.57**

*p <.05; **p <.01; ***p <.001; †Approximated F-values.

Notes: The table displays standardized regression coefficients (betas). *Age* is age in years. *Ethnicity* is coded 1 = non-white, 0 = white. *Education* is a scale of highest grade completed. *Income* is a scale of annual income clusters in varying increments ranging from 1 (less than $3,000) to 19 (more than $150,000). *Religious* is coded 1 = yes, 0 = not religious or religious but in a gay church. *Closet* is a 5-point scale ranging from 0 (definitely in the closet) to 4 (completely out of the closet). *Gay organization* is coded 1 = members in gay organizations, 0 = nonmembers. *Gay network* is the percentage of gay persons in the respondent's support network. *Read gay* is coded 1 = men who read gay newspapers regularly, 0 = those who do not. *Coupled* is coded 1 = coupled men, 0 = single men. ARC/ AIDS is coded 1 = men who were diagnosed with ARC or AIDS, 0 = men who were not.

TABLE 29.2 Distress Measures Predicted by Stigma Alone and by Stigma and Possible Confounding Variables

Dependent→ Independent Variables	Demoralization		Guilt		Suicide		AIDS-TSR		Sex Problems		All Distress Outcomes Multivariate Test with Confounders[†]
	Stigma Alone	With Confounders	Stigma Alone	With Confounders	Stigma Alone	With Confounders	Stigma Alone	With Confounders	Stigma Alone	With Confounders	
N	726	662	732	668	715	652	730	667	731	667	640
R^2	.03	.08	.02	.05	.01	.04	.02	.09	.00	.05	n/a
Stigma	.18***	.17***	.15***	.13***	.10**	.11**	.15***	.17***	.07	.07	4.91***
Age		−.06		−.11**		−.07		−.15***		.11**	6.15***
Ethnicity		.02		.02		.07		.08*		.03	1.85
Education		−.13***		−.04		−.02		−.10**		.02	3.21**
Income		−.04		.03		−.03		.10**		.04	3.68**

Religious	.05	.07	-.01	.03	-.02	1.05
Closet	-.04	-.10**	.03	.02	-.008	2.81*
Gay Organization	.05	.06	.05	.08*	-.05	1.90
Gay Network	.06	.03	.05	.07	.05	.72
Read Gay	.004	-.05	-.04	-.005	.007	.49
Coupled	-.04	.02	-.05	.08*	-.06	4.22***
ARC/AIDS	.09*	.01	.06	.10**	.11**	3.48**

*p < .05; **p < .01; ***p < .001; †Approximated F-values.

Notes: The table displays standardized regression coefficients (betas). *Age* is age in years. *Ethnicity* is coded 1 = non-white, 0 = white. *Education* is a scale of highest grade completed. *Income* is a scale of annual income clusters in varying increments ranging from 1 (less than $3,000) to 19 (more than $150,000). *Religious* is coded 1 = yes, 0 = not religious or religious but in a gay church. *Closet* is a 5-point scale ranging from 0 (definitely in the closet) to 4 (completely out of the closet). *Gay organization* is coded 1 = members in gay organizations, 0 = nonmembers. *Gay network* is the percentage of gay persons in the respondent's support network. *Read gay* is coded 1 = men who read gay newspapers regularly, 0 = those who do not. *Coupled* is coded 1 = coupled men, 0 = single men. ARC/AIDS is coded 1 = men who were diagnosed with ARC or AIDS, 0 = men who were not.

TABLE 29.3 Distress Measures Predicted by Prejudice and Possible Confounding Variables

Dependent→ Independent Variables	Demoralization		Guilt		Suicide		AIDS-TSR		Sex Problems		All Distress Outcomes Multivariate Test with Confounders[t]
	Prejudice Alone	With Confounders	Prejudice Alone	With Confounders	Prejudice Alone	With Confounders	Prejudice Alone	With Confounders	Prejudice Alone	With Confounders	
N	731	665	737	671	720	655	734	669	736	670	642
R^2	.03	.08	.01	.05	.01	.04	.03	.09	.00	.05	n/a
Prejudice	.16***	.19***	.07*	.11**	.12**	.11**	.17***	.17***	.04	.06	4.47***
Age		−.03		−.09*		−.05		−.13***		.12**	5.31***
Ethnicity		.03		.03		.07		.09**		.03	2.19*
Education		−.13**		−.03		−.01		−.09*		.02	3.05**
Income		−.05		.02		−.03		.09*		.04	3.51**

Religious	.05	.07	−.01	.03	−.02	1.09
Closet	−.10**	−.13***	−.002	−.03	−.02	3.19**
Gay Organization	.04	.05	.04	.06	−.06	1.65
Gay Network	.08*	.04	.06	.08*	.05	1.02
Read Gay	.01	−.04	−.04	.006	.009	.39
Coupled	−.05	.01	−.05	.07*	−.06	4.04***
ARC/AIDS	.06	−.006	.05	.07*	.10**	2.58*

p < .05; ** *p* < .01; *** *p* < .001; †Approximated F-values.

Notes: The table displays standardized regression coefficients (betas). *Age* is age in years. *Ethnicity* is coded 1 = non-White, 0 = White. *Education* is a scale of highest grade completed. *Income* is a scale of annual income clusters in varying increments ranging from 1 (less than $3,000) to 19 (more than $150,000). *Religious* is coded 1 = yes, 0 = not religious or religious but in a gay church. *Closet* is a 5-point scale ranging from 0 (definitely in the closet) to 4 (completely out of the closet). *Gay organization* is coded 1 = members in gay organizations, 0 = nonmembers. *Gay network* is the percentage of gay persons in the respondent's support network. *Read gay* is coded 1 = men who read gay newspapers regularly, 0 = those who do not. *Coupled* is coded 1 = coupled men, 0 = single men. *ARC/AIDS* is coded 1 = men who were diagnosed with ARC or AIDS, 0 = men who were not.

association of internalized homophobia, stigma, and prejudice events on distress and do not support the alternative hypothesis — that the effect of these stressors is indirect, through reduction of participation in and identification with the gay community.

The Combined Effect of Minority Stress   To test the combined effect of minority stress, the three minority stressors were added to regression models together. A multivariate regression of the combined effect of minority stress predicting psychological distress showed that each of the three stressors has an independent association with the five psychological distress outcomes considered simultaneously (internalized homophobia: Pillai's value = .1424, approx. F = 20.62, p = .001; stigma: Pillai's value = .0271, approx. F = 3.46, p = .004; prejudice: Pillai's value = .0311, approx. F = 3.99, p = .001).

Table 29.4 shows the combined effect of the three minority stressors on the five psychological distress measures considered individually. The table shows associations (betas), significance levels, and R^2 for four models: In Column 1, the effect of internalized homophobia alone was entered; in Column 2, the effect of stigma was added; in Column 3, the effect of prejudice events was added; and in Column 4, this combined effect was controlled by the confounding variables. Results show that, with the exception of sex problems, each of the minority stress measures had a significant independent association with distress, as indicated by the significant betas in each of the models and by the increase in explained variance with the addition to the model of each minority stress measure. The effects of minority stress on sex problems was mixed. While internalized homophobia consistently showed significant associations with sex problems, neither stigma nor prejudice showed a main effect for sex problems (Tables 29.2 and 29.3), and therefore did not add to the combined effect of minority stress in this analysis.

The results so far suggest a significant effect for minority stress on psychological distress. Judging from the R^2 reported, the contribution of minority stress is moderate. This would be expected, considering the myriad of additional factors — both endogenous and exogenous — that affect psychological distress. It should be noted that, at least with respect to demoralization, guilt, and AIDS-TSR, the effect size is comparable to, or larger than, the effect size typically detected for stressful life events (Rabkin and Struening 1976). To provide an additional assessment of the importance of the effect of minority stress, I also estimated the relative risk for distress of men with high, compared to low, levels of minority stress by calculating the odds ratio (Kelsey et al. 1986). Men who had experienced any discrimination

TABLE 29.4 Regression Models Including Internalized Homophobia, Stigma, and Prejudice, and Control Variables[a]

Model[†]→	1	2	3	4
Dependent Variables				
Demoralization				
IHP	.25***	.24***	.25***	.25***
Stigma		.16***	.15***	.14***
Prejudice			.16***	.17***
R^2	.06	.09	.12	.15
Guilt				
IHP	.31***	.30***	.30***	.30***
Stigma		.13***	.12***	.10**
Prejudice			.08*	.09*
R^2	.10	.11	.12	.13
Suicide				
IHP	.15***	.15***	.15***	.20***
Stigma		.09*	.08*	.09*
Prejudice			.12***	.10**
R^2	.02	.03	.05	.08
AIDS-TSR				
IHP	.24***	.23***	.24***	.31***
Stigma		.12***	.11***	.13***
Prejudice			.18***	.15***
R^2	.06	.07	.11	.20
Sex Problems				
IHP	.12**	.11**	.11**	.15***
Stigma		.06	.05	.05
Prejudice			.05	.05
R^2	.01	.02	.02	.07

*p <.05; **p <.01; ***p <.001; †Model 1 = IHP Alone; Model 2 = IHP and Stigma; Model 3 = IHP, Stigma, and Prejudice; Model 4 = IHP, Stigma, Prejudice, and Control Variables.
[a]Betas, significance level, and R^2.

or violence events, or who scored above the mean of either internalized homophobia or stigma, were classified as having high minority stress. Men who had experienced no discrimination or violence events, and who scored below the mean of both internalized homophobia and stigma, were classified as having low minority stress. Most men (N = 553, 75 percent) were classified as scoring high on this combined minority stress measure. The relative risk for high distress of those high in minority stress was then estimated. High levels of distress were defined in two ways: (1) "high distress," representing distress scores above the sample's mean; and (2) "very high distress," representing distress scores above one standard deviation above the mean. Using these definitions, two odds ratios were calculated for each of the five distress measures (Table 29.5). Minority stress was associated with high levels of distress by both definitions (with the exception of sex problems in the "very high distress" definition). Overall, men who reported high minority stress were two to three times more likely to have reported "high" and "very high" levels of distress than their counterparts, suggesting that minority stress is associated with a two- to threefold increase in risk for high levels of psychological distress.

Interactions Among Minority Stressors   In addition to assessing the additive effect of the three minority stress measures on distress, I assessed their interactive effects. I suggested earlier that self-blame attributions — indicated by high levels of internalized homophobia — would exacerbate the effects of expectations of stigma and actual prejudice events on psychological distress.

TABLE 29.5 Risk for High and Very High Distress Levels Associated with Minority Stress Odds Ratios (and 95% Confidence Intervals) Estimates

Definition of Distress →	1 High Distress $>\bar{X}$	2 Very High Distress $>\bar{X} + 1SD$
Distress Measure		
Demoralization	2.00 (1.41, 2.84)	1.98 (1.19, 3.28)
Guilt	3.08 (2.11, 4.51)	2.61 (1.43, 4.73)
Suicide	1.77 (1.15, 2.72)	2.12 (1.08, 4.18)
AIDS-TSR	2.53 (1.77, 3.61)	3.02 (1.67, 5.47)
Sex Problems	1.44 (1.03, 2.03)	1.71 (.93, 3.04)

This was tested by introducing the interaction terms of *internalized homo-phobia by stigma* and *internalized homophobia by prejudice* to regression equations testing the effect of stigma and prejudice, respectively, on distress. It was predicted that high stigma or prejudice along with high internalized homophobia will be more damaging than high stigma or prejudice with low internalized homophobia. This is because self-blame attributions are impli-cated in the former case, where men seem to justify their victimization (or expected victimization) — literally, "adding insult to injury."

Internalized homophobia interactions were significant in three of the ten regression models (Table 29.6). The multivariate analysis of internalized homophobia by stigma interaction was not significant (Pillai's value = .0120, approx. F = 1.51, p = .18), indicating that, overall, internalized homophobia does not modify the effect of stigma on psychological distress. The multivariate analysis of internalized homophobia by prejudice inter-action was significant (Pillai's value = .0212, approx. F = 2.69, p = .02). The significant individual interactions were those predicting demoralization and guilt, and there was a trend toward predicting suicide (Table 29.6). These interactions were consistent with the self-blame attributions hypoth-esis. They suggest that experiencing events of discrimination or violence is more painful when one agrees with the homophobic attitudes conveyed by the victimization event. By stigmatizing their own condition, it seems, such gay men "join their aggressors" and suffer further pain — feeling more guilty and more demoralized.

Discussion and Conclusions

I set out to study the effect of minority stress on the mental health of gay men by specifying and testing explicit minority stress processes. As predicted, the results indicated that internalized homophobia, expectations of rejection and discrimination (stigma), and actual events of discrimination and vio-lence (prejudice) — considered independently and as a group — predict psy-chological distress in gay men. Relative risk estimates suggested that minority stress is associated with a two- to threefold increase in risk for high levels of distress — clearly a substantial risk. Furthermore, I ruled out an alternative hypothesis that minority stressors affect distress by diminishing affiliations in the gay community, thus supporting the hypothesized direct effect for mi-nority stress.

Nevertheless, this cross-sectional analysis limits our ability to test the

TABLE 29.6 Regression Analyses Predicting Psychological Distress Interactions of IHP by Stigma and IHP by Prejudice[a]

Interaction Term→	IHP × Stigma			IHP × Prejudice		
Dependent:	N	Beta	p	N	Beta	p
Demoralization	662	–.20	.38	665	.28	.02
Guilt	668	–.49	.04	671	.27	.02
Suicide	652	.23	.34	655	.21	.09
AIDS-TSR	667	–.21	.36	669	–.06	.59
Sex Problems	667	–.38	.11	670	.14	.25

[a]In fully controlled models.

postulated causal role of minority stress. A plausible alternative explanation is that the causal relationships are reversed: that psychological distress increases internalized homophobia, perceptions of stigma, and reports of prejudice events (McCrae 1990; Watson and Pennebaker 1989). The multi-operationalism of minority stress and distress, however, allows detection of divergences and convergences in the results that help interpret causal relationships (Cook and Campbell 1979). Reversed causality arguments are more convincing regarding some findings than others. For example, it may be argued that demoralization increases the experience of minority stress, but it is less convincing that the domain-specific measures (e.g., suicidal ideation and behavior, or sex problems) cause minority stress. Similarly it is plausible that internalized homophobia is caused by distress, but this is a less convincing explanation for stigma, and hardly a viable explanation for objective reports of prejudice events (cf. Watson and Pennebaker 1989). This is especially illuminating when we consider that there were no associations between reports of prejudice events and internalized homophobia or stigma, and only a weak association between internalized homophobia and stigma. If minority stressors were indeed caused by distress, a significant association among them would have been inevitable because of the underlying common cause. While it is plausible that different causal relationships explain different parts of the results, the interpretation that minority stress is the causal agent leading to distress allows a more parsimonious explanation and is therefore more compelling (cf. Link 1987).

These findings contrast with previous evidence compiled on minority stress. When studies compared rates of disorder or distress between minority and nonminority groups, we found little evidence that minority stress is related to adverse mental health. Now that we have looked at specific, theoretically driven, minority stress processes, we do find an adverse role for minority stress processes in the mental health of gay men. Although the minority stress processes described here are specific to gay men, they are clearly applicable to other minorities as well. Further studies need to explicate minority stress processes and describe their relationship to distress in other minority groups. Certainly the issue of rates of disorder and distress cannot be sidestepped and will also have to be addressed. But if the present findings are convincing, we must address the question of rate differences with this evidence in mind. The issue thus becomes one of explaining why there are no differences in rates of disorder between minority and nonminority populations and how such findings could be consistent with the evidence that noxious social conditions do, in fact, have adverse mental health effects.

One clear path for reconciling the evidence, which most researchers who address the issue have suggested, may be termed *minority coping*. Researchers have proposed that, by actively coping with stigmatization, some — perhaps most — minority group members are protected from the ill effects of minority stress (Allport 1954; Garnets et al. 1990; Kessler et al. 1985; Neighbors 1984; Shade 1990; Weinberg and Williams 1974). In fact, this argument is implicit in the rationale of the present investigation, which presumes ingroup variation in the experience and effect of minority stressors. Minority coping may work in a variety of ways: by providing opportunities for social support, by affirming and validating minority persons' culture and values, and by allowing reappraisal and devaluation of the stigmatizing values of the dominant culture (Crocker and Major 1989; Garnets and Kimmel 1991; Jones et al. 1984; Shade 1990; Smith and Siegel 1985; Thoits 1985). Conceptually it is important to remember that minority coping must be considered at the group — rather than the individual — level. Individuals may differ in the degree to which they mobilize minority coping, but the coping options available to them are predetermined at the community level. Preliminary work suggests that even a generalized sense of connectedness to the gay community may prove an important factor in ameliorating and buffering minority stress in gay men (Meyer 1993). Further work on minority coping needs to specify mechanisms that alleviate minority stress and to develop appropriate measures. In addition, the present study demonstrates intragroup variation in minority stress but does not explain what accounts for the ability of many gay people to accept themselves and thrive in the face of societal oppression. Once the role of minority stress on mental health has been demonstrated, our attention must turn to studying environmental and personal factors that account for such variability.

This study also helps to shed some light on the association of minority status and socioeconomic status, and their effect on distress. It has been argued that minority status is related to adverse mental health effects, not because of the oppressive social environment of the minority person but because of economic disadvantages to which ethnic minority persons are typically subjected. This argument, articulated by Mirowsky and Ross (1980, 1989) among others (cf. Kessler and Neighbors 1986), states that it is economic inequality, rather than prejudice and discrimination, that is at the root of minority stress. But this argument defies a host of theoretical formulations (discussed earlier) that quite clearly specify an oppressive stigmatizing environment at the source of minority stress. The findings presented here suggest that a strong minority stress effect may be detected even in a sample of socioeconomically advantaged men.

Throughout the paper I have discussed the issue of minority stress as it applies to gay men. Similar minority stress processes likely play an important role in the mental health of lesbians as well (cf. Brooks 1981; de Monteflores and Schultz 1978; Sophie 1987). Nevertheless, generalizations from gay men to lesbians should be made with caution. This is primarily because lesbians are subjected to social stress and oppression related to both the homosexual and the gender aspects of their identity (Brooks 1981). The issue of dual stigmatizing identities also applies to gay men and lesbians of ethnic minorities (Garnets and Kimmel 1991). Further research is necessary to explore the effects of such multiple stigmatizations. In addition, it is necessary to assess the role of minority stress within the context of other stressors. General life events, role-related stress, and gay-specific stressors interact as individuals occupy increasingly complex roles in society (cf. Pearlin 1989).

Stress research organizes our understanding of the individual and society, and points to pathogenic factors (Young 1980). The minority stress perspective, which views social conditions as the source of morbidity and distress for minority persons, advances an ideological agenda that promotes social change toward a more egalitarian society. It is necessary to identify such socially induced stressful conditions because "the eventual control of disease caused by stress depends on understanding the social etiology of the stress" (Pearlin 1982:368). But there is great resistance to identifying socially induced sources of stress (Adams 1990) because of public policy implications that "often encounter the angry resistance of the power forces that get real benefit from the values being criticized" (Albee 1982:1046). From a public policy perspective, cumulative evidence of the negative effects of prejudice and discrimination may help mobilize social forces to abolish oppressive policies. Indeed, the argument that psychological disabilities result from racial prejudice and discrimination played an important part in the evidence presented to the U.S. Supreme Court preceding the 1954 school segregation decision (McCarthy and Yancey 1971). Identifying the stressful conditions that are related to antigay attitudes highlights the need for gay-affirmative programs in dealing with psychological distress in lesbians and gay men, and for public education and legislation in preventing antigay violence and discrimination (Berrill and Herek 1992). Further research on minority stress must address these public policy and public health recommendations as well as barriers to their implementation.

Acknowledgments

The author acknowledges the invaluable contribution of the late John L. Martin, who was the principal investigator of the study used in this paper, and whose vision and insight made this investigation possible. The author also thanks Bruce G. Link, Sharon Schwartz, Suzanne C. Ouellette, Mary Clare Lennon, Eugene Litwak, and Laura Dean.

Notes

1. The now obsolete diagnosis of ARC was used in 1987 in the presence of immunodeficiency symptoms (e.g., lymphadenopathy) but before the emergence of any of the diseases that qualified for diagnosis of full-blown AIDS. ARC/ AIDS status is included because of the importance of ARC or AIDS diagnosis and its plausible effects on distress. By 1987, when the data were collected, 249 of the men had been independently tested for HIV and 75 of them were HIV-positive; 43 men of the total sample were diagnosed with ARC or AIDS. ARC/ AIDS status, rather than HIV status, was used in the analyses because it more strongly predicted relevant variables than did HIV status, thus representing a stronger potential confounder.

References

Adams, P. L. 1990. Prejudice and exclusion as social traumata. In J. D. Noshpitz and R. D. Coddington, eds., *Stressors and the Adjustment Disorders*, pp. 362–93. New York: Wiley.

Albee, G. W. 1982. Preventing psychopathology and promoting human potential. *American Psychologist* 37:1043–50.

Allport. G. W. 1954. *The Nature of Prejudice*. Reading, Mass.: Addison-Wesley.

American Psychological Association. 1986. APA testimony on violence against lesbians and gay men. Statement of Gregory Herek before the United States House of Representatives, Committee on the Judiciary, Subcommittee on Criminal Justice.

Bell, A. P., and M. S. Weinberg. 1978. *Homosexualities: A Study of Diversity Among Men and Women*. New York: The Free Press.

Berrill, K. T., and G. M. Herek. 1992. Primary and secondary victimization in anti-gay hate crimes: Official response and public policy. In G. M. Herek and K. T. Berrill, eds., *Hate Crimes: Confronting Violence Against Lesbians and Gay Men*, pp. 289–305. Newbury Park, Calif.: Sage.

Bray, J. H., and S. E. Maxwell. 1985. *Multivariate Analysis of Variance*. Newbury Park, Calif.: Sage.

Brewin, C. R. 1985. Depression and causal attributions: What is their relation? *Psychological Bulletin* 98:297–309.

Brooks, V. R. 1981. *Minority Stress and Lesbian Women*. Lexington, Mass.: Heath.

Cass, V. C. 1984. Homosexual identity formation: Testing a theoretical model. *The Journal of Sex Research* 20:143–67.

Cohen, S. G. W. Evans, D. Stokols, and D. S. Krantz. 1986. *Behavior. Health, and Environmental Stress*. New York: Plenum.

Coleman, E., R. Brian, S. Rosser, and N. Strapko. 1992. Sexual and intimacy dysfunction among homosexual men and women. *Psychiatric Medicine* 10(2/3):257–71.

Coleman, E. 1982. Developmental stages of the coming out process. *Journal of Homosexuality* 7(2/3):31–43.

Cook, T. D., and D. T. Campbell. 1979. *Quasi-Experimentation: Design and Analysis Issues for Field Settings*. Boston, Mass.: Houghton Mifflin.

Crocker, J., and B. Major. 1989. Social stigma and self-esteem: The self-protective properties of stigma. *Psychological Bulletin* 96:608–30.

Dean, L., S. Wu, and J. L. Martin. 1992. Trends in violence and discrimination against gay men in New York City: 1984–1990. In G. M. Herek and K. T. Berrill, eds., *Hate Crimes: Confronting Violence Against Lesbians and Gay Men*, pp. 46–64. Newbury Park, Calif.: Sage.

Dohrenwend, B. P. 1976. Sex differences and psychiatric disorders. *American Journal of Sociology* 81:1447–54.

Dohrenwend, B. P., P. E. Shrout, G. Egri, and F. S. Mendelsohn. 1980. Nonspecific psychological distress and other dimensions of psychopathology: Measures for use in the general population. *Archives of General Psychiatry* 37:1229–36.

Dohrenwend, B. P., and B. S. Dohrenwend. 1969. *Social Status and Psychological Disorder: A Causal Inquiry*. New York: Wiley.

Dohrenwend, B. P., I. Levav, P. E. Shrout, S. Schwartz. Guedalia Naveh, Bruce Link, Andrew E. Skodol, and Anne Stueve. 1992. Socioeconomic status and psychiatric disorders: The causation-selection issue. *Science* 255:946–52.

Durkheim, E. 1951. *Suicide: A Study in Sociology*. New York: The Free Press.

Friedman, R. C. 1991. Couple therapy with gay couples. *Psychiatric Annals* 21:485–90.

Garnets, L., and D. Kimmel. 1991. Lesbian and gay male dimensions in the psychological study of human diversity. In J. D. Goodchilds, ed., *Psychological Perspectives on Human Diversity in America*, pp. 143–92. Washington, D.C.: American Psychological Association.

Garnets, L., G. M. Herek, and B. Levy. 1990. Violence and victimization of lesbians and gay men: Mental health consequences. *Journal of Interpersonal Violence* 5:366–83.

Goffman, E. 1963. *Stigma: Notes on the Management of Spoiled Identity*. Englewood Cliffs, N.J.: Prentice-Hall.

Gonsiorek, J. C. 1988. Mental health issues of gay and lesbian adolescents. *Journal of Adolescent Health Care* 9:114–22.

Gonsiorek, J. C. 1991. The empirical basis for the demise of the illness model of homosexuality. In J. C. Gonsiorek and J. D. Weinrich, eds., *Homosexuality: Research Implications for Public Policy*, pp. 115–36. Newbury Park, Calif.: Sage.

Hart, M., H. Roback, B. Tittler, L. Weitz, B. Walston, and E. McKee. 1978. Psychological adjustment of nonpatient homosexuals: Critical review of the research literature. *The Journal of Clinical Psychiatry* 39:604–8.

Herek, G. M., and K. T. Berrill. 1992. *Hate Crimes: Confronting Violence Against Lesbian and Gay Men.* Newbury Park, Calif.: Sage.

Herek, G. M., and E. K. Glunt. 1988. An epidemic of stigma: Public reactions to AIDS. *American Psychologist* 43:886–91.

Hetrick, E. S., and A.D. Martin. 1984. Ego-dystonic homosexuality: A developmental view. In E. S. Hetrick and T. S. Stein, eds., *Innovations in Psychotherapy with Homosexuals*, pp. 2–21. Washington D.C.: American Psychiatric Association Press.

Hetrick, E. S., and A.D. Martin. 1987. Developmental issues and their resolution for gay and lesbian adolescents. *Journal of Homosexuality* 14(1/2):25–43.

Hirschfeld, R.M.A., and C. K. Cross. 1983. Psychosocial risk factors for depression. Pp. 55–67 In National Institute of Mental Health, ed., *Risk Factors Research in the Major Mental Disorders*, pp. 55–67. Rockville, Md.: Department of Health and Human Services Publications.

Horowitz, M. J., N. Wilner, and W. Alvarez. 1979. Impact of event scale: A study of subjective stress. *Psychosomatic Medicine* 41:209–18.

Jones, E. E., A. Farina, A. H. Hestrof, H. Markus, D. T. Miller, and R. A. Scott. 1984. *Social Stigma: The Psychology of Marked Relationships.* New York: Freeman.

Joseph, H. 1986. Sampling gay men. *Journal of Sex Research* 22:21–34.

Kelsey, J. L., W. D. Thompson, and A. S. Evans. 1986. *Methods in Observational Epidemiology.* New York: Oxford University Press.

Kessler, R. C., R. H. Price, and C. B. Wortman. 1985. Social factors in psychopathology: Stress, social support, and coping processes. *Annual Review of Psychology* 36:531–72.

Kessler, R. C., and H. W. Neighbors. 1986. A new perspective on the relationship among race, social class, and psychological distress. *Journal of Health and Social Behavior* 27:107–15.

Lazarus. R. S., and S. Folkman. 1984. *Stress, Appraisal, and Coping.* New York: Springer.

Lemert, E. M. 1967. *Human Deviance, Social Problems, and Social Control.* Englewood Cliffs, N.J.: Prentice-Hall.

Link, B. G. 1987. Understanding labeling effects in the area of mental disorders: An assessment of the effects of expectations of rejection. *American Sociological Review* 52:96–112.

Link, B. G., and F. Cullen. 1990. The labeling theory of mental disorders: A review of the evidence. In J. Greenley, ed., *Mental Illness in Social Context*, pp. 75–105. Greenwich, Conn.: JAI Press.

Link, B. G., F. T. Cullen, J. Frank, and J. F. Wozniak. 1987. The social rejection of former mental patients: Understanding why labels matter. *American Journal of Sociology* 92:1461–1500.

Malyon, A. K. 1982. Psychotherapeutic implications of internalized homophobia in gay men. *Journal of Homosexuality* 7(2/3):59–69.

Marmor, J. 1980. Epilogue: Homosexuality and the issue of mental illness. In J. Marmor, ed., *Homosexual Behavior: A Modern Reappraisal*, pp. 391–401. New York: Basic Books.

Martin, J. L. 1987. The impact of AIDS on gay male sexual behavior patterns in New York City. *American Journal of Public Health* 77:578–81.

Martin, J. L. 1988. Psychological consequences of AIDS-related bereavement among gay men. *Journal of Consulting and Clinical Psychology* 56:856–62.

Martin, J. L. 1990. Drinking patterns and drinking problems in a community sample of gay men. In D. Seminara and A. Pawlowski, eds., *Alcohol, Immunomodulation, and AIDS*, pp. 33–47. Washington, D.C.: National Academy Press.

Martin, J. L. 1990. "Developing a Community Sample of Gay Men for an Epidemiologic Study of AIDS." *American Behavioral Scientist* 33:546–61.

Martin, J. L., and L. Dean. 1987. Summary of measures: Mental health effects of AIDS on at-risk homosexual men. Unpublished manuscript. Division of Sociomedical Sciences, Columbia University, School of Public Health.

Martin, J. L., L. Dean, M. A. Garcia, and W. E. Hall. 1989. The impact of AIDS on a gay community: Changes in sexual behavior, substance use, and mental health. *American Journal of Community Psychology* 17:269–93.

McCarthy, J. D., and W. L. Yancey. 1971. Uncle Tom and Mr. Charlie: Metaphysical pathos in the study of racism and personal disorganization. *American Journal of Sociology* 76:648–72.

McCrae, R. R. 1990. Controlling neuroticism in the measurement of stress. *Stress Medicine* 6:237–41.

Merton, R. K. [1957] 1968. *Social Theory and Social Structure*. New York: The Free Press.

Meyer, I. H. 1993. Prejudice and pride: Minority stress and mental health in gay men. Ph.D. dissertation, Division of Sociomedical Sciences, School of Public Health, Columbia University, New York.

Miller, B. J. 1992. From silence to suicide: Measuring a mother's loss. In W. J. Blumenfeld, ed., *Homophobia: How We All Pay the Price*, pp. 79–94. Boston, Mass.: Beacon.

Mirowsky, J., and C. E. Ross. 1980. Minority status, ethnic culture, and distress: A comparison of blacks, whites, Mexicans, and Mexican Americans. *American Journal of Sociology* 86:479–95.

Mirowsky, J., and C. E. Ross. 1989. *Social Causes of Psychological Distress*. Hawthorne, N.Y.: Aldine de Gruyter.

de Monteflores, C., and S. J. Schultz. 1978. Coming out: Similarities and differences for lesbians and gay men. *Journal of Social Issues* 34:59–72.

Moss, G. E. 1973. *Illness, Immunity, and Social Interaction*. New York: Wiley.

National Gay and Lesbian Task Force. 1991. *Anti-Gay/Lesbian Violence, Victimization, and Defamation in 1990*. Washington, D.C.: NGLTF Policy Institute.

Neighbors, H. W. 1984. The distribution of psychiatric morbidity in black Americans: A review and suggestions for research. *Community Mental Health Journal* 20:169–81.

Norusis, M. J. 1990. *SPSS Advanced Statistics User's Guide*. Chicago, Ill.: SPSS.

Nungesser, L. G. 1983. *Homosexual Acts, Actors, and Identities*. New York: Praeger.

Pearlin, L. I. 1982. The social context of stress. In L. Goldberger and S. Breznitz, eds., *Handbook of Stress: Theoretical and Clinical Aspects*, pp. 367–79. New York: Academic Press.

Pearlin, L. I. 1989. The sociological study of stress. *Journal of Health and Social Behavior* 30:241–56.

Perry, H. S., M. L. Gawel, and M. Gibbon. 1956. *Clinical Studies in Psychiatry*. New York: Norton.

Pettigrew, T. F. 1967. Social evaluation theory: Convergences and applications. *Nebraska Symposium on Motivation*, 241–304.

Pillard, R. C. 1988. Sexual orientation and mental disorder. *Psychiatric Annals* 18:52–56.

Rabkin, J. G., and E. L. Struening. 1976. Life events, stress, and illness. *Science* 194:1013–20.

Reiss, B. F. 1980. Psychological tests in homosexuality. In J. Marmor, ed., *Homosexual Behavior: A Modern Reappraisal*, pp. 296–311. New York: Basic Books.

Research and Decision Corporation. 1984. *Designing an Effective AIDS Prevention Campaign Strategy for San Francisco*. Report for the San Francisco AIDS Foundation.

Robins, L. N., and D. A. Regier. 1991. *Psychiatric Disorders in America: The Epidemiologic Catchment Area Study*. New York: The Free Press.

Rosenberg, M. 1979. *Conceiving the Self*. New York: Basic Books.

Saghir, M. T., and E. Robins. 1973. *Male and Female Homosexuality: A Comprehensive Investigation*. Baltimore, Md.: Williams and Wilkins.

Schur, E. 1971. *Labeling Deviant Behavior: Its Sociological Implications*. New York: Harper and Row.

Schwartz, S. 1991. Women and depression: A Durkheimian perspective. *Social Science and Medicine* 32:127–40.

Shade, B. J. 1990. Coping with color: The anatomy of positive mental health. In D. S. Ruiz, ed., *Handbook of Mental Health and Mental Disorder Among Black Americans*, pp. 273–89. New York: Greenwood.

Smith, A. J., and R. F. Siegel. 1985. Feminist therapy: Redefining power for the powerless. In L. R. Rosewater and L.E.A. Walker, eds., *Handbook of Feminist Therapy: Women's Issues in Psychotherapy*, pp. 13–21. New York: Springer.

Sophie, J. 1987. Internalized homophobia and lesbian identity. *Journal of Homosexuality* 14(1/2):53–65.

Sowa, C. J., and P. J. Lustman. 1984. Gender differences in rating stressful events, depression, and depressive cognition. *Journal of Clinical Psychology* 40: 1334–37.

Stein, T. S., and C. J. Cohen. 1984. Psychotherapy with gay men and lesbians: An examination of homophobia, coming out, and identity. In E. S. Hetrick and T. S. Stein, eds., *Innovations in Psychotherapy with Homosexuals*, pp. 59–73. Washington, D.C.: American Psychiatric Association Press.

Stryker, S., and A. Statham. 1985. Symbolic interaction and role theory. In G. Lindzey and E. Aronson, eds., *Handbook of Social Psychology*, pp. 311–78. New York: Random House.

Thoits, P. A. 1985. Self-labeling processes in mental illness: The role of emotional deviance. *American Journal of Sociology* 91:221–49.

Thomas, A., and S. Sillen. [1972] 1991. *Racism and Psychiatry*. New York: Citadel.

Troiden, R. R. 1989. The formation of homosexual identities. *Journal of Homosexuality* 17(1/2):43–73.

Tross, S., D. Hirsch, B. Rabkin, C. Berry, and J.C.B. Holland. 1987. Determinants of current psychiatric disorders in AIDS spectrum patients. In *Programs and Abstracts of the Third International Conference on AIDS*, p. 60. Washington, D.C., June 1–5.

Warheit, G., C. E. Holzer, and S. S. Arey. 1975. Race and mental illness: An epidemiological update. *Journal of Health and Social Behavior* 16:243–56.

Warren, C. 1980. Homosexuality and stigma. In J. Marmor, ed., *Homosexual Behavior: A Modern Appraisal*, pp. 123–41. New York: Basic Books.

Watson, D., and J. W. Pennebaker. 1989. Health complaints, stress, and distress: Exploring the central role of negative affectivity. *Psychological Review* 96: 234–54.

Weinberg, M. S., and C. Williams. 1974. *Male Homosexuals: Their Problems and Adaptations*. New York: Oxford University Press.

Williams, D. H. 1986. The epidemiology of mental illness in Afro-Americans. *Hospital and Community Psychiatry* 37:42–49.

Williams, J., J. Rabkin, R. Remien, J. M. Gorman, and A. A. Ehrhardt. 1991. Multidisciplinary baseline assessment of homosexual men with and without Human Immunodeficiency Virus Infection. II: Standardized clinical assessment of current and life-time psychopathology. *Archives of General Psychiatry* 48:124–30.

Wilson, J. D. 1992. Gays under fire. *Newsweek*. September 14, pp. 35–40.

Winkelstein, W., Jr., D. M. Lyman, and N. S. Padian. 1987. Sexual practices and risk of infection by the AIDS-associated retrovirus: The San Francisco Men's Health Study. *Journal of the American Medical Association* 257:321–25.

Young, A. 1980. The discourse of stress and the reproduction of conventional knowledge. *Social Science and Medicine* 14:133–46.

Part VIII

Status of Research, Practice, and Public Policy Issues in American Psychology

What is the appropriate response to the rage one feels about violence based on sexual orientation, blatant discrimination, deep-seated prejudices that are unfair, unjust, and unfounded, to the sexual prejudice and heterosexism that is endemic in our society?

Too often the response has been for lesbians, bisexuals, and gay men to internalize the stigma, rage, and despair. For much of modern Western history, same-gender sexual and affectional orientation has been an individual condition, variously labeled as a sin, sickness, or mental illness. With the beginning of the contemporary gay movement in 1969, a paradigm shift occurred that has altered homosexuality from an individual condition to an identity. The quotation from Harry Hay says it well:

> When I was putting together, back in 1948 to 1950, what would become the FIRST Mattachine Society, there wasn't as yet in the minds of my fellow Queers, let alone the American society at large, even the beginnings of such a concept as that of a GAY IDENTITY. Everywhere we were constantly being told . . . that we were heteros who occasionally performed nasty acts. . . .
>
> The tremendous leap forward in consciousness that was the Stonewall Rebellion changed the pronoun in Gay identity from "I" to "WE." (Hay 1990:5)

The emergence of a collective identity began with a police raid on the popular Stonewall Inn Bar in New York City, which led to several days of demonstrations and violent confrontations in the streets, and culminated in the formation of new political activist organizations. These events followed and were parallels to the successes of the civil rights movement and the women's movement. They built on existing lesbian and gay male organizations and an underground network of newspapers. As with the previous rights movements, individual oppression became reconceptualized as a collective struggle for equal rights and equal status to that of the dominant group — middle-class, able-bodied, white male heterosexuals.

This book is a result of the success of this collective movement within American psychology. Three examples of this new paradigm of lesbian, bisexual, and gay psychology are reprinted here. They represent the areas of psychology we have emphasized throughout this book: research, practice, and public policy.

The first article is the culmination of a long-term project. Morin (1977) documented the extent of heterosexual bias in psychological research up to the mid-1970s. For example, he noted then that the search for the cause, cure, and diagnostic cues for homosexuality were dominant themes; research that did not view homosexuality as an abnormality, or worse, was only beginning to emerge. The frustration about such obviously inaccurate and biased research led to the formation, in 1985, of a task force sponsored by the American Psychological Association (APA) Board of Scientific Affairs and the Board of Social and Ethical Responsibility in Psychology to develop guidelines for avoiding heterosexist bias in psychological research. The report of this task force, published in 1991 and reprinted here, reflects the new paradigm in psychology because it pointed out the fallacy of assuming that everyone is heterosexual or that important research questions should be phrased from the point of view of heterosexuals. Instead, it argued that "overcoming these biases . . . will lead to more ethical science, as we learn how better to respect the dignity and worth of individuals, to strive for the preservation of fundamental human rights, and to protect the welfare of our research participants."

Another long-term project is represented in the second article in this section. In 1975 the APA took a strong stance regarding bias toward lesbians and gay men, resolving that "homosexuality per se implies no impairment in judgment, reliability, or general social and vocational abilities" (Conger 1975). Recognizing that practice does not quickly follow policy change, a task force was formed in 1984 by the American Psychological Association's Committee on Lesbian and Gay Concerns (now Committee on Lesbian, Gay, and Bisexual Concerns) sponsored jointly by the APA's Board of Professional Affairs and the Board of Social and Ethical Responsibility in Psychology. The purpose of the task force was to investigate the range of bias that may occur in psychotherapy with lesbians and gay men. The results suggested that psychologists vary widely in their adherence to a standard of unbiased practices with gay men and lesbians (Garnets et al. 1991). Subsequent research found similar results (Dworkin 1992; Greene 1994; Fox 1996). As a result, several past presidents of the APA Division 44 (Society for the Psychological Study of Lesbian, Gay, and Bisexual Issues) and other practitioners labored for several years to draft guidelines for psychotherapy with lesbian, gay, and bisexual clients that would be approved by APA's Board of Directors and the Council of Representatives. This task was accomplished when the guidelines were approved in February 2000. In many ways this document is a model for other stigmatized groups and may do much to remove the stigma that mental health professions have long placed on homosexuality.

The third focus in this section is public policy. Despite great progress in some areas, unfortunate laws criminalize same-gender sexual behavior in some states, prohibit open lesbians and gay men from serving in the U.S. armed forces, and prevent extending marital benefits to same-gender couples. Likewise, the results of major court decisions have been mixed but often negative. Nonetheless, the arguments psychology raised regarding these issues have had some positive effect and have been reflected in a few court opinions (Bersoff and Ogden 1991; Patterson and Redding 1996). For example, in the mid 1990s Hawaii's Supreme Court ruled that the state's refusal to marry same-gender couples violated Hawaii's constitutional guarantee of equal protection. A court case followed to adjudicate the state's argument that it has a "compelling interest" in maintaining the original ban on same-sex marriages. Extensive scientific evidence was presented at the trial comparing gay and lesbian parents to heterosexual parents, and the children of gay and lesbian parents to the children of heterosexual parents; it consistently showed that lesbian mothers and gay fathers are as likely as heterosexuals to be good parents and to have no ill effects on their children because of their sexual orientation (Patterson 1995). It is probable that similar issues will again come before the courts and legislatures, and that APA will continue to file amicus briefs reviewing relevant research in support of the rights of lesbians, bisexuals, and gay men.

The use of psychology to influence public policy also reflects the new paradigm that being lesbian, bisexual, or gay is not a personal problem (or mental illness) but is a minority-group identity. Thus prejudice against gays, lesbians, and bisexuals is parallel to racial or religious prejudice. Similarly discrimination and hate crimes against homosexuals and bisexuals are parallel to other civil rights and privacy issues. Reconceptualizing sexual orientation as a social category — similar to race, religion, gender, or ethnicity — has proven to be a powerful way to change public attitudes and policy.

The final paper in this anthology concerns the role of psychology in the politics of legislation affecting lesbians, bisexuals, and gay men. Writing from the perspective of an openly lesbian California state legislator, Sheila James Kuehl provides a blueprint for action.

Contemporary Issue: What Do Lesbians, Gay Men, and Bisexuals Contribute to Society? Conversely, What Is the Cost to Society for the Various Forms of Legal Discriminations Against Bisexuals, Lesbians, and Gay Men?

The treatment of lesbians, gay men, and bisexuals by the U.S. armed forces is an example of blatant discrimination. The U.S. military policy of excluding gays and lesbians has a cost: It involves secrecy, deceit, hypocrisy, and the loss, perhaps, of superior personnel (Herek 1993; Herek, Jobe, and Carney 1996; Melton 1989; Wolinsky and Sherrill 1993).

Discrimination, prejudice, homophobia, and heterosexist bias affect not only lesbians, bisexuals, and gay men but everyone else as well. Society pays a price for rigid adherence to traditional gender roles, enforced by homophobia and violence based on sexual orientation, threats, and reciprocal fear and distrust. Society endures a further toll for the anti-sexual ideology that taints condoms, sex education, surveys of sexual behavior, and same-gender sexual relations with a broad brush of condemnation at the same time that the media glorifies erotic imagery, suggestive heterosexual television and movie themes (even involving unmarried teenagers), and violence of all kinds.

The emerging lesbian, bisexual, and gay affirmative paradigm in psychology can help our society evaluate the destructive impact of these outdated and misguided views and ideologies. On the one hand, it can suggest different models for examining the important issues of violence, sexuality, and AIDS prevention. Moreover, the ways that gay men, lesbians, and bisexuals have been innovative in their identities, intimate relationships, family relationships, gender roles, and sexuality can broaden our understanding of human experience and provide new models for heterosexuals. On the other hand, the new paradigm can reduce the constraints imposed by sexual prejudice and heterosexist bias on the general population. The resulting freedom may also affect sexism and racism, as we acknowledge our multi-cultural diversity and relish the richness it provides.

One approach for ending discrimination is to raise the broader question of what lesbians, bisexuals, and gay men contribute to our diverse society. It is provocative to apply this new paradigm to the inevitable threat to human survival that will result from worldwide overpopulation. It has been suggested that disease, war, or famine are the only solutions that nature can impose. We suggest another option: same-gender sexual attraction. This alternative clearly does not rule out propagation at adequate levels, but it can serve to limit it effectively and humanely, without disease, famine, or war, while maintaining loving relationships and affectional sexual behavior. Indeed, the long-term survival of our species may depend on a dramatic increase in the number of individuals whose lovemap includes a same-gender orientation.

References

Bersoff, D. N., and D. W. Ogden. 1991. APA Amicus curiae briefs: Furthering lesbian and gay male civil rights. *American Psychologist* 46:950–56.

Conger, J. J. 1975. Proceedings of the American Psychological Association, Incorporated, for the year 1974: Minutes of the annual meeting of the Council of Representatives. *American Psychologist* 30:620–51.

Dworkin, S. 1992. Some ethical considerations when counseling gay, lesbian, and bisexual clients. In S. Dworkin and F. Gutierrez, eds., *Counseling Gay Men and Lesbians: Journey to the End of the Rainbow*, pp. 325–34. Alexandria, Va.: American Association for Counseling and Development.

Fox, R. 1996. Bisexuality in perspective: A review of theory and research. In B. Firestein, ed., *Bisexuality: The Psychology and Politics of an Invisible Minority*, pp. 3–50. Thousand Oaks, Calif.: Sage.

Garnets, L. D., K. A. Hancock, S. D. Cochran, J. Goodchilds, and L. A. Peplau. 1991. Issues in psychotherapy with lesbians and gay men: A survey of psychologists. *American Psychologist* 46:964–72.

Greene, B. 1994. Lesbian and gay sexual orientations: Implications for clinical training, practice, and research. In B. Greene and G. M. Herek, eds., *Lesbian and Gay Psychology: Theory, Research, and Clinical Applications*, pp. 1–24. Thousand Oaks, Calif.: Sage.

Hay, H. 1990. Identifying as gay — there's the key. *Gay Community News*, April 22–28, p. 5.

Herek, G. M. 1993. Sexual orientation and military service: A social science perspective. *American Psychologist* 48:538–47.

Herek, G. M., and J. Jobe, and R. Carney, eds. 1996. *Out in Force: Sexual Orientation and the Military*. Chicago: University of Chicago Press.

Melton, G. B. 1989. Public policy and private prejudice: Psychology and law on gay rights. *American Psychologist* 44:933–40.

Morin, S. F. 1977. Heterosexual bias in psychological research on lesbianism and male homosexuality. *American Psychologist* 32:629–37.

Patterson, C. J. 1995. Lesbian mothers, gay fathers, and their children. In A. R. D'Augelli and C. J. Patterson, eds., *Lesbian, Gay, and Bisexual Identities over the Lifespan: Psychological Perspectives*, pp. 262–90. New York: Oxford University Press.

Patterson, C. J., and R. E. Redding. 1996. Lesbian and gay families with children: Implications of social science research for policy. *Journal of Social Issues* 52(2):29–50.

Wolinsky, M., and K. S. Sherrill, eds. 1993. *Gays and the Military: Joseph Steffan versus the United States*. Princeton, N.J.: Princeton University Press.

27 Avoiding Heterosexist Bias in Psychological Research

Gregory M. Herek, Douglas C. Kimmel, Hortensia Amaro, and Gary B. Melton

The social and behavioral sciences have an important role to play in increasing society's knowledge about and understanding of lesbians, gay men, and bisexual people. For example, empirical research by Kinsey and his colleagues (Kinsey, Pomeroy, and Martin 1948; Kinsey et al. 1953), Ford and Beach (1951), and Hooker (1957) demonstrated that homosexual behavior is fairly common in the United States and in other cultures, and is not inherently associated with psychopathology. These pioneering works continue to be cited today. Unfortunately the bulk of scientific research has ignored sexual orientation and behavior or has uncritically adopted societal prejudices against gay and bisexual people. For example, Morin (1977) reviewed *Psychological Abstracts* for the years 1967–74 and found that most published research on homosexuality treated it within the framework of a sickness model (for detailed discussions of the history of scientific research on homosexuality, see Bayer 1987; Bérubé 1989; Chauncey 1982; Lewes 1988).

Ever since 1975, when the American Psychological Association (APA) Council of Representatives adopted its resolution stating that "homosexuality per se implies no impairment in judgment, stability, reliability, or general social and vocational capabilities," the APA has taken a leading role among scientific organizations in "removing the stigma of mental illness that has long been associated with homosexual orientations" (American Psychological Association 1975:633). In 1986, for example, the APA submitted a brief amicus curiae to the United States Supreme Court in the case of *Bowers v. Hardwick*, using data from the social and behavioral sciences to argue for the elimination of state sodomy laws (Melton 1989). In 1988 the APA submitted a brief amicus curiae to the U.S. Ninth Circuit Court of Appeals in the case of *Watkins v. U.S. Army*, arguing that empirical data do not support the military's exclusionary policies toward lesbians and gay men (Melton 1989). In 1986 the APA provided testimony to a congressional committee summarizing scientific research on the sources, prevalence, and consequences of hate crimes against lesbians and gay men (Committee on the Judiciary 1986; Herek and Berrill 1990).

Recognizing a general need for gay-affirmative scientific research, the APA Board for Social and Ethical Responsibility in Psychology (BSERP), in 1985, convened a Task Force on Non-Homophobic Research. The task force was charged to "assemble and prepare materials that can be used for educating psychologists about techniques for preventing homophobic bias in research" (Burroughs 1985).[1] In fulfilling its charge, the task force focused on the problem of *heterosexist bias* in psychological research, which it defined as conceptualizing human experience in strictly heterosexual terms and consequently ignoring, invalidating, or derogating homosexual behaviors and sexual orientation, and lesbian, gay, and bisexual relationships and lifestyles.

In the present article, which is based on the final report of the task force, we describe some of the principal ways in which heterosexist bias can enter each stage of the research process, and we offer suggestions for avoiding such bias.[2] The discussion is organized as a series of questions that investigators can use to evaluate their own research projects. The questions are especially relevant to studies conducted with gay male, lesbian, or bisexual populations. Additionally we suggest that they be used for any research that (a) might incidentally include lesbians, gay men, or bisexual people in a sample of the general population; (b) might affect participants' attitudes, assumptions, or beliefs about sexuality, human relationships, or gay and bisexual people; or (c) might provide results relevant to a general understanding of sexuality, relationships, mental health, minority groups, or related topics.

Because the questions that follow can best be answered by well-informed researchers, we urge all psychologists to learn more about lesbians, gay men, and bisexual people. This self-education should not be restricted to library research and consultations with colleagues but should also include discussing research ideas and procedures with gay and bisexual women and men, and seeking information from gay community periodicals and other media. Although community consultations do not absolve researchers of primary responsibility for problems inherent in their procedures, they can help researchers to recognize or anticipate such problems and to respond to them sensitively (Melton et al. 1988).

Formulating the Research Question

1. *Does the research question ignore or deny the existence of lesbians, gay men, and bisexual people?* Failing to recognize that most adolescent and adult samples include some lesbians, gay men, and bisexual participants can weaken a research design. For example, equating interpersonal attraction with hetero-sexual attraction can cause a researcher to misapply theoretical concepts or to use experimental manipulations that are inappropriate for some partici-pants. By considering male-male and female-female attraction as well as female-male attraction, researchers open themselves to the possibility of a broader understanding of interpersonal attraction and its relation to cultural concepts of gender and sexuality. Similar comments can be made concerning psychological research in many other areas, including stress and coping (which could consider the stress faced by subjects whose sexual orientation is stigmatized), adolescent development (which could address specific chal-lenges gay adolescents face, such as coming out), and prejudice (which could consider how the social and psychological dynamics of heterosexism compare with racism, anti-Semitism, and other out-group attitudes).

2. *Does the research question devalue or stigmatize gay and bisexual peo-ple?* Even research questions that appear to be scientifically neutral can be biased by equating an exclusively heterosexual orientation with being "healthy" or "normal." In addition to its potential for reinforcing the stig-matization of lesbians, gay men, and bisexual people, such research can be scientifically weak because it limits inquiry to a single aspect of a multifac-eted phenomenon. For example, research on the development of *sexual orientation* (which treats heterosexuality, bisexuality, and homosexuality as equally requiring explanation) has the potential of improving scientific un-derstanding of human sexuality. In contrast, research is unlikely to yield scientifically important findings if it seeks a cause only for homosexuality and omits heterosexuality from the investigation. Such research also can perpetuate societal prejudices against people who engage in homosexual behavior. Psychological research intended to prevent development of ho-mosexual or bisexual identity, or to change or "cure" a homosexual or bi-sexual orientation once it has developed, is an even more dramatic example of heterosexist bias. Aside from the general failure of conversion therapies

in most cases, the ethics of such attempts are highly questionable (Davison 1991; Haldeman 1991).

3. *Does the research question reflect cultural stereotypes of lesbians, gay men, and bisexual people?* Lesbians, gay men, and bisexual people do not share any common characteristics apart from their sexual orientation. Nevertheless, numerous stereotypes persist about them (Adam 1978; Herek 1991). Erroneously assuming that gay or bisexual people constitute homogeneous groups can lead researchers to overlook the mediating influences of other important variables (age, race, gender, ethnicity, class, etc.). The assumption of homogeneity also can foster unwarranted generalizations about all gay or bisexual men and women from data that were obtained from a single nonrepresentative sample. It also can limit the choice of research topics. For example, few researchers have addressed the experiences of lesbian and gay male people of color, who often encounter both racism and heterosexism (see, e.g., Hidalgo and Hidalgo-Christensen 1976; Icard 1986). One probable reason for this deficit in the literature is that researchers have failed to recognize the racial and cultural diversity of the gay community.

4. *Does the research question implicitly assume that observed characteristics are caused by the subjects' sexual orientation?* The familiar principle that correlation should not be confused with causation applies to research with lesbians, gay men, and bisexual people. Phenomena should not be assumed to result from sexual orientation simply because they are observed in the gay community. Alcoholism, for example, is a serious problem in some sectors of the gay community. Attributing it to homosexuality per se, however, exemplifies the fundamental attribution bias (Ross 1977): It explains behavior entirely in terms of personal characteristics while ignoring situational factors (e.g., the sample was recruited from patrons of gay bars).

Sampling

1. *To what degree is the sample representative?* When results are to be generalized to the entire population of gay men, lesbians, and bisexuals, researchers should use standard sampling procedures in order to obtain the most representative sample possible (e.g., Sudman 1976). As with any attempt at probability sampling, researchers should be aware of factors that reduce the sample's representativeness. These include general limitations on any sample (e.g., random-digit dialing techniques exclude persons with-

out telephones from the sampling frame) as well as problems unique to a lesbian, gay male, or bisexual sample (e.g., because of societal stigma, an unknown proportion of eligible respondents will refuse to disclose their sexual orientation to an interviewer).

In the past, researchers often have assumed that lesbians, gay men, and bisexuals could not be sampled through probability methods because of their status as "hidden" minorities in the United States. Recently, however, survey items about sexual behavior and orientation have been successfully administered to probability samples in telephone interviews, face-to-face interviews, and self-administered questionnaires (Miller, Turner, and Moses 1990). These studies suggest that the problem of nonresponse in surveys of sexual behavior or orientation, although serious, may not be qualitatively different from that encountered with other samples. Researchers, therefore, should seriously consider probability sampling as a strategy for research in this area.

2. *If the sample is not a probability sample, does it include sufficient diversity to permit adequate assessment of relevant variables?* When convenience samples must be used, researchers should fully describe their recruitment procedures and sample characteristics, discuss possible sampling biases, and identify particular groups (e.g., ethnic, age, social class) that are likely to be over- or underrepresented. The negative effects of sampling by convenience can be offset to a limited extent by using a variety of recruitment strategies and by targeting diverse sections of the community. Unless bar patrons or political activists are the specific population of interest, for example, restricting recruitment efforts to those individuals will yield a highly selective sample. Instead, researchers should seek participants from throughout the community (e.g., at coffeehouses, bookstores, community centers, parent groups, political organizations, religious organizations, bathhouses, service-oriented programs, social clubs, and student organizations). Respondents can also be successfully recruited through advertisements in community publications and electronic media, and through exit polls at targeted voting sites (e.g., gay-identified neighborhoods).

3. *Is the sample appropriate for the research question?* When sampling gay and bisexual people, researchers should ensure that the sample's composition permits valid tests of hypotheses. This requires that researchers be familiar with the participants' communities. For example, a study of changes in gay men's sexual behavior since the outbreak of acquired immunodeficiency syndrome (AIDS) should be sufficiently diverse in terms of age, ethnicity, level of sexual experience, and relationship status (e.g., uncoupled, sexually exclusive relationship, sexually nonexclusive relationship).

Research Design and Procedures

1. *Is sexual orientation the variable of interest?* Sexual orientation should be carefully distinguished from such variables as gender identity and gender-role conformity. Specific sexual behaviors should be distinguished from the long-term pattern of attractions, behaviors, and identity known as "sexual orientation." In cross-cultural research, cultural influences on how members of other societies conceptualize sexual behavior should be considered; the categories associated with what is called sexual orientation in Western cultures may not be applicable to all societies (Herdt 1984; Herek 1989; Ortner and Whitehead 1981; Williams 1986).

2. *Is sexual orientation assessed appropriately?* The method of assessing sexual orientation and behavior should fit the sample and the research question. For example, different conclusions are likely to be reached with each of the following operationalizations: (a) self-labeling by respondents as gay male, lesbian, bisexual, or heterosexual; (b) self-reports of sexual behavior during a specified time period (e.g., the previous year, or since age eighteen); and (c) self-reports of sexual desires or fantasies during a specified time period. Additional differences will be observed if these questions are asked among different racial, ethnic, or language groups. For example, Peterson and Marin (1988) noted that black and Hispanic men may be more likely than white men to have engaged extensively in homosexual behavior while still considering themselves to be heterosexual.

Recruitment procedures should not be confused with assessment of sexual orientation or behavior, because all members of a particular group do not necessarily share the same sexual orientation. Just as samples of the general population should not be assumed to be entirely heterosexual, for example, samples of patrons of gay bars should not be assumed to be entirely gay. They may also include heterosexual and bisexual persons who patronize bars for various reasons (e.g., to socialize with friends, to dance, and so on).

3. *Are comparison groups appropriate to the research design?* Comparison groups should be carefully selected to avoid confusing other variables with sexual orientation. For example, comparing married women with lesbians confuses relational status with sexual orientation. The two groups are not comparable because (a) not all married women are heterosexual; (b) some lesbians are married to men; and (c) many lesbians are in committed relationships. Depending on the research question, any of the following might be appropriate comparison groups: married heterosexual women with un-

married heterosexual women; married heterosexual women with lesbians in an ongoing relationship; and single lesbians with lesbians in ongoing relationships.

4. *Do questionnaire items or interview protocols assume heterosexuality?* Researchers should avoid inappropriate use of standardized measures that equate heterosexuality with sexuality. Such instruments should be modified when possible or alternative instruments should be devised. For example, personality inventories that assess "need for heterosexuality" as a proxy for "need for sexual intimacy" do not accurately assess the experiences of lesbians, gay men, and bisexual people. Such measures also reinforce heterosexist assumptions among respondents. Generally questions should not use language that assumes the respondent's heterosexuality. For example, items concerning a respondent's romantic or sexual partner should not reflect unwarranted assumptions about that partner's gender. Nor should questions about marital status be assumed to yield complete information about respondents' committed relationships. Because marital relationships between two persons of the same sex are not legally recognized in the United States, lesbians and gay men who are involved in an ongoing same-sex relationship are legally single. Similarly attempts to obtain information about an individual's sexual behavior outside a primary relationship can be limited when only terms such as *premarital* or *extramarital* are used. In addition to providing data about only a limited range of behaviors, these terms define all sexuality in relation to a heterosexual marriage, thereby discounting sexual experiences and relationships with members of the same gender.

5. *Do the researchers' personal attitudes and feelings influence participants' responses?* Many lesbians, gay men, and bisexual people are justifiably suspicious of all psychological research, which historically has labeled them as sick. Unless researchers are well-informed, candid, and sensitive to such suspicions, they are likely to obtain incomplete or inaccurate responses. Research personnel's lack of knowledge about and comfort with homosexuality and bisexuality can be communicated to participants in subtle ways (e.g., interpersonal distance, nervous speech, unfamiliarity with slang) that can affect research outcomes. Thus whenever data collection explicitly includes information about sexual orientation or behavior, the members of the research team should educate themselves sufficiently so that they are familiar and comfortable with lesbian, gay male, and bisexual cultures.

Demand characteristics also can affect results when the researcher is openly lesbian, gay male, or bisexual. Participants may feel pressured to provide responses that are not accurate but that are socially desirable within their community. Because of the gay male community's emphasis on safer sex practices to avoid AIDS, for example, male respondents may be reluctant to admit to a gay researcher that they continue to engage in high-risk behaviors.

6. *Do experimental manipulations presume that participants are hetero-sexual?* Data collection procedures can evoke different responses from lesbian, gay male, and bisexual participants than from heterosexual respondents. For example, using "attractive male" confederates in a study of arousal and attraction will evoke different responses from lesbians and heterosexual women. Although the lesbians might well rate the confederate as attractive in an aesthetic sense, they are much less likely than the heterosexual women to translate this attraction into feelings of sexual arousal. Although random assignment of participants to conditions will help to avoid systematic biases in the data in such a situation, such biases might still intrude when small samples are used. Furthermore, using such a procedure conveys an assumption of heterosexuality to participants. Researchers could avoid such problems by advertising the study as one of heterosexual females, by asking lesbian participants to indicate their sexual orientation through an unobtrusive and anonymous procedure, or through simply including a manipulation check that assesses the participants' level of sexual arousal in the presence of the confederate. Generally, unless sexual orientation is an explicit variable in the research, procedures should be neutral concerning respondents' sexual orientations.

Protection of Participants

1. *Is information obtained about sexual orientation and behavior truly confidential, or what are the limits to confidentiality?* Because of the stigma attached to homosexuality in American culture, participants who disclose information about their sexual orientation or behavior to a researcher are at heightened risk for negative consequences if that information becomes known to others. At the same time, obtaining such information often is crucial to the success of empirical research that will have beneficial effects for gay communities and for society as a whole. Researchers should not be deterred from addressing issues of sexual orientation and behavior in their research but should develop procedures for protecting the participants' privacy and welfare. Researchers should carefully consider potential risks to respondents from possible public exposure and subsequent discrimination or harassment, as well as possible psychological stress resulting from requests

for disclosure, especially for participants who feel uncertain about their sexual orientation.

Researchers should make a special effort to learn the actual limits to confidentiality of their data, including potential legal requirements for involuntary release of data and legal means for protecting confidentiality. One strategy for protecting participants is to obtain a certificate of confidentiality pursuant to the Public Health Service Act (see Gray and Melton 1985). When audits are conducted by federal agencies, the researcher should attempt to have them conducted on-site; otherwise the data might become accessible under the Freedom of Information Act (Morris, Sales, and Berman 1981). If data are subpoenaed, the researcher should attempt to have the subpoena quashed or should contest it (see Gray and Melton 1985; Knerr 1982). Information about the limits of confidentiality and safeguards should be shared with participants.

Because of the risks to confidentiality, researchers should avoid keeping identifying information about their data when not absolutely necessary. If data must be identified for later matching in longitudinal or follow-up studies, researchers should use code names or numbers to eliminate the need for keeping names on file.

2. *Does the research procedure reinforce prejudice or stereotypes among heterosexual respondents?* If researchers decide to introduce homosexual or bisexual orientation into the procedure (e.g., through a manipulation), they should carefully evaluate the likely effect of such a manipulation on all respondents (heterosexual, bisexual, lesbian, and gay male). For example, if a study exposes participants to gay-related stereotypes, the researcher should develop careful debriefing procedures to ensure that respondents' stereotypes are not increased through their participation. Another example would be a study of person perception that includes a manipulation of a target person's sexual orientation. Again, researchers should use the debriefing period to educate respondents about lesbian, gay male, and bisexual issues, and to counter the effects of any negative stereotypes or prejudice that may have been communicated during the study.

3. *Does the procedure have negative effects on lesbian, gay male, or bisexual participants?* Research procedures that explicitly disparage lesbians, gay men, or bisexual people are objectionable on ethical grounds. More subtle assumptions by researchers that all subjects are heterosexual also are problematic both because they negate the experiences of lesbian, gay male, and bisexual participants and because they obscure the possible effects of a potentially important variable. When participants learn the study's purpose in

the debriefing session, they may feel that their experiences do not count —
that the researcher considers them to be merely a source of error variance.
Such communication can affect respondents' feelings of self-worth as well
as their level of respect for psychological research. Furthermore, such a
procedure can reinforce heterosexism by encouraging participants to see the
world exclusively in heterosexual terms.

4. *Does the recruitment procedure intrude inappropriately on potential participants' privacy?* In their quest for participants, researchers run the risk of
being overly intrusive in their recruitment procedures, and thereby inadequately safeguarding potential respondents' anonymity or confidentiality. For
example, researchers who recruit outside a gay bar or community center may
encounter patrons whom they know personally but who have not voluntarily
chosen to disclose their sexual orientation. Researchers should consult with
colleagues and community members about how best to protect respondents'
privacy and confidentiality in those situations. In general, the means of recruitment should be as unobtrusive as possible, with the level of intrusiveness
balanced against the possible benefits that will result from the study.

5. *Does the observation procedure intrude inappropriately on participants'
privacy?* Researchers conducting unobtrusive observation studies should attempt to obtain consent from participants. When such a study violates the
participants' expectation of privacy, consent is usually necessary to protect
the participants' autonomy and dignity. For example, following respondents
from a gay bar to their home would violate their privacy. Simple observation
in a public or semipublic setting is more ambiguous, depending on the study
and the kinds of observations made.

6. *Does the assessment of sexual orientation create stress for participants?*
Some participants may experience stress when asked about their sexual orientation and behavior. This is especially likely among those who have not
previously labeled themselves (even privately) as lesbian, gay male, or bisexual
and among those who are especially vulnerable to stigma or discrimination
(e.g., participants who are in the armed forces, institutionalized, concerned
with child custody, or are members of a culture that stigmatizes gay or bisexual
people more severely than the dominant culture does). Participants who are
concerned about their privacy and about possible discrimination if their sexual
orientation becomes known to others need protection as well as sensitive reassurance from the researcher concerning confidentiality.

To permit participants to give their informed consent before agreeing to
participate, researchers should inform them about the general nature of the
questions being posed. Debriefing procedures also should be designed to

detect and alleviate any damaging consequences of the research procedure. In addition to other standard debriefing practices, researchers should make certain that respondents understand the goals of the research and should be prepared to provide referrals to gay-affirmative counselors or information sources when appropriate.

Interpreting and Reporting Results

1. *Is an observed difference assumed to reflect a problem or pathology of lesbian, gay, or bisexual participants?* Simply because lesbians, gay men, or bisexual people are observed to differ from heterosexual respondents, it should not be assumed that this reflects a deficit. Value judgments should not be made about different experiences in childhood and adolescence, for example, simply because one pattern is prevalent among heterosexual adults and another is prevalent among lesbian and gay male adults. Similarly differences between heterosexuals and lesbian, gay male, or bisexual respondents within the normal range of psychological test scores should not in itself be judged as indicative of a deficit in one group (Gonsiorek 1991).

2. *Does the language reflect heterosexist bias?* When reporting results, researchers should carefully avoid heterosexist language, including characterizations that pathologize or ignore the experiences of lesbians, gay men, or bisexual people (see APA Committee on Lesbian and Gay Concerns 1991; Morin and Charles 1983).

3. *Are the limitations of the research findings stated appropriately?* As in all areas of psychological research, care should be taken when generalizing from the research sample to larger populations. If the research findings are applicable only to heterosexuals or to specific segments of the gay community (e.g., urban white males), this should be clearly stated in the abstract and throughout the research report.

4. *Has the researcher attempted to anticipate distortions or misinterpretations of findings by the lay public and in the popular media?* Scientific research on lesbian, gay male, and bisexual populations often is disseminated to the general public through the popular media. For example, studies of developmental or physiological differences between homosexual, bisexual, and heterosexual individuals have been widely reported in popular media as indicating the possible discovery of a presumed "cause" for homosexuality. Such reports usually are followed by immediate discussion of how to prevent or "cure" a homosexual orientation. Although misinterpretations of research

results in the mass media are beyond their direct control, researchers should nevertheless try to anticipate and prevent them. This can be accomplished, in part, by clearly discussing the limitations of results and methodology, taking care that interpretations do not go beyond the data, explaining the qualifications on findings, and interpreting the results for reporters in clear and unambiguous terms. Researchers should be particularly conscientious when their findings are released to the press before publication (as in some AIDS research), because their scientific colleagues cannot provide informed criticisms of the research.

5. *Have the results been disseminated to research participants or to the larger gay community?* After collecting data from the lesbian, gay male, and bisexual communities, researchers should disseminate the findings in understandable language to the members of those communities. This dissemination can be considered a partial repayment to the communities for participating in the research. It need not violate scientific rules regarding double or prior publication.

Creating an Intellectual Environment Free from Heterosexism

For the advancement of science and society, high-quality research is needed on a wide variety of issues related to sexual orientation. This article and the report (Task Force on Non-Heterosexist Research 1986) on which it is based signify the APA's commitment to foster such research. Further steps are also clearly needed, especially in the areas of publishing and graduate training.

Journal editors and reviewers should recognize the legitimacy of research involving sexual orientation, should evaluate such research with the same criteria used to evaluate research on other topics, and should not dismiss such research as overly specialized or as frivolous. We applaud the efforts that many APA journal editors have made to recruit reviewers from minority populations, including gay and bisexual people, and we encourage the continuation of these efforts.

Textbook authors and editors also have an obligation to avoid statements and explanations that are likely to reinforce heterosexism and foster negative self-images among lesbian, gay male, and bisexual students. For example, discussions of same-gender attractions should not be relegated to chapters on psychopathology and should not be concerned only with consideration of the causes of such orientations. Readers of textbooks should be taught that lesbian, gay male, and bisexual people have unique experiences and concerns that are appropriate topics of psychological study. Explicit mention of lesbian, gay male, and bisexual perspectives should be included for a wide variety of psychological topics, including human development, interpersonal attraction, health, attitudes, and stress and coping. Teachers and professors should actively seek textbooks that present an affirmative view of lesbians, gay men, and bisexual people, and should inform publishers that they are doing so.

Finally, non-heterosexist research will be facilitated by colleges and universities that sensitize their students and faculty to the concerns expressed in this article. In their hiring and promotion procedures, educational institutions should consider research associated with lesbian, gay male, and bisexual topics to be legitimate. Candidates for employment and promotion who conduct such research should be evaluated for the quality of their work and should not be discounted because of the subject matter. Regardless of their sexual orientation, students should be encouraged to conduct research on lesbian, gay male, and bisexual issues, and to recognize those issues in their research on other topics. Providing such encouragement should not be solely the responsibility of lesbian, gay male, and bisexual psychologists; rather, all psychologists should educate themselves to issues of sexual orientation relevant to their own field of expertise.

Conclusion

The science of psychology requires studying human behavior in all its diversity. It is most appropriate, therefore, that psychologists address issues relevant to sexual orientation in research with general samples and also conduct research with lesbians, gay men, and bisexual people from diverse cultural backgrounds. Because American society is heterosexist, however, research may reflect cultural ignorance, biases, and prejudices surrounding sexuality and sexual orientation. During the past fifteen years, psychologists and other social and behavioral scientists have taken significant steps toward rejecting the negative value assumptions underlying earlier views of sexuality and have begun to remove the stigma so long associated with homosexual and bisexual orientations. This has led to a new research paradigm that recognizes the legitimacy of lesbian, gay male, and bisexual orientations, behaviors, relationships, and lifestyles.

Because this affirmative approach is such a recent development in the social sciences, many implicit and overt prejudices remain to be overcome. Overcoming these prejudices will lead to better science, as researchers recognize the many ways in which heterosexist bias has influenced formulation of research questions, sampling procedures, methods and measures, and the interpretation of results. Overcoming these biases also will lead to more ethical science, as researchers learn how better to respect the dignity and worth of individuals, to strive for the preservation of fundamental human rights, and to protect the welfare of research participants.

Acknowledgments

This article is based on the final report of the APA Task Force on Non-Heterosexist Research (Douglas C. Kimmel, chair), which was convened by the Board for Social and Ethical Responsibility in Psychology (BSERP) in 1985. The authors (who constituted the task force) wish to thank Carol Burroughs, APA staff liaison, for her valuable assistance in completing the task force's mission. The authors also thank the many members of BSERP, the Committee on Lesbian and Gay Concerns, and the Board of Scientific Affairs, as well as the many APA members and staff who provided comments on the original task force report and earlier drafts of this article. We dedicate this article to the memory of our distinguished colleague and task force member, Barbara Strudler Wallston.

Notes

1. The task force included one representative each from the Board for Social and Ethical Responsibility in Psychology, the Board of Scientific Affairs, the Committee on Lesbian and Gay Concerns, and APA Division 44, as well as one additional expert from the field. It met in December 1985 and completed its report the following year (Task Force on Non-Heterosexist Research 1986). The task force chose from the outset to refer to itself as the Task Force on Non-Heterosexist Research and to title its report "Avoiding Heterosexist Bias: Guidelines for Ethical and Valid Research." The word *homophobia* was avoided for several reasons, including its implication that prejudice against gay men and lesbians is a form of psychopathology, and its focus on the individual rather than on the larger cultural context. For the present article, *heterosexism* is defined as an ideological system that denies, denigrates, or stigmatizes homosexual behaviors and gay, lesbian, and bisexual identities, relationships, and communities (see Herek 1990).

2. Researchers should display the same sensitivity to heterosexism as they do to other prejudices, such as those based on race, gender, age, and class. Valuable suggestions can be found in the report of the Ad Hoc Committee on Nonsexist

Research (Denmark et al. 1988), which addresses problems of sexist bias in empirical inquiry. Because sexist bias also can interfere with research on lesbian, gay male, and bisexual populations, that document is a useful supplement to the present article.

References

Adam, B. D. 1978. *The Survival of Domination: Inferiorization and Everyday Life.* New York: Elsevier.

American Psychological Association. 1975. Minutes of the Council of Representatives. *American Psychologist* 30:620–51.

American Psychological Association, Committee on Lesbian and Gay Concerns. 1991. Avoiding heterosexual bias in language. *American Psychologist* 46:973–74.

Bayer, R. 1987. *Homosexuality and American Psychiatry: The Politics of Diagnosis.* 2nd ed. Princeton, N.J.: Princeton University Press.

Bérubé, A. 1989. *Coming Out Under Fire: The History of Gay Men and Women in World War II.* New York: The Free Press.

Burroughs, C. 1985. Memorandum to members of the Task Force on Non-Homophobic Research from Carol Burroughs, Administrative Associate for Governance Affairs, American Psychological Association, November 28. On file at the American Psychological Association.

Chauncey, G., Jr. 1982. From sexual inversion to homosexuality: Medicine and the changing conceptualization of female deviance. *Salmagundi* 58–59:114–46.

Committee on the Judiciary. 1986. Anti-gay violence: Hearing before the Subcommittee on Criminal Justice of the Committee on the Judiciary, House of Representatives, serial no. 132, October 9. Washington, D.C.: U.S. Government Printing Office.

Davison, G. 1991. Constructionism and morality in therapy for homosexuality. In J. C. Gonsiorek and J. D. Weinrich, eds., *Homosexuality: Research Implications for Public Policy*, pp. 137–48. Newbury Park, Calif.: Sage.

Denmark, F., N. F. Russo, I. H. Frieze, and J. A. Sechzer. 1988. Guidelines for avoiding sexism in psychological research: A report of the Ad Hoc Committee on Nonsexist Research. *American Psychologist* 43:582–85.

Ford, C. S., and F. A. Beach. 1951. *Patterns of Sexual Behavior.* New York: Harper.

Gonsiorek, J. C. 1991. The empirical basis for the demise of the illness model of homosexuality. In J. C. Gonsiorek and J. D. Weinrich, eds., *Homosexuality: Research Implications for Public Policy*, pp. 115–36. Newbury Park, Calif.: Sage.

Gray, J. N., and G. B. Melton. 1985. The law and ethics of psychosocial research on AIDS. *Nebraska Law Review* 64:637–88.

Haldeman, D.C. 1991. Sexual orientation conversion therapy for gay men and lesbians: A scientific examination. In J. C. Gonsiorek and J. D. Weinrich, eds.,

Homosexuality: Research Implications for Public Policy, pp. 149–60. Newbury Park, Calif.: Sage.

Herdt, G. H., ed. 1984. *Ritualized Homosexuality in Melanesia.* Berkeley: University of California Press.

Herek, G. M. 1989. Sexual orientation. In H. Tierney, ed., *Women's Studies Encyclopedia*, 1:344–46. New York: Greenwood.

Herek, G. M. 1990. The context of anti-gay violence: Notes on cultural and psychological heterosexism. *Journal of Interpersonal Violence* 5:316–33.

Herek, G. M. 1991. Stigma, prejudice, and violence against lesbians and gay men. In J. Gonsiorek and J. Weinrich, eds., *Homosexuality: Research Implications for Public Policy*, pp. 60–80. Newbury Park, Calif.: Sage.

Herek, G. M., and K. Berrill, eds. 1990. Violence against lesbians and gay men. *Journal of Interpersonal Violence* (special issue) 5:3.

Hidalgo, H. A., and E. Hidalgo-Christensen. 1976. The Puerto Rican lesbian and the Puerto Rican community. *Journal of Homosexuality* 2(2):109–20.

Hooker, E. 1957. The adjustment of the male overt homosexual. *Journal of Projective Techniques* 21:18–31.

Icard, L. 1986. Black gay men and conflicting social identities: Sexual orientation versus racial identity. *Journal of Social Work and Human Sexuality* 4(1/2):83–93.

Kinsey, A. C., W. B. Pomeroy, and C. E. Martin. 1948. *Sexual Behavior in the Human Male.* Philadelphia: Saunders.

Kinsey, A. C., W. B. Pomeroy, C. E. Martin, and P. H. Gebhard. 1953. *Sexual Behavior in the Human Female.* Philadelphia: Saunders.

Knerr, C. R., Jr. 1982. What to do before and after a subpoena of data arrives. In J. E. Siever, ed., *The Ethics of Social Research: Surveys and Experiments*, pp. 191–206. New York: Springer-Verlag.

Lewes, K. 1988. *The Psychoanalytic Theory of Male Homosexuality.* New York: Simon and Schuster.

Melton, G. B. 1989. Public policy and private prejudice: Psychology and law on gay rights. *American Psychologist* 44:933–40.

Melton, G. B., R. J. Levine, G. P. Koocher, R. Rosenthal, and W. C. Thompson. 1988. Community consultation and socially sensitive research: Lessons from clinical trials of treatments for AIDS. *American Psychologist* 43:573–81.

Miller, H. G., C. F. Turner, and L. E. Moses, eds. 1990. *AIDS: The Second Decade.* Washington, D.C.: National Academy Press.

Morin, S. F. 1977. Heterosexual bias in psychological research on lesbianism and male homosexuality. *American Psychologist* 32:629–37.

Morin, S. F., and K. A. Charles. 1983. Heterosexual bias in psychotherapy. In J. Murray and P. R. Abramson, eds., *Bias in Psychotherapy*, pp. 309–38. New York: Praeger.

Morris, R. A., B. D. Sales, and J. J. Berman. 1981. Research and the Freedom of Information Act. *American Psychologist* 36:819–26.

Ortner, S. B., and H. Whitehead. 1981. *Sexual Meanings: The Cultural Construction of Gender and Sexuality*. Cambridge: Cambridge University Press.

Peterson, J., and G. Marin. 1988. Issues in the prevention of AIDS among black and Hispanic men. *American Psychologist* 43:871–77.

Ross, L. D. 1977. The intuitive scientist and his shortcomings: Distortions in the attribution process. In L. Berkowitz, ed., *Advances in Experimental Social Psychology*, 10:173–220. San Diego, Calif.: Academic Press.

Sudman, S. 1976. *Applied Sampling*. San Diego, Calif.: Academic Press.

Task Force on Non-Heterosexist Research. 1986. *Avoiding Heterosexist Bias: Guidelines for Ethical and Valid Research*. Washington D.C.: American Psychological Association.

Williams, W. L. 1986. *The Spirit and the Flesh: Sexual Diversity in American Indian Culture*. Boston: Beacon.

28 Guidelines for Psychotherapy with Lesbian, Gay, and Bisexual Clients

American Psychological Association

In 1975 the American Psychological Association (APA) adopted a resolution stating that "homosexuality per se implies no impairment in judgment, stability, reliability, or general social or vocational capabilities" (Conger 1975:633). This resolution followed a rigorous discussion of the 1973 decision by the American Psychiatric Association to remove homosexuality from its list of mental disorders (American Psychiatric Association 1974). More than twenty-five years later the implications of this resolution have yet to be fully implemented in practice (Dworkin 1992; Firestein 1996; Fox 1996; Garnets et al. 1991; Greene 1994b; Iasenza 1989; Markowitz 1991, 1995; Nystrom 1997). Many of these authors have suggested that there is a need for better education and training of mental health practitioners in this area. This document is intended to assist psychologists in seeking and using appropriate education and training in their treatment of lesbian, gay, and bisexual clients.[1]

The specific goals of these guidelines are to provide practitioners with (a) a frame of reference for the treatment of lesbian, gay, and bisexual clients; and (b) basic information and further references in the areas of assessment, intervention, identity, relationships, and the education and training of psychologists. These guidelines build on APA's (1992) "Ethical Principles of Psychologists and Code of Conduct,"[2] two other APA policies, and policies of other mental health organizations.

The term *guidelines* refers to pronouncements, statements, or declarations that suggest or recommend specific professional behavior, endeavors, or conduct for psychologists. Guidelines differ from standards in that standards are mandatory and may be accompanied by an enforcement mechanism. Thus these guidelines are aspirational in intent. Their aim is to facilitate the continued systematic development of the profession of psychology and to help ensure a high level of professional practice by psychologists. These guidelines are not meant to be mandatory or exhaustive and may not be applicable to every clinical situation. They should not be construed as definitive and are not intended to take precedence over the judgment of psychologists. These guidelines are organized into four sections: (a) attitudes toward homosexuality and bisexuality; (b) relationships and families; (c) issues of diversity; and (d) education.

Attitudes Toward Homosexuality and Bisexuality

Guideline 1. Psychologists understand that homosexuality and bisexuality are not indicative of mental illness.

For more than a century homosexuality and bisexuality were assumed to be mental illnesses. Hooker's (1957) study was the first to question this assumption. She found no difference on projective test responses between nonclinical samples of heterosexual men and homosexual men. Subsequent studies have shown no differences between heterosexual groups and homosexual groups on measures of cognitive abilities (Tuttle and Pillard 1991) and psychological well-being and self-esteem (Coyle 1993; Herek 1990; Savin-Williams 1990). Fox (1996) found no evidence of psychopathology in nonclinical studies of bisexual men and bisexual women. Furthermore, an extensive body of literature has emerged that identifies few significant differences between heterosexual, homosexual, and bisexual people on a wide range of variables associated with overall psychological functioning (Gonsiorek 1991; Pillard 1988; Rothblum 1994). When studies have noted differences between homosexual and heterosexual individuals regarding psychological functioning (DiPlacido 1998; Ross 1990; Rotheram-Borus, Hunter, and Rosario 1994; Savin-Williams 1994), these differences have been attributed to the effects of stress related to stigmatization on the basis of sexual orientation. This stress may lead to increased risk for suicide attempts, substance abuse, and emotional distress.

The literature that classifies homosexuality and bisexuality as mental illnesses has been found to be methodologically unsound. Gonsiorek (1991) reviewed this literature and found serious methodological flaws, including unclear definitions of terms, inaccurate classification of participants, inappropriate comparisons of groups, discrepant sampling procedures, an ignorance of confounding social factors, and questionable outcome measures. The results from these flawed studies have been used to support theories of homosexuality as mental illness or arrested psychosexual development or both. Although these studies concluded that homosexuality is a mental illness, they have no valid empirical support and serve as the foundation for beliefs that lead to inaccurate representations of lesbian, gay, and bisexual people.

All major American mental health associations have affirmed that homosexuality is not a mental illness. In 1975 APA urged all psychologists to "take the lead in removing the stigma long associated with homosexual orientations" (Conger 1975:633). The APA and all other major mental health associations subsequently adopted a number of resolutions and policy statements founded on this basic principle, which has also been embodied in their ethical codes (cf. American Association for Marriage and Family Therapy 1991; American Counseling Association 1996; Canadian Psychological Association 1995; and National Association of Social Workers 1996). In addition, this principle has informed a number of APA amicus curiae briefs (Bersoff and Ogden 1991).

Thus psychologists affirm that a homosexual or bisexual orientation is not a mental illness (APA 1998). "In their work-related activities, psychologists do not engage in unfair discrimination based on . . . sexual orientation" (APA 1992:1601). Furthermore, psychologists assist clients in overcoming the effects of stigmatization that may lead to emotional distress.

Guideline 2. Psychologists are encouraged to recognize how their attitudes and knowledge about lesbian, gay, and bisexual issues may be relevant to assessment and treatment and seek consultation or make appropriate referrals when indicated.

The APA Ethics Code calls on psychologists to "strive to be aware of their own belief systems, values, needs, and limitations and the effect of these on their work" (APA 1992, p. 1599). This principle is reflected in training programs and educational materials for psychologists. The APA Ethics Code further urges psychologists to evaluate their competencies and the limitations of their expertise — especially when treating groups of people who share distinctive characteristics. Without a high level of awareness about their own beliefs, values, needs, and limitations, psychologists may impede a client's progress in psychotherapy (Corey, Schneider-Corey, and Callanan 1993).

The assessment and treatment of lesbian, gay, and bisexual clients can be adversely affected by therapists' explicit or implicit negative attitudes. For example, when homosexuality and bisexuality are consciously regarded as evidence of mental illness, a client's homosexual or bisexual orientation is apt to be viewed as a major source of the client's psychological difficulties, even when sexual orientation has not been presented as a problem (Garnets et al. 1991; Liddle 1996; Nystrom 1997). When psychologists are unaware of their negative attitudes, the effectiveness of psychotherapy can be compromised by heterosexist bias. Herek (1995) defined heterosexism as "the ideological system that denies, denigrates, and stigmatizes any nonheterosexual form of behavior, identity, relationship, or community" (p. 321). Heterosexism pervades the language, theories, and psychotherapeutic interventions of psychology (Anderson 1996; Brown 1989; Morin 1977). When heterosexual norms for identity, behavior, and relationships are applied to lesbian, gay, or bisexual clients, their thoughts, feelings, and behaviors may be misinterpreted as abnormal, deviant, and undesirable. Psychologists strive to avoid making assumptions that a client is heterosexual, even in the presence of apparent markers of heterosexuality (e.g., marital status, because lesbian, gay, and bisexual people can be heterosexually married: Glenn and Russell 1986; Greene 1994a).

Another manifestation of heterosexism in psychotherapy is approaching treatment with a "sexual-orientation-blind" perspective. Like "color-blind" models, such a perspective denies the culturally unique experiences of a population — in this case, lesbian, gay, and bisexual populations — as a strategy for avoiding a pathologizing stance. However, when psychologists deny the culture-specific experiences in the lives of lesbian, gay, and bisexual people, heterosexist bias is also likely to pervade that work in a manner that is unhelpful to clients (Garnets et al. 1991; Winegarten et al. 1994). When psychologists are uninformed about the unique issues of lesbian, gay, and bisexual people, they may not understand the effects of stigmatization on these individuals and their intimate relationships.

Because many psychologists have not received sufficient current information regarding lesbian, gay, and bisexual clients (Buhrke 1989; Pilkington and Cantor 1996), psychologists are strongly encouraged to seek training, experience, consultation, or supervision when necessary to ensure competent practice with these populations. Key issues for practice include an understanding of human sexuality; the coming-out process and how variables such as age, gender, ethnicity, race, disability, and religion may influence this process; same-sex relationship dynamics; family-of-origin relationships; struggles with spirituality and religious group membership; career issues and workplace discrimination; and coping strategies for successful functioning.

According to the APA Ethics Code, psychologists "are aware of culture, individual, and role differences, including those due to . . . sexual orientation . . . and try to eliminate the effect on their work of biases based on [such] factors" (APA 1992:1599–1600). Hence psychologists are encouraged to use appropriate methods of self-exploration and self-education (e.g., consultation, study, and formal continuing education) to identify and ameliorate preconceived biases about homosexuality and bisexuality.

Guideline 3. Psychologists strive to understand the ways in which social stigmatization (i.e., prejudice, discrimination, and violence) poses risks to the mental health and well-being of lesbian, gay, and bisexual clients.

Many lesbian, gay, and bisexual people face social stigmatization, violence, and discrimination (Herek 1991). Living in a heterosexist society may precipitate a significant degree of stress for lesbian, gay, and bisexual people, many of whom may be tolerated only when they are "closeted" (DiPlacido 1998). Sexual minority status increases risk for stress related to "chronic daily hassles (e.g., hearing anti-gay jokes, always being on guard)" and to more serious "negative life events, especially gay-relevant events (e.g., loss of employment, home, custody of children, anti-gay violence and discrimination due to sexual orientation)" (DiPlacido 1998:140). Greene (1994a) noted that the cumulative effects of heterosexism, sexism, and racism might put lesbian, gay, and bisexual members of racial and ethnic minorities at special risk for social stressors.

Research has shown that gay men are at risk for mental health problems (Meyer 1995) and emotional distress (Ross 1990) as a direct result of discrimination and negative experiences in society. DiPlacido (1998) reported that research on psychosocial stress factors for lesbian and bisexual women is virtually nonexistent. She suggested that "some lesbians and bisexual women may be coping with stressors resulting from their multiple minority status in maladaptive and unhealthy ways" (DiPlacido 1998:141). Social stressors affecting lesbian, gay, and bisexual older adults, such as a lack of legal rights and protection in medical emergencies and a lack of acknowledgment of couples' relationships, particularly following the loss of a partner, have been associated with feelings of helplessness, depression, and disruption of normative grief processes (Berger and Kelly 1996; Slater 1995). Stress factors have been examined in lesbian, gay, and bisexual youth, for whom social vulnerability and isolation have been identified as prominent concerns. Social stressors affecting lesbian, gay, and bisexual youth, such as verbal and physical abuse, have been associated with academic problems, running away, prostitution, substance abuse, and suicide (Savin-Williams 1994, 1998). Antigay verbal and physical harassment has been found to be significantly more common among gay and bisexual male adolescents who had attempted suicide compared with those who had not (Rotheram-Borus et al. 1994). These stressors have also been associated with high-risk sexual behavior (Rotheram-Borus et al. 1995).

Lesbian, gay, and bisexual people who live in rural communities may experience stress related to the risk of disclosure because anonymity about their sexual orientation may be more difficult to maintain. Fears about loss of employment and housing may be more significant because of the limited opportunities within small communities. Less visibility and fewer lesbian, gay, and bisexual support organizations may intensify feelings of social isolation. Furthermore, lesbian, gay, and bisexual people may feel more vulnerable to acts of violence and harassment because rural communities may provide fewer legal projections (D'Augelli and Garnets 1995).

Given the real and perceived social and physical dangers that many lesbian, gay, and bisexual clients face, developing a sense of safety is of primary importance. Societal stigmatization, prejudice, and discrimination (e.g., antigay ballot initiatives or the murders of lesbian, gay, and bisexual individuals) can be sources of stress and create concerns about workplace and personal security for these clients (Fassinger 1995; Prince 1995; Rothblum and Bond 1996). Physical safety and social and emotional support have been identified as central to stress reduction (Hershberger and D'Augelli 1995; Levy 1992) among lesbian, gay, and bisexual people.

In addition to external stressors, Gonsiorek (1993) described the process by which many lesbian, gay, and bisexual people internalize negative societal attitudes. This internalization may result in self-image problems ranging from a lack of self-confidence to overt self-hatred (Gonsiorek 1993), depression (Meyer 1995; Shidlo 1994), or alcoholism and other substance abuse (Glaus 1988). Meyer and Dean (1998) showed that gay men scoring high on a measure of internalized homophobia were significantly more likely than less homophobic gay men to experience sexual dysfunction and relationship instability and to blame themselves for antigay victimization.

Psychologists working with lesbian, gay, and bisexual people are encouraged to assess the client's history of victimization as a result of harassment, discrimination, and violence. This assessment enables the psychologist to understand the extent to which the client's worldview has been affected by these abuses and whether any post-traumatic concerns need to be addressed. Furthermore, the psychological consequences of internalized negative attitudes toward homosexuality and bisexuality are not always obvious or conscious (Shidlo 1994). Therefore, in planning and conducting treatment, psychologists are encouraged to consider more subtle manifestations of these consequences, such as shame, anxiety, and low self-esteem, and to consider the differential diagnostic implications of such stressors, both historically and in a client's ongoing psychosocial context.

Guideline 4. Psychologists strive to understand how inaccurate or prejudicial views of homosexuality or bisexuality may affect the client's presentation in treatment and the therapeutic process.

Bias and misinformation about homosexuality and bisexuality continue to be widespread in society (APA 1998; Haldeman 1994). Because of the stigmatization of homosexuality and bisexuality, it is to be expected that many lesbian, gay, and bisexual people will feel conflicted or have significant questions about aspects or consequences of their sexual orientation (see Guideline 3). Fear of multiple personal losses — including family, friend, career, and spiritual community losses — as well as vulnerability to harassment, discrimination, and violence may contribute to an individual's fear of self-identifying as lesbian, gay, or bisexual. These factors have been considered central in creating a lesbian, gay, or bisexual person's discomfort with his or her sexual orientation (Davison 1991; Haldeman 1994). Many clients who are conflicted about or are questioning the implications of their sexual orientation seek psychotherapy to resolve their concerns. A psychologist who harbors prejudice or is misinformed about sexual orientation may offer responses to the questioning or conflicted client that may exacerbate the client's distress (see Guideline 2). Such a stance would consist of a psychologist's agreement with the notion that the only effective strategy for coping with such conflict or discrimination is to seek to change the lesbian, gay, or bisexual person's sexual orientation.

APA's (1998) "Appropriate Therapeutic Responses to Sexual Orientation" policy offers a framework for psychologists working with clients who are concerned about the implications of their sexual orientation. The policy highlights those sections of the APA Ethics Code that apply to all psychologists working with lesbian, gay, and bisexual clients. These sections include prohibitions against discriminatory practices (e.g., basing treatment on pathology-based views of homosexuality or bisexuality), a prohibition against the misrepresentation of scientific or clinical data (e.g., the unsubstantiated claim that sexual orientation can be changed), and a requirement for informed consent (APA 1992). Based on the APA Ethics Code, the "Appropriate Therapeutic Responses to Sexual Orientation" policy calls on psychologists to discuss the treatment, its theoretical basis, reasonable outcomes, and alternative treatment approaches. In providing clients with accurate information about the social stressors that may lead to discomfort with sexual orientation, psychologists may help neutralize the effects of prejudice and inoculate clients against further harm.

If psychologists are unable to provide this or other relevant information because of lack of knowledge or contravening personal beliefs, they should obtain the requisite information or make appropriate referrals (see Section 1.08 of the APA Ethics Code; APA 1992). Furthermore, when clients present with discomfort about their sexual orientation, it is important for psychologists to assess the psychological and social context in which this discomfort occurs. Such an assessment might include an examination of internal and external pressures on clients to change their sexual orientation; the presence or absence of social support and models of positive lesbian, gay, or bisexual life; and the extent to which clients associate homosexuality or bisexuality with negative stereotypes and experiences. These and other dimensions of sexual orientation discomfort are important for psychologists to explore, because the meanings associated with them are invariably complex. The role of psychologists, regardless of therapeutic orientation, is not to impose their beliefs on clients but to examine thoughtfully the clients' experiences and motives. Psychologists may also serve as a resource for accurate information about sexual orientation (e.g., by providing clients with access to empirical data on such questions as the development of sexual orientation or the relationship between mental health and sexual orientation).

Relationships and Families

Guideline 5. Psychologists strive to be knowledgeable about and respect the importance of lesbian, gay, and bisexual relationships.

Lesbian, gay, and bisexual couples are both similar to and different from heterosexual couples (Peplau, Veniegas, and Campbell 1996). They form relationships for similar reasons (Klinger 1996) and express similar satisfactions with their relationships (Kurdek 1995). The differences are derived from several factors, including different patterns of sexual behavior, gender role socialization, and the stigmatization of their relationships (Garnets and Kimmel 1993). Lesbian, gay, or bisexual people in relationships may seek therapy for reasons common to many couples or for reasons that are unique to those in same-sex relationships (Cabaj and Klinger 1996; Matteson 1996; Murphy 1994).

Common relationship problems, such as communication difficulties, sexual problems, dual-career issues, and commitment decisions, can be affected by societal and internalized negative attitudes toward same-sex relationships. Problems that present in therapy specific to lesbian, gay, and bisexual couples include disclosure of sexual orientation as a couple to family, work colleagues, health professionals, and caregivers; differences between partners in the disclosure process; issues derived from the effects of gender socialization in same-sex couples; and HIV status (Cabaj and Klinger 1996; Slater 1995). External issues, such as pressure from families of origin or current or former heterosexual partners, may also arise.

Parenting may present unique issues for lesbian, gay, and bisexual people (possible risks to child custody from previous heterosexual partners or grandparents, lack of legal rights for one of the parents, etc.). Changes in physical health may present unique issues, especially to older lesbian, gay, and bisexual couples (e.g., possible separation and loss of contact for partners in nursing homes or other inpatient settings).

Psychologists are encouraged to consider the negative effects of societal prejudice and discrimination on lesbian, gay, and bisexual relationships. It is important for psychologists to understand that, in the absence of socially sanctioned forms and supports for their relationships, lesbian, gay, and bisexual people may create their own relationship models and support systems. Therefore psychologists strive to be knowledgeable about the diverse nature of lesbian, gay, and bisexual relationships, and value and respect the meaning of these relationships.

Guideline 6. Psychologists strive to understand the particular circumstances and challenges faced by lesbian, gay, and bisexual parents.

Research has indicated no significant differences in the capabilities of lesbian, gay, and bisexual parents when compared with heterosexual parents (Allen and Burrell 1996; Bigner and Bozett 1990; Bozett 1989; Cramer 1986; Falk 1989; Gibbs 1988; Kweskin and Cook 1982; Patterson 1996a). However, lesbian, gay, and bisexual parents face challenges not encountered by most heterosexual parents because of the stigmata associated with homosexuality and bisexuality. Prejudice has led to institutional discrimination by the legal, educational, and social welfare systems. In a number of instances, lesbian, gay, and bisexual parents have lost custody of their children, have been restricted in visiting their children, have been prohibited from living with their domestic partners, or have been prevented from adopting or being foster parents on the basis of their sexual orientation (Editors of the *Harvard Law Review* 1990; Falk 1989; Patterson 1996b).

The primary difficulties that children of lesbian, gay, and bisexual parents face are associated with misconceptions about their parents that are held by society at large. Those in the legal and social welfare systems have raised three areas of concern about the impact that a parent's lesbian, gay, or bisexual orientation may have on children. These concerns include the influence of a lesbian, gay, or bisexual parent on a child's gender identity, gender role conformity, and sexual orientation. The body of research on lesbian mothers is currently considerably larger than that on gay fathers. In a comprehensive review of the literature, Patterson (1996b) concluded that there was no evidence of gender identity difficulties among children of lesbian mothers. She also reported studies indicating that gender role behavior among children of lesbian mothers was within normal ranges. Furthermore, children of lesbian, gay, and bisexual parents appear to be no different than peers raised by heterosexual parents in their emotional development and their likelihood of becoming homosexual (Bailey et al. 1995; Golombok and Tasker 1994, 1996).

Psychologists rely on scientifically and professionally derived knowledge and avoid discriminatory practices when conducting assessments for suitability for child custody, adoption, or foster parenting. Psychologists provide accurate information, and they correct misinformation in their work with parents, children, community organizations, and institutions (e.g., educational, legal, and social welfare systems).

Guideline 7. Psychologists recognize that the families of lesbian, gay, and bisexual people may include people who are not legally or biologically related.

The recognition of diverse family forms, including extended and blended families, is central to effective psychotherapy with ethnically and culturally diverse clients (Ho 1987; Thomas and Dansby 1985). For many lesbian, gay, and bisexual people, the primary partner or a network of close friends or both constitute an alternative family structure. In the absence of legal or institutional recognition, and in the face of societal, workplace, and familial discrimination, these alternative family structures may be more significant than the individual's family of origin (Kurdek 1988; Weston 1992). The importance of alternative family structures to lesbian, gay, and bisexual adults and youth is not always understood. Furthermore, these relationships have been devalued or denied by some psychologists (Garnets et al. 1991; Laird and Green 1996).

Social support is an important resource in a heterosexual couple's capacity to handle relationship distress (Sarason, Pierce, and Sarason 1990). People in same-sex relationships tend to derive less support in adulthood and old age from their families of origin than do their heterosexual counterparts (Kurdek 1991; Laird and Green 1996). Close relationships with a network of supportive friends also are considered by lesbian, gay, and bisexual youth to be extremely important. A strong friendship network has been viewed as pivotal in sexual identity exploration and development (D'Augelli 1991).

Given the importance of social support in overall relationship satisfaction and longevity, psychologists are encouraged to consider the importance of lesbian, gay, or bisexual alternative family relationships. Psychologists are also aware of the stress that clients may experience when their families of origin, employers, or others do not recognize their family structure. Therefore, when conducting assessments, psychologists are encouraged to ask clients to specify those they consider to be part of their family.

Guideline 8. Psychologists strive to understand how a person's homosexual or bisexual orientation may have an impact on his or her family of origin and the relationship to that family of origin.

Families of origin may be unprepared to accept a lesbian, gay, or bisexual child or family member because of familial, ethnic, or cultural norms; religious beliefs; or negative stereotypes (Chan 1995; Greene 1994b; Matteson 1996). The awareness of a family member's homosexuality or bisexuality may precipitate a family crisis that can result in the expulsion of the homosexual or bisexual member, rejection of the parents and siblings by the homosexual or bisexual member, parental guilt and self-incrimination, or conflicts within the parents' relationship (Griffin, Wirth, and Wirth 1996; Savin-Williams and Dube 1998; Strommen 1993). Even when reactions are positive, adjustments may be necessary to accommodate a new understanding of the lesbian, gay, or bisexual family member (Laird 1996). Many families face their own coming-out process when a family member discloses his or her homosexuality or bisexuality (Bass and Kaufman 1996; Savin-Williams and Dube 1998).

Families may need to adjust to the loss of hopes, perceptions, or expectations associated with the presumption of heterosexuality (Savin-Williams 1996). Families may also need assistance in developing new understandings of sexual orientation, in confronting the ways in which negative societal attitudes about homosexuality and bisexuality are manifested within the family, and in addressing difficulties related to societal stigmatization. Psychologists also are sensitive to the cultural variations in a family's reaction and ways of adapting to a lesbian, gay, or bisexual member. Local and national resources are available that can provide information, assistance, and support to family members (e.g., Parents, Family, and Friends of Lesbians and Gays; Children of Lesbians and Gays Everywhere).

Issues of Diversity

Guideline 9. Psychologists are encouraged to recognize the particular life issues or challenges that are related to multiple and often conflicting cultural norms, values, and beliefs that lesbian, gay, and bisexual members of racial and ethnic minorities face.

Racial/ethnic-minority lesbian, gay, and bisexual people must negotiate the norms, values, and beliefs regarding homosexuality and bisexuality of both mainstream and minority cultures (Chan 1992, 1995; Greene 1994b; Manalansan 1996; Rust 1996). Cultural variation in these norms, values, and beliefs can be a major source of psychological stress. There may be no one group or community to which a racial/ethnic-minority lesbian, gay, or bisexual person can anchor his or her identity and receive full acceptance.

This problem may be an even greater challenge for racial/ethnic-minority youth who are exploring their sexual identity and orientation.

In offering psychological services to racially and ethnically diverse lesbian, gay, and bisexual populations, it is not sufficient that psychologists simply recognize the racial and ethnic backgrounds of their clients. Multiple minority status may complicate and exacerbate the difficulties these clients experience. Clients may be affected by the ways in which their cultures view homosexuality and bisexuality (Gock 1992; Greene 1994c). The effects of racism within lesbian, gay, and bisexual communities are also critical factors to consider (Gock 1992; Greene 1994a; Morales 1996; Rust 1996). Sensitivity to the complex dynamics associated with factors such as cultural values about gender roles, religious and procreative beliefs, degree of individual and family acculturation, and the personal and cultural history of discrimination or oppression is also important. All these factors may have a significant impact on identity integration and psychological and social functioning (Chan 1995; Greene 1994a; Rust 1996).

Guideline 10. Psychologists are encouraged to recognize the particular challenges that bisexual individuals experience.

Bisexual adults and youth may experience a variety of stressors in addition to the societal prejudice resulting from same-sex attractions. One such stressor is that the polarization of sexual orientation into heterosexual and homosexual categories invalidates bisexuality (Eliason 1997; Fox 1996; Markowitz 1995; Matteson 1996; Ochs 1996; Paul 1996; Shuster 1987). This view has influenced psychological theory and practice as well as societal attitudes and institutions. As a result, bisexuality may be inaccurately represented as a transitional state. Although no evidence of psychological maladjustment or psychopathology has been found, bisexual individuals who do not adopt an exclusively heterosexual or homosexual identity may nevertheless be viewed as developmentally arrested or in other ways psychologically impaired (Fox 1996).

Negative individual and societal attitudes toward bisexuality in both the heterosexual and homosexual communities adversely affect bisexual individuals (Fox 1996; Ochs 1996). Such attitudes may be due to a lack of information about or access to a visible and supportive community of other bisexual individuals (Hutchins 1996). According to Hutchins (1996) and

Matteson (1996), information on community resources can facilitate the development and maintenance of positive bisexual identities.

Psychotherapy with bisexual clients involves respect for the diversity of their experiences and relationships (Fox 1996; Klein, Sepekoff, and Wolf 1985; Matteson 1996). Psychologists are encouraged to adopt a more complex understanding of sexual orientation, rather than a dichotomous model, in their approach to treatment (Matteson 1996).

Guideline 11. Psychologists strive to understand the special problems and risks that exist for lesbian, gay, and bisexual youth.

It is important for psychologists to understand the unique difficulties and risks that lesbian, gay, and bisexual adolescents face (D'Augelli 1998). Lesbian, gay, and bisexual youth may experience estrangement from their parents when they reveal their sexual orientation (Cramer and Roach 1988). When lesbian, gay, or bisexual youths have been rejected by their parents, they are at increased risk of becoming homeless (Kruks 1991), may resort to prostitution (Coleman 1989), and are at greater risk of HIV infection (Gold and Skinner 1992) and stress (Hershberger and D'Augelli 1995; Savin-Williams 1994). Youths who identify as lesbian, gay, or bisexual at an early age are also at increased risk of becoming victims of violence (Hunter 1990), even within their families (Harry 1989); of abusing substances (Garofalo et al. 1998); and of attempting suicide (Remafedi et al. 1998).

Such difficulties may also complicate the developmental tasks of adolescence (Gonsiorek 1991). The social stigmata associated with a lesbian, gay, or bisexual identity may also complicate career development and choice issues (Prince 1995). Perceived parental and peer acceptance has an important impact on lesbian, gay, and bisexual youths' adjustment (Savin-Williams 1989). Although peers and educators may be helpful in improving the psychosocial environment for these youths (J. Anderson 1994; Caywood 1993; Lipkin 1992; Woog 1995), they may not be useful if they lack the appropriate information and experience. When these potential sources of support are heterosexist, they may cause additional conflict and distress (Martin and Hetrick 1988; Telljohann and Price 1993).

Appropriate therapeutic strategies for work with lesbian, gay, and bisexual youths have been described in the professional literature (Browning 1987; Coleman and Remafedi 1989; Gonsiorek 1988; Ryan and Futterman 1998).

Psychologists strive to create a safe therapeutic context for youth to explore sexual orientation issues. Psychologists should be aware of the ways in which psychological, ethical, and legal issues involved in working with minors are made even more complex when working with lesbian, gay, and bisexual youths.[3]

Guideline 12. Psychologists consider generational differences within lesbian, gay, and bisexual populations and the particular challenges that lesbian, gay, and bisexual older adults may experience.

Psychologists are encouraged to recognize that (a) lesbian, gay, and bisexual people of different generations may have had significantly different developmental experiences; and (b) older lesbian, gay, and bisexual people grew into adulthood with peers who shared characteristics that may make them distinct as a generation (Kimmel 1995). Examples of factors influencing generational differences include changing societal attitudes toward homosexuality, the AIDS epidemic, and the women's and civil rights movements. These cohort effects may significantly influence gay identity development as well as psychological and social functioning (Fassinger 1997; Frost 1997; McDougal 1993).

Psychologists are encouraged to be aware of the special transitions and life tasks that lesbian, gay, and bisexual older adults face, such as normative changes in health, retirement, finances, and social support (Berger 1996; Slater 1995). In many respects, these issues are the same as those of heterosexual older adults (Kimmel 1995; Kirkpatrick 1989; Reid 1995; Slater 1995). However, clients' multiple minority status may exacerbate problems, and gender may create different issues (see Guideline 9; Quam and Whitford 1992; Turk-Charles, Rose, and Gatz 1996). Moreover, tasks relating to the end of one's lifespan are often complex for lesbian, gay, and bisexual older adults and can develop into crises because of psychosocial stressors and heterosexism (Adelman 1990; Berger and Kelly 1996). Older lesbian, gay, and bisexual couples present potential issues, particularly because they lack legal rights and protection that are afforded older heterosexual couples (see Guideline 5). Psychologists are encouraged to (a) be aware that state laws and regulations may affect their clients' rights; and (b) support clients in seeking legal consultation related to medical crises, financial crises, and death.

Older adults are a diverse group, and normative changes in aging may be positive as well as negative and are not necessarily related to pathology or a client's sexual orientation. There are several descriptions of positive adaptation to aging among lesbian, gay, and bisexual older adults (Friend 1990; Lee 1987) that may be helpful to psychologists treating these clients. Having already addressed issues of being a stigmatized minority may help older gay men, lesbians, and bisexual people to address ageism and transitions in old age (Fassinger 1997; Kimmel 1995).

Guideline 13. Psychologists are encouraged to recognize the particular challenges that lesbian, gay, and bisexual individuals experience with physical, sensory, and cognitive-emotional disabilities.

Lesbian, gay, and bisexual individuals with physical or sensory disabilities may experience a wide range of challenges related to the social stigmata associated with both disability and sexual orientation (Saad 1997). One concern is the extent to which the individual's self-concept is affected by social stigmata, which, in turn, may affect the individual's sense of autonomy and personal agency, sexuality, and self-confidence (Shapiro 1993). For example, people with disabilities may be particularly vulnerable to the effects of "looksism" (i.e., basing social value on physical appearance and marginalizing those who do not conform, for reasons of age, ability, or appearance, to socially constructed standards). Another area of concern relates to how physical disability affects a person's relationships with partners, family, caregivers, and health care professionals. Within partner relationships, there may be issues related to life management, including mobility, sexuality, and medical and legal decision making. Family support may not be available because of negative reactions to the person's sexual orientation (McDaniel 1995; Rolland 1994). There may also be stress associated with a lesbian, gay, or bisexual person's need to come out to caregivers and health care professionals (O'Toole and Bregante 1992).

Lesbian, gay, and bisexual people with disabilities may not have access to information, support, and services that are available to lesbian, gay, and bisexual people without disabilities (O'Toole and Bregante 1992). Lack of societal recognition for lesbian, gay, and bisexual people in relationships affects those with ongoing medical concerns, such as medical insurance coverage for domestic partners, family medical-leave policies, hospital visitation, medical decision making by partners, and survivorship issues (Laird 1993).

Saad (1997) has recommended that psychologists inquire about the person's sexual history and current sexual functioning, provide information, and facilitate problem solving in this area. Studies have reported that many lesbians and gay men with disabilities have experienced coercive sexual encounters (Swartz 1995; Thompson 1994). It may be important for psychologists to assess the extent to which the person may have experienced sexual or physical victimization. Finally, given the prejudice, discrimination, and lack of social support both within and beyond the lesbian, gay, and bisexual communities, it also may be important that psychologists recognize that when physical, sensory, or cognitive-emotional disabilities are present, social barriers and negative attitudes may limit life choices (Shapiro 1993).

Education

Guideline 14. Psychologists support the provision of professional education and training on lesbian, gay, and bisexual issues.

A gap remains between policy and practice in the psychotherapeutic treatment of lesbian, gay, and bisexual clients (Dworkin 1992; Fox 1996; Garnets et al. 1991; Greene 1994b; Iasenza 1989; Markowitz 1991, 1995; Nystrom 1997). Despite the recent addition of diversity training during graduate education and internship, studies have shown that graduate students in psychology often report inadequate education and training in lesbian, gay, and bisexual issues (Buhrke 1989; Glenn and Russell 1986; Pilkington and Cantor 1996) and that graduate students and novice therapists feel unprepared to work effectively with lesbian, gay, and bisexual clients (Allison, Crawford, Echemendia, Robinson, and Knepp 1994; Buhrke 1989; Graham et al. 1984). The gap between policy and practice can be addressed by including information regarding these populations in all training programs.

Faculty, supervisors, and consultants are encouraged to integrate current information about lesbian, gay, and bisexual issues throughout training for professional practice. Resources are available to assist faculty in including lesbian, gay, and bisexual content in their curricula (e.g., APA 1995; Buhrke and Douce 1991; Cabaj and Stein 1996; Croteau and Bieschke 1996; Greene and Croom 2000; Hancock 1995; Pope 1995; Savin-Williams and Cohen 1996). Psychologists who have expertise in lesbian, gay, and bisexual psychology may be used on a full-time or part-time basis to provide training and consultation to faculty as well as course and clinical supervision to students. Faculty and supervisors may be encouraged to seek continuing education course work in lesbian, gay, and bisexual issues.

Guideline 15. Psychologists are encouraged to increase their knowledge and understanding of homosexuality and bisexuality through continuing education, training, supervision, and consultation.

The APA Ethics Code urges psychologists to "maintain a reasonable level of awareness of current scientific and professional information . . . and undertake ongoing efforts to maintain competence in the skills they use" (APA 1992:1600). It is unfortunate that the education, training, practice experience, consultation, and supervision that psychologists receive regarding lesbian, gay, and bisexual issues have often been inadequate, outdated, or unavailable (Buhrke 1989; Glenn and Russell 1986; Graham et al. 1984; Pilkington and Cantor 1996). Studies have revealed psychotherapists' prejudice and insensitivity in working with lesbian, gay, and bisexual people (Garnets et al. 1991; Liddle 1996; Nystrom 1997; Phillips and Fischer 1998; Winegarten et al. 1994). Preparation for the provision of psychotherapy to lesbian, gay, and bisexual clients may include additional education, training, experience, consultation, or supervision in such areas as (a) human sexuality; (b) lesbian, gay, and bisexual identity development; (c) the effects of stigmatization on lesbian, gay, and bisexual individuals and couples, and their families; (d) ethnic and cultural factors affecting identity; and (e) unique career development and workplace issues that lesbian, gay, and bisexual individuals experience.

Guideline 16. Psychologists make reasonable efforts to familiarize themselves with relevant mental health, educational, and community resources for lesbian, gay, and bisexual people.

Knowledge of community resources has been found to be a factor that lesbian, gay, and bisexual clients consider in their selection of psychotherapists (Liddle 1997; Matteson 1996). The availability of lesbian, gay, and bisexual community resources varies dramatically according to location; thus it is helpful for psychologists to know that sources of information and support can be found at the local, regional, and national levels. Several authors have provided discussion and overviews of lesbian, gay, and bisexual communities (D'Augelli and Garnets 1995; Esterberg 1996; Hutchins 1996).

It is useful for psychologists to be aware of the nature and availability of lesbian, gay, and bisexual community resources for clients and their families. Of particular use are organizations that provide support to the parents, young and adult children, and friends of lesbian, gay, and bisexual clients (e.g., Parents, Family, and Friends of Lesbians and Gays; Children of Lesbians and Gays Everywhere); programs that provide special attention to the victims of hate crimes; programs for lesbian, gay, and bisexual youths; and groups that focus on parenting issues, relationships, or coming out. There are also professional organizations and groups for lesbian, gay, and bisexual people of color; groups for people with HIV issues; groups for socializing and networking in business; and groups that can provide spiritual assistance. Psychologists and clients can also use electronic resources such as Internet news groups, mailing lists, and web pages as valuable sources of information and support. In addition, certain businesses cater to lesbian, gay, and bisexual clientele. Psychologists who are unfamiliar with local lesbian, gay, or bisexual resources may obtain consultations or referrals from local agencies, state psychological associations, or the APA.

Editor's Note

These guidelines were adopted by the American Psychological Association, Council of Representatives, on February 26, 2000.

Author's Note

These guidelines were developed by the Division 44/Committee on Lesbian, Gay, and Bisexual Concerns Joint Task Force on Guidelines for Psychotherapy with Lesbian, Gay, and Bisexual Clients (JTF).

The JTF co-chairs were Kristin A. Hancock, Ph.D. (John F. Kennedy University, Orinda, Calif.), and Armand R. Cerbone, Ph.D. (independent practice, Chicago). The JTF members included Douglas C. Haldeman, Ph.D. (independent practice, Seattle); Christine M. Browning, Ph.D. (University of California, Irvine); Ronald C. Fox, Ph.D. (independent practice, San Francisco); Terry S. Gock, Ph.D. (Asian Pacific Family Center, Rosemead, Calif.); Steven E. James, Ph.D. (Goddard College, Plainfield, Vt.); Scott D. Pytluk, Ph.D. (independent practice, Chicago); and Ariel Shidlo, Ph.D. (Columbia University, New York).

Acknowledgments

The Joint Task Force on Guidelines for Psychotherapy with Lesbian, Gay, and Bisexual Clients wishes to acknowledge Alan K. Malyon, Ph.D., for his foresight regarding the need for guidelines and for initiating their careful development. In addition, the JTF is grateful to Catherine Acuff, Ph.D. (Board of Directors), for her vision, support, and skillful guidance. Her humor, wisdom, and negotiating skills were extraordinarily helpful throughout the development of these guidelines. The JTF also extends thanks to Ronald H. Rozensky, Ph.D. (Board of Professional Affairs); Lisa Robbin Grossman, Ph.D./JD (Committee on Professional Practice and Standards); and Daniel J. Abrahamson, Ph.D. (Board of Professional Affairs), for their thorough and thoughtful reviews and editorial suggestions; to Kate F. Hays, Ph.D., Harriette W. Kaley, Ph.D., and Bianca Cody Murphy. Ph.D. (Board for the Advancement of Psychology in the Public Interest), for their assistance in providing important feedback on several earlier versions of the guidelines; to Ruth Ullman Paige, Ph.D. (Board of Directors), Jean A. Carter, Ph.D. (Committee for the Advancement of Professional Practice); Laura S. Brown, Ph.D. (Division 35), and the many other American Psychological Association colleagues for the consultation and assistance they gave to this project: to the Board for the Advancement of Psychology in the Public Interest, the Board of Professional Affairs, the Committee on Lesbian, Gay, and Bisexual Concerns, and especially Division 44 for their kind support; to Clinton W. Anderson (Lesbian, Gay, and Bisexual Concerns Officer) for the hard work, patience, and counsel he provided to the JTF throughout this project: to Geoffrey Reed, Ph.D. (Assistant Executive Director for Professional Development), whose considerable knowledge and experience were brought to this project when it was most needed: and the Committee on Lesbian, Gay, and Bisexual Concerns' Task Force on Bias, whose work (published in the September 1991 issue of the *American Psychologist*) formed the basis for the development of these guidelines.

Notes

1. Throughout this document, the term *clients* refers to individuals across the life span, including youth, adult, and older adult lesbian, gay, and bisexual clients. There may be issues that are specific to a given age range, and, when appropriate, the document identifies those groups.

2. Hereafter, this document is referred to as the APA Ethics Code.

3. Psychologists should be aware of relevant federal and state laws, regulations, and professional standards that address these treatment issues, such as confidentiality and informed consent.

References

Adelman, M. 1990. Stigma, gay lifestyles, and adjustment to aging: A study of later-life gay men and lesbians. *Journal of Homosexuality* 20(3–4):7–32.

Allen, M., and N. Burrell. 1996. Comparing the impact of homosexual and heterosexual parents on children: Meta-analysis of existing research. *Journal of Homosexuality* 32(2):19–35.

Allison, K., I. Crawford, R. Echemendia, L. Robinson, and D. Knepp. 1994. Human diversity and professional competence: Training in clinical and counseling psychology revisited. *American Psychologist* 49:792–96.

American Association for Marriage and Family Therapy. 1991. *AAMFT code of ethics.* Washington, D.C.: Author.

American Counseling Association. 1996. ACA code of ethics and standards of practice. In B. Herlihy and G. Corey, eds., ACA *Ethical Standards Casebook*, 5th ed., pp. 26–59. Alexandria, Va.: Author.

American Psychiatric Association. 1974. Position statement on homosexuality and civil rights. *American Journal of Psychiatry* 131:497.

American Psychological Association. 1992. Ethical principles and code of conduct. *American Psychologist* 47:1597–1611.

American Psychological Association. 1995. *Lesbian and Gay Parenting: A Resource for Psychologists.* Washington, D.C.: Author.

American Psychological Association. 1998. Appropriate therapeutic responses to sexual orientation in the proceedings of the American Psychological Association, Incorporated, for the legislative year 1997. *American Psychologist* 53:882–939.

Anderson, J. 1994. School climate for gay and lesbian students and staff members. *Phi Delta Kappan* 76:151–54.

Anderson, S. 1996. Addressing heterosexist bias in the treatment of lesbian couples with chemical dependency. In J. Laird and R. J. Green, eds., *Lesbians and Gays in Couples and Families: A Handbook for Therapists*, pp. 316–40. San Francisco: Jossey-Bass.

Bailey, J., D. Bobrow, M. Wolfe, and S. Mikach. 1995. Sexual orientation of adult sons of gay fathers. *Developmental Psychology* 31:124–29.

Bass, E., and K. Kaufman. 1996. *Free Your Mind: The Book for Gay, Lesbian, and Bisexual Youth and Their Allies.* New York: Harper Collins.

Berger, R. 1996. *Gay and Gray: The Older Homosexual Man.* 2nd ed. New York: Harrington Park.

Berger, R., and J. Kelly. 1996. Gay men and lesbians grown older. In R. Cabaj and

T. Stein, eds., *Textbook of Homosexuality and Mental Health*, pp. 305–16. Washington, D.C.: American Psychiatric Press.

Bersoff, D., and D. Ogden. 1991. APA amicus curiae briefs: Furthering lesbian and gay male civil rights. *American Psychologist* 46:950–56.

Bigner, J., and F. Bozett. 1990. Parenting by gay fathers. In F. Bozett and M. Sussman, eds., *Homosexuality and Family Relations*, pp. 155–76. New York: Harrington Park.

Bozett, F. 1989. Gay fathers: A review of the literature. In F. Bozett, ed., *Homosexuality and the Family*, pp. 137–62. New York: Harrington Park.

Brown, L. 1989. Lesbians, gay men, and their families: Common clinical issues. *Journal of Gay and Lesbian Psychotherapy* 1(1):65–77.

Browning, C. 1987. Therapeutic issues and intervention strategies with young adult lesbian clients: A developmental approach. *Journal of Homosexuality* 14(1/2): 45–52.

Buhrke, R. 1989. Female student perspectives on training in lesbian and gay issues. *Counseling Psychologist* 17:629–36.

Buhrke, R. A., and L. G. Douce. 1991. Training issues for counseling psychologists in working with lesbians and gay men. *Counseling Psychologist* 19:216–39.

Cabaj, R., and R. Klinger. 1996. Psychotherapeutic interventions with lesbian and gay couples. In R. Cabaj and T. Stein, eds., *Textbook of Homosexuality and Mental Health*, pp. 485–502. Washington, D.C.: American Psychiatric Press.

Cabaj, R. P., and T. S. Stein. 1996. *Textbook of Homosexuality and Mental Health.* Washington, D.C.: American Psychiatric Press.

Canadian Psychological Association. 1995. *Canadian Code of Ethics for Psychologists.* Ottawa: Author. Retrieved November 18, 2000, from the World Wide Web: http://www.cpa.ca/ethics.html

Caywood, C. 1993. Reaching out to gay teens. *School Library Journal* 39(4):50.

Chan, C. 1992. Asian-American lesbians and gay men. In S. Dworkin and F. Gutierrez, eds., *Counseling Gay Men and Lesbians: Journey to the End of the Rainbow*, pp. 115–24. Alexandria, Va.: American Association for Counseling and Development.

Chan, C. 1995. Issues of sexual identity in an ethnic minority: The case of Chinese American lesbians, gay men, and bisexual people. In A. D'Augelli and C. Patterson, eds., *Lesbian, Gay, and Bisexual Identities over the Lifespan: Psychological Perspectives*, pp. 87–101. New York: Oxford University Press.

Coleman, E. 1989. The development of male prostitution activity among gay and bisexual adolescents. In G. Herdt, ed., *Gay and Lesbian Youth*, pp. 131–49. New York: Haworth.

Coleman, E., and G. Remafedi. 1989. Gay, lesbian, and bisexual adolescents: A critical challenge to counselors. *Journal of Homosexuality* 18(3/4):70–81.

Conger, J. 1975. Proceedings of the American Psychological Association for the year

1974: Minutes of the annual meeting of the Council of Representatives. *American Psychologist* 30:620–51.

Corey, G., M. Schneider-Corey, and P. Callanan. 1993. *Issues and Ethics in the Helping Professions.* 4th ed. Belmont, Calif.: Brooks/Cole.

Coyle, A. 1993. A study of psychological well-being among gay men using the GHQ-30. *British Journal of Clinical Psychology* 32:218–20.

Cramer, D. 1986. Gay parents and their children: A review of research and practical implications. *Journal of Counseling and Development* 64:504–7.

Cramer, D., and A. Roach. 1988. Coming out to Mom and Dad: A study of gay males and their relationships with their parents. *Journal of Homosexuality* 15(3/4):79–91.

Croteau, J., and K. Bieschke. 1996. Beyond pioneering: An introduction to the special issue on the vocational issues of lesbian women and gay men. *Journal of Vocational Behavior* 48:119–24.

D'Augelli, A. 1991. Gay men in college: Identity processes and adaptations. *Journal of College Student Development* 32:140–46.

D'Augelli, A. 1998. Developmental implications of victimization of lesbian, gay, and bisexual youth. In G. Herek, ed., *Psychological Perspectives on Lesbian and Gay Issues.* Vol. 4: *Stigma and Sexual Orientation: Understanding Prejudice Against Lesbians, Gay Men, and Bisexuals,* pp. 187–210. Thousand Oaks, Calif.: Sage.

D'Augelli, A., and L. D. Garnets. 1995. Lesbian, gay, and bisexual communities. In A. D'Augelli and C. Patterson, eds., *Lesbian, Gay, and Bisexual Identities over the Lifespan: Psychological Perspectives,* pp. 293–320. New York: Oxford University Press.

Davison, G. 1991. Constructionism and morality in therapy for homosexuality. In J. Gonsiorek and J. Weinrich, eds., *Homosexuality: Research Implications for Public Policy,* pp. 137–48. Newbury Park, Calif.: Sage.

DiPlacido, J. 1998. Minority stress among lesbians, gay men, and bisexuals: A consequence of heterosexism, homophobia, and stigmatization. In G. Herek, ed., *Psychological Perspectives on Lesbian and Gay Issues.* Vol. 4: *Stigma and Sexual Orientation: Understanding Prejudice Against Lesbians, Gay Men, and Bisexuals,* pp. 138–59. Thousand Oaks, Calif.: Sage.

Dworkin, S. 1992. Some ethical considerations when counseling gay, lesbian, and bisexual clients. In S. Dworkin and F. Gutierrez, eds., *Counseling Gay Men and Lesbians: Journey to the End of the Rainbow,* pp. 325–34. Alexandria, Va.: American Association for Counseling and Development.

Editors of the *Harvard Law Review.* 1990. *Sexual Orientation and the Law.* Cambridge, Mass.: Harvard University Press.

Eliason, M. 1997. The prevalence and nature of biphobia in heterosexual undergraduate students. *Archives of Sexual Behavior* 26:317–25.

Esterberg, K. 1996. Gay cultures, gay communities: The social organization of lesbians, gay men, and bisexuals. In R. Savin-Williams and K. Cohen, eds., *The*

Lives of Lesbians, Gays, and Bisexuals: Children to Adults, pp. 337–92. Fort Worth, Tex.: Harcourt Brace.

Falk, P. 1989. Lesbian mothers: Psychosocial assumptions in family law. *American Psychologist* 44:941–47.

Fassinger, R. 1995. From invisibility to integration: Lesbian identity in the workplace. *Career Development Quarterly* 14:148–67.

Fassinger, R. 1997. Issues in group work with older lesbians. *Group* 21:191–210.

Firestein, B. 1996. Bisexuality as a paradigm shift: Transforming our disciplines. In B. Firestein, ed., *Bisexuality: The Psychology and Politics of an Invisible Minority*, pp. 263–91. Thousand Oaks, Calif.: Sage.

Fox, R. 1996. Bisexuality in perspective: A review of theory and research. In B. Firestein, ed., *Bisexuality: The Psychology and Politics of an Invisible Minority*, pp. 3–50. Thousand Oaks, Calif.: Sage.

Friend, R. 1990. Older lesbian and gay people: A theory of successful aging. *Journal of Homosexuality* 20(3/4):99–118.

Frost, J. 1997. Group psychotherapy with the gay male: Treatment of choice. *Group* 21:267–85.

Garnets, L. D., K. Hancock, S. Cochran, J. Goodchilds, and L. Peplau. 1991. Issues in psychotherapy with lesbians and gay men: A survey of psychologists. *American Psychologist* 46:964–72.

Garnets, L. D., and D. Kimmel. 1993. Lesbian and gay male dimensions in the psychological study of human diversity. In L. Garnets and D. Kimmel, eds., *Psychological Perspectives on Lesbian and Gay Male Experiences*, pp. 1–51. New York: Columbia University Press.

Garofalo, R., R. Wolf, S. Kessel, S. Palfrey, and R. H. DuRant. 1998. The association between health risk behaviors and sexual orientation among a school-based sample of adolescents. *Pediatrics* 101:895–902.

Gibbs, E. 1988. Psychosocial development of children raised by lesbian mothers: A review of research. *Women and Therapy* 8:65–75.

Glaus, O. 1988. Alcoholism, chemical dependency, and the lesbian client. *Women and Therapy* 8:131–44.

Glenn, A., and R. Russell. 1986. Heterosexual bias among counselor trainees. *Counselor Education and Supervision* 25:222–29.

Gock, T. 1992. The challenges of being gay, Asian, and proud. In B. Berzon, ed., *Positively Gay*, pp. 247–52. Millbrae. Calif.: Celestial Arts.

Gold, R., and M. Skinner. 1992. Situational factors and thought processes associated with unprotected intercourse in young gay men. *AIDS* 6:1021–30.

Golombok, S., and F. Tasker. 1994. Children in lesbian and gay families: Theories and evidence. *Annual Review of Sex Research* 5:73–100.

Golombok, S., and F. Tasker. 1996. Do parents influence the sexual orientation of their children? Findings from a longitudinal study of lesbian families. *Developmental Psychology* 32:3–11.

Gonsiorek, J. 1988. Mental health issues of gay and lesbian adolescents. *Journal of Adolescent Health Care* 9:114–21.

Gonsiorek, J. 1991. The empirical basis for the demise of the illness model of homosexuality. In J. Gonsiorek and J. Weinrich, eds., *Homosexuality: Research Implications for Public Policy*, pp. 115–36. Newbury Park, Calif.: Sage.

Gonsiorek, J. 1993. Mental health issues of gay and lesbian adolescents. In L. Garnets and D. Kimmel, eds., *Psychological Perspectives on Lesbian and Gay Male Experiences*, pp. 469–85. New York: Columbia University Press.

Graham, D., E. Rawlings, H. Halpern, and J. Hermes. 1984. Therapists? Needs for training in counseling lesbians and gay men. *Professional Psychology: Research and Practice* 15:482–96.

Greene, B. 1994a. Ethnic minority lesbians and gay men: Mental health and treatment issues. *Journal of Consulting and Clinical Psychology* 62:243–51.

Greene, B. 1994b. Lesbian and gay sexual orientations: Implications for clinical training, practice, and research. In B. Greene and G. Herek, eds., *Psychological Perspectives on Lesbian and Gay Issues.* Vol.1: *Lesbian and Gay Psychology: Theory, Research, and Clinical Applications*, pp. 1–24. Thousand Oaks, Calif.: Sage.

Greene, B. 1994c. Lesbian women of color: Triple jeopardy. In L. Comas-Diaz and B. Greene, eds., *Women of Color: Integrating Ethnic and Gender Identities in Psychotherapy*, pp. 389–427. New York: Guilford.

Greene, B., and G. Croom, eds. 2000. *Psychological Perspectives on Lesbian and Gay Issues.* Vol. 5: *Education, Research, and Practice in Lesbian, Gay, Bisexual, and Transgendered Psychology: A Resource Manual.* Thousand Oaks, Calif.: Sage.

Griffin, C., M. Wirth, and A. Wirth. 1996. *Beyond Acceptance: Parents of Lesbians and Gays Talk about Their Experiences.* New York: St. Martin's.

Haldeman, D. 1994. The practice and ethics of sexual orientation conversion therapy. *Journal of Consulting and Clinical Psychology* 62:221–27.

Hancock, K. A. 1995. Psychotherapy with lesbians and gay men. In A. D'Augelli and C. Patterson, eds., *Lesbian, Gay, and Bisexual Identities over the Lifespan: Psychological perspectives*, pp. 398–432. New York: Oxford University Press.

Harry, J. 1989. Parental physical abuse and sexual orientation in males. *Archives of Sexual Behavior* 18:251–61.

Herek, G. 1990. Gay people and government security clearance: A social perspective. *American Psychologist* 45:1035–42.

Herek, G. 1991. Stigma, prejudice, and violence against lesbians and gay men. In J. Gonsiorek and J. Weinrich, eds., *Homosexuality: Research Implications for Public Policy*, pp. 60–80. Newbury Park, Calif.: Sage.

Herek, G. 1995. Psychological heterosexism in the United States. In A. D'Augelli and C. Patterson, eds., *Lesbian, Gay, and Bisexual Identities over the Lifespan: Psychological Perspectives*, pp. 321–46. New York: Oxford University Press.

Hershberger, S., and A. D'Augelli. 1995. The impact of victimization on the mental health and suicidality of lesbian, gay, and bisexual youths. *Developmental Psychology* 31:65–74.

Ho, M. 1987. *Family Therapy with Ethnic Minorities.* Newbury Park, Calif.: Sage.

Hooker, E. 1957. The adjustment of the male overt homosexual. *Journal of Projective Techniques* 21:18–31.

Hunter, J. 1990. Violence against lesbian and gay male youths. *Journal of Interpersonal Violence* 5:295–300.

Hutchins, L. 1996. Bisexuality: Politics and community. In B. Firestein, ed., *Bisexuality: The Psychology and Politics of an Invisible Minority*, pp. 240–59. Thousand Oaks, Calif.: Sage.

Iasenza, S. 1989. Some challenges of integrating sexual orientations into counselor training and research. *Journal of Counseling and Development* 68:73–76.

Kimmel, D. 1995. Lesbians and gay men also grow old. In L. Bond, S. Cutler, and A. Grams, eds., *Promoting Successful and Productive Aging*, pp. 289–303. Thousand Oaks, Calif.: Sage.

Kirkpatrick, M. 1989. Lesbians: A different middle age? In J. M. Oldham and R. S. Liebert, eds., *The Middle Years: New Psychoanalytic Perspectives*, pp. 135–48. New Haven, Conn.: Yale University Press.

Klein, F., B. Sepekoff, and T. Wolf. 1985. Sexual orientation: A multivariable dynamic process. *Journal of Homosexuality* 11(1/2):35–49.

Klinger, R. 1996. Lesbian couples. In R. Cabaj and T. Stein, eds., *Textbook of Homosexuality and Mental Health*, pp. 339–52. Washington, D.C.: American Psychiatric Press.

Kruks, G. 1991. Gay and lesbian homeless/street youth: Special issues and concerns. *Journal of Adolescent Health* 12:515–18.

Kurdek, L. 1988. Perceived social support in gays and lesbians in cohabiting relationships. *Journal of Personality and Social Psychology* 54:504–9.

Kurdek, L. 1991. Correlates of relationship satisfaction in cohabiting gay and lesbian couples: Integration of contextual, investment, and problem-solving models. *Journal of Personality and Social Psychology* 61:910–22.

Kurdek, L. 1995. Lesbian and gay couples. In A. D'Augelli and C. Patterson, eds., *Lesbian, Gay, and Bisexual Identities over the Lifespan: Psychological Perspectives*, pp. 243–61. New York: Oxford University Press.

Kweskin, S., and A. Cook. 1982. Heterosexual and homosexual mothers' self-described sex-role behavior and ideal sex-role behavior in children. *Sex Roles* 8:967–75.

Laird, J. 1993. Lesbian and gay families. In F. Walsh, ed., *Normal Family Processes*, 2nd ed., pp. 282–328. New York: Norton.

Laird, J. 1996. Invisible ties: Lesbians and their families of origin. In J. Laird and R. J. Green, eds., *Lesbians and Gays in Couples and Families: A Handbook for Therapists*, pp. 89–122. San Francisco: Jossey-Bass.

Laird, J., and R. J. Green. 1996. Lesbians and gays in couples and families: Central issues. In J. Laird and R. J. Green, eds., *Lesbians and Gays in Couples and Families: A Handbook for Therapists*, pp. 1–12. San Francisco: Jossey-Bass.

Lee, J. 1987. What can homosexual aging studies contribute to theories of aging? *Journal of Homosexuality* 13(4):43–71.

Levy, E. 1992. Strengthening the coping resources of lesbian families. *Families in Society* 73:23–31.

Liddle, B. 1996. Therapist sexual orientation, gender, and counseling practices as they relate to ratings of helpfulness by gay and lesbian clients. *Journal of Counseling Psychology* 43:394–401.

Liddle, B. 1997. Gay and lesbian clients? Selection of therapists and utilization of therapy. *Psychotherapy* 34:11–18.

Lipkin, A. 1992. Project 10: Gay and lesbian students find acceptance in their school community. *Teaching Tolerance* 1(2):25–27.

Manalansan, M. 1996. Double minorities: Latino, Black, and Asian men who have sex with men. In R. Savin-Williams and K. Cohen, eds., *The Lives of Lesbians, Gays, and Bisexuals: Children to Adults*, pp. 393–415. Fort Worth, Tex.: Harcourt Brace.

Markowitz, L. 1991. Homosexuality: Are we still in the dark? *Family Therapy Networker* 15(January/February):26–29, 31–35.

Markowitz, L. 1995. Bisexuality: Challenging our either/or thinking. *In the Family* 1(July):6–11, 23.

Martin, A., and E. Hetrick. 1988. The stigmatization of the gay and lesbian adolescent. *Journal of Homosexuality* 15(1/2):163–83.

Matteson, D. 1996. Counseling and psychotherapy with bisexual and exploring clients. In B. Firestein, ed., *Bisexuality: The psychology and politics of an invisible minority*, pp. 185–213. Thousand Oaks, Calif.: Sage.

McDaniel, J. 1995. *The Lesbian Couples' Guide: Finding the Right Woman and Creating a Life Together*. New York: Harper Collins.

McDougal, G. 1993. Therapeutic issues with gay and lesbian elders. *Clinical Gerontologist* 14:45–57.

Meyer, I. 1995. Minority stress and mental health in gay men. *Journal of Health and Social Behavior* 7:9–25.

Meyer, I., and L. Dean. 1998. Internalized homophobia, intimacy, and sexual behavior among gay and bisexual men. In G. Herek, ed., *Psychological Perspectives on Lesbian and Gay Issues*. Vol. 4: *Stigma and Sexual Orientation: Understanding Prejudice Against Lesbians, Gay Men, and Bisexuals*, pp. 160–86. Thousand Oaks, Calif.: Sage.

Morales, E. 1996. Gender roles among Latino gay and bisexual men: Implications for family and couple relationships. In J. Laird and R. J. Green, eds., *Lesbians and Gays in Couples and Families: A Handbook for Therapists*, pp. 272–97. San Francisco: Jossey-Bass.

Morin, S. 1977. Heterosexual bias in psychological research on lesbianism and male homosexuality. *American Psychologist* 32:629–37.

Murphy, B. 1994. Difference and diversity: Gay and lesbian couples. *Journal of Gay and Lesbian Social Services* 1(2):5–31.

National Association of Social Workers. 1996. *Code of Ethics of the National Association of Social Workers*. Washington. D.C.: Author. Retrieved November 18, 2000, from the World Wide Web: http://www.naswdc.org/code.htm

Nystrom, N. 1997. February. Mental health experiences of gay men and lesbians. Paper presented at the meeting of the American Association for the Advancement of Science, February, Houston, Texas.

Ochs, R. 1996. Biphobia: It goes more than two ways. In B. Firestein, ed., *Bisexuality: The Psychology and Politics of an Invisible Minority*, pp. 217–39. Thousand Oaks, Calif.: Sage.

O'Toole, C. J., and J. Bregante. 1992. Lesbians with disabilities. *Sexuality and Disability* 10:163–72.

Patterson, C. 1996a. Lesbian and gay parenthood. In M. Bornstein, ed., *Handbook of Parenting*, pp. 255–74. Hillsdale, N.J.: Erlbaum.

Patterson, C. 1996b. Lesbian and gay parents and their children. In R. Savin-Williams and K. Cohen, eds., *The Lives of Lesbians, Gays, and Bisexuals: Children to Adults*, pp. 274–304. Fort Worth, Tex.: Harcourt Brace.

Paul, J. 1996. Bisexuality: Exploring/exploding the boundaries. In R. Savin-Williams and K. Cohen, eds., *The Lives of Lesbians, Gays, and Bisexuals: Children to Adults*, pp. 436–61. Fort Worth, Tex.: Harcourt Brace.

Peplau, L., R. Veniegas, and S. Campbell. 1996. Gay and lesbian relationships. In R. Savin-Williams and K. Cohen, eds., *The Lives of Lesbians, Gays, and Bisexuals: Children to Adults*, pp. 250–73. Fort Worth, Tex.: Harcourt Brace.

Phillips, J., and A. Fischer. 1998. Graduate students? Training experiences with lesbian, gay, and bisexual issues. *Counseling Psychologist* 26:712–34.

Pilkington, N., and J. Cantor. 1996. Perceptions of heterosexual bias in professional psychology programs: A survey of graduate students. *Professional Psychology: Research and Practice* 27:604–12.

Pillard, R. 1988. Sexual orientation and mental disorder. *Psychiatric Annals* 18: 51–56.

Pope, M. 1995. Career interventions for gay and lesbian clients: A synopsis of practice knowledge and research needs. *Career Development Quarterly* 44:191–203.

Prince, J. 1995. Influences on the career development of gay men. *Career Development Quarterly* 44:168–77.

Quam, J., and G. Whitford. 1992. Adaptation and age-related expectations of older gay and lesbian adults. *Gerontologist* 32:367–74.

Reid, J. 1995. Development in late life: Older lesbian and gay lives. In A. D'Augelli and C. Patterson, eds., *Lesbian, Gay, and Bisexual Identities over the Lifespan: Psychological Perspectives*, pp. 215–40. New York: Oxford University Press.

Remafedi, G., S. French, M. Story, M. Resnick, D. Michael, and R. Blum. 1998. The relationship between suicide risk and sexual orientation: Results of a population-based study. *American Journal of Public Health* 88:57–60.

Rolland, J. 1994. In sickness and in health: The impact of illness on couples' relationships. *Journal of Marital and Family Therapy* 20:327–47.

Ross, M. 1990. The relationship between life events and mental health in homosexual men. *Journal of Clinical Psychology* 46:402–11.

Rothblum, E. 1994. "I only read about myself on bathroom walls": The need for research on the mental health of lesbians and gay men. *Journal of Consulting and Clinical Psychology* 62:213–20.

Rothblum, E., and L. Bond, eds. 1996. *Preventing Heterosexism and Homophobia.* Thousand Oaks, Calif.: Sage.

Rotheram-Borus, M., J. Hunter, and M. Rosario. 1994. Suicidal behavior and gay-related stress among gay and bisexual male adolescents. *Journal of Adolescent Research* 9:498–508.

Rotheram-Borus, M., M. Rosario, R. Van-Rossem, H. Reid, and R. Gillis. 1995. Prevalence, course, and predictors of multiple problem behaviors among gay and bisexual male adolescents. *Developmental Psychology* 31:75–85.

Rust, P. 1996. Managing multiple identities: Diversity among bisexual women and men. In B. Firestein, ed., *Bisexuality: The Psychology and Politics of an Invisible Minority*, pp. 53–83. Thousand Oaks, Calif.: Sage.

Ryan, C., and D. Futterman. 1998. *Counseling Gay and Lesbian Youth.* New York: Columbia University Press.

Saad, C. 1997. Disability and the lesbian, gay man, or bisexual individual. In M. Sipski and S. C. Alexander, eds., *Sexual Function in People with Disability and Chronic Illness: A Health Professional's Guide*, pp. 413–27. Gaithersburg, Md.: Aspen.

Sarason, I., G. Pierce, and B. Sarason. 1990. Social support and interactional processes: A triadic hypothesis. *Journal of Social and Personal Relationships* 7: 495–506.

Savin-Williams, R. 1989. Parental influences on the self-esteem of gay and lesbian youths: A reflected appraisals model. In G. Herdt, ed., *Gay and Lesbian Youth*, pp. 93–109. New York: Haworth.

Savin-Williams, R. 1990. *Gay and Lesbian Youth: Expressions of Identity.* New York: Hemisphere.

Savin-Williams, R. 1994. Verbal and physical abuse as stressors in the lives of lesbian, gay male, and bisexual youths: Associations with school problems, running away, substance abuse, prostitution, and suicide. *Journal of Consulting and Clinical Psychology* 62:261–69.

Savin-Williams, R. 1996. Self-labeling and disclosure among lesbian, gay, and bisexual youths. In J. Laird and R. J. Green, eds., *Lesbians and Gays in Couples and Families: A Handbook for Therapists*, pp. 153–82. San Francisco: Jossey-Bass.

Savin-Williams, R. 1998. " . . . and Then I Became Gay": Young Men's Stories. New
    York: Routledge.
Savin-Williams, R., and K. Cohen, eds. 1996. The Lives of Lesbians, Gays, and
    Bisexuals: Children to Adults. Fort Worth, Tex.: Harcourt Brace.
Savin-Williams, R., and E. Dube. 1998. Parental reactions to their child's disclosure
    of gay/lesbian identity. Family Relations 47:1–7.
Shapiro, J. P. 1993. No Pity: People with Disabilities Forging a New Civil Rights
    Movement. New York: Times Books.
Shidlo, A. 1994. Internalized homophobia: Conceptual and empirical issues in mea-
    surement. In B. Greene and G. Herek, eds., Psychological Perspectives on Les-
    bian and Gay Issues. Vol. 1: Lesbian and Gay Psychology: Theory, Research,
    and Clinical Applications, pp. 176–205. Thousand Oaks, Calif.: Sage.
Shuster, R. 1987. Sexuality as a continuum: The bisexual identity. In Boston Lesbian
    Psychologies Collective, ed., Lesbian Psychologies: Explorations and Chal-
    lenges, pp. 56–71. Urbana: University of Illinois Press.
Slater, S. 1995. The Lesbian Family Life Cycle. New York: The Free Press.
Strommen, E. 1993. "You're a what?": Family member reactions to the disclosure of
    homosexuality. In L. Garnets and D. Kimmel, eds., Psychological Perspectives
    on Lesbian and Gay Male Experiences, pp. 248–66. New York: Columbia Uni-
    versity Press.
Swartz, D. B. 1995. Cultural implications of audiological deficits on the homosexual
    male. Sexuality and Disability 13:159–81.
Telljohann, S., and J. Price. 1993. A qualitative examination of adolescent homo-
    sexuals' life experiences: Ramifications for secondary school personnel. Journal
    of Homosexuality 26(1):41–56.
Thomas, M., and P. Dansby. 1985. Black clients: Family structures, therapeutic is-
    sues, and strengths. Psychotherapy 22:398–407.
Thompson, D. 1994. The sexual experiences of men with learning disabilities having
    sex with men: Issues for HIV prevention. Sexuality and Disabilities 12:221–42.
Turk-Charles, S., T. Rose, and M. Gatz. 1996. The significance of gender in the
    treatment of older adults. In L. Carstensen, B. Adelstein, and L. Dornbrand,
    eds., The Handbook of Clinical Gerontology, pp. 107–28. Thousand Oaks, Ca-
    lif.: Sage.
Tuttle, G., and R. Pillard. 1991. Sexual orientation and cognitive abilities. Archives
    of Sexual Behavior 20:307–18.
Weston, K. 1992. Families We Choose. New York: Columbia University Press.
Winegarten, B., N. Cassie, K. Markowski, J. Kozlowski, and J. Yoder. 1994. Aversive
    heterosexism: Exploring unconscious bias toward lesbian psychotherapy clients.
    Paper presented at the 102nd Annual Convention of the American Psycholog-
    ical Association, August, Los Angeles.
Woog, D. 1995. School's Out: The Impact of Gay and Lesbian Issues on America's
    Schools. Boston: Alyson.

29 Seeing Is Believing: Research on Women's Sexual Orientation and Public Policy

Sheila James Kuehl

As a legislator, I call on my "knowledge" every day in deciding whether to favor or disfavor a particular bill, approach to the law, concept, or idea. How do I know what I know? And what part of what I "know" is really opinion, based on a murky brew of experience, bias, misinformation, factoids, and facts gleaned from newspapers, magazines, the Internet, surveys, and half-digested reports on research? Since more than four thousand bills cross my desk in every two-year legislative session, you can, more than likely, understand the sentiments of the anonymous wag who opined, "There are two things you never want to watch being made: sausages and law." However you may feel about lawmakers, once we are elected to any legislative body, we are expected to change the law for the better. "Better," however, is in the eye of the beholder, and so the eighty assembly members in the California Assembly and the forty senators in the State Senate legislate furiously, advocate vociferously, and attempt to persuade their colleagues to vote for the changes. This advocacy is done, primarily, through the use of research, testimony, and argument.

One of the first sermons I was given in law school went like this: If the law is on your side, pound the law; if the facts are on your side, pound the facts; if neither is on your side, pound the table. With the dearth of research on sexual orientation and especially on the experiences of women who are sexual minorities, little is left on both sides but a whole lot of table pounding. Inevitably, however, the law, whether in its present form or as we and others propose to change it, has great power to reward, punish, and protect people on the basis of their sexual orientation. Therefore, in order to make the law more responsive to the needs of sexual minorities such as lesbian, gay, bisexual, transgendered, or others, we must legislate.

The Legislature as Battleground

State legislatures, as well as the U.S. Congress, are a battleground on which social theories of fairness, equality, crime and punishment, the creation and protection of families, workplace safety, and a host of other issues collide and where ideas strive for ascendance, acceptance, and enactment. With the greater openness of sexual minorities in declaring or acknowledging their sexuality in public and with the election of openly gay and lesbian legislators, issues concerning women and sexuality have come to the fore in these public arenas. The questions raised by the presentation of these issues require answers based in research, and that has presented a significant problem to legislators. What is the research? How do we find it? How do we influence the choice of topics or considerations being studied?

For me, some of the answers may lie in my experience in the women's movement and especially in the movement to protect women against domestic violence. In the late 1970s I became drawn into early efforts to make the law more responsive to the needs of women who were being battered by their intimates. Such actions were not even a crime, and, when we set out to try to convince legislators that, indeed, these acts should be criminalized, we ran into a firewall of resistance. It was clear to me that, even though I had yet to work in any arena to change the law, social attitudes alone were powerful enough to shape women's experience in this area.

The mythologies concerning domestic violence influenced public policy, or the lack of it, in powerful ways. First, no one seemed to believe that domestic violence was widespread; rather, they believed that women made it up or that a few violent men in "lower" economic classes just lost their tempers and got carried away. Consequently there was no need, in their minds, for legislation. Although fact gathering was difficult, given the self-blaming and secretive nature of domestic violence, early research went a long way to prove that, indeed, this phenomenon was widespread.

Well then, the mythology went, women must bring it on themselves, and, indeed, other research was brought forward to show that domestic violence was actually "mutual combat" with both sides engaged in violent acts. Public policy then developed mutual restraining orders and arrested women for fighting back. Further research was needed to show that women could not inflict the same level of harm, did not initiate family violence, and so on. By continuing to tell the truth about women's lives, research drove public policy to swing back to a place where women might truly be protected. Perhaps the most intractable myth influencing public policy in this area was the belief that violence against a parent was not harmful to children unless they, too, were victims of the physical violence. It took years of research to change this fallacy, but, just this year, I introduced a bill that was signed into law stating that the court could take for granted, as a matter of law, that placing a child in the custody of a batterer was detrimental to the child. The batterer then has the burden of showing that it would be in the child's best interest to be with him or her. Lawmakers were convinced to vote for this bill by a multitude of studies examining the effects of domestic violence on children.

Social Beliefs About Sexual Minorities

In lawmakers' considerations surrounding sexual orientation, several issues come into play. Legislators have strong opinions, pro and con, about reproductive choice and similarly strong beliefs about gender equality. These beliefs tend to influence their thinking about sexual orientation as well. As those who oppose equality see it, sexual minorities do not appear to have procreation as the intent or result of their sexual activity, as married folk are supposed to have, and they are therefore part of a larger way of thinking about the immorality of nonreproductive sex. Policy makers who favor reproductive choice tend to see the treatment of sexual minorities more in the line of discrimination and equality law. On the other hand, legislators' views on sex and reproduction may not be the only concepts brought into play by these issues. By utilizing the rubric of sexual "preference," groups of people are stereotyped whether they engage in sexual acts or have simply indicated a preference and engage in no sexual activity. To buttress whatever arguments they may make, lawmakers utilize research, but they generally choose research that reflects their own beliefs.

Since the law is primarily engaged in drawing lines, the issue of definition is an important one and may or may not be amenable to solution by research. For example, I wanted to include transgendered people in California's hate crimes statute, but there were a number of issues involved in whether and when one could truly be considered "transgendered." Our solution was to focus on what the perpetrator believed about the victim, making it a crime based on gender when the perpetrator committed the crime because he or she thought the victim was behaving or appearing inappropriately for his or her gender. Although this may seem to be a weak resolution, it actually allowed us to refute, in law, the notion that the reason gay men were not deserving of protection was that they had abandoned their male privilege and chosen to identify with women. The issue of gender, long the underpinning of privilege, was addressed in law in a way that helped.

Other mythologies can, however, be overcome with careful, supportable research. A considerable body of social science research is available to separate myth from reality about sexual orientation. Social science researchers can use several strategies to influence public policy in this area.

First, researchers can distribute relevant empirical findings in places where legislators and policy makers are likely to read them. For example, Gregory Herek (1991) published an article entitled "Myths About Sexual Orientation: A Lawyer's Guide to Social Science Research" in a special issue of Tulane's law journal. In the article, Herek refuted eight common social myths about lesbians and gay men, for example, the belief that homosexuality is a form of mental illness, that lesbians and gay men are not capable of sustained relationships, and that gay people are detrimental to the morale, discipline, or efficiency of an organization or institution.

Second, researchers can testify as experts in legal and legislative decisions involving issues in which social myths are being used to deny basic civil rights such as same-sex marriage, child custody, adoption, or foster care (Patterson and Redding 1996).

Third, professional associations, like the American Psychological Association, can provide relevant research to legislators, adopt policy statements, and participate in amicus briefs concerning the civil rights of lesbians and gay men (see Bersoff and Ogden 1991).

Specific Areas of Law Amenable to Research

Generally the consideration given by legislators to an issue benefits enormously from the truth that research can reveal. Following are just a few areas where public policy has begun or can begin to affect treatment of sexual minorities under the law.

Education

Students in California public schools and community colleges are protected against harassment and discrimination on the basis of actual or perceived sexual orientation or the fact that someone thought they were be-having or appearing inappropriately for their gender. This new statute, unique in the country, was recently signed into law. The breadth of the law stems from the fact that we first amended the hate crimes statute and then incorporated that statute into the education code, but neither would have been possible without exhaustive studies about violence in schools and its impact on students' experiences, including dropping out, attempting suicide, and risking injury (D'Augelli 1998). This research revealed that students suffered violence on the basis of their "category": race, gender, national origin, ethnicity, disability, or sexual orientation. It was also important that the literature highlight the similarities between harassment and discrimi-nation against people in a variety of categories. Indeed, it underscored what most of us believed: that the actual category does not much matter; the purpose for the harassment or violence is to take power over someone else and to elevate one's own group through demonizing another.

The issue of curriculum in schools is also hotly contested, and certainly not simple where categories of people are concerned. Since no law mandates the teaching of anything having to do with social categories, but only pre-cludes curriculum that reflects adversely on different groups, the most useful research in this area might involve the "teaching tolerance" — type programs and whether they make a difference.

Health

In recent years there has been an explosion of health research but little of it, until recently, had anything to do with women. Current research that studies only women has been enormously helpful in providing medical so-lutions. However, social science research also has a part to play, primarily in revealing how access to health care coverage and treatment affects health and well-being, especially for women and, within the general category of women, for women with disabilities, women of color, immigrant women, and lesbians (see, for example, National Academy of the Sciences 1999, on lesbian health research). Each of these categories has differing health needs and access problems, not to mention problems of visibility.

Workplace Issues

Sexual harassment, both in the workplace and at school, has been among the most difficult issues to address in the law. Social attitudes have long held that sexual interplay in the office was harmless, even a good thing. Only when research showed the harmful effects of this harassment on the work experience, promotion, success, and mental health of women did the law began to prohibit such behavior as a form of sex discrimination. Similarly same-sex harassment at work was thought by many to be different from "sexual harassment" as the women's movement had come to define it, because the law had, essentially appropriately, blended the notion of gender with the notion of power in the workplace and recognized the powerful role that demands for sex, as well as the diminishment of workers by sexual innuendo, can play in keeping (mostly) women in their place at work. Further research revealed, however, that the problem was not gender alone but the intrusion of sexual demands and diminishment in the workplace because of being considered a sexual object. This led to the inclusion of same-sex harassment in the laws.

Workplace discrimination on the basis of sexual orientation was a bit easier to sell, because people, generally, were coming to the same conclusion they had reached when faced with racial or gender discrimination: People should be judged by their ability to do the job. The somewhat more intractable problem, however, was how much weight should be given to coworkers' opinions when deciding how to protect workers. The conclusion most legislators reached was that protection from discrimination was more important than giving weight to workers' discriminatory attitudes. Here, again, however, research played a part in showing that those who were less aggressive about asserting their opinions in the workplace generally favored evaluation based on merit and competence, not on categories.

Families

As the history of every other minority seeking equality and acceptance in this country attests, sexual minorities have the greatest difficulties in having their families recognized in the law. The weight of social opinion is still strongly against sexual minorities adopting, foster parenting, and marrying. This is an area where I believe the social sciences can really help, because it is not clear what constitutes the true basis of this public concern. Many of my colleagues seem to believe that marriage by sexual minorities threatens heterosexual marriage. This view is too deeply seated simply to dismiss as prejudice or religious fervor. Indeed, these individuals do not actually know why they believe this. Research, therefore, needs to be creative. What truth will help to dispel this myth? It may be simpler to counter negative attitudes about foster parenting and adoption that seem to stem from concerns about protecting children from sexual abuse. Research in this area has shown that children of lesbian mothers and gay fathers are not at greater risk for within-family sexual molestation than children raised by heterosexual parents. In fact, the great majority of adult perpetrators of sexual abuses are heterosexual men (American Psychological Association 1995).

Several factors are at play here. The primary concern seems to be the myth that gay men pose a threat to children. Women are invisible in this myth but suffer from it, perhaps because it is thought that they will not be able to protect children from their gay male friends. Another myth concerns the mental health of children who grow up with only a one-gender role model. This myth conveniently ignores the millions of single parents as well as the growing number of two-parent lesbian and gay male households in this country. Another myth concerns the notion that gayness is "catching" and that children will want to emulate their gay parents. Careful scientific research about the mental health of children and foster children of lesbian and gay male parents is enormously helpful. The results of research comparing gay and lesbian parents to heterosexual parents and the children of gay and lesbian parents to children of heterosexual parents consistently shows that negative stereotypes are not supported by the data. Lesbian mothers and gay fathers are as likely as heterosexuals to be good parents (Patterson 1995).

In the next few years several policy issues, in which research would be invaluable, are likely to gain prominence. These include workplace discrimination (e.g., a federal employment nondiscrimination act); domestic partner/same-sex marriage; gay, lesbian, and bisexual youths (e.g., managing harassment, school issues); the recognition of gay and lesbian families; and hate crimes.

The Role of Research

Legislators and their staff use research in three main ways:

1. *Support for an existing belief.* Sometimes I have an idea about a change in the law. The idea stems from my own experience, prejudice, a call from a constituent, or interest in a tangential issue raised by another legislator. I ask my staff to review the literature on the subject. For example, I wanted to protect gay and lesbian young people and those who were thought to be gay or lesbian from violence and harassment at school. When I began, I had only anecdotal evidence that such harassment took place. Jennifer Richard,

a member of my staff, began to collect stories in 1995, when I first introduced a bill to ensure such protection. Through the years that we fought to change our colleagues' minds about the problem, we began to see more organized data showing that this problem was widespread, identifying schools that had already adopted such policies and had improved outcomes, and demonstrating the effects of this violence on young gay and lesbian people. Finally, in 1999, a study from the Centers for Disease Control showed both the widespread nature of the problem and its unhealthful effects (see Safe Schools Coalition of Washington 1999). This prompted us to look for existing research and even to request that further research be done.

2. *Advocacy using existing research.* When advocacy groups bring an issue to me, they sometimes have extensive research to back up the efficacy of the desired change in the law, sometimes not. In my six years in the California Assembly, I have found that a bill has virtually no chance of being enacted without thorough research supporting the proposed change. Someone has to testify in at least four different committees on the need for the bill. Individual horror stories are helpful to move the hearts of legislators, but our minds are also needed to reach a conclusion about the bill. A good example is in the data on battered lesbians. Since little research existed on lesbians, as a class, being battered by their partners, there was no push to have the domestic violence laws apply to same-sex relationships or to attempt to convince shelters that this problem was serious enough to require that issues of sexual orientation be included in training protocols. The presentation of such data facilitated these necessary changes (Renzetti 1992). Another example involves the transgendered community. For years transgendered people insisted that they were the target of hate crimes based either on their transitional or ambiguous sexual appearance or on the perpetrator's knowledge of their status. Supporting data, however, were never sufficient even to convince my well-meaning colleagues of the problem. Last year, armed with new studies, I was able to convince the legislature that transgendered people, as a class, needed protection. Because the data also revealed that perpetrators most often acted out of animosity toward a perceived gender ambiguity, we amended the Penal Code to add crimes committed because the perpetrator thought the victim appeared or behaved inappropriately for his or her gender.

3. *Innovation in the law.* Let me state clearly here that *innovation* and *law* are two words rarely seen in the same sentence. By the time lawmakers arrive at a place where a majority agrees there is a problem, that something should be done about it, and that this particular bill is the correct solution,

society is usually way ahead of us. However, I believe it is possible for researchers in the social sciences to lead us in useful directions purely by their choice of issues. We have not seen very much on the dynamics of power unrelated to pure gender issues, as legislators understand them (that is, as men versus women). It has been difficult to educate legislators about the ways that gender stereotypes permeate attitudes about sexual minorities, and the close association between the two (see Kite 1994, for a review of this research). It may be possible to look at issues of power, economics, and morality in new and useful ways and to consider how social attitudes in these three areas shape the experience of disfavored people.

How Can a Researcher Offer Help to Legislators?

The approach I outline here for researchers wishing to offer help to legislators will be an imperfect one, as every legislator is different. However, each of us in elected office is called on to know something about an enormously broad range of issues. We serve on various committees. I, for instance, chair the Judiciary Committee and the Select Committee on Entertainment and the Arts, and serve on the Water, Parks, and Wildlife Committee, the Health Committee, the Appropriations Committee, the Local Government Committee, and the Revenue and Taxation Committee, which means I consider a few thousand bills a year. I vote for or against all bills when they come to the floor. On my staff are a few people who look into everything for me. They each have three or four areas of expertise. It is difficult for them to tell a researcher whether or not their research will be helpful. However, once original research is completed, if the researcher believes that a change in public policy could help to alleviate some problem, it is perfectly acceptable to inquire of the staff of some legislator as to whether that legislator might be interested in a particular area, or, if not, who might be interested. Take a chance.

Conclusion

Perhaps I am no closer to understanding how I know what I know. However, as with any other area of bias, faith, or belief, I am beginning to understand that bias, faith, and belief play a powerful role in the work of the 120 California legislators with whom I spend most of my working life. I suspect it is much the same with all the other states and with the Congress. One thing is clear: In order for legislators to move their colleagues to adopt a just and fair solution to a social problem, we need information and access to that information. The rest is up to you.

References

American Psychological Association. 1995. *Lesbian and Gay Parenting: A Resource for Psychologists*. Washington, D.C.: American Psychological Association.

Bersoff, D. N., and D. W. Ogden. 1991. APA amicus curiae briefs: Furthering lesbian and gay male civil rights. *American Psychologist* 46(9):950–56.

D'Augelli, A. R. 1998. Developmental implications of victimization of lesbian, gay and bisexual youths. In G. M. Herek, ed., *Stigma and Sexual Orientation: Understanding Prejudice Against Lesbians, Gay Men, and Bisexuals*, pp. 187–210. Thousand Oaks, Calif.: Sage.

Herek, G. M. 1991. Myths about sexual orientation: A lawyer's guide to social science research. *Law and Sexuality* 1:133–172.

Kite, M. E. 1994. When perception meets reality: Individual differences in reactions to lesbians and gay men. In B. Greene and G. M. Herek, eds., *Lesbian and Gay Psychology: Theory, Research, and Clinical Application*, pp. 25–53. Thousand Oaks, Calif.: Sage.

National Academy of Sciences, Institute of Medicine. 1999. *Lesbian Health: Current Assessment and Directions for the Future*. Washington, D.C.: National Academy Press.

Patterson, C. J. 1995. Lesbian mothers, gay fathers, and their children. In A. R. D'Augelli and C. J. Patterson, eds., *Lesbian, Gay, and Bisexual Identities over the Lifespan: Psychological Perspectives*, pp. 262–90. New York: Oxford University Press.

Patterson, C. J., and R. E. Redding. 1996. Lesbian and gay families with children: Implications of social science research for policy. *Journal of Social Issues* 52(2):29–50.

Renzetti, C. 1992. *Violent Betrayal: Partner Abuse in Lesbian Relationships*. Newbury Park, Calif.: Sage.

Safe Schools Coalition of Washington. 1999. Information from Web site: http://www.safeschools-wa.org/quant_cont.html

Acknowledgments

Part 1: The Meaning of Sexual Orientation

D. C. Kimmel and L. D. Garnets, What a light it shed: The life of Evelyn Hooker, in G. Kimble and M. Wertheimer, eds., *Portraits of Pioneers in Psychology*, vol. 4, pp. 253–67 (Washington, D.C.: American Psychological Association, 2000). Copyright 2000. Reprinted by permission of the American Psychological Association and Lawrence Erlbaum Associates.

J. M. Bailey, Biological perspectives on sexual orientation, in A. R. D'Augelli and C. J. Patterson, eds., *Lesbian, Gay, and Bisexual Identities over the Lifespan*, pp. 102–35 (New York: Oxford University Press, 1995). Copyright 1995. Reprinted by permission of Oxford University Press.

R. C. Fox, Bisexual identities, in A. R. D'Augelli and C. J. Patterson, eds., *Lesbian, Gay, and Bisexual Identities over the Lifespan*, pp. 48–68 (New York: Oxford University Press, 1995). Copyright 1995. Reprinted by permission of Oxford University Press.

L. M. Diamond and R. C. Savin-Williams, Explaining diversity in the development of same-sex sexuality among young women, *Journal of Social Issues* 56(2):297–313. Copyright 2000. Reprinted by permission of the Society for the Psychological Study of Social Issues and Blackwell Publishers.

Part 2: Psychological Dimensions of Prejudice, Discrimination, and Violence

G. M. Herek, The psychology of sexual prejudice, *Current Directions in Psychological Science* 9:19–22. Copyright 2000. Reprinted by permission of Blackwell Publishers.

M. E. Kite and B. E. Whitley, Do heterosexual women and men differ in their attitudes toward homosexuality? A conceptual and methodological analysis, in G. M. Herek, ed., *Stigma and Sexual Orientation: Understanding Prejudice Against Lesbians, Gay Men, and Bisexuals*, pp. 39–61 (Thousand Oaks, Calif.: Sage, 1998). Copyright 1998. Reprinted by permission of the Society for the Psychological Study of Lesbian, Gay, and Bisexual Issues and Sage Publications.

L. D. Garnets, G. M. Herek, and B. Levy, Violence and victimization of lesbians and gay men: Mental health consequences, *Journal of Interpersonal Violence* 5:366–83. Copyright 1990. Reprinted by permission of Sage Publications.

R. C. Savin-Williams, Matthew Shepard's death: A professional awakening, *Applied Developmental Science* 3:150–54. Copyright 1999. Reprinted by permission of Lawrence Erlbaum Associates.

Part 3: Identity Development and Stigma Management

P. C. Rust, Finding a sexual identity and community: Therapeutic implications and cultural assumptions in scientific models of coming out, in E. D. Rothblum and L. A. Bond, eds., *Preventing Heterosexism and Homophobia*, pp. 87–123 (Thousand Oaks, Calif.: Sage, 1996). Copyright 1996. Reprinted by permission of Sage Publications.

G. M. Herek, Why tell if you're not asked? Self-disclosure, intergroup contact, and heterosexuals' attitudes toward lesbians and gay men, in G. M. Herek, J. Jobe, and R. Carney, eds., *Out in Force: Sexual Orientation and the Military*, pp. 197–225 (Chicago: University of Chicago Press, 1996). Copyright 1996. Reprinted by permission of University of Chicago Press.

R. C. Savin-Williams, Lesbian, gay, and bisexual youths' relationships with their parents, in C. J. Patterson and A. R. D'Augelli, eds., *Lesbian, Gay, and Bisexual Identities in Families*, pp. 75–98 (New York: Oxford University Press, 1998). Copyright 1998. Reprinted by permission of Oxford University Press.

M. V. Badgett, Employment and sexual orientation: Disclosure and discrimination in the work place. *Journal of Gay and Lesbian Social Services* 4(3):29–52. Copyright 1996. Reprinted by permission of Haworth Press.

Part 4: Diversity Among Gay Men, Lesbians, and Bisexuals

B. Greene, Beyond heterosexism and across the cultural divide. Developing an inclusive lesbian, gay, and bisexual psychology: A look to the future, in B. Greene and G. L. Croom, eds., *Education, Research, and Practice in Lesbian, Gay, Bisexual, and Transgendered Psychology*, pp. 1–45 (Thousand Oaks, Calif.: Sage, 2000). Copyright 2000. Reprinted by permission of the Society for the

Psychological Study of Lesbian, Gay, and Bisexual Issues and Sage Publications.

T. Tafoya, 1997 Native gay and lesbian issues: The two-spirited, in B. Greene, ed., *Ethnic and Cultural Diversity Among Lesbians and Gay Men*, pp. 1–9 (Thousand Oaks: Sage, 1997). Copyright 1997. Reprinted by permission of the Society for the Psychological Study of Lesbian, Gay, and Bisexual Issues and Sage Publications.

E. Blackwood and S. E. Wieringa, Sapphic shadows: Challenging the silence in the study of sexuality, in E. Blackwood and S. E. Wieringa, eds., *Female Desires: Same-Sex Relations and Transgender Practices Across Cultures*, pp. 39–63 (New York: Columbia University Press, 1999). Copyright 1999. Reprinted by permission of Columbia University Press.

D. C. Kimmel, Identifying and addressing health issues of gay, lesbian, bisexual, and transgender populations in rural communities: Psychological perspectives. Paper prepared for the National Rural Health Association Conference, New Orleans, May 25, 2000. Copyright 2000. Reprinted by permission of author.

Part 5: Relationships and Families

L. A. Peplau and L. R. Spalding, The close relationships of lesbians, gay men, and bisexuals, in C. Hendrick and S. S. Hendrick, eds., *Close Relationships: A Sourcebook*, pp. 111–23 (Thousand Oaks, Calif.: Sage, 2000). Copyright 2000. Reprinted by permission of Sage Publications.

P. C. Rust, Monogamy and polyamory, in B. A. Firestein, ed., *Bisexuality: The Psychology and Politics of an Invisible Minority*, pp. 127–48 (Thousand Oaks, Calif.: Sage, 1996). Copyright 1996. Reprinted by permission of Sage Publications.

C. J. Patterson, Children of lesbian and gay parents, in T. H. Ollendick and R. J. Prinz, eds., *Advances in Clinical Child Psychology*, pp. 235–82 (New York: Plenum, 1997). Copyright 1997. Reprinted by permission of Kluwer Academic/ Plenum Publishers.

A. Y. Hom, Stories from the homefront: Perspectives of Asian American parents with lesbian daughters and gay sons, in R. Leong, ed., *Asian American Sexualities: Dimensions of the Gay and Lesbian Experience*, pp. 37–49 (New York: Routledge, 1994). Copyright 1994. Reprinted by permission of A. Y. Hom and the Asian American Studies Center, University of California, Los Angeles.

Part 6: Adolescence, Midlife, and Aging

K. Anhalt and T. L. Morris, Developmental and adjustment issues of gay, lesbian, and bisexual adolescents: A review of the empirical literature. *Clinical Child and Family Psychology Review* 1(4):215–230. Copyright 1998. Reprinted by permission of Kluwer Academic/Plenum Publishers.

D. C. Kimmel and B. E. Sang, Lesbians and gay men in midlife, in A. R. D'Augelli and C. J. Patterson, eds., *Lesbian, Gay, and Bisexual Identities over the Lifespan*, pp. 190–214 (New York: Oxford University Press, 1995). Copyright 1995. Reprinted by permission of Oxford University Press.

A. H. Grossman, A. R. D'Augelli, and T. S. O'Connell, Being lesbian, gay, bisexual, and 60 or older in North America, *Journal of Gay and Lesbian Social Services* 13(4):23–40. Copyright 2000. Reprinted by permission of Haworth Press.

Part 7: Mental Health

E. D. Rothblum, "Somewhere, in Des Moines or San Antonio": Historical perspectives on lesbian, gay, and bisexual mental health, in R. M. Perez, K. A. DeBord, and K. J. Bieschke, eds., *Handbook of Counseling and Psychotherapy with Lesbian, Gay, and Bisexual Clients*, pp. 57–79 (Washington, D.C.: American Psychological Association, 2000). Copyright 2000. Reprinted by permission of the American Psychological Association.

D.C. Haldeman, The practice and ethics of sexual orientation conversion therapy, *Journal of Consulting and Clinical Psychology* 62:221–27. Copyright 1994. Reprinted by permission of the American Psychological Association.

I. Meyer, Minority stress and the mental health in gay men, *Journal of Health and Social Behavior* 7:9–25. Copyright 1995. Reprinted by permission of the American Sociological Association.

Part 8: Status of Practice, Research and Public Policy Issues, in American Psychology

G. M. Herek, D. C. Kimmel, H. Amaro, and G. B. Melton, Avoiding heterosexist bias in psychological research, *American Psychologist* 46:957–63. Copyright 1991. Reprinted by permission of the American Psychological Association.

American Psychological Association, *Guidelines for Psychotherapy with Lesbian, Gay, and Bisexual Clients* 55(12):1440–51. Copyright 2000. Reprinted by permission of the American Psychological Association.

S. J. Kuehl, Seeing is believing: Research on women's sexual orientation and public policy. *Journal of Social Issues* 56(2):351–59. Copyright 2000. Reprinted by permission of the Society for the Psychological Study of Social Issues and Blackwell Publishers.

Index

adolescence, 563, 571–96
adolescents: adjustment issues of, 584–90; coming out, 577–78; conduct problems among, 588–89; dating, 577–80; high-risk sexual behavior among, 582–84; prevalence of minority sexual orientation, 575–76; risk and protective factors for, 591–93; school issues, 590; substance abuse among, 589–90; suicide attempts of, 584–88; victimization of, 580–82
adoption of children, sexual orientation and, 536–37
African-Americans: invisibility syndrome, 388–89; resilience of, 363–65; sexual orientation and, 375; social class and, 374–76. *See also* cultural diversity
aging, 565–68, 629–44; cultural differences and, 369; HIV/AIDS and, 640–41; issues, 439–40; loneliness and, 636; mental health and, 635; physical health and, 637–38; psychotherapy and, 770–71; self-esteem and, 635–36; sexual identity and,

641–42; sexual orientation and, 369–71; social support and, 638–40; socioemotional selectivity theory, 643–44; stress factors in, 761; substance use and, 638; suicide and, 637; victimization and, 640, 643
Allison, Dorothy, 376–78
Amazons of Dahomey, 414
American Psychiatric Association, 2, 40, 42
American Psychological Association, 2, 3, 16, 43–46; Committee on Lesbian, Gay, and Bisexual Concerns, 676, 734; resolutions on homosexuality, 44, 675–76
American Psychological Foundation, Wayne Placek Fund, 674
anthropology: bisexuality, 97–99; *mati* relationships, 411–12, 756; sexual orientation, 410–27
antigay hate crimes, 188–202
antigay verbal abuse, 195
Asian-American: parents of lesbians and gay men, 549–60. *See also* cultural diversity

Between Men~Between Women
Lesbian and Gay Studies

Lillian Faderman and Larry Gross, Editors

Richard D. Mohr, *Gays/Justice: A Study of Ethics, Society, and Law*

Gary David Comstock, *Violence Against Lesbians and Gay Men*

Kath Weston, *Families We Choose: Lesbians, Gays, Kinship*

Lillian Faderman, *Odd Girls and Twilight Lovers: A History of Lesbian Life in Twentieth-Century America*

Judith Roof, *A Lure of Knowledge: Lesbian Sexuality and Theory*

John Clum, *Acting Gay: Male Homosexuality in Modern Drama*

Allen Ellenzweig, *The Homoerotic Photograph: Male Images from Durieu/Delacroix to Mapplethorpe*

Sally Munt, editor, *New Lesbian Criticism: Literary and Cultural Readings*

Timothy F. Murphy and Suzanne Poirier, editors, *Writing AIDS: Gay Literature, Language, and Analysis*

Linda D. Garnets and Douglas C. Kimmel, editors, *Psychological Perspectives on Lesbian and Gay Male Experiences* (2nd edition)

Laura Doan, editor, *The Lesbian Postmodern*

Noreen O'Connor and Joanna Ryan, *Wild Desires and Mistaken Identities: Lesbianism and Psychoanalysis*

Alan Sinfield, *The Wilde Century: Effeminacy, Oscar Wilde, and the Queer Moment*

Claudia Card, *Lesbian Choices*

Carter Wilson, *Hidden in the Blood: A Personal Investigation of AIDS in the Yucatán*

Alan Bray, *Homosexuality in Renaissance England*

Joseph Carrier, *De Los Otros: Intimacy and Homosexuality Among Mexican Men*

Joseph Bristow, *Effeminate England: Homoerotic Writing After 1885*

Corinne E. Blackmer and Patricia Juliana Smith, editors, *En Travesti: Women, Gender Subversion, Opera*

Don Paulson with Roger Simpson, *An Evening at The Garden of Allah: A Gay Cabaret in Seattle*

Claudia Schoppmann, *Days of Masquerade: Life Stories of Lesbians During the Third Reich*

Chris Straayer, *Deviant Eyes, Deviant Bodies: Sexual Re-Orientation in Film and Video*

Edward Alwood, *Straight News: Gays, Lesbians, and the News Media*

Thomas Waugh, *Hard to Imagine: Gay Male Eroticism in Photography and Film from Their Beginnings to Stonewall*

Judith Roof, *Come As You Are: Sexuality and Narrative*

Terry Castle, *Noel Coward and Radclyffe Hall: Kindred Spirits*

Kath Weston, *Render Me, Gender Me: Lesbians Talk Sex, Class, Color, Nation, Stud-muffins . . .*

Ruth Vanita, *Sappho and the Virgin Mary: Same-Sex Love and the English Literary Imagination*

renée c. hoogland, *Lesbian Configurations*

Beverly Burch, *Other Women: Lesbian Experience and Psychoanalytic Theory of Women*

Jane McIntosh Snyder, *Lesbian Desire in the Lyrics of Sappho*

Rebecca Alpert, *Like Bread on the Seder Plate: Jewish Lesbians and the Transformation of Tradition*

Emma Donoghue, editor, *Poems Between Women: Four Centuries of Love, Romantic Friendship, and Desire*

James T. Sears and Walter L. Williams, editors, *Overcoming Heterosexism and Homophobia: Strategies That Work*

Patricia Juliana Smith, *Lesbian Panic: Homoeroticism in Modern British Women's Fiction*

Dwayne C. Turner, *Risky Sex: Gay Men and HIV Prevention*

Timothy F. Murphy, *Gay Science: The Ethics of Sexual Orientation Research*

Cameron McFarlane, *The Sodomite in Fiction and Satire, 1660–1750*

Lynda Hart, *Between the Body and the Flesh: Performing Sadomasochism*

Byrne R. S. Fone, editor, *The Columbia Anthology of Gay Literature: Readings from Western Antiquity to the Present Day*

Ellen Lewin, *Recognizing Ourselves: Ceremonies of Lesbian and Gay Commitment*

Ruthann Robson, *Sappho Goes to Law School: Fragments in Lesbian Legal Theory*

Jacquelyn Zita, *Body Talk: Philosophical Reflections on Sex and Gender*

Evelyn Blackwood and Saskia Wieringa, *Female Desires: Same-Sex Relations and Transgender Practices Across Cultures*

William L. Leap, ed., *Public Sex/Gay Space*

Larry Gross and James D. Woods, eds., *The Columbia Reader on Lesbians and Gay Men in Media, Society, and Politics*

Marilee Lindemann, *Willa Cather: Queering America*

George E. Haggerty, *Men in Love: Masculinity and Sexuality in the Eighteenth Century*

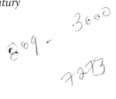

Andrew Elfenbein, *Romantic Genius: The Prehistory of a Homosexual Role*

Gilbert Herdt and Bruce Koff, *Something to Tell You: The Road Families Travel When a Child Is Gay*

Richard Canning, *Gay Fiction Speaks: Conversations with Gay Novelists*

Laura Doan, *Fashioning Sapphism: The Origins of a Modern English Lesbian Culture*

Mary Bernstein and Renate Reimann, eds., *Queer Families, Queer Politics: Challenging Culture and the State*

Richard R. Bozorth, *Auden's Games of Knowledge: Poetry and the Meanings of Homosexuality*

Larry Gross, *Up from Invisibility: Lesbians, Gay Men, and the Media in America*